SWITZERLAND

FODOR'S TRAVEL PUBLICATIONS

are compiled, researched, and edited by an international team of travel writers, field correspondents, and editors. The series, which now almost covers the globe, was founded by Eugene Fodor in 1936.

OFFICES

New York & London

Fodor's Switzerland:

Area Editors: Sara Cashen, Jennifer Stone, Margaret Studer-Walsh
Editorial Contributors: Robert Brown, Mark Heller, Kenneth Loveland, Irene M. Ritter, Tom Szentgyorgyi
Editor: Thomas Cussans
Executive Editor: Richard Moore
Editorial Assistant: Caz Philcox
Illustrations: Lorraine Calaora
Maps and Plans: Brian Stimpson, Swanston Graphics

FODOR'S®

SWITZERLAND 1988

(Including Liechtenstein)

FODOR'S TRAVEL PUBLICATIONS, INC.

New York & London

ISBN 0-679-01569-8
ISBN 0-340-41805-2 (Hodder & Stoughton)

MANUFACTURED IN THE UNITED STATES OF AMERICA
10 9 8 7 6 5 4 3 2 1

CONTENTS

FOREWORD

Switzerland remains an ideal country to visit, and for a variety of excellent reasons. It is exceedingly comfortable, with a bewildering range of fine hotels and restaurants in all price ranges. It is remarkably beautiful, with an astonishing range of landscapes: Alpine peaks, rolling meadows, mirror-like lakes, richly-historic towns and cities. It is also—perhaps this is almost the most compelling reason of all to visit it—a country supremely well adapted to the demands of modern tourism.

Switzerland can justly claim the parentage of modern tourism, a role that stretches back to the end of the 18th century. It was the Swiss landscapes that were the draw originally, and they had the People of Quality flocking from all over Europe, and even sometimes the New World. But hand in hand with the country's incomparable landscapes went a natural aptitude, a certain flair, on the part of the Swiss for welcoming guests, for making them comfortable, for feeding them memorably, for running hotels, for organizing excursions. The Swiss, in short, took to tourism as to the manner born.

It's hard to know exactly why the Swiss should be so gifted in the finer arts of hospitality. But the fact remains that this talent has not in any way deserted them today. Rather the opposite in fact. Never a people to rest on their not inconsiderable laurels, the Swiss have made ever more effective efforts to promote themselves and their country. Holiday Cards, discounts, special deals and off-peak rates galore are very much a fact of life for today's visitor.

But crucially, it is in the field of old-fashioned hospitality and courtesy that the Swiss continue to lead the way. Today's visitors, though hardly embarking on the voyage into the unknown that their great grandparents may have undertaken 100 years ago when they came here, can be absolutely sure that their welcome will be every bit as warm, and every bit as genuine. Switzerland for the tourist remains the heart of the matter of Europe.

* * *

The task of preparing this edition would not have been possible without the assistance of many friends in Switzerland, New York and London. We would like to thank especially Franz Blum of the Swiss National Tourist Office, and, above all, Sara Cashen, Jennifer Stone and Margaret Studer-Walsh, who have once more placed their expertise and hard work at our disposal.

* * *

All prices quoted in this guide are based on those available to us at the time of writing. In a world of rapid change, however, the possibility of inaccurate or out-of-date information can never be totally eliminated. We trust, therefore, that you will double-check to be sure of the latest figures.

Similarly, be sure to check all opening times of museums and galleries. We have found that such times are liable to change without notice, and you could easily make a trip only to find a locked door.

When a hotel closes or a restaurant produces a disappointing meal, let us know, and we will investigate the complaint. We are always ready to revise our entries for the following year's edition should the facts warrant it.

Send your letters to the editors of Fodor's Travel Publications, 201 E 50th Street, New York, N.Y. 10022. European readers may prefer to write to Fodor's Travel Guides, 9–10 Market Place, London W1N 7AG, England.

SWITZERLAND and LIECHTENSTEIN

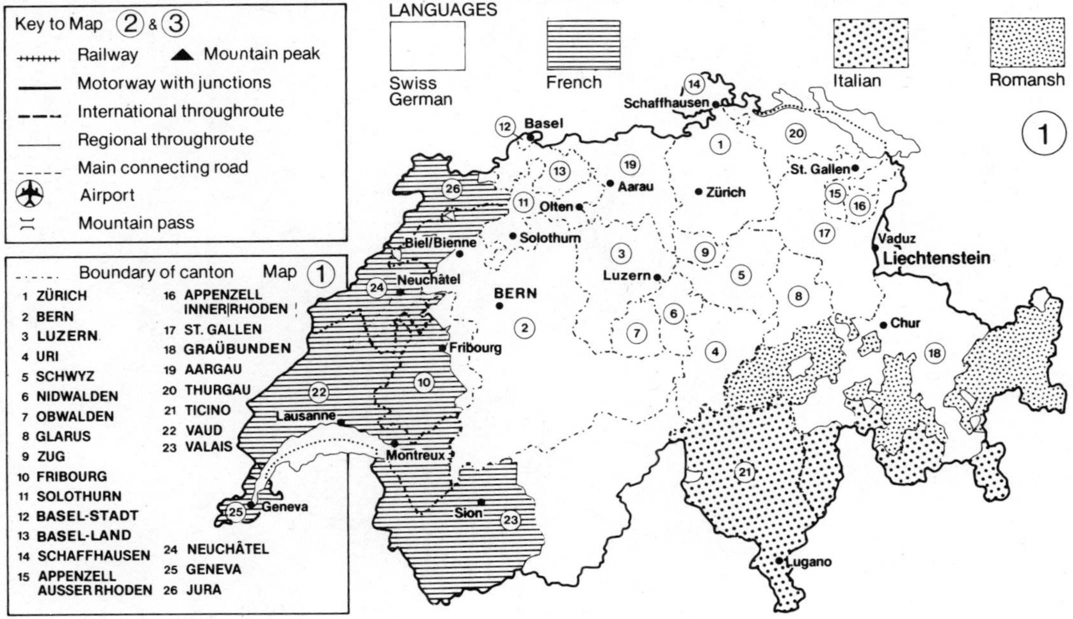

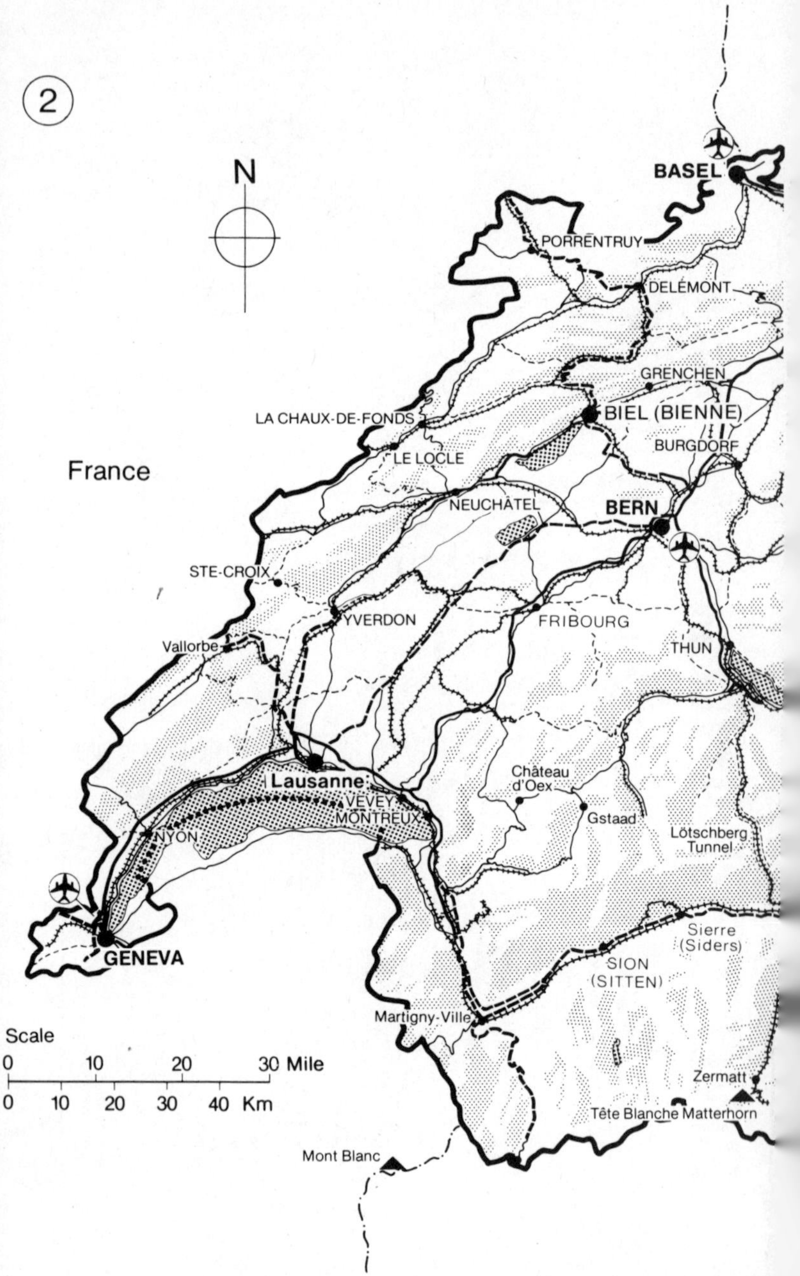
2
N
BASEL
PORRENTRUY
DELEMONT
GRENCHEN
BIEL (BIENNE)
BURGDORF
LA CHAUX-DE-FONDS
LE LOCLE
France
NEUCHÂTEL
BERN
STE-CROIX
YVERDON
FRIBOURG
Vallorbe
THUN
Château d'Oex
Lausanne
VEVEY
MONTREUX
Gstaad
NYON
Lötschberg Tunnel
GENEVA
Sierre (Siders)
SION (SITTEN)
Martigny-Ville
Scale
0 10 20 30 Mile
0 10 20 30 40 Km
Zermatt
Tête Blanche
Matterhorn
Mont Blanc

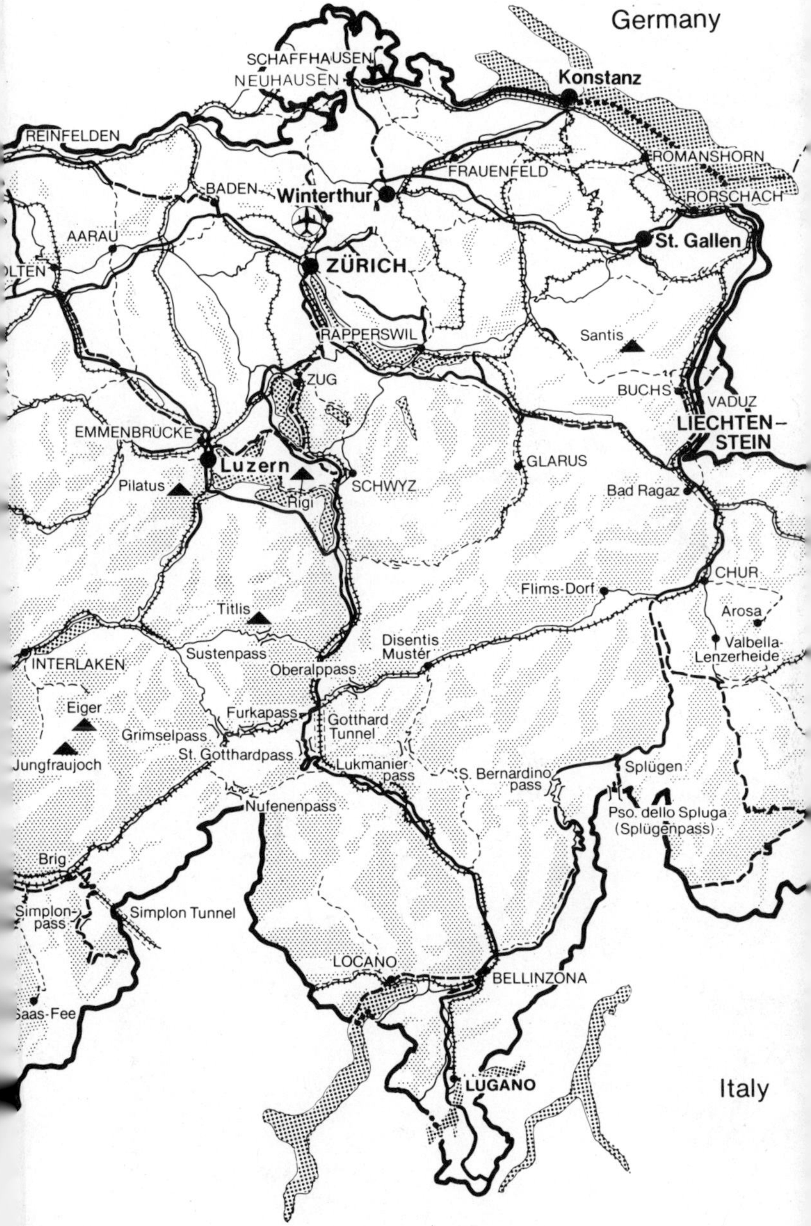
Germany
SCHAFFHAUSEN
NEUHAUSEN
Konstanz
REINFELDEN
ROMANSHORN
FRAUENFELD
BADEN
Winterthur
RORSCHACH
AARAU
St. Gallen
OLTEN
ZÜRICH
RAPPERSWIL
Santis
ZUG
BUCHS
VADUZ
LIECHTEN-
STEIN
EMMENBRÜCKE
Luzern
GLARUS
Pilatus
SCHWYZ
Rigi
Bad Ragaz
CHUR
Flims-Dorf
Titlis
Arosa
Disentis
Mustér
Valbella-
Lenzerheide
Sustenpass
INTERLAKEN
Oberalppass
Eiger
Furkapass
Gotthard
Tunnel
Grimselpass
Jungfraujoch
St. Gotthardpass
Lukmanier
pass
S. Bernardino
pass
Splügen
Nufenenpass
Pso. dello Spluga
(Splügenpass)
Brig
Simplon-
pass
Simplon Tunnel
LOCANO
BELLINZONA
Saas-Fee
LUGANO
Italy

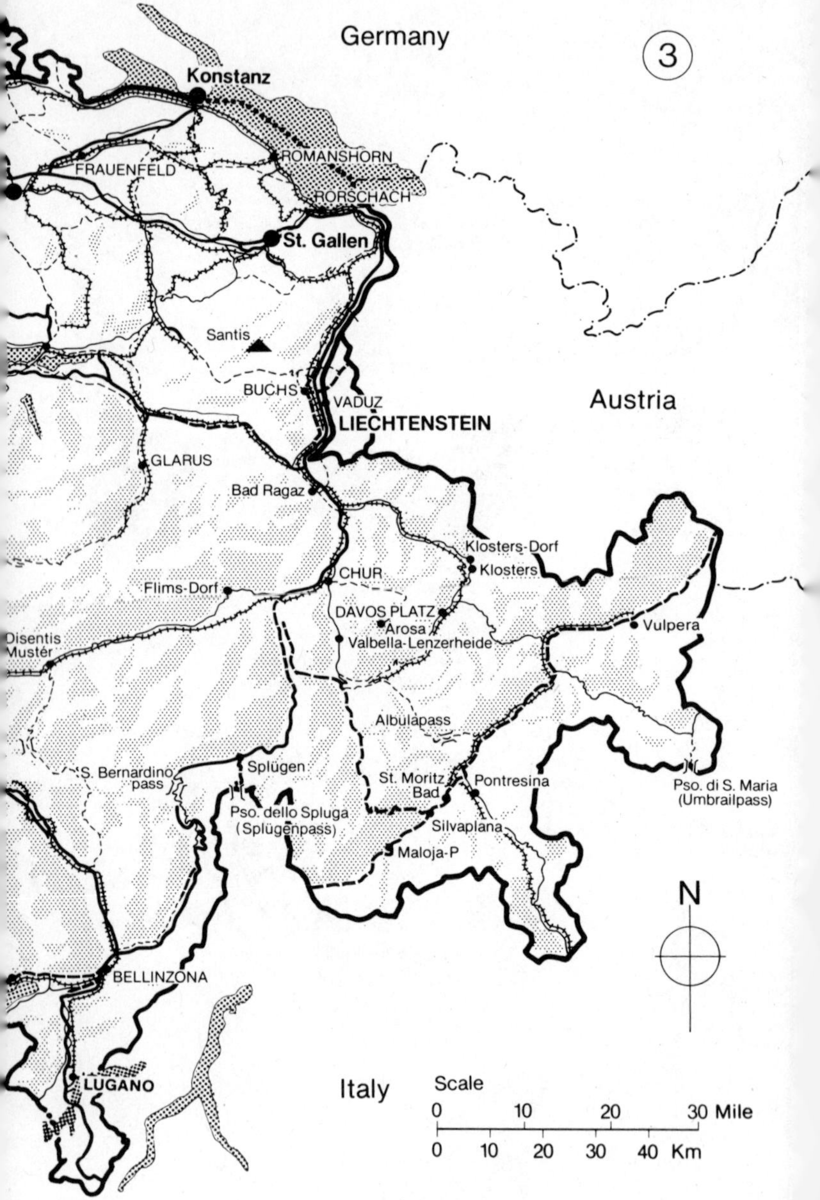

Germany
3
Konstanz
ROMANSHORN
FRAUENFELD
RORSCHACH
St. Gallen
Santis
BUCHS
VADUZ
LIECHTENSTEIN
Austria
GLARUS
Bad Ragaz
Klosters-Dorf
Klosters
CHUR
Flims-Dorf
DAVOS PLATZ
Arosa
Valbella-Lenzerheide
Vulpera
Disentis
Mustér
Albulapass
Splügen
S. Bernardino pass
St. Moritz Bad
Pontresina
Pso. di S. Maria
(Umbrailpass)
Pso. dello Spluga
(Splügenpass)
Silvaplana
Maloja-P
N
BELLINZONA
LUGANO
Italy
Scale
0
10
20
30 Mile
0
10
20
30
40 Km

FACTS AT YOUR FINGERTIPS

Planning Your Trip

NATIONAL TOURIST OFFICE. The major source of information for anyone planning a trip to Switzerland is the Swiss National Tourist Office, an organization of near legendary efficiency. They can supply information on all aspects of travel to and around Switzerland, from which type of vacation is best suited to your needs and purse, to the best and most economical ways of getting there. They produce copious amounts of information, much of it free and all of it useful.

Their addresses are:

In the U.S.: 608 Fifth Ave., New York, NY 10020 (212–757–5944); 250 Stockton St., San Francisco, CA 94108 (415–362–2260).

In Canada: Commerce Court West, PO Box 215, Toronto, Ontario M5L 1E8 (416–868–0584).

In the U.K.: Swiss Center, New Coventry St., London W.1 (01–734 1921).

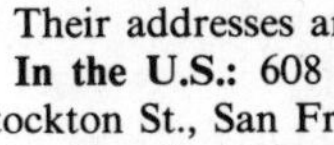

TOURS. The range of tours to Switzerland is immense, from fully escorted bus tours of almost the whole country—or combined with neighboring countries as well—to self-drive vacations around just one small corner. Gourmet, art, architecture, music, antiques, gardens, crafts, history, staying in a castle or chalet, plus a wide range of sports (though naturally with the emphasis on winter sports) are all catered for, and at prices to suit all pocket books.

Full details of all tour operators are available from the Swiss National Tourist Office and your travel agent, but we give a summary below of some of the more typical and a partial list of some of the better-known tour operators. All details are for 1987, so check for up-to-the-minute information.

Tours From the U.S.

Dial Switzerland Instant Reservations, one of the leading Swiss tour operators, offers a wide range of escorted and self-conducted tours, including the "Glacier Express Package," a self-conducted train tour through Zürich, St. Moritz, Geneva, and Zermatt. Included are all hotel bookings, a Swiss Holiday Card good for unlimited train, postal bus and lake steamer travel, lunches, and seat reservations on the "Glacier Express." Five- and nine-day packages are available; prices start at $456 (five days) and $750 (nine days). Also available from Dial Switzerland are ski tours (winter and summer), spa tours, and Rhine River Rafting, a two to three hour raft down the Rhine that is part of a visit to Laax, in Eastern Switzerland.

"Swiss Alpine Resorts," from Maupintour, is a 15-day tour beginning and ending in Zürich, with 18 stops in between, including Bern, Lausanne, Grindelwald, Zermatt, St. Moritz and Luzern. Also included are a ride on the "Glacier Express" and a trip to the Matterhorn. Costs range from $2,900 to $3,000. Another 15-day tour from Maupintour is "The Alps of Europe," which begins in Geneva and passes through Northern Italy and Austria before winding up in Zürich. Cost is $3,000 to $3,200.

For those interested in a truly deluxe tour of the Alps, Hemphill Harris offers an "Alpine Interlude," 22 days through Austria, Germany, Italy, France and with nine days in St. Moritz, Zermatt, Luzern and Bern. Highlights of the Swiss period include a trip up to the Diavolezza glacier and a visit to the United Nations' headquarters in Geneva. Cost is $6,660.

Also high on the luxury scale is the "Alpine Splendor" tour offered by Cunard Lines, operator of the *QE2.* The first five of the trip's 20 days are spent sailing from New York to Southampton, England, on the last great trans-Atlantic cruise liner. From Southampton the tour goes on to visit London, Brussels, Munich, Salzburg, St. Moritz, Zermatt, Chamonix, Geneva and Paris. Return is by air from Paris. Cost is approx. $3,400.

Pan Am offers "Alpine Bouquet", 15 days in Germany, Austria and Switzerland for $1,335 to $1,495.

U.S. Tour Operators. **American Express,** 822 Lexington Ave., New York, NY 10021 (212–758–6510).

Bennett Tours, 270 Madison Ave., New York, NY 10016 (212–532–5060).

Cortell Group, 770 Lexington Ave., New York, NY 10021 (212–751–4200).

Cosmos/Globus-Gateway, 95–25 Queens Blvd., Rego Park, NY 11374 (718–268–1700).

Cunard Lines, 555 Fifth Ave., New York, NY 10017 (1–800–223–0764).

Dial Switzerland Instant Reservations, 25 West 39th St., New York, NY 10018 (1–800–223–5105; in NY, 212–719–2255).

Extra Value Travel, 437 Madison Ave., New York, NY 10022 (212–750–8800).

Hemphill Harris Travel Corp., 16000 Ventura Blvd., Encino, CA 91436 (818–906–8086).

Journeyworld International Ltd., 410 East 51st St., New York, NY 10022 (212–752–8308).

Maupintour, 1515 St. Andrews Dr., Lawrence, KS 66044 (913–843–1211).

Pan Am, Pan Am Building, New York, NY 10017 (212–687–2600).

Tours from the U.K.

The range of tours available from the U.K. is even greater. Resorts and city vacations, two- and three-center vacations, bus and rail tours, self-catering and camping, motoring and go-as-you-please, walking and mountaineering, alpine flowers and painting, ornithology, Rhine cruises, even bridge vacations are all available. An equally wide range of winter sports vacations is also on offer.

U.K. Tour Operators. **Airtour Swiss,** 157 Praed St., London W.2 (tel. 01–724 2388).

American Express Holidays, Portland House, Stag Pl., London S.W.1 (tel. 01–834 5555).

Inghams Travel, 329 Putney Bridge Rd., London S.W.15 (tel. 01–789 6555).

Ramblers Holidays, Longcroft House, Frethern Rd., Welwyn Garden City (tel. 0707–331133).

Super Swiss Holidays, 4 Mays Court, London W.C.2 (tel. 01–379 7885).

Swiss Travel Service, Bridge House, Ware, Herts. (tel. 0920–3971).

Taber Holidays, 126 Sunbridge Rd., Bradford, West Yorkshire (tel. 0274–735611).

Thomson Holidays, Greater London House, Hampstead Rd., London N.W.1 (tel. 01–387 9321).

Travel Choice, 27 High St., Benson, Oxford 0X9 6RP (tel. 0491–37607).

CLIMATE. Switzerland is almost unique among European countries in having two quite separate tourist seasons: the winter sports season, which runs from around Christmas to the middle of April, and the summer season, which runs from around the beginning of May to the end of September.

Summer in Switzerland can be delightful. The weather is generally warm and very sunny, though of course the higher you go the colder it gets, especially at night. In many of the alpine valleys, however, it is frequently very hot. Spring and fall can also both be charming, the former especially for the profusion of wild flowers in the Alps. But both can also be rather dull and wet. The Swiss winter is cold everywhere. In the low-lying areas the weather is frequently damp and overcast, while in the Alps, though there are often brilliantly clear days, it is guaranteed to be very cold and very snowy.

Summer or winter, Switzerland is prone to an Alpine wind that blows from the south and is known as the *Föhn.* It gives rise to very clear but rather oppressive weather, particularly in the valleys, that the Swiss claim causes headaches and sundry other minor but irritating complaints.

The only exception to the general weather patterns of Switzerland is the Ticino, the Italian-speaking canton in the south of the country. Here, protected by the Alps, the weather is positively Mediterranean; even in winter it is significantly warmer than elsewhere.

Daily weather reports covering about 25 resorts are displayed in all major rail stations. Otherwise, you can check up on the weather by calling 162.

Average afternoon temperatures in degrees Fahrenheit and Centigrade:

Geneva	Jan.	Feb.	Mar.	Apr.	May	June	July	Aug.	Sept.	Oct.	Nov.	Dec.
C°	4	6	11	14	19	23	25	24	21	14	8	4
F	40	43	51	58	66	73	77	76	69	58	47	40
Lugano												
C°	6	9	13	17	21	26	28	28	24	17	11	7
F	43	48	56	63	70	78	83	82	75	63	52	45
Luzern												
C°	0	3	7	12	16	20	22	21	17	11	6	2
F	32	37	45	53	61	68	71	69	63	52	43	35

SPECIAL EVENTS. Twice a year the Swiss National Tourist Office publishes a free booklet—*Events in Switzerland.* Here are some you may not want to miss:

January. Notable for two sets of celebrations—the Schlittedas of the Engadine and the Vogel Gryff festival in Basel. The first is an informal excursion on fine Sundays when unmarried boys and girls in traditional costume go on delightfully decorated sleighs from one Engadine village to another. The Basel celebration, which in English would be the Feast of the Griffin, occurs in the middle of Jan. (not always on the same date, so inquire when it is to take place) and begins with the arrival by boat of the Wild Man of the Woods, who is greeted by the Lion and the Griffin; afterwards a mummers' parade keeps the streets lively for the entire day. Wengen stages the International Lauberhorn ski races.

February. Also marked by a folk fête, the burning of Old Man Winter (the Homstrom) at Scuol, in the Lower Engadine, usually on the first Sunday of the month. Carnival is wildest at Basel, where it begins with another mummers' parade on the Monday after Ash Wednesday. Luzern celebrates the Thursday before Ash Wednesday with its parade of the Fritschi family through the streets, when oranges are distributed to children, the carnival continuing into the following week. At the same time, Schwyz has a mummers' procession of harlequins, called Blatzli. In Ticino, at Mardi Gras, is the Festa del Risotto when risotto and sausages are served in the squares. International speed skating championships at Davos; horse racing on the frozen lake at St. Mortiz.

March. The month for Geneva's auto show and the Engadine Skiing Marathon, Maloja-Zuoz. Davos stages the Parsenn Derby international downhill ski race. Easter is celebrated in a number of Catholic communities by the footwashing ceremony on Maundy Thursday, and in Fribourg the bishop, in token of humility, kisses the feet of the faithful in the cathedral. Religious processions occur on Good Friday in many southern towns. Mendrisio's is a survival of a medieval Passion Play, and occurs on both Maundy Thursday and Good Friday. Annual Locarno Concerts (through June). Swiss Industries Fair at Basel.

April. The Landsgemeinde meetings, where you can see Swiss democracy at work in its oldest and most direct form, take place in Appenzell, Hundwil or Trogen, Sarnen, Stans and elsewhere. Other events in April are the Festa delle Camelie at Locarno, and the Sechseläuten festival of Zürich, when centuries-old guilds parade, and the Böögg, a straw scarecrow representing winter, is burned at the side of the lake; the blessing of horses, donkeys and mules at Tourtemagne (Valais) on April 23; and the pilgrimage from the Centovalli across the Italian frontier to the shrine of the Madonna di Rè on the 30th.

May. May Day is celebrated with particularly colorful ceremonies at Bad Ragaz (St. Gallen), Romainmôtier (Vaud) and Juriens (Vaud). At Cartigny (Geneva) the first Sunday in May is dedicated to the festival of the Feuillu, when the children who have been crowned King and Queen of the May lead a procession from house to house, and on the same day the Landsgemeinde is held at Glarus. Ascension is celebrated elaborately at Beromünster (Luzern), when priests carrying the sacrament ride on horseback around the district blessing the crops, a ceremony dating from 1509. Corpus Christi is observed at Appenzell by strewing carpets of flowers underfoot; at Kippel (Valais) by a procession headed by the Grenadiers of God, in 19th-century uniforms; and at Bulle, Romont, Fribourg, Châtel St. Denis, Einsiedeln, and Luzern by colorful rites and pageants. Around mid-May, Neuchâtel has its Musical Spring festival, and Lausanne starts its festival of music and ballet. Golden Rose Television Festival at Montreux.

June. Geneva makes a considerable to-do about the rose, exhibit 100,000 of them, and accompanying Rose Week with concerts, shows, amusements. If you want to see cows fight, this is the month when pitted against each other in the lower Valais. It's a month full of mu... Lausanne has its International Festival Weeks of music and ballet; Zürich, its International June Festival (music, opera, drama, etc.); Bern holds an Art Festival. If you want to look down at it all, go to Mürren for the International High Alpine Ballooning Weeks.

July. Weggis (near Luzern) has its Rose Festival, and this is the month to see crossbow shooting in the Emmental, and the famous William Tell play which starts at Interlaken and goes on through August. For those who can't get enough skiing in the winter there's the giant slalom on the Diablerets glacier and the summer ski race on Jungfraujoch. Montreux holds its International Jazz Festival.

August. The Geneva festival with a battle of flowers and much jollification takes place now. As does Luzern's music festival and the film festival at Locarno. Folklore is in full swing. Swiss wrestling in the Emmental and elsewhere, folkfests at Interlaken, the National Horse Fair with costumed riders on the strong Jura horses at Saignelégier, and the Menuhin festival at Gstaad. August 1 is the Swiss national day, with celebrations and lots of fireworks all over the country, but shops and offices mostly remain open.

September. Lausanne stages its big industrial and agricultural fair, the Comptoir Suisse, and the Knabenschiessen or boys' shooting contest, is held at Zürich. Einsiedeln has the Engelweihe, a religious festival marked by spectacular torchlight processions. Montreux and Ascona both have important music festivals.

October. There are vintage festivals everywhere, especially Lugano, Neuchâtel, and Morges. This month there are also Geneva's garden show and the picturesque fair of La Chaux-de-Fonds, the Braderie, a tremendous flea market without fleas, and the great Olma agricultural and dairy fair at St. Gallen. At Lausanne there's the Italian Opera Festival.

November. A month of open-air markets, dancing and kermesses, the most quaint being the Zibelemärit (Onion Market) of Bern.

December. The Spengler ice hockey tournament at Davos is one of the year's most notable sports events. Christmas merriment begins on St. Nicholas' Day, Dec. 6, with particularly colorful practices in the Goms Valley (Valais), Kaltbrunn (St. Gallen), Küssnacht and Arth, goes on through the riotous Escalade festival at Geneva on the 11th and 12th; and ends, after Christmas itself, with the noisy masquerades of St. Sylvester (New Year's Eve).

National Holidays 1988. January 1; April 1; April 4; May 12; May 23; Dec. 26. A number of cantons also observe January 2, May 1 and August 1.

SWITZERLAND

WHAT TO PACK. Travel light. Airline baggage allowances are based on size rather than weight. Outside first class, you may take free two pieces of baggage, provided that the sum of their dimensions—height plus length plus width—is not over 106 inches, and neither one by itself is over 62 inches. For first class the allowance is two pieces up to 62 inches each, total 124 inches. The penalties for oversize are severe. In any case, traveling light simplifies going through customs, makes registering and checking baggage unnecessary, lets you take narrow-gauge mountain trains with room for hand baggage only, and is a lifesaver if you go to small places where there are no porters. The principle is not to take more than you can carry easily yourself (unless you travel by car).

Clothes. Except at the most chic of international resorts you won't need formal evening dress. Nonetheless, women visitors staying at first-class and better medium-grade hotels will be glad to have something smart, but lightweight, for the evening, and men, a lounge suit. That said, elsewhere and on other occasions Switzerland is a country where you can get along most of the year on sports clothes, shifting with the seasons from the summer to the winter variety (and of the latter, in particular, you'll find a tempting selection in Swiss shops, though they are not cheap). In the summer, don't forget a sweater or two; high up in the mountains it grows chilly even on August evenings. Also something to drape over your bathing suit to protect yourself from the sun is advisable if you burn easily; there are a couple of thousand feet less of atmosphere than at sea level to screen you from the sun's rays.

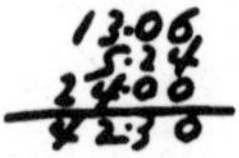

COSTS IN SWITZERLAND. Switzerland has an air of expensive plush and ingrained affluence that tends to discourage many potential vacationers. But the fact of the matter is that, while the country does have an admirably high standard of living, it is not expensive to visit. The reason for this apparently paradoxical state of affairs lies largely in the positively legendary efficiency of the Swiss. While much of the world has been grappling with the many-headed monsters of inflation, unemployment and recession, Switzerland has continued largely undisturbed on her quiet course of economic expansion and prosperity.

But while prices have remained so stable in comparison to those in the bulk of other western countries, services—what you actually *get* for your money that is—have emphatically not declined. The hotels are still as comfortable and as clean, the restaurants as excellent and welcoming, the trains as punctual and fast and, perhaps most important of all, the people as hospitable and courteous.

Of course you can still go to Switzerland and live as luxuriously and expensively as anywhere in the world—and where better to do so than in Switzerland?—but you can also have a splendid and delightful holiday, in either the summer or the winter, without sending your bank manager into paroxysms of rage or committing yourself to the poorhouse for the rest of your natural span.

Nonetheless, there are still some points to bear in mind if you want to keep costs down. Stay away from the really smart winter sports resorts such as St. Moritz, Davos, Arosa or Zermatt during the height of the winter season. These places are still genuinely expensive and prices, particularly for hotels and restaurants, can be very high. Similarly, the major cities, especially Zürich and Geneva, are significantly more expensive than most other areas of the country. So investigate some of the quieter and less well-known areas such as St. Gallen in the northeast or the Jura in the northwest where, incidentally, the skiing can be pretty good. Make a point of avoiding the more obviously expensive luxuries;

whiskey and other imported spirits are expensive, as are taxis and the more fashionable restaurants. And try to take advantage of the many excellent special deals offered by the Swiss National Tourist Office, not least the now-famed Swiss Holiday Rail Card which, for an extremely modest outlay, offers unlimited travel by rail and postal bus, as well as reductions on many lake steamers and cable cars. You really don't need to do a lot of traveling to make significant savings.

TAKING MONEY ABROAD. Traveler's checks are still the standard and best way to safeguard your travel funds; and you will usually get a better exchange rate in Switzerland for traveler's checks than for cash. In the U.S., many of the larger banks issue their own traveler's checks—just about as universally recognized as those of American Express, Cook and Barclays—as well as those of one or more of the other firms mentioned. In most instances there is a 1% charge for the checks; there is no fee for Barclays' checks. Some banks also issue them free if you are a regular customer. The best-known British checks are Cook's and those of Barclays, Lloyds, Midland and National Westminster banks. It is also always a good idea to have some local currency upon arrival for the airport bus, taxis, tips and so on. Some banks will provide this service; alternatively, contact Deak-Perera, 630 Fifth Ave., New York, NY 10111 (212–757–0100, call for additional locations). But try to get bills in smaller denominations—it is embarrassing to have local currency which you can't use.

Britons holding a Uniform Eurocheque card and check book—apply for them at your bank—can cash checks for up to £100 a day at banks participating in the scheme *and* write checks for goods and services (hotels, restaurants, shops, etc.) again for up to £100.

Credit Cards. All the major credit cards are generally, though by no means universally, accepted throughout Switzerland. In our hotel and restaurant recommendations we list which of the major cards—American Express, Diner's Club, MasterCard (incorporating Access and EuroCard), and Visa—are accepted by each establishment. But always be sure to check before reserving your room or ordering a meal that your particular piece of plastic is accepted. As a general rule, Visa is probably the most widely accepted, while practically all larger and more expensive establishments will take American Express. But make a point of checking.

For details of Swiss currency and changing money, see *Staying in Switzerland.*

PASSPORTS. Americans. All U.S. citizens require a passport for entry into Switzerland. Visas are not required. In the U.S., apply in person at U.S. Passport Agency Offices, local county courthouses or selected Post Offices. If you have a passport not more than eight years old you may apply by mail. Otherwise you will need:

—proof of citizenship, such as a birth certificate.

—two identical photographs, two inches square, in either black and white or color, on nonglossy paper and taken within the past six months;

—$35 for the passport itself plus a $7 processing fee if you are applying in person (no processing fee when applying by mail) for those 18 years and older, or, if you are under 18, $20 for the passport plus a $7 processing fee if you are applying in person (again, no extra fee when applying by mail);

—proof of identity such as a driver's license, previous passport, any governmental ID card, that includes a photo and signature.

Adult passports are valid for 10 years, others for five years; they are not renewable. Allow four to six weeks for your application to be processed, but in an emergency, Passport Agency offices can have a passport readied within 24–48 hours, and even the postal authorities can indicate "Rush" when necessary.

If you expect to travel extensively, request a 48- or 96-page passport rather than the usual 24-page one. There is no extra charge. When you receive your passport, write down its number, date and place of issue separately. If it is later lost or stolen, notify either the nearest American Consul or the Passport Office, Department of State, 1425 K St. NW, Washington, DC 20524, as well as the local police.

Canadians. Canadian citizens should apply in person to regional passport offices, post offices or by mail to Bureau of Passports, Complexe Guy Favreau, 200 Dorchester West, Montreal, P.Q. H2Z 1X4 (514–283–2152). A $21 fee, two photographs and evidence of citizenship are required. Canadian passports are valid for five years and are non-renewable.

Britons. Apply for passports on special forms obtainable from your travel agency or from the main post office in your town. The application should be sent to the Passport Office in your area (as indicated on the guidance form) or taken personally to your nearest main post office. It is advisable to apply for your passport four to five weeks before it is required, although in some cases it will be issued sooner. The regional Passport Offices are located in London, Liverpool, Peterborough, Glasgow and Newport. The application must be countersigned by your bank manager, or by a solicitor, barrister, doctor, clergyman or Justice of the Peace who knows you personally. You will need two photos. The fee is £15. A larger, 94-page passport can be obtained for an extra charge.

HEALTH AND INSURANCE. There is no free medical treatment in either Switzerland or Liechtenstein, and charges are high. For a clinic consultation expect to pay around Fr. 50, for a doctor's visit at least twice as much. And if you wind up in hospital, you can conservatively expect to pay approximately the same as at the most expensive deluxe hotel in the country. Medical expenses insurance is therefore pretty much essential for anyone planning a trip to Switzerland. If you are going on a winter sports holiday, it is vital.

The first thing to do when considering your insurance needs for an upcoming trip is to look at the coverage you've already got. Most major insurers (Blue Cross/Blue Shield, Metropolitan Life, etc.) treat sickness, injury and death abroad no differently than they treat them at home. If, however, you find that your existing insurance comes up short in some significant way (most do not cover the costs of emergency evacuation, for example); or if you would like help finding medical aid abroad, as well as paying for it; or if you would like coverage against those most vexing travel bedevilments—baggage loss and cancellation of your trip—then you may want to consider buying travel insurance.

Your travel agent will be a good source of information. She or he should have an idea of the insurance demands of different destinations; moreover, several of the traveler's insurance companies retail exclusively through travel agents. The American Society of Travel Agents endorses the "Travel Guard" plan, issued by The Insurance Company of North America. Travel Guard offers an insurance package that includes coverage for sickness, injury or death, lost baggage, and interruption or cancellation of your trip. Lost baggage coverage will also cover unauthorized use of your credit cards, while trip cancellation or interruption coverage will reimburse you for additional costs incurred due to a sudden halt (or failed start) to your trip. Cost depends on the plan chosen (there are four) and the length of your stay. A single person can get a week's coverage for $19; a family of four will pay $80 for the same length of time. For more information, talk to your travel agent, or Travel Guard, 1100 Center Point Dr., Stevens Point, WI 54481 (1–800–826–1300).

The Travelers Companies has a "Travel Insurance Pak," also sold through travel agents. It is broken down into three parts: Travel Accident Coverage (sickness, injury, or death); Baggage Loss; and Trip Cancellation. Any one of the three parts can be bought separately. Cost of the Accident and Baggage loss coverage depends on the amount of coverage desired and the length of your stay. Two weeks of accident coverage can cost approximately $20; baggage coverage for the same length of time costs $30. The cost of Trip Cancellation coverage depends on the cost of your travel; the rate is $5.50 per $100 of travel expenses. Again, your travel agent should have full details, or you can get in touch with the Travelers Companies, Ticket and Travel, One Tower Square, Hartford, CT 06183 (1–800–243–3174).

If an accident occurs, paying for medical care may be a less urgent problem than finding it. Several companies offer emergency medical assistance along with insurance. Access America offers travel insurance and the assistance of a 24-hour hotline in Washington, DC, that can direct distressed travelers to a nearby source of aid. They maintain contact with a worldwide network of doctors, hospitals and pharmacies, offer medical evacuation services (a particular problem if you're hurt in an out-of-the-way spot), on-site cash provision services (if it's needed to pay for medical care), legal assistance, and help with lost documents and ticket replacement. Access America offers its services through travel agents and Triple A. Cost ranges from $5–10 per day. For more information, Access America, 600 Third Ave., Box 807, New York, NY 10163 (1–800–851–2800).

Other organizations that offer similar assistance are:

Travel Assistance International, the American arm of Europ Assistance, offers comprehensive medical and personal emergency services. Costs range from $35 for a single person for eight days to $220 for a family over a year. Europ Assistance Worldwide Services, Inc., 1333 F St. N.W., Washington, DC 20004 (1–800–821–2828).

Carefree Travel Insurance, c/o ARM Coverage, Inc., 120 Mineola Blvd., Box 310, Mineola, NY 11510 (516–294–0220), offers insurance, legal and financial assistance, and medical evacuation through Inter.Claim.

International SOS Assistance, Inc., Box 11568, Philadelphia, PA 19116 (1–800–523–8930) charges from $15 a person for seven days to $195 for a year.

IAMAT (International Association for Medical Assistance to Travelers), 417 Center St., Lewiston, NY 14092 (716–754–4883); 188 Nicklin Rd., Guelph, Ontario N1H 7L5 (519–836–0102).

Note. Travelers to Switzerland interested in winter sports should take an especially close look at their policies. Skiing is not covered by most non-travel policies (though Access America and Travel Guard do cover it), and mountain climbing is covered by almost no policies at all. *Be sure to check before you leave.*

STUDENT AND YOUTH TRAVEL. Switzerland is particularly well attuned to the needs of young travelers, especially those who would like the chance to study there. Every student traveler should acquire an International Student Identity Card, which will insure that she or he can take advantage of the available half-price travel tickets, lodging discounts, and the like. It costs $10, and is available from the Council on International Educational Exchange (C.I.E.E.), 205 E. 42nd St., New York, NY 10017 (212–661–1414); or 312 Sutter St., San Francisco, CA 94108 (415–421–3473). In Canada the card is available from the Association of Student Councils, 187 College St., Toronto, Ont. M5T 1P7 (416–979–2406). CIEE also sponsors work exchange programs, volunteer services programs (through which young people receive room and board in exchange for community service-type work abroad), operates study centers abroad, and much more. Its subsidiary, Council Travel Services, operates an international network of travel agencies (21 in the U.S.) oriented toward student travel. They also publish the *Whole World Handbook* ($7.95 plus $1.00 postage), a listing of work and study opportunities. A complete description of their offerings is given in their *Student Travel Catalogue* ($1.00).

American Youth Hostels (A.Y.H.) is a similarly useful resource for student travelers, though its membership is by no means limited to them. Membership in A.Y.H. opens the doors to more than 5,000 hostels around the world, where you can usually stay for $4–10 per night. Membership costs $10 for those under 17 or over 60, and $20 for those in between. A.Y.H. also distributes the two-volume *International Youth Hostel Handbook* ($6.95 per volume), and has recently begun to organize escorted tours for its members. For further information on youth hostels in Switzerland, see *Youth Hostels* on page 18.

Other helpful organizations are the Institute of International Education (809 United Nations Plaza, New York, NY 10017; 212–883–8200) which is primarily concerned with study abroad, and the Educational Travel Center (438 North Frances, Madison, WI 53703; 608–256–5551).

College students should consider talking to their school's office of study abroad. A wide variety of programs exist that give college credit for foreign study. High school students interested in similar travel should get in touch with A.F.S. International (313 East 43rd St., New York, NY 10017; 212–949–4242). A.F.S. arranges international exchanges, giving high school students the opportunity to spend a summer, or full school year, abroad.

Within Switzerland, a number of organizations cater for student travelers. Foremost among them is the Swiss Student Travel Service (S.S.R.), Bäckerstr. 52, 8004 Zürich (tel. 01–242 3000). They organize a number of excellent-value tours to Switzerland and can also provide inexpensive accommodations in seven resort areas. The Experiment in International Living, Seestr. 167, 8800 Thalwil, can help find families for young people to stay with.

Private schools in Switzerland are numerous. For information on schools in French-speaking areas, write Fédération Suisse des Ecoles Privées, 40 rue des Vollandes, 1211 Geneva. For information on schools in German- and Italian-speaking areas, write Verband Schweizerischer Privatschulen, Postfach 3367, 3000 Bern 7.

The Swiss National Tourist Office can also provide much useful information. Their *Holidays and Language Courses* booklet details summer schools offering a wide variety of courses, from computing to cooking, as well as listing several international youth camps in the country offering stays for eight to 18 year-olds. Other Swiss National Tourist Office publications include *Holidays in Switzerland for Young People, Inexpensive Accommodations in Switzerland* and *Student Lodgings in Switzerland.*

Other specialists in student and youth travel are:

Arista Student Travel Assoc., 1 Rockefeller Plaza, New York, NY 10020 (212–541–9190).

Bailey Travel Service Inc., 123 East Market St., York, PA 17401 (717–854–5511).

Harwood Tours & Travel Inc., 2428 Guadalupe, Austin, TX 78705 (512–478–9343).

Intercollegiate Holidays Inc., 501 Madison Ave., New York, NY 10022 (212–355–4705).

Osborne Travel Service Inc., 3379 Peachtree Rd., N.E. Atlanta, GA 30326 (404–261–1600).

HINTS FOR HANDICAPPED TRAVELERS. Facilities in Switzerland for handicapped visitors are above average in comparison to many other European countries, if still variable (though where are they not?). The two major sources of information within Switzerland are the Schweizerische Arbeitsgemeinschaft für Körperbehinderte (S.A.K.), c/o Pro Infirmis, Postfach 129, 8032 Zürich; and the Schweizerischer Invalidenverband, Frohburgstr. 4, 4600 Olten 1. The former publishes various guides for the handicapped listing suitable accommodations, restaurants and excursions; the latter produces a hotel guide for the handicapped. Similarly, the Swiss National Tourist Office's annually revised *Swiss Hotel Guide* details all hotels with facilities for the handicapped.

Otherwise, major sources of information are: *Access to the World: A Travel Guide for the Handicapped,* by Louise Weiss, an outstanding book covering all aspects of travel for anyone with health or medical problems; it features extensive listings and suggestions on everything from availability of special diets to wheelchair accessibility. Order from Facts On File, 460 Park Ave. South, New York, NY 10003. The Moss Rehabilitation Hospital, 12th St. and Tabor Rd., Philadelphia, PA 19141, gives information on facilities for the handicapped in many countries and also provides toll-free numbers of airlines with special lines for the hearing impaired; they can also provide listings of tour operators who arrange vacations for the handicapped. But for a complete list of tour operators, write to the Society for the Advancement of Travel for the Handicapped, 26 Court St., Brooklyn, NY 11242.

In the U.K., contact Mobility International, 43 Dorset St., London W.1; the National Society for Mentally Handicapped Children, 117 Golden Lane, London E.C.1; the Across Trust, Crown House, Morden, Surrey (they have an amazing series of "Jumbulances," huge articulated ambulances, staffed by volunteer doctors and nurses, that can whisk even the most seriously handicapped across Europe in comfort and safety). But the main source in Britain for all advice on handicapped travel is the Royal Association for Disability and Rehabilitation (R.A.D.A.R.), 25 Mortimer St., London W.1.

LANGUAGE. Language in Switzerland is a complicated matter. Yet as ever the Swiss contrive to make it easy for the tourist. There are four official languages: German (or more properly Schwyzerdütsch, the Swiss variant of German, though high German is also spoken), French, Italian and Romansch. This last is spoken only in Graubünden in the southeastern corner of the country, and though a number of groups are active in promoting its use it is not likely to be encountered by many visitors. It is, in truth, a dying language artificially preserved. Italian is spoken only in the Ticino, the canton to the south of the Alps, while French is spoken only in the more westerly parts of the country, in those areas around Lac Léman and in the cantons of Fribourg, Jura, Neuchâtel and Vaud. But the large majority of the population (74%) speak Schwyzerdütsch. Notices in all public places appear in French, German and Italian.

But if anyone feels alarmed at the prospect of having to cope with not one but three foreign tongues simultaneously they need not worry. First, German is very much the predominant language (only 20% of the population speak French and only 4% speak Italian). Secondly, the divisions between the various language areas are distinct and it is most unusual to encounter more than one language simultaneously. But, and more to the point, English, the lingua franca of the modern world, is spoken widely. All tourist offices will have at least one person who speaks English (probably more), and the same goes for hotels, restaurants, airlines and rail road personnel. But if you can master a few phrases your efforts will be warmly appreciated by the Swiss.

TIME. Switzerland is six hours ahead of Eastern Standard and one hour ahead of Greenwich Mean Time.

Getting to Switzerland

FROM THE U.S. By Air. Four airlines provide direct service from the U.S. to Switzerland: Swissair, Pan Am, American Airlines and TWA. Swissair departs from New York, Boston, Atlanta and Chicago; Pan Am and TWA from New York only; American Airlines fly from Chicago. Geneva and Zürich are the favored destinations. One can, of course, also catch a flight to another major European city, and there pick up a flight on most of the major European carriers to Switzerland.

Note that airlines have begun to beef up security on international flights considerably. That translates into a substantially longer time getting on and off a plane. Be sure to leave yourself plenty of time at the airport arriving and departing. Note that many airlines now levy a security charge of $25–35.

Pan Am, Pan Am Bldg., New York, NY 10017 (212–687–2600).
Swissair, 608 Fifth Ave., New York, NY 10020 (718–995–8400).
TWA, 605 Third Ave., New York, NY 10016 (212–290–2141).

Fares. The ever-changing puzzle of international air fares is best put together with the help of a travel agent, who can unearth the most recent bargain, and book your flight for you, at no charge. There are, however, a few things about fares you should know before setting out. For instance, you should shop around. Pan Am, TWA and American Airlines are challenging the virtual monopoly of Swissair who are now working closely with Delta Airlines in response, opening up plenty of new opportunities for travelers. Remember too that Switzerland is a gateway to the rest of Europe, so that even if you are planning a trip somewhere else, it may be worth a visit here before moving on.

Tickets generally come in four categories. In descending order of expense these are: First Class; Business; Economy; and APEX. The first three are usually sold without restrictions. They can be bought at any time, used at any time, and cancelled or changed at any time. They are distinguished from one another by where they seat you on the plane, and what sort of perquisites are attached to your travel (e.g., free champagne, transportation to and from the airport, etc.).

They are also all quite expensive compared to the fourth, APEX. APEX tickets are always round trip, seat the passenger in the economy section, and are subject to several conditions. They must be bought well in advance of the flight (7–21 days), they limit the times and days one can fly; and they restrict the length of your travel; there is usually a minimum stay of seven days, and a maximum of three months, attached. Nonetheless they are inexpensive compared to the other tickets and good value. In mid-1987, a round trip First Class ticket New York–Zürich cost $3,228; an Economy ticket, $1,506; and an APEX ticket, $776–876.

For even greater savings, tickets on charter flights are sometimes available. Check with your travel agent. There are also a number of ticket brokers who sell seats on flights ordered by tour operators that are not completely booked. Note that these tickets are usually available only on very short notice. Among the brokers are: *Stand-Buys Ltd.,* 311 West Superior, Ste. 414, Chicago, IL 60610 (312–943–5737); *Moments Notice,* 40 East 49th St., New York, NY 10017 (212–486–0503); *Discount Travel Intl.,* 114 Forest Ave., Narberth, PA 19072 (215–668–2182); and *Worldwide Discount Travel Club,* 1674 Meridian Ave., Miami Beach, FL 33139 (305–534–2082).

FROM THE U.K. By Air. Switzerland is easily accessible by air from all parts of Britain, and services are improving all the time. From London (Heathrow) to Zürich there are a minimum of seven non-stop flights daily, operated by Swissair/British Airways. The flying time is around one hour 35 minutes. From London (Gatwick) services are operated by Dan Air. Swissair/British Airways also operate direct flights to Zürich from Birmingham and Manchester.

Services to Geneva have greatly improved. There are now at least six non-stop flights daily by British Airways/Swissair from London (Heathrow). The flying time is one hour 40 minutes. From London (Gatwick) there are direct flights by British Caledonian and Dan Air.

Basel airport (Basel/Mulhouse) is just across the French border at St. Louis and has a service of three non-stop flights from London (Heathrow) on weekdays. These are run by British Airways/Swissair. The federal capital, Bern, has flights on several days a week by Dan Air from Aberdeen and Newcastle, both of which can be boarded at London (Gatwick) en route. If you want to go to Lugano there no direct services but there are frequent connecting flights from Zürich operated by Crossair. Both Zürich and Geneva airports are now directly linked to the Swiss rail network, with through express trains to all parts of the country. Bags can be checked through to your final destination using the Welcome Luggage system—no toting bags! Ask for details at any SNTO.

Fares. Fares to Switzerland from London are excellent value for money—especially at the tourist end of the market. For 1988 a full fare scheduled return to Geneva or Zürich will work out at around £110. Fares to Bern and Basel are slightly higher. Euro-budget tickets are valid for one year, no break of journey is allowed and they must be paid for at the time of reservation and cannot subsequently be altered. Slightly cheaper are Excursion return tickets, valid for up to one month. A Saturday night must be included in the stay and again no break of journey is allowed. Slightly cheaper still is the PEX fare—for which the number of seats available is restricted. It has the same general conditions as the Excursion ticket except that it is valid for three months. The cheapest fare is the APEX return; this is also valid for three months and has the same conditions as the others but must be booked one month before departure. It is also possible to obtain discounted tickets for scheduled flights from many travel agents or tour operators; savings can be considerable and it pays to shop around. Also, especially in winter, tour operators offering skiing package holidays often have spare seats on their charter flights which can be obtained very cheaply. For these scan the Classified Ads in newspapers like *The Times, The Sunday Times, The Standard* and *The Mail on Sunday.* But be sure to check all the costs quoted and ask about extras. Not all are as cheap as they seem at first sight.

FROM THE U.K. By Train. Access to Switzerland by rail is excellent, and with recent improvements in the European rail system journey times have been much reduced. From Britain, you have a choice of several routes depending on which part of Switzerland you are visiting, what you want to see and do on the way and, of course, on your budget.

The classic route to northern Switzerland is from London (Liverpool Street) to Basel, sailing from Harwich to the Hook of Holland and then via Cologne to Basel and Zürich. Unfortunately the TEE "Rheingold" no longer runs so the route has lost much of its magic. However, the journey can be made using the new air-conditioned EuroCity expresses. Board the evening boat train from Liverpool Street station to Harwich and sail overnight to the Hook of Holland which is reached in the early morning. Then catch the Eurocity "Loreley" which runs through to Basel and on to Lugano and Chiasso via Luzern. This train takes the scenic route along the banks of the Rhine and has full restaurant facilities. Advance reservation is obligatory.

An alternative route to the above is from London to Basel via Ostend, Brussels, Luxembourg and Strasbourg. The channel crossing from Dover to Ostend is on the speedy Jetfoil which allows you to complete the entire journey in one day, leaving London (Victoria) at 8:15 in the morning and arriving in Basel at 10:43 P.M. The journey from Ostend is in two stages, first to Brussels (Midi Station), then change to the EuroCity train "Edelweiss" for the run to Basel. The Edelweiss leaves at 4:09 P.M. giving you about 2 hours in Brussels. There is a supplement for travel on the Jetfoil and it is advisable to reserve seats for the whole trip in advance. The route can also be covered by using the conventional ferry service from Dover to Ostend, but the extra time taken for the Channel crossing means that the journey cannot be completed in one day.

The most rapid route from London to Switzerland is via Paris. The journey to Geneva, Lausanne and Bern can be completed comfortably in one day. Services are now so fast that it is possible to leave London (Victoria) at 10 in the morning and be in Geneva/Lausanne before 10 P.M. the same evening. The route is best considered in two sections: from London to Paris; and from Paris to Switzerland.

1. From London to Paris. There is a choice of several routes and combinations of transport. The quickest is by the Citylink rail–hovercraft–rail service operated by Hoverspeed from London (Victoria) to the Gare du Nord in Paris. The first stage of the journey is by train to Dover Priory Station where you transfer to the Hoverport for the cross-Channel "flight" to Boulogne. The hovercraft terminal there has its own railway station and it is a simple matter to change to the French Turbotrain for the fast run to Paris. By this route and combination of transport the journey to Paris takes under five and a half hours.

There are several other options open for the run to Paris, although most do not arrive there in time to catch trains which will get you to Switzerland the same evening. For example, Hoverspeed operate a coach and hovercraft service from London to Paris, the City Sprint service. Alternatively, you can go by train from London (Victoria) to Dover Western Docks, then by Sealink ferry to Calais (Gare Maritime) and thence by train to Paris (Gare du Nord). For travelers with heavy luggage this is the best all year round route. During the summer only there is a service from Calais to Venice; accordingly, there is no need to change trains and stations in Paris. On its way through Switzerland this useful train stops at Vallorbe, Lausanne, Montreux and Brig. However, during the winter the train runs in two halves, first from Calais to Paris (Gare du Nord) and then from the Gare de Lyon, making it necessary to transfer between stations at Paris. Another London to Paris possibility is from London (Victoria) to Folkestone Harbor, then by British Ferries to Boulogne (Gare Maritime) and on to the Gare du Nord. This is a useful summer-only route and takes around eight and a half hours to Paris.

Finally, for the traveler looking for something different. Travel in ritzy style by taking the recently resurrected and very luxurious "Venice–Simplon–Orient Express" from London, either to Paris or right through to Zürich. The train operates twice a week during the summer and gets you to Zürich in the early morning the day after leaving London. For this you must book well in advance. Details from: Orient Express, Suite 1235, One World Trade Center, New York, NY 10048 (800–223–1588, in NY 212–938–6830), or Sea Containers House, 20 Upper Ground, London S.E.1.

2. From Paris to Switzerland. The journey from Paris to the Swiss cities of Geneva, Lausanne and Bern has been revolutionized by the introduction of the magnificent *Train à Grande Vitesse* (TGV) and the construction of a new line exclusively for its use. As a result, journey times have been dramatically reduced. From Paris (Gare de Lyon) there are five TGVs a day to Geneva and four to Lausanne; traveling time in both cases is now a mere three and a half hours. In addition, a new through TGV service runs daily to Neuchâtel and Bern as part of the EuroCity network. The evening departure from Paris at 6.06 P.M., the "Champs-Elysées", reaches Bern a little after 10.30 P.M. A great improvement! Connections to all other major Swiss cities are excellent and frequent. For details of these services contact either the Swiss National Tourist Office or French Railways. Note that it is necessary to book in advance for all TGVs and that a supplement is payable on most services. Further details are available in the useful *Traveler's Guide to TGV* produced by French Railways.

Fares. These vary widely depending on your route, the length of the channel crossing and type of accommodations, on ship or train, if traveling overnight. Fares for 1988 were not available at the time of writing, but every year the Swiss National Tourist Office publishes a full list—Fares list A—available free. They will also give a quotation for the complete through fare to any destination. If you have a Swiss Holiday Card (details of which are given in *Getting Around Switzerland,* page 22) you need only buy a ticket to the Swiss Frontier. Return tickets are valid for two months. Young people (under 26) should investigate the reduced rail fares offered by Transalpino Travel. They are able to offer a choice of routings—even with their discount fares breaks of journey are allowed. Transalpino Travel, 71 Buckingham Palace Rd, S.W.1 (tel. 01–834 9056/6283).

FROM THE U.K. By Car. There are many drive-on, drive-off car ferry services across the Channel, but only a few are suitable as a means of getting to Switzerland. The situation is complicated by the different pricing systems operated by ferry companies and the many off-peak fares, and by the fact that the French charge tolls on some of their motorways; these add up, particularly if you drive long distances. To avoid the tolls, many people take a northerly route through Belgium or Holland and Germany where motorways are free. The crossings for this route are: Felixstowe, Dover to Zeebrugge;

Sheerness to Vlissingen; Dover to Ostend; and Ramsgate to Dunkirk. All these Continental ports have good road connections and Switzerland can be reached in one day's hard driving.

The short crossings from Dover and Folkestone to Calais and Boulogne do not give an ideal landfall in France for a fast journey to Switzerland. The first kilometers towards Paris are slow—even though the autoroute now reaches Nordausques a few kilometers from the coast. Once Paris has been reached then the *Periphérique* (ring road) around the capital has to be negotiated—not for the faint hearted! On the motorway from Paris to Switzerland and the south of France, the *Autoroute du Soleil,* tolls have to be paid. Travelers going the French route should consider using the sailings from Portsmouth to Le Havre as road connections on both sides of the Channel are excellent. To use the Swiss motorways an extra tax is payable—either in advance or at the border. 1987 price was Fr. 30. Contact the S.N.T.O. for details for 1988.

Fares. These vary considerably according to season, journey time and length of vehicle. However, the approximate cost of crossing the Channel by one of the short sea routes in high summer, with an average vehicle of 14 ft. (4.5 meters) and two adult passengers, works out at around £95 one way. But traveling off peak, i.e. early morning or late evening, or in June and September, costs can be reduced.

FROM THE U.K. By Bus. International bus services to Switzerland are virtually nonexistent. International Express member Eurolines operate a service from London to the French side of Geneva via Paris. The bus runs daily during the summer leaving London in mid-afternoon and arrives in Geneva (Annemasse) late the following morning. The round trip fare to Geneva works out at around £90. Details from International Express, The Coach Travel Centre, 13 Regent St., London SW1Y 4LR (tel. 01–439 9368). However, there are a large number of bus tour operators who run inclusive holidays from the U.K. to Swiss resorts.

CUSTOMS ON ARRIVAL. There are two levels of duty-free allowance for visitors to Switzerland. Residents of non-European countries may import: 400 cigarettes or 100 cigars or 500 grams of tobacco; plus, two liters of alcoholic beverage below 15° and one liter of alcoholic beverage in excess of 15°. Residents of European countries may import: 200 cigarettes or 50 cigars or 250 grams of tobacco; plus, two liters of alcoholic beverage below 15° and one liter of alcoholic beverage in excess of 15°. These allowances are for those aged 18 and over only.

There are no restrictions on the import or export of any currency.

Staying in Switzerland

SWISS CURRENCY. The monetary unit in Switzerland is the Swiss franc, generally written as either Fr. or Sfr. It is divided into 100 *rappen* (in French-speaking areas *centimes*). There are notes of 10, 20, 50, 100, 500, and 1,000 francs, and coins of 5, 10, 20 and 50 *rappen,* and 1, 2 and 5 francs.

The rate of exchange at the time of writing (mid-'87) was Fr. 1.45 to the U.S. dollar and Fr. 2.45 to the pound sterling. These rates will change before and during 1988.

Changing Money. You can change money at all banks in Switzerland, though note that traveler's checks generally get a better rate than cash. Banks are open Monday through Friday 8:30–4:30 or 5. In addition, there are *bureaux de change* at all the main airports and rail stations; these normally stay open much longer than regular banks, though offering rates just as good. Many hotels and even some restaurants will also change money for you, but unless you're cashing traveler's checks already in Swiss francs, likely as not you'll get a much less favorable rate of exchange.

HOTELS. Swiss hotels are the envy of hoteliers the world over, and for excellent reasons. At all price levels they are spotlessly clean, impeccably run and excellent value for money. At the top end of the scale you will find luxury and superb service unequalled almost anywhere else in the world. And at the lower end of the scale, though frills and extras are obviously fewer, you are guaranteed shelter at the very least, but are more likely to encounter both extremely hospitable service, and not inconsiderable comfort. There are not many bad hotels in Switzerland.

For anyone planning to do much traveling around in Switzerland, it is well worth while getting the official *Swiss Hotel Guide,* available free from all Swiss National Tourist Offices and most regional and local tourist offices. It lists all members of the Swiss Hotels Association—approximately 80% of the country's hotels—and gives full details of all establishments listed. For those on a budget, the Swiss National Tourist Office also publishes a guide to *Inexpensive Accommodations in Switzerland.*

All major towns and many rail stations and airports have accommodations offices. Most charge a small fee, but it is unlikely that they will not be able to find you a bed for the night even if it is only in a private house.

Prices. We have divided all the hotels in our listings into four categories: Deluxe (L), Expensive (E), Moderate (M), and Inexpensive (I). These grades are determined solely by price.

Two people in a double room can expect to pay:

Deluxe (L)	Fr. 250 and up
Expensive (E)	Fr. 180 to 320
Moderate (M)	Fr. 110 to 180
Inexpensive (I)	Fr. 70 to 110

Note that in many larger cities and towns a considerable number of Expensive hotels may cost *more* than the lowest price level we have designated for Deluxe hotels. The reason for this seeming contradiction is simple. Many of these city-center hotels, especially businessmen's hotels, though very expensive, can't in all conscience be graded Deluxe, despite their high cost. Likewise, there are a good many Deluxe hotels in less expensive areas of the country offering extremely high levels of service and comfort for less than these city-center hotels. By the same token, Deluxe hotels in the larger cities and the most fashionable resorts can easily start at much more than Fr. 250, with top prices peaking at around Fr. 500 a night for two. In all cases, however, check the price of your room *before* booking in.

Credit Cards. The initials AE, DC, MC, and V at the end of each hotel entry in our listings refer to the credit cards accepted by each establishment. They stand, respectively, for American Express, Diners Club, MasterCard (incorporating Access and EuroCard), and Visa.

Hotel Chains. Among the most delightful places to stay—and eat—in Switzerland are the aptly named Romantik Hotels and Restaurants. The Romantik group now have hotels throughout northern Europe (and even a few in the States), with a good number in Switzerland itself. All are in atmospheric and historic buildings—an essential precondition of membership—and are personally run by the owners, with the emphasis on excellent food and service. A detailed brochure listing all Romantik Hotels and Restaurants is available at $7.50 (including mailing) from Romantik Hotels Reservations, P.O. Box 1278, Woodinville, WA 98072 (206–485–6985; for reservations call 1–800–826–0015).

Among other good hotel chains in Switzerland, though less unusual, are the Ambassador Swiss Hotels, affiliated to Best Western International. They have around 100 hotels, most in the Moderate and Expensive grades. They offer hotel-to-hotel reservations, excellent-value packages and the usual range of conference facilities. In Switzerland call 031–23 44 45 for reservations. Less expensive accommodations are offered by the Check-In group, with rates averaging around Fr. 50 a night for two. Further details are available from the Swiss National Tourist Office or your travel agent.

CHALETS. There are thousands of furnished chalets or apartments of all sizes and price levels throughout Switzerland. Off season, a simple but comfortable chalet-apartment sleeping four people could be rented for about Fr. 50 per person per week. But during the high season, a deluxe one sleeping five or six costs nearly ten times as much. Many travel agents can make rental arrangements for you, often incorporating reduced-rate travel. You can get an illustrated brochure describing many hundreds of chalets and apartments from Swiss Touring Club, Wasserwerkgasse 39, 3000 Bern 13; UTO-Ring AG, Beethovenstrasse 24, 8022 Zürich; or Inter Home, Buckhauserstrasse 26, 8048 Zürich, or 383 Richmond Rd., Twickenham TW1 2EF, England. In the U.S., contact Villas International, 71 West 23 St., New York, NY 10010 (212–929–7585).

Climbers and mountain walkers can find accommodations in a series of mountain huts throughout the Alpine areas. A full list of huts is available from the Schweizer Alpen-Club (S.A.C.), Helvetiaplatz 4, 3005 Bern.

YOUTH HOSTELS. Since Switzerland is essentially a country where outdoor vacations are a special feature and facilities for youth exchange on an international scale are encouraged, it follows that it is well supplied with youth hostels, with a chain of nearly 100 spread throughout the land. Administered by the Swiss Youth Hostels (Schweizerischer Bund für Jegendherbergen, Wildhainweg 19, 3001 Bern), all are affiliated to the International Youth Hostels Association and are open to anyone holding a valid International Youth Hostel Membership Card, though priority is given to those under 25. Nonmembers can obtain cards at any Swiss Youth Hostel. Rates range from about Fr. 4 to Fr. 15 per night and sometimes include an obligatory charge for breakfast. You must have a sleeping bag to use a Youth Hostel, but most Hostels will hire them. Advance reservations are always recommended.

To join the International Youth Hostels Association, contact American Youth Hostels, P.O. Box 37613, Washington, DC 20013 or, in Canada, the Canadian Hostelling Association, 333 River Rd., Place Vanier, Tower A, Vanier City, Ottawa, Ontario K1L 8H9. In the U.K. contact YHA Services Ltd., 14 Southampton St., London W.C.2.

CAMPING. Switzerland is an ideal country for campers, with approximately 450 sites throughout the country. All are classified from one to five stars according to amenities, location, etc. Rates vary widely, but average out at around Fr. 15 per night for a family of four, plus car or camper. Lists of camp sites are available from the Federation of Swiss Camping Clubs, Habsburgerstr. 35, 6000 Luzern, or the Swiss National Tourist Office.

To stay in most European camp sites you must have an International Camping Carnet, a certificate of third party (public liability) insurance. This is available from any national camping association within Europe, or from the National Campers and Hikers Association, 4804 Transit Rd., Bldg. 2, Depew, NY 14043 (716–668–6242); in the U.K. apply to the Camping and Caravan Club Ltd., 11 Lower Grosvenor Pl., London S.W.1.

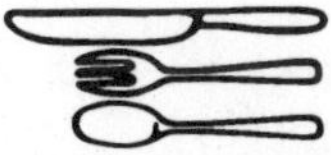

RESTAURANTS. As with hotels, so with restaurants. Standards throughout Switzerland are uniformly high. And though you can eat as expensively—and as well—here as anywhere in Europe, the country also has a wealth of reasonably priced and small eating houses serving delicious food. As a general rule, German food predominates in the German-speaking parts of the country, while in the French and Italian areas, French and Italian food respectively are the norm. But for a fuller picture of Swiss cuisine, see our *Food and Drink* chapter.

Prices. We have divided all the restaurants in our listings into three categories: Expensive (E), Moderate (M), and Inexpensive (I). These grades are determined solely by price.

Approximate prices per person, not including wine

Expensive (E)	Fr. 50 and up
Moderate (M)	Fr. 25 to 50
Inexpensive (I)	Up to Fr. 25

Note that many Swiss restaurants, especially the more expensive, offer set-price menus at lunch that work out significantly less expensive than eating *à la carte.* Likewise, a number of chain restaurants, notably the excellent Mövenpick chain, often have more than one price range, making the same restaurant Inexpensive *and* Expensive simultaneously: make sure you go to the right part of the restaurant. All restaurants, however, are obliged by law to display their menus and prices in the window. Be sure to check them before going in.

Credit Cards. The initials AE, DC, MC, and V at the end of each restaurant entry in our listings refer to the credit cards accepted by each establishment. They stand, respectively, for American Express, Diners Club, MasterCard (incorporating Access and EuroCard), and Visa.

TIPPING. There are few occasions when you will have to tip in Switzerland. By law, an automatic service charge of 15% is included in all hotel, restaurant, cafe, bar, and hairdressers' bills. Similarly, most taxis will also automatically include this charge, but check the notice in the cab: not all do. Generally, then, you need only leave a tip if you feel the service has been exceptional.

Otherwise, tip baggage porters at hotels Fr. 2 to 4; washroom and cloakroom attendants about 50 centimes or Fr. 1; and leave about Fr. 2 for your hotel maid. Station porters are rare birds, so if you find one tip him well. Baggage wagons are plentiful at airports and most train stations.

MAIL. Current mail rates for letters (all mail goes airmail) are: to the U.S. Fr. 1.70, to western Europe Fr. 0.90, rest of Europe Fr. 1.10; postcards are Fr. 1.10 to the U.S., and 80 centimes to Europe. Post offices are open from 7:30 to 12, and 1:45 to 6:30 Monday to Friday, and on Saturday from 7:30 to 11 A.M. Principal post offices in some cities close later.

You can have mail forwarded to any post office in Switzerland by marking it "poste restante" and addressing it to any town or resort with a post office (almost all of them in other words). All unclaimed mail is returned to the sender if not collected within 30 days. Bring your passport with you to claim.

TELEPHONES. The Swiss telephone system is excellent. You can direct dial most places in the world, and everywhere within Switzerland itself. There are booths with operators in attendance in all post offices and rail stations in larger towns and cities; instructions are provided in English. Dialing and area codes are listed in the front (pink) pages of telephone books. Lower rates apply between 5 and 7 P.M., after 9 P.M. and at weekends. For information and inquiries, dial 111.

Useful telephone numbers: 120—tourist news (summer only); 120—snow and avalanche reports (winter only); 144—ambulance; 160—exchange rates; 162—weather reports; 163—driving conditions; 190—international operator.

CLOSING TIMES. Usual shop hours are 8 to 12:15 and 1:30 to 6:30 Monday to Friday (4 on Saturday). In Zürich and Bern shops stay open at midday. In Geneva the larger shops stay open during lunch, but smaller ones close. Many shops throughout Switzerland close on Monday mornings. Bank hours vary slightly from place to place, but are generally 8:30 to 4:30 or 5. Business hours are 8 to 12 and 2 to 5.

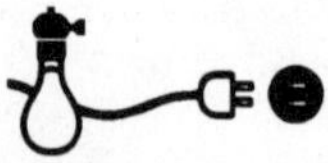

ELECTRICITY. Voltage in Switzerland is 220v. Adding to the problem for visitors from the U.S. and Canada, sockets here are also different. If you plan to use an electric hairdryer or razor, or any other item of electrical equipment in Switzerland, buy an adaptor/transformer before you leave, and make sure it is suitable for continental plugs.

NEWSSTANDS. Known as kiosks in Switzerland, newsstands can be found near rail stations, tourist attractions and busy street corners. They offer all kinds of necessary supplies, from paperbacks to Swiss chocolates. A wide variety of reading materials is generally available, with the English-language magazines and newspapers grouped together. Also usually for sale: cigarettes, candy of all kinds, tissues, envelopes and writing material, and souvenirs. Kiosks frequently sell soft drinks, ice cream and other snacks as well. Those selling postcards usually sell the necessary stamps.

Opening hours vary, but they are usually longer than shop hours and often include weekend service. Attendants, most of whom speak English, are good sources of local information and are used to dealing with travelers.

LAVATORIES. Lavatories in Switzerland, even in the simplest spots, are usually modern, and invariably clean. Look for a W.C. sign, or (in French, German and Italian speaking areas respectively) *Toilettes, Toiletten* or *Gabinetti.* Ladies: *Dames* or *Femmes; Damen* or *Frauen; Signore* or *Donne.* Gentlemen: *Hommes* or *Messieurs; Herren* or *Männer; Signori* or *Uomini.* Public lavatories are at stations, cable car termini and the like, and near major tourist attractions and features. Otherwise they are not very common. Use those in cafés, gas stations, department stores, etc. Normally free but might need a 20 centime coin.

Getting Around Switzerland

BY AIR. Given the excellence of rail and road links in Switzerland, and the relatively small size of the country, internal air travel is very much the exception rather than the rule here. However, some 20 flights daily, linking most main towns and cities, especially those in the Ticino, are operated by Crossair. A flight over the Alps in one of their small but comfortable planes can be the experience of a lifetime. Crossair also have services to a number of neighboring countries. Prices are reasonable.

For further information, contact Crossair, P.O. Box 630, 8058 Zürich Airport, or your travel agent.

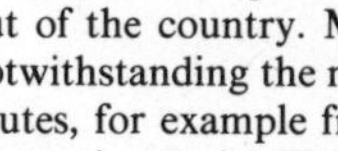

BY TRAIN. The Swiss public transport system is probably the best in the world. Despite its complex web of private and public transport companies and the extensive and equally complex links between train, bus, boat and mountain transport, the system functions as one smooth and immensely well-oiled body. The proverbial notion that you can set your watch by Swiss trains is not so far off the mark. And certainly Switzerland is perhaps the only country in Europe where it isn't always necessary to have a car to get the best out of the country. Many of the Swiss intercity trains are very fast indeed—notwithstanding the mountainous terrain they have to traverse. In fact on some routes, for example from Lausanne to Sion or Bern to Brig, it is best to catch a stopping train (Train Regional or *Regionalzug*) in order to appreciate the scenery. The steep gradients, sharp curves, long tunnels (much of the Swiss rail system represents a triumph of engineering) also mean superb views. And what the trains may lack in speed, they make up for in reliability and cleanliness.

Anyone contemplating a vacation in Switzerland using public transport should avail themselves of a number of essential purchases. One is a copy of the official timetable *(Offizielles Kursbuch* or *Indicateur Officiel),* price Fr. 8.50. Don't be put off by the appearance of this volume. It may be the size of a thick paperback but, despite being written in four languages (English, French, German and Italian), it is beautifully clear and easy to understand. The timetable gives schedules of the state network, the private railways, lake steamers, postal buses, main cable cars and also details of the bus and tram routes in main towns and cities.

Also very useful is the Kummerly and Frey Rail Map of Switzerland, which includes postal coach routes, lake steamers and town plans. Both the map and the timetable can be purchased from any Swiss National Tourist Office. However, the most useful purchase you can make, especially if you plan to do quite a bit of traveling, is the Swiss Holiday Rail Card. Of course, if you also intend to travel elsewhere in Europe by train, you will probably find that the Eurail Pass (see below for details), perhaps with the addition of a Postal Coach Holiday Season Ticket, is your best bet. But for travel in Switzerland only, the Holiday Card is unbeatable value.

The card gives unlimited travel for periods of 4, 8 or 15 days or one month on all trains of the Swiss Federal Railways, and on nearly all private railways, lake steamers and postal coaches. In addition it gives reduced fares on many mountain railways and cable cars. (But if you are in any doubt as to precisely on which routes you qualify for reductions, the map on the reverse of the card marks them all clearly.) The first class card costs Fr. 215, Fr. 250, Fr. 300 and Fr. 420 for 4 days, 8 days, 15 days and one month respectively. The second class card costs Fr. 145, Fr. 170, Fr. 205, Fr. 285, respectively, for the same periods.

The card is only available to non-Swiss residents and must be purchased outside Switzerland, either through travel agencies or from any office of the Swiss National Tourist Office or Swissair.

There are also a series of Regional Holiday Tickets. These are good for train, postal bus and steamer travel and are valid for 15 days. They also permit unlimited travel, but only in the area for which they are good. But unlike the main Rail Card, you are allowed to travel free for only 5 out of the 15 days of the card's validity. On the remaining 10 days, you must pay half-fare. These regional cards are, with some exceptions, for second class travel only, and are available from April 1st to October 31st for the following regions: Montreux/Vevey, Central Switzerland. From May 1 to October 31: Chablais Region, Sarganserland/Walensee, Graubünden. March 1 to October 31: Locarno/Ascona, Lugano. Prices vary considerably so that it is best to check with your tourist agency or directly on arrival in Switzerland at the very competent tourist offices. One thing is for sure, if you obtain one it will make your trip to Switzerland much cheaper and therefore more enjoyable.

There is also a family rail ticket that enables a group of adults and children to travel at reduced rates. This is particularly useful for short stays: enquire at any rail station. All these cards conspire to make rail travel in Switzerland an extremely viable proposition, especially as the trains are otherwise very expensive; there are very few reductions. However, children under six travel free and those under 16 travel at half-fare.

The Eurailpass. A Eurailpass is a convenient, all-inclusive ticket that can save you money on over 100,000 miles of railroads, and railroad-operated buses, ferries, river and lake steamers, hydrofoils, and some Mediterranean crossings in 16 countries of Western Europe. It provides the holder with unlimited travel at rates of: 15 days for $280, 21 days for $350, 1 month for $440, 2 months for $620, 3 months $760; a 2nd class Youthpass (anyone up to the age 26) is available for $310 for 1 month and $400 for 2 months. Children under 12 go for half-fare, under 4 go free. These prices cover first-class passage, reservation fees, and surcharges for the EuroCity expresses. Available to U.S., Canadian and South American residents only, the pass must be bought from an authorized agent in the Western Hemisphere or Japan *before* you leave for Europe. Apply through your travel agent or the Swiss National Tourist Office.

Excellent value as the Eurailpass is, remember that it is essentially for those who plan to do a lot of traveling, over considerable distances and in several countries. The Eurail pass is *not* valid on many of the important privately owned narrow gauge networks which serve some of the main resort areas in Switzerland; neither does it cover the alpine Postbuses. If you plan to stay mostly inside Switzerland you'll do better with one of the special plans offered by the Swiss railways for that country only.

Preserved Steam Trains. The Swiss are addicted to the romanticism of steam train travel, especially when it is combined with excellent food and wine aboard a vintage rail car. This is a delightful enough prospect at the best of times, but when you also add beautiful and often dramatic scenery viewed at a sedate pace, you have the makings of a perfect day out. As ever, the Swiss have it organized to a fine art.

Every spring the Swiss National Tourist Office produces a booklet listing those lines that operate steam trains. These fall into three groups. First, those which operate steam trains to a regular timetable for public travel on certain Sundays of the month, usually from June to the end of September. Second, those which run steam locomotive-hauled trains once or twice a year (for which it is best to book in advance). Third, there are those which have operational steam engines, but only run them for groups hiring a complete train. The railways below are those which are of scenic interest, are easily accessible and on which you could see steam operation during even a short stay in Switzerland.

Chemin de Fer Touristique Blonay-Chamby. A museum line, run by enthusiasts, is situated on the hillside above Vevey and Montreux. The three kms. (two miles) route is operated using steam and electric traction. It can be reached by taking the Montreux Oberland Bahn from Montreux to Chamby or the line from Vevey to Blonay. For details of operating dates, see Table 105 (blue pages) in the Swiss Federal Railway timetable.

Brienzer-Rothorn-Bahn. Climbs the Rothorn from Brienz. This is the last mountain railway in Switzerland using steam locomotives in normal service. Operates from June to October.

Vitznau-Rigi-Bahn. Rack-and-pinion railway that runs from Vitznau on the shores of the Vierwaldstättersee almost to the summit of Mt. Rigi. The views from the summit itself are spectacular. Steam services operate on the first and third Sundays of every month from June to September. But if you want a really special day out, make use of the "Full Steam Ahead" excursion. You travel by historic paddle steamer to Vitznau from Luzern and then go by steam train up the Rigi. After lunch, you return to Weggis and continue by paddle steamer to the Swiss Transport Museum on the lakeside at Luzern.

Regionalverkehr Bern Solothurn operate a very efficient network of narrow-gauge suburban railways serving the Bern area. During the summer a steam special is run on the second Sunday of each month. Start your journey on the RVB platforms in the Bern main station and travel the short distance to Worblaufen, a modern suburb where the steam trips begin. The first, in the morning, is on the line to Worb; in the afternoon go to Solothurn. Both are attractive routes running through a mixture of garden suburbs and fields.

Rhaetische Bahn. This is part of one of the largest meter gauge railway systems in Europe (the other principal parts being the Furka Oberalp and the Brig-Visp-Zermatt railways). The railway had in fact largely dispensed with steam engines as long ago as 1922, but two 2-8-0 locomotives (Nos. 107 and 108) have been maintained in working order for special trains. Public excursions are run on several Sundays from May to August and make a circular trip that takes in Landquart, Klosters, Davos, Filisur, Thusis, Chur and back to Landquart. It is an unforgettable day out; the views are magnificent.

It is also occasionally possible to travel on main lines behind steam locomotives. Swiss Federal Railways maintain some five engines for operation at festivals and displays, but they are usually only advertised locally.

The Mikado 1244 preservation society have restored a Liberation 2-8-0 built by the Montreal Locomotive Works in Canada in 1947 for French Railways (SNCF). This magnificent machine is based at Rapperswil and hauls several trains a year; they often include opulent former Orient Express coaches. Book well in advance, and have dinner on the train! Details from Verein Mikado 1244, Postfach 4106, Therwil.

Finally, the Swiss Transport Museum in Luzern is well worth a visit. The museum covers the complete spectrum of transport in Switzerland from aircraft, through lake steamers, railways and postal coaches and includes exhibits on telecommunications. A large section of the museum is devoted to the development of the railway network including a superb automated model railway of the famous Gotthard route.

Lake Steamers. Swiss Federal Railways provide regular year-round services on a number of lakes, among them: Léman, Bodensee, Zurich, Neuchâtel, Bienne, Morat, Thun, Brienz, Lugano and Maggiore. Sailings are reduced out of season—see the official rail timetable for details or ask at the Tourist Office.

POSTAL BUSES. The postal bus network is excellent, and connects central towns with places off the rail network. The buses are a bright buttercup yellow and still have the traditional and delightful three-tone coach horn of days of yore as a warning to other drivers as they approach hairpin bends. If you have not got one of the Holiday Cards giving unlimited travel on both the railways and postal coaches it may be worth buying the Postal Coach Holiday Season Ticket. This is valid for one month and gives free travel on three days, which you can choose as you go along, and half price travel for the rest of the month. Also look out for the Postal Coach Weekly Cards which give unlimited travel over a section of the network. They are available for the following districts: Sion, Sierre, Oberwallis, Ilanz, Thusis, Appenzell, Toggenburg, and the Principality of Liechtenstein. You buy the tickets at the local post office on arrival. And watch out for the booklets which give details of easy (and not so easy) walks which can be made using one of the postal coaches to return you to your base. Finally keep an eye open for special day or half-day tours; these are invariably good value.

BY CAR. Switzerland has two associations which can be of service to the visiting motorist—the Automobile Club de Suisse (ACS), Wasserwerkgasse 39, Bern, and The Touring Club (TCS), rue Pierre Fatio 9, Geneva 3, both of which have branch offices throughout the country. The TCS operates a 24-hour breakdown and patrol service. Your own automobile club can make contact with either of these two, but ask the Swiss National Tourist Office, before you leave, to give you their tourist map, a marvel of condensation, which on a single sheet gives you a route map for the entire country.

Swiss roads are usually well-surfaced but are mostly winding and hilly, not to say mountainous. It is not really possible to achieve high average speeds, and when estimating likely travel times it is sensible to take a close look at a map. There may be only 20 miles between one point and another, but there could also be a mountain pass among them. There is a well-developed motorway network, but it still has some noteworthy gaps, as for instance in the south along the east–west line roughly between Lugano and Lausanne. When the snows are down this makes motoring in the south a time- and petrol-consuming business, and the snows may well be down until the end of May. However, brilliantly engineered roads and tunnels make north–south travel a delight at any time.

Some mountain passes have railway tunnels beneath them through which cars can be transported by train, the passengers remaining in the cars—a rather curious experience, and often very cold. The latest pride and joy of the Swiss is the St. Gotthard road tunnel, opened in September 1980. At just over nine miles, it is the longest of its kind in Europe and represents a magnificent feat of engineering. The other long Swiss tunnel, the Great St. Bernard, levies a toll of Fr. 15 to 34 according to wheelbase. Useful information on the mountain passes, tunnels, use of chains and many other things is available in the leaflet *Switzerland by Car* obtainable from Swiss National Tourist Offices. From Jan. '85 motorists have been required to display a special tax disc costing Fr. 30 if they wish to drive on the motorways. A second disc is needed for towed caravans or trailers. Discs are good for one year of unlimited use.

Information of use to tourists is also broadcast daily, in English, at around 7 P.M. on Channel 1 Swiss Radio, and a daily tourist information bulletin is available on the Swiss telephone system by dialing 120; or 140 for round-the-clock motoring advice and emergency assistance; a road conditions bulletin is issued from 8 A.M. onwards on 163.

If you take your own car to Switzerland the only documents you need are the car's registration papers and a valid driving license (minimum age 18), but it is wise to have an insurance Green Card. Caravans require the usual Customs documents (obtainable through your motoring organization). You drive on the right. In built-up areas the speed limit is 50 k.p.h. (30 m.p.h.). On motorways it is 120 k.p.h. (75 m.p.h.) and on all other roads, except where clearly marked to the contrary (e.g., motorways), there is a strictly enforced speed limit of 80 k.p.h. (50 m.p.h.). It is compulsory to wear seat belts and children under 12 years old must not be carried on the front seats.

In Switzerland, as in most European countries, vehicles coming from the right normally have priority, and will expect it. The exceptions are on main roads marked by a yellow diamond sign, or by a blue road sign. In such cases *you* have priority over traffic coming from the right—but do *not* take it for granted.

Driving on sidelights only is no longer permitted in any circumstances. Vehicle lights—main, dipped or fog—must be on when traveling in heavy rain or poor visibility, while in road tunnels dipped headlights are obligatory at all times. Police are authorized to collect fines on the spot, *and they do.*

On mountain roads, which are marked with a road sign showing a yellow posthorn on a blue background, the yellow postal buses have priority over all other vehicles. Such buses have a distinctive three-note horn that is used liberally to announce their approach around blind corners and narrow turns: when you hear it, allow as much passing room as the size of your car permits. If the road is too narrow for you and the bus to pass, you must follow the instructions of the driver as to backing up, pulling to one side, etc.

Traffic going *up* a mountain road has priority over all traffic, except postal coaches, going *down.* A useful booklet, *Handbook of Swiss Traffic Regulations,* is obtainable at customs offices, price Fr. 5.

Along mountain roads, where snow chains are frequently needed (and sometimes compulsory) in the winter, there is an established service to equip cars with them. Snow chain service posts are identified by signs bearing the words *Service de Chaînes à Neige.* Chains can be hired throughout Switzerland.

If your automobile breaks down, assistance can be hired through the local telephone exchange (ask operator for *Autohilfe*). Roadside repairs or towage are free to motorists with international touring documents.

Major Alpine Passes. Except in midsummer, it is advisable to check road and weather conditions before starting across any of the major passes. The sun may be shining down where you are, but that's no guarantee that snow and ice aren't turning the pass itself into a nightmare of poor visibility and slick surfaces, or that highway repairs won't necessitate one-way traffic along certain stretches that will delay you for hours. Both of the Swiss automobile clubs issue daily bulletins, otherwise dial 163 for constant road reports. With most of the important passes, somewhere on the approach road there is a prominent notice stating whether the pass is open or closed.

Swiss Touring Club mechanics in black-and-yellow cars patrol the most frequented mountain passes: St. Gotthard, Susten, Furka, Grimsel, Julier, Simplon, Flüela, Mosses, Pillon, etc.

Bernina. This pass, connecting St. Moritz with Tirano, across the Italian border, is among the most scenic in Switzerland, and is traversed by rail as well as highway. The principal attraction is the exquisite Piz Palü, with its sensational glacier, which is seen just beyond the 2,345 meter (7,700 ft.) summit of the pass. From Poschiavo onward, the atmosphere is distinctly Italian.

The pass is open most of the winter. Maximum gradient 10%. The narrow-gauge Bernina Railway takes three hours for the trip.

Great St. Bernard. The granddaddy of all Swiss passes. Although best known for the legendary lifesaving dogs kept by the monks from the famous hospice, the Great St. Bernard connecting Martigny with Aosta (Italy) is historically one of the most important passes in Europe. It was known and used by the Celts, and later, but long before the birth of Christ, by the Romans. The old pass road, which reaches a height of 2,470 meters (8,100 ft.), is relatively easy driving for an Alpine pass, having a maximum gradient of about 10%, but is narrow in parts. The summit section is usually closed about mid-Oct. to mid-June, but a fine six-kms. long (three and three quarter miles) tunnel, which burrows some 680 meters (2,000 ft.) under the summit, now enables the crossing to be made throughout the year although chains may be necessary in winter.

There is a Swiss postal bus service from Martigny to the hospice, June–September, two and a half hours; an Italian one from the hospice to Aosta, two hours.

Julier, Maloja. The approach roads for both of these passes connect at Silvaplana, near St. Moritz. Open the year round, they provide an excellent connection between Graubünden and Italy, starting at Chur and passing through Lenzerheide and Silvaplana. On both, the highway is excellent and kept relatively free of snow in winter, although in January and February chains are recommended. The scenery is less rugged than along the western passes but no less pleasing. The countryside is heavily wooded even though the summits of both passes rise above 1,900 meters (6,000 ft.).

Julier: modern, well engineered; maximum gradient 12%. *Maloja:* modern road; gentle, easy ascent from Silvaplana; much steeper–9%–with hairpins coming from Italy.

Postal buses run from St. Moritz to Lugano, an all-day excursion and one of the most rewarding trips you can make in Switzerland.

Oberalp, Furka, Grimsel. These three connecting passes constitute the primary east–west Alpine traverse, crossing the northern approach to the St. Gotthard at Andermatt. The Oberalp, 2,040 meters (6,700 ft.), begins at Disentis near the source of the Rhine and is the boundary between the cantons of Graubünden and Uri. The Furka, 2,440 meters (8,000 ft.), between Andermatt and Gletsch, affords a sensational view of the 13 km.-long (eight miles) Rhône Glacier, and at the western end connects with the Grimsel Pass road leading to the Bernese Oberland. The Grimsel, 2,163 meters (7,100 ft.), was known to be in use as early as the 13th century. The principal attraction now is the 304 meter-long, 115 meter-high Spitallam Dam, one of Europe's outstanding engineering feats. The whole Oberalp-Furka-Grimsel area is noted for the beauty of its wild flowers in summer.

Furka: open mid-June to mid-Oct.; hairpin bends but mostly good road; heavy weekend traffic; maximum gradient 10%. *Grimsel:* open mid-June to mid-Oct.; modern surface, comparatively easy, heavy weekend traffic; maximum gradient 10%. *Oberalp:* open mid-June to end Oct.; narrow road, mostly good surface; numerous hairpins; max. gradient 10%.

St. Gotthard. A pass of considerable historic importance, the 2,102 meter (6,900 ft.) St. Gotthard, leading from the northern cantons to the Ticino, was traversed by carriage as early as 1775 by an Englishman named Greville. Until the railroad tunnel was completed in 1880 the pass was the principal route between central Europe and Italy. Today it is a good road and, since the completion of a new by-pass avoiding the top 25 hairpins, a moderately easy drive. However, a 14 km. (nine miles) road tunnel under the pass was opened in September 1980 making it unnecessary to use the pass unless you actually want to. Also as a result of this new tunnel, the car rail service has been stopped. The tunnel is toll free. Pass usually open mid-May to mid-Oct. Max. gradient 10%.

San Bernardino. This new tunnel, almost four miles long under the old San Bernardino pass, has given this route added importance. The old road, although fairly easy, maximum gradient 10%, was usually closed mid-Oct. to June over its 1,071 meter (6,800 ft.) summit. With the new tunnel, this route connecting central Graubünden with Bellinzona and Lakes Lugano and Maggiore is now open throughout the year.

Simplon. This major route between Switzerland and Italy was completed at the beginning of the 19th century at the order of Napoleon. When the railway tunnel—the longest in the world—was opened in 1905 Napoleon's road over the pass lost much of its importance. Recently, the road—which reaches 2,080 meters (6,500 ft.)—has been much improved. As a result of new tunnels and snow galleries it is now open throughout the year and, as Alpine passes go, is a relatively easy drive. Cars can also be carried on trains through the rail tunnel between Brig and Iselle.

Swiss postal buses join Brig and Domodossala in Italy, a three-hour trip.

Susten. An alternative to the Furka/Grimsel pass route is the Susten, which connects Wassen, north of the St. Gotthard, and Andermatt with Meiringen. This is a first-class highway, the pride of all the Swiss Alpine passes. The Susten region is a favorite of mountain climbers. A quarter-mile tunnel underpasses the summit of the Susten.

Open mid-June to late Oct.; magnificently engineered; easy to drive; heavy weekend traffic; maximum gradient nine %.

There are several buses a day from Meiringen to Susten, a three and a half hour trip.

Other Alpine Passes. **Brünig.** 1,005 meters (3,300 ft.). Usually open all year. Good surface, not too many hairpins. Maximum gradient eight %.

Flüela. 2,375 meters (7,800 ft.). Usually open during the winter, with a toll. Not too difficult. Maximum gradient 10%.

Forclaz. 1,525 meters (5,000 ft.). Usually open throughout the year. Good surface most of way. Maximum gradient eight %. Chains required in winter.

Jaun. 1,493 meters (4,900 ft.). Usually open most of the year, with chains. Good surface, but narrow. Maximum gradient 10%.

Klausen. 1,950 meters (6,400 ft.). Open from mid-June to mid-Oct. Some sharp turns, gravel over summit. Maximum gradient nine %.

Lukmanier. 1,920 meters (6,300 ft.). Open May to end Oct. Good surface. Maximum gradient nine %.

Mosses. 1,432 meters (4,700 ft.). Usually open all year. Relatively easy, modern road. Maximum gradient eight %.

Nufenen. 2,468 meters (8,100 ft.). Fairly narrow approach roads lead to new construction over summit. Maximum gradient 10%. Open June to end Sept.

Ofen (or **Fuorn**). 2,163 meters (7,100 ft.). Usually open throughout year. Good surface, relatively easy. Maximum gradient 10%. Chains.

Pillon. 1,525 meters (5,000 ft.). Usually open throughout year. Fairly easy. Maximum gradient nine %. Chains.

Splügen. 2,102 meters (6,900 ft.). Open June to mid-Oct. Good surface but many hairpins and tunnels. Maximum gradient nine %.

Umbrail. 2,498 meters (8,200 ft.). Open late June to mid-Oct. Switzerland's highest pass, narrow and well-supplied with hairpin turns. Gravel surface otherwise not overly challenging. Maximum gradient nine %.

Alpine Tunnels. Alpine rail tunnels, through which cars and their occupants are carried by train, make possible year-round transit of the Simplon, Furka, Lötschberg and Albula passes; detailed information on timetables, charges and fares obtainable from the Swiss National Tourist Office or regional tourist offices. In addition, there are four splendid road tunnels—the Great St. Bernard, Mont-Blanc, San Bernardino and the St. Gotthard.

Albula. Rail tunnel Tiefencastel to Samedan. Automobiles about Fr. 82 one way, including driver. Up to eight-seaters; passengers Fr. 17 in 2nd class, Fr. 27 in 1st. Trains run about six times a day the year round.

Furka. Rail tunnel opened in 1982. From Oberwald to Realp. The newest Swiss rail tunnel provides all-year access for both motorists and rail travelers between the Valais and Central Switzerland/the Grisons. The car-carrying shuttle runs hourly and costs Fr. 33 for car and driver.

Great St. Bernard. Road tunnel. Martigny (Switzerland) to Aosta (Italy). Almost four miles long. The first Alpine road tunnel to be built. Tolls levied according to wheelbase; from 15 to 22.50 for car. Drivers are requested to carry either Swiss or Italian money for the payment of tolls.

Lötschberg. Rail tunnel. Automobiles Fr. 40 irrespective of length. Charges are for the journey Kandersteg to Brig, and includes vehicle and up to eight passengers remaining in it during journey. (See below for the Brig-Iselle section through Simplon.)

Mont Blanc. Road tunnel opened in 1965. Connects France (Chamonix, near Geneva) with Italy (Courmayeur). For cars, tolls are based on wheelbase, and range from 50 to 270 French francs. Payment must be made in French, Swiss or Italian currency.

San Bernardino. From Hinterrhein to San Bernardino. A six km. (four miles) long road tunnel beneath the old pass. Connects the Grisons with Ticino, Lakes Lugano and Maggiore. No toll charges.

Simplon. Rail tunnel. Brig to Iselle (Italy). Automobiles Fr. 37 irrespective of length; includes vehicle and up to eight passengers remaining in it during journey.

Kilometers into Miles. This simple chart will help you to convert to both miles and kilometers. If you want to convert from miles into kilometers read from the center column to the right, if from kilometers into miles, from the center column to the left.

Miles		*Kilometers*	*Miles*		*Kilometers*
0.6	1	1.6	37.3	60	96.6
1.2	2	3.2	43.5	70	112.3
1.9	3	4.8	49.7	80	128.7
2.5	4	6.3	55.9	90	144.8
3.1	5	8.0	62.1	100	160.9
3.7	6	9.6	124.3	200	321.9
4.3	7	11.3	186.4	300	482.8
5.0	8	12.9	248.5	400	643.7
5.6	9	14.5	310.7	500	804.7
6.2	10	16.1	372.8	600	965.6
12.4	20	32.2	434.9	700	1,126.5
18.6	30	48.3	497.1	800	1,287.5
24.8	40	64.4	559.2	900	1,448.4
31.0	50	80.5	621.4	1,000	1,609.3

Leaving Switzerland

V.A.T. REFUNDS. Switzerland charges a 6.2% "turnover" tax on all goods. This is automatically included in the price of your purchase. Nonresidents may claim this back at the time of purchase (though for administrative reasons not all shops can do this) or the shop will send a refund to your home. In order to qualify for the refund, you must sign a form at the time of purchase and present it to the Swiss customs on departure. All shops that deal regularly with visitors from overseas are familiar with this procedure.

CUSTOMS ON RETURNING HOME. Americans. U.S. residents may bring in $400 worth of foreign merchandise as gifts or for personal use without having to pay duty, provided they have been out of the country more than 48 hours and provided they have not claimed a similar exemption within the previous 30 days. Every member of a family is entitled to the same exemption, regardless of age, and the exemptions can be pooled. For the next $1,000 worth of goods a flat 10% rate is assessed.

Included in the $400 allowance for travelers over the age of 21 are one liter of alcohol, 100 non-Cuban cigars and 200 cigarettes. Only one bottle of perfume trademarked in the U.S. may be brought in. However, there is no duty on antiques or art over 100 years old. You may not bring home meats, fruits, plants, soil or other agricultural products.

Gifts valued at under $50 may be mailed to friends or relatives at home, but not more than one per day of receipt to any one addressee. These gifts must not include perfumes costing more than $5, tobacco or liquor.

If you are traveling with such foreign-made articles as cameras, watches or binoculars that were purchased at home or on a previous trip, either carry the receipt or register them with U.S. Customs prior to departure.

Canadians. In addition to personal effects, and over and above the regular exemption of $300 per year, the following may be brought into Canada duty free: a maximum of 50 cigars, 200 cigarettes, two pounds of tobacco and 40 ounces of liquor, provided these are declared in writing to customs on arrival. Canadian Customs regulations are strictly enforced; you are recommended to check what your allowances are and to make sure you have kept receipts for whatever you may have bought abroad. Small gifts can be mailed and should be marked "Unsolicited gift, (nature of gift), value under $40 in Canadian funds." For other details, ask for the Canadian Customs brochure, *I Declare.*

British Customs. There are two levels of duty free allowance for people entering the U.K.; one, for goods bought outside the EEC or for goods bought in a duty free shop within the EEC; two, for goods bought in an EEC country but not in a duty free shop.

In the first category you may import duty free: 200 cigarettes or 100 cigarillos or 50 cigars or 250 grammes of tobacco (*Note* if you live outside Europe, these allowances are doubled*);* plus one liter of alcoholic drinks over 22% vol. (38.8% proof) or two liters of alcoholic drinks not over 22% vol. or fortified or sparkling or still wine; plus two liters of still table wine; plus 50 grammes of perfume; plus nine fluid ounces of toilet water; plus other goods to the value of £32.

In the second category you may import duty free: 300 cigarettes or 150 cigarillos or 75 cigars or 400 grammes of tobacco; plus one and a half liters of alcoholic drinks over 22% vol. (38.8% proof) or three liters of alcoholic drinks not over 22% vol. or fortified or sparkling or still wine; plus five liters of still table wine; plus 75 grammes of perfume; plus 13 fluid ounces of toilet water; plus other goods to the value of £250 (*Note* though it is not classified as an alcoholic drink by EEC countries for Customs' purposes and is thus considered part of the "other goods" allowance, you may not import more than 50 liters of beer).

In addition, no animals or pets of any kind may be brought into the U.K. The penalties for doing so are severe and are strictly enforced; there are *no* exceptions. Similarly, fresh meats, plants and vegetables, controlled drugs and firearms and ammunition may not be brought into the U.K. There are no restrictions on the import or export of British and foreign currencies.

SWITZERLAND AND THE SWISS

Heritage and Achievement

by
KENNETH LOVELAND

The biggest challenge Switzerland has to face is its own reputation. Every visitor arriving for the first time does so with a picture ready formed in the mind, either from carefully selected postcards sent by friends on holiday, or from films, from classic tales of travel or from legends.

The Swiss have always been able to rely on other people to do their advertising for them. Poets, painters, musicians, Mark Twain, Queen Victoria—they all did their bit before the tourist explosion happened. Switzerland is the one country about which we can all claim authority before we have ever been there. The image having been established, Switzerland has to live up to it.

Mostly it does. Here is one of the remaining places on earth where arriving really does justify traveling hopefully. Yet here we encounter the Swiss paradox. It is fatally easy to be wrong about Switzerland.

Delight at discovering the Swiss idyll can cause us to stop right there, to be happy with the half of the truth that is about places, and neglect the other half, which is about people. When we spare time for that other half, we uncover contradictions, and some of the ideas we have brought along in our luggage have to be thrown away. Tidily, of course, for Switzerland is a tidy place.

Memory may be allowed the luxury of recalling some of the goods Switzerland puts in its shop window. I remember a day when I sat on a rocky ledge high above the Vierwaldstättersee. Below, steamers chugged their way from Vitznau across to Beckenried, from Brunnen down to Weggis, slashing the turquoise of the lake with minute wakes of white. Snow-clad peaks reached defiantly into an azure sky, green meadows were dotted with wild flowers, cowbells tinkled in happy indiscipline in the valley below. I ate my sandwiches enthralled, ravenous after a walk round the plateau of Klewenalp. Surely this was the Switzerland of the imagination?

There was a day when the sun was hot on the waterside terraces of Montreux, all flowers and sophistication, with the splendor of primitive nature watching from the distant mountains, the vineyards rising in orderly rows, an overlay of French style and elegance subtly suggested all around, and into a lazy mind ghosts intruded. Could this be Stravinsky and Diaghilev arguing out some new idea for the Russian ballet? Was that Tchaikovsky, out on an afternoon walk from Clarens, whence he fled after his disastrous marriage? By Lake Geneva—the visitor soon learns to call it Lac Léman—so much inspiration was born. How could it be otherwise?

Another day, clearly etched in the mind, happened in the Ticino. It was early October in Locarno. The roses had not yet retired, the summer flowers were still in profusion. Yet the trees were changing color, the streets were thick with the russet and gold of fallen leaves and, beyond, the snows were glistening white. There had been minestrone and pasta for lunch in a genial, noisy restaurant in a lakeside village. The chestnut festival awaited us. Three seasons were exchanging greetings amid a riot of color, and Italian brio was tempered with Swiss efficiency.

Days like these are dangerous. They can drug curiosity. And when the drug has worn off, and logic intrudes into the hour of recovery, *the* question starts to nag. In such a land, where three old European cultures of such marked contrast all form part, each with its inherited language, can there possibly be a national character? There is, and it expresses itself in ways that are positive but quiet. We should go in search of it.

Dispelling Illusions

Switzerland is a land which disproves the theory, cherished by propagandists, that you cannot have a national identity without a national language. If there was a national language here, it would be Romansch. According to the sympathies of the person you ask, Romansch is either dead, dying or recovering. But even those who claim that it is gathering strength would be hard put to claim for it much commercial viability. It is kept alive by sincere enthusiasts, which is the way of such things, but when I last sought definite statistics, I was told that it is the first language of no more than one percent of the population. For 74 percent, the first language is German, for 20 percent French and for four percent Italian. Mathematicians will point to a missing one percent, proof that Switzerland still attracts immigrant minorities.

This is the point at which to dispel, or at least modify, a long-standing legend that the Swiss all speak English. Not all of them do, and I have waited more than once in an attractive backwater village while an obliging landlady fetched a daughter who had progressed to high-school English. But mostly, they do speak English, and this is one of the features that makes Switzerland an ideal place for English-speaking visitors dipping a cautious first toe into the waters of European travel. So is the general desire to get things right.

It is, incidentally, an English with occasional American overtones. Americans will be reassured, British slightly surprised, to learn, at Zürich's fine airport station giving quick access to all the principal cities, that the next train arrives, not at platform four, but track four.

Two more illusions to be dispelled. After days spent walking through pine forests, following mountain tracks, hiking through meadows with only photogenic cows for company, it is easy to support the impression that Switzerland is under-populated and that most of its people must be farmers. Untrue. The average distribution of population works out at more than six times as many people per square kilometer as in the United States, and only seven percent of them are engaged in agriculture or forestry. Machinery tops the employment figures, chemical industries are next, and third place is taken by tourism—which must be another reason for approaching a Swiss holiday with confidence.

Peace, Perfect Peace

Harry Lime made one of the biggest mistakes about Switzerland when he delivered his cynical defense of violence while going round the great wheel of Vienna's Prater. Look at the cruel history of Italy, he argued, and the glories of art it produced. Look at Switzerland. Hundreds of years of peace, and what did it produce? The cuckoo clock!

Now, though Switzerland has produced no Shakespeare, no Mozart, no Michelangelo, the Swiss record in the creative arts is not insignificant, and in appreciation of them it is higher than most. The nations which produce the artists are not necessarily those with the widest taste. I have sat appalled in the countries which produced Beethoven and Haydn while audiences have mustered only grudging applause for masterpieces which happened not to be German or Austrian. I have been dismayed many times by the apathy of Italian audiences towards works which were part of the mainstream of world music but not part of their national tradition. But, on the other hand, I have often felt the audience at the Luzern Festival to be the most receptive and broad-minded in Europe, witness to an informed cosmopolitanism which is a healthy thread running through Swiss artistic life.

Where Harry Lime really got it wrong was in that crack about peace. True, the last time the Swiss were involved in a war with a foreign power was during the Napoleonic campaigns, though there have been conflicts at home, including the armed dispute between Catholics and Protestants in 1847. But Swiss nationhood had first to be bought with blood and fire.

Back home, the holiday over, it is easy to nod approval at the text books which claim that the William Tell legend is only partly true. But it is another thing to deny it when you are standing in front of Richard Kissling's defiant statue, in the square at Altdorf, where they will tell you he shot the apple from his son's head and braved Gessler. It is a cold-blooded disbeliever who does not feel the pulse quicken in the valley where the men of the cantons gathered to destroy Gessler's troops. If it was good enough for Schiller and Rossini, it is good enough for me. Only an unromantic cynic can walk the lush green plateau of the Rütli, and not warm to the thought of the representatives of the founder cantons taking their oath.

A long time ago? So it was. But it was on this same ground, they say, that the Swiss commanders gathered in 1940 when, surrounded by Axis powers, they decided on a plan of defense. Switzerland was not involved in the actual fighting of the two major wars in Europe during the 20th century—but she was not untouched by them. There were the hardships caused by the blockades of the first, there was the proximity of the second. The help given to Allied airmen and escaped prisoners of war during that time is a matter of history.

Peace and absence of war are not quite the same thing, as the world is beginning to learn. Realists ever, the Swiss determination to protect a hard-won independence is one of the strongest indications of a national character. It comes as a shock to the uninformed to learn that this nation with a reputation for peace has compulsory military service.

It was brought home to me when I was waiting for a train in Bern one Saturday morning. Surely I knew that uniformed figure, pack on back, rifle slung, boots polished? I did. It was a prominent businessman off to do his national service. Did he have to, I asked? Yes, he replied gloomily, and you could see that Sunday lunch was on his mind. Then, as the train came in, he brightened. "I am, in fact, a very good shot with a rifle," he proclaimed defensively.

In Switzerland, only disability or residence abroad qualify for exemption from military service, which must be bought with a personal tax. Every young Swiss man has an initial course of 17 weeks at the age of 20, and is allocated after basic training to the unit with which he will work in future. There will be recurring refresher courses of three weeks until he is 36, of two weeks each after that. The military obligation lasts until 55 for officers, until 50 for other ranks.

Even in years when he is not called for national service, he is not allowed to forget it. His equipment is always somewhere around the house, for the Swiss soldier is the only one in the world who keeps his rifle, ammunition, gas mask and other gear at home—he has to produce it for regular inspection and attend marksmanship courses.

Hardly what you would expect in a peace-loving nation. So as the train pulled out I asked the question. "Why, if you never have a war, do you need such a large trained army?"

He lowered the window. "That," he shouted, "is why we never have a war."

Tolerance and Enlightenment

So the Swiss are prepared to defend their own rights. They have, of course, always been generous in their championship of the rights of others. I was walking past the place Molard in Geneva one morning when a plaque above an ancient gateway caught my eye. *Geneva, cité de refuge,* it read. So it has been, a city of refuge down the centuries.

What an assorted company they make, those refugees who came to Geneva. Here came Calvin, Knox and other fugitives from persecution at the time of the Reformation, and one of Geneva's finest statues catches them in a mood of collective disapproval, a stern "Thou Shalt Not" about to be delivered. De Beze, though, looks as if his mind is on other things. After all, he did marry his mistress before joining the Presbyterians.

What would the Calvinists have thought of some of those who came after them? Byron, in disgrace with London society and accused of incest with his half-sister Mrs. Leigh; Shelley, his marriage with Harriet Westbrook disintegrated; Liszt, with his mistress the Countess d'Agoult; Wagner, on the run from husbands, creditors and politicians. Defenders of the word and freedom of thought, Voltaire, Victor Hugo, Balzac and others passed through the town where Rousseau himself was born. And in our own century, Geneva's role as the home of the League of Nations, then the United Nations, and as the birthplace of the Red Cross have won for it and the nation of which it is part a name as the protector of humanities. Tolerance is one word which comes to mind. Enlightenment is another.

All of which makes it rather odd that women in Switzerland should have had to wait so long for the vote. It did not come their way until 1971.

One day, while shopping in the vegetable market for a picnic, I took my courage in both hands and asked a woman if she felt deprived at not having the vote. "And what would I do with it?" she demanded. Waving a hand at a stall of mushrooms and tomatoes, "Would it buy me any more of these?"

The awful truth is that I cannot recall a Swiss woman ever telling me that she felt deprived at not participating in elections. No doubt some did. Neither have I spoken to any who feel that their lives have changed dramatically since women's suffrage was introduced. No doubt some do. I shrink before the impending assault of women's rights campaigners, but can only report. Switzerland seems to be the same happy, well-run country that it was before. Yet a little voice persists. Was it not odd that the land of humanities kept its women waiting so long?

In fact, there are still corners where they are not yet allowed to take part in cantonal elections, particularly where such elections are conducted in the open air by a show of hands (*Landsgemeinde*).

Transports of Delight

One senses a reluctance to change which contrasts oddly with the Swiss reputation for grasping the nettle of progress in other things. But one detects also a readiness to compromise. This is demonstrated practically in the partnership of state and private enterprise in the transport system, a genius for making the best of both worlds.

At a time when we hear of state-owned airlines plunging into deficit, it comes as a surprise to know that Swissair, the national carrier and a superb advertisement for Swiss standards everywhere it flies, is not, in fact, state-owned and actually makes a profit. Roughly two-thirds of its share capital is in private hands, and only about 30 percent in the hands of government institutions and local authorities. There is no direct government subsidy.

When we turn to the railways, the private sector is even more prominent. Spend a holiday in Switzerland, and you are almost certain to travel at some time or another on a private railway. They may have pulled up a few lines and put down one or two others since writing, but in round figures, something like three-fifths of the network is state-owned, and the rest is operated by 97 private railways.

Over the state lines run the crack expresses and an intricate design of local services. To this the private lines are an indispensable complement, reaching into delectable backwaters and adding to the personality of the areas they serve. I have had some wonderful experiences on the private lines of Switzerland, and if I remember the Montreux–Bernese-Oberland railway especially, it's just that this is the one that comes to mind at the moment.

I was commuting between the Festivals of Luzern and Montreux. It was a glorious September day, golden and mellow, and I changed to the Montreux–Bernese-Oberland line at Zweisimmen. The line curved its way in and out of the mountains, taking steep gradients in its stride, giving unforgettable views of proud mountain peaks and sylvan valleys. Then, suddenly, we passed through clouds, and there was the blue spread of Geneva's lake below—there was Montreux, there was the Château de Chillon, immortalized by Byron, its gaunt walls washed by the waters of the lake, there were the sun-kissed vineyards, there were fields ablaze with wild narcissi. It was as though a master magician had suddenly drawn back the curtain on the unexpected and the exotic.

The triumphs of engineering and organization that have gone into the making of the Swiss railway design can be measured in statistics. We can be astonished to know that there are more than 5,000 kilometers of railway in such a small country, that Mount Pilatus (which Queen Victoria ascended on a mule the first time she went there) has the steepest rack and pinion railway in the world with a maximum gradient of one in two. We are impressed to learn that the Jungfrau railway's Jungfraujoch terminus stands at 11,333 feet, and is the highest anywhere in the world. We can thrill to the thought of the adventurous pioneering and engineering that gave Switzerland some of the longest tunnels, the 12 miles of the Simplon, the nine miles each of the Gotthard and the Lötschberg. The figures are a permanent record of the determination of a small nation to conquer a difficult terrain.

But what cannot be measured in statistics in the joy that Swiss railways, and particularly those mountain ascents, have given to millions of passengers. When Queen Victoria was helped from her mule at the top of Pilatus, she would have been rewarded by a panorama of the green Swiss lowlands, the Vierwaldstättersee looking like a star-shaped mirror, and the ice-capped peaks of the Bernese Oberland—the Eiger, the Mönch, the Jungfrau—brilliant in the sunshine. You will find similar experiences at the top of most mountain railways in Switzerland. Statistics retreat at the memory.

I have often climbed into one of the red cars of the Rigi railway and watched Vitznau shrink into a dot as we rose ever higher. Not so long ago, I saw in a museum a notice announcing that for Fr. 16, you could hire a horse to take you to the top. That was in the 18th century. You could also be carried there in a sedan chair. But in 1871, they built the rack and pinion railway, and it's now the oldest of its kind in Europe.

It has long been electrified, but when the centenary was celebrated in 1971, they fetched out of retirement one of the splendid old steam engines that had been specially designed for the gradients in the early days of the line, and we savored the nostalgic smell of hot oil and felt ourselves to be a little corner of history relived as the old engine with the upright boiler puffed her way to the top.

No matter how much more efficient the railways are now that the steam engines have been put out to grass, a slice of romance has gone with them. The Swiss have a sentimental regard for them, and you will find some among other relics of their transport system preserved in the fine Luzern Transport Museum, worth a day's browsing. During the summer, steam returns on several of the lines. When last I went up Rigi, I was delighted on leaving the steamer at Vitznau to see an engine belching smoke at the head of a line of carriages. It was like coming home. The Swiss know that, given the chance, we can be just as sentimental as they are, and steam can add a dimension of romance.

They call Rigi the singing mountain. Mark Twain might have had another name for it. The story is that, pursued by ardent Alpine horn blowers, he paid them off generously only to find their numbers doubled at the next village. The news had spread.

Rigi I love, Pilatus too. Wagner would have had a magnificent view of both. He took the villa at Tribschen, just outside Luzern (it is a well-kept museum today) and there wrote parts of *The Mastersingers, Siegfried,* and *Twilight of the Gods,* as well as the *Siegfried Idyll,* a combined Christmas and birthday present for Cosima. I like to think that some of the most turbulent passages in the *Ring* might have been written with memories of days when storms swept the lake, and lightning flickered around the tops of Pilatus and Rigi.

Today, when one watches the Cisalpin rush out of the Simplon tunnel on its way from Paris to Milan, or stands on Basel station marvelling at the way they break up and re-form through expresses from all parts of Europe, it's amusing to recall that one of the practical reasons for the start of Swiss railways in 1847 was the liking of the Zürich aristocracy for hot buns with their breakfast. The buns were made at Baden, and an important assignment for Switzerland's first railway, 23 kilometers from Zürich to Baden, was to ensure that the buns arrived in time for breakfast. Out of such priorities grew one of the finest railway systems in the world.

The Varied Fabric

The Swiss are proud of their railways. They are, in fact, proud of anything to do with transport, and have a quite touching affection for it. It's an affection that's easy to share, whether it is lavished on the railways, the yellow postal buses or those lovely old paddle steamers with the beautifully engraved prows and majestic lines, sailing down the lakes with all the elegance of swans. For me, drifting from one lakeside settlement to another on an old-fashioned steamer with a tall funnel is an ideal form of escape. The Switzerland of statistics and business acumen slips out of sight, and the romance is enhanced when a village band comes on board, or perhaps a choir in national costume, on the way to a folk festival.

Switzerland is rich in these folk festivals, and you can be quickly caught up in them. There are the grape harvest festivals of Valais; the beribboned cows on their way to their winter quarters in a score of villages; Alpine traditions jealously preserved—Luzern's Martinmas Goose; the cheese distribution in the Justis valley; the risotto meals of the Ticino; religious festivals. Colorful costumes, masks, processions, dancing, quaint old customs are all part of celebrations which can be riotous, sometimes devout.

In the remote regions of Appenzell, I have been awakened by the drum heralding the dawn of carnival day; in Schaffhausen, I've been hauled on to the platform to become part of carnival itself. You need to know a little about local politics to get the best out of carnival. Much of it is involved in the lampooning of local figures, the burlesquing of recent events. The cartoon of a year's affairs passes before your eyes. And suddenly, another myth is exploded. Who said the Swiss have no sense of humor? They have, and what is more, they can stand being on the receiving end of the joke. At carnival time, the most unlikely people have to.

I was once told you can judge a nation by its capital. Experience makes me doubtful. But the Swiss, as a nation, are happily represented by Bern. On the one side, a city of fine shops and a transport center that is a model of 20th-century planning; on the other, the old town: graceful arcades that remind one of Italy, 11 decorated fountains in the old streets that lead from the Kramgasse to the Marktgasse, the onion market, the signs of the guilds, the medieval facades, geraniums tumbling from the window boxes, the 16th-century astronomical clock and, at the end of it all, the bears, Bern's very special pets, part of the town's history and celebrated on its coat of arms, regularly going through their performances in the pit watched by admiring children of all ages—Swiss sentiment beginning to show again.

You can step backwards in time so easily in Bern. So you can in Basel, by old Father Rhine, and in Zürich, where the quiet of medieval squares contrasts so strangely with the city's fame as a business center.

In Engelberg too, though in a different way; here it is not fanciful at all to imagine the shades of ecclesiastics dead for centuries, nor whimsical for the ear to catch the chants of forgotten monks in the grounds of the Benedictine monastery beneath the mountains. Here is peace of a kind that transcends time, and atmosphere is all. So it is at Einsiedeln, when I once sat hushed while a procession of pilgrims, their long journey over, filed slowly into the monastery and fell to prayer. It had been happening there for a thousand years.

But we started by looking, in a practical and reasoned way, for the Swiss national character, and we have been seduced from the path by the beauty of the country, by its diversity—just as we predicted would happen.

Yet in letting the fancy wander, in deserting hard facts for romance and color remembered, perhaps we have discovered something.

Perhaps a picture has emerged of a national character which is welcoming and is no less sincere because it is experienced: a peaceable demeanor with a strong streak of realism, and a firm willingness to stand up for itself. A personality wary of change for its own sake but open to persuasion and prepared to compromise, proud of achievement and jealous of heritage, be it from God or man. There is a surprising vein of sentimentality and a touch of poetry which can be aroused by such matters as the snows of the Jungfrau turning from white to pink in the sunset. There's quite a sense of fun, too, and a feeling for the fine things of life.

On the whole, just the kind of person to be found living in a land where distinctive cultures overlap—a place of dramatic mountains, time-soaked cities, busy industry, placid lakes, noisy carnivals and massive forest silences. He is the product of a small state with an amazingly varied fabric. May he never have to bring the equipment out of the cupboard to defend it. For Switzerland is contentment—a vanishing commodity in an angry world.

THE CONFEDERATION THAT WORKS

A Synopsis of Swiss History

by
KENNETH LOVELAND

Wander the slopes of Klewenalp above the Vierwaldstättersee on a still spring day, gaze across the placid waters beneath, and it is easy to identify Switzerland as a land of peace. Wander on a mile or so and you are reminded that for much of the time Switzerland has been nothing of the kind. Here is the Rütli, the meadow where legend avers that the men of the three forest cantons, Uri, Schwyz and Unterwalden, met to plot the overthrow of their Habsburg landlords. A few miles away is the site of the battle of Sempach, where the Habsburgs were routed. All around is the country of the William Tell story. Some scholars may doubt its authenticity, but it would hardly help the Swiss tourist industry if they were proved right. True or false, it reinforces fact. Swiss peace was won with violence and war.

From Romans to Habsburgs

Swiss history begins with the traces of settlements from the Alpine Stone and Neolithic Ages in the cantons of Graubünden and Schaffhausen, and relics of the Early Iron Age by the Lac de Neuchâtel. The first inhabitants of Switzerland in recorded history were the Helvitii in the northwest and the Rhaetians in the southwest.

The Roman conquest began as early as 107 B.C. when the Roman armies burst through the St. Bernard Pass on their way to Gaul. Subjection under Julius Caesar began in 58 B.C. but was never total. Christianity was introduced gradually from the fourth century A.D.

The ancestors of the modern Swiss were the Germanic tribes who gradually drove the Romans back home. The Alemanni settled in the east around 406, the Burgundians in the southwest about 443. The boundaries between the two are roughly those still existing between the German and French language areas. But Latin remained the language spoken in Rhaetia, and in this one traces the roots of Romansch, the fourth, and minority, language of Switzerland and still spoken in Graubünden today.

Charlemagne (768–814) included most of the area in his great empire. When it broke up, Burgundy extended its territories to Lac Léman, while eastern Switzerland went to the Franks. The Burgundian rule was constructive and wise, and agriculture and crafts flourished. Rudolph III of Burgundy gave his lands to the ruler of the Holy Roman Empire, and when he died, Conrad II, who had been crowned emperor at Peterlingen in 1032, formally took them over. All the Alpine lands were now part of the empire.

Central control was loose, and powerful dynasties within Switzerland snatched what lands they could for themselves. The Dukes of Zähringen were the most successful, winning all the land between Lac Léman and Bodensee, founding Fribourg (1178) and Bern (1191) to strengthen their hold. But Berthold V died childless in 1218, and in moved the vultures, not only neighboring states, but the petty barons of the empire, bishops as well, as it became clear that territory was up for grabs. Duke Peter of Savoy came off best, successfully invading the land around Lac Léman and beyond. As his troops reached as far as the Bernese Oberland, he imported military experts and architects from England, from the court of Henry III, to leave a trail of protecting castles. One was Chillon, still jutting today into Lac Léman near Montreux. Peter died in 1268, brave in war and wise in counsel, a man whose foresight prepared the way for his family's later even more widespread influence, culminating in acceptance of the throne of the new Italy in the 19th century.

But a formidable figure already barred the road to the east. The Savoy armies had gone as far as they could. The Habsburg family, from their seat at Aargau, east of Zürich, had gradually risen to riches and power, particularly under Count Albert IV. His son Rudolph greatly expanded their influence, laying the foundations of the sprawling empire which was to play such an important part in European history right down to the early 20th century. By the time he died in 1291, the house of Habsburg was the supreme overlord of central Europe and the Alps.

Rudolph was elected emperor of Germany in 1273. The title had become almost an empty one since the empire was mostly made up of greedy squabbling nobles. But Rudolph brought them sternly to heel, encouraged economic growth and generally goes into history as a firm but enlightened ruler. Even so, there was unrest under his landlords in German-speaking Switzerland, and he had been dead no more than a few days when it came to a head. The leaders of Uri, Schwyz and Unterwalden met secretly (at the meadow of Rütli, says legend), and the first Perpetual League of the Three Forest States was formed. From this the Swiss Confederation was to grow, and its inaugural document is preserved today in the canton of Schwyz.

The Rise of the Swiss Confederation

However the Habsburgs might be strengthening their hold elsewhere in Europe, in Switzerland they were on the retreat. This is the time of William Tell. Perhaps he is only a legend. Perhaps if he existed at all, he was not as important as romance makes out. But it was good enough for Schiller, good enough for Rossini, and that statue in the market place at Altdorf is pretty convincing stuff. So let's not spoil a good yarn. What is important is that the kind of exploits attributed to him illustrate the historical fact of how the power of the Habsburgs was whittled away by skirmishes and guerilla warfare.

Not that they took it lying down. Duke Leopold decided to put a stop to all this. But his troops were routed by the Confederation at Morgarten (1315), and Leopold's aggression merely proved the excuse for the men of the Confederation to make their intentions public. This they did in the Pact of Brunnen (today a fashionable lakeside holiday center, just across the water from the historic Rütli). Revolt spread like wildfire, and Luzern (1332), Zürich (1351), Glarus and Zug (1352), then Bern (1353) joined the three.

Leopold II decided to teach the Swiss a lesson once and for all, but he too had to retire licking his wounds. His troops were driven back at Sempach (1386) and Näfels (1388). The Habsburgs signed a peace pact for 20 years in 1394.

A peace pact with a defeated Habsburg leader was recognition indeed for the Confederation. It meant confidence as well. As soon as the 20 years expired they were at the Habsburgs again and seized Aarau and Thurgau. The Swiss blood was up, and in Appenzell and Graubünden the feudal grip of bishoprics was thrown off. From this time, too, dates the birth of Swiss industry, the Swiss devotion to education and the development of identifiably Swiss literature and the arts.

Europe watched the rise of the Swiss with a mixture of interest and apprehension. The French king Louis XI, ever cunning in diplomacy, decided to turn it to good account. He had a running quarrel with Charles the Bold of Burgundy, who was also in conflict with the Habsburgs. Louis suggested that the Swiss should make friends with the Austrians and if they really wanted to carry on fighting somebody, they might like to give the Habsburgs a hand against Burgundy. The

Swiss fell for the idea and did both. They increased their military prestige and influence by giving Charles a good hiding at Grandson and Morat. Making the most of a winning streak, they went on to invade the Vaud, which at the time owed allegiance to Savoy.

The vassals liberated had become conquerors themselves. They had learned, too, just how to make chances to expand out of what looked like virtuous causes. Swiss farmers complained that their cattle had been stolen by the agents of the Duke of Milan, so he was next on the list. The Valle Leventina was seized. Swiss fingers were probing south of the Alps. But power has its dangers no less than servitude. Sharing out the spoils is always a sensitive business and when it came on the agenda of the Council of Stans it began to look as though it would lead to civil war.

It was solved by a decision which may seem odd in the 20th century but which worked well at the time, and may not be without its lesson. Despairing of reaching an agreement round the table, the council consulted a much respected mystic and hermit, Niklaus von Flüe. Make it up and stay pals was his advice. Surprisingly they did just that.

Fribourg, Solothurn, Basel, Schaffhausen, and finally Appenzell all joined the Confederation and Swiss independence was recognised after victory over the Empire at Dornach (1499), as a result of which the Confederation was freed from the imperial tax.

But the niggling dispute with Milan refused to go away. The first three forest cantons seized Bellinzona. Then surprisingly, the Swiss made friends with the Duke of Milan and helped him by sweeping the French from the plains of Lombardy, generously reestablishing the Sforza dynasty. The Swiss really were top of the fighting league. But a hard new truth awaited, although in the light of what followed, it could be counted a valuable experience. In 1515 at Marignano, a Swiss force of 20,000 faced a combined French and Venetian army of 60,000. They were defeated, not so much by force of numbers (numerical inferiority had never worried the Swiss greatly) but because the enemy was armed with the most modern artillery.

The Swiss retired to consider this. Clearly, warfare was moving into a time of more sophisticated weaponry. And equally clearly, a small nation could not hope to compete with the great powers who could afford it. Best to keep away and let the big boys sort their wars out for themselves. So the Swiss publicly announced their intention of renouncing further territorial expansion.

Prophesying Peace

It must rank with the most forward-looking and intelligent decisions any government ever made. And it heralded expansion in other directions. The Swiss at home now directed their energies towards commercial improvement, and the arts of peace. They had, too, a major export. Nobody denied the Swiss their courage and fighting qualities. Many had rueful cause to admit them. Very well, they would place their soldiers for hire. And for centuries to come, the leading powers engaged highly professional groups of Swiss mercenaries to fight their wars. These regiments were commanded by Swiss officers and flew Swiss flags. They were never part of the national armies beside which they fought. Their bravery and total dedication to the employers who hired them were both legendary. When the mob stormed the royal palace in Paris on August 10, 1792, the Swiss guards died to a man. Even today, the Pope's Vatican guards are still Swiss.

From the early 16th century, the structure of Swiss society was established. With no inherited nobility, Switzerland had drawn its leaders from patrician families. Now, in a changed climate, their descendants became the captains of trade and commerce, writing the rules from which Swiss prosperity was to grow.

Not that all was peace at home. Religion, that traditional excuse for bloodshed, oppression and intolerance, split the nation as the disputes of the Reformation spread. The north followed the teachings of Martin Luther and Ulrich Zwingli; the forest cantons remained solidly Catholic. Geneva began its role as a city of refuge, and there John Calvin preached his uncompromising doctrine. Savoy, thoroughly alarmed, marched against Geneva. Bern, ever ambitious, seized the chance to take up arms, allegedly to help Geneva, claiming to be "liberating" the Vaud.

But gradually the religious differences were sorted out. Switzerland skillfully avoided involvement in the Thirty Years War, and when that ended with the Treaty of Westphalia at Munster in 1648, an important clause of the Treaty was the confirmation by all signatories of Switzerland as a sovereign and, very important, a *neutral* state.

But in the ensuing centuries, Swiss domestic life was embittered by the anomaly that splits so many lands today. The rich grew richer, the poor grew poorer, and the rich were richest in communities like Bern and Zürich, the poor poorest in the rural areas. A few patrician families seemed to have the best of things in the cities, and ruled in a way that protected their privileges.

Revolutions spread, and were always crushed ferociously. Looking back five centuries, the peasants must have wondered whether they were really any better off under Swiss landlords than they had been under the Habsburgs. In the civil war of 1653, they were ruthlessly punished. In 1728 Davel, the hero of the Vaud, was executed by the Bernese. Local risings continued as the century went on. Yet, curiously, to the rest of Europe, on the outside looking in, Switzerland appeared a haven of peace. The great powers, after all, had their own problems, beside which the Swiss insurrections seemed minute.

So as early as the last quarter of the 17th century we can see the first signs of a tourist industry that much later was to become such a shining jewel in the Swiss economic crown. Jean-Jacques Rousseau (1712–1788), the Geneva-born writer and philosopher, drew attention to the beauties of Lac Léman with *Julie, ou la nouvelle Héloise* (1759) with its setting in Montreux and Chillon. Others extolled the glory of the Alps. Visitors came to find out for themselves, and found a retreat from their troubles at home. The first trickle of travelers had begun.

From Revolution to Referenda

France was where the greatest revolution against the established order was to explode, and France was on the doorstep. The revolutionary waves that emanated from France broke on the shores of Swiss politics with a resounding crash. "Liberty and Equality" sounded sweet in the ears of those who were steadily being deprived of the former and certainly had not much of the latter. Basel, Geneva and Zürich rose against their masters. In 1798 the people of the Vaud threw off their Bernese overlords and declared an independent state (the Lemanic Republic, they called it).

This all suited the French and Napoleon. In March 1798, France invaded, annexing the Vaud and Bern. This meant the end of the Confederation. The French government established in its place the Helvetic Republic, a satellite state which it proclaimed "one and indivisible" though there was little doubt who was boss. It did, though, have a uniform Swiss currency system (with Latin inscriptions so as not to upset the language groups).

Like most artificially created states, it was doomed from the start. Its highly concentrated design was contrary to the Swiss preference for local self-government and there were too many conflicting factions jostling for top positions. In 1803 Napoleon admitted that it was not working, and in the Treaty of Mediation restored the former cantonal system, with Aargau, Graubünden, St. Gallen, Ticino, Thurgau and Vaud as new members. Legislative powers were vested in a diet presided over by a Landamann, appointed annually. The diet declared Switzerland neutral. This hardly bothered the Austrians, who marched in with 160,000 men. In 1813, the diet abolished the overlordship of France, and, seeing the possibilities, formerly powerful cantons like Zürich and Bern began forming a line to see what they could pick up and restore their former positions.

Enter now an unlikely figure in the shape of Alexander I of Russia, determined to see that right was done by the smaller cantons. At this stage of the game at least, Alexander was a liberal reformer. Moreover, he knew Switzerland and was sympathetic to it. His tutor had been a Swiss republican and a follower of Rousseau. At the Congress of Vienna in 1815 he urged the diet to adopt federation. They did. Valais, Geneva and Neuchâtel were added, and the Congress guaranteed Switzerland's independence and permanent neutrality.

Religious controversy split the Swiss in the mid 19th century, culminating in civil war between the Protestant and the seven Roman Catholic cantons, who had formed a separatist league following the suppression of some monasteries. The federal army, led by General Dufour, defeated the Catholics in November 1847.

The flood of revolutions that swept across Europe in the following year could hardly leave Switzerland untouched. A new constitution was agreed by the 22 cantons. Bern became the capital; the country's national government and relations with foreign powers were to be conducted by an upper and lower chamber; while all the cantons retained their own councils, but undertook not to form mutual alliances.

This constitution was revised considerably in 1874. Mostly, the changes were sensible in the light of the experience of the previous quarter of a century, and involved the responsibilities of the federal government, which were widened particularly as regards military matters. Compulsory free schooling was introduced, though its application remained a matter for the cantons. Two important liberties were introduced, that of initiative and that of referendum. By the first, any citizen could propose a new law to the federal assembly if he could produce 100,000 signatures in support, and by the second 50,000 signatures could be enough to compel the government to submit an issue to referendum. In the years following, the commercial and industrial expansion of Switzerland advanced and was consolidated, its engineering achievements in conquering difficult terrain astonished the world, and international acceptance of its role as a center for the encouragement of education, the arts and humanitarian objectives won illustrious prestige.

The 20th Century

World War I found Switzerland sandwiched between battling nations of both sides. But Swiss neutrality was strictly maintained. And as a neutral, Switzerland could still follow its now widely acknowledged mission as a land of mercy and help relieve suffering. Red Cross units were organized, and wounded escapees and prisoners of war permitted to be interned there.

The League of Nations arose from the ashes of war, a beacon of optimism for a disillusioned world, with its headquarters at Geneva. Switzerland joined in 1920, the first year, with an important clause protecting her neutrality in that she was not required to take part in any military sanctions proposed by the league, nor should she permit preparations for them to be carried out on Swiss soil. She was nonetheless expected to take part in economic and financial sanctions. From this she was released by the league on May 14, 1938.

Between the wars, Switzerland's rapid economic progress, humanitarian aims, industrial achievements and quickly widening tourism, together with a reputation for efficient administration, greatly enhanced her prestige. The Swiss took note of the gathering war clouds as Nazi arrogance became ever more ominous; and on August 28, 1939, the total mobilization of the frontier and air defenses was ordered to ensure an immediate response should neutrality need to be defended.

It never was, though bombs fell inadvertently on Swiss territory on several occasions, notably in 1940 at Geneva and Lausanne, and in 1944 heavily on Schaffhausen. Rationing was introduced, but Switzerland still exercised her role of mercy, for which many escaped British and, later, American, prisoners were grateful.

At the end of World War II, Switzerland did not join the United Nations, but nevertheless became an active member of UNESCO (the United Nations Educational Scientific and Cultural Organization) whose stated aims of promoting collaboration in these fields, and furthering universal respect for justice and human rights obviously coincided with Switzerland's own objectives. (In 1986 Switzerland went to the polls to decide whether to enter the United Nations as a full member, but voted against as this, many felt, had implications running contrary to Switzerland's now widely accepted and understood neutrality.)

Switzerland took part in the Marshall Plan after the war, though seeking no American aid for herself, and entered on another period of highly successful commercial, industrial and financial expansion during which social services were increasingly developed (general old-age pensions were introduced in 1948), unemployment virtually eradicated, and education and the arts consistently encouraged.

A creative partnership of private and public ownership became firmly established. The only nationalized utilities are those of post office, telegraph, telephone and main railways, the Swiss Federal Railroads, of which the Swiss, who have something of a passion for transport, are rightly proud. Other services (buses, gas, branch railways, etc.) are either private or municipal enterprises or a mixture of both, sometimes with a cantonal subsidy. Hydroelectric power plants are owned by private companies under federal or cantonal grant.

Switzerland has become a byword for efficiency, something which more and more visitors are discovering at first hand. Even the most remote regions have now opened their doors to tourism, and in doing so, have ensured that natural beauty remains unspoiled. Much of Switzerland's progress and economic security can be attributed to wise industrial labor relations. Though in 1986 the nation's strikes increased by 100 per cent. From two to four.

Switzerland Today

Defense. Peaceful Switzerland may be today, but it is a nation prepared to defend itself and the principles for which it stands. Every able bodied male is a soldier. At 19, he is medically examined for fitness and, if passed, begins military service the following year with 120 days at a toughening recruiting center. He takes full kit and uniform with him at the end, must keep it in good order, and before 36, serve ten three-week refresher courses. Recruits hoping to become N.C.O.s serve an additional 148 days, as do intending officers. Their duties cease at 50 and 55 respectively.

Men exempted from military duty do not escape entirely. They are expected to serve in the auxiliary forces (air raid wardens, ambulance service, etc.) or pay an annual tax. Fire service is compulsory up to 45 (including foreign male residents) but may be replaced on payment of a local fire tax instead.

The role of Switzerland as the neutral custodian of important arteries of communication running through her territories has been acknowledged by successive international treaties as far back as Westphalia (1648), through to Vienna (1815), Versailles (1920) and 1939.

Government. The structure of administration is roughly that agreed in 1874. The Federal Assembly comprises a lower and upper chamber, the first a National Council elected on the basis of proportional representation (one member for every 22,000 people), the second a States Council (not unlike the U.S. Senate) with two representatives from each canton. The Federal Council has seven members, elected for four years. A woman made it for the first time in 1984. Presidencies of the Council, and of the federation, rotate annually.

Each canton is a sovereign republic, with its own government composed of executive and legislative sections. They control most cantonal affairs. Jura, the French speaking area of Bern, was the last to achieve full cantonal status (on January 1, 1979), bringing the total to 23. The Jura has its capital at Delémont.

Federal and cantonal elections are held every four years. Not until 1971 did women win the federal vote (though they seem not to have missed it much before then). It was left to the cantons to decide whether to follow suit in local elections and most did. But not in part of Appenzell where women still have no vote, and appear not to feel very deprived.

Mountainous Appenzell—where the men wear rings in the right ear and smoke the handsomely decorated *Lendeauerli* pipe (it's smoked upside down)—is one of the areas where they hold open-air parliaments and decide issues on a show of hands. These Landsgemeinde date back to the 13th century, and include picturesque rituals of processions, bands and singing. Old traditions and crafts refuse to die. Despite the smooth efficiency, financial prosperity and shrewd commonsense of modern Switzerland, inside every Swiss there beats a romantic heart.

CREATIVE SWITZERLAND

A Collision of Cultures

Switzerland, in many ways, is the most European of all European countries, rich in history and tradition, prosperous, elegant, civilized. One has only to walk through the lively and affluent streets of Geneva, an international city *par excellence,* or around the chic streets of Zürich or Bern, to be aware of the many-centuried layers which have combined to make Switzerland one of the most intriguing, sophisticated and culturally varied countries in the West.

All of Europe, it seems, is here.

As befits a prosperous and stable country, cultural activities are everywhere in evidence. L'Orchestre de la Suisse Romande in Geneva ranks high among the leading European orchestras; the Schauspielhaus in Zürich boasts one of the finest classical theater companies in Europe; Bern, the federal capital, is home to a whole host of museums, ranging from the Kunsthaus, which houses the Klee collection (the largest and most important of its kind in the world) to, at the opposite end of the scale, the Swiss Alpine Museum. The medieval cities of Basel—home to one of the oldest and most respected Universities in Europe—Luzern, St. Gallen, Bern itself, Fribourg and Neuchâtel all contain a multitude of marvelous buildings from practically every period of the country's history. And throughout the last 500 years Switzerland has been home to some of the most advanced and influential of philosophers, teachers, artists and writers of Europe.

But, extraordinarily, this cultural crossroads has failed to produce any extended body of work that one can confidently call a Swiss school of painting or music, literature or architecture. How can one explain this strange cultural vacuum?

The unique geographical and political nature of Switzerland goes a long way toward providing the answer. Switzerland lies at the meeting point of three great European countries, and thus at the meeting point of three powerful European cultures—France to the west, Germany to the north and Italy to the south, each with a long and rich heritage of national creativity. As might be expected of a small country surrounded by such very powerful neighbors, Switzerland has long been susceptible to their influence, all the more so in that it is only in relatively recent years that Switzerland has enjoyed real internal political unity, without which a national identity is hard to attain.

As a consequence of this three-way pull, there has been a natural tendency, still very much in evidence today, for Swiss artists to gravitate toward, and become a part of, the very well-established cultures of these countries.

The Cultural Exodus

The most extreme example of this cultural dominance occurs in literature. A francophone Swiss writer, for example, writing in French, automatically becomes part of the French literary tradition. Similarly, a German-Swiss writer, because he writes in German, becomes part of the German literary tradition. Hermann Hesse, winner of the Nobel Prize for literature in 1946 for his novel *The Glass-Bead Game,* though a naturalized Swiss, is always considered a German writer. This is not simply because he was born in Germany but because, writing in German, he could hardly be considered anything else. Similarly, Friedrich Dürrenmatt, perhaps the most important Swiss playwright of this century, is generally considered a German author first and a Swiss second. Without a unifying Swiss language, the possibility of a body of native Swiss literature is something of a contradiction in terms.

There is, however, one fairly important exception. Though the Swiss-Germans mostly speak pure German, their everyday spoken language is a dialect known as Schwyzerdütsch (literally Swiss-German). This is not spoken outside Switzerland. Consequently, any Swiss-German writer who elects to write in Swiss-German, and proclaim his Swissness, necessarily confines himself to a limited readership and can seem rather parochial.

The exigencies of language have created a more extreme situation for Swiss literature than the circumstances affecting the other arts, but much the same sort of dilemma faces the painter, architect or sculptor as faces the writer. Even in the 20th century—when, following the establishment of a very much more obvious national identity, one might expect to find native schools of Swiss art growing up and establishing themselves positively—nearly every single Swiss artist of international stature has been drawn to the established cultural milieu of his or her parent culture and has subsequently become firmly identified with it.

Le Corbusier (1887–1966) and Alberto Giacometti (1901–1966)—probably the two most important and influential Swiss artists of the 20th century—both spent the majority of their adult lives in France and are, to all intents and purposes, French artists. Le Corbusier, apart from belonging to an avowedly international school of architecture, claimed that he owed his cultural allegiance exclusively to France. Switzerland, for the most part, is noticeably lacking buildings by him.

Among slightly less well-known Swiss artists of the 20th century one finds a similar natural inclination to leave Switzerland in favor of the more stimulating and varied cultural climate abroad. The sculptor Jean Tinguely (b. 1925), whose exploding and disintegrating "animated" sculptures have raised more than their fair share of artistic eyebrows the world over, followed Giacometti's example and settled in France, where he still works.

The composer Arthur Honegger (1892–1955), the leading Swiss composer of the 20th century, despite training at Zürich Conservatory, nonetheless spent most of his life in Paris where, with Francis Poulenc and others, he founded the avant garde musical group Les Six in 1917. Another important Swiss composer, Frank Martin (1890–1974), a leading figure of the post-war musical world, lived in Holland for long periods.

To trace these trends further back, to the 19th century, the painter Arnold Böcklin (1827–1901), though born in Switzerland, was trained in Germany, Flanders and Paris and subsequently spent many years in Munich and Rome. It is difficult not to see him as a German painter first and foremost.

The Baroque and Beyond

Before the 19th century, with Switzerland unified not even in name, this pattern is more pronounced and, from time to time, more confused. The painter Henry Fuseli (1741–1825), whom the Swiss have long claimed as one of their most important artists, spent his entire working life outside Switzerland. In fact it is difficult to see how any convincing case for considering him a "Swiss" artist can be made, except by virtue of his birth. He trained in Berlin and London before journeying to Rome where he remained for eight years before returning to London. It was in London that he enjoyed his greatest success, which included full membership of the Royal Academy in 1790. He was highly thought of among artistic circles and his powerful, nightmare visions, poised somewhat incongruously between neo-Classicism and the fully blown Romantic proved highly influential. His pupils included Constable and Landseer and he was highly admired by Blake.

Francesco Borromini (1599–1667), the most idiosyncratic and original architect of Roman High Baroque, presents a remarkably similar case. Like Fuseli he was born in the Ticino, the Italian-Swiss part of the country. But having traveled to Rome in his early 20s, he remained there for the rest of his life and is completely identified with the Italian Baroque.

The painters Conrad Witz (1400/10–1444/6) and Hans Holbein the Younger (1497/8–1543), both extremely influential, have stronger claims to be considered Swiss, but they are by no means convincing. Witz lived and worked in Basel and subsequently Geneva—at that time not a member of the Helvetic Confederation, though in other respects very closely allied to it—and it was there he painted his one extant masterpiece, *The Miraculous Draught of Fishes,* the background of which contains the first specifically recognizable landscape in Western painting. The greater part of his working life was spent in Switzerland, and the Swiss landscape was crucially important to his development of landscape painting, but Witz was born in Germany, where he received his early training, and the dominant influences on him were the Van Eyck brothers, who were Flemish. So the degree to which Witz can be considered a specifically Swiss painter is certainly debatable.

Holbein, too, was born not in Switzerland but in Germany. His father was an accomplished portrait painter and, as a young man, Holbein worked in his studio. He left Germany and settled in Basel, becoming a citizen in 1520, though in 1517 he left briefly to visit Italy. It was in Basel that he met the Dutchman, Erasmus, in 1523, the greatest of all the Humanist philosophers. Despite the fact that Holbein enjoyed great success as a portraitist and painter of religious pictures in Basel and that his style was consolidated there, much of his most successful and characteristic work was done in London for Henry VIII during two trips to England, the first from 1526 to 1528, the second from 1532 to 1536. Similarly, the dominant influences on him were Flemish and Dutch. And it is also interesting that his strikingly penetrating and psychologically charged portraits attracted only the lamest of imitators and disciples in Switzerland itself whereas his influence in Germany was very much more pronounced.

The Land As Influence

Ironic though it may perhaps seem, Switzerland's most distinctive and famous geographical feature, the Alps, Europe's largest mountain range, has also played its part in preventing the development of Swiss culture. Over 50 percent of the total land area of Switzerland is alpine, and about half of those alpine areas are entirely nonproductive. Until the coming of the railways in the latter part of the 19th century, many alpine communities were entirely isolated even from their immediate neighbors for long periods during the winter months. For much of the country's past the Alps were the province of the peasant farmer and shepherd. Consequently, much of Switzerland's heritage centers around folk art and peasant culture.

A great deal of this is extremely attractive and ingenious: the delightfully painted and carved wooden houses of the Engadine, for example, the weird but wonderful Alphorn, today very much a national symbol, even the much-maligned cuckoo clock. Similarly, there are a number of festivals which owe their origins to peasant celebrations—the world-famous Fête des Vignerons held every 25 years at Vevey, or the Unspunnen Festival of Alpine Herdsmen, which draws vast crowds.

Folk music is still very popular in Switzerland and the visitor is likely to come closest to uncovering a genuinely Swiss atmosphere at one of the many festivals held in the summer. Folk music, of a sort, is also evident in one of the most instantly recognizable Swiss traditions, yodelling. But though this thriving heritage of popular culture may be both enduring and characteristic of Switzerland, it cannot really be considered a positive contribution to European cultural traditions. Folk art, however enjoyable it may be, is by definition derivative and decorative. It lacks the spiritual and intellectual content that the creation of great art must inevitably generate.

A Comfortable Culture

But the prevalence of a peasant culture and the dominance of Switzerland's neighbors cannot completely account for the strange lack of home-grown cultural achievement. There is another crucially important factor: the character of the Swiss themselves. Though it is always dangerous to generalize about a people, there is nevertheless no doubt that at heart the Swiss are an extremely sober and bourgeois people, fond of their creature comforts and dedicated to prosperity, banking and railway timetables. In the German-speaking areas in particular, the conspicuously conservative and careful attitudes one encounters do seem at odds with the probing imagination necessary for artistic endeavor.

In many ways this is rather paradoxical. The stability, peace and prosperity that the bourgeois attitudes of the Swiss have created might well be expected to have encouraged rather than to have stifled artistic life. The predominantly comfortable culture of Flanders and Holland in the 17th century, for example, produced Rubens, Rembrandt, Vermeer, Hals, Cuyp, the Ruisdaels, Van Dyck, the Brueghels and a score of other extraordinary painters. The arts always prosper during times of plenty—indeed this is an essential ingredient—and it is a Romantic myth to believe that there is something fundamentally incompatible between art and material wealth or that the reckless spirit of the artist must have turmoil and unrest to drive him on. Nearly all the most productive periods in the history of art have coincided with periods of peace and prosperity. But not apparently in Switzerland. Why this should be so to quite the extent it is remains a mystery. It is undeniable that there is in Switzerland's distinctive brand of bourgeois thinking something fundamentally inimical to the creation of art—although it provides rich soil for the growth of cultural awareness and the enjoyment of art in all its forms.

Craftsmanship in Print

But if the sobriety of the Swiss has inhibited the creative arts, it has paid dividends where craftsmanship is concerned. Since the Reformation the excellence of Swiss craftsmanship has been acknowledged both in Europe and, latterly, through the world at large. In more recent times this expertise has reached its highest peak in sophisticated feats of engineering and technology. Watches are perhaps the best-known example. But from the standpoint of the arts, the finest flowerings of Swiss craftsmanship are found in printing in all its forms.

The first great period—it has been described as Switzerland's golden age—came in the 16th century when Holbein, Niklaus Manuel (1484–1530), Tobias Stimmer (1539–1584) and the extraordinary Urs Graf (1485–1527), poet, draughtsman, engraver, painter and mercenary, began a rich and longlasting tradition of skillful and sophisticated drawing and printmaking. The 17th and 18th centuries saw a number of competent draughtsmen and printers continue this tradition, though none of outstanding merit emerged. But in the 19th century Switzerland enjoyed something of a renaissance in printmaking, the principal and most influential figure being Rudolphe Toepffer (1799–1846), an engaging character who, among his other achievements, is credited with the development of the strip cartoon. His humorous and satirical lithographs, fluid and delicate, are today enjoying a well-deserved revival.

In the 20th century there are only a few figures to compare with the distinguished graphic artists of the past—and among those few Hans Erni must rank high—but the country is nonetheless a world leader in color printing in general and the printing of fine art posters in particular. There are a number of celebrated and sophisticated printing plants and many of Europe's leading artists of the 20th century have taken advantage of these facilities. They include Arp, Chagall, Henry Moore, Kokoschka and many others.

Patronage Par Excellence

Switzerland's bourgeois affluence has led to the establishment of a large number of cultural institutions. Being wealthy, Switzerland is consequently also rich in art. It is a curious fact that there is more art per capita in private hands in Switzerland than in any other country in the world. Among the outstanding private collections are three of particular excellence: that of Baron Heinrich Thyssen in Lugano (Villa Favorita), which ranks among the finest anywhere in the world; the Oskar Reinhart collection in Winterthur which includes Goya's last, unfinished, work as well as a very large number of French, Flemish and Dutch masterpieces; and the Hahnloser collection, now divided between Winterthur and Bern and which features 19th- and 20th-century works, many by artists who were close personal friends of Dr. Hahnloser. Three private collections of this sustained excellence in a country the size of Switzerland are eloquent testimony to the commitment—and spending power—of the country's private collectors. All three collections, however, were formed before the war, and it is doubtful if even the most assiduous and affluent collector could amass anything comparable today.

The federal and cantonal museums, despite their scale and numbers, do not for the most part rank among the leading European galleries, though there are exceptions. The Kunstmuseum in Basel, for example, contains important works by Holbein and Witz as well as a large collection of 19th- and 20th-century French paintings, including a fine collection of pictures by Ferdinand Leger. The Bern Kunstmuseum is home to the Klee collection, certainly the most representative in existence, as well as to a number of very beautiful Kandinskys. The rest of the collection is, however, undistinguished. Zürich is the site of the third most important gallery in Switzerland. It organizes consistently stimulating and imaginative exhibitions of modern work, as well as possessing a large and important permanent collection that includes a number of Monet's enormous *Water Lilies* panels.

The Intellectual Heritage

Switzerland also has a thriving and varied intellectual heritage. In fact this fecund intellectual tradition may well constitute Switzerland's most persuasive claim to cultural importance. Basel, home to Erasmus and Holbein at the beginning of the 16th century, was the first city in Switzerland to rise to intellectual prominence, though during the same period the fiery presence of the Frenchman Jean Calvin in Geneva and Ulrich Zwingli in Zürich, both preaching the new doctrine of the Reformed church, ensured that Switzerland remained in the forefront of new ideas in Europe, as well as playing a leading role in the Reformation.

In the 18th century two other Frenchmen, the philosophers Jean Jacques Rousseau and Voltaire, continued this tradition of intellectual excellence. Both were forced to flee France as a result of their championing of enlightened thought and liberal ideas and both settled in French-Switzerland. (Rousseau was to proclaim himself proudly a "citizen of Geneva.") At the end of the 18th century Switzerland enjoyed a brilliant period intellectually. Zürich was the "little Athens of the north"; Geneva a cauldron of new political liberalism, "the political laboratory of Europe." The Académie of the Vaud, a Protestant college founded during the Reformation, held courses on diplomacy and civil administration—unknown elsewhere—and supplied diplomats, administrators and tutors to many European courts, most especially in Germany.

This period also saw the emergence of one of the handful of truly original and influential thinkers Switzerland has produced—the pedagogue, visionary and humanist, Heinrich Pestalozzi (1746–1827). His revolutionary approach to education, based on methods one can only call psychological, though he predated the discovery of psychology as a science by almost 75 years, and his precocious social conscience, allied to his insistence on the importance of love as the mainspring of all successful human relations, single out Pestalozzi as a man genuinely before his time.

Of the legion of botanists, chemists, philosophers, educators and men of letters that distinguish Switzerland's story in the latter part of the 19th century and into the 20th century, two men deserve special mention. Jacob Burckhardt (1818–1897), the historian whose work on the Italian Renaissance dramatically altered perceptions of that period as well as initiating a new approach to art history, and the psychologist Carl Jung (1875–1961), now considered the founder of a legitimate alternative to Freud's system of psychoanalysis, since he placed more emphasis on what he felt to be the naturally religious character of the human soul, and displayed a creative flexibility in his thought that outreached the rigid doctrinaire legacy of the Viennese master.

The Brain Drain in Reverse

Switzerland has attracted a large number of foreign exiles, especially since the end of the 18th century. A fair percentage of them have been artists and intellectuals of the highest caliber. This trend can be traced originally to the early 16th century, with the presence of Witz, Holbein and Erasmus in Basel. But it is not until the arrival of Rousseau and Voltaire in Geneva around 1760, both of them coming to Switzerland as exiles from the Ancien Régime in France, that the notion of Switzerland as a place of exile for the dispossessed of Europe began to take firm shape. With the subsequent confirmation in the Constitution of 1848 of neutrality and tolerance as the bedrock of Swiss foreign policy, the number of exiles in Switzerland swelled dramatically, though for much of the remainder of the 19th century these were principally political rather than artistic refugees.

However, the innumerable European artists that poured into Switzerland in the early 19th century were basically tourists, inspired largely by Rousseau's powerful polemics on the glories of the dramatic Alpine landscape. Hardly a single major figure from this period did not at some time or another visit Switzerland, many staying for lengthy periods, among them the English historian Gibbon, author of *The Decline and Fall of the Roman Empire,* who settled in Geneva, and the Frenchwoman Madame de Staël. Her château at Coppet on the shores of Lac Léman became a focal point of liberal thought in Europe. It was she who first propounded the notion of a Europe without frontiers where the free exchange of ideas would not only be possible but actively encouraged; prophetic indeed.

Other giants of the Romantic age who came to Switzerland were—Goethe; his fellow German Schiller, who gave fictional flesh to the greatest of all Swiss folk heroes, William Tell, in his play of the same name; Byron, still looked upon in Switzerland as the very embodiment of the Romantic ideal, largely as a result of his poem, *The Prisoner of Chillon,* which celebrated the six-year incarceration of Bonivard in the Château de Chillon during the Reformation; and Keats and Shelley (whose wife Mary wrote *Frankenstein* in Switzerland in 1816).

Among the many painters who drew inspiration from the towering misty peaks and gushing waterfalls of the Swiss landscape, perhaps the most famous was Turner who, during a number of visits, sketched, drew and painted the Alps in every weather and all lights, seeking to extract the maximum of mystery and majesty from their mighty masses. The many albums of prints he produced proved essential visual complements to the literary outpourings inspired by the Alps for the People of Quality throughout Europe.

Two later 19th-century visitors to Switzerland were the German composer Richard Wagner and the philosopher Friedrich Nietzsche, both having made life more than a little hot for themselves in their native lands. Wagner began his massive operatic epic, *The Ring of the Nibelung,* in Zürich and, during a later stay in Luzern, completed *The*

Mastersingers of Nuremburg. Nietzsche taught at Basel University and conceived the idea for his Zarathustra and Superman during a holiday in the Engadine.

In the 20th century—largely as a result of the vast upheavals caused by World War I, the Russian Revolution, the rise to power of the Nazis and World War II—a large number of exiles, principally, but not exclusively, German, settled in the safe bourgeois bosom of Switzerland. Among the most distinguished were Einstein, who did much of the groundwork for his Theory of Relativity in Bern; the novelist Hermann Hesse; the playwright Bertolt Brecht; Thomas Maria Rilke, perhaps the leading German 20th-century poet; the innovatory Russian composer Stravinsky; and the Russian painter Kandinsky who lived for a time in Bern, when Paul Klee was there.

Klee, in fact, of all these artists, has the best claim to be considered Swiss. Not only was he born in Bern, though of German parents, he long nurtured a fervent hope of obtaining Swiss citizenship, though this was never to be. However, at the same time it has to be said that his most productive periods were all spent in Germany where he was a member of the Blau Reiter group, "founders," as it were, of abstract painting. He also enjoyed a long and fruitful association with the Bauhaus in Weimar (Prussia), until its dissolution by the Nazis the leading avant garde art school in Europe.

This influx of refugees, both political and artistic, led to one extraordinary simultaneous gathering of unlikely figures in Zürich in 1916. These were Hans Arp and Tristan Tzara—co-founders of Dada, the anti-art, anti-bourgeois movement—Lenin and Trotsky—fathers and prime movers of the Russian Revolution—and James Joyce, *enfant terrible* of English literature. Tom Stoppard's successful play, *Travesties,* is based on this strange concatenation of characters.

Today, foreigners have continued to make Switzerland their home, but their motives have been influenced more by favorable tax concessions than persecution at home.

Switzerland Performs

Music is a universal language, transcending the limitations of tongue. Appropriately, the multilingual Swiss are great listeners. That is not to imply that they do not produce great performers, but that their programs are designed without the narrow prejudices which sometimes invade nations with greater creative classical traditions, and without the inborn reservations of some of their audiences.

A winter tour of their opera houses can be a stimulating experience, and since the country is so concentrated and well-connected it can be undertaken in a few days. It is something for the visitor who has out-grown mere worship of stars—there will not be many of these—but who has come to understand opera as a team integration of singing with imaginative production and design, meaningful orchestral playing and intelligent acting.

Geneva's Grand Théâtre, rebuilt after a disaster in which a fire scene rehearsal became too realistic, is a handsome theater casting its net wide for its repertory and staging mostly new productions of established works. Zürich's Opernhaus has an enterprising policy judiciously mixing in tradition and, like Geneva, combining it with a school where maturing young singers can get practical experience, producing many famous names. Bern's Stadttheater achieved international recognition when in 1981 it staged a modern-dress *Rigoletto* which exemplified the Swiss spirit of innovation, and the Stadttheaters of Basel and St. Gallen are others where exciting things can happen. The Swiss opera seasons run from early fall to summer.

Orchestral music abounds. Every city has its permanent symphony orchestra and if we single out one for special mention, it does not mean that the others, such as the Zürich Tonhalle formed in 1867, are unimportant. But L'Orchestre de la Suisse Romande in Geneva, through their numerous recordings, have carried the flag of Swiss excellence to the four corners of the world. Formed in 1918, they were conducted for almost half a century by the great Ernest Ansermet, famed for the lucidity of his Stravinsky performances. The orchestra retains its high international esteem.

A remarkable ensemble is the Basel Chamber Orchestra, formed in 1926 by the enthusiastic Paul Sacher when he was only 20. He still conducts it—his youthful vigor was astonishing at the golden jubilee concerts—and the orchestra still specializes in contemporary music. Among the composers who have written specially for it have been Britten, Bartok, Stravinsky, Prokofiev, Honegger, Martinu, Martin, Tippett, Hindemith and more recently, Henze and Berio. Some list.

Swiss festivals abound for the summer visitor, and the most important is Luzern, begun by Toscanini and Walter in 1938, and still playing host to the world's top orchestras and conductors every August in the concert hall by the lake. It is a favorite summer date for music lovers.

Montreux in September follows a similar design. It includes the Clara Haskil piano competition, and stages some of its events in such picturesque settings as the Château de Chillon. Other festivals of note are Zürich (June), where the accent is on opera, and Gstaad (August), enjoying an illustrious association with Yehudi Menuhin. But the visitor should also keep an eye open for the less publicized festivals in small towns which often yield unexpected delights and unfamiliar music in lovely old Baroque churches.

If we have concentrated on operas and concerts, it is because they present few problems of communication. But it should be added that most Swiss communities have healthy drama companies, and though a limited command of the local language may blunt the message it need not obscure it. You could, for example, enjoy a play of Dürenmatt with only minimal German, follow his de-bunking of inbred conservatism and out-dated pomposity, and emerge feeling you have enjoyed a Swiss Ibsen.

In the summer there are numerous special festival productions. One of the most famous, which takes place every five years, is Einsiedeln's *Welttheater,* with its theme of the life and death of man, played out in the great arena that forms a natural open-air theater in front of the Benedictine monastery. Altdorf ensures that the motto on the William Tell statue ("The story of William Tell will be told as long as the mountains stand") becomes an annual reality by staging Schiller's drama in the town from which the Swiss patriot fought.

Ballet is performed regularly throughout the year and there are workshops and experimental theater wherever you find the conventional stage. Plenty of specialist theaters, too, such as the puppets of St. Gallen, Fribourg and Geneva.

A Cultural Calendar

Here are the most important cultural events in the Swiss calendar, taking place every year at about the same time—

March/June	Locarno	The Locarno Concerts
April/June	Lugano	The Lugano Concerts
April	Montreux	International Choral Festival
April/beg. May	Montreux	*Golden Rose of Montreux* International TV Festival
April/beg. May	Bern	International Jazz Festival
May/June	Lausanne	Lausanne International Festival
June	Zürich	International June Festival Weeks
Mid-June	Bern	Bern Art Weeks
July	Montreux	International Jazz Festival
Mid-July	Braunwald	Braunwald Music Week
July/August	Interlaken	William Tell Festival Plays
Mid-July/ mid-August	Engadine	Engadine Concert Weeks
July/September	Sion	Tibor Varga Music Festival
Mid-August/ beg. September	Luzern	International Festival of Music
Mid-August	Geneva	*Fête de Genève* (Geneva Festival)
August	Locarno	Locarno International Film Festival
August	Gstaad	Yehudi Menuhin Festival
September	Montreux-Vevey	Montreux-Vevey International Music Festival
September/October	Ascona	Ascona Music Festival Weeks
2nd half September	Geneva	International Competition for Musical Performers
End September	Diablerets	International Alpine Film Festival
October	Zürich	International Jazz Festival
Mid-October	Lausanne	Italian Opera Festival

SKIING IN SWITZERLAND

Downhill All the Way

by
MARK HELLER

English-born Mark Heller has been skiing since 1921. He has written 15 books on the subject, as well as writing regularly on skiing for the Guardian *newspaper.*

Winter sports were conceived and born of British parentage in the village of St. Moritz in the winter of 1864–5. Midwife to this momentous event was Swiss hotelier Johannes Badrutt of the Kulm hotel. In the fall of 1864 four English visitors bade farewell to their host, Badrutt, lamenting their return to the cold, misery and mists of an English winter. In a moment of inspired madness, Badrutt enthused over the wonders of sunshine and snow in the Engadine and invited his four guests to spend the winter with him. If it was not everything he promised, their stay was to be entirely free. In December they returned, bringing with them ten other friends, including two ladies and at least two Americans. They arrived, roasted and snow-blind, after a spectacular 12-hour sleigh journey over the Julier Pass from Chur. They stayed until the snows began to melt in March, spending their days skating, tobogganing and walking. They were not disappointed.

The next 40 years or so saw a steady but undramatic growth in winter visitors to Switzerland, though by no means all came for the winter sports. Davos and Arosa, for example, specialized in sanatoria for tuberculous patients. But St. Moritz attracted skaters and lugers, while Kandersteg became popular among the British as a skating center. Despite the travel difficulties and the eccentricty of the venue, wintering in Switzerland began to attract the attention of the fashionable press, with St. Moritz in particular a favored resort, not least as a rival to the South of France (where a subtle shift in the climate was beginning to make the once-balmy Mediterranean weather distinctly unwelcoming). But the winter sports themselves were strictly a subsidiary attraction, an amusing diversion at best, for all except the serious, rather puritanical exponents of the British school of skating. Skiing hardly figured at all, remaining the domain of a few hardy pioneers—"plank hoppers" they were called—who were viewed with a mixture of comic disbelief and disdain. Considering their incompetence, perhaps this wasn't so surprising.

The Plank Hoppers Persevere

By this date skiing was, in fact, comparatively widespread in most of Switzerland. Konrad Wilde is credited as being the first person to use skis in Switzerland, in a small township called Mitlodi in 1868. Before then, skis were totally unknown in Switzerland. In the following ten years or so, a number of other experimenters also brought skis to the Alps. Many of them were Norwegians from the Oslo and Telemark regions of Norway, generally considered the home of skiing. Skiing had been known in Scandinavia for about 6,000 years, where it was used as a means of winter transport, chiefly by hunters and, occasionally, by the Scandinavian armies.

Among the plank hoppers were Englishman Gerald Fox and his cousin, who experimented with Norwegian skis in Grindelwald in the 1870s. Similarly, following the Great Exhibition in Paris in 1878, where Finnish skis were exhibited and on sale, one Dr. Paulcke and the brothers Brangger among others brought similar skis to Davos. They hoped to emulate Christoph Iselin and his friends, who had crossed the Pragel Pass near Glarus on skis in 1884.

Having no practical knowledge of skis, however, progress was far from smooth. Even the Norwegians who claimed to be able to ski were defeated by what they claimed was the excessive steepness of the Swiss hills. Dr. Paulcke didn't have much more luck. He had a Norwegian valet who he assumed would be able to teach him. To his disgust he discovered that not all Norwegians were born skiers. (He consigned his boards to the attic where, some years later, they were discovered by his son; he was to become one of the great pioneers of skiing, in 1897 making the first ski crossing of the Bernese Oberland). The Brangger brothers meanwhile had another problem. They couldn't read the Finnish instructions with their skis.

Nonetheless, the plank hoppers persevered, and, by a combination of instinct and common sense, painfully taught themselves the rudiments of skiing. That they were not immediately successful is made uncomfortably clear by the fact that it was to be several years yet before anyone discovered how to make turns on these primitive, unwieldy skis. The basic technique was to go in a straight line until you fell down, whether by accident or design. Despite these handicaps, in 1884 the Branggers nonetheless managed to cross the Maienfelder Furka above Davos to Arosa, still a very respectable ski expedition today. They repeated the expedition the following year, this time in the company of Arthur Conan Doyle. He wrote an account of their adventures in the *Strand Magazine,* the world's first piece of ski journalism. The word was spreading.

Right across the Alps enterprising eccentrics were discovering the potential of skis. At this time it was the British who still led the way, taking the first tentative steps toward organizing the sport, elevating it from the realms of curiosity to an established winter sport. In Davos the Richardson brothers founded the Davos English Ski Club, a move that lead indirectly to the foundation of the Ski Club of Great Britain in 1903. Likewise, in the Bernese Oberland, Caulfield was laying the foundations for a serious scientific study of skiing techniques. In 1911 the first downhill race was staged, from Plaine Morte to Crans.

Coming Down Comes Up

By 1914 winter sports had become big business. All the main resorts now had year-round rail links. Likewise, the number and range of hotels open in winter had increased dramatically. Facilities for skating, tobogganing and walking expanded at a similar rate. Skiing, however, remained something of a specialized sport, the poor relative of winter sports. Though, for example, the hills around St. Moritz, Davos and Arosa all had ski tracks, equipment and clothing continued to be woefully inadequate.

Skiing as a competitive and, above all, downhill sport blossomed only after 1918 when the British returned to their familar winter resorts. The reason for its comparative unpopularity up to this point was that, despite the advances in techniques and understanding of the sport, skiing was still considered essentially an adjunct to walking and mountaineering, the winter ascents of summer routes, a walk in the mountains on skis followed by a painful and difficult descent.

By the end of World War I, however, the emphasis was to change dramatically. What became important was not going uphill on your skis but coming downhill. The breakthrough came in Mürren in the Bernese Oberland when Englishman Arnold Lunn, charismatic and energetic champion of the Ski Club of Great Britain, persuaded the operators of the little Allmenhubel funicular to run it in the winter. Once you could get up your hill easily, what then became important was coming back down it again. Almost overnight the entire concept of skiing was transformed. Downhill skiing was born.

The boost in popularity skiing received was tremendous. Throughout the '20s and into the '30s more and more rail lines, funiculars and cable cars were kept open through the winter as the search for the longest, steepest and fastest downhill runs intensified. In 1928, for example, St. Moritz—host that year of the second Winter Olympics—built the Corviglia extension to the Chanterella funicular, making the Corviglia ski slopes accessible for the first time. In 1932, Davos went one better, opening the first funicular designed specifically for downhill skiers, in the process opening the entire Parsenn area to skiers. Similarly, Engelberg built the cable car from Gerschnialp to Trübsee, putting itself firmly on the skiing map. Most significant of all was the opening in December 1934 of the world's first T-bar lift on the Bolgen nursery slopes at Davos. Simple to use, the now ubiquitous T-bar proved the final technical breakthrough. Where before a 20-minute slog uphill was rewarded by a one-minute descent, now you could glide up the hill perched on the wooden, anchor-shaped bar in less than five minutes. It was an invention that hurtled downhill skiing from a popular but nonetheless still faintly eccentric sport, still something of a minority interest, to the forefront of all winter sports.

How the Resorts Grew

Parallel to this explosion in the popularity of skiing was the equally dramatic growth of the winter resorts themselves, a process that the Swiss managed with characteristic aplomb. Switzerland had of course long been popular in the 19th century as a summer destination. Accessible mountain villages had sprouted magnificent Victorian and Edwardian hotels, vast baronial edifices, the Victorias, Edens and Reginas. The local inns—the Bärens, Adlers, Krones and Schlussels—likewise grew, adding new bedrooms and dining rooms. The local farmers also found a new role, guiding the summer visitors up to their grazing meadows, a source of income far greater than ever their cows could provide.

When the skiing vogue arrived, these mountain communities adjusted just as readily. They were not slow to realize that the usual hibernation they endured in the winter could now be turned decisively to their advantage. Thus was the first generation of ski resorts born.

The second generation was not slow in coming. Little villages, off the main rail lines, linked to the outside world only by snowbound roads, soon found that with a little pressure on the Post Office to run a regular bus service from the nearest rail station, a few refurbished rooms in the local inn and the modest cost of a T-bar they could attract not only weekend visitors from nearby towns but foreign guests who stayed for weeks. Among these second generation resorts were Braunwald, Flums and Wildhaus in eastern Switzerland, Stoos and Rigi in Central Switzerland, and Saanenmöser and Hasliberg in canton Bern, to name just a few. They quickly became more than just a secret ski-hideaway for some eccentric Englishmen and equally enthusiastic Swiss. By the end of the '30s, Switzerland had more than 100 ski resorts, catering to visitors from England, Holland, Germany, and Italy. This pattern of development needed little refinement after World War II, expanding with ease to cope with over a million visitors annually.

Today, as the popularity of skiing has continued to grow, Switzerland has generally resisted the temptation to construct purpose-built resorts in otherwise empty mountain country. Only four such resorts have in fact been built: Hoch Ibrig near Einsiedeln in Central Switzerland, and Anzère, Thyon and Haute Nendaz in the Valais. Some have complained, however, that the rapid and rather uncontrolled developments of resorts like Verbier in the Valais and Caax and Savognin in Graubünden come very close to a third generation of ski resort. But the Swiss, ever aware of the need to husband their assets prudently, through strict conservation controls and zoning laws, are very unlikely to allow the type of purely financial, speculative developments that have so scarred the mountainsides of the Savoie and Tarentaise in France.

Equally unusual in Switzerland are lift-linked resorts, neighboring resorts with adjoining lift systems across passes, ridges and summits. Geography largely accounts for this, but strong local loyalties and conservation measures are also important. Those that do exist are notable largely because of their scarcity. The oldest are Davos and Klosters, both of which share the extensive Parsenn ski fields. Likewise Wengen and Grindelwald are similarly linked—by the rail link that climbs the Kleine Scheidegg from both sides of the pass—though the logical link over the Mannlichen is relatively recent. The slightly tenuous link between Verbier, Haute Nendaz, Nendaz and Thyon is wholly artificial, while the long-distance lift journey from Arosa, via Lenzerheide, Parpan, Futschellas and Reinwaldhorn to Chur, though sensible on a map, is a considerable undertaking, rarely carried out. Skiing in Switzerland in other words is essentially a single resort activity, though this in no way means restricted or limited skiing.

A couple of other factors—geographical and historical—have also conspired in shaping the nature of Swiss ski resorts. First, farming history has decreed that today's resorts are either on a valley shelf or floor, at an altitude of never less than 1,000 meters (3,280 ft.) and never more than 1,800 meters (5,900 ft.), the timber line. Both these limits were set by the requirements of alpine farming. As a general rule of thumb, those villages lying below 1,400 meters (4,600 ft.) will have ski areas that rarely exceed 3,000 meters (9,840 ft.), while those above 1,400 meters will frequently have access to the high Alps and glaciers above 3,500 meters (11,300 ft.).

Farming has also helped determine the terrain of Switzerland's ski fields. In very general terms, these are the upper grazing meadows, communally owned by the local parishes and lying between the timber line at 1,800 meters and the level of permanent snow on the north facing slopes, around 2,800 or 3,000 meters. These slopes are still actively grazed in the summer, giving relatively rock-free and open surfaces, without the maze of erosion gullies and dangerous cliffs characteristic of certain other areas of the Alps, and with firm, short grass. Also characteristic are the farmers' dairy and hay huts and, at about 2,000 meters (6,560 ft.), their associated living quarters. Many of these double as restaurants in the winter and, in a few cases, huts for skiers, complete with bunk beds. These "Schwendi" have become one of the most characteristic hallmarks of skiing in Switzerland, not least because of the universal practise of flying the Swiss flag from those open for business.

One final characteristic of Swiss ski resorts worth mentioning is that the descent from the timberline to the village is frequently narrow and steep, often not much more than an icy path through the woods. Though much money and effort has been expended in widening and "softening" these home runs, they remain an unavoidable part of skiing in Switzerland.

Which Resort?

Graubünden. This is the oldest of Switzerland's ski regions, extending over what can loosely be called the Rhaetian alps in the extreme eastern corner of the country, and running from Chur in a shallow triangle to the Austrian and Italian frontiers. It divides into two main areas. One, the Prätigau range, site of Davos, Klosters and Arosa; two, the Bernina range a little further south, site of St. Moritz, Pontresina and the numerous small villages of the upper Engadine that lie along the chain of lakes that make up the course of the river Inn.

The skiing varies surprisingly greatly between the main centers. Davos, for example, boasts probably the largest coherent ski domain in the world, the Parsenn, extending from the summit of the Weissfluh at 2,836 meters (9,300 ft.) to Kublis, at an elevation of 820 meters (2,690 ft.) 18 kms. (11 miles) away and Klosters, 1,260 meters high (4,150 ft.). It includes one of the most difficult runs in the world, the Gotschnagrat. In addition, Davos also has access to three further mountains, the Pischahorn, Brämabühl and Rhinerhorn. Arosa, by contrast, a little to the east of Davos, boasts the sunniest and most comfortable intermediate slopes in Switzerland, while St. Moritz, away to the south, for all its fame is a very scattered, if extensive and high, domain, serving all the villages of the upper Engadine. Here, there is access to two glaciers—the Corvatsch at 3,456 meters (11,430 ft.) and the Diavolezza at 2,977 meters (9,770 ft.)—as well as to the extensive, if repetitive, ski areas of the Corviglia/Piz Nair/Trais Flur complex.

In all, Graubünden lays claim to a further 37 listed ski resorts, in addition to those already named. For the most part, these are small, intimate, family-style resorts of considerable charm. They are patronized almost exclusively by the Swiss themselves, and the skiing is not particularly testing.

To generalize about Graubünden, it is an open, ski-anywhere region, with good intermediate and upper intermediate skiing and, except for Davos and St. Moritz, very well suited to beginners.

The Bernese Oberland. Though probably the best-known ski area of Switzerland, the Bernese Oberland nonetheless boasts only 31 resorts. Once again it is geography that has restricted the skiing, for the greater part of this region is occupied by the giants of the Oberland: the Jungfrau massif and the great glaciers that fall from this giant mountain chain. Best known of these resorts are the historical trio of Wengen, Grindelwald and, their near neighbor, Mürren. Dominated by the dark face of the Eiger and the soaring ice cliffs of the Jungfrau, the skiing in the linked resorts of Wengen and Grindelwald is open, almost entirely treeless and, for the intermediate performer, provides long, exciting and relatively undemanding runs where verticals of 1,000 meters (3,280 ft.) and more from the Kleine Scheidegg, Eigergletscher or Männlichen can be skied for a week without ever repeating yourself. Mürren, on the other hand, separated from these twins by the precipitous Lauterbrunnen valley, is very much the specialist's ski home where, with local knowledge and despite the relatively small verticals that are immediately available, there are so many hidden routes through the open pine forests, that there are top class skiers who have been visiting this resort for a generation or more without ever tiring of its variety. And for those who are looking for big ski excitement, there is the Schilthorn, with its revolving restaurant providing a cinemascope view of the peaks and glaciers of the Oberland before you attempt the gruelling Inferno run down 1,600 vertical meters (4,250 ft.) to Lauterbrunnen.

The Bernese Oberland consists of more than just the famous Jungfrau resorts, however. Away to the west and tucked up the picturesque Frutigtal is Adelboden, star ski resort of the '20s and '30s, though now making a comeback among more leisurely skiers; it also has the advantage of being linked to an equally well-known little resort, Lenk. Only a few miles away is a little group of resorts whose fame has extended far beyond the confines of winter sports: Gstaad and its less fashionable satellites Saanen, Schonried, Saanenmöser and, just over the border in canton Vaud, Chateau d'Oex. This is not high alpine country so much as friendly farming land, with open, free-swinging skiing, well served by lifts and the efficient rail link of the Montreux–Oberland–Bernois rail line. With the exception of wealthy and exclusive Gstaad, this is a friendly region, very popular with the Swiss families who flock here from Bern and Lausanne, and ideal for beginners, children and grandmothers alike, all of whom will find as much happy skiing as their more active relations can on the long steep slopes of the Videmanett or Hornfluh.

The Valais. With 47 listed ski centers this is the most dramatic of all Swiss ski areas. Pride of place must go to Zermatt, probably the best known winter resort in the world, if only by reason of that singular mountain the Matterhorn. The skiing here is long and demanding, with Himalayan scale scenery and, unique among Swiss resorts, no nursery slopes within walking distance of the village. It's not a place for beginners. But advanced skiers will find little cause for complaint. There are three distinct ski areas: the Schwarzsee-Theodul glacier, boasting the highest lift in Europe, the Klein Matterhorn, just a few meters short of the magical 4,000 meter mark (13,123 ft.); the Gornergrat-Stockhorn area; and the somewhat lower but more difficult mid-winter area of the Sunegga-Rothorn pistes. Zermatt is generally at its best in the spring, for it is only then that the high, long runs—the Stockhorn, Klein Matterhorn/Theodul and the glorious Ventina route into Italy—are open and safe. In addition to all of which, the region also boasts probably the best collection of mid-mountain restaurants in the country.

For a completely different ambiance and scenery, Verbier, away to the northwest, an unplanned sprawl of apartments and chalets, caters to the ever-increasing demand for continuous and instant skiing. This is provided in plenty, from the almost unskiable difficulties of the high alpine slopes of the Mont Fort and the Col des Gentianes to the gentlest and longest of nursery areas on the south-facing slopes of the Savoleyres. The resort is also lift-linked into Haute Nendaz, Thyon, Veysonnaz and Mayence de Riddes. If you are clever, and lucky, you can complete the long circuit back to Verbier in a tiring day, but should you miss the bus in Nendaz that takes you to Riddes, you will find yourself saddled with a very expensive taxi ride, or a night in the Rhône valley.

On the north side of the Rhône valley, the long, sunny shelf that accommodates the contiguous villages of Crans, Montana, Vermala and Aminoma is the base for skiing on the steep and broken slopes that drop down from the hidden expanse of the old captive glacier called the Plaine Morte. This is the start of one of the great runs of Switzerland, the trail that drops from 3,000 to 1,500 meters (9,840 to 4,900 ft.) in one continuous route that more or less follows that of the world's first downhill race, the Kandahar, run in 1911. Only a few ski miles away and, since its creation, threatening a ski link with Crans, is the purpose-built resort of Anzère with limited skiing, good nursery areas and attractive architecture.

For those who do not want the famous or the fashionable, the Rhône valley can provide a long list of small, unspoilt villages, each with very respectable skiing. Chandolin, St.-Luc, Grimentz and Zinal in the Val d'Anniviers figure on few travel brochures but all are worthy of a short stay, while the isolated villages of the Lotschental—Kippel, Wiler and Blatten—once threatened with massive commercialization, are once again quiet, almost primitive Alpine communities where century-old customs are more important than *après ski.* Belalp, Riederalp and Bettmeralp, bordering the foot of the Aletsch glacier, once only sleepy summer hamlets, have built themselves ski lifts and cross-country trails and, while certainly not in the five-star league, have a charm and isolation which captivates all skiers who visit them. They are the best examples of the variety of skiing that can be found in the apparently hostile and barren regions of the high Alps.

Eastern and Central Switzerland. Lastly, from a downhill skier's point of view, there are the diverse list of resorts loosely grouped in Eastern and Central Switzerland. With the exception of Engleberg and, perhaps, Andermatt, they are virtually unknown outside Switzerland and have mostly tailored themselves to local Swiss requirements. They are all basically mid-winter resorts, low-lying at around 1,000 meters (3,280 ft.) with ski fields rarely extending above 2,200 meters (6,220 ft.), but nevertheless offering clear verticals of 1,000 meters and more. Some are essentially family resorts, such as Braunwald above the Linthal, carless and unsophisticated. By contrast, the Toggenbrug resorts—Alt St. Johann, Unterwasser and Wildhaus, all very popular with weekend and day skiers from Zürich—are small hotel-villages providing some quite spectacular skiing on the open grazing slopes of the Kurfirsten mountains. From their summits, there is the startling, plunging view of the Walensee more than 1,000 meters below, while the skiing on the northern slopes back into the valley is much more exciting than the trail maps might suggest.

Mountaineering and Cross Country

Although mid-winter ski-touring has been virtually displaced by the unbiquitous ski lifts, gondolas and cable cars, Switzerland is still a mecca for the serious ski mountaineer, who combines skiing skills with those of the rock and ice mountaineer, exploring the highest of the great Alpine peaks, his skis carrying him safely and swiftly over the long glaciers. The main centers for ski mountaineering are Saas Fee—start of the classical Haute Route to Chamonix—Zermatt, Pontresina, gateway to the Bernina range, and Andermatt, with gives access to the Gotthard massif. Professional guides are recommended for anyone new to the techniques of glacier and high Alpine skiing. All the main centers run regular spring excursions, lasting two days or more, and culminating in week-long traverses. The specialist skis and boots can be hired in all the ski mountaineering centers.

Cross country skiing is popular throughout Switzerland, with all resorts maintaining machine prepared *loipes,* or tracks. Certain areas of the country have specialized in this branch of the sport, notably the Jura in western Switzerland. Based on the towns of Neuchâtel, La Chaud de Fonds, and Le Locle, extensive marked routes extend the length of the Jura chain. There are similarly well organized routes around Gruyères in canton Fribourg and around Einsiedeln in Central Switzerland. A comprehensive guide, *Ski Wandern,* published by the Swiss Ski Federation, lists all the marked routes as well as accommodations available on the long distance tracks.

Summer skiing is available above Crans on the Plaine Morte, in Saas Fee, Zermatt, the Corvatsch above St. Moritz, on the Diavolezza above Pontresina, the Jungfraujoch and on the Titlis above Engelberg. In addition to these locations, depending on snow conditions, there is limited summer skiing on the Diablerets above Gstaad and on the Sustenpass above Meiringen. The most extensive and interesting summer skiing is on the Felskinn/Mittel Allalin between 3,500 meters (11,480 ft.) and 2,700 meters (8,860 ft.) with a total of about 20 kms. (12 miles) of prepared trails.

Ski Schools and Hire

The Swiss Ski School is federally controlled, but organized on a cantonal basis. Instructors are all multi-lingual, with the majority speaking English. Schools are organized into six classes, determined by ability. Half-day instruction is always available, and most ski schools have reduced rates for five half-day courses. Nonetheless, it is the policy of the Swiss Schools to encourage visitors to take all-day courses. The standard of instruction is high, if a little conservative in outlook, with the emphasis on giving pupils the greatest ski pleasure rather than a concentrated course of ski didactics. 1986 costs for six half-day lessons were between Fr. 72 and 96.

The hire of skis and boots is of a generally high standard, with costs fairly uniform across the country. Seven days' ski hire runs about Fr. 117, and seven days boot hire about Fr. 42. Buying equipment outright in Switzerland is expensive, though more moderate prices can often be found in the large towns, particularly near the end of the skiing season.

Lift costs vary considerably, making it difficult to generalize. As a rule, however, the higher you go the more it costs, though the number of available lifts on a single pass does not influence the price as much. The following costs for a seven-day non-transferable pass applied in 1986: Anzère, seven lifts, Fr. 147; Saas Fee, 23 lifts, Fr. 210; Crans, 34 lifts, Fr. 169; Zermatt, 29 lifts, Fr. 224; Verbier, 66 lifts, Fr. 252.

Few of the lifts are button or Poma design, the greatest number being the conventional T-bar. Although chairlifts are not uncommon, and some very modern versions can be found—Arosa for example has four-seater lifts with slow loading and unloading speeds—gondolas are the preferred type, not least for their high ground clearance. Cable cars are the universal choice for extreme altitude lifts. Lines are moderately disciplined and, with certain notorious exceptions, not excessive. (Verbier, Zermatt and St. Moritz are probably the worst in this respect).

Looking Back?

And what, one might ask, has happened to those old, traditional winter sports? The luge runs are given over to racing cars, the ice rinks have disappeared into great sports halls—though Davos still maintains the world's largest natural ice rink—and the winter walkers can now go only to Arosa, St. Moritz and Zermatt. Indeed, few now come to Switzerland merely to skate or go curling, though at the same time there is no major resort where these sports aren't available.

On the other hand, you can hang glide in Arosa and St. Moritz, go horse racing in Davos, Arosa and St. Moritz, ballooning in Gstaad, and play indoor tennis just about everywhere. Interestingly, however, more than half the winter visitors to Arosa, St. Moritz and Zermatt do not come for the skiing, or indeed any sort of winter sport. For them perhaps, Switzerland's traditional appeal as a land of rest, relaxation, comfortable hotels and good food still outweighs the revolution that has transformed the grazing lands of the Alps.

SWISS FOOD AND DRINK

Cuisine? . . . Kochkunst? . . . Cucina?

by
IRENE M. RITTER

English-born Irene Ritter has lived in Switzerland for many years. She has written regularly for numerous English-language publications in Switzerland, including the Swiss edition of the Reader's Digest.

When Harry Schraemli, who knows all there is to know about Swiss gastronomy, tells me that Swiss cuisine does not exist, I confess to being a bit taken aback. But think for a moment. Switzerland is really no more than a conglomeration of elements which belonged at different times to Germany, Austria, France and Italy. Perhaps the idea that diversity, fragmentation even, is the keynote of Swiss cooking, even to the point where Swiss cooking as such can be said not to exist, is not so wild after all. You could even go further, and claim that the very diversity brought about by Switzerland's historical and geographical circumstances, and the regionalism they have naturally spawned, have proved greatly beneficial to Switzerland's gastronomic evolution.

So what are these factors that have ganged up on Swiss cooking and made it such a splintered, divided affair? First, of course, are the influences of her neighbors, Germany, Austria, France and Italy. Thus, food in German-speaking Switzerland bears a marked resemblance to its counterparts in Germany, especially southern Germany, and Austria. Similarly, French-speaking Switzerland, once part of Burgundy, has kept a marked preference for French cuisine, while the Italian-speaking Ticino, down in the south, still inclines to Lombardy.

Two other factors—both, again, geographical and historical—have also played an important part. The first reflects Switzerland's traditional position as a land of transit, a land criss-crossed throughout its history by foreign travelers, among them traders in spices, all of whom left their mark on Swiss cooking. (In similar vein, Swiss mercenaries, whose legendary fighting qualities made them prized soldiers throughout Europe, also brought new recipes and tastes to their native land). The second reason is even more basic. Think of all the mountains and the countless valleys between them—today no less than 26 cantons with over 3,000 municipalities—each sporting its own brand of local pride and, of course, local cooking. Is it any wonder that the emphasis should be on local specialties and regional cooking?

Putting on the Ritz

Of the myriad influences that have shaped Switzerland's cooking, and notwithstanding the fact that German-speaking Switzerland is by some way the largest part of the country, the greatest culinary influence, particularly in more recent times, is France and its great chefs. The greatest of them all was Auguste Escoffier, who, together with the Swiss hotelier Cesar Ritz, made gastronomic history. Their partnership began at the Hotel National in Luzern, before continuing on to glory in London at the Savoy and Carlton hotels. As tourism in Switzerland generated great dynasties of hoteliers—the Seilers in Zermatt, the Badrutts in St. Moritz—Swiss chefs were also to be found in nearly every luxury hotel in the world. Not only were they excellent cooks, they had one especially valuable asset: they were trustworthy. Today, Swiss master chef Henry Haller is at the White House, Anton Mosimann at the Dorchester hotel in London, Werner Vögeli at the Swedish court, and many others in kitchens of greater and lesser fame in countries near and far.

While French cooking dominates Switzerland's hotel gastronomy, it has also, to a certain extent, influenced the Swiss housewife. Today she cooks better than ever, and, also a French influence, despite her modern aids and gadgets, nostalgia is taking over. It's back to grandma and her recipes.

Eating Habits

The Swiss day begins with *café complet,* continental breakfast of coffee and hot milk, and bread or rolls with butter, cheese and jam. The main cooked meal is at midday, when husbands and schoolchildren come home for lunch. From noon to 1:30 factories, offices and shops, except some downtown in main cities, close. The evening meal by contrast is generally a light affair, often no more than *café complet.* But the average Swiss not infrequently treats themself to dinner out. Celebrations and entertaining often take place at a restaurant.

The Swiss of all classes are discriminating eaters, a fact reflected in the range and number of restaurants, from the luxury temples of gastronomy to simple country inns, where the decor may not be as fancy but the food is excellent and ample. Regional specialties are chalked up on a blackboard outside, or marked on a menu in a glass case near the door. Fixed-price menus with the day's choice offer excellent value, often at lower prices than eating *à la carte.*

Meats

Meat, despite its high price, is the backbone of a Swiss meal. The Swiss consume great quantities annually and portions are always generous. Though game in the fall provides interesting and unusual dishes—venison in particular—year round veal is Switzerland's finest meat: pale and tender, and very often the choice for a festive meal. *Geschnetzeltes Kalbfleisch* (or *émincé de veau*), a dish of thinly sliced veal in a cream sauce, is highly acclaimed in the gourmet world.

The Swiss regard sauces as an all-important accompaniment to meat dishes, and cutlets or roasts are served in a richly flavored wine or cream sauces. Stewed and jugged meats of all kinds rank high on favorite menus. Even variety meats such as tripe, kidneys and liver make specialty dishes in recipes handed down from frugal grandmothers.

But it is the sausage that stretches the household budget. Beef, veal and/or pork, fresh or smoked, fried, boiled or grilled, sausages come in any number of variations. You can even buy *Bratwürst* by the meter. Cold ready-sliced sausages and cured hams, meatloaf, pies and open sandwiches in aspic are displayed at the butcher's counter in a manner so decorative as to whet even the most reluctant appetite. The highlight of sausage eating is in the village inns at the "Metzgete," when you will get black pudding, liver and pork sausages fresh from the farm.

Fish

Fish in landlocked Switzerland means freshwater fish from the numerous lakes, rivers and streams. But, despite its abundance, fish is more a delicacy than a staple. It has a fine subtle flavor, and is always served fresh. You will find many excellent fish restaurants along the shores of all the lakes and rivers, where you can try out the local specialties to the accompaniment of the appropriate white wine.

Perch—called *Egli* in Swiss German, *perche* in French, *pesce persico* in Italian—a fish of excellent flavor, is found in most lakes and some rivers. So are various kinds of dace (*Felchen, Albeli, Balchen/fera, palée, bondelle/coregono, bondella*), pike *(Hecht/brochet/luccio)* and carp (*Karpfen/carpe/carpa*). Lake Lugano has eel (*agone*), and the *omble chevalier,* an exquisite char, a kind of salmon trout. Trout itself (*Forelle/truite/trota*) is served in many restaurants all over Switzerland. Most trout are bred, but if you can get them the best are those from mountain streams. In the cool months the Rhine has grayling

(*Aesche*), a type of trout, and winter is the season for *Rötel,* a delicious red-bellied char found only in the Zugsee. In the Middle Ages, the Zugsee was very rich in *Rötel,* which was exacted as a fee by the feudal barons and local monasteries. It is still tradition today for the cantonal government to dine on the first catch of *Rötel,* while on St. Andrew's Day the fishermen take their *Rötel* to the friars at the Franciscan monastery.

Fruit and Vegetables

When the potato came to Switzerland in the 17th century it was treated with great suspicion. Only when it was understood that the poisonous part was *above* the earth and the tubers *beneath* it were edible, did the potato proliferate. Swiss Germans call it the *Erdöpfel,* the earth apple. And where would the thrifty Swiss housewife be without it? Shredded and fried golden brown, *Rösti* is a real Swiss-German dish, and comes in at least nine versions. To prove just how versatile the humble earth apple can be, in some cantons it is even combined with the tree apple.

Orchards abound in Switzerland. Apples and pears were an early Swiss peasant food, used fresh, cooked or dried, or fermented into cider and brandy. And nearly a century ago when Dr. Bircher-Benner opened a private clinic in Zürich he so prized the nutritional value of the *entire* apple—grated with skin, core and pips—added to cereals in milk, plus berries and more, than a new dish was born: the famous Swiss *Müesli.* Today *Birchermüesli* is a Swiss national dish, served in cafes and tea-rooms throughout the country.

Wholefoods are in fashion and Swiss housewives buy more and more fruit and vegetables organically grown without chemicals. Likewise, despite the supermarkets, the small food store still survives. Nearly every town has an open-air market once or twice a week, where local farmers sell their own produce and rows of stands present flowers, fruit, vegetables, eggs and poultry neatly arranged. Many markets are held on a lake or river shore, a tradition which dates back to the days when farmers brought their produce by boat, and you will generally find the fish market on the water's edge.

Cheese

About one quarter of Switzerland's livestock spends the summer months, from June to September, munching the succulent grass of the alpine pastures. Herdsmen are responsible for the cattle owned by the farmers, who stay in the lowlands. As milk cannot be taken down to the valley farms before it turns sour it is made into cheese. In the fall, the cheeses are then divided into equal piles at the cheese store up on the mountains, with every herd owner receiving his share. Although the farmers keep much of the cheese, a good choice does come on to the market.

There are many kinds of alpine cheese, all varying in taste and quality according to the pasture and the way they are made. But though they rarely appear on the cheese board of a city restaurant, you will find them in village inns, and most cheese shops carry an interesting selection.

Emmentaler and *Gruyère* are the two best known Swiss cheeses—and often confused. *Emmentaler* is the one with the big holes (or "eyes"), from the Emmental in canton Bern. It used to be made only on the alpine pastures, but today it comes from cooperative dairies in the lowlands. As the milk reaches the dairies very quickly, it is still fresh and can be turned into cheese without chemical additions. The legendary holes are created quite naturally as carbonic acid gas inside the ripening cheese is unable to escape. This is also how it gets its nutty taste.

Sbrinz from Central Switzerland is the oldest and hardest Swiss cheese, and was probably the one the Romans liked so much. In Eastern Switzerland the soft green *Schabzieger* from the canton Glarus is a specialty that has been made in the same way for over 500 years. *Toggenburger,* a hard cheese, comes from the alps of St. Gallen and is the only Swiss sour-milk cheese. Canton Appenzell cheese is hard and comes in two types: full-fat or pungent. The Jura produces a delicately flavored *Tête de Moine,* best eaten scraped with a cheese plane, and the Valais specializes in a mountain cheese called *Bagnes.* The harder *Vacherin* comes from Fribourg, but the soft creamy *Vacherin Mont d'Or* is made in the mountain dairies of the Joux valley in canton Vaud. Both Fribourg and Vaud make variants of a small soft cheese called *Tomme,* and the Ticino has three varieties of *Piora.* Processed cheese is a Swiss invention, mostly based on *Emmentaler,* but many other varieties have ham, herbs and wine added for flavoring.

Should you, like an American lady I met on a hot summer's day, want to buy cheese, choose the hard or processed kind. She had traveled by train with a plastic bag full of soft cheese. With the bag on the luggage rack above her she sat in solitary state as everybody moved away, more or less discreetly sniffing at her in disgust. Now the bag hung outside her hotel window and she was leaving for Italy by bus the next morning. Yes, I inherited the sticky pungent mess . . . and my family was treated to an unusually rich and tasty cheese tart for supper!

Hot open-faced cheese tarts followed by cold fruit tarts and coffee and hot milk make a popular meal. You can buy man-size triangular portions of tart or small, round tartlets in most bakeries, especially on a Friday, which used to be the Roman Catholic meatless day. The famous cheese *fondue* is, preferably, a cool season meal where you sit round the pot dunking bread cubes into creamy bubbling cheese. The cantons of Neuchâtel, Fribourg, Valais, Vaud and Geneva each has its own particular blend of cheese, wine and flavoring, and each claims to be the genuine *fondue.* Be that as it may, the *fondue* mixture must stay hot and if a gentleman loses his bread cube in it his forfeit is a bottle of wine, whereas a lady pays with a kiss . . . to whom she chooses! White wine or hot tea is the usual accompaniment, though half-way through it is customary to assist digestion with a glass of *Kirsch* brandy. But *never* drink beer, water or other cold drinks with or after a *fondue.*

Soup

Whether it was a forerunner of the *fondue* or just plain milk soup that saved the day on the battlefield at Kappel in 1529, remains a historical moot point. The fact is that the warring Catholics and Protestants alike lay down their arms and dipped their spoons into the pot. Soup-eating is a deeply ingrained Swiss habit. Nearly always the meal starter, soup is quite often the meal itself. Meat, bread, vegetables, eggs, pasta, dumplings, flour, potatoes, cheese—all go separately, combined, or as the imagination dictates into the soup. It is hardly surprising that packaged soups were invented in Switzerland. In the 1880's when women had to work in the factories, Julius Maggi, a flour miller, created a complete dehydrated soup mixture to make cooking easier. Today, Maggi's chief competitor is Knorr and they each produce an incredible number of soups ready for the table in less than 15 minutes.

Bread and Confectionery

If soup is the prop and mainstay of Swiss eating, bread runs it very close. A choice of over 200 different breads has made the Swiss selective breadeaters. They like their bread crisp of crust and well leavened. While the French- and Italian-speaking Swiss prefer white bread, the Swiss Germans like to choose among the dark wholemeal and any of the multiple flour and grain combinations. Each canton has a particular variety of bread and local bakers all over the country make their own specialties. All baker's shops carry a substantial selection of freshly baked loaves, rolls, buns, and *Gipfeli* (croissants). Some bread is factory made, but for the most part the accent is on private bakeries. Handmade bread is a matter of pride and Swiss bakers are amazingly creative, a process actively aided by the celebrated Swiss Bakery School in Luzern.

The crowning glory of baking is confectionery, and here the Swiss really do excel. Although many baker's shops sell plain cakes and pastries, it is in the *Konditorei, pâtisserie* or *pasticceria*—the pastry shop and tearoom—that you can best indulge in these wondrously luscious creations. Pastry-making is a fine art, which the Engadine bakers learned and practised in Venice in the Middle Ages. Obliged to emigrate because of poverty and bad soil in Graubünden, they soon became famous, and indeed were much praised because their weights were accurate and they did not dilute the brandy. They opened coffeehouses and confectioneries in Venice, and their reputation for excellence and integrity went with them as they moved to Austria, Germany, Poland, Russia, and Egypt. Some of the pastry shops still exist and are kept by their descendants. In 1792 the brothers Josty, confectioners who also came from Graubünden, began making chocolates in Berlin and in 1819 François-Louis Cailler opened the first chocolate factory in Vevey. Since then it has been chocolates galore. They heralded the Swiss sweet tooth, splendid in fancy desserts topped in a swirl of whipped cream, the dot on the "i" of Swiss gastronomy.

Regional Specialties

Many traditional recipes relate to some event in history or are linked to some folklore custom. In the following lists, although the typical dishes are ascribed to their canton of origin, they are probably available elsewhere, perhaps in another version.

German Swiss Cantons. Bern. The *Berner Platte* is great classic among the national dishes—an assortment of boiled beef, tongue, broiled ham, pork chops, sausages, bacon, with sauerkraut, beans and potatoes. *Wine:* Twanner or Salvagnin.

Crisp, feather-light meringues filled with fresh whipped cream are a specialty of the Emmental.

Zürich. The traditional meal of the Zürich town councillors, normally eaten following a meeting, is *Zürcher Ratsherrentopf,* veal and beef fillets, calf's liver, kidneys and sweetbreads, bacon and vegetables. *Wine:* Clevner Stadtberger or Dôle.

Geschnetzeltes nach Zürcher Art is the famous sliced veal and cream dish, served with Zurich-style *Rösti. Wine:* Aigle or Ermitage.

Zug. *Zuger Hechtli,* pike fried in batter. *Wine:* Dorin or a Swiss-German white wine. *Zuger Kirschtorte* is a sponge cake soaked in Kirsch between Japonais layers.

St. Gallen. *St. Galler Bratwürst,* special veal sausage, generally served with onions and *Rösti.*

Aargau. *Schnitz und Drunder* is a dried-apple-and-potato casserole with diced smoked ham. *Rüeblitorte* is a fluffy carrot sponge cake.

Luzern. *Luzerner Chügelipastete* is a puff-pastry pie filled with diced veal and pork, sausage meat dumplings, raisins soaked in Kirsch, mushrooms, in a brown sauce. *Wine:* a Riesling-Sylvaner or a Dorin.

Solothurn. *Mistchratzerli nach Ambassadoren Art* are stuffed young cockerels. *Wine:* Salvagnin or Dôle.

Solothurn and **Schwyz.** *Saurer Mocken* is marinaded braised beef, served with noodles or mashed potato. *Wine:* a Pinot Noir.

Unterwalden. *Ziegerkrapfen'* are pear fritters.

Basel. The *Basler Leckerli* are famed honey and almond cookies.

Appenzell. Here try the spiced honey cake called *Biber.*

Graubünden. *Tuorta de Nusch Engiadinaisa* is a rich walnut pie from the Engadine.

Both the *Bündnerfleisch* in Graubünden and the viande sechée in the Valais are the genuine well-known air-dried beef of delicate flavor served sliced wafer-thin. In Appenzell and Glarus the beef is marinaded in cider before it is air-dried and known as *Moschtbröckli.*

In the fall game season: *Rehpfeffer,* jugged venison, and *Rehrücken,* saddle of venison, are both generally served with stewed apples topped with cranberries, chestnuts, red cabbage and *Knöpfli,* small dumplings. *Wine:* Dôle.

French Swiss Cantons. Geneva. The lake fish *omble chevalier* served in special Genevese cream sauce. *Wine:* Perlan.

Vaud. *Filets de perches aux amandes* are perch fillets topped with almonds. *Wine:* a Dorin or Fendant. *Papet Vaudois* is a traditional dish of creamed leek eaten with either smoked pork, cabbage or liver sausage. Wine: a *Dorin* or *Salvagnin.* The recipe for the *Malakoff* cheese fritters made in Vinzel, on Lac Léman, was brought home by a mercenary soldier who fought in the Crimean war. *Wine:* Vinzel. Fried *Tomme,* the small cheese is served very hot oozing its creamy center. *Wine:* white Lavaux or red Salvagnin.

Valais. Raclette makes a convivial meal as the Bagnes cheese is melted and scraped off onto the plate, eaten with baked potatoes and pickles. *Wine:* Fendant.

Jura and **Neuchatel.** *Truites du bief,* a dish of river trout with mouseline sauce. *Wine:* Villette. A specialty is fried river carp. *Wine:* Auvernier. *Marc sorbet* is a refreshing dessert.

Fribourg. The *fondue moitié-moitié* is made with half *Gruyère* and half *Vacherin* cheese, and the *fondue au Vacherin* is made with water instead of wine, and boiled potatoes instead of bread for dunking. *Ragoût d'agneau à la bénichon* is lamb stewed with grapes, served with caramelized pears and mashed potatoes. *Wine:* Pinot. Vermicelles is a sweet chestnut cream piped onto crushed meringue and topped with whipped cream.

The Ticino. *Minestrone* is a filling vegetable soup containing beef and bacon, macaroni or rice, sprinkled with grated cheese. A variant is *Busecca* with tripe instead of beef. *Capretto alla Locarnese* is pot-roasted kid. *Stufato alla Luganese* is beef stewed in Marsala. *Coniglio arrosto alla Ticinese* is rabbit casserole in Marsala sauce. *Wine:* Merlot.

Polenta (maize meal), "*gnocchi*" (small dumplings), *risotto,* noodles or spaghetti, are typical accompaniments to principal dishes or make a light meal on their own. *Zabaione* is a warm dessert of egg foam whipped in Marsala. *Amaretti* are light macaroon type cookies with a gently bitter taste.

WINES AND SPIRITS

Plain fresh water rarely appears on a Swiss dining table unless requested. With motorists mindful of alcohol content, soft drinks and mineral water are, needs must, becoming more common although most Swiss do like beer or wine with their meals.

Without wine a gourmet meal would be incomplete and a festive occasion unthinkable. Swiss wine, however, is expensive. The high cost of living in Switzerland and the unremitting work involved in cultivating vineyards on more or less steep slopes make production a costly affair. And, as Swiss wine production accounts for only about a third of domestic cosumption, little of it is exported, so you will have to taste it on the spot.

Swiss wines vary tremendously in bouquet and savor, and the following listings are by no means exhaustive. By far the most important wine-growing region is French-speaking Switzerland, in the Valais and on shores of Lac Léman and lake Neuchâtel. The leading grape in this whole area is the white Chasselas, which yields very different wines, known in the Valais as Fendant, in Vaud as Dorin, in Geneva as Perlan and in Neuchâtel as Chasselas. Some specialty wines come from the Riesling-Sylvaner grape. Red wines from the Gamay and Pinot Noir (Blue Burgundy) grapes are marketed as Dôle in the Valais, Salvagnin in Vaud, and Pinot Noir in Neuchâtel.

Valais Vintages. The Fendant is a rather heady white of delicious bouquet. Special wines are: Malvoisie, Ermitage, Arvine and Amine. Johannisberg is from the Sylvaner grape. Rare wines are Heïda, from Europe's highest vineyard at 1,100 meters (3,600 ft.) near Visperterminen, and Vin du Glacier made in the Rhône valley and left to mature for ten to 15 years in the vaults of high alpine villages.

The farther east you go up the Rhône valley, the more the Pinot Noir grape gains ground. Blended in different amounts to attain the desired taste, aroma and color, the Pinot Noir and Gamay result in Dôle, the most popular quality red wine. Only a wine which has more than 83 degrees sugar content in the Oechsle scale of measurement can be called a Dôle. Wines that do not reach this mark are sold under the name of Goron, with lesser alcohol content. Pinot Noir and Gamay are unblended.

Vaud Vintages. From Geneva to Lausanne the area of La Côte along Lac Léman is known for its light dry wines such as Féchy, Mont-sur-Rolle and Vinzel. Along the Swiss Riviera from Lausanne to Montreux, the terraced vineyards of Lavaux produce rich and fruity wines: Dézaley, Epesses, Saint-Saphorin. Where the Rhône meets the end of the lake, the Chablais wines, Aigle and Yvorne, are strong and smooth. The ancient castle of Aigle houses a fascinating wine museum.

Geneva Vintages. Perlan wines are light and refreshing. Try Le Mandement and Satigny.

Neuchâtel Vintages. Here the wines are mostly white, light and sparkling. The criterion for a good Neuchâtel vintage is that it forms a star in the glass as it is being poured out. The labels are: Auvernier, Pinot Gris, a light rosé Oeil de Perdrix and red Cortaillod.

German Switzerland. The wine-growing areas of German Switzerland are much smaller, the wines in short supply and of local importance only. The red wines are mostly from Pinot Noir grapes and the white from Riesling-Sylvaner. The largest areas are cultivated in Zürich and Schaffhausen, but the cantons of Aargau, Thurgau, St. Gallen and the Rhine valley of Graubünden also produce excellent wines.

The Ticino. Sunny Ticino is ideal for wine growing. The red Merlot is a fruity wine with a pleasant bouquet. A fiery Grappa brandy is distilled from the grape pressings, while the nonalcoholic grape-juice sold all over Switzerland is made from Ticino Americano grapes.

Spirits

Distilling fruit brandies is a very old Swiss tradition. A brandy which has become very popular is Williamine, made from the fragrant Williams pear and much milder than Träsch, made from cider pears. Old-established white brandies are the Pflümli, made from plums, and Kirsch, made from cherries, which in no way should be confused with the sweet liqueur Cherry Brandy. The strong brandies made from Alpine herbs and flowers, Enzian and Chrüter, are taken neat to aid digestion.

Try a Swiss brandy in hot sweet coffee served in a glass and called *Kafi fertig* or *Kafi Buffet*—it's a delicious drink which will warm the cockles of your heart.

ZÜRICH

Home of the Gnomes

"Zürich's relationship to the world is not of the spirit, but of commerce," remarked Swiss psychologist C. J. Jung of his adopted city. And indeed Switzerland's largest city is, first and foremost, a dynamic center of banking and business. You'll find no nostalgia here for a past filled with kings and queens so much as a discreet but real pride in the city's pragmatic and hard-headed approach to life and finely tuned capacity for changing with the times.

It is this down to earth attitude that has made Zürich one of the world's leading financial centers. Strolling through the well-kept streets, it is impossible not to become almost immediately aware of the sheer affluence of the place, and of Zürich's love affair with finance. The city is littered with banks and sundry other financial institutions. No teller raises an eyebrow if you want to buy an over-the-counter kilo of gold. Money and precious metals are a commodity here, much like wheat or sugar, say, in other places. The remarkable success the city's financiers have enjoyed has not always been appreciated by everyone who does business with them, however. During just one of many difficult moments for the pound sterling in the mid '60s, the English somewhat resentfully coined the term "Gnomes of Zürich" to describe what some saw as those secretive and sly Swiss bankers, supposedly manipulating world currencies in backrooms.

In fact the secret of Zürich's phenomenal success and affluence is simple: hard work, the city's only natural resource as its citizens are fond of pointing out. More than anything else, what prompts and regulates the "Zürcher," as the other Swiss know them, is the good old fashioned Protestant work ethic. You will meet it here naked and unashamed. The Zürcher got the idea from Huldrych Zwingli, a terrifying Reformation preacher in the 17th century, and they have lived by it ever since.

Hand in hand with all this hard work goes a certain native caution, a reluctance to take anything for granted, least of all their own success. This is not exactly humility, rather a profound appreciation of the precariousness of success and the attendant risks of collapse and ruin, however unlikely such a scenario may seem to visitors. Ostentation is rigorously shunned. Thus the president of a leading bank will likely as not ride to work in the same spotless blue tram that his secretary takes. (The saying goes that if you see a Rolls Royce in Zürich there'll be a foreigner behind the wheel). Likewise, the sons and daughters of the rich are expected to settle down early at a respectable job, adding to the assets so assiduously accumulated by their fathers. One further example: the morning rush hour in Zürich begins around seven o'clock; the evening rush hour ends around seven.

One natural result of Zürich's financial and industrial clout is that they have conspired to make the city the unofficial capital of Switzerland. This is not a development that the country's other cantons have necessarily welcomed. It has long been a basic tenet of Switzerland's political philosophy that decentralization is essential for social stability, and the view that the town on the Limmat is politically pushy is reasonably widespread. It is undeniable that Zürich has successfully accumulated considerable influence in spheres other than financial, particularly education. The Federal Institute of Technology and the Jung Institute are just two among many highly prestigious educational institutions in the city.

It would be quite wrong, however, to give the impression that the Zürcher are only interested in high finance. It has been remarked elsewhere that though Switzerland may not be able to boast a striking cultural or artistic heritage, being rich in money the country is also correspondingly rich in art. Zürich accordingly has a remarkably active cultural life. On the one hand, high quality opera, concerts and art exhibits are commonplace; on the other, you'll find a vital, extremely forward-looking approach to modern art forms, theater and music. Not so many years ago, the city was rudely disturbed by riots as Zürich's young people pressed for increased subsidies for rock concerts. With one eye on the city's reputation for harmony and order, the city fathers, who no doubt preferred opera themselves, stepped in to ensure that these demands were met. The city's artistic role does not end here, however, for where Zürich is concerned commerce cannot be far away. It is no surprise to learn that Zürich is also a leading center of the international art market, with an extraordinary range of private galleries.

Zürich Overview

Visitors are often surprised by the beauty of Zürich, perhaps imagining it one vast high-tech banking hall, all chrome and computers. The city's location is, however, delightful. It sits astride the river Limmat where it flows into the Zürichsee, the lake of Zürich. The charming Old Town, comprising a substantial portion of the city center, is full of beautifully restored historic buildings and narrow, hilly alleys. In the distance snowclad peaks overlook the sweeping waters of the blue lake. Turn-of-the-century mansions dominate the lake shore, with numerous parks adding a generous helping of green to the landscape. (The city employs an army of gardeners who see to it that the profusion of flowers and shrubs live up to Switzerland's cared-for reputation). Zürich lays claim to only three high-rise buildings, and even they are small by U.S. standards. And there are no dominating palaces from yesteryear, no record of previous imperial or dynastic glory. In keeping with its solid bourgeois character, Zürich is human in scale.

Leafing Through History

Few summer bathers taking a dip in the Zürichsee realize that they could be swimming over a 6,500 year old village. The earliest known Zürchers lived around 4500 B.C. in small houses perched on stilts by the lakeside. These early inhabitants were primarily hunter-gatherers, though they also planted wheat and kept cattle and pigs. Underwater archeologists have discovered a wealth of prehistoric artifacts stretching over thousands of years. Delicate Stone Age pottery, Bronze Age necklaces, bracelets and charms made from boar fangs, bear teeth and animal skulls have all been found. Many of these fascinating discoveries are now on display at the Schweizerisches Landesmuseum, the Swiss National Museum near the Hauptbahnhof, the main rail station. In all, there are thought to be 34 Stone and Bronze Age settlements scattered around the lake.

In the 1st century B.C., the Romans, attracted by Zürich's central position, built a customs house on a hill overlooking the Limmat. In time, the customs house became a fortress, remains of which can still be seen on the Lindenhof, a square in the center of the city. The Romans were also to provide Zürich with its patron saints. Legend has it that the Roman governor beheaded the Christian brother and sister, Felix and Regula, on a small island in the river. The martyrs then picked up their heads, waded through the water and walked up a hill before collapsing where the main church of Zürich now stands, the Grossmünster.

After the Germanic Alemanni, ancestors of the present day Zürchers, drove out the Romans in the 5th century, the region gradually diminished in importance until the Carolingians built an imperial palace on the Limmat four centuries later. Louis the German, grandson of Charlemagne, then founded an abbey here, making his daughters the first abbesses. It was built on the site of what is now the Fraumünster, today in a square near the Bahnhofstrasse, Zürich's main street. The first mention of "Zürich" dates from about this time (c. 845). At this point the town's significance seems to have been chiefly as a convenient halfway point for the rulers of the Holy Roman Empire to meet envoys from Italy. Indeed the German emperors regularly held court on the Lindenhof.

Despite the imperial presence, Zürich was never really to develop into a town of kings and palaces. Indeed, even at this early stage in its history, commerce played a leading role. By the 12th century, Zürich had already acquired a reputation as a wealthy settlement populated by diligent merchants making their fortunes from weaving silk, wool and linen, and tanning leather. By 1336 this merchant class had become too powerful for an impoverished aristocracy and an up-and-coming band of tradesmen. A charismatic aristocrat, Rudolf Brun, allied himself with the tradesmen to overthrow a town council controlled by the rich merchants. The 13 guilds Brun and the tradesmen then set up never really lost their power till the French Revolution at the end of the 18th century. (Even today, membership of a guild bestows considerable prestige: every year prominent businessmen dress up in medieval costumes for the guilds' traditional march through the streets to the impressive guildhalls that still dominate the Old Town's architecture).

Shortly after the Brun rebellion, Zürich threw in her lot with the Everlasting League of Uri, Schwyz, Unterwalden and Luzern, the nucleus of what was to become the Swiss Confederation. More than a century of intermittant warfare followed as the League struggled, for the most part successfully, with the Habsburgs, rulers of the Holy Roman Empire. Simultaneously, Zürich was pursuing her own political ambitions, doing all she could to expand her hold over what is now the canton of Zürich.

Defeat by the French in 1515 at the Battle of Marignano brought a sudden and traumatic end to the town's expansion and growing prosperity, a crisis greatly exacerbated by the coming of the Reformation. This, however, was the moment of truth for Zürich. Chief among the leading exponents of the Reformed, Protestant, church was Zwingli, the great preacher of fire and brimstone. Though he was subsequently to be killed fighting the Catholics, Swingli was to prove the decisive influence on Zürich, the man who taught the Zürchers their love of thrift and hard work.

The city's economic and cultural growth continued apace throughout the 17th and 18th centuries, a process aided by the influx of Protestant refugees from France and the Italian-speaking areas of Switzerland. These Huguenots were only the first of a long line of stimulating foreigners who were to seek refuge in the city. It was from Zürich that the exiled Lenin set out in his closed rail carriage to Moscow in 1917. And it was in Zürich that, at the same time, exiled French artist Hans Arp proclaimed the birth of a new art movement—later to become famous as Dada—that would "heal mankind from the madness of the age."

The beginnings of this cultural flowering date from the 18th century when Johann Jakob Bodmer and Johann Jakob Breitinger turned the town into something of an intellectual mecca. So successful were they that the German poet Ewald von Kleist was moved to write in 1752,

"Zürich is assuredly an incomparable place, not only on account of its admirable situation, which is unique in the world, but also due to the good and clever people who live there. As one meets three or four people of taste and intelligence in the great city of Berlin, there are in tiny Zürich 20 or 30." Since then Zürich has had an admirable reputation as a literary city, producing a number of significant writers both in the last century and in this, as well as playing host to a long line of distinguished literary figures from other countries, among them Thomas Mann, James Joyce and Thornton Wilder.

Nonetheless, by the mid 19th century, Zürich was still no more than just one of several equally important Swiss towns. But by the end of the century, she had become unquestionably the leading city in the country. What had happened? The answer is one Alfred Escher, a politician and financial genius who singlehanded dragged Zürich into the modern age.

Escher established the city as a major banking center, in addition to vigorously championing the development of the Federal Railways, the city's University, and pushing through the construction of the rail tunnel under the Gotthard Pass. His dynamism and farsightedness have marked the city ever since.

The going has not always been smooth, for all the air of businesslike efficiency and calm that characterize Zürich today. Though Switzerland remained neutral in both world wars, the country suffered enormous hardship in both. And the years after World War I were to prove particularly severe, marked by widespread rioting and industrial unrest. But with characteristic aplomb and shrewdness, the Zürchers turned even these setbacks to their advantage. Lead by industrialists from the canton of Zürich, who pointed out the futility of industrial disorder, a Peace Pact was signed in the '30s with the Swiss Labor Unions. Fifty years on, the pact remains valid.

Exploring Zürich

Zürich is easy to discover on foot. A walk through the city center on either side of the Limmat gives the essential feel of Zürich's comfortable mixture of old world charm and elegant modernity.

Start off from the busy Hauptbahnhof, the main rail station, an impressive 19th-century pile with high, wide halls. (When opened in 1871, one description has it that, "An admiring crowd wandered through the huge halls and brightly lit waiting rooms, with their heavily upholstered seats, mirrors, bouquets and splashing fountains, and marveled not least at the luxury of the buffets and the noble appearance of the toilets.") Pick up a map from the tourist office here. Unless you have a yen to dice with the trams and ferocious traffic outside the station, head down into the underground shopping mall and follow the signs for the Bahnhofstrasse, Zürich's principal boulevard.

The Bahnhofstrasse is justifiably famous for its tempting shops and cafes, and indeed the farther you stroll along it the more evident its atmosphere of understated wealth becomes, and the more expensive the shops. Intriguingly, and perhaps lending credence to the idea that the Zürcher instinctively tends to throw smokescreens round his real pur-

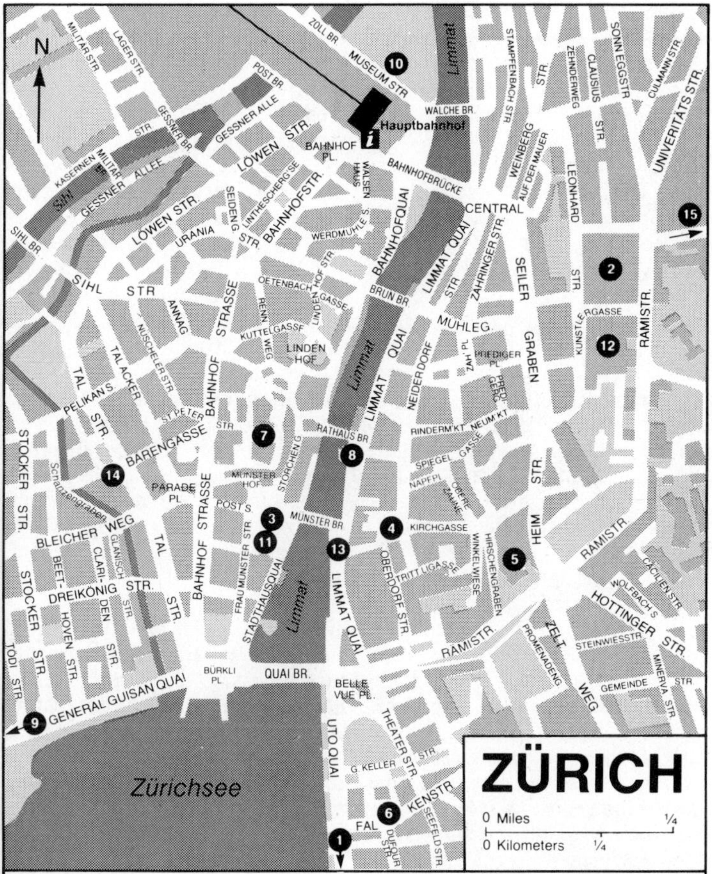

Points of Interest

1 Centre Le Corbusier
2 Federal Institute of Technology
3 Fraumünster
4 Grossmünster
5 Kunsthaus
6 Opernhaus
7 Peterskirche
8 Rathaus
9 Rietberg Museum
10 Schweizerisches Landesmuseum
11 Stadthaus
12 University of Zürich
13 Wasserkirche; Helmhaus
14 Wohnmuseum
15 Zoo

i Tourist Information

pose, at least as far as money is concerned, the Bahnhofstrasse is also the heart of the country's banking network. Not that the casual visitor would know it. The only apparent sign of the phenomenal wheeling and dealing that takes place continually behind these tranquil facades, where pressurized bankers conclude giant deals, are the figures that chase each other endlessly across computer screens, flashing share prices and the latest news. Even more intriguing is the thought that the vaults housing one of the world's great treasure troves are actually under your feet. For Zürich is one of the world's most important precious metals markets, rivaled only by London. And these vaults under the Bahnhofstrasse are where much of the gold and silver is kept.

A quarter of the way up the Bahnhofstrasse take off to your left into the Rennweg, and turn left again into the Fortunagasse, a charming medieval street which leads to the Lindenhof. With a few steps you have moved out of the world of high finance and elegant shops and deep into history. On this quiet square, overlooking the Old Town on both sides of the river, are the remains of the original Roman customs house and fortress, and the imperial medieval residence. There's also a fountain here, put up in 1912, commemorating the day in 1292 when Zürich's women saved the city from the Habsburgs. As the story goes, the town was on the brink of defeat as the imperial Habsburg aggressors moved in. Determined to avoid this humiliation, the town's women donned armor and marched to the Lindenhof. On seeing them, the enemy thought they were faced with another army and promptly beat a strategic retreat. Today, the scene could hardly be less martial, as young mothers sit with their babies in the sun and men play chess on a giant board.

From the Lindenhof a maze of medieval alleys leads off to your right. Among them, in one of the loveliest medieval squares in Switzerland, is the Peterskirche, whose 13th-century tower is reputed to have the largest clockface in Europe. The Peterskirche is the oldest parish church in Zürich: though the present building dates back only to the early 13th century, there's been a church on this site since the 9th century. The existing building has, however, been considerably added to over the years. The tower, for example, was extended in 1534 (when the clock was added), while the nave was rebuilt in 1705. Plays are often performed on the steps during the summer.

But walk down to the river from the Lindenhof and follow its course till you come to the Fraumünster. The church itself dates from the 13th century, but stands on the site of Louis the German's original 9th-century abbey, the remains of which may be visited on request. The Romanesque, or pre-Gothic, choir has stained glass windows by the Russian-born artist Marc Chagall, a long-time fan of Zürich, while Swiss sculptor and painter Augusto Giacometti executed the fine painted window in the north transept. The lofty north tower was completed in 1732.

In the same square are two lovely guildhalls. These are the Zunfthaus zur Waag, meeting place of the linenweavers and hatmakers, dating from 1637, and the Baroque Zunfthaus zur Meise, a rather more aristocratic looking building erected for the city's wine merchants in the 18th century. Today, it is the home of the ceramics collections of the Swiss

National Museum, the Landesmuseum, with a particularly strong collection of 18th-century porcelain.

From here, head back to the Bahnhofstrasse to the Paradeplatz, a focal point of the city's tram network. It's also the site of one of the most celebrated cafes in cafe-conscious Zürich, Sprüngli. This is the place to glimpse chic Zürich society, from young bankers to glamorous housewifes, settling into one of Sprüngli's famous chocolate truffles. Fortified by one of these delicious concoctions, continue down the Bahnhofstrasse which, as it nears the lake, opens out into a vista of boats, wide waters and distant peaks. Cross over Bürkliplatz to the Quai Bridge and the most glorious sight in the city: on one side, the majestic sweep of the lake, on the other the medieval town. It's particularly memorable at night when the floodlit buildings are reflected in the inky waters, their images broken only by the quiet rustle of the wind or the slow drifting of a sleeping swan.

The East Bank

There is a different feel to the Zürich you encounter on crossing over to the east bank: the place becomes somehow less dignified and more lively. If you turn to your right here where the Quai Bridge runs into Bellevue Platz you come to the Opera House, which has a considerable reputation for the high quality of its performances. Alternatively, you can continue straight ahead up the Rämistrasse to the Kunsthaus, the Zürich Art Museum. The museum has excellent permanent collections, but is particularly strong in its Swiss material, boasting the largest group of paintings in the world by late 18th-century, early 19th-century Romantic Füssli and almost 100 works by the Swiss 19th-century painter Hodler. In addition, there is an excellent modern collection with Munch, Picasso and the Dadaists well to the fore. First class changing exhibits are a regular feature.

But for a first walk, head along the river to the imposingly gaunt Grossmünster, whose stern 11th-century exterior looks out over the chic boutiques, singles hangouts, art galleries and movie theaters of this part of town. On the south tower, a squatting figure of Charlemagne stares out with equal disapproval. (You can see the 500-year-old original statue of the Carolingian emperor in the crypt). The interior of the Grossmünster is appropriately dour and forbidding, an apt setting, you feel, for the fire-and-brimstone sermons of Zürich reformer Huldrych Zwingli in the 16th century. The present building is mostly late 11th, early 12th century, but, as with the Peterskirche, for example, or the Fraumünster, there's been a church on this site since the 9th century, though very little remains of this today. A contemporary touch is provided by the stained glass, again the work of Giacometti.

Head back down the steps to the Limmat and the Münster Bridge, site of the 18th-century Helmhaus, the open court of which was originally a cloth market. Attached to the Helmhaus is the 15th-century Wasserkirche, the Water Church, one of the most beautiful and delicate late-Gothic churches in Switzerland. Here, too, the stained glass is by Giacometti. The land on which both buildings stand was an island until 1839. Then, it was joined to the river bank when the Limmatquai was extended. It was on this spot that the martyrs Felix and Regula were beheaded by the Romans.

A series of guildhalls jot the Limmatquai at this point. Today, they have mostly been converted into restaurants, each with the fascination of centuries-old traditions complementing their excellent food. There is the 13th-century Gesellschaftshaus zum Rüden, the noblemen's hall and one of the major landmarks of Zürich, where today's dinner guests dine under a magnificent 300-year-old wooden ceiling. Then there is the charming Zunfthaus zur Zimmerleuten, built for the town's carpenters in 1708, and the appealing Zunfthaus zur Saffran, built in 1723, where the haberdashers came to discuss the business of the day.

Over the road from the latter is the late 17th-century Rathaus, the Town Hall, a fine Baroque building sitting in the Limmat. Its interior has been preserved largely as it was when first built; indeed the Banqueting Hall, with its richly decorated stucco ceiling, is one of the most beautiful Baroque rooms in the country. This elegant building is not simply for show, however. The Parliaments of both the city and the canton of Zürich meet here still. And it was here, during the youth riots of the early '80s, that the city fathers (and a mother) were trapped as demonstrators beseiged the building for many hours, demanding additional finance for rock concerts and the like. Though not normally open to the public, you may attend the meetings of the cantonal and city Parliaments on Monday mornings and Wednesday afternoons respectively.

It's a good idea to take off from here into the alleys and streets to your right where the Old Town meanders through a captivating jigsaw puzzle of tiny houses, many dating back to medieval times. Among the best and most interesting streets are the Rindermarkt, Neumarkt, Napfplatz and Kirchgasse. Rindermarkt 9 was for many years home of Gottfried Keller, commonly considered Switzerland's national poet and novelist. The house became famous in his novel *Der Grüne Heinrich* (*Green Henry*); opposite is a restaurant, Zur Opfelchammer, where the 19th-century writer used to eat. The Rindermarkt joins the picturesque Neumarkt, the most interesting point of which is the tiny square formed by the junction of the Rindermarkt, Neumarkt and Spiegelgasse. Here, there's a fine early Gothic tower, the Grimmenturm, rising above a charming medieval building, now a popular restaurant, the Kantorei.

Head up the Spiegelgasse, and you come to the Napfplatz, a truly medieval square with a little tower. This, interestingly, was used in the 14th century by Zürich's bankers. From the Napfplatz, take the Obere Zäune and head up to the Kirchgasse, a broad medieval thoroughfare packed with antique shops, galleries and book stores. This takes you back to the Grossmünster or the Limmatquai, depending which route you take.

If you had walked parallel to the river and not up into the maze of the Old Town, you would pass through Niederdorf, Zürich's red-light district. Here you'll find numerous late night bars, and, in summer, the streets busy with people strolling through the warm nights. Zürich's ladies of the night have a certain Swiss pragmatism when it comes to identifying potential clientele, meaning that it's always comfortable to walk around here.

The northern end of the Niederdorf leads into Central Square, from where a quaint cable car, leaving at frequent intervals, climbs up to the University and the neighboring Federal Institute of Technology—very useful if you don't fancy the stiff climb up to the University. From the University there's a fine view over the city.

Alternatively, for those who want to dig into Swiss history, walk over the Bahnhof Bridge to the Landesmuseum, the Swiss National Museum, housed in a curious Victorian structure just to the right of the Hauptbahnhof as you cross the bridge.

EXCURSIONS—Lake and River

In good weather there's no more enjoyable excursion from Zürich than a trip on the Zürichsee on one of the many lake steamers that leave from the Bürkliplatz. You can take a long trip of around four to five hours down the lake to Rapperswil, whose romantic castle dominates the skyline, or just a short lunchtime trip around the northern end of the lake. (The regular lunchtime boat, leaving at 12:10 and returning at 1:15, is enduringly popular). If sitting on a boat and looking at the scenery leaves you cold, however, there are several evening sailings—once a week there's a fondue party—with dancing, drinking and eating.

The Zürichsee is pretty rather than spectacular. There are none of the dramatic crags that plunge precipitately into the ice cold waters of the Vierwaldstättersee, for example. But this domesticity has a charm of its own. The banks rise in gentle slopes, in the midst of which are numerous pretty villages and villas. To the east are lofty wooded hills, with the Alps a striking background.

Heading down the lake from Zürich, you pass first a park on the east bank—the left—where the Zürchers stroll on summer days. The Zürichhorn, as it is known, is dotted with sculptures, among them a typically eccentric kinetic piece in iron by Swiss artist Jean Tinguely and a contrastingly monumental work by Henry Moore. The Centre le Corbusier is also here, with its colorful, freestanding building, the last work of the great Swiss architect and apostle of modernism.

Past the Zürichhorn, the east bank of the lake is known as the Gold Coast as its sunnier aspect has long made this a desirable address among the wealthiest of Zürich's citizens. Yet the famous have by no means neglected the other side of the lake: the writers Thomas Mann and Conrad Ferdinand Mayer both lived in Kilchberg, for example. The villages on both sides of the lake, however, have naturally tended to spread and grow together, yet each remains a proud entity in itself, with a complete infrastructure of local government, police and taxation.

The first stopping place of interest after leaving Zürich is Meilen, a pretty little town with a 15th-century church. It was here, in the winter of 1853, when the lake was unusually low, that teacher Johannes Aeppli discovered the first evidence of prehistoric habitation of the area. The exact site of these early excavations is today underwater again, but further traces of these early Zürchers, in the form of piles driven into the lake bed to support houses, can be seen at Wetzikon, a few miles from Meilen. Here what was once part of the lake shore has become a peat moor.

Another town along the lake is Stäfa, once well-known as a producer of silk, but now principally a wine-producing center. Here Goethe stayed for a time in 1797 when writing his play *Jery and Bately,* inspired by the Swiss scenery. Nearly opposite Stäfa is the little island of Ufenau, which has a ruined church and the grave of Ulrich von Hutten, an associate of Luther. He had fled to Zürich from his persecutors to seek the protection of Zwingli.

Rapperswil, its monastery and castle etched against the sky, is seen long before the steamer reaches its snug little harbor. The castle was originally built around 1200, though the present building dates from 1354. The original building was destroyed by the Zürcher in 1350 in retribution for the people of Rapperswil plotting the sacking of Zürich with the Habsburgs. Other features of interest here are the Rathaus, the Town Hall, with a fine carved Gothic portal and, inside, a colossal old wrought-iron stove, and the monastery. This is a fairly recent addition to the town, but its tall spire adds greatly to the picturesque appearance of Rapperswil, with its many medieval houses. Be sure also to check out the fish restaurants on the lakeside promenade.

Finally, a variation on a trip on the Zürichsee is provided by the little boats that make the short trip down the Limmat in the center of Zürich from the Landesmuseum to the Zürichhorn.

Land Excursions

Switzerland is so compact that most points of interest can be reached with ease in less than a day. Zürich is particularly well suited as a center for day trips. Trains leave regularly for Basel, Bern, Luzern, St. Gallen and Schaffhausen. In the immediate vicinity of the city there are also a number of interesting places to visit on a day trip. (We give further details of excursions from Zürich in the *Practical Information* that follows).

A few miles to the north of Zürich is Winterthur. Though primarily an industrial center, it lays claim to both a long and distinguished history and the possession of a notable art collection. The city's origins can be traced back to A.D. 294. During the Middle Ages it became a mecca for craftsmen before falling under the yoke of Zürich. Manuscripts, paintings, furniture and everyday items chronicle the city's development at the Heimatmuseum, the local museum.

Of significantly greater interest, however, is the Sammlung Oskar Rheinhart, the Oscar Rheinhart Collection, a magnificent collection of Old Masters and 19th-century French paintings. The pictures hang in the lovely home where Rheinhart himself lived, the domestic nature of their setting adding enormously to an appreciation of them. Housed in the Stiftung Oskar Rheinhart, or Oskar Rheinhart Foundation, are a further 600 works by Swiss, German and Austrian artists of the 18th, 19th and 20th centuries which the great collector donated to Winterthur.

For a complete change of pace, visit the Technorama der Schweiz, the Swiss Technical Museum, a museum reflecting Winterthur's long tradition of manufacturing and technical innovation.

Winterthur itself has a carefully preserved Old Town, alive with late-Gothic and Renaissance buildings that bear witness to a long and proud history.

The surrounding countryside is also rich in medieval castles, though check with the tourist office before starting your trip that they are open. The best known is that at Kyburg above the river Töss. First mentioned in 1027 as belonging to the Counts of Kyburg, it passed to the Habsburgs in 1264. In 1452 the castle came under the auspices of the canton of Zürich, in whose authority it remains today. Of particular interest is the Romanesque chapel, with frescoes from the 14th and 15th centuries. But the whole complex is deeply impressive, and strongly medieval in atmosphere.

A further three castles can also be easily visited from Zürich, though if you take them all in on one day it makes a very full day. Leave Zürich on the N1, the main expressway to Bern. Turn off the expressway at Baden, itself a famous spa town, 22 kms. (14 miles) from Zürich and take the highway to Brugg, route 3. Here, take route 5 south to the spa town of Schinznach, a further 10 kms. (six miles) on. Here, ask the way to Schloss Habsburg, the castle that gave the famous imperial family their name. Dating back to 1020, the castle was once rather more imposing than it is today. But enough remains to give an impression of the famous family's beginnings.

About six kms. (four miles) south of Schloss Habsburg is Lenzburg, site of one of the most impressive castles in Switzerland; indeed its dominating silhouette is visible from many miles around. Founded in the 11th century, it was greatly extended and added to over the years. Today, it boasts architecture from practically every period of Swiss history up to the 18th century. *Raison d'être* and explanation of its magnificence was its crucial location along one of Switzerland's most important east–west arteries of communication and domination of the fertile lowlands of the river Aare.

About 10 kms. south of Lenzburg is Boniswil, site of one the prettiest castles in Switzerland, Hallwil am See. Dating back to the 11th century and surrounded by a water-filled moat, it is a fascinating complex with a fine view of the Halwiler See.

From Boniswil it is an easy drive back to Zürich via Lenzburg and then route 25 and route 1.

PRACTICAL INFORMATION FOR ZÜRICH

GETTING TO TOWN FROM THE AIRPORT. Zürich airport (Kloten), the country's principal international airport, has a main line rail station beneath its terminal buildings. There are regular and fast services into Zürich itself, all of which go to the main rail station, the Hauptbahnhof, in the center of town; the trip takes about 10 minutes. Fare is around Fr. 4.20. You can also get through trains from Kloten to Aarau, Baden, Basel, Bern, Bienne (Biel),

Geneva, Lausanne, Luzern, Olten, St. Gallen, Solothurn, Winterthur and Zug. Trains run from around 6 A.M. to midnight. Taxis into town are unjustifiably expensive.

TOURIST OFFICES. The main branch of the Zürich Tourist Office (Verkehrsbüro Zürich) is at Bahnhofplatz 15 in the main rail station (tel. 01–211 40 00). The office is open Nov. to Feb., Mon. to Thurs. 8–8, Fri. 8–10, Sat. and Sun. 9–6; Mar. to Oct., Mon. to Fri. 8–10, Sat. and Sun. 8–8:30. There are also branches at Zürich Airport in Terminal A (tel. 01–816 40 81) open 11–8, and in Terminal B (01–814 40 81) open 8–5.

Services offered include information about Zürich and surroundings, hotel reservations in Zürich and other places in Switzerland, city tours and strolls through the Old Town, excursions, all-inclusive arrangements, car hire, guides and hostesses, tram and bus ticket information. The tourist office has a good selection of pamphlets filled with useful information including *Zürich News* detailing what's on.

HOTELS. Zürich has an enormous range of hotels, from some of the most chic and prestigious in the country, all the way down to modest guesthouses. Standards in all price ranges are high even at the very lowest end of the scale. Despite having long had a reputation as the most expensive of all Swiss cities, especially for hotels, prices are no longer disproportionate in comparison to other major centers. This being Switzerland, however, prices are still not exactly low, but you can be very sure that you get what you pay for: quality and service remain as high as ever.

During the week, when Zürich is filled with visiting businessmen, the centrally located hotels are often booked out. Book ahead, or arrive in Zürich on a weekend if possible. On the way into town, there are pleasant hotels, particularly along the lake. Staying near the water in these lakeside villages can be a lovely experience if the weather is right. These small hotels often have good restaurants.

If you do find yourself stuck, the Zürich tourist office will help in finding a bed.

Deluxe

Atlantis Sheraton, Döltschiweg 234 (tel. 01–463 00 00). 460 beds. The remote location—a good 20 minutes outside town center—is more than compensated for by the quiet and attractive surroundings. Modern building with good restaurant and indoor pool. AE, DC, MC, V.

Baur au Lac, Talstr. 1 (01–221 16 50). 220 beds. One of the world's finest hotels, enjoying a very central location at the southern end of the Bahnhofstrasse by the lake. There's a lovely garden with a pavilion for lunch and drinks in summer; the grill room is much favored by businessmen. Rooms are hard to come by during the week, but generally easier at weekends. AE, V.

Dolder Grand Hotel, Kurhausstr. 65 (tel. 01–251 62 31). 300 beds. Long recognized as one of the world's top hotels and a regular haunt of the super wealthy. The atmosphere throughout is deeply luxurious, with high-ceilinged reception rooms and many interesting architectural features. The airy, elegant restaurant has fine service, and cuisine to match; outdoor dining in summer is an additional bonus. Swimming pool and tennis courts. Located above the city—about 10 minutes from the center (20 minutes in rush hours)—so may be a bit out of the way for those who prefer a downtown location. AE, DC, MC, V.

Eden au Lac, Utoquai 45 (tel. 01–47 94 04). 75 beds. A charming mansion on the lake near the Opera House. Intimate atmosphere with an old-world tinge. Restaurant adds to its charms. AE, DC, MC, V.

Savoy Baur en Ville, Poststr. 12 (01–211 53 60). 150 beds. Elegant and attractive older hotel located in the heart of the Bahnhofstrasse; lately renovated. Popular small bar and good cafe with sidewalk tables in summer from which to watch the passing parade. AE, DC, V.

Zürich, Neumühlequai 42 (01–363 63 63). 400 beds. Modern, efficient and comfortable high-rise hotel across the river from the main rail station. Fitness club and indoor pool complete the many facilities. AE, DC, MC, V.

Expensive

Ascot, Tessinerplatz 9 (tel. 01–201 18 00). 122 beds. Recently reopened after extensive renovations. Attractive, with good restaurant. AE, DC, MC, V.

Carlton Elite, Bahnhofstr. 41 (tel. 01–211 65 60). 110 beds. Somewhat dark reception hall, but it's very convenient and with good service. Its English pub is popular with the bankers working nearby. AE, DC, MC, V.

Continental, Stampfenbach 60 (01–363 33 63). 250 beds. Modern and comfortable, if located in a rather unexciting area, but within a few minutes of the center. AE, DC, MC, V.

Glärnischhof, Claridenstr. 30 (tel. 01–202 47 47). 120 beds. Just off the Bahnhofstrasse within easy reach of shopping, lake and river. Pleasant restaurant. AE, DC, MC, V.

Neues Schloss, Stockerstr. 17 (tel. 01–201 65 50). 96 beds. Newly renovated and comfortable. Off the Bahnhofstrasse, well-situated for the Tonhalle (concert hall). Elegant, French restaurant. AE, DC, MC, V.

Nova-Park, Badenerstr. 420 (tel. 01–491 22 22). 1000 beds. Very lively and modern ambiance, with varied facilities. Kindergarten for tiny guests; art exhibits; music in the bar; indoor pool and health club. Slightly off the beaten track and in a dull area, but tram connections make center reachable in a matter of minutes. DC, MC, V.

Schweizerhof, Bahnhofplatz 7 (tel. 01–211 86 40). 150 beds. Opposite the main rail station. Very few double rooms. Primarily for businessmen or others traveling on their own. Charming restaurant discreetly hidden away on the first floor. Atmospheric bar. AE, DC, MC, V.

St. Gotthard, Bahnhofstr. 87 (tel. 01–211 55 00). 200 beds. Busy, no-nonsense business-type hotel near main rail station. A range of restaurants including a steakhouse, sidewalk cafe, gourmet fish restaurant and popular bar where you can eat. AE, DC, MC, V.

Zum Storchen, Weinplatz 2 (tel. 01–211 55 10). 110 beds. Former guildhall overlooking the river and Old Town. Famed particularly for its restaurant; one of the great experiences in Zürich is sitting on the terrace here for dinner, overlooking the water; very few tables, so book. AE, DC, V.

Moderate

Adler, Rosengasse (tel. 01–252 64 30). 70 beds. Comfortable and convenient. Reader recommended. AE, DC, MC, V.

Belvoir, Säumerstr. 37 in Rüschlikon (tel. 01–724 02 02). 52 beds. Overlooking the lake with a magnificent view, around 10 minutes from town. Children will enjoy the easy atmosphere. Restaurants.

Florhof, Florhofgasse 4, (tel. 01–47 44 70). 56 beds. In University district with a certain quaint charm. Favored by writers and academics. Good restaurant. AE, DC, MC, V.

Franziskaner, Niederdorfstr. 1 (tel. 01–252 01 20). 40 beds. Convenient for those who want to enjoy the pleasures of Zürich's nightlife. Well-run hotel with restaurant. AE, DC, MC, V.

Glockenhof, Sihlstr. 31 (tel. 01–211 56 50). 168 beds. Very convenient and popular with tourists. AE, DC, MC, V.

Kindli, Rennweg/Pfalzgasse 1 (tel. 01–211 59 17). 30 beds. In the center of town with a lively folklore restaurant. Loads of atmosphere. AE, MC.

Löwen, Seestr. 153 in Kilchberg (tel. 01–715 43 02). 32 beds. On the lake road into Zürich about 10 minutes from center. Lovely position, pleasant restaurant.

Inexpensive

Ascona, Meinrad-Lienert-Strasse 17 (tel. 01–463 27 23). 30 beds; no rooms with bath. Out of the center, but generally recommended.

Italia, Zeughausstr. 61 (tel. 01–241 05 55); no rooms with bath. Simple accommodations in the largely Italian district of Zürich. Restaurant is very popular with artists and writers.

Linde Oberstrass, Universitätstr. 91 (tel. 01–362 21 09). 14 beds; no rooms with bath. Traditional inn within a short tram ride of the center. Local restaurant with good Swiss food.

Splendid, Rosengasse 5 (tel. 01–252 58 50); no rooms with bath. Centrally located in Zürich's nightlife district. V.

Vorderer Sternen, Bellevueplatz (tel. 01–251 49 49). 20 beds; no rooms with bath. Popular restaurant with local specialties. AE.

Boarding Houses

St. Georg, Weberstr. 11 (tel. 01–241 11 44). 58 beds; one with bath. Comfortable building renovated in 1986, convenient for the center. Breakfast and dinner.

Titlis, Rütistr. 44 (tel. 01–252 73 59); 15 beds, none with bath. A family house in a residential district above the town. Breakfast only.

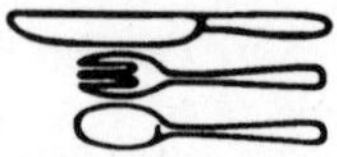

RESTAURANTS. Zürich has more than 1,000 restaurants, offering everything from local specialties, fine French, Italian and Spanish cuisine to Asian dishes. The Swiss may not look very fat but don't be fooled: they love to eat. For example, in most typically German-Swiss restaurants you are likely to be handed a large second helping immediately you've finished the first. However, in recent years, a number of top restaurants have moved toward a variation of *nouvelle cuisine,* with meals composed of a succession of tiny portions. Here, you need have few worries for your waistline, if not for your pocketbook. It's as well always to reserve as well ahead as possible for the more expensive spots.

Zürich specialties include *Zuri-Gschnätzlets* (diced veal in a white wine sauce), *Kutteln nach Zürcher Art* (tripe with onions, mushrooms and white wine), *Leberspiesschen* (liver with bacon and sage) and *Rösti* (fried sliced potatoes). You can order open wines, which are cheaper than bottled. Often a restaurant has its own house wine; again generally a good bet.

The restaurants below represent no more than a small selection of Zürich's rich range of eating places. Note that many cafes also serve light meals at reasonable prices.

Expensive

Agnes Amberg, Hottingerstr. 5 (tel. 01–251 26 26). Supervised to the last detail by one of the best chefs in Switzerland. Decor on the over-elegant side, but service is excellent. Typical menu consists of a series of tiny dishes cooked with fresh ingredients, the whole beautifully presented. Indeed presentation and quality, not quantity, are what you're paying for. Deluxe prices. AE, DC, MC, V.

Chez Max, Seestrasse 53, Zollikon (tel. 01–391 88 77). Worth the short drive from the city to sample the extraordinarily imaginative offerings of owner/chef Max Kehl. Among specialties are a series of dishes improbably marrying Japanese and French cuisine. A gourmet's mecca for years despite the steep prices.

Conti, Dufourstrasse 1 (tel. 01–251 06 66), an elegant establishment with sophisticated cuisine behind the Opera House. From 10 P.M., a special after-theater menu. In the less expensive corner, journalists from the prestigious *Neue Zürcher Zeitung* newspaper nearby take time off from their typewriters. AE, DC, MC, V.

Eichmühle, Neugutstrasse 933, Wädenswil (tel. 01–780 34 44). A good 30 minutes from Zürich in rustic surroundings. Chef Paul Wannewetsch has resolutely resisted the siren calls of *nouvelle cuisine* in favor of a substantial, almost regal, *Grand Cuisine* of yesteryear. Surroundings are intimate and welcoming, and service very special. A unique experience, but hidden in the country the restaurant is a little hard to find. Get exact instructions from your hotel. AE, DC, MC, V.

Haus zum Rüden, Limmatquai 42 (tel. 01–47 95 90). A guildhall overlooking the Limmat River where you dine in a late-Gothic hall under an ornamented wooden ceiling. French cuisine. DC, V.

Kronenhalle, Rämistrasse 4 (tel. 01–251 66 69). Typically Swiss-German recipes presented by motherly waitresses. Unique in that diners sit surrounded by famous paintings by such artists as Picasso, Matisse, Vlaminck, Bonnard and Utrillo. This was James Joyce's favorite Zürich restaurant. AE, DC, V.

Kunststuben, Seestrasse 160, Küsnacht (tel. 01–910 07 15). Somewhat out of town on the lake, but proprietor Horst Petermann is a superb chef who insists on using only the freshest and finest ingredients. Book weeks ahead.

Nouvelle, Erlachstrasse 46 (tel. 01–462 63 63). Surrealistic decor by Swiss artist Hansrudi Giger provides an offbeat setting for the French dishes which black-coated waiters serve with solemnity. AE, DC, MC, V.

Piccoli Accademia, Rotswandstr. 48 (tel. 01–241 62 43). One of the best Italian restaurants outside Italy. Photos of guests from the theater and movies look down from the walls with written appreciations of the fine food. It pays to ask what the daily special is. DC, MC.

Rebe, Schützengasse 5 (tel. 01–221 10 65). A few steps from the main rail station. Perfectly prepared French cuisine long popular with Bahnhofstrasse bankers and businessmen. DC, MC.

Zunfthaus zur Schmiden, Marktgasse 20 (tel. 01–251 52 87). Dating back to the 16th century, a sumptuous Renaissance and Baroque interior. Sophisticated German-Swiss cuisine. AE, DC, MC, V.

Moderate

La Bouillabaise, Hotel St. Gotthard, Bahnhofstrasse 87 (tel. 01–211 83 17). Popular fish restaurant where the local business community likes to lunch.

Le Dézaley, Römergasse 7 (tel. 01–251 61 29), near the Grossmünster cathedral. A charming restaurant with Swiss specialties, including *fondue.*

Mère Catherine, Im Nägelihof am Rüdenplatz (tel. 01–69 22 50). Lively French restaurant in the heart of the Old Town. Value for your money.

Mövenpick, locations all over town. Restaurant chain offering excellent value for money and wide range of specialties. AE, DC, MC, V.

Münsterhof, Münsterhof 6 (tel. 01–211 53 07). Cozy little restaurant in a 600-year-old building with medieval frescoes on the walls. A substantial Swiss menu. AE, DC, MC.

Obere Flühgasse, Flühgasse 69 (tel. 01–53 11 10). For summer nights when you want to sit in a tranquil garden out of the center of town. Book first. Swiss specialties, with delicious homemade desserts. AE.

Rosenhof, Weberstrasse 14 (tel. 01–242 85 97). Slightly off the beaten track in a business district, though not far from the center, this restaurant is well worth the effort to find. Excellent Italian dishes. AE, MC.

Vorderer Sternen, Theaterstrasse 22, am Bellevue (tel. 01–251 49 49). A truly Zürich restaurant, with Swiss specialties, conveniently located near movie houses and the opera. Very good value for your money, and accordingly has many regulars.

Zeughauskeller, Bahnhofstrasse 28a (tel. 01–211 26 90). Loads of atmosphere, with arms and armor on the walls recalling the days when the town's arsenal was kept here. A typical beer restaurant, though also with wines, and solid, reliable local specialties and inexpensive dishes.

Zunfthaus zur Saffran, Limmatquai 40 (tel. 01–47 67 22). An impressive guildhall dating back to 1723 with wide windows and rich stucco ceilings. Swiss dishes. AE, DC, MC, V.

Zunfthaus zur Zimmerleuten, Limmatquai 40 (tel. 01–252 08 34). Waitresses in folk costumes, rich Swiss cuisine and the Baroque hall with views over the river make this a deeply atmospheric experience. Located in the carpenters' guildhall. V.

Inexpensive

Augustiner, Augustinergasse 25 (tel. 01–211 72 10). A country pub on the elegant Bahnhofstrasse; popular with bankers. AE, DC, MC, V.

Bauschänzli, Stadthausquai. Open only in summer. Lovely location on the edge of the lake near the Quai Bridge.

Bierhalle Kropf, In Gassen (tel. 01–221 18 05). Just off the Bahnhofstrasse, a favorite eating place for students and office workers. DC.

Brasserie, main rail station (tel. 01–211 15 10). Quick service and reliable food in a turn-of-the-century hall with a lot of charm. AE, DC, MC.

Cooperativo, Strassburgstr. 5 at Werdplatz (tel. 01–241 44 75). Somewhat out of the center but popular with families, journalists and workers from nearby offices. Italian food.

Hinterer Sternen, Freieckgasse 7 (tel. 01–251 32 68). Right in the center of the movie and theater area at the Bellevue; simple restaurant with good food.

Mensa, Rämistrasse 71, and Mensa Polyterrasse, Leonhardstr. 34. Student restaurants with rock bottom prices.

Migros, locations all over town. Switzerland's largest chain of supermarkets; all have restaurants where the emphasis is very much on good, inexpensive food. No alcohol.

Silberkugel, locations all over town. Swiss fast-food chain. Reliable and quick service. No alcohol.

Weisses Kreuz, Falkenstrasse 27 (tel. 01–251 49 50). Nothing fancy and a rather mixed clientele, but the food is tasty.

CAFES. Cafes form a central part of Zürich life. Here you'll find the Zürcher reading the papers, meeting their friends or just taking time off from shopping. You can sit over tea or coffee as long as you like; there is no hurry. All cafes offer light snacks so that you can have your lunch in one. Delicious cakes and pastries are a common treat.

Cafe Münz, Münzplatz 3 (tel. 01–221 3027). A wonderfully crazy cafe, though extremely chic for all that, just off the Bahnhofstrasse where sculptures and mobiles by Swiss artist Jean Tinguely whizz and whirl from the ceilings and walls.

Investor's Club, Nüschelerstr. 9 (tel. 01–211 26 60). Filled—as you might imagine—with investors and bankers studying the stock exchange pages while monitors flicker the latest financial news above their heads. Waitresses can provide you with the latest precious metals and currency developments as well as coffee and cream cakes.

Odéon, Limmatquai 2 (tel. 01–251 16 50). Turn-of-the-century bar where Lenin used to sit when in Zürich exile before the Russian Revolution. The cafe was also popular with the iconoclastic Dada artists of the same period. There's a bar here too, open till 2 A.M.

Schober, Napfgasse (tel. 01–251 80 60). One of the prettiest cafes in the world, located right in the heart of Zürich's Old Town. In the tiny shop, tables are piled high with mouth-watering cakes and chocolates in ribboned boxes.

Sprüngli, Bahnhofstrasse 21 (tel. 01–211 07 95). Elegant and fashionable meeting place for downtown shoppers and workers. Chic Zürich congregates here en masse.

BARS. Zürich has some pleasant bars. The **Kronenhalle** bar, Rämistrasse 4, is attached to one of the best restaurants in town, but it is an entity in itself. In the elegant atmosphere, white-coated barmen greet the town's "in" people with their well-mixed cocktails. Some of the city's traditional hotels have wonderfully comfortable bars, such as the **Storchen,** Weinplatz 2, and the **Schweizerhof,** opposite the main rail station. Then there is the **James Joyce Pub,** Pelikanstr. 8, the Dublin hangout, where the poet drank, transported to Zürich, or the **Carlton Pub** in the Carlton Elite Hotel at Bahnhofstr. 41, with an English atmosphere which seems to go down with the locals. The **Old Fashion Bar,** Fraumünsterstr. 15, and **Le Philosoph,** im Nägelihof am Rüdenplatz, draw a lively singles' crowd. At the **Casa Bar,** Münstergasse 30, alternating bands play jazz from 8 P.M.

GETTING AROUND. By Bus and Tram. Buses and tram services are excellent. Most services start from the main rail station, the Hauptbahnhof, in the center of town. Buy tickets from the machine at the stop before boarding. There is a one-day season ticket which is good for all trips on the Zürich network. A free booklet with full details and maps (in English) is available from all city transit offices (VBZ).

By Taxi. Taxis are expensive and not recommended unless you are in a real hurry.

By Bicycle. Bicycles are available for hire at the rail station.

On Foot. Zürich is a city to walk in. Places of interest are close together. Get a map at your hotel or from the tourist office and generally follow the route outlined in our main "Exploring Zürich" text.

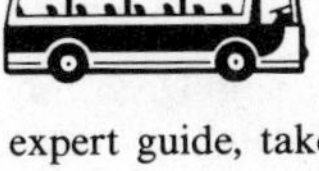

TOURS AND EXCURSIONS. For further details of all tours in and around Zürich contact the tourist office in the main rail station. Walking tours around the Old Town, lasting two-and-a-half hours and accompanied by an expert guide, take place twice daily June through September on Tuesday,

Thursday and Saturday. A more unusual, though no less popular tour is down the Bahnhofstrasse and around many of the city's historic buildings and quarters on a gold-painted tram. This leaves four times daily on Wednesdays, Fridays and Sundays from May 7 through October 19.

River and lake trips are legion. River trips, leaving every 30 minutes from the Swiss National Museum, April through October, take visitors through the heart of the city and out into the lake. For trips on the Zürichsee, boats leave regularly from Bürkliplatz at the southern end of the Bahnhofstrasse. There are trips of varying duration, the most interesting and lengthy being to Rapperswil at the southern end of the lake.

Excursions from Zürich. From Zürich day excursions are available by bus or rail throughout the summer to points of interest all over Switzerland. From the Zürich tourist office, buses leave for the Jungfrau and Bernese Oberland, the St. Gotthard and the Italian-speaking area, Mt. Pilatus and Luzern, Liechtenstein and Lac Léman (Lake Geneva). As tours do not take place every day, check before planning.

MUSEUMS AND GALLERIES. Though not perhaps a great "museum town," Zürich nonetheless boasts a fairly wide range of museums, some of international stature. The city is especially rich in modern and contemporary art, in part at least the result of reasonably wide-scale patronage of new artists by industrialists and bankers, many of whom have collections of their own. But of equal importance is the rapid growth of Zürich as a major art dealing center, with more than 100 private galleries dotted throughout the city. It has become almost a commonplace to hear the *cognoscenti* claim that there is now little in London or Paris that cannot be seen in Zürich.

Haus "Zum Rech", Neumarkt 4 (tel. 01–69 20 81). Intriguing exhibit for those drawn to the architectural history of Zürich. A model of the city around 1800 is on permanent display. Open Mon. to Fri. 8–6, Sat. 8–11:30.

Jacobs Suchard Kafee-Museum, Seefeldquai 17/Feldeggstrasse (tel. 01–385 12 83). For those interested in the history of coffee, intriguingly chartered through objects, graphics and pictures. Open Fri. 3–6, Sat. 10–4.

Kunsthaus (Art Museum), Heimplatz 1 (tel. 01–251 67 65). Fine collection of 19th- and 20th-century sculpture and painting. Of particular interest are a number of works by Alberto Giacometti and the Zürich "concrete" art school including Max Bill, Graeser and Lohse. Open Mon. 2–5, Tues. to Fri. 10–9, weekends 10–5.

Museum Bellerive, Höschgasse 3 (tel. 01–251 43 77). Beautifully displayed jewelry, glass, textiles and crafts. Exhibits change regularly. Open Tues. to Sun. 10–12 and 2–5; closed Mon.

Museum Rietberg, Gablerstr. 15 (tel. 01–202 45 28). One of the world's leading non-European art museums with 2,000 objects. India, Indochina, China and Africa are well represented. Complete collections of Japanese ink drawings. The collection is set in a lovely 19th-century villa. Open Tues. to Sun. 10–5, Wed. 5–8; closed Mon.

Sammlung E.G. Bührle (Bührle Collection), Zollikerstr. 172 (tel. 01–55 00 86). Private collection of the industrialist family Bührle. World renowned for its magnificent 19th-century French paintings. Valuable works by Courbet, Manet, Degas, Renoir, Cezanne, Toulouse-Lautrec, Gauguin and van Gogh. In a villa above the town, the collection is reached on tram 2 or 4. Open only on Tues. and Fri. 2–5 and the first Friday of the month 2–8 P.M.

Schweizerisches Landesmuseum (Swiss National Museum), Museumstr. 2 (tel. 01–221 10 10). A look at Swiss history, with fascinating pre-Romanesque and Romanesque church art; glass paintings from the 15th to 17th centuries; complete rooms furnished as in the 15th to the 18th century; splendid ceramic stoves; gold and silver from Celtic times; weapons from the 9th to the 18th century. Open Tues. to Fri. and Sun. 10–12 and 2–5, Sat. 10–12 and 2–4, closed Mon. Entry free.

Städtische Galerie zum Strauhof, Augustinergasse 9 (tel. 01–216 31 39). Changing exhibits by contemporary Swiss artists charmingly displayed in an Old Town house. Open Tues. to Fri. 10–6, Thurs. 10–9, closed Sun. and Mon.

Völkerkundemuseum (Ethnology Museum), Pelikanstrasse 40 (tel. 01–221 31 91). Set in a lovely garden, the museum offers much of interest to fans of Indonesian East Asian and African art. Open Tues. to Fri. 10–12 and 2–5, Sat. and Sun. 11–4, closed Mon.

Wohnmuseum (Museum of Domestic Art), Bärengasse 22 (tel. 01–211 17 16). Alternating exhibits show how people lived from the 17th through the 19th centuries. Open Tues. to Fri. and Sun. 10–12 and 2–5, Sat. 10–12 and 2–4, closed Mon. Entry free. At the same address is a charming collection of dolls by the Swiss puppet artist Sasha Morgentahler. Housed in lovely 17th-century buildings.

Zürcher Spielzeugmuseum (Zürich Toy Museum), Fortunagasse 15/Corner Rennweg (tel. 01–211 93 05). For those traveling with small children this could be worth a visit. It is right in the center of town and shows the collection of the Franz Carl Weber toy store. Open Mon. to Fri. 2–5.

Winterthur

Sammlung Oskar Reinhart (Collection Oskar Reinhart), Haldenstr. 95 (tel. 052–23 41 21). Magnificent private collection of 19th-century French painters and Old Masters. Open daily 10–4, closed Mon.

Stiftung Oskar Reinhart (Foundation Oskar Reinhart), Stadthausstr. 6 (tel. 052–84 5172). Important 18th-, 19th- and 20th-century paintings by Swiss, German and Austrian artists. Open daily 10–12 and 2–5, closed Mon. morning.

Technorama der Schweiz (Swiss Technical Museum), Technoramastr. 1 (tel. 052–27 77 21). Fine technological museum with well-displayed exhibits. Somewhat out of the center. Open daily 10–5.

HISTORIC BUILDINGS. All Zürich's major buildings and historic sites are easily reached on foot or by a comfortable train ride. A number, the guildhalls chief among them, are not open for sightseeing as such having been converted into restaurants (meaning that the best way to see them is to eat there). Entrance to most historic buildings is free.

Fraumünster, Münsterhof. Elegant Gothic church on the site of the 9th-century convent. Stained glass by Chagall and Giacometti adds a contemporary touch. Open Mon. to Sat. 10–12:30 and 2–5. Closed Sun.

Gesellschaftshaus zun Rüden, Limmatquai 42. Former aristocratic guildhall and one of the major landmarks of the city. Today it's a restaurant with impressive Gothic hall with beamed and decorated ceiling.

Grossmünster, Grossmünsterplatz. The most dominant building on the Zürich skyline, dating back originally to the Carolingian period. Open Mon. to Sat. 10–4, Sun. after services.

Haus zum Rechberg, Hirschengraben 40. The most important private mansion in the city, built in 1759. Headquarters in turn of both the French and the allied generals in the Napoleonic wars; in 1815 Austrian Emperor Franz I stayed here. Large gardens and terraces. Visits allowed.

Peterskirche, St. Peterhofstatt. Oldest parish church in the city, and boasting the largest clock face in Europe. In tranquil square on the west bank of the Old Town.

Rathaus (Town Hall), Limmatquai 55. Impressive, late-Renaissance civic building on island in Limmat, site of the parliament building of both the city and canton of Zürich. Not normally open to public but the proceedings of the cantonal parliament and city parliament may be attended on Monday mornings and Wednesday afternoons respectively.

Stadthaus (City Hall), Stadthausquai 17 (tel. 01–216 31 11). Impressive turn-of-the-century building with lovely enclosed courtyard. Changing art exhibits of Swiss interest. Now houses part of the city administration. Open Mon. to Fri. 8–6.

Wasserkirche and **Helmhaus,** Limmatquai 31. Adjoining buildings by the Limmat on what was, until 1839, an island in the river. The Wasserkirche is generally considered one of the most beautiful late-Gothic churches in Switzerland, while the Helmhaus, formerly a law court and linen market, stages art exhibits. Open Tues. to Sun. 10–6, Thurs. 10 A.M.–9 P.M., closed Mon.

Zünfthaus zur Meisen, Münsterhof. Imposing Baroque guildhall built for the city's wine merchants in 1757. Fine interior is complemented by the ceramic collection of the Landesmuseum (the National Museum). Open Tues. to Fri. and Sun. 10–12 and 2–4, Sat. 10–12 and 2–6, closed Mon.

Zunfthaus zur Saffran, Limmatquai 54. Richly decorated haberdashers' guildhall dating from 1723. Today a restaurant.

Zunfthaus zur Schmiden, Marktgasse 20. The smiths' guildhall, dating largely from 1520, though the original building is very much older. Restaurant on the first floor, richly decorated guild room on the second floor with late-Gothic wooden ribbed ceiling.

Zunfthaus zur Zimmerleuten, Limmatquai 40. Baroque carpenters' guildhall dating from 1708. Today a restaurant.

ZOO. Located on Zurichbergstrasse 222 (tel. 01–255 54 11). One of Europe's outstanding zoos with 2,100 animals from every quarter of the globe and enjoying an international reputation for breeding wild animals away from their natural habitats. A little out of the center but easily reached on trams 5 and 6. Open daily from 8–6; guided tours on Sun. at 10.

SHOPPING. Directly opposite the rail station is the Bahnhofstrasse, one long curve of fashionable shops leading all the way down to the lake. Considered by many to be one of the most elegant shopping streets in the world, the imaginative window displays offer even those who do not wish to buy real enjoyment. (To refill empty wallets, there are plenty of banks along the way.) Shops are usually open from 8 or 9 until 6:30 P.M. (Sats. to 4), and there is late-night shopping on Thursdays till 9. Sales are held in January, June and July.

Zürich women are very demanding shoppers. This has resulted in a very high quality in the stores. Consequently, you may just pick up a fashion item here which you might not be able to find in the more famous centers of London, Paris and Rome.

The Bahnhofstrasse is particularly noted for its fine jewelry shops and expensive fashion stores. Two department stores, **Jelmoli,** just off the street at Seidengasse 1, and **Globus** at Löwenplatz are well worth a visit. At Bahnhofstrasse 66, you find the main shop of **Bally,** the famous Swiss shoe company, which also sells other fashion items. **Les Ambassadeurs,** with a beautifully exhibited range of watches, is next door. **Franz Carl Weber's** toy shop is at Bahnhofstrasse 62. The jewelry and watch shop of **Bucherer** is usually filled with tourists at Bahnhofstrasse 50. Down the road a bit is **Grieder,** an elegant fashion shop for men and women. Towards the lake at Bahnhofstrasse 2 is the **Schweizer Heimatwerk** for souvenirs, with a further branch at Rudolf Brun-Brücke, a bridge crossing the Limmat further back towards the station.

In the small streets off the Bahnhofstrasse you find expensive boutiques, jewelry, cheese and chocolate shops. **Teuscher** at Schlüsselgasse 2 is the prettiest chocolate shop possible. It changes decorations with the seasons, reflecting the rebirth of spring to the festivities of winter.

On the other side of the river, shops are usually less expensive. On the Limmatquai are found clothing stores and the traditional souvenir and watch shops. In the alleys behind, original boutiques, gold and silversmiths and quaint bookshops make for a stimulating stroll. Kirchgasse has antiques and Neumarkt unique little jewelry shops.

Souvenirs to watch out for include the Swiss army knife, with its multitude of gadgets from bottle opener to scissors. Others: watches, chocolates, fabrics, jewelry.

Colorful vegetable and fruit markets take place on several days during the week. The easiest for you to get to is probably at Bürkliplatz at the lake end of the Bahnhofstrasse. It takes place on Tuesday and Friday from 6–11 A.M. On Saturdays from 7–4; at the same spot there is a flea market crowded with Zürcher looking for bargains.

MUSIC, MOVIES AND THEATERS. Zürich spends considerable sums subsidizing music and theater throughout the year. In June there is a festival with a wealth of top performances. At the end of that month and lasting into July, on the lakeside at Mythenquai, the Zürcher-Spektakel takes place. In circus tents set up on the lawns, avant-garde, experimental and way-out performers from around the world put on their acts. This lively and relaxed event has become one of the most popular and important cultural events in the city.

Music. Tonhalle (Concert Hall), Gotthardstr. 5 (tel. 01–201 15 80). The Tonhalle orchestra has long been famous for its performances of the German Romantics, including Brahms and Schumann, though seasons in recent years have covered a wider repertoire. Visiting guests include such names as Yehudi Menuhin. For major performances, buy your tickets as early as possible, as concerts can be booked. From the outside the Tonhalle holds little architectural interest as it has been changed considerably since Brahms opened the then new concert hall with his *Song of Triumph* in 1895. However, the hall itself is fairly attractive.

Opernhaus (Opera House), Schillerstrasse 1 (tel. 01–251 69 22). Zürich's opera has a world reputation for its ambitious performances, indeed it is justly renowned for its lavish and beautiful staging. Associated with Wagner, he conducted his works here over many years, including the *Flying Dutchman* and *Tannhauser.* (Zürich audiences were quick to recognize Wagner's talent and he achieved recognition here earlier than other places.) The Opera House was reopened last year after a costly renovation which highlighted its turn-of-the-century dignity and added a practical modern wing with a very charming restaurant.

Movies. The Zürcher are enthusiastic moviegoers. Movies are usually in the original language, which means that English-speaking visitors do not have to sit through a dubbed show. Films range from the latest releases through studio movies for a limited audience, to the greats of yesteryear. There are movie houses in several sectors of the city, and a concentration on the Limmatquai side of the river.

Information on theaters is available in *Zürich News,* a weekly bulletin found at the Tourist Office or in hotels. In the streets there are posters with the movie programs. Local newspapers also tell you what is on. Advance bookings are made for major concerts and the theater at the Billettzentrale (Ticket Center), Werdmühleplatz (tel. 01–221 22 83). Open Mon. to Fri. 10–6:30, Sat. 10–2.

Theaters. Schauspielhaus (Theater House), Rämistrasse 34 (tel. 01–251 11 11). The main theater in Zürich has a hard job satisfying popular taste and that of the sophisticated critics who would like to see more adventurous plays. Nevertheless, it has done a very good job recently of balancing between traditional and new theater. The staging is often stunning. Performances are, however, in German. The Schauspielhaus earned a considerable reputation in World War II, when it was practically the only German stage where performances were not censored. Refugee players, fleeing the Nazis, brought the Zürich stage to an illustrious peak.

In addition to the Schauspielhaus, there are several smaller theaters in Zürich. They include: **Theater am Neumarkt** (Neumarkt Theater), Neumarkt 5 (tel. 251 44 88), with contemporary plays; **Theater an der Winkelwiese** (Winkelwiese Theater), Winkelwiese 4 (tel. 01–252 10 01), often experimental; **Theater am Hechtplatz** (Hechtplatz Theater), tel. 01–252 32 34, a range of musicals and plays including the occasional performance in English.

NIGHTLIFE. A visitor can hardly miss the traditional nightlife area of Zürich, around the Niederdorf. This is a street which runs parallel to the Limmat on the other side from the rail station. Here, there are plenty of bars, striptease establishments and music. It is also the red light district. However, choosing the right place can prove difficult.

Nightclubs and discos close around 2 P.M. Ask your hotel about private clubs which open around 10 and close about 4. As they come and go, it is difficult to recommend any with confidence. Generally, night spots without a special licence must be closed by midnight.

Every night there is a folklore evening at the **Swiss Chalet,** Kindli, Rennwag/ Pfalzgasse 1 (tel. 01–211 41 82). A happy atmosphere filled with yodeling, dancing and Alpine music with the deep tones of the traditional alphorn.

For those looking for a traditional nightclub atmosphere with show, the following are recommended: **Terrasse,** Limmatquai 3 (tel. 01–251 10 74); **Red House,** Marktgasse 17 (tel. 01–252 11 10); **Tabaris,** Rämistrasse 6 (tel. 01–47 41 98).

Zürich has any number of discos. The most exclusive is the **Diagonal,** at the Hotel Baur au Lac, which is only open to members and hotel guests. The **Birdwatcher's Club,** Schützengasse 16 (tel. 01–211 50 58) is an elegant hangout where a man at the door looks potential guests up and down to see that they come up to scratch. **Club of Clubs** at Nova Park Hotel, Badenerstr. 420 (tel. 01–491 22 22) is fun. **Le Petit Prince,** Bleicherweg 21 (tel. 01–201 17 39) is small and intimate. And if you are stuck at the airport, the **Blackout Airport** disco (tel. 01–814 10 87) is worth a visit.

From May 1 to Oct. 31, a bus leaves from the Zürich Tourist Office for a "Zürich by Night" tour which includes folklore, and for those who want to extend the night, some nightclubbing.

SPECIAL EVENTS. Sechselauten ushers in spring, with a colorful festival which transforms Zürich's center into a carnival of fancy costumes donned for the occasion by the town's leading citizens. On the third or fourth Sunday in April, festivities begin with a children's parade. On Monday, their fathers take to the streets, marching first to where they burn the "Böögg," a huge cotton-wool snowman symbolizing winter. Then it is back for a feast at the guildhalls. Through the night, carrying burning torches, these descendants of medieval craftsmen walk through the Old Town visiting each other.

SPORTS. Although winter sports are not on your doorstep in Zürich, there are skiing possibilities within a reasonable distance. In summer, swimming in the lake is well provided for and there are many other sports on hand. The Zürich tourist office can help with information, as well as brochures.

Golf. Two golf courses nearest to the city center are the *Dolder Golfclub* with 9 holes and par 60 (tel. 01–47 50 45) and *Golf and Country Club Zürich* in Zumikon with 18 holes and par 72 (tel. 01–918 00 51).

Rowing, Sailing and Motor Boats. Available for hire without license.

Skating. The "Heuried" and "Dolder" artificial ice rinks, open October to March.

Skiing. The nearest region, Hoch-Ybrig, is an hour away. Choice of five skilifts and two chairlifts. **Cross-country Skiing** on the 12 km. (7.5 miles) trail on the Albiskamm, around 20 minutes from the center of Zürich. Tel. 01–201 24 24 for state of the trail.

Swimming. Several possibilities in Lake of Zürich. Public indoor pools in bad weather.

Tennis. Courts by the hour at 10 municipal and many private courts.

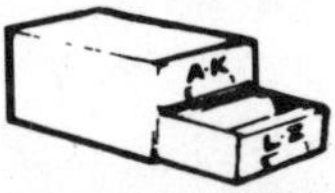

USEFUL ADDRESSES. All-Night Pharmacist. *Bellevue Apotheke,* Theaterstr. 14 (tel. 01–252 44 11). **Medical and Dental Emergency Service** (tel. 01–47 47 00).

Car Hire. *Avis,* Gartenhofstr. 17 (tel. 01–242 20 40), also at Zürich Airport (tel. 01–813 00 84); *Budget Rent-a-Car,* Tödistr. 9 (tel. 01–201 26 70), Zürich Airport (tel. 01–814 38 04); *Europcar,* Badenstr. 812 (tel. 01–432 28 20), Zürich Airport (tel. 01–813 20 44); *Hertz,* Lagerstr. 33 (tel. 01–241 80 77), Zürich airport (tel. 01–814 05 11).

Child-Minding Service. Big stores have crêches where children can be left while you shop (tel. 01–211 37 86).

Consulates. *American,* Zollikerstr. 141 (tel. 01–55 25 66). *British,* Bellerivestr. 5 (tel. 01–47 15 20).

Lost Property Office. Werdmühlestrasse 10, tel. 01–216 51 11. Open Mon. through Fri. 7:30–5:30.

Travel Agents. *American Express,* Bahnhofstrasse 20 (tel. 01–211 83 70); *Kuoni,* Bahnhofplatz 7 (tel. 01–221 34 11).

EASTERN SWITZERLAND

Charm and Creature Comforts

Eastern Switzerland is rich in variety, rich in tradition—and just plain rich! Yet despite the obvious prosperity, the region retains an air of other-worldliness. Everywhere you will see past and present interwoven. Houses—new as well as old—with frescoes and carved-wood balconies; turrets, roofs, and entire walls made of wood shingles so delicate that, when weathered, they look almost like fur.

But although the old customs are as much a part of life today as they were centuries ago, time has not entirely stood still. In St. Gallen, for instance, the largest town in Eastern Switzerland, a modern textile industry has ensured that this charming little town has not been passed by the technological advances of the late 20th century. Nonetheless the fact remains that many tourists have been slow to appreciate the myriad attractions of Eastern Switzerland, and that as a result it has managed to retain much more of its regional personality than some of the more well developed areas of the country. One happy side effect of this is that prices are often lower here than in the more famous parts of the country.

The region lies to the east of Zürich and comprises the cantons of Glarus, Schaffhausen, Thurgau, St. Gallen and—cocooned within the latter, and itself divided into two half-cantons (Innerrhoden and Ausserrhoden, or Inner and Outer Rhoden)—Appenzell. The Principality of Liechtenstein is also a part of the area administratively. However, as it is also a separate country in its own right, albeit a very tiny one, it is not covered in this chapter.

Within this area, the landscape varies from the snowcapped peaks of Mount Säntis, almost 2,500 meters (8,200 ft.) high, through the mountain valleys and the rolling hills of Appenzell, to the shores of Bodensee, Lake Constance. To the east and the north is the Rhine, separating Switzerland from Liechtenstein, Austria and Germany.

Towns range from the delightful St. Gallen to spas such as Bad Ragaz, and scores of summer and winter resorts. Some smaller towns, notably Appenzell, played a big part in forming the Swiss Confederation. In Appenzell itself, and in Glarus, the picturesque Landsgemeinde, or open-air parliament can still be seen.

Exploring St. Gallen

As well as being Switzerland's largest eastern city, St. Gallen is also an excellent center for tourists, since in addition to its own attractions, it provides easy access to Bodensee, the Säntis mountains, and the Appenzell country. The town itself lies less than an hour from Zürich by train, and balances its role as an important, modern textile center with a medieval cultural heritage. Its origins date back to 612, when the Irish missionary Gallus laid the foundations of an abbey that was to become a major cultural center of medieval Europe. The abbey itself was largely destroyed during the Reformation, but in its magnificent Rococo library, the Stiftsbibliothek (dating from the 18th century), containing over 100,000 volumes, visitors can see illuminated manuscripts which are over 1,000 years old.

The valley town of St. Gallen, which grew up in a semicircle around the abbey walls, owed allegiance to the abbot until the early 15th century when, by making an alliance with the farmers of Appenzell, the citizens gained political freedom. Religious freedom followed a century later with the Reformation, brought to the area by the humanist Vadin, whose statue can be seen in the market place. As a Protestant town St. Gallen then formed an independent miniature state surrounded by monastic territory. This lasted until the French Revolution, at the end of the 18th century, when the present canton was founded and the monasteries secularized. The abbot's former residence is now the seat of government and the local parliament.

The splendid twin-towered Rococo cathedral, built in 1756, is the town's most imposing building; its superbly restored interior fairly scintillates with light and color. On the northern side of the cathedral lies the old quarter whose ancient houses are rich in oriel windows and frescoes. By way of contrast it is worth visiting the new Municipal Theater and University; both are almost stark in their simplicity, but conceived with great imagination. St. Gallen's long connection with textiles is traced in the Textile Museum in Vadianstrasse, which houses examples of lace and embroidery made in the town from the 16th century onwards. The collection includes many pieces worn by famous European courtiers, and some stunning examples of modern work. The town is also well provided with parks and gardens, and one of the most interesting is the Peter and Paul Deer Park, where you can see ibex, chamois, stags, marmots, deer, and wild boar; and of course wonderful alpine views.

About 11 kms. (17 miles) west of St. Gallen is Wil, a beautiful 700-year-old town, once part of the estates of the Abbey of St. Gall. The massive 15th-century residence of the Bishop-Princes, the Hof zu Wil, still dominates the old Hofplatz but now houses the local museum. From the terrace of St. Nicolas church you may see the Vorarlberg, Säntis, Churfirsten and Glärnisch Alps.

A good half-day excursion from St. Gallen is to the cable car at Schwagalp, which lies about 32 kms. (20 miles) south from the town. This will take you up Mount Säntis to within a few meters of the summit, and from there—weather permitting—you will have incredible views of the Alps, and far beyond. There is a restaurant and small hotel near the summit.

Resorts and Spas

A popular resort area in canton St. Gallen is the Toggenburg Valley, which runs in a great curve between Mount Säntis and Wil. In the fine alpine surroundings of the Upper Toggenburg, beside the river Thur, are the neighboring resorts of Wildhaus, Unterwasser and Alt-St. Johann, skiing centers in the winter and the starting points for excursions in the Churfirsten and Alpstein mountains in summer. Wildhaus is the birthplace of Swiss reformer and fire-and-brimstone preacher of the Reformation, Ulrich Zwingli, whose house can still be visited. Lower down the valley, also on the river Thur, are the adjacent resorts of Krummenau, Ebnat-Kappel, Nesslau and Neu-St. Johann. A secondary road leads eastwards from the latter, through the spa and winter sports resort of Rietbad, to Schwägalp.

The southern slopes of the Churfirsten mountains, across which there are no roads, drop steeply to become the northern shores of the Walensee, a deep, 16 kms.-long (10 miles) gash in the mountains. At the western end of the lake is Weesen, a quiet little resort noted for its mild climate. Six kms. (four miles) away, along the northern shore, is the winter sports center of Amden. Opposite, running along the southern shore, is a spectacular road which travels through a number of small resorts to the lakeside village of Unterterzen. This is the lower terminal for the cable railway which goes up to Tannenbodenalp, and the Flumserberg health resort and winter sports area, a picturesque region of mountain slopes which looks across the end of the Walensee to the Churfirsten mountains. You can also reach it by steep roads that wind upwards from Flums, a small town situated in the valley that runs from the east end of the Walensee to the Rhine, near Bad Ragaz. At Flumserberg you can go on one of the world's longest cableways; over a distance of nearly two miles, a procession of little four-seater cabins climbs steadily up to Leist (2,056 meters, 6,750 ft.).

Bad Ragaz, with its beautiful golf course, is a well-run and well-established resort in a quiet mountain setting beside the Rhine. As well as having a modern spa establishment, the town is also equipped as a winter resort, and there is a cablecar running up to Pardiel (1,630 meters, 5,350 ft.), and a connecting lift to Laufboden (2,224 meters, 7,300 ft.). An excellent range of hotels complements these facilities. Just a little way south of Bad Ragaz is Bad Pfäfers, a beautiful little Baroque spa located in a dramatic canyon and extensively renovated in 1983/4. Its waters have been known since 1038. Bad Pfäfers is only open May through October, however.

From both Pardiel and (more particularly) Laufboden there are outstanding views, and in summer the latter is the starting point for the "Five Lakes" walk, which takes in five beautiful mountain lakes. In complete contrast, the famous walk (you can now go by minibus part of the way) up the Tamina Gorge will give you a dramatic taste of a journey to the center of the earth. Deep down in the gorge a narrow path winds along under overhanging rock sides. In places they touch to form a natural bridge. It's best in May or June when the snows are melting and water roars down the gorge in a tumbling, tempestuous torrent. At the end of the path is the hot spring from which over a million gallons of healing waters a day come up, at over 32°C. (90°F.), to be piped down to the spa at Bad Ragaz. The healing properties of the waters were known many centuries ago. Then, it is said, luckless patients were lowered into the waters by a rope from the top of the chasm!

Appenzell

Another delightful trip from St. Gallen is to Appenzell, in the canton of the same name. A narrow gauge railway takes you in about half an hour via the mountain village resorts of Teufen and Gais. Canton Appenzell had until recent times almost no communications with the surrounding provinces, and so has retained many of its ancient customs. It is one of three cantons (including Glarus, Ob- and Nidwalden) where the Landsgemeinde is still held. This is an open-air town meeting where each male citizen votes personally on all the laws, budgets, and taxes imposed by his administrators. Those taking part can be distinguished by the sword which they carry, a symbol of the right to vote. It is one of the few surviving examples of direct (as opposed to representative) democracy.

The assembly takes place on the last Sunday in April in the towns of Appenzell (every year), Hundwil (years with odd numbers), and Trogen (years with even numbers). Trogen is also the home of Kinderdorf Pestalozzi, a group of houses in which more than 200 orphans from many countries are educated together in an effort to bridge differences of language, religion and outlook.

The Appenzell countryside is rich, covered with fruit trees and meadows. As might be expected in such a fertile land, dairying is the major industry. In the spring, when the herds are driven up to the mountain pastures, picturesque festivals are held, while in the fall, when they come down to the valleys again, the cow with the greatest milk yield during the year is fêted and decked with flowers. Hand embroidery is also a specialty of the Appenzell, and few tourists leave without buying some. But don't expect to find many bargains: the local people are very well aware of the value of their work. In the town of

Appenzell itself, the old town hall, dating from 1561, with its folklore museum, is worth seeing.

A delightful side trip can be made up the Schwende Valley, by railway or road, to the resort of Wasserauen. From here it is only a short walk to the Seealpsee, one of the loveliest mountain lakes in Switzerland. From Wasserauen you can also take a cable car up the Ebenalp (1,645 meters, 5,400 ft.), where there is a splendid viewing point. Similar, equally rewarding, trips can be taken to the summits of the Hoher Kasten (1,800 meters, 6,000 ft.) near Brülisau; and the Kronberg (1,676 meters, 5,500 ft.) at Jakobsbad.

You can return to St. Gallen from Appenzell by a different, slightly longer route, via the resort of Urnasch and Herisau—capital of the half-canton of Appenzell/Ausserrhoden.

Glarus

To the south of canton St. Gallen is the secluded canton of Glarus, which is marked on its southern border by Mount Tödli, 3,626 meters (11,900 ft.) high. The principal road to the little town of Glarus itself runs alongside the river Linth, which winds southwards through the canton in its own deep valley. Scattered along it you will find a series of small industrial towns, though they do not interfere with the beauty of the valley itself. This provides a good foretaste of what you may expect throughout the rest of the canton: alpine pastures, snow-covered peaks, mountain lakes—from the diminutive Ober-See to the equally beautiful Klöntaler-See—figs, vineyards, chamois, and marmots; all wrapped in an aura of isolation.

All this can be found less than 20 kms. (13 miles) from Glarus, the cantonal capital. This is a small industrial town whose buildings almost all date from after 1861, the year of a disastrous fire. Here, in the disproportionately large Zaunplatz the citizens gather every year on the first Sunday in May, to take part in the Landsgemeinde, the open-air parliament.

Schaffhausen

Schaffhausen, capital of the northernmost canton of Switzerland, is an easy train ride or drive from Zürich or St. Gallen. England's William Cox wrote of the local people, "Here, every person has the mien of content and satisfaction. The cleanliness of the homes and the people is peculiarly striking, and I can trace in all their manners, behavior and dress some strong outlines that distinguish this happy people from neighboring nations. Perhaps it may be prejudice, but I am the more pleased because their first appearance reminds me of my own countrymen, and I could think for a moment that I am in England." It is certainly true that the people of Schaffhausen are far less inhibited and more easy going than most Swiss. The reason they give is that they are not surrounded by mountains, which are said to have a tendency to make the mountain dweller introspective and silent. Another reason may be the fine red wines produced by the region!

A city of about 36,000 inhabitants, Schaffhausen has preserved, like most towns in this area, a medieval aspect. From the early Middle Ages, it was an important depot for river cargoes, as these had to be loaded and unloaded there because of the natural barrier created by the waterfall and rapids. The name Schaffhausen is probably derived from the "skiffhouses" ranged along the river bank. Rising picturesquely from the water's edge, Schaffhausen, with its numerous oriel windows and fountains, has such an air of antiquity that it is sometimes called the Swiss Nürnberg.

The town is dominated by the 16th-century Schloss Munot, perched on a hilltop seemingly made for the purpose. A covered passage links this formidable fortress to the rest of the town, and there is a fine view from its massive tower. In some of the winding streets of the older sections of the town, there are some interesting frescoed houses, notably the Haus Zum Ritter in the Vordergasse, with its 16th-century frescoes by Tobias Stimmer. The Münster, a Romanesque basilica dating from the 11th century, is, however, the chief architectural feature of Schaffhausen. In a small courtyard off the cloisters stands a famous old bell (cast in 1468) that inspired Schiller to write his *Lied von der Glocke.* The adjacent monastery of All Saints (zu Allerheiligen) has been transformed into a national museum—the Museum Allerheiligen—one of the most important in Switzerland.

Neuhausen and the Falls

On the northern bank of the Rhine, Neuhausen and Schaffhausen, with a combined population of over 40,000, are for all practical purposes the same town, the former being the industrial section. Neuhausen's factories, which make among other things arms, railroad cars and aluminum products, derive at least part of their power from the famous Rhine falls on the southern fringe of the town. Probably the most impressive waterfall in central Europe, it is easy to understand how it inspired an enthusiastic description by John Ruskin. Just above the falls the river is around 150 meters (500 ft.) wide, and the drop itself—taken in three giant leaps—measures almost 25 meters (80 ft.). The flow of water can reach over 1,200 tons a second; and in the huge rock basin below the falls it seethes and boils angrily.

Probably the best view of the falls is from the grounds of Schloss Laufen, almost directly above them on the southern shore. In the castle itself, there is a collection of Swiss carvings worth half an hour of the visitor's time. A path leads down from the castle to a small tunnel in the rock and on to Känzeli, a wooden platform beside the falls. Descending again, you enter through a massive doorway to the Fischetz, another platform overhanging the cascade. You'll need a raincoat here, for the spray is quite heavy. Alternatively, from the center of Schaffhausen a 15-minute bus ride will take you to Neuhausen. There, a walk of a couple of hundred yards down a steep lane will bring you to a fine viewpoint on the northern side of the falls. Nearby there's a good restaurant, and a picturesque little Fischerstube, or fisherman's museum, where souvenirs of great salmon catches from the river are to be seen.

The falls are best viewed early on a sunny morning, when the rainbows are all around, or at sunset. On moonlit nights, the effects are exquisite, and often in summer the falls are illuminated to provide an eerie and quite different aspect.

En Route to Konstanz

From Schaffhausen, many visitors prefer to go on by river steamer to Konstanz and Kreuzlingen, a splendid trip taking about four hours. There are boats two or three times a day, depending on the season. The train and highway both follow the same route and, of course, take less time.

Leaving Schaffhausen, the steamer passes the old convent of Paradies on the starboard side. Nearby, is the spot where the Austrian army under Archduke Charles is said to have crossed the Rhine in 1799; and farther on, near Diessenhofen, is the historic crossing point used by the French army in 1800, before the battle of Hohenlinden. The scenery along the river banks changes continually: forests and vineyards, trim little medieval villages, and stern old fortified castles. Diessenhofen, called Gunodorum by the Romans, has a lovely old clock tower and houses dating from the 16th and 17th centuries.

Stein-am-Rhein, where the river starts to widen out as it approaches the Bodensee, is one of the most picturesque medieval towns in Switzerland. Near the northern shore is the old hilltop castle of Hohenklingen, approached by a steep road. From the battlements, you can get a superb view of the river, the lake beyond, and the surrounding countryside, as well as the little gem of the town below. Lining the streets of Stein-am-Rhein, particularly the main street (Hauptgasse) and the town hall square (Rathausplatz), is an unrivaled collection of quaint houses rich in oriel windows and elaborate frescoes. The town hall has a museum of arms and stained glass, much from the 16th and 17th centuries, which is also well worth a visit.

The 15th-century Sonne, distinguished by a medieval emblem of the sun, provides delightful surroundings in which to enjoy a good dinner or simply a glass of white Steiner or red Rheinhalder wine, both native to the region. Immediately below is a fountain with a statue of a Swiss mercenary leaning on his pike, surrounded by beds of flowers. All the houses opposite are adorned by their owners' coats of arms painted in bright colors.

A short distance up the river, past the last bridge over the Rhine before Bodensee, is the Benedictine monastery of St. George, built in 1005 and well-preserved. A curious old monument with a lovely cloister, it also has a small museum open to the public and featuring some fine examples of woodwork and old paintings. As the river widens into the Untersee—the southwestern branch of Bodensee—the boat passes the Isle of Werd, on which you can see the beautiful old chapel of St. Othmar. Opposite lies the village of Eschenz, the castles of Freudenfels and Liebenfels, and the one-time monastery of Oehningen. On the Swiss side, at the foot of a chain of hills, picturesque villages succeed one another. Between Mammern and Steckborn, in a small bay, is the little summer resort of Glarisegg, located in the middle of a large natural park. Steckborn is dominated by the imposing Turmhof Castle, built in 1342, and has some fine old houses, including the Baronenhaus and the Gerichtshaus.

In the middle of the Untersee is the German island of Reichenau, about three kms. (two miles) long and one and a half kms. (one mile) wide. Charles the Fat, great-grandson of Charlemagne, was buried there. The island has three small villages—Mittelzell, Unterzell and Oberzell—and there is an interesting Romanesque basilica at Niederzell. On the Swiss side of the lake, and behind the village of Mannenbach (nearly opposite Reichenau), is the castle of Arenenberg. There, from 1818, Hortense de Beauharnais, formerly Queen of Holland, lived with her son, who was later to become Emperor Napoleon III. After the fall of the Empire, Empress Eugénie stayed there for some time before giving it to the canton of Thurgau in 1906. Nowadays, it is a museum containing numerous souvenirs of the Second Empire. Nearby are two additional châteaux with Napoleonic memories. In Salenstein, which was at one time the traditional residence of the Abbot of Reichenau and which dates from the 12th century, the Duchess of Dino, a companion of Hortense de Beauharnais, went to live in 1817. Eugensberg Castle was built four years later by Eugène de Beauharnais, the son of the Empress Joséphine, and born before she married Napoleon.

Not far beyond Ermatingen, the Untersee quickly narrows to become, at Gottlieben, a riverlike channel which, on the other side of the German city of Konstanz, joins the main body of the lake. The Dominican monastery at Gottlieben is where the Protestant reformers John Huss and Jerome of Prague were imprisoned in the 15th century by order of the Emperor Sigismund and Pope John XXII. Pope John was himself confined in the same castle a few years later.

Konstanz—Over the German Border

The German city of Konstanz (population about 170,000), with its Swiss suburb of Kreuzlingen, dominates the straits. It is on the Swiss side of the lake, but in 1805 was ceded to Baden by the Treaty of Pressburg. In Roman days it was known as Constantia. As a focal point for many of the main alpine passes into Italy it achieved early significance as a trading center, and has had a long and turbulent history. Together with the Gottlieben monastery, it is alive with memories of John Huss, burnt at the stake in 1415 by order of the Council of Konstanz. His house in the Hussenstrasse bears his effigy, and in the cathedral, visitors can see the spot on which he stood when the sentence was delivered. Kneeling before his accusers, he cried, "Lord Jesus, forgive my enemies." Those who revere his memory say that the stone on which he knelt always remains dry, even when those around it are damp. Protestantism having gained the upper hand only temporarily in the 16th century, Konstanz is now mainly Catholic.

The Münster, or cathedral, of Konstanz, was founded in 1052, but did not begin to assume its present form until the start of the 15th century. The Gothic tower at the west end was erected in 1850. From the platforms around the openwork spire, there is a magnificent view of the town, the lake, the valley of the Rhine and the Austrian mountains. The oak doors of the chief entrance are decorated with reliefs by Simon Haider, dating from 1470 and representing scenes in the life of Christ. The nave is supported by 16 monolithic pillars, and the choir stalls are handsomely carved. The cathedral contains the tomb of Robert Hallam, Bishop of Salisbury, and in the ancient crypt, there is a representation in stone of the Holy Sepulcher.

Other points of interest in Konstanz include the Konzilgebäude, where the Council of Konstanz held its sittings; the Renaissance town hall (Rathaus), with historical frescoes on its facade; the Rosgarten Museum, notable for its prehistoric Roman and medieval collections; and the monument to Count Zeppelin, whose famous airships were built near Friedrichshafen on the other side of the lake. In the market square stands the house in front of which the Emperor Sigismund gave Frederick of Nürnberg the "March" of Brandenburg in 1417. And another old house, inscribed with the words "Curia Pacis," is said to be where peace was signed between Barbarossa and the Lombardy city-states in 1183. Outside the town is the Field of Bruhl, where John Huss was burned at the stake in 1415 and Jerome of Prague a year later. The spot is marked by a rough monument of stones.

Konstanz is a good center for excursions, with steamer services to many of the towns and resorts around Bodensee itself and on Ueberlinger See, its northwestern branch. You can get steamers in the adjacent Swiss town of Kreuzlingen for excursions to the Untersee and down the Rhine to Schaffhausen.

If it were not for the frontier stations in the connecting streets, it would be difficult to know where the German city of Konstanz ends and Swiss Kreuzlingen begins. There is no difficulty in walking from one to the other, but a valid passport is necessary (although, in some cases, an identity card is accepted). Kreuzlingen, much smaller than Konstanz, has a picturesque old quarter. In what was formerly an Augustine priory, founded in the 10th century by Bishop Conrad of Konstanz, there is now a teachers' training college. The original building was destroyed during the Thirty Years' War and the present structure built shortly afterwards. In the chapel a magnificent piece of woodcarving, the Passion of Kreuzlingen, contains many hundreds of separate sculptured figures, all the work of one anonymous Tirolean craftsman. Also on view is an embroidered vest, adorned with pearls, presented to a local dignitary by the medieval antipope Pope John XXIII, when he came to Konstanz in 1414.

Bodensee

Known sometimes as Lake Constance, Bodensee is about 65 kms. (40 miles) long and 15 kms. (almost 10 miles) wide; making it second in size only to Lac Léman (Lake Geneva). Since it is not protected by mountains it is turbulent in stormy weather and even on fine days is apt to be hazy. Thus it has a gloomy, brooding aspect, in contrast to the jewel-like quality of other Swiss lakes; but many visitors find that this makes it more romantic. Certainly it abounds in lore of a more lurid type than is usual in Switzerland—tales of smuggling and fleeing refugees, rather than poetry and William Tell. One of these stories relates that after World War II a group of contraband runners were found to be operating a submarine in its waters, and running a highly profitable trade between Germany and Switzerland. The local geography favors this sort of thing, since the frontiers of three countries—Switzerland, Austria, and Germany—run down the middle of the lake.

Turning to more everyday activities, Konstanz provides excellent opportunities for fishing (either trout or whitefish), and is frequented by over 70 species of birds. From its shores can be seen both the Appenzell and the Vorarlberg Alps, the latter in Austria.

The German island of Mainau, the former home of the Grand Duke of Baden and also the residence of Prince Lennart Bernadotte, (nephew of the late King Gustav VI Adolf of Sweden), is about 6 kms. (4 miles) north of Konstanz. Connected to the mainland by a bridge, it can be reached from Konstanz either through a wood or by lake steamer. It has a remarkable garden of subtropical vegetation, reminiscent of the most beautiful Italian gardens, a product of the exceptionally mild climate of the area.

On the opposite shore of Bodensee, again in Germany, is the town of Friedrichshafen, a pleasant town with a population of around 53,000, a castle that was formerly the summer home of the Kings of Württemberg, and a notable exhibition of Zeppelin mementos in the municipal museum. Farther along the lake, still on the German side, is the splendidly situated little town of Lindau with some 25,000 inhabitants. Approached by rail over a causeway or by road over a long bridge, Lindau was once a powerful fortress, an Imperial city and, in ancient times, the site of a Roman fortification. Its town hall, although much restored in 1887, dated from the 15th century.

Back to Switzerland

After our brief excursion to some of the German parts of the lake, let us return once more to Switzerland, at Kreuzlingen. From here, heading southeast along the shore of the lake, you come first to Bottighofen, and then to Münsterlingen, which has a former Benedictine convent, founded in the 10th century although rebuilt in the 18th. It is now a hospital for the canton of Thurgau. A little beyond it, on a hill overlooking the lake, is the pretty village of Altnau; then in rapid succession, Güttingen, Kesswil, Uttwil and, finally, Romanshorn. The latter is a small industrial town and an important ferry port for Friedrichshafen, but also a surprisingly pleasant place with fine views of the mountains of Switzerland and Austria.

Halfway to Rorschach, the town and resort of Arbon (known to the Romans as Arbor Felix) lies on a little promontory jutting out into the lake and surrounded by lovely meadows and orchards. It was a Celtic town before the Romans came in the year 60 B.C. and built military fortifications. There is a medieval chateau, which is now public property and so open to visitors. The St. Gallus church, with its fine stained-glass windows, and St. Martin's church are both worth seeing. The latter is late-Gothic and has an interesting collection of relics dating from the days of the Romans.

Rorschach

Rorschach, in the canton of St. Gallen and with 10,000 inhabitants, is the largest port on the Swiss side of the lake. It is on a small, well-protected bay at the foot of the Rorschacherberg, a beautiful 883 meters (2,900 ft.) mountain covered with orchards, pine forests and little meadows. Rorschach carries on a thriving trade with Germany, and the imposing Kornhaus, built by the convent of St. Gallen in 1746, indicates what was for generations the nature of that trade. The Baroque building has an interesting little folklore museum. There is also a Baroque village church dating from 1667.

There are some good excursions from Rorschach. On the surrounding hills, there are several old castles, and a good road leads to the ancient abbey of Mariaberg, built by the abbots of St. Gallen and now used as a school. Nearby is St. Anna Castle, long inhabited by the lords of Rorschach and restored during the early part of the last century. Although it is not open to visitors, the Duke of Parma's chateau of Wartegg, formerly the summer residence of the Prince of Hohenzollern, is worth seeing from outside. The ascent of the Rossbüchel, 959 meters (3,150 ft.), is rewarded with an excellent view of the Rhätikon and Vorarlberg mountains.

There are two railroad stations in Rorschach, the main station and another smaller one, by the port in the town center, from which the cogwheel trains climb up to Heiden. Only five and a half kms. (three and a half miles) long, the train's route ascends through lovely orchards, past old castles and over a number of viaducts, disclosing beautiful views of the valleys, mountains and the upper Rhine. Heiden itself is 790 meters (2,600 ft.) high, and is situated on a sunlit terrace surrounded by meadows and nicely wooded hills. The village was almost entirely destroyed by fire in 1838 and was rebuilt to a uniform pattern (but in traditional style), so that it has a neat charm. It is a well-known health resort, with carbonic acid and brine baths, electrotherapy, massage and other treatments. It also has a famous Kursaal with frequent concerts. Henri Dunant, founder of the Red Cross, spent many years working in the local hospital.

Another interesting trip from Rorschach is to St. Margrethen, where, in 1900, the Swiss and Austrian governments undertook important engineering works to regulate the Rhine's flow. Two long cuts were made, one at St. Margrethen, and another, a little farther south, between Altstätten and Diepoldsau. These enable the river to flow straight into Bodensee instead of winding around the countryside to join the lake at Altenrhein.

From Rorschach, the end of this tour, both rail and road links lead to Zürich, via St. Gallen, or through Bad Ragaz to Graubünden.

PRACTICAL INFORMATION FOR EASTERN SWITZERLAND

TOURIST OFFICES. The main regional, cantonal, tourist offices can supply you with information on sightseeing, accommodations, public transport and so on. They are often closed over lunch so time your visit for the morning or afternoon. **Appenzell Ausserrhoden,** Verband Appenzell Ausserrhodischer Verkehrsvereine, Dorf 33, Stein (tel. 071–59 11 59). **Appenzell Innerrhoden,** Kur- und Verkehrsverein Appenzell Innerrhoden, Hauptgasse 19, Appenzell (tel. 071–87 41 11). **Glarus,** Verkehrsverein Glarnerland und Walensee, Kirchweg 18, Glarus (tel. 058–61 13 47). **Schaffhausen,** Kant. Verkehrsvereinigung Schaffhausen, Vorstadt 12, Schaffhausen (tel. 053–5 51 41). **St. Gallen,** Fremdenverkehrsverband des Kt. St. Gallen, Bahnhofplatz 1a, St. Gallen (tel. 071–22 62 62). **Thurgau,** Thurgauische Verkehrsvereinigung, Arboner Str. 2, Amriswil (tel. 071–67 68 51).

HOTELS AND RESTAURANTS. Nearly all the hotels in our listings below have a wide range of rooms, a good many of which may well fall into a lower grading than that given here. Generally, however, prices in Eastern Switzerland are significantly lower than in most other areas of the country.

In the smaller towns, the choice of hotels and restaurants is significantly reduced, but service is almost always reliable, and the setting often spectacular. It is also possible to rent chalets or apartments for group or family accommodations throughout much of the region. Contact tourist offices for more information.

AMDEN. *Arvenbuel* (M), tel. 058–46 12 86. 70 beds. Sauna, solarium, table tennis, kitchenettes in rooms, ideal for children. AE, DC. *Parkhotel Arvenbühl* (M), tel. 058–46 19 19. 120 beds. Sauna, solarium, indoor pool. AE, DC, MC, V. *Bellevue* (I), tel. 058–46 11 57. 50 beds. Heated outdoor pool. *Rössli* (I), tel. 058–46 11 94. 25 beds. DC, MC.

Restaurant. *Rossli* (M), tel. 058–46 11 94. Hotel restaurant; good for local specialties. DC, MC.

APPENZELL. *Appenzell* (M), Landsgemeinde-Platz (tel. 071–87 42 11). 31 beds. Charming new hotel. AE, DC, MC. *Hecht* (M), tel. 071–87 10 25. 70 beds. Sauna, central but quiet. DC, MC, V. *Löwen* (M), tel. 071–87 21 87. 58 beds. Central. AE, DC, MC. *Romantik Hotel Säntis* (M), tel. 071–87 87 22. 60 beds. Historic building, riding. AE, DC, MC, V.

Restaurant. *Romantik Hotel Säntis* (M), tel. 071–87 87 22. Hotel restaurant with excellent local specialties, river trout and Appenzell wines. AE, DC, MC, V.

ARBON. *Metropol* (M), tel. 071–46 35 35. 70 beds. Beside Bodensee, with roof garden, outdoor pool and sailing school. DC, MC, V.

BAD RAGAZ. *Quellenhof* (L), tel 085–9 01 11. 200 beds. In park with cure facilities, golf and tennis. AE. *Cristal* (E), tel. 085–9 28 77. 90 beds. Indoor pool and sauna, near station. AE, DC, MC, V. *Grand Hotel Hof Ragaz* (E), tel. 085–9 01 31. 160 beds. Cure facilities, comfortable. AE, V. *Lattmann* (M), tel. 085–9 13 15. 120 beds. Cure facilities, sauna, park. AE, DC, MC. *Ochsen* (M), tel.

085–9 14 28. 50 beds. Central, with gymnasium. AE, DC, MC, V. *Park* (M), tel. 085–9 22 44. 95 beds. AE, DC, V. *Quelle* (I), tel. 085–9 11 13. 25 beds. Central, garden, terrace, diet meals. *Traube* (I), tel. 085–9 14 60. 35 beds. Small hotel in own grounds, ideal for children. V.

Restaurants. *National* (M), tel. 085–9 13 04. Famous for veal soufflé and game in season. V. *Paradies* (M), tel. 085–9 14 41. Fish specialties; closed Jan., Feb. and Tues. AE, DC, MC, V.

BRAUNWALD. *Alpina* (M), tel. 058–84 32 84. 60 beds. Quiet, marvelous view from restaurant. AE, V. *Bellevue* (M), tel. 058–84 38 43. 100 beds. Tennis, sauna, indoor pool, ideal for children. *Niederschlacht* (M), tel. 058–84 36 84. 80 beds. Indoor pool. AE, DC, MC. *Tödiblick* (M), tel. 058–84 12 36. 25 beds. Quiet, in park. V.

Restaurants. *Alpenblick* (I–M), tel. 058–84 15 44. Hotel restaurant; scampi, snails, and steaks. AE, DC, MC, V. *Rubschen* (I–M), tel. 058–84 15 34. French cuisine.

DEGERSHEIM. *Krone* (M), tel. 071–54 24 54. 45 beds. With casino. *Kurhaus und Bad Sennrüti* (M), tel. 071–54 11 41. 110 beds.

FLUMSERBERG. *Cafrida* (M), tel. 085–3 11 93. 24 beds. Known for its restaurant. *Gauenpark* (M), tel. 085–3 31 31. 64 beds. Indoor pool, skittles. AE, V. *Alpina* (I), tel. 085–3 12 32. 51 beds. Quiet and in own grounds. AE.

Restaurants. *Gamperdon* (M), tel. 085–3 16 21. Good hotel restaurant. MC. *Gauenpark* (M), tel. 085–3 31 31. Hotel restaurant. AE, MC, V.

GLARUS. *Glarnerhof* (M), tel. 058–61–41–06. 50 beds. New in Dec. 1986. Historic building, central and quiet. AE, DC, MC, V. *Rössli* (I), tel. 058–61 16 46. 18 beds. AE, MC. *Stadthof* (I), tel. 058–61 63 66. 17 beds. Central, with facilities for the handicapped. MC.

HEIDEN. *Krone-Schweizerhof* (M), tel. 071–91 11 27. 60 beds. With indoor pool, central and in own grounds. V. *Linde* (I), tel. 071–91 14 14. 30 beds. Central, quiet. MC.

HORN. *Bad Horn* (M), tel. 071–41 55 11. 65 beds. Lakeside hotel in own grounds. AE, DC, MC, V.

KREUZLINGEN. *Bahnhof-Post* (I), Nationalstr./Bahnhofstr. (tel. 072–72 79 72). 65 beds. Near station; restaurant has specialties. AE, DC, MC, V. *Elmont-Plaza* (I), Löwenstr. 23 (tel. 072–72 68 68). 22 beds. AE, DC, MC, V. *Emmishofen* (I), Konstanzerstr. 73 (tel. 072–72 60 60). 16 beds. Quiet, superior (I) hotel with two skittle alleys. AE, DC, V.

Restaurants. *GasthausBurg* (I–M), tel. 072–75 18 22. Closed Wed. all day, Thurs. to 5 P.M. AE, V. *Schäffli* (I–M), tel. 072–72 22 28. In town center, quiet garden.

NEUHAUSEN. *Bellevue* (M), tel. 053–2 21 21. 55 beds. Overlooking Rhine falls. AE, MC, V.

RAPPERSWIL. *Schwanen* (M), tel. 055–21 91 81. 44 beds. Centrally located historic building. AE, MC, V. *Speer* (I), tel. 055–27 17 20. 24 beds. Small, quiet, atmospheric. AE, MC, V.

Restaurants. *Eden* (E), tel. 055–27 12 21. Hotel restaurant; gastronomic menus, with excellent fish and meat specialties. MC, V. *Hirschen* (M), tel. 055–27 66 24. Fillets of perch, Hainanese Mah Mee, soufflé Grand Marnier. V.

RAPPERSWIL-BOLLINGEN. *Schiff Motel* (I), tel. 055–28 38 88. 18 beds. Delightful small hotel in attractive building, own beach. DC, MC.

ROMANSHORN. *Parkhotel Inseli* (M), tel. 071–63 53 53. 70 beds. Central but very quiet, in own grounds. AE, DC, MC, V. *Seehotel* (I), tel. 071–63 42 94. 30 beds. Quiet, in own grounds beside lake; breakfast only. DC, V.

RORSCHACH. *Waldau* (L), Seebleichestr. (tel. 071–43 01 80). 70 beds. Very quiet and comfortable; indoor and outdoor pool, indoor tennis, sauna and gymnasium. MC, V.

Restaurant. *Bahnhofbuffet* (M), Bahnplatz (tel. 071–41 60 25). Terrace on lake, own wines and fish specialties. AE, DC, V.

ST. GALLEN. *Einstein* (E), Berneggstr. 2 (tel. 071–20 00 33). 120 beds. In beautifully restored 150-year-old building, once an embroidery factory, with elegant interior, fashionable bar and recommended restaurant. AE, DC, MC, V. *Metropol* (E), Bahnhofplatz 3 (tel. 071–20 61 61). 52 beds. Comfortable, near station. AE, DC, MC, V. *Walhalla* (E), Bahnhofplatz (tel. 071–22 29 22). 82 beds. Also near station. AE, DC, MC, V.

Continental (M), Teufenerstr. 95 (tel. 071–27 88 11). 62 beds. Central. AE, DC, MC, V. *Dom Garni* (M), Webergasse 22 (tel. 071–23 20 44). 65 beds. Comfortable and friendly, near cathedral; breakfast only. AE, DC, MC, V. *Sonne Rotmonten* (M), Guisanstr. 94 (tel. 071–24 43 42). 50 beds. AE, MC, V. *Ekkehard* (I), Rorschacherstr. 50 (tel. 071–22 47 14). 50 beds. Central, quiet and comfortable; bowling. AE, DC, MC.

Restaurants. St. Gallen is famous for its small restaurants situated on the second floor of houses in the old town. Charming eating places include: *zum Goldenen Schafli,* Metzgergasse 5 (tel. 071–23 37 37); *Baumli* (I), tel. 071–24 31 44). AE, DC, V. Recommended for good food is *Stadtkeller* (E), Spisergasse 15 (tel. 071–22 00 88). DC. Best hotel restaurants are found at the *Einstein* (E), Berneggstr. 2 (tel. 071–20 00 33); the *Metropol* (E), Bahnhofplatz 3 (tel. 071–20 61 61); and the *Walhalla* (M), Bahnhofplatz (tel. 071–22 29 22). AE, DC, MC, V.

SCHAFFHAUSEN. *Fischerzunft* (E), Rheinquai 8 (tel. 053–5 32 81). 24 beds. AE, MC. *Bahnhof* (M), Bahnhofstr. 46 (tel. 053–5 40 01). 80 beds. AE, DC, MC, V. *Kronenhof* (M), Kirchhofstr. 7 (tel. 053–5 66 31). 50 beds. AE, DC, MC, V. *Promenade* (M), Fäsenstaubstr. 43 (tel. 053–4 80 04). 70 beds. AE, DC, MC.

Restaurants. *Schloss Taverne Herblingen* (E), Schloss Str. (tel. 053–3 35 15). Excellent food, in castle. AE. *Gerberstube* (M), Bachstr. 8 (tel. 053–5 21 55). Italian food in 16th-century Guildhall. AE, DC, MC, V.

TROGEN. *Krone* (I), tel. 071–94 13 04. 22 beds. Small hotel in historic building. AE, DC, MC, V.

UNTERWASSER. *Säntis* (M), tel. 074–5 28 11. 64 beds. Indoor pool, sauna. AE, DC, MC, V. *Sternen* (M), tel. 074–5 24 24. 118 beds. Evening dancing, fishing. AE, DC, MC, V. *Traube* (I), tel. 074–5 11 12. 45 beds. Fitness room, sauna, solarium, steam bath; specialty restaurant; historic building.

VALENS. *Kurhotel Valens* (M), tel. 085–9 37 14. 40 beds. Very quiet, cure facilities. AE, MC

WEESEN. *Parkhotel Schwert* (M), tel. 058–43 14 74. 45 beds. Quiet, central, marvelous view from restaurant. V.

WILDHAUS. *Acker* (E), tel. 074–5 91 11. 150 beds. Indoor pool, sauna, gymnasium, ideal for children. AE, DC, MC, V. *Alpenrose* (M), tel. 074–5 21 21. 90 beds. Quiet situation near Lake Schwendi, with sauna, keep fit room and solarium. *Sonne* (M), tel. 074–5 23 33. 50 beds. Indoor pool and sun terrace. AE, DC, MC. *Toggenburg* (M), tel. 074–5 23 23. 50 beds. Sauna, solarium, fitness room. AE, DC, MC, V.

Restaurant. *Toggenburg* (M), tel. 074–5 23 23. Hotel restaurant; Italian specialties. AE, DC, MC, V.

WIL. *Schwanen* (I), Obere Bahnhofstr. 21 (tel. 073–22 01 55). 30 beds. Central, grill and snack bar. V.

GETTING AROUND. Eastern Switzerland is not the easiest part of the country to get around. Take your time and plan your trip carefully. Unless you are traveling by car you will probably need to use a combination of transport facilities, especially to reach out-of-the-way places.

By Train. Trains connect all the major towns, with excellent links between Zürich and St. Gallen and Schaffhausen. Combined with the postal bus system this is a very good way of getting around. For train schedules inquire at any train station or tourist office.

By Car. Traveling by car is ideal in this part of Switzerland, with much of the sightseeing away from the beaten track in small towns and villages. Roads are generally good, and exploring the back roads is recommended. There is an expressway linking Zürich and St. Gallen, and from St. Gallen down the Rhine Valley. Good regional maps are available from gas stations and tourist offices.

By Bus. Where the trains don't run, postal buses often do, though they may make trips only a couple of times a day. Plan your trip having consulted the official Swiss transportation timetable, available from any tourist office.

By Boat. There are many boat trips on Bodensee, and one also on the Walensee. Services are more frequent in the summer; for details contact local tourist offices.

Sightseeing Data

APPENZELL/STEIN. Appenzeller Schaukäserei (Appenzell Cheese Dairy), Stein (tel. 071–59 17 33). Here you can watch Appenzell's famous cheese in the making, and taste it. Open daily 9–11 and 1–3.

BRAUNWALD. Alpine Rosenprüfanlagen (Alpine Rose Gardens). Roses are grown and tested to see how they react in alpine conditions. Especially beautiful in the flowering season.

DEGERSEHEIM. Retonio's Magic Casino, Hauptstr. 81, Degersheim (tel. 071–54 24 54). Optical illusions, magic theater, museum and bar, freak show. Reservations obligatory for all shows.

FRAUENFELD. Kartause Ittingen, superb former Trappist monastery situated five kms. (three miles) north of Frauenfeld. Baroque and Rococo 16th-century church, art museum of canton Thurgau (tel. 054–21 90 21) showing local 19th- and 20th-century artists; good restaurant (tel. 054–21 90 21) which can be packed on busy days. Open all year, Tues. to Fri. 2–5, Sat. and Sun. 10–12 and 2–5.

HEIDEN. Henry Dunant Museum, ask at the tourist office (tel. 071–91 10 96) for directions. Dunant founded the Red Cross. Open daily 9–5.

LIPPERSWIL. Conny Land, tel. 054–63 28 88. Moonwalk, dolphin and sealion shows.

RAPPERSWIL. Heimatmuseum (Regional Museum), Brenyhaus am Herrenberg (tel. 055–27 71 64). Important folklore and ethnic collections. Open Easter Mon. to mid-Oct., Sat. to Thurs. 2–5, closed Fri.

Knie's Kinderzoo (Knie Children's Zoo), tel. 055–27 52 22. Dolphin show, 400 animals from all over the world, elephant and pony rides, feeding and touching of animals allowed. Open mid-Mar. to beginning of Nov., 9–6.

ST. GALLEN. Historisches Museum (Historical Museum), Museumstr. 50 (tel. 071–24 78 32). Outstanding cultural and historical collections including arms, flags and silverwork. Open Tues. to Sat. 2–4, Sun. 10–12 and 2–4.

Stiftsbibliothek (Monastery Library), Klosterhof 6d (tel. 071–22 57 19). Changing exhibits and 2,000 medieval books in exquisite Baroque room.

Textilmuseum, Vadianstr. 2 (tel. 071–22 17 44). Open Mon. to Fri. 10–12 and 2–5, closed Sun.; Apr. through Sept. also open Sat.

SALENSTEIN. Napoleon Museum, Schloss Arenenberg (tel. 072–64 18 66). 16th-century house beside Bodensee, bought by Queen Hortense in 1817 and filled with Napoleonic memorabilia. Napoleon III grew up here. Open May to Sept., Tues. to Sun. 9–12 and 1.30–6, closed Mon.; winter, same days 10–12 and 1:30–4, Apr. and Oct. closes at 5.

SCHAFFHAUSEN. Museum Allerheiligen, Klosterplatz 1 (tel. 053–5 43 08). Manuscripts, arts and crafts including stained glass, gold- and silverwork, costumes, arms, flags and uniforms. Interesting contemporary exhibitions. Open Tues. to Sun. 10–12 and 2–5, closed Mon. **Hallen für Neue Kunst** (Halls for Contemporary Art), Baumgartberstr. 23. Tel. 053–5 25 15 for information on opening hours. Open generally May–Oct., Tues. to Sat. 3–5, Sun. 11–3, but subject to change.

URNÄSCH. Appenzeller Brauchtum (Appenzell Folklore Museum), Dorfplatz (tel. 071–58 23 22). Collection illustrating the life of the Alpine herdsman, with woodcarvings, naive art and farmhouse furniture. Open July to Oct., daily 2–5; Apr., May and June on Wed., Sat. and Sun. 2–5; closed Nov. to Mar.

WILDHAUS. Zwinglihaus, tel. 074–5 21 78. Birthplace in 1484 of Zürich's Protestant reformer Huldrich Zwingli. Open Tues. to Sun. 2–4, closed Mon. Closed completely from April 21 to May 27.

SHOPPING. The region can provide you with many typical Swiss souvenirs. In Appenzell you will find rural gifts: cowbells of all sizes, naive paintings of country life, wood carvings of sheep, dogs and cows, as well as lovely dolls. There is a good selection in *Tabak Klarer,* A. de Gass, 9050 Appenzell (tel. 071–87 11 23).

The St. Gallen textile industry is famous for its quality and originality, and supplies many of the world's couturiers. You can buy lovely materials in the little shops attached to some of the embroidery manufacturers in St. Gallen.

WINTER SPORTS. Eastern Switzerland is dotted with resorts catering to downhill and cross-country skiers, as well as to those who prefer tobogganing, skating and curling. **Amden,** 900–1,600 meters (3,000–5,300 ft.); 1 chairlift, 4 lifts, 1 children's lift, 20 kms. (12 miles) of downhill runs, 12 kms. (7 miles) of cross-country trails. Ski school, skating on natural ice rink, walking paths.

Bad Ragaz, 517 meters (1,700 ft.); 2 cable cars, 3 lifts, 12 kms. (7 miles) of downhill runs, 3 kms. (2 miles) of cross-country trails. Ski school.

Braunwald, 1,250–1,900 meters (4,250–6,230 ft.); 1 funicular railway, 1 cable car, 3 chair lifts, 2 lifts, 20 kms. (12 miles) of downhill runs, 6 kms. (4 miles) of cross-country trails, 20 kms. (12 miles) of well-kept mountain trails, skating, curling, ski bob, toboganning. Ski school, car-free.

Flumserberg, 1,000–1,310 meters (3,300–4,300 ft.); 1 cable car, 2 chair lifts, 16 lifts, 80 kms. (50 miles) of downhill runs, 52 kms. (32 miles) of cross-country trails, 20 kms. (12 miles) of mountain trails, skating, curling, ski bob, night skiing. Ski school.

Heiden, 820 meters (2,700 ft.); 3 lifts, less than 1 km. of downhill ski runs but 18 kms. (11 miles) of cross-country trails and 50 kms. (31 miles) of ski hiking trails. Ski school.

Unterwasser, 910 meters (3,000 ft.); 1 funicular railway, 1 cable car, 4 lifts, 47 kms. (29 miles) of downhill runs, 18 kms. (11 miles) of cross-country trails, 15 kms. (9 miles) of ski hiking trails, ski bob, tobogganing. Ski school.

Wildhaus, 1,098 meters (3,650 ft.); 4 cable cars, 8 lifts, 50 kms. (31 miles) of downhill runs, 45 kms. (28 miles) of cross-country trails, 30 kms. (19 miles) of ski hiking trails, skating, curling. Ski school.

LIECHTENSTEIN

Postage-Stamp Principality

Crossing over from the world's oldest living democracy into a monarchy that is the last remnant of the Holy Roman Empire is the easiest thing in the world for anyone driving along the Swiss Rhine valley, between Bodensee and Graubünden. You turn east at the right moment, cross a bridge, and there you are, smack in the middle of the realm of His Highness, Franz Josef II, Maria Alois Alfred Karl Johann Heinrich Michael George Ignatius Benediktus Gerhardus Majella, Prince von und zu Liechtenstein, Duke of Troppau and Jaegerndorf, and last of the hundreds of reigning kings, princes, dukes, and counts who once populated the map of the Holy Roman Empire.

His Highness rules as a constitutional monarch over only 160 square kms. (62 square miles) and about 27,000 loyal subjects, but don't let appearances fool you. Liechtenstein may look like nothing more than an oversized Alpine resort, with its gentle wooded hills in the north, fertile Rhine valley in the west, and craggy mountains in the east. But it is actually a complete state, with a sound and diversified economy and a prosperous, German-speaking people who can easily afford their friendly smiles and easy going ways, considering their glowing state of affairs.

Liechtensteiners insist that their case is different from other miniature states. They are not just the product of rivalries from great powers, a buffer zone between France and Spain like Andorra; nor are they tolerated only for curiosity's sake, as San Marino is by Italy; neither are they in danger of being swallowed by a bigger power if they lose their ruler, as in Monaco. They could depose their prince any day and continue as a free republic. But they won't because the house of Liechtenstein has proved a lucky charm.

A Hobby for the Man Who Has Everything

It all started at the end of the 17th century, when a wealthy Austrian prince, Johann Adam von Liechtenstein, bought up two bankrupt counts in the Rhine valley, united their lands, and in 1719 obtained an imperial deed, creating the Principality of Liechtenstein. In January 1969, Liechtenstein celebrated its 250th anniversary.

At that time the Liechtenstein family was already a power in the Holy Roman Empire. From the time of Hugo of Liechtenstein, a knight in the 12th century with a modest castle near Vienna, their wealth and power had grown consistently. In 1608 they were elevated to Princes of the empire, and when Johann Adam bought his new lands in the Rhine valley, he was already one of the richest men in Europe. The new principality was but a small fraction of the land all over the Austro-Hungarian Empire that belonged to the Liechtenstein family. Yet it suited his purpose to have a moderate-sized territory and thus qualify for a vote in the Diet of the Princes.

The new principality became the hobby of the wealthy Liechtenstein family. Although they spent most of their time at the glittering imperial court of Vienna or on their estates in Austria, Bohemia, Moravia, and Hungary, they spent most of their money on Liechtenstein. The champion spender was probably Prince Johann II, who reigned for a full 71 years (almost a record) until his death in 1929. He gave away the equivalent of about 75 million Swiss francs of his private fortune, some to charity, but most of it to make Liechtenstein a better place to live in. Known as John the Good, he also established an art gallery that today enjoys an international reputation. Of greater significance, in 1921 he oversaw the introduction of Liechtenstein's constitution under which she became a modern, democratic monarchy. Despite the seeming contradiction, the government of Liechtenstein has proved remarkably stable, with authority vested equally in the Prince and the people—though the Prince nonetheless retains substantial powers: he has the right to call, adjourn and dissolve the national parliament; similarly, the Prince must approve every act of parliament before it can become law.

Contrary to the popular impression, Liechtensteiners do pay taxes, but these are moderate by international standards and are one of the reasons for Leichtenstein's economic boom since World War II. The principality has little difficulty finding capital for investments and has become the seat of numerous international holding and finance corporations, 50,000 of them by some estimates. The income from this economic boom is amply sufficient to make up for the former large subsidies from the private fortune of the princes.

The old saying that the Liechtenstein family may have a Principality on the Rhine, but a kingdom in Bohemia, is no longer true. World War I threatened misfortune in view of Liechtenstein's close links with the crumbling Austro-Hungarian Empire, but the little country bailed out just in time in 1918 and started the drift towards Switzerland that ended in the complete customs and monetary union of 1924. The Liechtenstein family recovered most of its fortune, then scattered over the new states that succeeded the Austro-Hungarian monarchy. From land, castles, jewelry, and the fabulous Liechtenstein gallery they diversified their holdings into industry and blue-chip stock.

The situation looked much gloomier after World War II when communist Czechoslovakia and Hungary expropriated the land holdings of the Prince and offered a "final settlement" of only about six or seven per cent of the actual value. Prince Franz Joseph II, who had succeeded his childless uncle Franz I in 1938, proudly declined to sell what he regarded as his inalienable rights for some ready cash. But the Liechtenstein family is by no means impoverished. They still own large estates in Austria, the choicest vineyards in Liechtenstein, their art gallery, and a bank at their capital, Vaduz, which is doing brisk business with all the foreign corporations in town.

The Prince and His Family

Under these circumstances, nobody will doubt the sincerity of the prayers and congratulations that echoed through Liechtenstein in the summer of 1956, when 15,000 people, almost as much as the official population at that time, gathered twice at Vaduz. First they celebrated the 50th birthday of their ruler (he was born on August 16th 1906, at one of the family's Austrian castles, Frauenthal in Styria,) and then the 150th anniversary of Liechtenstein's sovereign independence. This first came in 1806 when Austria's Emperor Franz II gave up his Imperial Crown, thus dissolving the Holy Roman Empire, to which Liechtenstein had previously owed allegiance. In 1815 Liechtenstein joined the German Confederation but once again, in 1866, it regained the full sovereign independence which it still enjoys to this day.

Although Liechtensteiners could be sure of continuing as an independent state (and a prosperous one) even without a prince, they have no wish to do so and are understandably eager to leave things as they are. Fortunately they are spared one headache, the question of succession. The Liechtensteins are a prolific stock, and history knows no instance when His Highness' loyal subjects were worried about being left with a vacant throne. In the few cases of childless reigning princes there were always plenty of brothers or nephews around.

One of those nephews is the present prince—Franz Joseph II, 12th ruling prince of Liechtenstein. Approaching his 88th birthday in 1984, the Prince formally handed over to his eldest son and heir—Prince Johann—many of the day-to-day responsibilities of the monarchy.

In the tradition of his house Franz Joseph II was the eldest of eight children and is the doting father of four sons and a daughter: Hereditary Prince Johann Adam Pius, Prince Philipp Erasmus, Prince Nikolaus Ferdinand, Prince Franz Josef Wenzel and Princess Nora

Elisabeth. Their father has been careful to educate them in the democratic ways proper to the constitutional monarch of a small, freedom-loving country. The children were sent to the public elementary school at Vaduz, together with other Liechtensteiners. The boys then went on to Vienna's Catholic Schotten Gymnasium, Franz Josef's own prep school, where many generations of Liechtensteiners were educated by the learned padres of the Scottish Brothers order.

Vaduz and Its Castle

Objectively speaking, Vaduz castle, although outwardly a jewel of medieval architecture, was at one time anything but an inviting place to live in. Starting in 1905 the gloomy, thick-walled fortress on a cliff overlooking Vaduz was completely renovated, and today it really is fit for a prince, lavishly furnished with costly antiques, tapestries, and valuable works of art. The famous Gothic bedroom contains furniture already antique when Columbus sailed for America.

But with all the money and care that went into redecorating the castle, Franz Josef II was the first reigning prince to take up permanent residence there. When Franz Josef succeeded his uncle in 1938, he was 32 and still unmarried, but the Liechtensteiners relaxed and rejoiced with him when their new ruler met the Countess Georgina Wilczek in Vienna. The phlegmatic, taciturn prince was properly impressed by vivacious "Gina," one of the reigning belles of Viennese aristocracy. Legend has it that he first met her in a modern version of Andersen's fairytale about the princess and the swineherd, when she was pressed into the Nazi labor service during the war and had to work on a farm. In any case, they were married on March 7th 1943, and to all appearances have lived happily ever after.

The prince leaves the ruling of his country to a democratically elected diet of 15 deputies, but works away at increasing his country's fortune and his own. Friends say he would have made an excellent investment banker, and he knows quite a lot about agriculture and forestry too, holding a university degree as a forestry engineer.

At the same time Princess Gina gave Liechtenstein a court, an institution that was sorely missed for many decades. The princess completed the new regime that started with the redecoration of the castle by making it the center of Liechtenstein's life. A continuous stream of guests from Liechtenstein and abroad and frequent return visits of members of the royal family to the homes of local notables have given tiny Vaduz a taste of society and have forged strong bonds between the people and their ruler. The Princess has also helped found a number of social and charitable institutions, such as the Liechtenstein Red Cross and a foundation for the aged.

There is still a considerable difference between Vaduz and most other courts, even certain small ones. The prince dislikes pomp. Donning a fancy uniform with gold braid or playing with crown and scepter would seem perfectly ghastly to him. Even the jubilee stamps, issued on the occasion of his 50th birthday, show him with only an ermine-collared cape and a heavy gold chain as signs of his office, over a simple white tie and tails . . . there is no sign of the crown.

The royal family follows an unostentatious life, shunning Cadillacs and Rolls-Royces and preferring cars of medium size. This kind of life strikes just the right note with Liechtenstein's hardworking, sober-minded citizens. They have much of the democratic no-nonsense attitude of the neighboring Swiss, but they gladly combine it with a little sparkle from the faint imperial glitter that still hangs over their other neighbor, Austria.

The Role of Switzerland

The political marriage of the principality with republican Switzerland has proved advantageous in every way. Except for Swiss economic policy, which extends to Liechtenstein more or less automatically by way of the customs union, there is absolutely no Swiss interference in Liechtenstein's politics and Liechtenstein is perfectly free to dissolve the customs, monetary, and postal union any time. Switzerland also represents Liechtenstein abroad; the only Liechtenstein minister accredited to a foreign government is the one at the Swiss capital, Bern. But the Swiss can act only with Liechtenstein's consent. They cannot enter into any agreement affecting Liechtenstein against that country's will.

Military service was abolished as long ago as 1868. Liechtenstein's present armed might consists of three dozen regular police and some three dozen men in an auxiliary police force. In those dangerous years before and during World War II, when Hitler annexed Austria and wanted to unite all German-speaking countries into one Reich, Swiss influence, along with the Prince's own urgent diplomatic efforts, succeeded in keeping Liechtenstein out of the conflict, but there was no attempt to press Liechtenstein into reintroducing military service.

Since the war Liechtenstein has participated in Switzerland's economic boom. The farm population has shrunk from 60 percent of the total 30 years ago to three percent now. Forty-five percent of the population is engaged in industry and the craft trades, and exports have swelled from 15 million Swiss francs in 1950 to more than one billion Swiss francs in 1984. Already, about one-third of Liechtenstein's residents are foreigners. Today, the Liechtenstein government is even a little wary of new investments because there are no longer sufficient Liechtensteiners to fill all jobs. Another problem was the protection of the landscape. The government has succeeded there. The factories (their products range from calculating machines to false teeth) are tucked away unobtrusively, and with their clean, white-and-glass facades look more like modernistic hotels.

So the Liechtensteiners continue to get the best of two worlds, a democratic freedom, peace, and prosperity like their Swiss neighbors, and a feeling of security from a dignified prince, a heartening symbol of their independence, who gives much to his country and seeks little in return. Visiting Liechtenstein for its scenery is pleasant, but even more rewarding is the experience of being among people who have found a secure balance in a world of imbalance, a formula for taking the best of old worlds and new alike and making it into a way of life that is today all too rare.

Exploring Liechtenstein

Like ancient Gaul, Liechtenstein is divided into three parts: first the so-called lowlands, about 16 square kms. (six square miles) of wooded hills in the north; next, the flat Rhine valley in the southwest with its eastern slope rising towards the first ridge of mountains; and lastly the mountainous area between the first ridge and the second one which forms a natural border with Austria.

Exploring Liechtenstein, you should start at the capital, Vaduz, about halfway between the northern and southern extremities of the country. Vaduz is the political and natural center of the flat, fertile country along the Rhine, and with just under 5,000 residents, it is also the most populous community. About three-quarters of Liechtenstein's population live in the five communal districts from Schaan, where road and railroad cross the Rhine from Switzerland to Balzers in the south, where you can cross back into Switzerland via a bridge or via the scenic Luziensteig road on the eastern bank.

The 14 kms. (nine miles) of road from Schaan to Mäls, the southernmost hamlet, are Liechtenstein's economic showcase. Neat farms, inns, houses, old churches and new schools line the road. Through the gaps on one side you can see the Rhine flats with their rich fields and orchards; on the other, creeping up the wooded slopes, are vineyards and the villas of the wealthy.

The villa quarter of Vaduz is growing steadily. Low taxes make the principality a pleasant dwelling place for people who have or earn good money without being bound to a certain spot by their jobs. Successful novelists and playwrights form a strong group among the "new Liechtensteiners".

The guarded castle of Vaduz completely dominates the town. Perched on a cliff about 90 meters (300 feet) high, it can easily be reached either by car along the road which climbs up from the northern end of Vaduz towards the mountains, or in half an hour on foot. The interior of the castle is out of bounds for tourists since it is occupied by the royal family and an almost continuous stream of guests. Still, the castle should be seen from up close. Originally built in the 12th century it was burnt down by troops of the Swiss Confederation in the Swabian Wars of 1499 and partly rebuilt in the following centuries, until a complete overhaul that started in 1905 gave it its present form. The walls are, in places, 12 feet thick. There is another medieval building about ten minutes on foot from the center of town, the Rotes Haus, once a fortress for bailiffs of a Benedictine monastery in Switzerland. It too can only be viewed from the outside.

Around Vaduz

For pleasant walks off the main road try one of the paths down to the Rhine, about half an hour, and then along the river on one of the two embankments. A covered wooden bridge, closed to cars, houses artists' exhibits in summer. Right in the middle of the bridge is the border with Switzerland. Alternatively, if you go in the opposite direction, a 40-minute climb up the hill will bring you to a romantic ruin tucked away in the forest, the Wildschloss, once the seat of robber-barons. Cutting across the slope horizontally you reach the village of Schaan via the scenic Fürstenweg (Prince's Path) in less than an hour.

Schaan, about three kilometers (two miles) north of Vaduz, offers the same choice of walks down to the Rhine and up the mountains, as does Triesen, also three kilometers from Vaduz, but to the south. Overlooking Triesen is the old stone and wood St. Mamertus Chapel from where there is an extensive view. Between Balzers and Mäls, the two southernmost villages, rises a steep hill bearing Gutenberg Castle, another splendid medieval fortress. It is located on a prehistoric cult site and can be reached by a footpath with slate steps that protrude from the hillside. Numerous artifacts testify to continuous settlement in this region since around 3000 B.C. Unfortunately, like Vaduz, Gutenberg Castle can be admired only from the outside.

From Vaduz (456 meters, 1,500 feet high) two good but sometimes narrow roads twist and climb steeply up into the mountains past the solidly romantic Vaduz castle (where there's a roadside parking place) and a succession of splendid views across the Rhine valley. At 883 meters (2,900 feet) you pass the little town of Triesenberg, settled during the 13th century by immigrants from the Valais in southwest Switzerland. Beyond the town the road continues to wind upwards and after a couple of kilometers a side road sheers off to the left towards the mountain hotels of Masescha, at 1,250 meters (4,100 feet) and Gaflei. Masescha, Gaflei, nearby Silum and Triesenberg, all clinging to the steep side of the Rhine valley, are unpretentious, do-it-yourself skiing centers in winter and lovely centers for walks in summer.

Gaflei, at 1,460 meters (4,800 feet) is the starting point of the Fürstensteig or Prince's Climb, a path along the highest ridge between the Rhine and the Samina Valley. Winding among and around several peaks between 1,800 and 2,000 meters (5,904 and 6,560 feet) high, it provides a relatively comfortable way of feeling like Sherpa Tenzing without doing any really dangerous climbing. The climb is named after Prince John II, who had the path cleared and made safe in 1898. A pair of good shoes is all you need, but don't try the Fürstensteig if you're apt to feel giddy looking down a sheer drop of a couple of thousand feet or so.

Back at the road junction above Triesenberg, if you now drive on towards the mountains you'll shortly pass through a kilometer tunnel under the first mountain ridge and emerge near the village of Steg (1,300 meters, 4,265 feet). Situated in a completely different setting—a high alpine valley, wild, impressive and with rushing mountain streams—Steg in winter is a simple, no-frills skiing center. In summer it becomes an excellent starting point for a wide choice of not-overstrenuous mountain hikes. One is the hike following the Samina river downstream (northwards) and then turning right up the Valorsch valley to Malbun, a roughly semi-circular excursion. Another is up the Samina valley to the Bettlerjoch pass (1,950 meters, 6,400 feet) along a tolerable track, broad enough for jeeps to take provisions up to the Joch alpine shelter, but forbidden to all other motor vehicles.

At the upper end of the Samina Valley experienced climbers can try one of Liechtenstein's highest peaks, the Grauspitz, Schwarzhorn or Naafkopf, each about 2,560 meters (8,400 feet) high.

If you now take the excellent new road which winds eastwards up easy grades beyond Steg you will find that in little more than a couple of miles it ends abruptly at Malbun (1,580 meters, 5,200 feet) a rapidly expanding village nestling on the floor of a huge mountain bowl. Hitherto little known outside Liechtenstein, in the last few years Malbun has begun to make modest impact on the international winter sports scene thanks to the splendid variety and proximity of slopes and the generous network of chairlifts and skilifts which serve them. For beginners it is outstanding, and it was here that the Prince of Wales and Princess Anne learned to ski while they were staying with the princely family at Vaduz castle. Winter finished, Malbun turns into an unpretentious summer resort for those who want complete rest or healthy exercise, plenty of fresh air, and comfortable quarters at a realistic price.

Incidentally, the only way to visit Austria from Liechtenstein via the mountains, without too much climbing, is provided by the path from Malbun to Sareiserjoch (1,860 meters, 6,100 feet) the border pass. If you're a glutton for exercise you'll find it takes about two hours on foot.

There's a regular bus service between Vaduz and Malbun, but if possible go by car—especially in summer. The return journey can take well under two hours including brief viewing stops en route, but leave more time if you can. Provided the weather's good, you'll want to linger.

The part of Liechtenstein least known to tourists is the "lowland" area in the north, which, despite its name, has some fair-sized and very attractive hills. The area is rich in archeological finds. The Holy Cross Chapel on the Rofenberg near Eschen was formerly a place of execution and public assembly. A Roman settlement has been excavated in Nendeln, and discoveries around Gamprin have provided evidence of New Stone Age culture. The "Historishce Höhenweg Eschnerberg" (historical Eschner mountain path) offers an illustrated history of the people who lived in the region over the years.

The 13th-century ruins of the Schellenberg fortresses, the Obere and Untere Burg, are fun to explore, especially for children. It's worth driving up to the Schellenberg hills, almost 1,000 meters (3,280 feet) high, where you can get fine views of the broad, flat valley of the Rhine with its steep sides, and gaze at an almost uninterrupted panorama of peaks—the mountains of Liechtenstein, Switzerland and Austria. From your viewpoints you will be able to see most of the little Principality we have just visited.

PRACTICAL INFORMATION FOR LIECHTENSTEIN

TOURIST OFFICES. The principal tourist office for the whole of Liechtenstein is the Liechtenstein National Tourist Office, Städtle 38, P.O. Box 139, FL–9490 Vaduz (tel. 075–21443 or 66288); open Mon. to Fri. 8–12 and 1:30–5, closed Sat. and Sun. In addition there are local tourist offices in the following towns: **Vaduz,** Städtle 37, FL–9490 Vaduz (tel. 21443); open Mon. to Fri. 8–12 and 1:30–5:30, Sat. 9–12 and 1–4 (except Oct. to Apr.). **Malbun,** FL–9497 (tel. 26577); open Mon. to Wed., Fri., Sat., 9–12 and 1:30–5, closed Thurs. and Sun. and during low season (May and Nov., 1–15 Dec.). **Triesenberg** "Dorfzentrum," FL–9497 Triesenberg (tel. 21926); open Tues. to Sat. 1:30–5:30, closed Sun. and Mon.

GETTING TO LIECHTENSTEIN. By Train. Although a number of European expresses cross Liechtenstein, none stop here. The best way to get here then is to take a train to the little station at Buchs in canton St. Gallen or Sargans, a little further away, and then take the excellent connecting post bus into Vaduz. Taxis are available from both Buchs and Sargans, but they are much more expensive. The bus from Buchs takes about 15 minutes, from Sargans about 45 minutes. If you are coming from Austria, there is a good train service to Feldkirch on the Austrian border. From Feldkirch there are similarly good post bus services into Liechtenstein. A weekly season bus ticket is available, allowing holders to make an unlimited number of journeys on all post bus routes in the country as well as to neighboring places across the border. The ticket can be obtained from any Liechtenstein post office or at the post offices in Buchs and Sargans and the train station in Sargans.

By Car. The N13 motorway runs along the Rhine frontier of Liechtenstein and extends all the way to Bodensee in the north and past Chur in the south. To the west, motorways go most of the way to Zürich, Bern and Basel. Automobile travel within Liechtenstein is ideal.

By Air. The nearest airport is Kloten, outside Zürich, about 130 kms. (80 miles) or one-and-a-half hours by car from Vaduz.

FORMALITIES. None, if you enter Liechtenstein from Switzerland. There are no customs checks. All travel documents valid for Switzerland are also valid for Liechtenstein. Entering Liechtenstein from Austria, the formalities are the same as for entering Switzerland. Swiss customs officials and border police do the checking at the Liechtenstein–Austria border. For tourists eager to get their passports filled with stamps from different nations, the official "Fürstentum Liechtenstein" seal can be obtained at the National Tourist Office or the Prince's Art Gallery (cost: Fr. 1).

Money. The Swiss franc is Liechtenstein's legal tender. Swiss currency regulations and rates of exchange also apply to Liechtenstein.

MAIL AND TELEPHONE. The Swiss postal system extends to Liechtenstein, with one exception: mail posted in Liechtenstein must bear Liechtenstein stamps and indeed the country is famous for finely engraved stamps and frequent new issues. (If you have philatelists among your friends, heavy correspondence is indicated.) The mail, telegram and telephone rates are, of course, the same as Switzerland. Liechtenstein belongs to the automatic Swiss phone system. Any Swiss phone number can be reached by simple dialing without the aid of an operator. In the same way you can phone any Liechtenstein number from Switzerland by dialing 075 (the Liechtenstein area code) and then the listed number.

HOTELS AND RESTAURANTS. Liechtenstein benefits in the field of tourism from a very effective, extensive national organization. It boasts some 100 establishments in the hotel and restaurant trade, most of them smaller, family concerns. There are no deluxe hotels in Liechtenstein, and most of the best ones are in Vaduz and along the Rhine valley. A Liechtenstein specialty are the mountain inns, all at least 4,000 feet (1,220 meters) up and all accessible by road. Although, with one or two exceptions, simple and unpretentious, they are recommended to anyone seeking peace, quiet and fresh air. It's possible to rent chalet or vacation apartments for group or family accommodations, and two alpine huts are open to the public; contact the tourist offices for more information.

Hotel prices are usually reasonable. The gradings given in our listings are general, and some hotels have a wide range of rooms with different prices. For specific information, check with the hotel beforehand.

Many hotels have their own restaurants, and breakfast is usually included in the hotel price. The cuisine is Swiss with Austrian overtones.

BALZERS. *Post* (I), Im Höfle 45 (tel. 41208). 14 beds. Small, with bowling and garden restaurant. AE, V. *Römerhof* (I), Egerta 432 (tel. 41960). 12 beds. Small and inexpensive, with hotel bar and disco.

Restaurants. *Engel,* Im Höfle 18 (tel. 41201). Simple, good food. *Roxy,* Landstrasse 435 (tel. 41282). Snack bar with dancing, reasonable prices.

BENDERN. *Deutscher-Rhein* (I), tel. 31347. 26 beds. Quiet rooms, restaurant with view.

ESCHEN. *Brühlof* (I), Essanestrasse 499 (tel. 31566). 23 beds. *Eintracht* (I), Essanestrasse 40 (tel. 31356). 5 beds. Very small with quiet rooms.

Restaurants. *Haldenruh,* Simsgasse 68 (tel. 31233). Regional and Italian cooking. *Pinocchio,* Bendernstrasse 508 (tel. 33008). Basic fare.

GAMPRIN. *Waldeck* (I), tel. 31463. 60 beds. Very quiet location, bowling, good for families (with kindergarten). Hotel bar with occasional musical entertainment. AE, DC, V.

MALBUN. *Gorfion* (M–E), tel. 24307. 72 beds. Indoor pool, garden, disco. AE, DC, V. *Malbunerhof* (M–E), tel. 22944. 60 beds. Medium-sized hotel with indoor pool, sauna and bowling. AE, DC, V. *Montana* (M), tel. 27333. 30 beds. Central; sauna, hotel bar and restaurant. AE, DC. *Alpenhotel Malbun* (I), Malbun 235 (tel. 21181). 50 beds. Indoor pool, central location, particularly suitable for families. *Walserhof* (I), Malbun 435 (tel. 23396). 13 beds. Central with restaurant. No showers in rooms.

Restaurants. *Gorfion,* tel. 24307. Hotel restaurant; twice weekly candlelight suppers with farmers' buffet, fondue *bourguinonne.* AE, DC, V. *Scesaplana,* tel. 24544. Regional cuisine.

MASESCHA. *Berggasthof Masescha* (I), Masescha 133 (tel. 22337). Seven beds. Restaurant with view. No showers in rooms.

NENDELN. *Engel* (M), Churer Str. 26 (tel. 31260). 43 beds. Hotel bar and restaurant, garden. AE, DC, V. *Landhaus* (I), Churer Str. 189 (tel. 32011). 27 beds. Grill restaurant, hotel bar with occasional musical entertainment. AE, DC, V.

SCHAAN. Three kms. (nearly two miles) from Vaduz. *Schaanerhof* (M), in der Ballota 3 (tel. 21877). 75 beds. With indoor pool, sauna and facilities for the handicapped. AE. *Dux* (I), Duxweg 31 (tel. 21727). 17 beds. Quiet location, sauna, facilities for the handicapped. Restaurant with view. AE, DC, V. *Linde* (I), Feldkircher Str. 1 (tel. 21704). 35 beds. Quiet and central.

Restaurants. *Post,* Bahnhofstr. 14 (tel. 21718). *Rössle,* Landstr. 48 (tel. 21707). Basic fare.

SCHELLENBERG. Restaurant. *Wirthschaft zum Löwen,* Im Winkel 53 (tel. 31162). Traditional restaurant in a lovely setting. Local specialties.

SILUM. *Berggasthof Silum* (I), tel. 21951. 19 beds. Quiet location, hotel restaurant. Very reasonable.

STEG. *Hotel Steg* (I), Steg 274 (tel. 22146). 24 beds. Quiet rooms, hotel bar and restaurant. V.

TRIESEN. *Landgasthof Schatzmann* (I), Landstr. 779 (tel. 29070). 19 beds. Restaurant with view, hotel garage. AE, V. *Meierhof* (I), Meierhof 326 (tel. 21836). 56 beds. Outdoor pool, facilities for the handicapped, camping. AE, DC.

Restaurants. *Gasthof Schäfle,* Landstr. 13 (tel. 21502). Good, simple food, game in autumn. *Mittagsspitze,* Lawena (tel. 23642). Various fondues.

TRIESENBERG. *Kulm* (I), Dorfzentrum (tel. 28777). 46 beds. Good family hotel. AE, V. *Martha Bühler* (I), Sennwies 450 (tel. 25777). 17 beds. AE, DC, V.

Restaurants. *Edelweiss,* Jonaboda 245 (tel. 21904). Basic fare. *Samina,* Rotenboden 220 (tel. 22339).

VADUZ. *Park-Hotel Sonnenhof* (E), Mareestr. 29 (tel. 21192). 50 beds. Quiet hotel with sauna and indoor pool, five minutes from town; fine gardens and superb view. DC, V. *Real* (M–E), Städtle 21 (tel. 22222). 15 beds. Central, small and highly recommended; excellent food. AE, DC, V. *Schlössle* (M), Schlossstr. 68 (tel. 25621). 48 beds. Quiet location; sauna, hairdresser. AE, DC, V. *Landhaus Prasch* (M), Zollstr. 16 (tel. 24663). 44 beds. Sauna, indoor pool, exercise room. AE, DC, V. *Engel* (I), Städtle 13 (tel. 21057). 38 beds. Central, inexpensive hotel with friendly service. AE, DC. *Vaduzerhof* (I), Städtle 3 (tel. 28484). 54 beds. Central location, with bar and restaurant. AE, DC.

Restaurants. *Engel,* Städtle 13 (tel. 21057). Hotel restaurant; international cuisine, reasonable prices. Terrace dining, music every evening. AE, DC, V.

Linde, Kirchstr. 2 (tel. 21034). Basic fare, reasonably priced. AE, DC. *Löwen,* Henengasse 35 (tel. 21408). Historical building with view of castle. Local and regional dishes. *The Old Castle Inn,* Aeulestr. 22 (tel. 21065). Atmospheric, with warm food served until 1 A.M. AE, DC, V. *Real,* Städtle 21 (tel. 22222). Excellent hotel restaurant, with regional and French cuisine. AE, DC, V. *Torkel,* Hintergass 9 (tel. 24410). Named after impressive wooden wine press from 17th century. Five minutes' walk from town center, owned by the Prince and surrounded by his vineyards. International and local dishes, wine tasting from 2–5 P.M. Rather expensive. AE, DC. *Cafe Wolf,* Städtle 29 (tel. 22818). Snacks only. AE.

NIGHTLIFE. There are movie houses in Balzers and Vaduz. The **Gorfion** and **Turna** hotels in Malbun, the **Römerkeller Bar** in Balzers, and the **Derby Bar** in Schaanwald offer dancing. In Vaduz, the hotels **Real, Schlössle** and **Vaduzerhof** have bars. The hotel **Landhaus** in Nendeln and **Waldeck** in Gamprin sometimes offer musical entertainment.

At the **Theater am Kirchplatz** (TaK) in Schaan, plays, concerts and dance performances are presented (tel. 24169 or 21431, season Sept. to June).

MUSEUMS AND GALLERIES. Liechtenstein National Museum. Städtle 43, Vaduz (tel. 22310). Historical finds and ancient coins from Liechtenstein, church carvings and items from the Prince's private arms collection. Open May to Sept. daily 10–12 and 1:30–5:30; Oct. to Apr. Tues. to Sun. 2–5:30.

The Prince's Art Gallery and the State Art Collection. Städtle 37, Vaduz (tel. 22341). Largely as a result of the Prince's decision to allow part of his world-famous private collection to be on public display, visitors to Vaduz can enjoy art exhibits unmatched by any other community of similar size. Paintings, sculptures, *objets d'art* and weapons that have been systematically acquired over the centuries are exhibited in well-lit, attractive display rooms. Previous exhibits have featured works of Rubens, Italian art, German painting and the Viennese Biedermeier. A new, more spacious arts center is under development. Open Apr. to Oct. daily 10–12 and 1:30–5:30; Nov. to Mar. daily 10–12 and 2–5:30.

Postage Stamp Museum. Städtle 37, Vaduz (tel. 66259). One-room facility where visitors can browse through 300 frames of Liechtenstein stamps and learn about their design. Liechtenstein has issued its own stamps since 1912, and their artistic worth is recognized worldwide. Open daily 10–12 and 2–6. Free entrance.

Walser Museum. Dorfzentrum, Triesenberg (tel. 21926). Exhibits on the cultural history of the people who travelled from the upper Valais to settle in Triesenberg in the 13th century. Includes farming and craft tools, old pastoral huts and wood sculptures. Open year round, Tues. to Sat. 1:30–5:30. During June–Aug. also on Sun. 2–5.

SPORTS. Although relatively unknown, **Malbun** is ideal for winter sports and has a near certainty of good snow. An excellent network of four ski lifts and two chairlifts, rarely congested except at high season weekends, serves 20 kms. (12 miles) of runs. Ski school, rental equipment and guides available.

Steg is well known for its cross-country skiing and offers 14 kms. (nearly nine miles) of trails including a 1.7 km. lighted trail.

Vaduz and **Schaan** have an open-air swimming pool—Mühleholz—open from May to Sept.

As in Switzerland, walking and hiking are favorite pastimes here; there are 150 kms. (93 miles) of marked paths in the alpine area and 120 kms. (74 miles) in the valley. Maps and descriptions are available at tourist offices.

SPECIAL EVENTS AND ACTIVITIES. Adjacent to the post office in Vaduz is the **Official Philatelic Service** of the Liechtenstein government, where subscriptions for Liechtenstein's famous stamp issues can be ordered. In 1982, 93,000 collectors subscribed to the series; proceeds accounted for a substantial part of the nation's finances.

Winetasting is possible in the "Hofkellerei des Fürsten von Liechtenstein" (The Prince's Wine Cellars). Address: Feldstrasse 4, Vaduz (tel. 21018). Depending on the year, Liechtenstein's total vintage ranges between 60,000 and 90,000 liters, most of the red burgundy type. Grapevines, brought by the Romans to Liechtenstein, take up about 35 acres (14 hectares) of the country's land.

Excursions by horse-drawn carriage are available daily from the town hall in Vaduz. Various routes organized on request. Contact Fuhrhalterei Franz Beck, Zollstrasse 71, FL–9494 Schaan (tel. 21753 or 24724).

On "Funken Sonntag" (Spark Sunday) the communities of Liechtenstein are aglow with huge bonfires, symbolizing the burning of winter. Celebrated at the beginning of Lent (after the Carnival), the holiday is the occasion for a contest between the towns to see which one can build the largest bonfire. Branches, scrap wood and logs are piled high, and some enthusiasts even employ cranes to reach greater heights.

The International Masters Courses in Music have been organized since 1971 by the Liechtenstein School of Music. The annual two-week event, usually at the end of July, features instruction and concerts in Vaduz and other town centers.

The National Holiday is celebrated on August 15th jointly with Prince Franz II's birthday, with fireworks and entertainment.

Feldkirch, just over the border in the Austrian state of Vorarlberg, is an attractive outing. The old city quarter is well preserved with descriptive historic plaques, arcades and decorated facades. The old and the new are cleverly blended; chic shopping malls and the city's castle coexist well.

Werdenberg, at the north end of the Swiss town of Buchs, is a picturesque, tiny village at the foot of the Castle of the Counts of Werdenberg (open Apr. to Oct., Tues. to Sun. 9:30–5). Its wooden houses have low doorways, inscriptions and multicolored decorative patterns; piles of chopped wood in winter attest to a traditional heating system. Wandering through the narrow streets is like going back in time to the 17th or 18th century.

GRAUBÜNDEN

Winter Playground of the World

The canton of Graubünden (or Grisons, as it is also known) rivals the Bernese Oberland as the Swiss region most familiar to winter sports lovers. Here you will find such famous resorts as Arosa, Davos, Flims, Klosters, Lenzerheide, Pontresina, Scuol-Tarasp-Vulpera, and the vast conglomeration of St. Moritz and its satellites. Here the Engadine, the mountain-bordered valley of the river Inn and its chain of lovely lakes, cuts a 25-mile-long swath across the southern part of Graubünden.

A land of contrasts, Graubünden has a rich cultural tradition and a vivid history, as well as scenic wonders that leave the visitor groping for superlatives. It has some of the highest and most rugged mountain chains in Europe, a host of silvery Alpine lakes, trout-filled rivers, and no fewer than 150 valleys sheltering a race of hardy peasant folk who are as independent and proud as they are hospitable.

Covering about 7,250 sq. kms. (2,800 sq. miles), Graubünden is the largest canton in Switzerland, occupying more than one-sixth of the country. Originally the people were known as the "gray confederates," and it is from this that the name Graubünden derives. A little more than half the population of 160,000 speak Schwytzerdütsch, one-third Romansch, and the remainder an Italian dialect.

The recorded history of the area goes back as far as 600 B.C., when an Etruscan prince named Rhaetus invaded the area and renamed it, unsurprisingly, Rhaetia. It became a Roman province, Rhaetia Prima, in 15 B.C., and graves of Rhaetians who fought in the Roman armies have been found as far away as Libya. The region allied itself with the Swiss Confederation in the 15th century, although it was not until 1803 that it officially entered the Confederation, becoming the 18th Swiss canton. During the Thirty Years' War in the 17th century Graubünden was invaded at various times by the armies of Austria, Spain and France, all of whom sought to control the strategically important passes leading to Italy.

The region's economy rests mainly on cattle, wood, and, most importantly, tourism. Internationally it owes its reputation to a few, highly sophisticated, winter playgrounds, patronized by the rich and famous. However, there are 100 holiday resorts throughout the region, which cater to all types of interests and budgets.

Exploring Graubünden

The canton is served by the highly efficient Swiss road system, and public transport is provided by the bright yellow post buses. In addition there is a rail network, centering on the Rhaetian narrow gauge line. This fascinating little railway runs for 386 kms. (240 miles), using some 480 bridges and 117 tunnels. It is possible to combine a trip on this line—using some bus connections—with a circular tour of the canton. Alternatively the trip can be completed by car.

Begin by traveling north on the Rhaetian railroad, from the provincial capital of Chur to Landquart, and then east to Klosters and Davos. From Davos take the Flüela Pass road to Susch, and then head northeast, by either bus or train, to Scuol. From here you can take a diversion, again by bus, to the castle of Tarasp. From Scuol head southwest to St. Moritz, where there is another possible side trip, to Muottas Muragl. Back on the main route take the bus north to Tiefencastel, traveling via the Julier Pass. Here, rejoining the Rhaetian railway, you loop westwards to Thusis and Reichenau, and back to Chur.

This tour takes a good 12 hours' traveling time, so that with stopovers it should be undertaken only if you can devote at least two full days to it. However, by eliminating the trip from Susch to Scuol and Tarasp, and returning directly to Chur from St. Moritz via the Albula Pass, the tour could, at a pinch, be shortened to a one-day jaunt. But by rushing hell-bent through Graubünden you will miss much of the region's fascination and get only a superficial glance at its fabulous scenery, something for which you may find it hard to forgive yourself when you return home.

Chur

The little town of Chur, capital of Graubünden, is generally considered the oldest continuously settled site in Switzerland; there are traces of habitation as far back as 2,500–3,000 B.C. The Romans had a settlement here too which they founded in 15 B.C. and called Curia Ra-

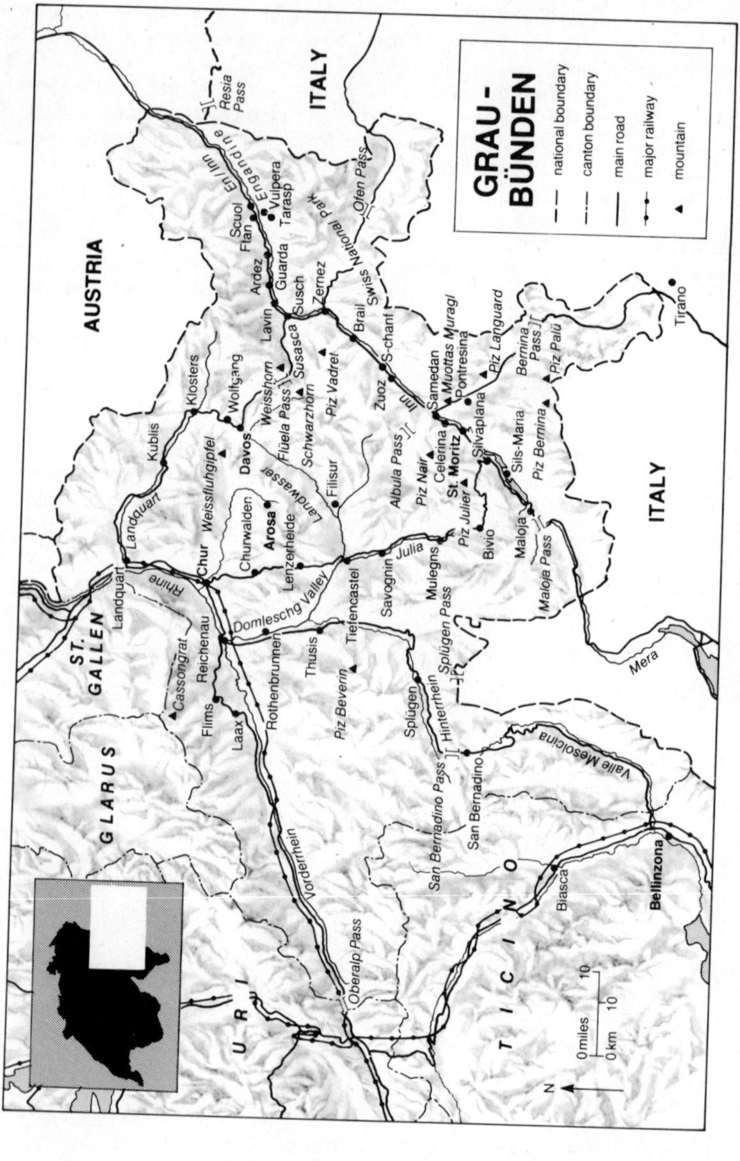
GRAU-
BÜNDEN
national boundary
canton boundary
main road
major railway
mountain
AUSTRIA
ITALY
ITALY
ST. GALLEN
GLARUS
URI
TICINO
Resia Pass
En/Inn
Engadine
Scuol
Ftan
Vulpera
Tarasp
Ardez
Guarda
Lavin
Susch
Zernez
Ofen Pass
Swiss National Park
Brail
S-chanf
Zuoz
Susasca
Piz Vadret
Flüela Pass
Weisshorn
Schwarzhorn
Klosters
Wolfgang
Davos
Kublis
Weissfluhgipfel
Landwasser
Filisur
Landquart
Chur
Arosa
Churwalden
Lenzerheide
Albula Pass
Piz Nair
Celerina
St. Moritz
Samedan
Muottas Muragl
Pontresina
Piz Languard
Bernina Pass
Piz Palü
Piz Bernina
Silvaplana
Sils-Maria
Piz Julier
Bivio
Maloja
Maloja Pass
Julia
Savognin
Mulegns
Tiefencastel
Rhine
Reichenau
Domleschg Valley
Thusis
Rothenbrunnen
Piz Beverin
Splügen Pass
Splügen
Hinterrhein
Cassongrat
Flims
Laax
San Bernadino Pass
San Bernadino
Valle Mesolcina
Mera
Tirano
Vorderrhein
Oberalp Pass
Biasca
Bellinzona
0 miles 10
0 km 10
N

etorum. It was used to protect the Alpine routes leading to Bodensee in the north. This camp was situated on the rocky terrace in the portion of the town south of the river. From about the 4th century, Chur was ruled by the Catholic bishops, who, in 1170, were raised to the status of bishop-princes. But in the 15th century, the irate inhabitants forced the ruling bishop-prince to give up much of his political power over the town. This process continued through the decades until, by 1526, Chur had become a city free from temporal domination of the bishops and subject only to the Holy Roman Emperor.

Today, Chur is a modern, well-developed town, with a population of around 37,000. It lies at the entrance to the Schanfigg valley, within a ring of wooded mountains; and the river Plessur runs through the town before joining the Rhine a mile and a half downstream. From here a road and rail network extends in all directions, making Chur a good starting point for any day trips into Graubünden.

Much of the city still retains its medieval character. Narrow streets, cobble-stoned alleys, hidden courtyards and quaint and ancient buildings abound, punctuated by massive structures such as the 12th-century cathedral with its splendid, 14th-century high altar, the 15th-century St. Martin's church notable for its stained glass, the Rathaus and the Bishop's Palace. Red or green footprints painted on the sidewalks lead the visitor on two itineraries (described in the city's free brochure) which take in most of the sights. Each walk lasts about an hour; more if you linger.

From Chur, the route follows the fertile Rhine valley downstream through vineyards, wheat fields and orchards. At Landquart, leave the Rhine and go through the dramatic Chlus gorge, following the river Landquart upstream. After a long, winding but gentle ascent past a number of resort villages, including Saas and Mezzaselva (with Spa Serneus down in the valley to the right), you come to Klosters-Dorf and Klosters.

Klosters

Klosters, once a group of hamlets, is now a small town in a valley bordered by mountains. With some 3,500 inhabitants, it is a typical Graubünden village, which has achieved special popularity as a well-equipped summer and winter sports resort. With Davos, it shares access to the long Parsenn slopes that are said to provide some of the best ski runs in the world. Tobogganing is believed to have originated here. It also has a heated outdoor swimming pool.

Named for the cloisters of a now extinct monastery, Klosters also has a pretty church with a clock tower. It is decorated with the coat of arms of Graubünden, showing a wild man pulling a fir tree out of the ground on one side, and a complacent apple tree on the other.

Klosters attracts young people who take their winter sports seriously, perhaps because it is smaller and has a more intimate atmosphere than its sister resort, Davos. The excellence of its children's ski school draws many families who rent chalets or apartments during the holidays. The starting point for the best of the Klosters-Parsenn ski-runs is the Weissfluhjoch, reached by cable car from the town to the Gotschnagrat and then, after a short ski-run, by another cable car. The run back to Klosters is almost 10 kms. (over six miles) long, dropping down almost 1,500 meters (5,000 ft.). The variety of runs from the Weissfluhjoch and Gotschnagrat is almost unlimited, but the best known are the ones that lead north to Küblis or south to Wolfgang. The Madrisa ski slopes, reached by the Albeina gondolas, are popular with both skiers (there are several well-placed lifts) and, weather permitting, sunbathers.

The rail line to Davos crosses the river Landquart by a lofty bridge, climbs through some stately pine forests, and then through Wolfgang, a skiing center, before dropping down again to the Davosersee and the town of Davos itself. Sir Arthur Conan Doyle put in a good deal of time in Davos, and Robert Louis Stevenson finished *Treasure Island* here in 1881.

Probably the most famous name among Swiss winter resorts is still that of St. Moritz, to which we shall come presently, but Davos—like Arosa and Gstaad—is pushing it hard.

Davos

Davos—in reality Davos-Dorf, with its indistinguishable Siamese-twin resort of Davos-Platz—owes its fame to the rise of skiing as the sport *à la mode* among the smart set in all western countries. Fanatic skiers supposedly find in Davos the world's most perfect terrain—the Parsenn run.

Davos lies at one end of the Davos Valley, running parallel to and northwest of the upper Engadine, and separated from it by the Albula chain of mountains, some of which are over 3,000 meters (10,000 ft.) high. On the opposite side of the valley is the Strela chain, dominated by the Weissfluhjoch. The open, sun-bathed slopes of this range provide the magnificent skiing that attracts devotees of the sport from all over the world. The Parsenn funicular railway takes skiers from Davos up to Weissfluhjoch, over 2,700 meters (9,000 ft.) high, and the upper end of the Parsenn run. From there they can ski down over vast, open snowfields to the town, a drop of around 1,000 meters (3,500 ft.). Or, striking off to the northeast, they come to Davos' neighboring resort—Klosters. Another funicular, combined with a gondola, goes to Strela. There's a lift to Rinerhorn (2,286 meters, 7,500 ft.), and a couple of dozen other mountain railways, cable cars and assorted lifts. Nearby is the well-equipped Brämabüel-Jakobshorn ski area, reached by cable car and lift.

Long before the skiing craze gave Davos international fame the place had a considerable vogue as a health resort. Its ideal situation from the standpoint of altitude and climate attracted tuberculosis sufferers as early as 1865, and it still has several of the finest sanatoria in Switzerland. With 12,000 inhabitants, Davos is even larger than St. Moritz, and it has more hotels and pensions, not counting the rest homes, health clinics and indoor swimming pools.

In addition to its unrivaled ski-runs, Davos also boasts a truly magnificent ice rink on which hockey matches and exhibitions of international caliber are staged throughout the winter. It is overlooked by a vast and well appointed terrace. There are two fine ski schools, either eminently capable of instilling in the novice sufficient skill to accomplish a fair sized *schuss* within a few days. As in some other Swiss resorts, the runs are constantly patrolled by guards who will set you right side up if you happen to do a nosedive into a snowdrift. Furthermore, the mountainsides are dotted with little inns and taverns, where toes can be thawed out and courage fortified with a jigger of Kirsch. English-speaking visitors who mistrust such foreign concoctions will even find their favorite brands of whisky at most of these places (though at a steep price). It is also the Mecca of cross-country skiers. Over 70 kms. (45 miles) of prepared trails across stunning landscapes make up a varying and ideal terrain for cross-country skiers.

In summer, Davos is pleasant, but no more so than dozens of other Swiss resorts, and it is considerably less picturesque than a great many of them. It offers sailing and swimming in the Davosersee, trout fishing in either the lake or the river Landwasser and its tributaries, mountain climbing with experienced guides, golf on an 18-hole course, and skating, from June to October, on the open-air ice rink.

The resort is dominated by the steeple of a pretty, late-Gothic church, while the city hall, part of which dates from the 17th century, has some interesting stained-glass windows and coats of armor. There is a medical institute where much effective research has been carried out by Swiss scientists into the problems of tuberculosis, and on top of the Weissfluh another group of scientists has established an institute for the study of snow conditions and avalanches.

Toward the Engadine

From Davos, the road leads over the Flüela Pass to Susch in the Engadine, a distance of 11 kms. (18 miles). It's a relatively easy drive, as Alpine passes go, with no gradient steeper than 1 in 10, and comparatively few hairpin bends. Although the highway reaches an altitude of 2,377 meters (7,800 ft.), it is normally open to traffic in winter.

At first the road climbs gently. As it rises dense larch forests give way first to pine trees, then to firs, and finally, above the timber line, to a rocky, desolate waste of boulders and jutting cliffs, much of it snow-covered except in summer. It's impressive rather than beautiful scenery. Ahead, on the left, are the rocky slopes of Weisshorn, (3,078 meters, 10,100 ft.), with Schwarzhorn, (3,139 meters, 10,300 ft.), to the right, perennial snowcapped guardians of the pass. Towards the summit, even in August, the traveler may find himself driving through a light snowstorm. He will pass between two small lakes: the Schottensee and the Schwarzsee.

At the summit itself is the Flüela Hospiz, a picturesque wooden chalet with a windmill, offering refreshments and a night's lodging at reasonable rates, though few tourists would care to spend much time in this barren, formidable spot.

The descent takes the motorist through a narrow valley crossing the Susasca, in sight of the 3,180 meter (10,600 ft.) Piz Vadret, to the base of the great Grialetsch glacier, a spectacular mass of ice and snow that serves as a reminder that this entire country was, long ago, hidden under a vast sheet of ice. The road winds downward, crossing the torrential river Fless, and finally reaches Susch on the river En. The En, which eventually flows into the Danube, gives its name to this beautiful valley, the Engadine, "the narrow place of the En." Because of its chain of popular resorts, to many people the name of the Engadine is more familiar than that of Graubünden, the canton of which it is only a constituent (but important) part.

The Lower Engadine

One need only enter an Engadine house to be acutely conscious of its atmosphere and the almost painful state of cleanliness that exists within. The simple but solid facades, with their wonderful lattices and balconies, always prove attractive to foreigners, and their owners spare nothing to make them more picturesque. The deep windows are rich with flowers—geraniums, begonias and carnations—and flowering vines climb over the latticework. In winter, tiny bags of suet for the birds hang beside the windows.

The people of the Engadine are a proud lot. There is a story about a queen, traveling incognito, who once tried to buy a copper kettle that took her fancy as she was visiting the home of an Engadine peasant. The man didn't want to sell, and an aide drew him aside to tell him that the lady was a ruling queen, not accustomed to having her wishes denied. "Very well," said the peasant, with a haughty gesture even the queen could not match, "I'll *give* her the kettle. But it is not for sale."

Susch, where the Flüela Pass road joins the main highway traversing the Engadine, is a quaint little place. The homes and other buildings here are all modern in construction if not in style, for the part of the village that lies on the left bank of the En was destroyed by fire in 1925, only the Evangelical Church being saved. Despite the latter's Roman tower, most of it is comparatively new, dating from 1515. During a restoration in 1742, the late Gothic style of its windows was changed, but in 1933, on the evidence of recently discovered fragments, they were restored to their original form. Susch is sheltered by the magnificent Piz d'Arpiglias, towering above it like a sentinel.

From Susch, our route follows the river En northeast to Scuol; a portion of the trip that can be made by road or rail. It passes through several rocky gorges, through which the En tumbles in turbulent fashion, and then emerges into flower-filled plains with a pleasant chain of attractive hamlets: Lavin, Guarda, Ardez, and the quaintly named Ftan.

Guarda, a beautiful village, is under federal protection, to ensure that the peasant dwellings with their two-tone, etched ornamentation, called *sgraffiti,* remain unchanged. A narrow lane from Guarda leads through Bos-cha to Ardez. In Ardez, dominated by the ruins of Schloss Steinsberg, are more of the graceful *sgraffiti* wall decorations, as well as some fine Italian ironwork, imported from Venice. Ftan, on a secondary road running higher up the hill, but parallel to the main highway, has a colorful old tower with a copper steeple. You'll get a good view, too, of Schloss Tarasp, which is on the other side of the river En.

Scuol-Tarasp-Vulpera

Scuol, Vulpera, and Tarasp, three villages with a combined population of 2,000, form what is effectively one holiday and health resort complex, whose waters are reputed to be highly beneficial to sufferers from liver complaints. Most of the visitors are Swiss or German, but an increasing amount of British and Americans are arriving every year. Beautifully located in the open valley of the river En whose grass covered and wooded sides are backed by mountains, Scuol-Tarasp-Vulpera have hitherto been highly popular summer resorts. Now, thanks to a network of gondola cars and skilifts, and unobstructed south facing slopes, they are taking on a new role as winter sports resorts as well.

From Scuol and Vulpera, a bus goes up to the historic Schloss Tarasp in half an hour, or the trip makes a nice hike of about an hour and a half. It is a real dream castle, pure white, perched on top of a sheer cliff some 152 meters (500 ft.) above the valley. Notice the Austrian coats of arms, slit windows, painted shields and double walls. The main tower and chapel date from the 11th century, when it was the stronghold of the knights of Tarasp. Long a source of discord between the powerful Bishop of Chur and the Count of Tirol, it became the seat of the Austrian governors until the last century, when Graubünden joined the Swiss Confederation. Some years ago, it was sold to a toothpaste manufacturer who spent three million Swiss francs (over a million dollars) restoring it and then gave it to the Prince of Hesse.

The Swiss National Park

From Tarasp, you can only return along the road to Susch. But instead of turning to go over the Flüela Pass again, you can continue up the valley, along the banks of the river En, to St. Moritz. Six and a half kms. (four miles) past Susch is the village of Zernez. Close by is the entrance to the Swiss National Park. Patterned after the national parks in the United States, this was created in 1914 by a federal decree stating, rather self-consciously perhaps, that "an island of untouched primitive natural existence is to develop here in the midst of the seething waves of civilization." The phraseology seems a bit extreme in view of the tranquility of the surroundings, for here the waves of civilization don't seethe very hard. Within the limits of the 180 square kms. (70 square mile) park there is absolute protection for plants and animals; no shot can be fired, no flower picked, no tree cut down, and it is forbidden to camp or light fires. There is not even the sound of a cowbell since cattle can't be pastured in the park. Herds of chamois roam over the rocks, roebuck feed under the larch trees, deer drink from the transparent, icy streams. The ibex, historic emblem of Graubünden, is also to be seen.

The park lies in a mountainous region, the cleft of the Ofen Pass dividing it in two. But although the highest peak is little more than 3,150 meters (10,330 ft.), the mountains are extremely rugged, and the valleys, filled with rocky debris, among the wildest in the Alps. There are numerous hanging glaciers. Nevertheless, walking about the park is a delight, if a hilly one, for there are prepared paths, clearly marked, and visitors must follow them. The season lasts from about the middle of June, after the snow has melted, until it returns in the fall.

The park is the richest region in the Alps for flowers because of its great differences in altitude, its varying rock types and formations, and its position astride the boundary between eastern and western Alpine flora. You'll see many rare plants that are to be found nowhere else in Switzerland as well as alpenroses, edelweiss, dwarf roses, valerian, mountain poppies, primroses, Alpine grasses, shrubs, and almost every variety of meadow flower and Alpine tree. The flowers are normally at their best in the second half of June. Then, although this may vary slightly according to the severity and timing of the preceding winter, the place is a riot of color: gentian, fiery red catchfly, violets of every shade, saxifrage, white Pyrenean and Alpine ranunculus, and a host of other flowers forming a kaleidoscope of bright color in the most superb natural setting.

But the Swiss National Park is not a solitary, floral oasis. Almost wherever you go in the Engadine, you'll find an abundance of wild flowers, and by mid-May, unless it is a late winter, the valleys will be covered with millions of crocuses and soldanella. They are followed by anemones, and, as these fade, the blue gentians start to bloom. Towards the end of June, when the haymaking begins, the beauty of the lower meadows is somewhat spoiled, but the flowers of the high pastures and the mountains remain throughout the summer with a coloring far more intense than anything at the lower altitudes. Remember though, that all except the commonest wild flowers are protected by strict cantonal laws. It is forbidden to pick or remove them in large quantities—"large quantities" being officially defined as more than ten flowers.

All the way from Scuol, the route has been closely following the river En, as it has done since it crossed the Austrian frontier (24 kms., 15 miles the other side of Scuol) to enter the lower Engadine. And it continues to do so through the upper Engadine and past St. Moritz, to the river's source near Maloja. It's a lovely ride, the road climbing and twisting gently but steadily, with peaks, often snowcapped, to either side, and the river gushing in foaming torrents below. The villages are all lovely, and there are many old churches and, not least, some splendid examples of Engadine houses.

The Upper Engadine

After Zernez, the road passes Schloss Rietberg, owned by the Planta family. The Planta crest, a bear's paw, is a familiar sight in Graubünden, and members of the family still live there. They rose to importance subsequent to 1295, when they were named hereditary bailiffs to the bishops of Chur.

Just beyond Zernez, near Brail, you will pass from the lower to the upper Engadine, then through the surprisingly named little resort of S-chanf to Zuoz. Spare a short while here, for Zuoz, a small winter sports and summer resort as well as an education center, is noted for its Engadine houses, many of which were constructed for the Planta family, this village being their home. Indeed, you'll see the family emblem on top of the fountain in the main square. The Planta bear's paw is also a frequent decoration in the little church with its tall tower and needle-like spire.

Samedan and Celerina

A few miles farther on, you'll come to Samedan and Celerina, two charming Engadine villages that, if it were not for their vast difference in character, might be called suburbs of St. Moritz. From Samedan you have a magnificent view of the Bernina chain of mountains: Piz Bernina, 4,050 meters (13,300 ft.); Piz Palü and Piz Roseg at 3,900 meters (12,900 ft.); Piz Morteratsch, 3,750 meters (12,300 ft.); Piz Tschierva, 3,500 meters (11,700 ft.); Piz Corvatsch, 3,440 meters (11,300 ft.); Piz Rosatsch, 3,100 meters (10,200 ft.); and many others. Samedan also has a golf course and is close to the Upper Engadine airport.

The trip up to Muottas Muragl should not be missed, since it provides a superb view over the lovely valley of the En. A funicular goes in 15 minutes from Punt Muragl, between Samedan and Pontresina, to the summit; reaching an altitude of 2,450 meters (8,050 ft.)—700 meters (2,300 ft.) above the valley floor. From the top you will get an eagle's eye view of St. Moritz, the nearby watershed of Piz Lunghin, and the chain of lakes which stretches almost 16 kms. (10 miles) towards Maloja. Within about 450 meters you will also find the sources of the river Mera, flowing southwest to lake Como and the Adriatic: the river En, which runs through the Engadine to meet the Danube and the Black Sea; and a stream which winds north into the river Julier, and so to the Rhine and the North Sea. Understandably the Engadine is called the "roof of Europe."

The mountain panorama forms a full semicircle, between Piz Languard in the southeast and Piz Kesch in the northwest. In the south, near the white peak of the famed Piz Palü, the highest mountains in the Bernina group may be seen, including Piz Bernina itself, above the dark mass of Piz Chalchagn. The wide ridge of Piz Tschierva and the pointed Piz Roseg follow and then the glacier world of the Sella group, above the cleft of the Roseg valley. In the foreground are the massive blocks of Piz Rosatsch and Surlej, and farther behind the lovely Piz La Margna, while the peaks of the Bergell mountains loom over the Maloja Pass. The west side of the valley is bounded by Piz Lagrev, flanked by Piz Julier and Piz Albana, which in turn give way to Piz Nair and the wild and rocky tower of Piz Ot. Deep down on the left, just out of sight, is Pontresina, where the Bernina and Roseg valleys meet, and to the right, in the En valley, is Celerina.

Celerina, St. Moritz's little brother, is a first-rate ski resort in its own right with the additional advantage of easy access to all the winter sports facilities of its more celebrated neighbor. The renowned Cresta run, mecca for bobsledders, ends here.

Among the main attractions of the upper Engadine are the many mountain railroads and cableways. Whether it's for a climbing excursion or just for an afternoon's walk, you can go from St. Moritz to Corviglia by funicular and from there by cableway to Piz Nair, a wonderful 3,000 meters (10,000 ft.) mountaintop viewpoint that has a restaurant and cafe. On the terrace you can admire the fabulous view while sunbathing in a deckchair with a glass of your favorite potion close at hand. You can go from Celerina by cableway to Val Saluver or, as we have seen, by funicular to Muottas Muragl; from Pontresina by chairlift to Alp Languard; from Bernina by cableway to Diavolezza or to Piz Lagalb; from Surlej, between Lakes Champfêr and Silvaplana, to Piz Corvatsch (over 3,300 meters, 10,800 ft.); and from Sils to Furtschellas.

St. Moritz

What eastern Switzerland lacks in large cities is more than made up for with places bearing world-famous names. Foremost among them is a little village whose natural beauties and health giving baths have caused it to grow into one of Europe's most famous resorts—St. Moritz. The average visitor thinks of St. Moritz, the site of the 1928 and 1948 Winter Olympics and the setting for dozens of films, as something of a world capital. If he goes there during the winter season, when the plush hotels are crowded with what remains of European nobility, statesmen, film stars and Arab oil sheiks, he will not be disappointed. But in summer the town does lose some of its glitter, and prices are appreciably less than in winter. Many people consider that St. Moritz is at its best during this relatively low season—the end of June and beginning of July—since the mountains and pastures are covered with spring flowers.

It has been fashionable for quite some time. Bronze relics uncovered in 1907 and now on view in the Engadine Museum at St. Moritz indicate that the healing qualities of its waters were known at least 3,000 years ago, long before Rome was founded. The Romans had a settlement there, and later—exactly when is not known—a church was founded on the site and dedicated to Mauritius, one of the early Christian martyrs. The first historical reference to the town was in 1139; and in 1537 Paracelsus, the great Renaissance physician, described in detail the health-giving properties of the St. Moritz springs. It is said that toward the end of the 17th century the Duke of Parma led a retinue of 25 followers over the mountain passes to take the waters; the first of a still-continuing parade of royal visitors seeking to rejuvenate their jaded livers by drinking from the bubbling fount of Piz Rosatsch. In 1747, a description of the town speaks of the presence of the mineral water itself, from which the town's fame originally came. It was vividly described by a German visitor in 1793. "It puckers lips and tongue like the sharpest vinegar, goes to the head, and is like champagne in the nose."

St. Moritz grew into a major tourist resort in the last century after the bed of the En was altered to prevent the river from destroying the mineral spring. This early engineering feat was carried out by subterfuge. The elders of the village were opposed to the "new-fangled" development, so, when they were all away at a cattle market in Tirano, the younger men voted for the project in a town meeting and had it started by the time they returned. Then the first of the big luxury hotels was built, and by 1859 *Il Fögl Ladin,* the Romansch-language newspaper now published in Samedan, proudly announced that "the unheard-of number of 450 visitors" had come during the year. A half century later, in 1910, the same newspaper more calmly recorded that 10,000 people had visited St. Moritz.

The elders apparently learned their lesson, for ever since they have devoted themselves to improving the resort and its facilities. After Edison had displayed his electric light at the Paris Exhibition of 1878, it was introduced in St. Moritz by Johannes Badrutt, one of Switzerland's great hoteliers, and the man who more than anyone made Switzerland popular as a winter destination. Six years later, St. Moritz pioneered in winter sports with the construction of the first toboggan run—the Cresta—which, as it happened, started on Badrutt's own grounds. Then, in 1895, Philipp Mark, president of the local tourist bureau, gave one of the first ski-jumping exhibitions on a jump he had built himself in St. Moritz. The Olympic jump, with a height of 141 meters (465 ft.) from takeoff to landing run, was made for the 1928 Winter Olympics—an era when winter sports were regarded as a somewhat curious activity indulged in by the eccentric few with time to spare for a winter holiday and purses big enough to pay for it.

Twenty years later—1948—when the Winter Olympics were again held in St. Moritz, the resort became the first site to have staged them twice. Undoubtedly these two events were partially responsible for the superb facilities which have made St. Moritz synonymous with winter sports.

Around St. Moritz

The town itself is located at an altitude of 1,856 meters (6,090 ft.), in the upper Engadine valley on the shores of the lovely sky-blue lake of St. Moritz. The latter is the northernmost of a chain of four lakes around which are scattered a number of resorts that give the upper Engadine much of its charm. The other three are lakes Champfer, Silvaplana and Sils. Through all of them flows the En, here an infant river which rises nearby. The valley is enclosed by parallel mountain ranges, the Bernina chain on the southeast and the Julier chain to the northwest.

The resort is in three parts—St. Moritz-Dorf, situated on a mountain terrace 60 meters (200 ft.) above the lake; St. Moritz-Bad charmingly located at the end of the lake; and Champfer-Suvretta. When, towards the end of the 19th century, the fashion for spas began to wane, St. Moritz-Bad began to take a back seat to St. Moritz-Dorf, the sparkling winter resort. But in recent years St. Moritz-Bad has staged a comeback by laying heavy emphasis on skiing and other winter sports. In 1973 it started a new direct aerial cableway to Signal, feeding the Plateau Nair lift, and in 1976 a splendid spa complex was opened. Unfortunately one of the side effects of this growth has been a rash of unsympathetic modern building, much of which has little architectural merit. The charming little lakeside resort is beginning to look like a Costa Moritza, but its popularity is assured.

As a town, St. Moritz-Dorf has only minor attractions. There is a leaning tower, all that remains of an old village church built in 1573, and the Segantini Museum, which contains some important works by Giovanni Segantini, the 19th-century Italian artist who settled in Graubünden and became a distinguished painter of Alpine life and scenery. Outside is the Olympic Stone listing all the medal winners at the St. Moritz Winter Olympics. The Engadine Museum, in addition to the relics of prehistoric times previously mentioned, has an interesting collection of Engadine furniture. On the modern side, the town has some of the most fashionable shops in Switzerland.

Distractions at St. Moritz are virtually unlimited for the active sportsman, in either winter or summer. It is a skier's paradise, of course, and also offers wonderful ice skating, bobsledding, and riding and horse racing on the frozen lake. In summer, there's swimming, skating, summer skiing, sailing, riding, mountain climbing, golf, tennis and, in the river En and the 25 lakes, some of the best fishing in Switzerland. Serious connoisseurs of night life and gambling may be a little bored, although in a modest way both are available. The ice rink is open all year.

On lake Silvaplana, barely six kms. (four miles) from St. Moritz, is the Engadine village of Silvaplana, the first of the unspoiled village resorts outside the St. Moritz complex. Next comes Sils-Baselgia, little more than a couple of excellent hotels, and the tiny village of Sils-Maria, where Nietzsche wrote *Thus Spake Zarathustra.* Peace, quiet and good hotels are keynotes at Maria. Its summer highspots are horse-drawn bus excursions up the beautiful Fex valley, or gentle mountain hiking amid breathtaking scenery. In winter its attraction is skiing without queueing via the Furtschellas cable car; and always the life and amenities of St. Moritz can be reached easily and quickly.

Pontresina

Half a dozen miles east of St. Moritz, and below our earlier viewpoint on Muottas Muragl, is another famous summer and winter resort, Pontresina; one of whose greatest assets is its altitude, since at about 1,828 meters (6,000 ft.), it is only marginally lower than St. Moritz itself. Amply provided with fine hotels, Pontresina has everything the holidaymaker could desire. It stands at the center of a network of 200 kms. (124 miles) of well-kept paths, some of them passing spectacularly alongside the glaciers that descend from the snow-covered mountains above. If walking is too tame for you, there are plenty of guides to take you mountaineering. Or you can sit under the shaggy pines of the Tais woods and listen to the morning concerts given daily from June through September. There is golf at the nearby 18-hole golf course, tennis, swimming in a splendid indoor pool, trout fishing in streams and lakes, two of which are free, a gymnasium, summer skiing and horse riding. The most popular excursion is by horse-drawn bus up the Val Roseg, a delightful high Alpine valley. It takes about an hour each way, and there's a good restaurant at the terminus.

In winter, Pontresina turns to skiing. Just behind the village is the Alp Languard lift; the first level being for beginners, the second recommended only for moderately good skiers. At Bernina, about eight kms. (five miles) up the valley by train or bus, are the high rise cable cars to Diavolezza and Lagalb, but the latter's for piste-bashers only. Pontresina is a major ski-touring center with 50 mapped-out tours. It's got a modern cross-country skiing center, skating, curling and, for those who don't ski, special routes kept open for winter walking. From Pontresina, too, it is easy to get to any of the various cable cars, mountain railways and lifts in the Upper Engadine.

From Pontresina, the Bernina Railroad follows the old Bernina post road over the pass to Tirano, in Italy. It runs through magnificent countryside; wild and somewhat grim on the north side of the summit, quickly changing to lush meadows and trees on the southern descent—an indication of the warmer, Italian-type climate.

Although our itinerary at the start of this chapter planned a return from St. Moritz to Chur by post bus over the Julier Pass, there is an alternative, and a very attractive one, too. For you can go back by the Rhaetian Railroad through the Albula tunnel and down the Albula valley via Filisur, Tiefencastel and Thusis—a fantastic journey in which the gallant little train twists and weaves its way among outstandingly fine mountain scenery well matched by the engineering skill of the railway's constructors. But our planned route is by road over the Julier Pass, which, incidentally, is kept open throughout the winter. From St. Moritz the road goes southwest through Champfer to Silvaplana, where the Julier road branches northward. If you miss the turning you'll be on the road which goes all the way to lake Como; very nice, but not what we have in mind.

The Julier Route

The Julier route is one of the three great Alpine passes (the Great St. Bernard and the Splügen are the other two) that are known to have been used by the Romans, though even in those days, the Julier was favored because of its immunity from avalanches. The present road, built between 1820 and 1826, is dominated by three mountains, Piz Julier, Piz Albana, and Piz Polaschin, and near the top it is marked by two pillars, around one and a half meters (five ft.) high, which are said to be the remains of a Roman temple. Initially the climb is steep, giving a fine view of the Upper Engadine lakes, but it levels out before reaching the summit at 2,286 meters (7,500 ft.). Here there is a souvenir shop and parking place, and the Julier Hospice, where refreshments can be obtained.

The first village of any importance after leaving Silvaplana is Bivio, which is about eight kms. (five miles) beyond the summit, at an altitude of 1,780 meters (5,850 ft.). A former Roman settlement named Stabulum Bivio, it is called Bivio in Italian and in German, and Beiva in Romansch, and those who live here speak all three languages. From here the road follows the banks of the turbulent river Julia through splendid rocky gorges and over tempestuous cascades to Mulegns and Savognin, passing the artificial Lake of Marmorera, built to store water for hydroelectric power stations.

Savognin is an unpretentious winter sports resort with sunny slopes served by a good network of gondola cars and lifts going up to 2,700 meters (8,900 ft.). It's got a fine indoor pool and a dozen or more good hotels. In summer there are splendid signposted mountain walks, gondola cars and lifts giving easy access to the higher ones. For several years Savognin was the residence of the celebrated painter Segantini. The district and its people are well represented in his works which you'll see everywhere—but only reproductions; originals are very expensive.

Nine kms. (six miles) farther on is Tiefencastel, called Casti in Romansch, and where the river Julia flows into the Albula. The village was entirely destroyed by fire in 1890, but above the "new" one the tall white church of St. Ambrosius still stands out beautifully against the background of fir trees that cover the encroaching hills. A short distance from Tiefencastel is Vazerol, where there is a monument commemorating the oath of eternal union sworn by the "Free Leagues" of the Swiss Confederation in 1471.

At Tiefencastel you can either take the direct road to Chur via Lenzerheide and Churwalden, or go on a more circuitous route by Thusis.

Lenzerheide, which almost adjoins Valbella, is a charming winter and summer resort at an altitude of 1,524 meters (5,000 ft.). It enjoys long hours of sunshine and is virtually free of fog because of its situation in a high valley open to the south. It has two seasons, June to September (mountain climbers prefer the latter month) and mid-December to April.

Although the Lenzerheide-Valbella area is specially good for the intermediate grade skier, one of its principal attractions is the number of practice slopes which nature has thoughtfully provided for beginners. Another is the unusually good assortment of cable cars and lifts, including of course the cable car which runs up to Parpaner Rothorn, an altitude of 2,860 meters (9,400 ft.).

The range of facilities provided at this resort is nothing if not comprehensive. It has an 18-hole golf course, seven tennis courts, horse-riding, swimming and rowing on its little lake, fishing in the Julia and Albula rivers, and a good indoor swimming pool at the Posthotel Valbella. Guided mountain trips are organized every week during July and August, and free botanic excursions start one month earlier. If you want to explore the countryside on foot, a map of the various routes is available at the resort.

But if you have not made too many stops since leaving St. Moritz, the day will still be young and the longer route by way of Thusis and Reichenau will prove inviting. You can go by train, bus or car.

Tiefencastel to Flims

The rail trip from Tiefencastel to Thusis is particularly interesting from an engineering point of view, since this section of the Rhaetian Railroad passes through 16 tunnels, one of them over five kms. (three and a half miles) long. There are also 27 bridges or viaducts. One of these is the celebrated Solis Viaduct, the center arch of which is 41 meters (137 ft.) across, and 89 meters (293 ft.) high. The route is wonderfully scenic, threading through spectacular gorges and canyons, interspersed with peaceful valleys and pine forests for contrast.

Thusis, easily the most important town of the Domleschg Valley with about 1,700 inhabitants, is surrounded by high mountains and thick forests. It has a late-Gothic church, dating from 1506, and in the center of the woods, an open-air lido. The town is the starting point for climbers seeking to conquer the Piz Beverin. Here the river Albula joins the Hinterrhein (or Upper Rhine). Perched on the rocky heights guarding the entrance to the Via Mala are the ruins of the old Schloss Hohenrhaetien. The famous Via Mala, an ancient and dramatic road writhing along the bottom of a deep ravine, has now been replaced by a fine new one that eliminates the old bottlenecks. The route runs south through Andeer to the Splügen and San Bernardino passes, the latter of which has now been bypassed by a tunnel. The town of San Bernardino is a small winter resort.

From Thusis, you enter the fertile Domleschg Valley, through which the Upper Rhine flows to join the Lower Rhine (Vorderrhein) at Reichenau. This valley is one of the most scenic of the area, with numerous old castles, charming villages and blossoming orchards. Houses seen here are typical of the entire Graubünden: high, stuccoed structures with red-tiled roofs and small-paned windows set deep into the thick walls as protection against the cold. There is frequently a wooden balcony-porch running around the house at the second story, with gracefully carved railings invariably bordered with masses of flowers.

Rothenbrunnen, which comes next, means mineral waters containing iron. The town has a children's home, and there are old castles all over the place. In the triangle formed by the junction of the Upper Rhine and the Lower Rhine Schloss lies Reichenau, which has a long and fascinating history. Built in the 14th century, it was in 1793 the refuge of the then-exiled future King of France, Louis-Philippe. He lived there under the name of Professor Chabaud. Later it passed into the hands of the Plantas, the family which owned so many of the castles in Graubünden.

From Reichenau-Tamins—a twin village lying on both banks of the river—it is only nine and a half kms. (six miles) to Chur, our starting point, via the attractive village of Ems. However, if you have time it is well worthwhile making a detour westward to Flims, a summer and winter resort in the Bündner Oberland. This region extends from Reichenau along the Vorderrhein (or Lower Rhine), and runs as far as Oberalp—near Andermatt.

Located at an altitude of 1,127 meters (3,700 ft.), Flims is set on a south-facing terrace overlooking the Rhine valley. The village itself is in two adjacent sections: Flims-Dorf, which consists mostly of villas built among the meadows; and Flims-Waldhaus, in the pine trees and containing most of the hotels. Perhaps the greatest summer asset of Flims is the Caumasee, a small lake fed by warm springs that make it possible to swim there as early as June. In winter, aerial cableways to Cassonsgrat (2,636 meters, 8,650 ft.) and Grauberg FIL 15 7 1640 (2,224 meters(2,224 meters,well as several ski lifts serve the broad snowfields above the village. A mile or so down the road from Waldhaus is Laax, a nice little village with a couple of small lakes. More important, it's a relatively new but up-and-coming skiing center with some excellent top, medium grade and first class hotels. Close to Laax are the cable cars to Crap Sogn Gion (2,209 meters, 7,250 ft.), and Crap Masegn (2,483 meters, 8,150 ft.), with a well-planned system of linking ski lifts.

Chur to Arosa

From Chur you can strike east by rail or road towards the center of the circle we have just completed. It's a dead-end route, both rail and road stopping at the third of the three major resorts of Graubünden—Arosa. It's an idyllic high-altitude village about 1,800 meters (6,000 ft.) above sea level. Aside from the invigorating atmosphere and clean, crystal-clear air that this altitude guarantees, Arosa has gained the reputation of being an unusually friendly resort. The largest of its many hotels is moderately sized so there is none of the chilling formality or impersonal efficiency sometimes found in mammoth establishments.

The accent is on freedom. It's not compulsorily dressy, nor deliberately fashionable, but it can be smart if one wants it that way. In the top hotels a few men may wear dinner jackets, but if they do it's because they want to, not because they have to. It follows that Arosa has fallen heir to some of those who find the winter elegance, ostentation, and glitter of St. Moritz just a trifle overbearing.

One of Arosa's specialties is a sport that has always appealed to the upper crust—horseracing. But here it is on snow and ice, and in winter. For although Arosa is an excellent summer resort, it is more fashionable in winter, and more popular. This is hardly surprising, since the ski runs are among the best in Switzerland for beginners, intermediates and experts. There is always enough snow and, unlike many resorts, one can ski back right down into the village. With over 25 kms. (15 miles) of runs, cross-country skiing has also become popular in recent years. Arosa has over 70 hotels and pensions. These can accommodate about 6,000 visitors. Over 6,000 more guests (mostly families) can be lodged in furnished apartments and chalets.

It would be hard to say whether Arosa offers the visitors more in summer or winter. In the former, there is the bathing beach on the little lake, with a swimming instructor at hand, and some of the hotels which open in summer have indoor pools. There are several tennis courts, tennis halls, an artificial ice rink (ice hall), and a nine-hole golf course, as well as fishing on either of two lakes, and boats for hire. And there are concerts, dances and a seemingly endless program of varied entertainment and sporting events.

In winter, the broad skiing fields above the tree line are made accessible to everyone by a good network of cleverly located skilifts and linking runs. There is also a well-known cable car running to Weisshorn, (2,650 meters, 8,700 ft.); and gondola cars will take you to Hörnli (2,500 meters, 8,200 ft.). The resort claims to have over 70 km. (47 miles) of piste, and the ski school, which has over 100 instructors, is one of Switzerland's largest. Curling, skating and ice hockey take place on several rinks (natural and artificial), the Obersee Ice Stadium having a roofed grandstand for spectators. For non-skiers (and 50% of Arosa's winter visitors are just that) there are many miles of carefully prepared paths for winter walking, and if you hanker after something different you can take the popular Arlenwald Road sleigh ride. And winter and summer you have a wide selection of entertainment and can enjoy magnificent mountain scenery which is as elegant as the resort itself.

PRACTICAL INFORMATION FOR GRAUBÜNDEN

TOURIST OFFICES. The principal tourist office for Graubünden is the Verkehrsverein Graubünden (VVGR), Alexanderstr. 24, Postfach, 7001 Chur (tel. 081–22 13 60). In addition there are local tourist offices in the following towns: **Davos,** Kur- und Verkehrsverein, Promenade 65, 7270 Davos-Platz (tel. 083–3 51 35). **Klosters,** Kur- und Verkehrsverein, 7250 Klosters (tel. 083–4 18 77). **St. Moritz,** Kur- und Verkehrsverein, 7500 St. Moritz (tel. 082–3 31 47).

The Graubünden Tourist Office has a permanent representative in the U.S.: Tony Haeusler, 506 61st St., Suite 205, West New York, NJ 07093 (tel. 201–227–0546).

HOTELS AND RESTAURANTS. Though Graubünden is liberally provided with hotels, prices tend to be high in both summer and winter, especially in peak seasons. During these periods you will also need to make reservations well in advance. Many hotels, especially in resorts, tend to close between the main summer and winter seasons.

AROSA. *Arosa Kulm,* tel. 081–31 01 31. 250 beds. At the top end of town and well placed for Hörnli gondolas and Carmenna lift. AE, DC, V. *Savoy* (L), tel. 081–31 02 11. 220 beds. Indoor pool. AE, DC, MC, V. *Tschuggen Grand* (L), tel. 081–31 02 21. 245 beds. All facilities at this luxurious spot. *Alexandra Palace* (E), tel. 081–31 01 11. 200 beds. Modern and extremely smart. AE, DC, MC, V. *Des Alpes* (E), tel. 081–31 18 51. 70 beds. Quiet and central. AE, DC. *Bellavista* (E), tel. 081–31 24 21. 160 beds. Superior hotel with indoor pool. *Eden* (E), tel. 081–31 18 77. 160 beds. Very comfortable. AE, V. *Excelsior* (E), tel. 081–31 16 61. 126 beds. Indoor pool. *Golfhotel Maran* (E), tel. 081–31 01 85. 120 beds. Every sporting facility, including golf. AE, DC, V. *Park* (E), tel. 081–31 01 65. 190 beds. Grand and comfortable. *Raetia* (E), tel. 081–31 02 41. 85 beds. Very comfortable and modern. AE, DC, MC, V. *Waldhotel National* (E), tel. 081–31 13 51. 180 beds. In own garden, very quiet; indoor pool and sauna. AE, DC, V.

Alpensonne (M), tel. 081–31 15 47. 70 beds. V. *Alpina* (M), tel. 081–31 16 58. 55 beds. *Belri* (M), tel. 081–31 12 37. 35 beds. Quiet location. *Belvédère-Tanneck* (M), tel. 081–31 13 35. 70 beds. Quiet and central. *Streiff* (M), tel. 081–31 11 17. 75 beds. Garden. *Vetter* (M), tel. 081–31 17 02. 40 beds. *Ramoz* (M), tel. 081–31 10 63. 32 beds. Modest, terrace, skittles.

Restaurant. *Central* (M), tel. 081–31 15 13. Try the *scampi maison* or the rack of lamb *à la Sarladaise.*

BAD SCUOL. *Romantik Guardaval* (E), tel. 084–9 13 21. 90 beds. Historic and atmospheric building, furnished in local style, central but quiet. *Bellaval* (M), tel. 084–9 14 81. 55 beds. Good family hotel. *La Staila* (I), tel. 084–9 14 83. 10 beds. Ideal for children.

CELERINA. *Cresta Kulm* (E), tel. 082–3 33 74. 80 beds. Quiet location. AE, DC, MC, V. *Cresta Palace* (E), tel. 082–3 35 64. 150 beds. Indoor pool and many winter sports facilities. AE, DC, MC, V. *Misani* (M), tel. 082–3 33 14. 50 beds. Good restaurant. V. *Posthaus* (M), tel. 082–3 22 22. 35 beds. Modest.

CHUR. *Chur* (M), tel. 081–22 21 61. 70 beds. Sauna, dancing. AE, MC, V. *Duc de Rohan* (M), tel. 081–22 10 22. 60 beds. Indoor pool, elegant restaurant. AE, DC, MC, V. *Freieck* (M), tel. 081–22 17 92. 80 beds. Quiet and central. AE, DC, MC, V. *Posthotel* (M), tel. 081–22 86 44. 80 beds. Centrally located, facilities for the handicapped. No restaurant. AE, DC, MC, V. *Romantik Hotel Stern* (M), tel. 081–22 35 55. 90 beds. 300-year-old building, beautifully restored, furnished in regional style. AE, DC, MC, V.

Drei Könige (I), tel. 081–22 17 25. 60 beds. Suitable for families. AE, DC, MC, V. *Rebleuten* (I), tel. 081–22 17 13. 20 beds. Historic building with atmospheric restaurant and diet meals. MC, V.

Restaurants. *Duc de Rohan,* tel. 081–22 10 22, has several (E) restaurants. The *Stern* hotel/restaurant (E), tel. 081–22 35 55, can also be recommended for local food and wines. AE, DC, MC, V.

DAVOS. At **Davos-Dorf.** *Flüela* (L), tel. 083–6 12 21. 130 beds. Extremely grand, with every amenity and very good restaurant. AE, DC, MC, V. *Derby* (E), tel. 083–6 11 66. 120 beds. Comfortable and quiet. AE, MC, V. *Meierhof* (E), tel. 083–6 12 85. 125 beds. Central, in own grounds. AE, DC, MC, V. *Meisser* (E), tel. 083–5 23 33. 40 beds. Central, but in own grounds and very quiet. AE, DC, V. *Parsenn* (M), tel. 083–5 32 32. 75 beds. Central, opposite Parsenn railroad. AE, DC, V. *Sporthotel Herrmann* (M), tel. 083–5 17 37. 45 beds. Central. V. *Trauffer* (M), tel. 083–5 36 46. 14 beds. Bed and breakfast, with restaurant and pastry shop downstairs. AE, MC.

At **Davos-Platz.** *Steigenberger Belvédère* (L), tel. 083–2 12 81. 240 beds. Newly renovated. Luxurious with all facilities. AE, DC, MC, V. *Sunstar-Park* (L), tel. 083–2 12 41. 400 beds. Quiet, in own grounds with indoor pool, sauna, squash and many other facilities. AE, DC, MC, V. *Golfhotel Waldhuus* (E), tel. 083–6 11 31. 100 beds. Tennis, indoor pool. AE, DC, MC. *Morosani Posthotel* (E), tel. 083–2 11 61. 160 beds. With Pöstli-Bar and dancing; the "in" place to meet. DC, V. *Ochsen* (E), tel. 083–3 52 22. 67 beds. Family-run hotel with pleasant restaurant, and own horse-drawn coaches. AE, DC, MC. *Schatzalp* (E), tel. 083–3 58 31. 170 beds. Mountain hotel a few hundred meters up by funicular train, with indoor pool and other luxuries. AE, DC, MC. *Schweizerhof* (E), tel. 083–2 11 51. 150 beds. AE, DC, MC.

Restaurants. *Davoserstübli* (E) and *Jenatschstube* (E), tel. 083–3 68 17. French cuisine, members of the Rôtisseurs chain. *Flüela-Post* (E), tel. 083–6 12 21. Recommended cuisine. *Bistro Gentiana* (M–E), tel. 083–3 56 49. Fondues, snails, and good meat dishes. *Des Alpes* hotel, tel. 083–6 12 61, has several good restaurants (M–E) and is open all the year. AE, DC. *Molino* (I), tel. 083–5 34 44. Snacks and à la carte, reasonably priced.

At **Davos-Laret. Restaurant.** *Tschiery's Landhaus* (E), tel. 083–5 21 21. Try the menu Campagnard—country fare at its best. Also reasonably priced rooms.

FLIMS. *Parkhotel Waldhaus* (L), tel. 081–39 01 81. 300 beds. In beautiful grounds with many sports facilities and all comforts. AE, DC, V. *Adula* (E), tel. 081–39 01 61. 180 beds. Indoor pool, garden, good restaurant. AE, DC, MC, V. *Schweizerhof* (E), tel. 081–39 12 12. 80 beds. Attractive grounds, sporting facilities. DC, V. *Aparthotel Des Alpes* (E), tel. 081–39 01 01. 160 beds. Indoor tennis. MC, V. *National* (M), tel. 081–39 12 24. 46 beds. Comfortable and central. AE, MC, V. *Schlosshotel* (M), tel. 081–39 12 45. 60 beds. Central with good restaurant. DC, MC, V. *Cresta* (I), tel. 081–39 13 02. 80 beds. Central, but quiet location.

Restaurants. *Stiva* (M–E), tel. 081–39 26 26, with open fireplace, and *Las Valettas* (M–E), tel. 081–39 26 26, are both in Hotel Crap Ner in Flims-Dorf. *Albana Sporthotel* (I), tel. 081–39 23 33, has three restaurants plus pizzeria, terrace and pub, near skilifts and cableways. DC, MC, V.

KLOSTERS. *Aaba Health* (L), tel. 083–4 81 11. 115 beds. Modern, central, some sports facilities. AE, DC, MC. *Silvretta* (L), tel. 083–4 13 53. Grill room. AE, DC, MC, V. *Alpina* (E), tel. 083–4 41 21. 130 beds. Every facility, with apartments for families and swimming pool. Directly opposite station. *Chesa Grischuna* (E), tel. 083–4 22 22. Small and charming with good restaurant. 42 beds. AE, DC, MC, V. *Pardenn* (E), tel. 083–4 11 41. 130 beds. Indoor pool, sauna, bowling and other attractions. V. *Walserhof* (E), tel. 083–4 42 42. Small with enormous charm and outstanding restaurant. 21 beds. AE, DC, MC, V. *Kurhotel Bad Serneus* (M), tel. 083–4 14 44. 60 beds. Quiet location, cure facilities. *Rustico* (M), tel. 083–4 12 93. 21 beds. Comfortable and friendly sporting hotel, with billiard room, sauna, garden terrace, squash by arrangement; recommended. DC, MC.

Restaurants. *Walserhof* (E), tel. 083–4 42 42. Creative dishes. AE, DC, MC, V. *Chesa Grischuna* (E), tel. 083–4 22 22. AE, DC, MC, V. *Steinbock* (M), tel. 083–4 16 36. DC, V. *Rufinis* (M), tel. 083–4 13 71. Atmospheric, serving local specialties; bar and dancing. DC, MC, V. *Pizzeria Vereina* (I), tel. 083–4 11 61. Large buffet with hot and cold dishes.

LAAX. *Happy Rancho Sporthotel* (E), tel. 086–3 01 31. 250 beds. Exceptionally well-equipped with two pools, tennis, sauna and solarium. AE, DC, MC, V. *Crap Sogn Gion* (M), tel. 081–39 21 92. 75 beds. Indoor pool, sauna and bowling. *Sporthotel Larisch* (M), tel. 086–3 47 47. 70 beds. Indoor pool, and sauna nearby; facilities for the handicapped. AE, DC. *Sporthotel Signina* (M), tel. 081–39 01 51. 154 beds. Indoor pool, tennis, dancing indoors and in the open air. AE, DC, MC, V.

Restaurants. *Sporthotel Larisch* (M), tel. 086–3 47 47, has a large rustic restaurant and *Bündnerstube* with garden terrace, serving fondues, and fresh trout. AE, DC.

LENZERHEIDE. *Grand Hotel Kurhaus Alpina* (E), tel. 081–34 11 34. 160 beds. Central, comfortable and smart; indoor pool. AE. *Guarda Val in Sporz* (E), tel. 081–34 22 14. 80 beds. Rooms in renovated old alpine herdsmen's huts, with all comforts. Restaurant (E) serves local specialties. AE, DC, MC, V. *Schweizerhof* (E), tel. 081–34 11 81. 200 beds. Smart and expensive. DC, MC, V. *Lenzerhorn* (M), tel. 081–34 11 05. 40 beds. Central, garden; dancing and entertainment in the evening. Restaurant specializes in fondues. AE, DC, MC, V. *La Palanca* (M), tel. 081–34 31 31. Charming rustic rooms, with facilities for the handicapped; atmospheric restaurant serving fine food. AE, DC, MC. *Scalottas* (I), tel. 081–34 16 66. 24 beds. Some rooms in (M) price category. AE.

Restaurant. *Grotto Pizzeria Da Elio* (I–M), tel. 081–34 33 36. Homemade pasta.

At **Lenzerheide-Valbella.** *Posthotel Valbella* (L), tel. 081–34 12 12. 160 beds. Indoor pool, sauna, tennis. AE, DC, MC, V. *Valbella-Inn* (L), tel. 081–34 36 36. 100 beds. Indoor pool, sauna, curling, tennis, facilities for children. AE, DC, MC, V. *Kulm* (M), tel. 081–34 11 80. 40 beds. Central, in own grounds, also has facilities for children. AE, DC, MC, V.

Restaurant. *Romana* (I), tel. 081–34 16 16. Local specialties and homemade ice cream.

MALOJA. *Maloja Kulm* (M), tel. 082–4 31 05. 45 beds. Historic building at top of the pass, very quiet. AE, DC, MC, V.

PONTRESINA. *Kronenhof-Bellavista* (L), tel. 082–6 01 11. 200 beds. Grand hotel with ice rink, tennis and good restaurant. MC. *Rosatsch* (E), tel. 082–6 77 77. 90 beds. Centrally located; sauna. DC, V. *Walther* (E), tel. 082–6 64 71. 120 beds. Facilities include ice rink, tennis courts and sauna. AE, DC, MC, V. *Bernina* (M), tel. 082–6 62 21. 80 beds. Central, in own grounds; good restaurant. AE. *Sporthotel Pontresina* (M), tel. 082–6 63 31. 160 beds. AE, DC, V. *Schweizerhof* (M), tel. 082–6 64 12. 130 beds. MC, V. *Bahnhof-Chesa Briotta* (I), tel. 082–6 62 42. 31 beds. No rooms with bath. Simple.

ST. MORITZ. *Badrutt's Palace* (L), tel. 082–2 11 01. 380 beds. Central, but with spacious grounds and marvelous views at the back. Very expensive, with every amenity and sports facilities. AE, V. *Carlton* (L), tel. 082–2 11 41. 200 beds. Long famed for quiet elegance and service. AE, DC, MC, V. *Kulm* (L), tel. 082–2 11 51. 300 beds. A little out of the center with incredible views and price tags; indoor pool and sauna. AE, MC, V. *Suvretta House* (L), tel. 082–2 11 21. 360 beds. About a mile out of town in lovely grounds; very expensive. *Crystal* (E), tel. 082–2 11 65. 160 beds. Also has (M) rooms. Central, with sauna. AE, DC, MC, V. *Schweizerhof* (E), tel. 082–2 21 71. 150 beds. Many facilities include gymnasium. DC, MC, V. *Steffani* (E), tel. 082–2 21 01. 130 beds. Central; bowling. AE, DC, MC, V.

Bellevue (M), tel. 082–2 21 61. 80 beds. Riding, sauna. AE, DC, MC. V. *National* (M), tel. 082–3 32 74. 43 beds. AE, V. *Soldanella* (M), tel. 082–3 36 51. 60 beds. In own grounds, reasonable. AE, DC, V. *Sporthotel Bären* (M), tel. 082–3 36 56. 95 beds. In own grounds with indoor pool and sauna. *Granita* (I), tel. 082–3 36 29. 22 beds. Simple hotel with garden.

Restaurants. *Rôtisserie des Chevaliers* (M–E), tel. 082–2 11 51. Excellent. V. *Engiadina* (M), tel. 082–3 32 65. Cheese specialties. *Steinbock* (I), tel. 082–3 60 35. French cuisine and Italian specialties. DC.

SAMEDAN. *Des Alpes* (E), tel. 082–6 52 62. 64 beds. AE, MC, V. *Bernina* (E), tel. 082–6 54 21. 110 beds. Tennis and dancing. AE, DC, V. *Quadratscha* (E), tel. 082–6 42 57. 60 beds. Indoor pool. AE, DC, V. *Donatz* (M), tel. 082–6 46 66. 32 beds. Golf, ice skating and curling. DC, V. *Hirschen* (M), tel. 082–6 52 74. 45 beds. Historic building in town center. AE. *Sporthotel* (M), tel. 082–6 53 33. 50 beds. In own grounds. AE, DC, V.

Restaurant. *Le Pavillon* (M), Bernina hotel (tel. 082–6 54 21). For mouth-watering delicacies. V.

SAVOGNIN. *Bela Riva* (E), tel. 081–74 24 25. 38 beds. New hotel with a lot of charm. *Cresta* (E), tel. 081–74 17 55. 120 beds. Large hotel with indoor and outdoor tennis, indoor pool, sauna, bowling. DC, MC, V. *Danilo* (M), tel. 081–74 14 66. 70 beds. Central, with night club. DC, MC, V. *Piz Mitgel* (M), tel. 081–74

11 61. 42 beds. Central. Restaurant serves Swiss specialties. V. *Pianta* (I), tel. 081–74 11 05. 30 beds. No rooms with showers. Popular restaurant. DC.

S-CHANF. *Park Hotel Aurora* (M), tel. 082–7 12 64. 70 beds. Quiet hotel in own grounds, with bowling and facilities for children. *Scaletta* (I), tel. 082–7 12 71. 40 beds. Quiet, central; bowling. V.

SILS-MARIA. *Waldhaus* (L), tel. 082–4 53 31. 220 beds. Indoor pool, tennis; ideal for children. MC, V. *Maria* (M), tel. 082–4 53 17. 60 beds. Sailing school, ice rink, curling. *Privata* (M), tel. 082–5 42 47. 39 beds. Central; suitable for families with children. *Schweizerhof* (M), tel. 082–4 57 57. DC, MC.

At **Sils-Baselgia.** *Margna* (E), tel. 082–4 53 06. 110 beds. Tennis and sauna. *Chasté* (M), tel. 082–4 53 12. Small and simple. *Chesa Randolina* (M), tel. 082–4 52 24. 65 beds. Quiet.

SILVAPLANA. *Chesa Guardalej* (L), tel. 082–2 31 21. 220 beds. Swimming pool, sauna, solarium, squash, fitness room, ice rink, curling; congress hall. *Albana* (E), tel. 082–4 92 92. 50 beds. Sauna and gymnasium. AE, DC, V. *Julier* (E), tel. 082–4 81 86. 120 beds. Adequate. AE, V. *Sonne* (E), tel. 082–4 81 52. 90 beds. Sailing, skating and dancing, all in quiet surroundings. AE, DC, MC. *Arlas* (M), tel. 082–4 81 48. 26 beds. Small hotel. *Chesa Grusaida* (M), tel. 082–4 82 92. 29 beds. AE, DC, V.

SPLÜGEN. *Posthotel Bodenhaus* (M), tel. 081–62 11 21. 85 beds. 250-year-old building in mountain village. Napoleon, Queen Victoria and Tolstoy are said to have stayed here. Indoor pool. AE, DC.

TARASP-VULPERA. *Schweizerhof* (L), tel. 084–9 13 31. 300 beds. Excellent facilities, open summer and winter; reader recommended. AE, DC. *Villa Silvana* (E), tel. 084–9 13 54. 45 beds. Sports and cure facilities. AE, DC, V. *Schlosshotel Chasté* (E), tel. 084–9 17 75. 30 beds. V. *Waldhaus* (E), tel. 084–9 11 12. 150 beds. Quiet but expensive, with cure facilities, tennis, golf and pool; closed in winter. AE, V. *Tarasp* (M), tel. 084–9 14 45. 48 beds. Central but quiet, with ice rink. MC, V.

Restaurant. *Chasté* (M), tel. 084–9 17 75. Excellent. Try the sole fillets à la Champs Elysées.

ZUOZ. *Engiadina* (E), tel. 082–7 10 21. 71 beds. Central location, with tennis, pool, sauna, curling and dancing. AE, V. *Crusch-Alva* (M), tel. 082–7 13 19. Small and central.

GETTING AROUND. By Train. Rail lines in Graubünden are surprisingly extensive—and always scenic. Among the most spectacular lines are the "Glacier Express," which climbs its way over the Alps from St. Moritz to Zermatt in the Bernese Oberland; the equally dramatic "Bernina Express," which crosses the Alps to the south and Italy; and the "Engadine Express," which runs from Chur to the Swiss National Park in the lower Engadine.

A number of good-value rail vacation tickets are available, giving unlimited travel on all rail routes and on many cable cars. Details from the Rhaetian Railroad, Bahnhofstr. 25, 7002 Chur (tel. 081–21 91 21), or any rail station.

By Bus. Postal bus services are frequent and extensive, with a network totalling over 1,000 kms. (620 miles). A number of bus excursions are also available, as are good-value holiday tickets and reductions for families. Details from any bus station, post office or local tourist office.

By Car. Roads throughout Graubünden are excellent, despite the often inhospitable terrain (though this does have the advantage of ensuring dramatic scenery virtually throughout the region). Car hire is available in all larger towns and resorts.

Hiking. The entire region is laced with walking and hiking trails, many following centuries-old paths between villages and towns, and a number used since the Roman period. In addition, Graubünden has a series of magnificently scenic mountain walks. Maps, etc., are available from all tourist offices.

SIGHTSEEING DATA. Graubünden is primarily a region of superb mountain scenery, and most sightseeing here tends naturally to concentrate on this aspect rather than on museum-going, for example. Nonetheless, there is a handful of museums and other places of interest. Among them the following:

AROSA. Heimatmuseum Schanfigg (Local Museum), Kirchliweg (tel. 081–31 33 13). Modest regional museum illustrating economic and social development of Graubünden. Open Jan. to Mar., Tues. and Fri. 2:30–4:30; June 20 to Sept. 20, Mon., Wed. and Fri. 2:30–4:30.

CHUR. Bündner Kunstmuseum (Graubünden Art Museum), Postplatz (tel. 081–22 17 63). Paintings and sculptures from the 17th century to the present, including important collection of Swiss works by Giacometti, Kauffmann and Engadine artist Segantini. During exhibitions open daily except Mon., 10–12 and 2–5.

Dom Museum Kathedrale (Cathedral Museum), Hof 18 (tel. 081–22 23 12). Religious objects from the 4th to the 18th centuries. Appointments necessary (tel. 081–22 92 50).

DAVOS. Kirchner Museum, Postgebäude (tel. 083–3 64 84). Small and important museum devoted to Ernst Ludwig Kirchner, leading German Expressionist painter. Open Tues., Wed., Sat. and Sun. 4–7 in winter. May to Oct., on same days, 4–6.

DAVOS-MONSTEIN. Bergbaumuseum Graubünden (Mining Museum), Schmelzboden (tel. 082–3 57 12). Open mid-June to mid-Oct., Wed. and Sat. 2–4.

SPLÜGEN. Heimatmuseum Rheinwald (Local Museum), von Schorsch Haus (tel. 081–62 11 38). Small museum charting life—particularly farming—in Graubünden. Open end Dec. to mid-Apr., and June to Oct. Tues., Thurs. and Sat. 3–5.

SPORTS. Tennis, swimming and golf (five courses) are popular summer sports, and Graubünden offers many opportunities for hiking—however, bear in mind that the weather can be unreliable. Details of these from local tourist offices.

Canoeists can enjoy day and half-day excursions on the exciting upper reaches of the Rhine from Flims and Laax, from May through Sept. Call 086–3 41 41 or 086–3 41 42.

Mountain climbing is a major summer activity—but only of course for the experienced who should also go with a local guide. There are climbing schools at Klosters (tel. 083–4 36 36), Davos (tel. 083–5 26 24) and Pontresina (tel. 082–4 55 63).

WINTER SPORTS. Graubünden is a veritable paradise for winter sports enthusiasts. Many of the resorts here number among the best, and most famous, in the world. Facilities everywhere are excellent.

Arosa, 1,815 meters (5,955 ft.); 3 cable cars, 13 lifts, 70 kms. (43 miles) of downhill runs, 35 kms. (22 miles) of cross-country tracks, ski-hiking, skating, curling and ski bob. Ski school (downhill and cross-country) and skating school.

Celerina, 1,724 meters (5,656 ft.); 2 funiculars, 3 cable cars, 18 lifts, 60 kms. (37 miles) of downhill runs, 15 kms. (9 miles) of prepared cross-country tracks. Ski schools.

Chur, 600 meters (2,000 ft.); 3 cable cars, 3 lifts, 18 kms. (11 miles) of downhill runs, 3 kms. (2 miles) of cross-country trails, tobogganing, skating. Ski schools.

Davos, 1,560 meters (5,118 ft.); 3 funicular railways, 8 cable cars, 29 lifts, 320 kms. (199 miles) of downhill trails, 70 kms. (43 miles) of cross-country tracks, skating rinks, tobogganing trails and prepared runs, curling. Ski schools (downhill and cross-country).

Flims, 1,095 meters (3,600 ft.); 1 cable car, 5 chair lifts, 25 lifts, 220 kms. (137 miles) of downhill trails, 45 kms. (28 miles) of cross-country tracks, tobogganing, ski bob, curling. Ski schools.

Klosters, 1,220 meters (4,000 ft.); 2 funicular railways, 1 cable car, 22 lifts, 160 kms. (99 miles) of downhill runs, 40 kms. (27 miles) of cross-country trails (3 kms. lit at night), skating, curling, walking paths. Ski schools.

Laax, 1,050 meters (3,444 ft.); 6 cable cars, 25 lifts, 220 kms. (137 miles) of downhill runs—highest starting point is 3,050 meters (10,000 ft.), 63 kms. (39 miles) of cross-country tracks, tobogganing, skating, 35 kms. (22 miles) of well-kept walking paths. Ski schools.

Lenzerheide, 1,480 meters (4,856 ft.); 3 cable cars, 34 lifts, 155 kms. (96 miles) downhill runs, 50 kms. (31 miles) of cross-country tracks (2 kms. lit at night), 30 kms. (18 miles) of ski-hiking trails, ski bob, tobogganing, skating, curling. Ski schools.

Maloja, 1,817 meters (5,960 ft.); 2 lifts, 12 kms. (7 miles) of downhill runs, 58 kms. (36 miles) of prepared cross-country ski trails, skating, curling. Ski schools (downhill and cross-country).

Pontresina, 1,820 meters (5,970 ft.); 1 funicular railway, 2 cable cars, 11 lifts, 87 kms. (54 miles) of downhill runs, 120 kms. (75 miles) of cross-country trails, 38 kms. (24 miles) of ski-hiking trails, 9 open curling rinks, ski bob. Ski schools.

St. Moritz, 1,856 meters (6,090 ft.); 2 funicular railways, 6 cable cars, 47 lifts, 400 kms. (249 miles) of downhill runs, 150 kms. (93 miles) of cross-country trails, 20 kms. (12 miles) of special ski bob runs, tobogganing, curling, skating. Ski schools.

Samedan, 1,728 meters (5,670 ft.); 1 funicular railway, 3 lifts, 16 kms. (10 miles) of downhill runs, 120 kms. (75 miles) of cross-country trails, 17 kms. (11 miles) of ski-hiking trails. Ski schools (cross-country and downhill).

Savognin, 1,220 meters (4,000 ft.); 2 cable cars, 14 lifts, 80 kms. (50 miles) of downhill runs, 35 kms. (22 miles) of cross-country trails, 4 kms. (2 miles) of tobogganing runs, 2 kms. of cross-country trails at 1,800 meters (5,600 ft.) in Radons.

S-chanf, 1,672 meters (5,486 ft.); 1 lift, 60 kms. (37 miles) of cross-country ski trails, 3 kms. (2 miles) of downhill runs.

Silvaplana, 1,816 meters (5,958 ft.); 2 cable cars, 7 lifts, 36 kms. (22 miles) of downhill runs, 123 kms. (76 miles) of cross-country trails, 20 kms. (12 miles) of ski-hiking trails, 14 curling rinks, ski bob. Ski school (downhill).

Splügen, 1,465 meters (4,810 ft.); 7 lifts, 22 kms. (14 miles) of downhill runs, 30 kms. (19 miles) of cross-country tracks, skating. Ski schools.

Zuoz, 1,750 meters (5,740 ft.); 3 lifts, 20 kms. (12 miles) of downhill and cross-country trails, 18 kms. (11 miles) of ski-hiking trails, tobogganing. Ski schools.

LUZERN AND CENTRAL SWITZERLAND

Historic Heart of a Nation

To enter Luzern is to approach the heart of historic Switzerland, for the deeply indented shoreline of the Vierwaldstättersee, the lake of the Four Forest Cantons or, simply, lake Luzern, was the cradle of the Swiss Confederation. To the Swiss, the names of Rütli, Brunnen, and Altdorf—all places near the lake—recall the pact signed in 1291 between the clans of Schwyz, Unterwalden and Uri.

This is also the area in which William Tell is said to have lived: it was at Altdorf, or so the legend has it, that the famous archer was forced by the Habsburg bailiff, Gessler, to shoot an apple from the top of his son's head with a crossbow. As with all good legends this one has little basis in fact. But that hardly seems to matter, and its hero has made a splendid subject for many plays and monuments, as well as an opera and countless souvenirs.

But Altdorf is by no means the only famous town in the area, and the charms of Rigi, Pilatus, Bürgenstock, and of course Luzern itself, cultural and tourist capital of Central Switzerland, have been well known to visitors for over a century. Central Switzerland is made up of five cantons: Uri, Schwyz, the two half-cantons of Unterwalden—

Obwalden and Nidwalden—Zug and Luzern. It boasts majestic mountain scenery, more than a dozen charming lakes and historically the most important north–south trade route in Europe, the famous St. Gotthard Pass over the Alps.

Luzern

During the early Middle Ages, Luzern's role was as a vassal city of the House of Habsburg, and at the outbreak of the conflict between the Swiss and the Austrians she was unwillingly forced to fight against her mountain neighbors. After the defeat of the Habsburg army at Morgarten in 1315, the city felt it necessary to maintain friendly relations with the Confederates, since she had a growing reputation as a marketing and trading center to protect. In consequence it was for economic reasons, as well as to assert their individual rights, that the citizens of Luzern signed—in 1332—a pact of perpetual alliance with the founder members of the Confederation.

From that time on, although it did not shake off the final traces of Habsburg rule until after the victory at Sempach in 1386, Luzern shared the martial fervor of the Swiss, participating in all their conflicts with the outside world. But although a free, and fairly prosperous city, Luzern never acquired the same degree of power and wealth as her great allies: Basel, Bern, and Zürich. And until fairly recent times, the canton and its capital remained something of a quiet and relatively unknown backwater.

The town itself lies at the foot of the mountain slopes, and the natural charm of its surroundings is enhanced by the many 15th- and 16th-century buildings which still remain. Also worth seeing is the city hall, and of course the famous covered wooden bridges, with which Luzern is so often associated. Luzern has never had much in the way of industry, not even participating in the embroidery, spinning, weaving and wood and ivory carving that were, until some 40 years ago, the principal activities in much of the rest of Central Switzerland. As a result, the town depends chiefly on tourism for its not inconsiderable prosperity.

Exploring Luzern

Like several Swiss cities, Luzern is built at the end of a lake. To be more accurate, it is at the head of a large bay, for lake Luzern (or Vierwaldstättersee, as you will usually see it referred to locally) is so tortuous in outline that it is difficult to say where the end is. From the lake, the river Reuss flows through the town, before being joined on the far side by the river Emme. The two 14th- and 15th-century covered wooden bridges, the 17th-century Altes Rathaus—the Old Town Hall with its impressive roof and masonry—and the delightful Old Town, all help to create an atmosphere of medieval solidity. This impression is further enhanced by the picturesque Weinmarkt, the Fritschi fountain on Kapellplatz, and the ancient city walls topped by watch towers. In and around the old quarter is a maze of charming, narrow and traffic-free streets and little squares bordered by lovely old buildings. There are also plenty of enticing shops.

The Kapellbrücke (Chapel Bridge), the larger of the two covered bridges, crosses the river diagonally from the old St. Peter's chapel, past the octagonal Wasserturm (water tower) to the southern bank. The paintings on the timber ceilings of this bridge represent scenes from Luzern's history. Those on the other bridge, the Spreuerbrücke (or Mill Bridge), are typically medieval and illustrate a grim dance of death.

If you cross either of these two bridges, or the busy 19th-century Seebrücke, you'll come to the new town on the south side of the river Reuss. Here, close together, are the lake steamer landing stages, the railroad station, the Kunsthaus and, next to the Municipal Theater, the splendid Jesuit church, a Rococo masterpiece and one of the most beautiful churches in Switzerland. Built between 1666 and 1677, it is known for its sacristy and 18th-century stucco work. The penitential robe of St. Niklaus von Flüe (more on him later) is displayed in one of the side chapels. Around the corner from the church in Pilatusstrasse is the city tourist office, and two minutes away is the Gothic Franciscan church, built around 1300, with its Baroque chapels.

No visit to Luzern is complete without a trip to the famous Löwendenkmal, the Lion Monument. As much a Luzern trademark as the Kapellbrücke, this is the much praised dying lion designed by Thorwaldsen and carved out of the living rock by Ahorn in 1820–21. Dedicated to the Swiss Guards of Louis XVI who died after defending the Tuileries during the French Revolution in 1792, the 30-foot lion, lying in a niche hewn out of the cliffside, forms a unique and surprisingly moving memorial. It is close to the Gletschergarten, the Glacier Garden, a remarkable natural phenomenon discovered in 1872 by geologists who unearthed huge potholes created by glacier water during the Ice Age as well as many fossils. There's an Alpine and Ice Age Museum attached.

As a contrast, there are the attractive lakeside gardens and quays, with their magnificent views which give visitors a foretaste of the mountain and lake scenery that lies in store for them. The old fortified Musegg wall with its nine towers, which originally enclosed the whole city, offers splendid vantage points over the city. Parts of the wall, together with the Schirmer, Mannli and Zyt towers, are open to the public from May to October.

Excursions from Luzern

As an excursion center Luzern has few rivals. Among the shorter trips is a two-and-a-half-hour conducted bus tour of the town and its surroundings taking in the beautifully situated Richard Wagner Museum at Tribschen, just outside the town. There, souvenirs and relics of the great maestro have been reverently assembled, together with a fascinating collection of musical instruments. In the center of town, there is a small but excellent collection of Picassos in Am Rhyn-Haus, next to the Old Town Hall. And on the north side of the lake, a little outside the center, is the world-famous Swiss Transport Museum, the Verkehrshaus. Buses take the holidaymaker to Meggen or Horw. There

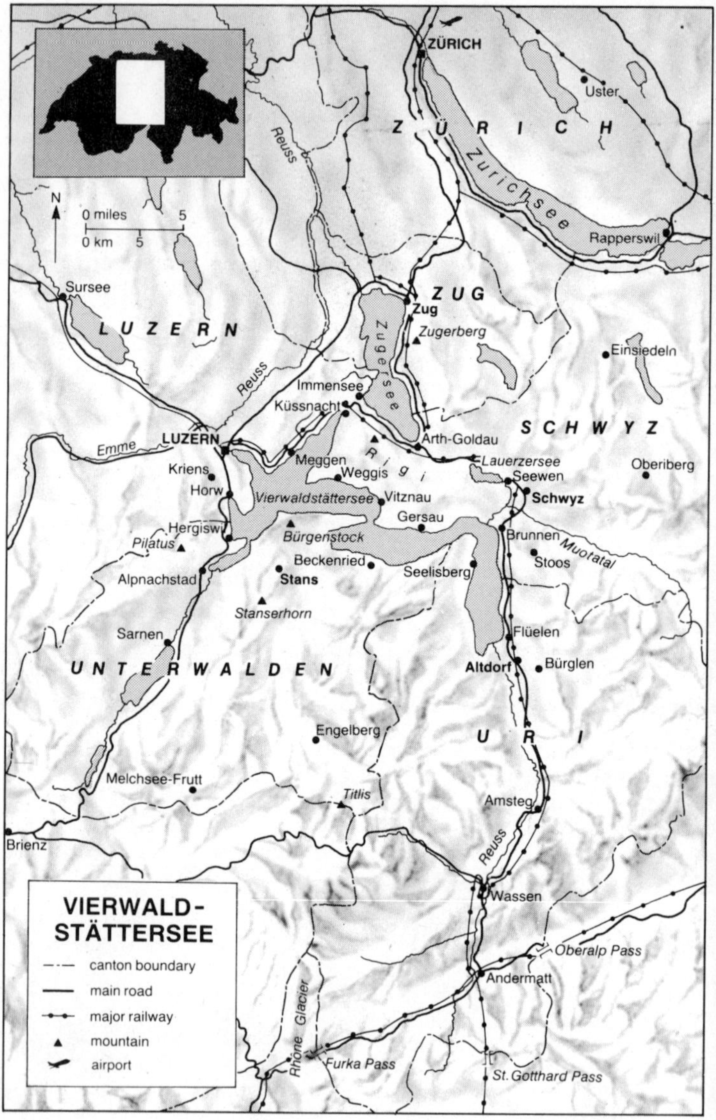
ZÜRICH
Uster
Z Ü R I C H
Zurichsee
Rapperswil
Reuss
N
0 miles 5
0 km 5
Sursee
L U Z E R N
Z U G
Zug
Zugersee
Zugerberg
Einsiedeln
Immensee
Küssnacht
Reuss
S C H W Y Z
LUZERN
Emme
Arth-Goldau
Meggen
Rigi
Lauerzersee
Oberiberg
Kriens
Weggis
Seewen
Horw
Vierwaldstättersee
Vitznau
Schwyz
Gersau
Hergiswil
Bürgenstock
Brunnen
Muotatal
Pilatus
Beckenried
Stoos
Alpnachstad
Stans
Seelisberg
Stanserhorn
Sarnen
Flüelen
U N T E R W A L D E N
Altdorf
Bürglen
Engelberg
U R I
Melchsee-Frutt
Titlis
Amsteg
Brienz
Reuss
Wassen
VIERWALD-
STÄTTERSEE
canton boundary
main road
major railway
mountain
airport
Oberalp Pass
Andermatt
Rhône Glacier
Furka Pass
St. Gotthard Pass

is a fine Museum of Swiss Folk Costumes and Folklore—Trachten und Heimatmuseum—at Utenberg.

Then there are Luzern's two neighboring mountains—Rigi (1,798 meters, 5,900 ft.) to the east of the city and 2,100-meter (7,000 ft.) Pilatus to the south. The summits of both can be reached easily.

Luzern, indeed, presents the tourist with a problem: which to choose from an almost bewildering selection of day and half-day excursions by train or lake steamer. To pick, almost at random, a mere dozen places, there are—in alphabetical order—Altdorf (capital of canton Uri and much involved in the William Tell legend); Brunnen (famed for the views from its lakeside promenades); Bürgenstock (from which you can look vertically down to the lake); Einsiedeln (pilgrimage center with its notable Abbey church); the pleasant winter sports and summer resort of Engelberg; little Immensee on the Zugersee; Kleintitlis and its glacier, over 3,000 meters (9,900 ft.) high; Klewinalp (high above the Vierwaldstättersee; the historic field of Rütli; the little city of Schwyz (which guards Switzerland's priceless archives); Schönbüel (2,010 meters, 6,600 ft.) and Zürich (Switzerland's largest city). High on your list, too, should be a slow boat journey down the lake, crisscrossing from place to place and presenting you with a panorama of constantly changing beauty. On the other hand, if you want to stay put and steep yourself in cultural activities, what better than Luzern during its International Festival of Music? Then, every day for three weeks towards the end of August, there are performances by outstanding artists.

Lakes, Mountains and Legends

Everyone knows the story of William Tell, the apple on his son's head and the well-aimed arrow, and no visitor to Central Switzerland will leave without hearing much more about him. But perhaps only a handful of the tourists who gaze respectfully up at his impressive statue in front of Altdorf's medieval tower have the vaguest idea whether he really existed. They can hardly be blamed, since most Swiss, to whom he is a national hero, don't know either.

Unfortunately, most historians discount the Tell story as mere legend. They point out that although much has been written about it through the ages, the story is either contradictory or at variance with historical fact, and there are no valid records to prove the existence of Tell, his son, the apple, or even the tyrant Gessler. But take heart. Whether there is any truth in the legend or not, all are agreed that broadly speaking, a situation such as that described in *The Story of William Tell* by Friedrich Schiller did exist in Central Switzerland during the 13th century. A proud and independent people were being oppressed by their Austrian overlords, and the spirit of rebellion was rife. All this contributed to the signing of a pact of perpetual cooperation and mutual assistance in 1291, an event in which William Tell is popularly believed to have played a major part.

Thus, although there may be no more truth in this legend than in any other, it is a fair allegory of the times, and those visitors who go to Altdorf every year to pay tribute to the hero's memory are not making an empty gesture.

It is easy to see that the spirit of the hardy old archer lives on in the hearts of the people of this region. They're soft spoken, friendly and tolerant of the views of others, but at the same time carry themselves with a dignity that allows no doubt about their independence.

The William Tell country is the area of Central Switzerland surrounding lake Luzern, the Vierwaldstättersee, and it is certainly one of the most beautiful summer holiday regions Switzerland has to offer. It has established a reputation for winter sports, the leading resorts being Andermatt, Stoos and Engelberg. From the top of Gemsstock, approached by cable car from Andermatt, it is said that you can see 600 alpine peaks.

Andermatt is near the meeting point of three alpine passes: the Gotthard, the Furka and the Oberalp, and is thus linked by road to the four points of the Swiss compass. It is also where the Rhône and Rhine valleys almost meet. If you have a car, try to experience one of these passes at firsthand. At the top of the Furka Pass is the Rhône glacier, where there is an ice grotto to explore. The Furka–Oberalp railway also passes through here providing a fabulous journey between the Rhône Valley and Graubünden. Every day, summer and winter, there are through carriages all the way from Zermatt to St. Moritz, providing one of the world's most memorable rail journeys.

Smart white steamers—some of them beautifully kept and picturesque old paddle-steamers—ply the Vierwaldstättersee and provide an ideal means of transport for exploring the region, assuming that you are not in too much of a hurry. The lake itself is the fifth largest in Switzerland, with a surface area of 113 sq. kms. (44 sq. miles), and a long and varied coastline, so that a journey on board one of the slow-moving steamers takes some time. In fact, if you are going to explore all the little towns and resorts that are worth seeing, several days will be required.

Leading off the Vierwaldstättersee in almost every direction are valleys, from most of which branch off yet more valleys, all with a charm of their own and all worth exploring if you have the time. You'll always be in the presence of mountains, and again and again you will come across lakes, sometimes tiny ones high in the mountains, sometimes larger ones like the Zugersee, lake Zug.

Pilatus and Rigi

The greater part of Central Switzerland can be explored from Luzern. One of the most popular excursions is to Mount Pilatus, over 2,100 meters (7,000 ft.), and the highest peak in the immediate vicinity. One route is to go by train or lake steamer to Alpnachstad and thence by the electric Pilatus Railway, claimed by its owners to be the steepest cogwheel railway in the world. Sometimes up gradients of nearly 1 in 2, the red trains take 30 minutes to climb the 1,693 meters (5,560 ft.) to the summit station. The trains run only during the summer. Another way of getting to the top is to take a trolley bus from Luzern to the suburb of Kriens and there join one of the procession of little, four-seat cable cars which take you over mountainside meadows and among trees on an eerily silent, half-hour trip to Fräkmüntegg (1,400 meters,

4,600 ft.). There you change to a cable car, seating up to 40 people, for the final climb up the near vertical rock face to the summit. This service runs all year round.

If you wish, you can go by one route and return by the other, as the terminals of both the cable car and the Pilatus Railway are in the same building, which is perched giddily in a saddle between two of the Pilatus peaks. Above the terminals is the Bellevue Hotel, a modern circular structure which many visit to watch, from their bedrooms, the sunrise or sunset. Close by is the older, traditional style Pilatus-Kulm Hotel. It takes little more than ten minutes to climb from the terminals, up steep but well-prepared paths and steps, to the top of the two nearest peaks. From either, and from the various paths and tunnels cut out of the rock, there are magnificent views. To the north the view extends to the Black Forest in Germany; east to the Säntis range and Bodensee; and southeast to Graubünden. In the south are the Alps, and to the northwest the Jura.

Pilatus owes its name, according to one legend, to Pontius Pilate, whose body, it is said, was brought there after the Crucifixion by the devil, and whose ghost, when disturbed, demonstrates displeasure by bringing storm and destruction to Luzern. Not unnaturally, to avoid any such happening the town put a ban on anyone climbing the mountain. This lasted until after the Middle Ages. Unfortunately, historians of greater reliability aver that this is nonsense and that the name comes from *pileatus,* or "hair covered," because of the way wisps of cloud often stream from the summit like wind-blown hair.

Certainly Pilatus was the cradle of mountain climbing. Ban or no ban, it has, for centuries, been climbed by a steadily increasing number of mountaineers. The first primitive inn was built at the top in 1856, and Queen Victoria rode to the summit of the mountain on muleback some 12 years later. You may not find a mule, but if you want to climb on foot the easiest route is from Hergiswil and it will take you about five hours to get to a well-deserved drink on the Kulm Hotel terrace.

After the trip to the top of Pilatus you should plan to go on the next clear day to Mount Rigi. You may ask what you can see from the top of Rigi that you can't from the top of old Hair Covered. In fact you'll find the two mountains have very different personalities. Pilatus is stern, forbidding and grandiose, with an enigmatic charm; while Rigi (despite its height of 1,798 meters, 5,900 ft.) seems a friendly, almost welcoming little mountain. There's grass at the summit, and the slopes are covered with trees and lush pastureland where in summer obviously contented cows graze to a cacophony of cowbells. You may not see as far from its summit, but the views are more attractive.

There are two electric rack-and-pinion railways leading up to the top of the Rigi. One runs from the pretty little resort of Vitznau on the northern shore of the Vierwaldstättersee; the other from Arth-Goldau, around the other side of the mountain at the southern tip of the Zugersee. These railways were built by competing companies back in the 1870's, and it was a race to see which outfit would get its line to the top first and capture the lion's share of the lucrative tourist business. The Vitznau line won, but that from Arth-Goldau gets its fair share of trade as its lower terminal, on the main St. Gotthard railway, is more accessible. Vitznau can be reached only by steamer and road, although there is a cable car from Weggis up to Rigi-Kaltbad, where you can join the Vitznau train to the top.

Visitors who want to see everything can go up one way and down one of the others, but whichever route you take the view is equally impressive. If you're the athletic type and want to try it on foot, start from Küssnacht, which is at the end of the northern arm that protrudes from the Vierwaldstättersee. It will take a good three hours and you will be puffing when you get to the top. But nobody will give you a medal for your pains, as the climb is considered strictly child's play in Switzerland. Mark Twain recounts in *A Tramp Abroad* how he labored up the path in the dark so as to be at the top of Rigi for the much vaunted sunrise, but was so tired when he got there that he fell asleep and didn't wake up until sunset. Not realizing how time had flown, he thought for a moment that the sun had changed direction. Even though he may only have seen the sunset, Twain describes the view in enthusiastic terms.

At the top of Rigi is another Kulm hotel, with a restaurant and a terrace where, on summer afternoons, there may be a Swiss boy or girl yodeling and playing the accordion. Even if you don't normally care for yodelers, they make wonderful background music for the lovely view of the lake and distant Alps. Near the Rigi-Kaltbad-First station (1,432 meters, 4,700 ft.), is the Hostellerie Rigi, a modern hotel. Not surprisingly, they have a Mark Twain Bar. There is a host of trails winding down through the meadows and woods of the Rigi and its companion hills, and in winter these become ski-runs that are popular with beginners, if not exciting enough for advanced enthusiasts.

The Bürgenstock and Stans

Having taken in the views from the top of Pilatus and Rigi, you may consider you've had your fill of heights. If so, you are going to miss half the fun for we haven't yet been to Bürgenstock, to the Stanserhorn, or to Mount Titlis.

The Bürgenstock, a mountain ridge jutting out into the Vierwaldstättersee, isn't particularly high but it rises so steeply from the water that the view of the lake and surrounding area from the top is strikingly beautiful—which probably explains why, for at least part of the year, many famous people, including film stars and world-famous musicians, live here. Although you can drive to Bürgenstock up a steep, narrow road from Stansstad, the most interesting and dramatic way is to make the 30-minute steamer trip from Luzern to Kehrsiten, where a funicular will take you 456 meters (1,500 ft.) above the lake to a group of hotels. This may not surprise you since the Swiss have a habit of crowning their peaks with a hotel or two. But this is rather different, since there are five—with a nine-hole golf course thrown in! Even if you are not going to stay in any of them, it is worth glancing inside since they are decorated in a style which, even by Swiss standards, is luxurious.

Mr. Frey, the owner of the three largest hotels, has combed the world for artistic treasures to furnish his mountain palaces, and a stroll through the various salons and reception halls is much like visiting a fine museum or art gallery, except that the hospitality is better.

Afterwards, unless you've no head for heights, you should walk along the cliff path (about 15 minutes) to the Hammetschwand electric lift, which, in next to no time, will waft you up the almost vertical cliff face to the summit, some 165 meters (540 ft.) higher. From there, if the weather has been kind to you, you'll see most of the Vierwaldstättersee, part of the Jura mountains, and a splendid selection of Alps.

Just to the south of Bürgenstock are Stans and the valley of the Engelberg Aa. Stans is rich in historical memories, and Engelberg is one of the country's outstanding resorts in both winter and summer. There are also two more mountains to climb—by funicular, of course. They are the Stanserhorn and mount Titlis.

The journey to Stans from Luzern is an easy one which can be completed via the Engelberg railway, or by road. The town is the capital of the half-canton of Nidwalden, and is a pleasant little summer resort with an interesting early Baroque church. From Stans you can choose between an 1893 funicular and an ultramodern cablecar to get to the top of the Stanserhorn (1,888 meters, 6,200 ft.), for a fine alpine view and the inevitable restaurant.

In the past the town has been associated with three of Switzerland's great heroes. The first is Arnold von Winkelried, who engineered the victory of the Confederates over Leopold II at the battle of Sempach in 1386. The Austrians, armed with long spears, formed a Roman square so that the Swiss, wielding axes and halberds, couldn't get in close enough to do any damage. Shouting "Forward, Confederates, I will open a path!" von Winkelried threw himself on the spears, clasping as many of them as he could to his breast, thus effectively giving his compatriots an opening into the square. Early pictures of this original kamikaze action make him look like a human pincushion.

The next great name in Stans is that of a hermit, Niklaus von Flüe, who was born in Flüeli, no more than ten miles to the south. It was just a century after Arnold von Winkelried had laid down his life for liberty that Niklaus also saved the Confederation, although through wise counsel rather than soldierly sacrifice. When the Confederates fell to quarreling over the spoils of the Burgundian wars, he came to the town and mediated in their disputes at the Diet of Stans in 1481. He was canonized in 1947.

The third name to conjure with is that of Heinrich Pestalozzi, the father of modern education. Although he was not born here, it was in Stans, after nearly 2,000 of its inhabitants had been massacred by the French in 1798, that this great humanist gathered together the homeless children, practising the educational theories that are now famous.

Stans is one of the few Swiss cantonal capitals still to hold the Landesgemeinde in traditional fashion in an outdoor ring, with citizens voting by hand on important cantonal matters. Their grand affair of direct democracy takes place on the last Sunday in April.

Engelberg

The train journey south from Luzern to Engelberg takes about an hour; and after leaving the lakeside the track runs through orchards, meadows, and along the canyon of the river Aa, before finally reaching the wide valley in which the village lies. It is a quiet, unspoilt place, clustered around a Benedictine monastery (founded in 1120) whose library contains some rare manuscripts dating from the 11th century—and earlier. As a resort the village is popular in both summer—for those who want to get away from it all and relax—and winter. It boasts a fine selection of slopes, served by an efficient network of funiculars, cable cars, chairlifts, and skilifts.

Towering above Engelberg is the permanently snow-covered peak of mount Titlis. At 3,200 meters (10,500 ft.) high, it is Central Switzerland's highest peak. A must for visitors—although the trip is not cheap—is the sensational ascent to Kleintitlis (3,017 meters, 9,900 ft.), which is just below the summit. From Engelberg a funicular will take you up to the first of a series of three cable cars, the last stage going directly over the Titlis glacier and its apparently bottomless crevasses to the top station. There, from the sun terrace, the glass-enclosed viewing hall or the restaurant you'll see an Alpine panorama (if you have chosen a clear day) which will leave a lasting memory. The trip is not recommended for people with heart trouble; at 3,000 meters (10,000 ft.) the air is pretty thin. But otherwise you need have no worry. The Swiss are a careful people and take safety precautions very seriously. For example, on the funiculars there are periodic inspections during which huge weights are put in the cars, which are hauled halfway up the incline; then the cable is loosened to see whether the brakes will hold. They have to be able to stop the car within a few feet. All of which is a comforting thought as your little train climbs up a railway as steep as a roof, or as your cable car creeps silently up a seemingly ridiculously thin cable slung between mountain peaks.

Around the Vierwaldstättersee

Having climbed some of the more notable peaks in this area comfortably and without effort (there are others, with and without funiculars and cable cars, if you want them), you may now prefer to take a more normal view of things, such as going to Altdorf to see where William Tell is said to have shot his famous arrow; to Schwyz, the cradle of Switzerland; and of course, on a steamer trip down the lake.

There are three routes to Altdorf from Luzern. The fastest is along the new highway, a journey of about half an hour. But you can also go by steamer all the way to Flüelen at the extreme end of the lake (it takes about three hours) and thence by bus for the short distance to Altdorf. The final route is via the Gotthard railway, about an hour's journey. From Luzern the train follows the lake to the end of the Küssnacht basin, then goes along the southern shore of the Zugersee and next past the smaller Lauerzersee before coming to Schwyz-Seewen, six minutes by bus from the historic town of Schwyz, to which we shall return in a moment. Less than five kms. (three miles) beyond Schwyz-Seewen the train meets up again with the Vierwaldstättersee at the resort of Brunnen and then follows the lake shore to Flüelen for Altdorf. Between Brunnen and Flüelen, and always close to the railway, is the remarkable Axenstrasse, a road cut out of the cliffs which, along this part of the lake, rise almost sheer from the water.

Whether you go by train or lake steamer, or out one way and back the other, depends on time available. But if at all possible try to make at least one trip by steamer between Luzern and Flüelen. And try, too, to stop off at the town of Schwyz—15 minutes by bus from the steamer landing stage at Brunnen, and much less from Schwyz-Seewen railroad station.

Historic Schwyz

Schwyz, capital of the canton of the same name, should be visited by everyone interested in Swiss history. A quiet, dignified little place, it seems conscious of the fact that it is one of the oldest and most historic towns in Switzerland, that it gave the country both its name and its flag, and that it is entrusted with Switzerland's most precious archives. It was here in the 14th century that the word Schweiz (German for Switzerland) was first recorded as the name of the mountain Confederacy which grew to become Switzerland.

Traces of an independent settlement at Schwyz have been found as far back as the Bronze Age (2500–800 B.C.); but by the 13th century the inhabitants, like much of the rest of what is now Central Switzerland, were under the rule of the House of Habsburg. Discontent was rife. In 1291 they joined with the folk of neighboring Uri and Unterwalden in the famous Oath of Eternal Alliance. You can see the beautifully scripted and sealed original of the documents, battle flags and paintings of the period in Schwyz's Bundesbrief-Archiv, an impressively simple concrete building completed in 1936.

Schwyz has several notable Baroque churches and a large number of fine old patrician homes dating from the 17th and 18th centuries, not least being the Redinghaus, with its magnificent interior and fine stained glass. Curiously, many of these splendid houses owe their origin to the battlefield. The men of Schwyz had a reputation as fine soldiers and in the 16th and 17th centuries were in considerable demand in other countries as mercenaries. They went abroad, fought in the many battles of the period, collected what in those days was handsome pay, returned home, and with the money built many of the houses you can see today.

From Schwyz it is only a ten-minute bus ride to Schlattli. There, a funicular (said to be Switzerland's steepest) will take you to a height of 1,310 meters (4,300 ft.), and to the hamlet of Stoos on a cozy mountain plateau. Boasting several lifts, some going up to over 1,800 meters (6,000 ft.), Stoos in winter is a first-rate, although unsophisticated, winter sports resort. In summer it turns into a hideaway for those seeking peace and quiet (Stoos has no roads, no cars) among alpine meadows and wildflowers, and with magnificent scenery. Down in the Muotta valley, and not very far from Schlattli, are the ruins of the

Suvorov Bridge, over which the French, under Masséna, and the Russians, under Suvorov, fought a major battle in 1799. Farther along the valley you can visit the vast Hölloch Caves. Already over 80 kms. (50 miles) of caves and corridors have been explored but they remain strangely unexploited although the public can go in for a couple of kilometers.

Einsiedeln, Sacred and Secular

From Schwyz it is a pleasant trip of 29 kms. (18 miles) northward to Einsiedeln. On the way you can make a side trip to a small mountain lake, the Ägerisee; passing, near Sattel, the famous battlefield of Morgarten. There, in 1351, Swiss peasants were victorious against troops of Frederick of Austria, an event which helped create modern Switzerland.

Einsiedeln is both a summer and winter resort, but it is not from this that the town's real fame comes. Most notably it is the home of the Black Madonna of Einsiedeln, and therefore one of Europe's most important centers of pilgrimage. She is housed in the abbey church of the Benedictine monastery. Secondly, on September 14th every year the great Festival of the Miraculous Dedication takes place, complete with torchlight processions. Further celebrations take place once every five years, when *The Great World Theater,* a religious drama written by Don Pedro Calderón, is performed in front of the abbey church with a cast of 700, all amateurs living in Einsiedeln. The play, first performed before the Court of Spain in 1685, is a drama of life and the problems of man. For generations the monks of the monastery have coached these amateur actors for their parts in this and other religious plays. Lastly, as if this was not enough to ensure Einsiedeln's reputation, Paracelsus, the eminent Renaissance physician, was born in the district.

The monastery of Einsiedeln was founded, like the Grossmünster in Zürich, during the time of Charlemagne. Meinrad, a Hohenzollern count and Benedictine monk, seeking to pursue his devotions in solitude, selected the site as being the most remote he could find. He built a little chapel for the image of the Virgin (which had been given to him by the abbess of Zürich), and since food was scarce in the region, two ravens kindly supplied him with the necessities of life. He lived for a while in peace, but some men who thought he possessed hidden treasures murdered him. The ravens followed the slayers to Zürich. Bent on justice being done, the birds attracted so much attention to the men by shrieking round their heads that they were detected and punished. The monastery was built over Meinrad's grave. When it was completed in the year 946 the Bishop of Konstanz was invited to consecrate it, but as he began the ceremony a voice was heard crying out in the chapel three times, "Brother, desist: God Himself has consecrated this building." A papal bull acknowledged the miracle and promised a special indulgence to pilgrims.

Through the ages the monastery of Einsiedeln has been destroyed by fire on several occasions, each time to be rebuilt, but always the Black Madonna has been saved. When Napoleon's armies plundered the church, hoping to carry off the sacred image, it had already been taken to the Tirol in Austria for safe keeping. Today the Madonna is housed in a black marble chapel just inside the west entrance to the church. Seen from a distance its color appears to be a rich bronze, not black, and there is something quaint and gentle about the figure, splendidly arrayed in jewels, which lends it a curious grace. The abbey church itself, built by Caspar Moosbrugger in 1735 and decorated by the famous brothers Egid Quirid and Cosmos Damian Asam, is one of the finest late-Baroque churches of its kind, the impressive simplicity and grace of the exterior contrasting vividly with the exuberance of its richly ornate interior. In front of the church is a huge square, the conspicuous centerpiece being a gilded statue of the Virgin surmounted by a large gilded crown. Round the base, water trickles from 14 spouts, and pilgrims, to be sure of good luck, traditionally drink from each one in turn.

The Vierwaldstättersee by Boat

If you decide to take the lake steamer from Luzern one of the boat's first calls will be at Weggis, a town noted for its mild, almost subtropical climate. In 1897 Mark Twain stayed here. Behind the resort you'll notice the aerial cableway which goes up to Rigi-Kaltbad, and opposite it, on the other side of the lake you will see the Hammetschwand elevator going to the top of Bürgenstock. After stopping at Vitznau, lower terminal of the Rigi cogwheel railway, the steamer sails through the giant gateway formed by the promontories of Bürgenstock and Vitznauerstock to call at the resort of Beckenried on the other side of the lake. From here there's a cable car to Klewenalp (1,600 meters, 5,250 ft.), a small winter sports and summer resort in a wonderful position overlooking the lake. The steamer again crosses the lake, this time to the little resort of Gersau, which, from 1332 to 1798, was an independent republic—the world's smallest. The boat's next port of call is Treib on the Seelisberg peninsula (look for the beautifully decorated chalet, still an inn, beside the jetty) before she returns to the northern shore and the resort of Brunnen, famed for the lovely views from its lakeside promenades. It is through the rocky mass of the Seelisberg that the new Seelisberg road tunnel (nine and a half kms., six miles long) was driven, providing, together with the St. Gotthard road tunnel a swift new route across the Alps. At Brunnen the steamer turns south around the Seelisberg peninsula to enter the last basin of the Vierwaldstättersee, the Urnersee, at the end of which is Flüelen. Now in succession come three points of major interest to those who revere the Tell saga and the Oath of Eternal Alliance—the Schillerstein (on the right as you pass the peninsula), the Rütli meadow (a little farther on, just above the Rütli landing stage), and Tellsplatte (on the other—eastern—side of the lake).

The Schillerstein, a natural rock obelisk sticking nearly 26 meters (85 ft.) up out of the lake, bears the simple dedication "To the author of *Wilhelm Tell,* Friedrich Schiller. 1859." The Rütli meadow is where the Confederates of Schwyz, Unterwald and Uri are said to have met on the night of November 7th 1307 to renew the 1291 Oath of Eternal

Alliance. Now it is a national shrine and every year, on August 1st, their Independence Day, Swiss citizens gather in the meadow in remembrance of the Oath—at night the sky glows with the light of hundreds of bonfires on the mountain tops. Tellsplatte, at the foot of the Axen mountain, is the rocky ledge onto which the rebellious archer leaped to escape from the boat in which the bailiff Gessler was taking him to prison, pushing the boat back into the stormy waves as he did so. The Tell chapel, much rebuilt in 1881, contains four frescoes which show the taking of the oath on the Field of Rütli, Tell shooting the apple on his son's head, Tell's escape, and Gessler's death.

From Flüelen it is only a short distance to Altdorf where, in the town's main square, Tell is said to have performed his feat. With true Swiss caution, he had a second arrow, reserved for the heart of the tyrant should the first miss its mark. The whole drama, as told by Schiller, is enacted every second or third summer in Altdorf's William Tell Theater, and in nearby Bürglen there's a William Tell Museum.

Zug

Before leaving Central Switzerland let us return to our starting point, Luzern, for a quick look at the second largest lake in the region, the Zugersee, less than two kms. from the Küssnacht arm of the Vierwaldstättersee. It's about 22 kms. (14 miles) long, and lies on the edge of Switzerland's most steeply mountainous region. Unlike the other lakes in the area only its southern shore rises sharply; in the north it has no more than gently rising hills.

A road hugs the shore round most of the lake. In the northeast is the lakeside town of Zug, capital of its namesake canton (the smallest in the Confederation). Although with much modern development—the town, despite its improbable name, is the headquarters of many multinational corporations—it is an ancient walled city with a distinctly medieval air, enhanced by massive towers and by the delicate spires of the 15th to 16th-century church of St. Oswald. In the town hall, an early 16th-century building with Gothic carvings, there are exhibits of gold and silver work, embroideries, wood carvings, stained glass, paintings, and with the flag said to have been held aloft to the last by Wolfgang Kolin. He perished in 1422 in the battle of Arbedo, where 3,000 Swiss valiantly tried to hold off 24,000 Milanese soldiers. There's a fountain in his honor in Kolinplatz.

From the Zugerberg (974 meters, 3,200 ft.) overlooking the town there is a famous view taking in the peaks of Jungfrau, Eiger, Mönch, Finsteraarhorn and, nearer at hand, Rigi and Pilatus. But if, after your tour, you are tired and have had enough of heights, you need go no farther than Zug's quayside promenades. The view there may not match up to that from the Zugerberg but it is still a pretty respectable one and you should be able to pick out several peaks which, earlier on in our tour of central Switzerland, appeared before you in wide-screen close-up.

PRACTICAL INFORMATION FOR LUZERN

TOURIST OFFICE. The Luzern tourist office (Verkehrsbüro) is located at Pilatusstr. 14, CH-6002 Luzern (tel. 041–51 71 71). It is open Mon. to Fri. 8–12 and 2–6, Sat. 9–12. They can advise on city tours and excursions and have an accommodations service. They also offer guided walks of the city, Apr. through Sept., Mon. through Sat., at 10 A.M.; tours start from the tourist office.

HOTELS. Luzern has a positive surfeit of hotels in all price categories, and the visitor should have no difficulty in finding a room, even at the height of summer, when many hotels are given over to tour groups. Note that a number of hotels are closed in winter.

Nearly all the hotels in our listings have a wide range of rooms, a good many of which may well fall into a lower grading than that which we give here. The best advice is always to check beforehand with the hotel. Nearly all hotels have restaurants, and a number of the more expensive have two or three.

All hotels are obliged to give visitors a copy of the town's official tourist guide which, apart from giving details of restaurants, excursions, museums and the like, is good for reductions on some excursions and booking tennis courts.

Deluxe

Carlton Hotel Tivoli, Haldenstr. 57 (tel. 041–51 30 51). 180 beds. Lakeside hotel with considerable comfort; tennis and nightclub. Open Apr. through Nov. only. AE, DC, MC, V.

Grand Hotel National, Haldenstr. 4 (tel. 041–50 11 11). 150 beds. Superbly situated on the lakeshore; suites fit for a king, ordinary rooms for a crown prince; one of the country's very top hotels. Sauna, indoor pool, hairdresser; excellent food. AE, DC, MC, V.

Palace, Haldenstr. 10 (tel. 041–50 22 22). 300 beds. Spacious hotel that faces the lake across a tree-lined promenade; famous and luxurious. Has excellent restaurant, the *Mignon.* AE, DC, MC, V.

Schweizerhof, Schweizerhofquai 3 (tel. 041–50 22 11). 245 beds. Traditional elegance in this old, centrally located hotel; very quiet, with facilities for children. Three restaurants, of which *Rotonde* is first class. AE, DC, MC, V.

Expensive

Des Balances, Metzgerrainle 7 (tel. 041–51 18 51). 150 beds. Quiet, old-world hotel in atmospheric building; central location. AE, DC, MC, V.

Château Gütsch, Kanonenstr. (via Sentimattstr.-Kreuzstutz), tel. 041–22 02 72. 75 beds. Queen Victoria stayed in this historic hotel; very quiet with splendid views and outdoor pool. AE, DC, MC, V.

Europe Grand Hotel, Haldenstr. 59 (tel. 041–30 11 11). 300 beds. Quiet and comfortable with attractive view of the lake. Open Apr. through Oct. only. DC, MC, V.

Montana, Adligenswilerstr. 22 (tel. 041–51 65 65). 120 beds. Hillside location with magnificent views and its own private cable car; quiet and highly recommended. Open Apr. through Oct. only. AE, DC, MC, V.

Moderate

Des Alpes, Rathausquai 5 (tel. 041–51 58 25). 80 beds. Close to the river, very quiet, with good restaurant. AE, DC, MC, V.

Astoria, Pilatusstr. 29 (tel. 041–24 44 66). 250 beds. Panoramic rooftop terrace and bar; facilities for the handicapped; highly recommended. AE, DC, MC.

Flora, Seidenhofstr. 3 (tel. 041–24 44 44). 280 beds. Central but quiet; good restaurant, nightclub. AE, DC, MC, V.

Johanniter, Bundesplatz 18 (tel. 041–23 18 55). 90 beds. In historic building; sauna and fitness room. AE, DC, V.

Luzernerhof, Alpenstr. 3 (tel. 041–51 46 46). 116 beds. Central, with facilities for the handicapped, hairdresser, bar and good restaurant. AE, DC, V.

Park, Morgartenstr. 13 (tel. 041–23 92 32). 60 beds. Central, close to station, but quiet; good-value restaurant. DC, MC.

Rebstock, St.-Leodegar-Str. 3 (tel. 041–51 35 81). 50 beds. Attractive building in the heart of the Old Town by the cathedral. Has an excellent outdoor restaurant. AE, DC, MC, V.

Inexpensive

Alpina, Frankenstr. 6 (tel. 041–23 00 77). 55 beds. Basic, but conveniently located in the middle of town. AE, DC, MC, V.

Bären, Pfistergasse 8 (tel. 041–22 10 63). 50 beds. Central location; no rooms with bath; breakfast only. Open Mar. to Oct. only. AE, DC, V.

Goldener Stern, Burgerstr. 35 (tel. 041–23 08 91). 24 beds. Central, with restaurant. AE.

Kolping, Friedenstr. 8 (tel. 041–51 23 51). 180 beds. Quiet and central, suitable for families; restaurant. AE, DC, V.

Pickwick, Rathausquai 6 (tel. 041–51 59 27). 23 beds. Central, with terrace and bar; breakfast only. DC, MC, V.

Spatz, Obergrundstr. 103 (tel. 041–41 10 75). 32 beds. Breakfast only. AE, V.

SSR Touristenhotel, St.-Karli-Quai 12 (tel. 041–51 24 74). 80 beds. Central, run by Swiss Student Travel Service. AE, DC, V.

Steghof, Voltastr. 2 (tel. 041–44 43 43). 80 beds. Bar and restaurant. AE, DC, MC.

Villa Maria, Haldenstr. 36 (tel. 041–31 21 19). 20 beds. In own grounds and very quiet; breakfast only. Open Apr. to Oct. only.

Weinhof, Weystr. 12 (tel. 041–51 12 51). 54 beds. Central, with bowling and restaurant. AE, DC, V.

Weisses Kreuz, Furrengasse 19 (tel. 041–51 60 23). 25 beds. No rooms with bath or shower; very inexpensive restaurant.

RESTAURANTS. Luzern is something of a gourmet's paradise and the town fairly bristles with restaurants. The more expensive are as good as any you will find in Switzerland, while the less expensive offer extremely good value for money, frequently in highly atmospheric and always attractive surroundings. The food everywhere is excellent and our list is no more than a selection. The older part of the town in particular has many worthwhile, inexpensive spots.

Expensive

Arbalète French Restaurant, Pilatusstr. 1 (tel. 041–23 08 66). Restaurant of the hotel *Monopol.* Fine French cuisine. AE, DC, MC.

Chez Marianne, zum Raben, Kornmarkt 5 (tel. 041–51 51 35). Four excellent restaurants, all quite different in character and cuisine, in delightfully converted old building by the Old Town Hall. Highly recommended; book ahead.

Le Manoir, Bundesplatz 9 (tel. 041–23 23 48). Splendid, atmospheric French restaurant in the new part of town. Highly recommended. Closed Mon. AE, DC, V.

Le Mignon, Haldenstr. 10 (tel. 041–50 22 22). Magnificent restaurant in the *Palace* hotel. Best to book ahead.

Old Swiss House, tel. 041–51 61 71. In converted house near the Lion monument; recommended. DC, MC, V.

Le Rotonde, Schweizerhofquai 3 (tel. 041–50 22 11). Sophisticated restaurant of the *Schweizerhof* hotel, with delightful view of the lake.

Von-Pfyffer-Stube, Haldenstr. 4 (tel. 041–50 11 11). In the *Grand Hotel National;* first class.

Moderate

Le Lapin, Museggstr. 2 (tel. 041–51 52 53). In the hotel *de la Paix;* excellent food, but can be a little expensive.

Fritschi, Sternenplatz 5 (tel. 041–51 16 15). Upstairs; reader-recommended. AE, DC, V.

Kunsthaus-Kongresshaus, Bahnhofplatz (tel. 041–23 28 16). Near the boat landing stage at the Strandbad; facilities for the handicapped; attractive garden terrace. AE, DC, MC, V.

Li Tai Pe, Furrengasse 14 (tel. 041–51 10 23). Popular Chinese restaurant. AE, DC, V.

Walliser Spycher, Eisengasse 15 (tel. 041–51 29 76). In the heart of the Old Town close by the Kornmarkt; *the* place for *fondue* and *raclette.* AE, MC, V.

Wilden Mann, Bahnhofstr. 30 (tel. 041–23 16 66). Luzern's most famous restaurant, in business since 1517; in the hotel of the same name. AE, DC, V.

Inexpensive

Hubertus, Hertensteinstr. 32 (tel. 041–51 25 50). In the Old Town, atmospheric and noisy, with excellent Italian food. DC, MC, V.

Ilge, Pfistergasse 17 (tel. 041–22 09 17). Hotel restaurant; good Swiss-German food. AE, V.

Mövenpick, Pilatusstr. 14 (tel. 041–23 62 50), opposite the tourist office, and Grendelstr. 19 (tel. 041–51 52 22), in the Old Town. Both provide the traditionally reliable food expected of the chain, and also have more expensive menus. AE, DC, MC, V.

Schiff, Unter der Egg 8 (tel. 041–51 38 51). In hotel of the same name; remarkable value, highly recommended. AE, V.

Zunfthaus zu Pfistern, Kornmarkt 4 (tel. 041–51 36 50). Historic building; also has more expensive dishes. AE, DC, MC, V.

MUSEUMS AND GALLERIES. Am-Rhyn-Haus, Furrengasse 21, next to Town Hall (tel. 041–51 17 73). Built in the early 17th century by a former mayor of Luzern, this building now houses a collection of works by Picasso from the last 20 years of his life. Open Apr. to Oct., daily 10–6; Nov. to Mar., Fri. to Sun. 11–12 and 2–5.

Bourbaki Panorama, Lowenstr. 18 (tel. 041–50 22 50). Somewhat faded but still imposing painted panorama scenes from the Franco-Prussian War of 1870–71. May not be to everyone's taste. Open Mar., April and Oct. daily 9–5, May to Sept. daily 9–6.

Elektrische Modelleisenbahn (Electric Model Railway), at Dietschiberg outside town beyond the Lion Monument, and a must for train buffs. 1,000 meters (3,280 ft.) of track scaled down (1:10). Open May to mid-Oct., Tues. to Sun., 2–5 (weather permitting).

Gletschergarten (Glacier Garden), Denkmalstr. 4, by the Lion Monument (tel. 041–51 43 40). Extraordinary evidence of the glaciers that once covered the whole of the Luzern region. The attached museum has a world-famous relief of the Alps. Open May to mid-Oct., daily 8–6; Mar., Apr. and mid-Oct. to mid-Nov., daily 9–5; mid-Nov. to Feb., Tues. to Sun. 10:30–4:30.

Kunsthaus (Museum of Fine Art), Robert-Zünd-Str. 1, near rail station (tel. 041–23 10 24). Representative collection of Central Swiss art and sculptures from the Middle Ages to the present day; 19th-century Swiss landscape paintings; 19th- and 20th-century European paintings. Open Tues. and Thurs. to Sat. 10–12 and 2–5, Wed. 10–9, Sun. 10–5.

Naturhistorisches Museum (Natural History Museum), Kasernenplatz 6 (tel. 041–24 54 11). Just by the southern end of the Spreuebrücke. Attractive museum with geology, minerals, fossils, flora and fauna of Central Switzerland carefully documented and displayed. Open Tues. to Sat. 10–12 and 2–5, Sun. 10–5.

Richard Wagner Museum, Wagnerweg 27 (tel. 041–44 23 70). Delightfully located villa on the south side of the lake where the maestro lived from 1866 to 1872. Contains many mementoes of the composer and a collection of old instruments. Open mid-Apr. to mid-Oct., Tues. to Sat. 9–12 and 2–6, Sun. 10:30–12 and 2–5; winter open Tues., Thurs., Sat. and Sun.

Trachten und Heïmatmuseum (Museum of Swiss National Costume and Folklore), Utenberg (tel. 041–36 80 58). Colorful national costumes; in the same building as the Federal Yodelers' Club! Open Easter to Oct., daily 9–5:30.

Verkehrshaus (Swiss Transport Museum), Lidostr. 5 (tel. 041–31 44 44). On the north side of the lake and easily reached by public transport or on foot (about 30 minutes from the rail station). Outstandingly fine collection of rail locomotives and carriages, airplanes, cars and ships, as well as many working models. It also has Switzerland's first (and only) planetarium and a building for aerospace exhibits. Three restaurants and the Hans Erni Museum are attached. Open Mar. to Oct., daily 9–6; Nov. to Feb., daily 10–4.

SHOPPING. Luzern is proud of the fact that it has one of the finest medieval shopping centers in Europe (a boast that Bern may dispute!). The narrow, twisting cobbled streets of the Old Town are traffic-free and ideal for window shopping, whatever your taste. But be wary of souvenir shops, most of which sell overpriced and tatty goods. Try not to miss Weggisgasse, Kapellgasse and Rathausquai. On Tuesdays and Saturdays, open-air markets are held under the arcades of the Altes Rathaus (Old Town Hall), and there is a flea market every Saturday in summer on Untere Bergstrasse.

Opening hours are 8–12 and 2–6:30, 5 on Saturdays. In summer many shops also stay open later in the evenings, and open on Sunday mornings after 11 A.M.

MUSIC, MOVIES AND THEATERS. Music. The International Music Festival is held every year at the end of August, and runs for about three weeks. Performances are given mostly at the Kunsthaus. Performers are frequently world famous. For further information write *Internationale Musikfestwochen,* Postfach, CH–6002 Luzern. Concerts are also given in the Kunsthaus during the rest of the year—details from the tourist office.

Movies. Luzern has nine movie theaters. Films are almost always in the original language.

Theaters. The principle Luzern theater is the **Stadttheater,** Theaterstr. 2 (tel. 041–23 66 18/23 66 19). Performances are given in German. For details of current productions contact the tourist office.

NIGHTLIFE. Surprisingly perhaps for a town as sober as Luzern, the nightlife is pretty lively. Many of the more exotic spots are concentrated in the Old Town, an area similar to the Niederdorf in Zürich. Small discos and clubs are the norm, and, as there is little to distinguish one from another, the best bet is to walk around and see what takes your fancy. We list here some of Luzern's more long-lived and popular clubs. **San Francisco,** Haldenstr. 21 (tel. 041–51 19 61), along the north side of the lake by the cathedral, has a floor show and dancing. A successful disco is the **Disco Club,** Seidenhofstr. 3 (tel. 041–24 44 44), in the Flora hotel just off Pilatusstr., where they also present folklore shows (yodeling, accordions, and lots of thigh slapping). The **Des Alpes** hotel, Rathausquai 5 (tel. 041–51 58 25), north of the river, has a similar folklore restaurant. A more unusual folklore show is given on board the **Nightboat,** Seestr. 106 (tel. 041–47 44 46), which, as its name suggests, is a lake boat. It leaves every evening in summer from the quay by the station.

The most sophisticated nightlife in Luzern is to be found at the **Casino,** Haldenstr. 6 (tel. 041–51 27 51), on the northern shore of the lake. You can play *boule* in the Gambling Room, disco the night away in the **Black Jack** club, watch an international show in the **Red Rose** (i.e., watch a strip show) or have a meal in **Le Chalet** while watching a folklore display.

SPECIAL EVENTS. Throughout the region in summer, there are yodeling contests and other traditional gatherings. Worth seeing are the "Schwinger" festivals, where powerful locals practise a form of wrestling and contend for titles. Carnival is celebrated with fervor in Luzern and Schwyz.

SPORTS. Full details of all clubs and sports facilities are available from the tourist office. **Golf.** There is an 18-hole golf course at the Allemand, Horwerstr. 99 (tel. 041–41 23 98). Call in advance.

Tennis. Courts are available at the Lido, Haldenstr. (tel. 041–31 31 37); at the Allemand, Horwerstr. 99 (tel. 041–41 23 98); and at the Kunsteisbahn (tel. 041–44 61 66). All open Apr. through Sept. Demand for courts is great, and it is essential to book well in advance.

Swimming. You can swim in the lake at the Lido, and there are many other opportunities to swim in this spectacular stretch of water at the villages bordering it.

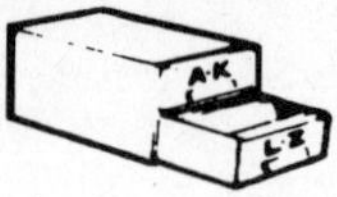

USEFUL ADDRESSES. Car Hire. *Avis,* Zürichstr. 35 (tel. 041–51 32 51); *Europcar,* Horwerstr. 81 (tel. 041–41 11 23); *Hertz,* Maihofstr. 101 (tel. 041–36 02 77).

Travel Agent. *American Express,* Schweizerhofquai 4 (tel. 041–50 11 77).

PRACTICAL INFORMATION FOR CENTRAL SWITZERLAND

TOURIST OFFICES. The principal tourist office for the whole of Central Switzerland is the Verkehrsverband Zentralschweiz, Alpenstr. 1, Luzern (tel. 041–51 18 91). The office is open Mon. to Fri. 8–12 and 2–6.

There are also local tourist offices at: **Schwyz,** Postplatz 9 (tel. 043–21 34 46); and **Zug,** Bahnhofstr. 23 (tel. 042–21 00 78). Many of the smaller towns and villages of Central Switzerland also have local information offices open in the summer only; most close at lunch.

Hotels and Restaurants

ALTDORF. *Bahnhof* (I), Bahnhofplatz 2 (tel. 044–2 10 32). 40 beds. No rooms with bath or shower; central and very inexpensive, with bowling and facilities for children. *Goldener Schlüssel* (I), Schützengasse 9 (tel. 044–2 10 02). 44 beds. Historic building in the heart of this historic town. Suitable for families, with restaurant. DC, V.

Restaurant. *Höfli* (I), Hellgasse 20 (tel. 044–2 21 97). Closed Wed.

AMSTEG. *Stern und Post* (M), Gotthardstr. (tel. 044–6 44 40). 70 beds. One-time Post House; atmospheric and good value, with hotel bar and excellent restaurant. AE, DC, MC, V.

ANDERMATT. *Krone* (M), Gotthardstr. 64 (tel. 044–6 72 06). 85 beds. Central; sauna and gymnasium. AE, DC, MC, V. *Monopol-Metropol* (M), Gotthardstr. 43 (tel. 044–6 75 75). 60 beds. Indoor pool and terrace restaurant. AE, DC, MC, V. *Bergidyll* (I), Gotthardstr. 39 (tel. 044–6 74 55). 36 beds. Central; diet meals; bar. AE, MC, V.

Restaurant. *Drei Könige* (M), Gotthardstr. 69 (tel. 044–6 72 03). Hotel restaurant. Lantern-lit grill room. Cheese, Chinese and *Bourguignonne* fondues. AE, DC, MC, V.

BRUNNEN. *Seehotel Waldstätterhof* (E), Waldstätterquai 6 (tel. 043–33 11 33). 180 beds. Lakeside location with extensive grounds; tennis, facilities for the handicapped, and good restaurant. AE, DC, MC, V. *Bellevue au Lac Kursaal* (M), Axenstr. 2 (tel. 043–31 13 18). 100 beds. On lakeside, quiet and comfortable; nightclub. AE, DC, MC, V. *Parkhotel Hellerbad* (M), tel. 043–31 16 81. 134 beds. Central but quiet, with cure facilities, tennis and gardens. AE, DC, MC, V.

Restaurant. *Weisses Rössli* (I), Bahnhofstr. 8 (tel. 043–31 10 22). Hotel restaurant. Indonesian rice specialties, fondues. MC.

BÜRGENSTOCK. *Grand Hotel* (L), tel. 041–63 25 25. 130 beds. Golf, tennis, indoor and outdoor pools, sauna, bowling; on the expensive side. Famous meeting place of the stars. AE, DC, V. *Park Hotel* (E), tel. 041–63 25 45. 100 beds. In own grounds, with many facilities including restaurant. AE, DC, V. *Waldheim* (M), tel. 041–63 23 83. 70 beds. In own grounds with great view, pool, fitness and games rooms; special food available. AE, V.

EINSIEDELN. *Drei Könige* (M), Klosterplatz (tel. 055–53 24 41). 110 beds. Nightclub, terrace restaurant. AE, MC, V. *Katharinahof* (I), Ilgenweidstr. 6 (tel. 055–53 25 08). 58 beds. Central but very quiet hotel in own grounds; sauna. Open Mar. to Nov. AE, DC, MC, V. *Pfauen am Klosterplatz* (I), Hauptstr. 89 (tel. 055–53 45 45). 40 beds. Centrally located. AE, DC, MC, V. *St. Josef* (I), Ilgenweidstr. 2 (tel. 055–53 21 51). 26 beds. Small and central. Open March to Oct. only. *Storchen* (I), Hauptstr. 79 (tel. 055–53 37 60). 60 beds. Central and quiet. AE, DC, MC, V.

ENGELBERG. *Ring-Hotel* (E), Schwandstr. 91 (tel. 041–94 18 22). 110 beds. *Bellevue Terminus* (M), Bahnhofplatz (tel. 041–94 12 13). 120 beds. Quiet, in own grounds with tennis court. AE, DC, MC, V. *Crystal* (M), Dorfstr. (tel. 041–94 21 22). 45 beds. Central and quiet, family hotel. AE, DC, MC, V. Good family hotel in own grounds. AE, DC, MC, V. *Alpenklub* (I), Dorfstr. 5 (tel. 041–94 12 43). 16 beds. Central and rather superior (I) hotel. Nightclub; breakfast only. AE, DC.

Restaurant. *Hess* (I–M), Dorfstr. 50 (tel. 041–94 13 66). Good hotel-restaurant. DC.

FLÜELEN. *Flüelerhof-Grill Rustico* (I), Axenstr. 38 (tel. 044–2 11 49). 45 beds. Quiet, with great views; grill restaurant. DC, V. *Hostellerie Sternen* (I), Axenstr. 6 (tel. 044–2 18 35). 30 beds. Central and quiet. AE, V. *Tourist* (I), Höhenstr. 32 (tel. 044–2 15 91). 70 beds. Historic building beside lake; facilities for the handicapped. AE, DC, V.

GERSAU. *Seehof-du-Lac* (M), tel. 041–84 12 45. 35 beds. Lakeside location with restaurant. *Beau-Rivage* (I), Seestr. 38 (tel. 041–84 12 23). 55 beds. Central, with pool, gym and terrace restaurant. AE, MC, V.

HERGISWIL. *Belvedere AG am See* (M), Seestr. 18 (tel. 041–95 01 01). 100 beds. Very quiet lakeside hotel in own grounds. AE, DC, MC, V. *Pilatus am See* (M), Seestr. 34 (tel. 041–95 15 55). 100 beds. Large lakeside hotel with indoor pool and sauna. AE, DC, V.

KUSSNACHT AM RIGI. *Engel* (I), Hauptplatz 1 (tel. 041–81 10 57). 20 beds. Centrally located, once the town hall (dates from 15th century) and meeting place of the local parliaments. Open March to Nov. only. AE, DC, V. *Seehotel Drei Könige* (I), Luzernerstr. 35 (tel. 041–81 10 69). 22 beds. Very quiet and inexpensive, with tennis and sailing; restaurant. AE, DC, V.

MELCHSEE-FRUTT. *Glogghuis* (M), tel. 041–67 11 39. 140 beds. Central, quiet, with indoor pool, sauna and fitness room, tennis; bar. *Reinhard am See* (M), tel. 041–67 12 25. 130 beds. Lakeside hotel with skating and curling in winter; nightclub and grill. Closed Oct., Nov., May and June. AE, DC, MC, V.

OBERIBERG. *Posthotel* (M), tel. 055–56 11 72. 60 beds. In own grounds, comfortable; nightclub. AE, DC, MC, V.

PILATUS. *Bellevue* (I), tel. 041–96 12 55. 50 beds. Near the summit of the mountain at about 2,000 meters (nearly 7,000 ft.), so very quiet (as may be imagined). AE, V. *Pilatus-Kulm* (I), tel. 041–96 12 55. 40 beds. Almost as high up the mountain. AE, V.

RIGI. *Bellevue* (M), tel. 041–83 13 51. 85 beds. At Rigi-Kaltbad, with fantastic view. AE, V. *Hostellerie Rigi* (M), tel. 041–83 16 16. 115 beds. Also at Rigi-Kaltbad, with indoor pool, sauna, tennis, bowling, and restaurant with similarly fine view. AE, DC, MC, V. *Rigi Kulm* (I), tel. 041–83 13 12. At the summit (1,800 meters, 5,906 ft.).

SCHWYZ. *Wysses Rössli* (M), Hauptplatz 3 (tel. 043–21 19 22). 46 beds. Centrally located historic building. AE, DC, MC, V. *Hirschen* (I), Hinterdorfstr. 14 (tel. 043–21 12 76). 26 beds. Small and central. AE, DC.

SEELISBERG. *Bellevue* (M), tel. 043–31 16 26. 75 beds. Very quiet hotel in own grounds with sauna and special facilities for the handicapped. AE, V.

STANS. *Regina* (I), Bahnhofstr. 2 (tel. 041–61 31 73). 25 beds. Central, breakfast only. *Stanserhof* (I), Stansstaderstr. 20a (tel. 041–61 41 22). 55 beds. Comfortable, well-equipped hotel; bowling.

STOOS. *Sporthotel Stoos* (M), tel. 043–21 15 05. 110 beds. Indoor pool, tennis, ice rink; suitable for families, with facilities for children. AE, DC, MC, V. *Klingenstock* (I), tel. 043–21 52 12. 45 beds.

VITZNAU. *Park-Hotel* (L), Kantonsstr. (tel. 041–83 13 22). 170 beds. Sophisticated, very comfortable lakeside hotel, with waterskiing, tennis, indoor pool and sauna. V. *Seehotel Vitznauerhof* (M), Hauptstr. (tel. 041–83 13 15). 100 beds. Very quiet lakeside hotel in own grounds, with tennis and facilities for the handicapped. AE, DC, MC, V. *Alpenrose* (I), Hauptstr. (tel. 041–83 13 77). 60 beds. Comfortable, beside lake; with bowls. Open April to Dec. only. AE, DC, MC, V. *Schiff* (I), Husenboden (tel. 041–83 13 57). 16 beds. No rooms with bath or shower. Also on lake, small hotel with nightclub.

WEGGIS. *Albana* (E), Luzernerstr. (tel. 041–93 21 41). 100 beds. Lakeside location; ideal family hotel. Open March to Oct. AE, DC, V. *Beau-Rivage* (E), Gotthardstr. (tel. 041–93 14 22). 80 beds. Many facilities, including pool; reader-recommended. Open April to Oct. AE, DC, V. *Park* (E), Hertensteinstr. (tel. 041–93 13 13). 105 beds. Beautiful location in lakeside park, with boating, swimming and tennis. Open April to Oct. AE, V.

Central am See (M), tel. 041–93 12 52. 70 beds. Smack on lake, with heated pool; excellent value; editor-recommended. AE, DC, V. *Rigi am See* (M), Seestr. (tel. 041–93 21 51). 60 beds. Comfortable hotel by lake. Open April to Oct. V. *Rössli* (M), Ägeristr. 2 (tel. 041–93 11 06). 60 beds. Central, but with very quiet rooms; facilities for the handicapped; grill restaurant. AE.

ZUG. *City Hotel Ochsen* (M), Kolinplatz (tel. 042–21 32 32). 72 beds. In the heart of town, in historic building. AE, V. *Rosenberg* (M), Rosenbergstr. 33 (tel. 042–21 43 43). 60 beds. Quiet, in own grounds with good view. AE, V.

Restaurants. *Aklin* (I–E), Am Zytturm (tel. 042–21 18 66). Excellent. AE, DC, MC, V. *Hirschen* (I–M), Zeugstr. 11 (tel. 042–21 29 30). AE, DC, MC, V.

GETTING AROUND. By Train and Bus. The whole area has many railways, some part of the national system, others privately owned, as well as numerous mountain and cable railways, plus funiculars. Add to this the excellent post-bus routes and the Luzern city transport and there is no problem in getting about.

The Regional Holiday Season Ticket, issued in summer by the transport companies of the area, is valid for 15 days. With this, you have unlimited travel for five days, and pay half-fare for the other ten—ideal for sightseeing.

By Car. The road network around the Vierwaldstättersee is excellent, and there are motorways running the length of the southern side of the lake and extending north to Schwyz and Zug. All secondary roads are good, and many provide spectacular views. The remarkable Seelisberg and St. Gotthard road tunnels (nine kms. and 17 kms.—six and eleven miles—long respectively), opened in 1980, have enormously speeded up access across the Alps to southern Switzerland; there are no toll charges. But the roads can get very busy.

By Boat. The Vierwaldstättersee has a very good network of steamers with a couple of old-timer paddlesteamers still going strong. They connect virtually every community on the lakeside. The larger boats have full restaurant facilities and even most of the smaller ones offer refreshments. As elsewhere in Switzerland, they link, where practical, with both the train and post-bus services. The roundtrip/excursion tickets offer best value for money. Services are frequent in the peak season with, for example, hourly departures from Luzern, but in the off-peak season services are limited so check on availability when you arrive.

Sightseeing Data

ALTDORF. Historisches Museum (Historical Museum), Gotthardstr. 18 (tel. 044–2 19 06). Local art, weapons, textiles. Open Easter to Sept., Tues. to Sun. 9–11 and 1–5.

BÜRGLEN. Tell Museum, tel. 044–2 41 55. Documents, exhibits and art connected with William Tell.

EINSIEDELN. Kloster (monastery). Open daily 1:30–6.

GELFINGEN. Schloss Heidegg (Heidegg castle), tel. 041–85 13 25. 12th-century castle with three floors of 17th- and 18th-century furnishings; chapel and rose garden. Open Apr. to Oct., daily 9–12, 1:30–5, closed Mon. mornings.

MUOTATAL. Höllochhöhlen (Hölloch Caves). Bus from Brunnen or Schwyz. Subterranean gorges, rock formations and glacier patterns. Tours from Easter through Oct., daily at 10, 11, 1, 2, 3 and 4.

SCHWYZ. Bundesbriefarchiv (Archives of the Federal Charters), tel. 043–24 11 24. In town center. Original documents of the Confederation dating from 1291 to 1513, including the Letter of Alliance, regarded as Switzerland's foundation charter. Open daily 9:30–11:30 and 2–5.

STANS. Historisches Museum (Historical Museum), Stansstaderstr. (tel. 041–61 17 81). Paintings, religious items, costumes and weapons. Open mid-Mar. to Oct., Wed. to Mon. 9–11 and 2–5.

ZUG. In der Burg Museum, Kirchenstr. 11 (tel. 042–25 32 97). Collections in historic fortress, including religious art, crafts and tools. Open Tues. to Fri. 2–5, Thurs. 7 P.M.–9 P.M., Sat. and Sun. 10–12 and 2–5.

WINTER SPORTS. With the exception of Andermatt, Engelberg and Stoos, the ski resorts of Central Switzerland attract relatively few foreign visitors. They are primarily nonfashionable, inexpensive resorts jammed at weekends with Swiss from nearby Luzern and Zürich. But during the week you can enjoy unbelievable freedom on the slopes and skilifts. However, beware Saturdays, Sundays and holidays unless skiing means so much that you are prepared to wait an hour or more for a cable car or lift. Because of the relative lack of elevation, some resorts (Andermatt, Engelberg, Melchsee-Frutt and, possibly, Stoos excepted) have a fairly short winter season.

Andermatt, 1,450 meters (4,750 ft.); 2 cable cars, 6 lifts, 43 kms. (27 miles) of downhill runs, 20 kms. (12 miles) of cross-country trails; tobogganing, curling, skating. Ski schools.

Einsiedeln, 915 meters (3,000 ft.); 6 lifts, 3.5 kms. (2 miles) of downhill runs, 45 kms. (28 miles) of cross-country trails, 16 kms. (10 miles) of ski-hiking trails, 2 kms. of tobogganing tracks; curling. Ski schools.

Engelberg, 1,030 meters (3,380 ft.); 2 funicular railways, 7 cable cars, 15 lifts, 45 kms. (28 miles) of downhill runs, 23 kms. (14 miles) of cross-country trails, 3.5 kms. (2 miles) of toboggan runs, skating. Ski schools.

Hoch-Ybrig, 1,050–2,200 meters (3,445–7,218 ft.); 15 cable cars and lifts, 50 kms. (31 miles) of downhill runs, 30 kms. (17 miles) of cross-country trails, night skiing. Ski school.

Hospental, 1,435 meters (4,715 ft.); 1 lift, 8 kms. (5 miles) of downhill runs, 16 kms. (10 miles) of cross-country trails. Ski school (downhill).

Luzern, 450 meters (1,470 ft.); a big center for sightseeing and nightlife, but limited to curling and skating as far as outdoor winter sports go.

Lungern, 725 meters (2,380 ft.); 2 cable cars, 2 lifts, 8 kms. (5 miles) of downhill runs, 6 kms. (4 miles) of cross-country trails, tobogganing, skating. Ski schools.

Melchsee, 1,920 meters (6,300 ft.); 2 cable cars, 5 lifts, 32 kms. (20 miles) of downhill runs, 18 kms. (11 miles) of cross-country trails, 10 kms. (6 miles) of ski-hiking trails. Ski schools.

Oberiberg, 1,130 meters (3,700 ft.); 1 cable car, 3 lifts, 5 kms. (3 miles) of downhill runs, 2 kms. of cross-country trails, 15 kms. (9 miles) of ski-hiking trails.

Rigi, 1,310 meters (4,300 ft.); 2 funicular railways, 2 cable cars, 5 lifts, 25 kms. (16 miles) of downhill runs, 14 kms. (9 miles) of cross-country trails, 5 kms. (3 miles) of ski-hiking trails, curling, ski bob. Ski schools.

Schwyz, 520 meters (1,700 ft.); 3 cable cars, 9 lifts, 50 kms. (31 miles) of downhill trails, 8 kms. (5 miles) of cross-country tracks, 6 kms. (4 miles) of ski-hiking trails, tobogganing. Ski schools.

Sörenberg, 1,666 meters (5,465 ft.); 2 cable cars, numerous lifts, 43 kms. (27 miles) of downhill trails, 25 kms. (16 miles) of cross-country tracks.

Stoos, 1,310 meters (4,300 ft.); 1 cable car, 6 lifts, 15 kms. (9 miles) of downhill trails, 8 kms. (5 miles) of cross-country tracks, 3 kms. (2 miles) of ski-hiking trails, curling. Ski schools.

Wilen-Sarnen, 485 meters (1,600 ft.); a cross-country ski center—15 kms. (9 miles) of trails for both cross-country and ski-hiking. Cross-country ski school.

Zug, 435 meters (1,430 ft.); 9 kms. (6 miles) of cross-country trails, 17 kms. (11 miles) of ski-hiking trails, curling. Ski schools.

BASEL

Enlightened City of Commerce

The significance of Basel—a significance out of all proportion to its modest population of 178,000—can be gauged almost immediately by a glance at a map of Europe. For the city lies at the meeting point of Germany, France and Switzerland, straddling the river Rhine where it bends north to flow between Germany and France to Holland and the North Sea. Basel, in other words, enjoys the well-nigh unique combination of proximity to two great European countries *and* a strategic location on northern Europe's most important waterway.

The Rhine has long explained the city's mercantile importance. Today, half of Switzerland's imports come through Basel and, believe it or not, Basel is also headquarters of the country's ocean-going merchant navy, all 30 ships of it. (Jokes about Switzerland's navy are legion, but, possibly adding credence to the belief that the Swiss can make any commercial venture viable, landlocked Switzerland ranks 66th among the world's maritime nations). Needless to say, however, it is the traffic up and down the Rhine itself that is of crucial importance to the Swiss, and Basel in particular. More than 400 Rhine cargo boats are registered in the city, while some eight million tonnes of cargo pass through Basel annually. The city is more than just a staging post, however. There is considerable industry here, not that you'd know it walking through the spotlessly neat industrial area. Among the major industrial concerns here are three of the world's most important chemical companies: Ciba-Geigy, Hoffman-La Roche, and Sandoz.

This being Switzerland, hand in hand with all this commerce goes finance. Though not on the scale of Zürich, Basel is still a financial and banking center of international significance. And central to the city's financial doings is the Bank of International Settlements. Here, every month the world's bankers meet, in secret, to discuss the latest global financial news.

But commerce is only half of what makes Basel tick. The closeness of France and Germany has always given the city an international and cosmopolitan flavor. 17,000 French and German commuters cross daily into Basel. Likewise, the Baslers think nothing of whipping across the frontiers to have lunch in a French restaurant or a German inn. In a similar vein, Basel's airport—Mulhouse—is actually in France, while both France and Germany have rail stations in Basel, with all the appropriate customs and immigration facilities. Symbol of this tri-national relationship is the Dreiländerpfahl, literally the "three-country-post," a rocket-like construction by the Rhine marking the spot where France, Germany and Switzerland meet. Walk round it and in half-a-dozen steps you'll have been in three countries.

It may well be this international quality that accounts for the third and, in many ways, the most interesting characteristic of Basel: her long and distinguished intellectual and artistic heritage. Indeed, Basel legitimately lays claim to the title of intellectual capital of Switzerland. For many centuries, the city's wealth has been channeled into supporting the arts and sciences, as the extensive network of museums, all originally enriched by private collections, makes clear. The oldest university in Switzerland, founded in 1460, is here. Likewise, Basel boasts the oldest publicly owned art collection in Europe; this dates from 1661 and contains the largest collection of paintings by Holbein the Younger in the world. Today, this priceless collection is in the Kunstmuseum, Basel's art museum. This tradition of municipal patronage has continued into the present. In the '60s the Baslers voted to buy two pictures by Picasso for the then princely sum of nearly nine million francs. (The painter was so delighted by this generosity that he gave several more works to the city.) These too are in the Kunstmuseum.

Basel Background

It all began about 2,000 years ago. The Celts were the first people to settle here, building a small settlement on the hill where the Münster, Basel's cathedral, now stands. In 44 B.C. the Romans planned to establish a town at the site of the present city of Augst, 12 kms. (seven miles) east of Basel. The murder of Julius Caesar delayed the project until A.D. 15 but on its completion it was called Colonia Augusta Raurica.

By the 3rd century A.D. the Romans had moved their town to the site of the Münster, the better to defend themselves against attack by maurauding German tribes. A Roman document dating from 374 records the name of the town as Basilia. In 401, however, the Romans abandoned Basilia, driven away by the increasingly aggressive Germans. Despite the growing spread of Christianity—by the early 5th century Basel had a bishop—it was not until Henry II, Holy Roman Emperor, took Basel under his wing in the 11th century and incorporated it into the Holy Roman Empire, that stability returned.

Henry built the original cathedral—on the site of a church which had been destroyed by a raiding band of Hungarian horsemen in 916—and established Basel as one of the centers of his court. In 1006 the bishop of Basel was made ruler of the town, and throughout the Middle Ages these prince-bishops gained, and exerted, enormous temporal, as well as spiritual, power. Today, Basel's flag, with its black bishop's staff, is a potent reminder of the long years when these powerful lords of the church governed from the Münster.

All the while, however, the city's traders and merchants profited from Basel's strategic site on the Rhine, enriching the town and themselves and slowly prising loose the restrictive hold of the city's prince-bishops. But more than trade flowed up and down the Rhine. As Basel became rich in commerce, so she also became rich in ideas. Geography had long since made the city a natural meeting point, for thinkers and politicians as much as for merchants. And in 1431 this status was officially recognized, so to speak, when the Council of Basel, an ecumenical conference on church reform, was convened in the city. It was to last a full 17 years. During it, Basel consolidated her role as an intellectual and political center of European significance as secular and ecclesiastical princes alike poured into the city.

Among those attending the conference was one Enea Silvio Piccolomini, later Pope Pius II. It was he who, as Pope, gave permission for the university to be built. With it, Basel's leading role as an intellectual center was assured.

The 100 years or so from the calling of the Council in fact marked a highwater mark in the city's intellectual affairs. And it was a glorious period. Basel became one of, if not the, leading centers of Renaissance thought and art north of the Alps. Artists such as Konrad Witz, Dürer, Urs Graf and Holbein the Younger all lived and worked in the city for varying periods. Similarly, numerous philosophers, the great Dutch humanist Erasmus chief among them, settled in the city. And all the while Basel grew rich on the swelling crest of Renaissance trade.

Union with the Swiss Confederation in 1501 and the adoption of the teachings of the Reformation some 30 years later further strengthened the city's security and prosperity: the former because by now the armies of the Confederation had more than demonstrated their superiority over the Holy Roman Empire; the latter because newly Protestant Basel welcomed a flood of Protestant refugees from Italy, France and Holland who brought with them the silk-weaving skills that made Basel a prosperous textile center.

The Thirty Years War in the 17th century—a cataclysmic religious struggle that devastated vast areas of Germany—though potentially disastrous for Basel and the Swiss was, perhaps characteristically, turned to shrewd advantage by Switzerland, a process in which Basel, in the person of her Lord Mayor, played a leading role. Having managed to avoid being sucked into the war, the Swiss were nonetheless invited to the peace negotiations by the victorious French, whose armies had been greatly assisted by Swiss mercenaries. Johann Rudolf

Wettstein, Basel's Lord Mayor, managed to obtain from both the Habsburgs and the French formal recognition of Swiss neutrality. He argued that Switzerland's central location in Europe and consequent control of numerous strategic rivers—the Rhine of course included—and Alpine passes was such as to make her guaranteed neutrality vital to the stability and prosperity not only of Switzerland but of Europe as a whole. Thus was Switzerland's legendary neutrality confirmed.

Basel's happy path to greater prosperity continued largely unchecked through the 18th and into the 19th centuries, the French Revolution and Napoleonic wars notwithstanding. Indeed perhaps the only setback of consequence suffered by Basel was the granting of independence to the rural areas around the city in 1833. This made Baselstadt—the city canton of Basel itself—the smallest canton in Switzerland at 37 square kms. (14 square miles). This decision to make what is now Baselland an independent territory—or at least a half-canton with divided political representation at national level—is one the city came to regret. Nonetheless, despite attempts by Basel at reunification, the people of Baselland have clung to their independence.

Today, though the third most important financial and banking center in Switzerland (after Zürich and Geneva) and home to the second most important bank in the country, it is the chemical and pharmaceutical industries on which the city's prosperity rests. Here again Basel's intellectual tradition has played a significant role. Basel university has always had a reputation as a center of innovation and research, ever since, indeed, it was visited by Paracelsus in 1526. Enormous sums are spent on research by the chemical companies, research that has sustained their leading roles in biotechnology today and that has helped make Basel the second most important economic center in Switzerland after Zürich.

Exploring Basel

Basel is a city with an atmosphere entirely its own. Perhaps, the best way to capture it is to sit at a terrace cafe beside the Rhine or stroll along the tree-lined Rheinweg, a pleasant riverside esplanade backed by elegant old houses pressed one against the other. Look across the great river as it swirls through the heart of the city. You'll notice the odd little gondola-like ferryboats, attached to a high wire, crossing silently from shore to shore, powered only by the swift current of the river. Silhouetted against the sky are the pencil-thin towers of the Münster, Basel's cathedral; behind and around it a maze of pretty old lanes and busy streets.

Begin your exploration at the tourist office, down the hill from the Münster at Blumenrain 2, in the Old Town. The whole of the Old Town lies in Gross-Basel, or Greater Basel, the commercial, cultural and intellectual center. The opposite, east, bank is Klein-Basel, Little Basel, a tiny Swiss enclave surrounded entirely by German territory, and the industrial quarter of the city.

Six bridges link the two halves of the city. The most historic, just around the corner from the tourist office, is the Mittlere Rheinbrücke, the Middle Rhine Bridge. At its western end, by a cafe, is a facsimile

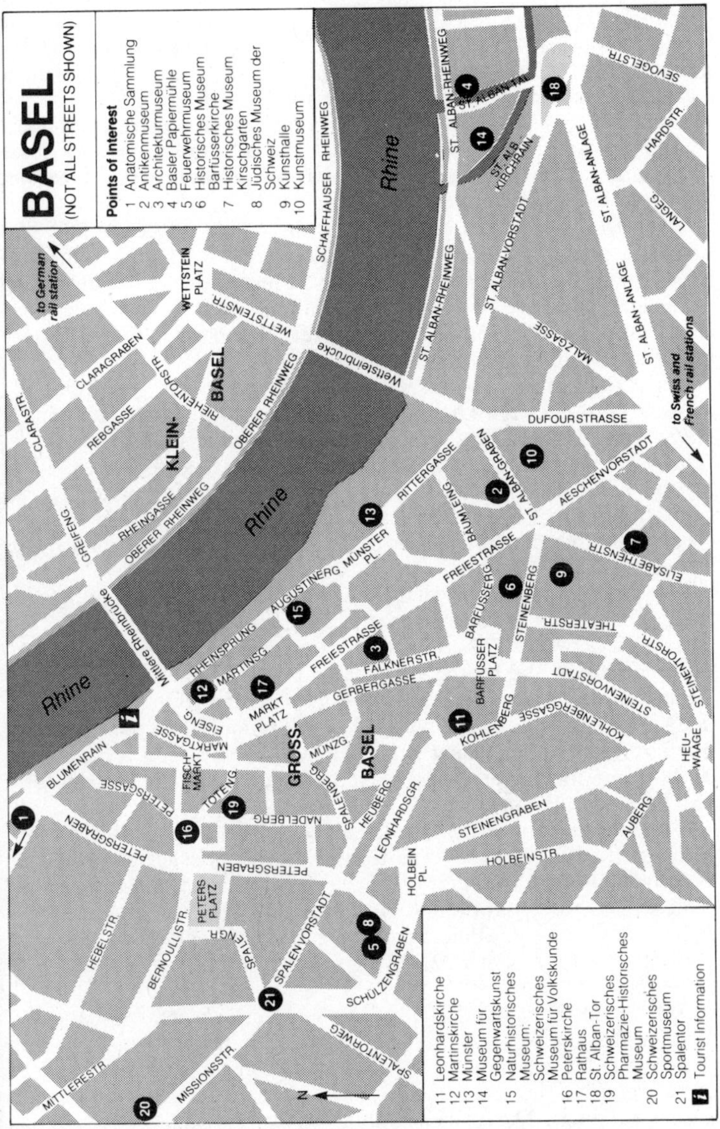
BASEL
(NOT ALL STREETS SHOWN)
Points of Interest
1 Anatomische Sammlung
2 Antikenmuseum
3 Architekturmuseum
4 Basler Papiermühle
5 Feuerwehrmuseum
6 Historisches Museum Barfüsserkirche
7 Historisches Museum Kirschgarten
8 Jüdisches Museum der Schweiz
9 Kunsthalle
10 Kunstmuseum
11 Leonhardskirche
12 Martinskirche
13 Münster
14 Museum für Gegenwartskunst
15 Naturhistorisches Museum; Schweizerisches Museum für Volkskunde
16 Peterskirche
17 Rathaus
18 St. Alban-Tor
19 Schweizerisches Pharmazie-Historisches Museum
20 Schweizerisches Sportmuseum
21 Spalentor
Tourist Information
Rhine
KLEIN-
BASEL
GROSS-
BASEL
to German rail station
to Swiss and French rail stations
Mittlere Rheinbrücke
Wettsteinbrücke
WETTSTEIN PLATZ
WETTSTEINSTR.
CLARASTR.
CLARAGRABEN
REBGASSE
RIEHENTORSTR.
GREIFENG.
RHEINGASSE
OBERER RHEINWEG
SCHAFFHAUSER RHEINWEG
ST. ALBAN-RHEINWEG
ST. ALBAN-TAL
ST. ALB. KIRCHRAIN
ST. ALBAN-VORSTADT
ST. ALBAN-ANLAGE
SEVOGELSTR.
HARDSTR.
LANGEG.
MALZGASSE
DUFOURSTRASSE
RITTERGASSE
BAUMLEING.
ST. ALBANGRABEN
AESCHENVORSTADT
ELISABETHENSTR.
FREIESTRASSE
MUNSTER PL.
AUGUSTINERG.
RHEINSPRUNG
MARTINSG.
FALKNERSTR.
GERBERGASSE
BARFÜSSERG.
STEINENBERG
THEATERSTR.
BARFUSSER PLATZ
STEINENVORSTADT
STEINENTORSTR.
KOHLENBERG
KOHLENBERGGASSE
HEUWAAGE
MARKT PLATZ
EISENG.
MARKTGASSE
BLUMENRAIN
FISCHMARKT
TOTENG.
MUNZG.
SPALENBERG
HEUBERG
LEONHARDSGR.
NADELBERG
PETERSGASSE
PETERSGRABEN
PETERS PLATZ
STEINENGRABEN
HOLBEINSTR.
HOLBEIN PL.
AUBERG
HEBELSTR.
BERNOULLISTR.
SPALENG.
SPALENVORSTADT
SCHÜTZENGRABEN
SPALENTORWEG
MISSIONSSTR.
MITTLERESTR.
N

of the notorious Lällekönig, the "Tongue King." He stares fiercely across the river at Klein-Basel, sticking out his tongue at it. The Lällekönig doesn't have it all his own way, mind you. Every year during Klein-Basel's Vogel Gryff festival, a bird-like figure dances onto the bridge and gives the Lällekönig a view of his backside. Festivals play an important part in the life of Basel, particularly the riotous Fasnacht celebration in February or March. Beginning at 4 A.M. with a burst of drums and pipes, the town is transformed as groups in grotesquely beautiful costumes take to the streets. The celebrations last for three days and combine ceremony and carnival in about equal measure, albeit with a strongly satirical twist.

Back to the sightseeing: walk onto the Mittlere Rheinbrücke and there's a sweeping view of the Rhine, bordered by the many medival buildings of the Old Town. Retrace your steps and turn left up a steep little alley called the Rheinsprung. Climb up the hill toward the Münster past 15th- and 16th-century houses. Number 11 housed Basel's university when it was first founded in 1460.

Turn right at Archivgasslein and you come to Martinskirche, the church of St. Martin. Outside it, there's a typical Basel fountain. It dates from the 16th century and depicts a warrior dressed for battle. The Martinskirche is a late Gothic building, dating from 1451. Parts of the lower section of the tower, however, are from the original church, built in 1225, making it the oldest parish church in the city. Today, the church, with its near perfect acoustics, is used primarily for concerts.

Head along the Martinsgasse, on your left, to the elegant courtyards of the Blaues and Weisses Haus, the Blue and the White House. They were built between 1762 and 1768 for two of the city's most successful silk merchants, the brothers Lukas and Jakob Sarasin. In 1777 the Emperor Joseph II of Austria was a guest in the Blue House. But in 1814 even this was topped when Czar Alexander of Russia, Emperor Franz of Austria and King Friedrich Wilhelm of Prussia met in the Blue House for dinner. There's another fine view of the houses from the Rheinsprung alley.

From here, turn left and you arrive at the Augustinergasse. At number 2 is the entrance to both the Naturhistorisches Museum, the Natural History Museum, and the Schweizerisches Museum für Volkskunde, the Swiss Ethnological Museum. The latter houses one of the world's foremost ethnological collections, though sadly only a selection of the museum's 32,000 objects can be displayed at any one time.

The Augustinergasse leads on to the Münsterplatz, the cathedral square. It's one of the most satisfying architectural ensembles in Europe, its fine townhouses set well back from the striking red of the cathedral. The present cathedral stands on the site of a number of earlier buildings. The earliest church was Carolingian, built in the 9th century. This was destroyed in 917 when Basel was sacked by the Hungarians. It was replaced by an Ottonian building, of which several traces have been found. This in turn was replaced by a more substantial cathedral built by Henry II, Holy Roman Emperor, and consecrated in 1019. In the 12th century Henry's church was itself replaced by the present late-Romanesque, or pre-Gothic, building.

As happened to most of Europe's great cathedrals, substantial sections of the building were rebuilt over the centuries as tastes changed or, occasionally, fires or other disasters destroyed parts of it. Thus the main entrance and outer aisles were rebuilt in the Gothic period, as were the towers and the choir following an earthquake in 1356. The facade of the north transept, by contrast, St. Gall's Door or the Galluspforte, looks much as it did when first built 800 years ago. It is, in fact, one of the oldest carved portals in German-speaking Europe. Inside, look for the impressive tomb of Queen Anna and her son Charles, dating from around 1285, the font, dating from 1465, and the pulpit, 1485. Also of interest are the tomb of Erasmus, and the medieval murals in the crypt. A magnificent view rewards those energetic enough to climb up the tower.

Fountains, Museums and Churches

From the Münsterplatz, head down the Rittergasse, past its elegant villas and courtyards, to a crossroads. Ahead of you is St. Alban-Vorstadt. This leads to the St. Alban-Tor, one of the original medieval city gates, parts of which date from the 13th century. Running off St. Alban-Vorstadt and leading down to the Rhine is St. Alban-Rheinweg. At number 60 is the Museum für Gegenwartskunst, the Museum of Contemporary Art. The museum was the gift of Hoffman-La Roche heir Maja Sacher, a Swiss Peggy Guggenheim. The collections are essential viewing for anyone with a taste for contemporary art. (Intriguingly, the building, partly set in an atmospheric 19th-century factory, has a stream flowing through it).

Another of the small streets running off the Rittergasse, St. Alban-Graben, contains the Kunstmuseum, Basel's justifiably celebrated art museum. The museum is probably most famous for its collection of Old Masters, including of course the collection donated to Basel in 1661 by Basilius Amerbach—the Amerbach Kabinett—which contains the world's largest collection of paintings by Hans Holbein the Younger. But the Kunstmuseum has also benefited greatly from donations by other prominent Baslers down the years. For a museum of its size, the collections are astonishingly rich. Of equal interest are the 20th-century collections, with Picasso, Braque, Gris, Léger, the German expressionists, American abstract expressionists and many others strongly represented.

Head on to the next crossroads. Here too you are faced with a choice. Straight ahead, at Steinenberg 7, is the Kunsthalle, the Basel Art Gallery. This presents regular exhibits of high quality by contemporary artists. Ask at the tourist office to find out what's showing. Just beyond is the Carnival Fountain. A number of Swiss cities—Zürich, Bern, and Basel among them—are filled with delightful medieval and Renaissance fountains. In the '60s, Basel not unreasonably decided to continue the tradition by commissioning a brand new fountain from Swiss sculptor Jean Tinguely. Characteristically, the maverick Swiss artist created a delightful and witty assembly of moving objects from old scrap metal and, seemingly, anything else he could lay his hands on.

Alternatively, rather than heading down Steinenberg, you can try Elisabethenstrasse, site of the Haus zum Kirschgarten at number 27, otherwise known as the Historisches Museum Kirschgarten. The mansion that forms the museum contains interiors from other 18th- and 19th-century houses, as well as fine collections of porcelain, silver, glass, and many other objets d'art.

However, if you can avoid the temptations of the Kunsthalle, Tinguely and the Haus zum Kirschgarten, it's probably best to continue your exploration of the Old Town by turning right into Freiestrasse, one of the major shopping streets in Basel, and from there left into the Barfüssergasse.

Dominating the Barfüsserplatz is a church, the Barfüsserkirche, or, poetically, the Bare Feet Church. Today, it is the Historisches Museum, Basel's History Museum. It's not the first church on this site. That was built around 1250 by the Franciscans who had just settled in Basel. But it was destroyed in a fire in 1298. The present building dates from the following century, the 14th. Some 500 years later it was deconsecrated and suffered the ignominy of becoming a warehouse. But in 1894 it was granted a new lease of life when it was turned into a museum. Generally felt to be one of the most important and beautiful Franciscan buildings north of the Alps, the church's harmonious interior provides a perfect setting for the many fascinating objects that chart the city's history from the Celts to the present. Among the collections is the Münster treasury, the richest and most valuable in Switzerland.

Just above the Barfüsserplatz is the Leonhardskirche, the church of St. Leonard, reached through a tree-lined churchyard. The body of the church is late Gothic but the crypt is Romanesque, some 900 years old. Interestingly, the west end of the church is built into the medieval city walls.

Continuing along the Heuberg street you enter one of the loveliest sections of old Basel. A network of small roads and alleys thread through the quarter, lined with charming houses from many periods: Gothic, Renaissance, Baroque and Biedermeier. To the left, where the Heuberg joins Spalenvorstadt, is the Holbein Fountain. Created by an unknown 16th-century stonemason, it depicts a group of dancing farmers—the figures were copied from a drawing by Holbein, hence the name—while above is a bagpipe player, a figure copied from an engraving by Dürer. As with most of the city's historic fountains, the original has had to be moved to the shelter of the History Museum to avoid the ravages of pollution; this fountain is only a replica.

The Spalenvorstadt leads to the 14th-century Spalentor, another of the city's medieval city gates. Spalengraben leads from here past the university buildings to Petersplatz, site of the Peterskirche, the church of St. Peter. Parts of the building date from the 13th century, the choir and the central west door among them.

Round the back of the Peterskirche is an alley, the Totengässlein. It leads to the Marktplatz, the heart of Basel, but is also interesting as the site of the Schweizerisches Pharmazie-Historisches Museum, a museum dedicated to the evolution of the Swiss pharmaceutical industry.

Marktplatz

The Marktplatz, no less perhaps than the Münsterplatz, lays claim to being the historic heart of Basel. Towering over it all is the Rathaus, the town hall, an exotic early-Renaissance pile built to honor the city's entry into the Swiss Confederation in 1501 (though only the middle section of the tri-partite facade was actually built then, between 1504 and 1514 to be exact). A massive clock with figures of the Madonna, the Emperor Henry II and his wife Kunigunde adorns the center of the facade, while all around are a series of colorful and decorative frescoes, the work of Hans Bock who painted them between 1608 and 1611. They extend into the inner courtyard and into the reception hall of the Council Chamber, the Regierungsratsaal. Also running around the courtyard are a series of inscriptions, one declaring ringingly "Freiheit ist über Silber und Gold"—Freedom is above silver and gold, not a sentiment likely to impress the Swiss banking community.

The Marktplatz itself, lined with shops and restaurants, is still the scene of a lively market most mornings when the Baslers come to buy vegetables, fruit and flowers. Also here is the Geltenzunft, the wine merchants' guildhall. Built between 1562 and 1578, it is one of only a handful of genuine Renaissance buildings in the city.

Leading off the Marktplatz are the Freiestrasse and Gerbergasse, two of Basel's major shopping streets. On the opposite side of the square is the Marktgasse, an alley that leads to the Fischmarkt, site of the medieval city's fishmarket. Today, it is known principally for its fountain, though, again, the original is in the History Museum. It depicts the Virgin Mary, St. Peter and St. John the Baptist. Unusually tall among Switzerland's fountains, it dates from 1390.

Continue down to the Rhine from here and you arrive again at the Mittle Rheinbrücke, back where we started.

Excursions from Basel

The easiest and most popular trip from Basel is to Augst, the little town 12 kms. (seven miles) up the Rhine founded by the Romans in the first century A.D. It's easily reached by road, but much more enjoyably by boat. There are once-weekly departures in summer from outside the Drei Könige hotel in the center of Basel. The return trip is by train. To add to the day you can have lunch in an atmospheric 500-year-old guesthouse.

The Roman ruins of Colonia Augusta Raurica, as the Romans called Augst, have been surprisingly well preserved, with substantial portions of the ancient town walls and gates, streets, water pipes and heating systems all in evidence. The 2nd-century theater has been restored and stages open-air plays and concerts in the summer. There's an interesting museum as well—the Römermuseum—that includes a reconstructed Roman house which makes vividly clear the way of life of the Romans. The museum is also home to a substantial treasure trove, unearthed only in 1962. The objects, dating mostly from the 4th century, are believed to have been buried by the Romans in 350 to protect them from the ravages of the Alemanni, the German tribes who drove the Romans out of Switzerland. Silver plates, bowls, goblets, spoons, statues and toilet articles are all on show, as are a collection of coins thought to depict the Emperor Constantine or one of his sons.

Around Baselland

Much of Baselland, the canton to the south of Basel itself, consists of highly prosperous agricultural countryside, with a mild climate and fertile soil. A sprinkling of castles, several spas and a number of pretty little towns and villages complete this bucolic scene.

An excursion in the immediate vicinity of Basel takes in Arlesheim and its neighboring village of Dornach. Arlesheim is little more than 15 minutes' drive from Basel itself, down route 18, the highway to Delemont. It's a tranquil village, surrounded by woods, cherry orchards and castles up in the hills. Focal point of the village is the Baroque church in the exquisite town square. Built by the Bishop of Basel in 1681, the church has a remarkable organ. It was constructed by the great Johannes Andreas Silbermann of Strasbourg in the early 18th century and is now the only example of his work in Switzerland. Also worth noting are the choir stalls, the high altar and the stucco decoration.

Neighboring Dornach is the home of the anthroposophical movement, founded by Rudolf Steiner and centering on man rather than God while nonetheless acknowledging all religions equally. Chief point of interest is Steiner's Goetheanum, a remarkable concrete construction built in the '20s that houses the Free University of Spiritual Arts. The building is visible from a considerable distance, and is intended to reflect anthroposophical thought. Guided tours through the mysterious structure are available, while courses, conferences and stage performances are held regularly.

A finishing touch to this mini-excursion is provided by the drive to Gempen, seven kms. (four miles) away. Here, take the footpath up to Gempenfluh, 760 meters (2,350 ft.) high for a magnificent view northwards up the Rhine valley over Basel as far as distant Strasbourg on the French-German border.

Aarau, Olten and Solothurn

The principal destination of this excursion is the Baroque town of Solothurn, jewel of the northwest and easily reached from Basel in about 40 minutes on the expressway. But a more enjoyable and leisurely trip is via Aarau and Olten.

To reach Aarau take the expressway out of Basel—the N3—passing by Rheinfelden, itself an important spa and the navigable limit of this stretch of the Rhine, to just beyond the little town of Frick. Here you turn south onto route 24 to climb over the 620 meter (1,900 ft.) Staffelegg pass to Aarau.

Aarau, capital of the canton of the same name and built over the river Aare, was founded around 1240 by Count Hartman IV of Kyberg as a bulwark against his enemies in the west. The Old Town has been carefully preserved and consists of a happy mixture of Renaissance and Baroque townhouses, many of the latter prettily decorated, and the whole conspiring to give the town a cosy, country-town atmosphere. Of particular interest is the medieval Rathaus, the town hall, the oldest parts of which date back to the founding of the town in the 13th century. There's a fine view of the town and its splendid houses from the bridge over the Aare.

A few miles up river is Schönenwerd, famous for its beautiful 12th-century church and as the home of Bally shoes. Appropriately, there's a shoe museum here, though it's only open on the last Friday of every month.

A further eight kms. (five miles) brings you to Olten. Today, it's an important railroad center. But there's still much of interest to see here in the old part of the town, not least the quaint old wooden bridge over the Aare that leads to the Old Town. A series of characteristic and attractive townhouses are grouped around the 16th-century tower of the Rathaus. Olten also boasts the Herberg zum Goldenen Löwen, a guest house rebuilt in the 18th century but whose origins stretch back fully 500 years.

Just to the south of Olten lies the little town of Aarburg, known chiefly for its imposing 11th-century castle. But our route continues down the Aare a further 34 kms. (21 miles), through Hägendorf, with its Devil's Gorge, Oensingen, site of the 13th-century castle of Neu-Beckburg, to Solothurn.

Perched on the banks of the Aare, Solothurn, capital of canton Solothurn, is an idyllic town of patrician houses, picturesque squares and fountains, towers and ancient gates. Though both a Celtic and Roman settlement, it was not until the 12th century that the town rose to any sort of promience when the Dukes of Zähringen extended and rebuilt the city walls, incorporating within them both the monastery of St. Ursen and the area originally settled by the Romans, the Castrum, where the majority of the townsfolk lived and worked. The town received a further boost in the 16th century. Then, the French chose Solothurn as the seat of their ambassador to the Swiss Confederation. Solothurn was to remain an ambassadorial city in fact from 1530 to 1792, and these 250 years of courtly presence gave the city the elegant, worldly atmosphere that so distinguishes it today; indeed, elegance and tranquility remain very much the hallmark of this pretty country town.

Start off your stroll at the cathedral of St. Ursen, rebuilt between 1762 and 1773, replacing the original medieval monastery. The cathedral possesses a remarkable treasury containing a series of gold religious objects and fine textiles; it may be visited only by appointment, however. The cathedral stands in the Zeughausplatz, a fine Baroque square. At number 1 is one of Europe's finest collections of ancient arms and armor. Originally the town armory, today it is home to a huge collection of uniforms, weapons, flags, artillery and suits of armor, including one that spits at you when you lift the face-guard. Also in the cathedral square is the 500-year-old Rathaus, where the French ambassadors and representatives of the Swiss Confederation used to meet. Today, it is the seat of the Solothurn cantonal government.

Behind the cathedral is the Baseltor, a fine early-Renaissance city gate, dating from 1504.

Other points of interest in the town are the Jesuitkirche—the Jesuit's church—in the Hauptgasse, with a beautiful late-Baroque interior; the Marktplatz, dominated by a 12th-century clock tower, with later 15th-century astronomical sections showing day, month and year; and the Landhaus, down by the Aare, where wine used to be unloaded from the river boats. But Solothurn is preeminently a place for wandering in, past fountains, through squares, along streets small and large, taking your time and drinking in the charming atmosphere.

From Solothurn, there are two routes back to Basel. You can take the expressway, or, if your sightseeing appetite has not yet been entirely satisfied, you can take the prettier and slower route 12. This passes through Balsthal, with the impressive ruins of Neu-Falkenstein nearby, and Liestal, capital of canton Baselland, and boasting a late Gothic church and Rathaus.

Alsace and the Black Forest

Alsace in France and the Black Forest in Germany are so close that a visit to either is a natural excursion from Basel. The tourist office has regular tours.

A visit to Alsace usually takes in Ottmarsheim, with its very unusual 11th-century church; Old Colmar, with a former monastery containing an altarpiece painted by Mathias Grünewald shortly before the Reformation; the walled village of Eguisheim; and a drive through the Vosges mountains.

Black Forest excursions can easily cover Freiburg with its renowned Gothic cathedral; Münstertal's famous Baroque church; the thermal spa of Badenweiler; and Titisee, where the cuckoo clock comes from. Contrary to popular belief, the cuckoo clock is not a Swiss invention.

PRACTICAL INFORMATION FOR BASEL

GETTING TO TOWN FROM THE AIRPORT. Basel shares its airport with the French city of Mulhouse, and indeed the airport itself is actually in France. There is a regular bus service to and from the airport from the rail station in the center of town. This takes around 15 minutes and costs Fr. 5 per person. Customs formalities between France and Switzerland are minimal.

TOURIST OFFICES. The main Basel tourist office (Verkehrsbüro Basel) is at Schifflande 5, 4001 Basel (tel. 061–25 50 50); open Mon. to Fri. 8:30–6, extended to 9 P.M. on Thurs., Sat. 8:30–1. In addition there is a Tourist Information Office at the rail station (tel. 061–22 36 84); open daily 9–12:30 and 1:30–7, Sun. 2–6. Both offices can help with a wide range of information on the city and region, hotel reservations, city tours and excursions, all-inclusive arrangements, guides and hostesses, public transport and car hire, and so on. They also publish a magazine—available only in German, however—called *Basel Aktuell.*

Hotel reservations can also be made through the Zentraler Logierdienst (Central Accommodation Service), Messeplatz 7, 4058 Basel (tel. 061–26 77 00); open Mon. to Fri. 8–12, 1–6. There is another branch at the rail station near the tourist office; open Mon. to Fri. 8–12, 1.30–6.

For information on Solothurn, contact the Verkehrsbüro Region Solothurn (Solothurn Regional Tourist Office), Kronenplatz, 4500 Solothurn (tel. 065–22 19 24 and 22 19 26); open Mon. to Fri. 9–12 and 2–6.30, Sat. 8–12.

HOTELS. Basel has a wide range of hotels covering the spectrum from super deluxe to reasonably priced, though the city has no guesthouses. As elsewhere in Switzerland standards and quality are very high. Be sure always to book as far ahead as possible, however. The city has a significant number of trade fairs which fill its hotels to bursting point. Although these are concentrated in the spring and fall the Art Fair in June and the annual influx of tourists in July and August more than take up the slack. In addition, many hotels raise their prices considerably during the peak periods.

For details of hotels and restaurants elsewhere in the Basel region, see the end of this chapter.

Deluxe

Drei Könige am Rhein, Blumenrain 8 (tel. 061–25 52 52). 124 beds. This is one of Europe's grand hotels with a vengeance, with a history dating back to 1026 and a list of distinguished guests ranging from Conrad II, Holy Roman Emperor, in the 11th century, to King Farouk of Egypt in the '50s. But though long on history and with a premium on luxury and fine service, the Drei Könige is in no sense an intimidating place to stay. Rather, the emphasis here is on comfort, old world charm and, almost, a certain cosiness (though this does not prevent it being the most expensive hotel in Basel). Dinner on its famous terrace overlooking the Rhine ranks high among its legendary delights. Located by the Mittlere Rheinbrücke. AE, DC, MC, V.

Euler Grand, Centralbahnplatz 14 (tel. 061–23 45 00). 100 beds. Near the rail station and straight opposite the Bank of International Settlements. Full of tradition and very comfortable. Rooms recently renovated and, despite the busy traffic outside, very quiet. Excellent restaurant and popular bar. AE, DC, MC, V.

Hilton, Aeschengraben 31 (tel. 061–22 66 22). 368 beds. Conveniently located within a short walk of the rail station, this is a modern, well-run hotel with every comfort. The interior is elegant, and the rooms generously proportioned. Sauna, swimming pool, nightclub and two restaurants. AE, DC, MC, V.

International, Steinentorstr. 25 (tel. 061–22 18 70). 350 beds. Modern hotel, though with a distinctly personal touch. Of the three restaurants, the *Charolaise* is considered one of the best in town. Health club, with large swimming pool and sauna, completes the many facilities. AE, DC, MC, V.

Le Plaza, Riehenring 45 (tel. 061–32 33 33). 450 beds. Newest and largest of the modern hotels. Located in Klein-Basel, it is preeminently a businessman's hotel, and very convenient for Basel's regular fairs. Good restaurants and popular bar with dancing. AE, DC, V.

Schweizerhof, Centralbahnplatz 1 (tel. 061–22 28 33). A few steps from the rail station, this is one of Basel's traditional luxury hotels. Run by the same family for three generations. The renovated and quiet rooms looking onto the inner courtyard are particularly recommended. AE, DC, MC.

Basel, Münzgasse 12 (tel. 061–25 24 23). 105 beds. Located in the heart of town and particularly convenient for shoppers. Rooms are comfortable and varied, while the Fürsten, or Prince's, suite is especially well appointed. Three restaurants, of which the *Baslerkeller* gets top marks. AE, DC, MC, V.

Europe, Clarastr. 43 (tel. 061–26 80 80). 250 beds. Comfortable modern hotel right by the trade fair buildings. Two restaurants, with *Les Quatre Saisons* ranking among the city's best. AE, DC, MC, V.

Merian am Rhein, Rheingasse/Greifengasse 2/4 (tel. 061–25 94 66). 75 beds. Attractive location in Klein-Basel. Good restaurant serving Basel specialties. AE, DC, MC, V.

Victoria am Bahnhof, Centralbahnplatz 3–4 (tel. 061–22 55 66). 170 beds. Long established traditional hotel opposite the rail station. Good restaurant with reliable Swiss-German specialties. AE, DC, MC, V.

Moderate

Alexander, Riehenring 85 (tel. 061–26 70 00). 100 beds. Comfortable hotel near trade fair grounds. Pleasant restaurant, bowling bar and dancing. AE, DC, MC, V.

Bristol, Centralbahnstr. 15 (tel. 061–22 38 22). 55 beds. A well-run hotel with a personal touch. Conveniently located near rail station. AE, DC, MC, V.

Cavalier, Reiterstr. 1 (tel. 061–39 22 62). 48 beds. Sensible and comfortable hotel near the airport. AE, DC, MC, V.

City-Hotel, Henric Petri-Str. 12 (tel. 061–23 78 11). 130 beds. Centrally located and good value. AE, DC, MC, V.

Krafft am Rhein, Rheingasse 12 (tel. 061–26 88 77). 78 beds. Pretty and atmospheric hotel in Klein-Basel overlooking the Rhine. AE, DC, MC, V.

Spalenbrunnen, Schützenmattstr. 2 (tel. 061–25 82 33). 45 beds. Excellent Old Town location directly opposite the Holbein Fountain. AE, DC, MC, V.

Inexpensive

Rochat VCH, Petersgraben 23 (tel. 061–25 81 40). Near university and convenient for both sightseeing and shopping.

Stadthof, Gerbergasse 84 (tel. 061–25 87 11). 16 beds; no rooms with bath. Very inexpensive, and conveniently located in the Old Town.

Steinenschanze, Steinengraben 69 (tel. 061–23 53 53). Popular with young travelers. Rooms without bath are very reasonable; those overlooking the garden cost more, but are very quiet.

RESTAURANTS. Basel has a wide variety of restaurants of many different types and as many different price levels, though the most expensive can be very expensive. At the same time many smaller restaurants offer sturdily reliable food and very good value for money.

Food here has naturally been strongly influenced by both French and German cooking, to the extent that you may well feel inclined to hop over to either or both France and Germany for lunch or dinner, as indeed many of the Baslers do. Among the city's specialties are asparagus, from Alsace, a spring-time delicacy that comes in many tempting recipes. Salmon, for which the city was famous in the Middle Ages, though no longer found in the Rhine, is still a definite Basler specialty. Likewise, try some of the city's famous *Mehlsuppe* (Flour Soup), a traditionally warming dish still popular among the city's revelers as they wait in the early hours of a wintry Monday morning for the start of the Fasnacht celebrations.

Expensive

Bruderholz, Bruderholzallee 42 (tel. 061–35 82 22). One of Switzerland's finest French restaurants. Presided over by chef Hans Stucki, the food at times nears perfection. Located in an elegant villa; you can dine in the garden in summer. AE, DC, V.

Charolaise, in Hotel International, Steinentorstr. 25 (tel. 061–22 18 70). High quality classical cuisine, with excellent changing gourmet menu. AE, DC, MC, V.

Chez Donati, St. Johanns-Vorstadt 48 (tel. 061–57 09 19). Here French and Italian cuisine successfully meet. Renowned for black-and-white truffle dishes.

Drei Könige am Rhein, Terrasse, Haltingerstr. 104 (tel. 061–32 34 78). Excellent hotel restaurant recommended by gourmets. AE, DC, MC, V.

Euler, Hotel Euler, Centralbahnplatz 14 (tel. 061–23 45 00). Dignified and traditional hotel restaurant, particularly famous for fish dishes. AE, DC, MC, V.

Les Quatre Saisons, Clarastr. 43 (tel. 061–26 80 44). Restaurant of the hotel Europe in Klein-Basel and one of the finest in town. The emphasis is very much on ingredients fresh that day from the market. AE, DC, MC, V.

Schützenhause, Schützenmattstr. 56 (tel. 061–23 67 60). Delightful historic building specializing in traditional Basel specialties. Try the *Basler Herrenschnitzel* (veal in breadcrumbs with ham and goose liver). AE, DC.

Moderate

Baslerkeller, in Hotel Basel, Münzgasse 12 (tel. 061–25 24 23). Basel specialties in an atmospheric cellar in the *Hotel Basel.* AE, DC, MC.

Charon, Schützengraben 62 (tel. 061–22 99 80). 200-year-old wine tavern with really good food. AE.

Drachen, Aeschenvorstadt 24 (tel. 061–23 69 20). Comfortable restaurant with Swiss, French and Italian dishes. AE, MC, V.

L'Escargot, at the Basel central rail station (tel. 061–22 53 33). Excellent French cuisine in Alsatian style. Reasonably priced smaller dishes. AE, DC, MC, V.

Zum Goldenen Sternen, St. Alban-Rheinweg 70 (tel. 061–25 23 54). This claims to be the oldest restaurant in Switzerland. Dating from 1506, the building originally stood in the town center at Aeschenvorstadt before it was rebuilt on the Rhine. Loads of atmosphere with good food. AE, DC, MC, V.

Kunsthalle, Steinenberg 7 (tel. 061–23 42 33). Restaurant for the arty crowd near the Stadttheater and part of Art Gallery complex. Swiss and Italian dishes. AE, MC.

Pfauen, St. Johanns-Vorstadt (tel. 061–25 32 67). Great selection of fish dishes in a relaxed atmosphere. DC, MC, V.

Safranzunft, Gerbergasse 11 (tel. 061–25 19 59). Guildhall with a famous "Bacchus" fondue with 14 trimmings. AE, DC, MC, V.

Schlüsselzunft, Freiestr. 25 (tel. 061–25 20 46). Local cuisine in an historic guildhall; worth a visit for the building alone. DC, MC.

St. Alban Eck, St. Albanvorstadt 60 (tel. 061–22 03 20). 500-year-old restaurant with excellent food to satisfy a variety of budgets. Plenty of atmosphere. AE, DC, MC, V.

Walliserkanne, Gerbergasse 50 (tel. 061–25 70 17). Popular restaurant with cosy ambiance and consistently attractive specialties. Serves some of the best *rösti* (fried potatoes) in Switzerland.

Inexpensive

Börse, Marktgasse 4 (tel. 061–25 87 33). Conveniently opposite the tourist office; very reasonable prices.

Brauner Mutz, Barfüsserplatz 10 (tel. 061–25 33 69). Biggest beer hall in Basel, usually filled with locals enjoying plain cooking of good quality.

Löwenzorn, Gemsberg 2 (tel. 061–25 42 13). Lovely old inn with a garden restaurant. Grill dishes at low prices. AE, DC, MC.

Zum Schnabel, Trillengässlein 2 (tel. 061–25 49 09). One of the oldest beer haunts in Basel. Particularly lively before and during Fasnacht. DC, MC.

Stadtkeller, Marktgasse 11 (tel. 061–25 72 51) and **Steinenpick,** Steinentorstr. 25 (tel. 061–22 18 70) offer very good value for those traveling on a budget. AE, DC, MC.

Out of Town

Schloss Binningen (E), Binningen, Schlossgasse 5 (tel. 061–47 20 55). 16th-century chateau, 5 minutes by car from the center of Basel. Lovely historic setting and fine cuisine. AE, DC.

Schloss Bottmingen (E), Bottmingen, Schlossgasse 9 (tel. 061–47 15 15). Beautiful little castle, surrounded by water, about 15 kms. (9 miles) from Basel. AE, MC.

BARS. Atlantis, Klosterberg 13 (tel. 061–23 34 00). Popular with young jazz fans. **Bar-Café des Arts,** Steinenberg 7 (tel. 061–22 36 19). Chic spot near the Kunsthalle. **Club 59,** Steinenvorstadt 33 (tel. 061–23 14 59). Pianist plays attractive music. **Euler Bar,** in *Euler Hotel,* Centralbahnplatz 14 (tel. 061–23 45 00). Aristocratic meeting place for the Baslers, much frequented by bankers and businessmen. **Hotel Drei Könige Bar,** Blumenrain 8 (tel. 061–25 52 52). Luxuriously comfortable bar in Switzerland's oldest hotel. **Old City Bar,** in *Hilton* hotel, Aeschengraben 31 (tel. 061–22 66 22). Well-appointed and comfortable; with pianist.

GETTING AROUND. By Train, Tram and Bus. Buy your tram and bus tickets at the machines (these also have maps of the transport network). A good value 24-hour ticket, giving unlimited travel on all bus and tram lines, is also available, again from the vending machines. However, if you don't have enough change or do not know how to use the machines, go into the centrally located office of the Basler Verkehrsbetriebe BVB (Basel Transport Authority) at Barfüsserplatz, and buy your ticket there.

Tickets good for one day's unlimited travel on all public transport within the Basel region, including 628 kms. (390 miles) of train routes, are also available from the BVB office and at the rail station and major post offices. Maps of the network are printed on the reverse of the tickets.

By Taxi. As in all major cities in Switzerland, taxis are expensive.

On Foot. Basel is a delightful city to walk around; indeed this is without doubt the best means of experiencing the city. Maps from your hotel or tourist offices.

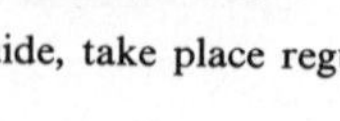

TOURS AND EXCURSIONS. For further details of all tours and excursions in and around Basel, contact the tourist office. Walking tours around the Old Town, lasting about two hours and accompanied by an expert guide, take place regularly in summer, though not every day, so check times carefully with the tourist office. There's also a regular bus tour of the city, taking in all the major sites, including those around the harbor; this lasts approximately one and three-quarter hours.

There is a once-weekly trip up the Rhine to Augst, site of the Roman settlement. The return trip is made by train. The tourist office also arranges regular bus trips to Alsace and the Black Forest; these generally last half a day.

MUSEUMS AND GALLERIES. For the size of the town, Basel has an extraordinarily large number of museums, an accurate reflection of the city's long and impressive cultural and intellectual heritage. The range of museums is equally impressive, extending from the Art Museums to such unlikely institutions as the Fire Brigade Museum and the Anatomy Collection.

Altes Zeughaus Waffen Museum (Weapons Museum), in Solothurn, Zeughausplatz 1 (tel. 065–23 35 28). Magnificent collection of weapons from Solothurn's historic arsenal. Open summer, Tues. to Sun. 10–12 and 2–5; winter, Tues. to Fri. 2–5, Sat. and Sun. 10–12 and 2–5.

Anatomische Sammlung (Anatomy Collection), Pestalozzistr. 20. Dating from 1589 this unusual museum contains, among many curiosities, the skeleton of a criminal executed in the 16th century. Open Sun. 10–12.

Antikenmuseum/Sammlung Ludwig (Museum of Antiquities/Collection Ludwig), St. Alban-Graben 5 (tel. 061–22 22 02). Ancient Greek, Etruscan and Roman works; the only museum in Switzerland dedicated exclusively to the classical period. Exceptionally fine Greek and Roman marble statues, bronze statues and gold jewelry. Open Tues. to Sun., 10–12 and 2–5.

Architekturmuseum (Architecture Museum), Pfluggässlein 3 (tel. 061–25 14 13). New museum in the heart of the shopping district, with changing exhibits of architectural interest. Open Tues. to Fri. 10–12 and 2–6:30, Sat. 10–4, Sun. 10–1.

Feuerwehrmuseum (Fire Brigade Museum), Kornhausgasse 18. Fascinating collection of old fire-fighting devices. Open Sun. 2–5.

Basler Papiermühle (Book Museum and Museum of the History of Paper), St. Alban-Tal 35. Located in a former paper mill and boasting a 15th-century water-driven stamping mill and many other medieval papermaking implements.

Museum für Gegenwartskunst (Museum of Contemporary Art), St. Alban-Rheinweg 58 (tel. 061–23 81 83 and 22 08 28). In a wonderful 19th-century factory on the Rhine with modern building attached. Windows look out on the atmospheric river area, creating a fascinating tension between the old and the new. Major works of minimalist and concept art. Open Mon., Wed. to Sun. 10–12 and 2–5. May to Oct. same days 10–5.

Historisches Museum Barfüsserkirche (Historical Museum), Barfüsserplatz (tel. 061–22 05 05). The history of Basel through the centuries, reflected in beautiful objects in the wonderful setting of a medieval church. Valuable Gothic tapestries, sculptures, altars, coins and weapons, plus the Münster treasury, the richest in Switzerland. Open Mon., Wed. to Sun. 10–5.

Historisches Museum Kirschgarten (Historical Museum), Elisabethenstr. 27 (tel. 061–22 13 33). A must for those interested in domestic life through the ages. A fine collection of furniture, porcelain, glasses, clocks and toys, displayed in a series of period interiors in an 18th-century house. Open Tues. to Sun. 10–12 and 2–5. May to Oct., Tues. to Sun. 10–5.

Jüdisches Museum der Schweiz (Swiss Jewish Museum), Kornhausgasse 8 (tel. 061–25 95 14). Excellent Jewish museum with wide range of religious objects. Basel was the site of the first Zionist Congress, organized by Herzl, the father of modern Zionism, in 1897. (The tourist office produces an interesting brochure detailing Jewish places of interest in and around the city). Open Mon. and Wed. 2–5, Sun. 10–12 and 3–5.

Katzen Museum (Cat Museum), in the Basel suburb of Riehen at Baselstr. 101. 10,000 feline objects assiduously collected by two cat lovers. Open Sun. 10–12 and 2–5.

Kunsthalle Basel (Basel Art Gallery), Steinenberg 7 (tel. 061–23 48 33). Regular, and frequently challenging, exhibits by contemporary artists. Open daily 10–5, Wed. 10–9:30 P.M.

Kunstmuseum (Museum of Art), St. Alban-Graben 16 (tel. 061–22 08 28). One of the world's best, and oldest, collections of Old Masters, with superb collection of Holbeins in particular. The Modern and contemporary departments are equally strong, with examples of practically every important 19th- and 20th-century artist. Open Tues. to Sun. 10–5.

Kupferstichkabinett (Collection of Prints and Drawings), St. Alban-Graben 16 (tel. 061–23 18 55). Department of the Kunstmuseum containing magnificent collection of drawings and other graphic works from the 15th century to the present. Works by particular artists can be requested in the reading room. Open Tues. to Fri. 9–12 and 2–6, Sat. 9–12 and 2–5.

Römermuseum Augst (Roman Museum in Augst), Augst near Basel (tel. 061–83 11 87). Roman remains from Augusta Raurica including a collection of silver plates and coins, a reconstructed Roman house and nearby amphitheater. Open Mon. 1:30–6, Tues. to Sun. 10–12 and 1:30–6; Nov. to Feb. closes at 5.

Schweizerisches Schiffahrtsmuseum (Swiss Navigation Museum), Wiesendamm 4, Kleinhüningen harbor (tel. 061–65 08 08). Fascinating models and displays tell the story of Rhine navigation through the ages. Open daily 10–12 and 2–5; Nov. to Feb., Tues., Sat. and Sun. only, 10–12 and 2–5.

Schweizerisches Sportmuseum (Swiss Sport Museum), Missionsstr. 28. Skates from many periods, 17th-century skis, historic bicycle collection. Open daily 2–5 and Sun. 10–12 and 2–5.

Spielzeug- und Dorfmuseum (Toy and Village Museum), Baselstr. 34, Riehen suburb (tel. 061–67 28 29). The toy collection of the Swiss Folklore Museum, housed in a 17th-century building. Open Wed. and Sat. 2–5, Sun. 10–12 and 2–5.

Museum für Völkerkunde (Ethnological Museum), Augustinergasse 2 (tel. 061–25 82 82). Excellent collections from Asia and the Americas, including internationally famous textiles. Open Tues. to Sun. 10–12 and 2–5. May to Oct., Tues. to Sun. 10–5.

HISTORIC BUILDINGS. The major sights of Basel can all be seen in a comfortable stroll through the Old Town. There is no charge for entering churches. Additional information is available from the Basel tourist office.

Barfüsserkirche (Franciscan church), Barfüsserplatz. Beautiful 14th-century Franciscan church, boasting the tallest choir on the Rhine after Köln cathedral. Now the Historical Museum. Open Tues. to Sun. 10–12 and 2–5. Open Mon., Wed. to Sun. 10–5.

Dreiländereck (Three Countries' Corner). Meeting place of France, Germany and Switzerland, marked by pillar the Dreiländerpfahl. To reach it, take tram 14 from Marktplatz to Kleinhünningen (25 minutes). Cross the river Wiese and continue along the Hochbergerstrasse to the Schiffahrtsmuseum. Then walk for about 15 minutes along the Westquaistrasse to the Café Zur Weiten Fahrt. Nearby is the elevator which takes you up to the Terrace overlooking the exact meeting place. Elevator operates Mar. through Oct., daily 10–12 and 2–5; Nov. through Feb., Sat. and Sun. only 10–12 and 2–5; price is Fr. 1.

Leonhardskirche (St. Leonhard's church), Leonhardskirchplatz. Most important late-Gothic, single-nave church in the Upper Rhine region; Romanesque crypt. Romantic setting in Old Town. Open daily 8–6.

Martinskirche (St. Martin's church), Martinskirchplatz. 15th-century church in the Old Town, the oldest parish church in Basel. Now used only on special occasions, including concerts.

Münster (Cathedral), Münsterplatz. Historic red sandstone cathedral dating back to 1019. On the site of the earliest settlement in Basel. Inside are renowned Romanesque reliefs, the 13th-century tomb of Anna of Habsburg and the 16th-century tomb of Erasmus. Open summer, Mon. to Fri. 10–6, Sat. 10–12 and 2–5, Sun. 1–5; winter 10–12 and 2–6. Tower open Mar. to Oct. only (Fr. 1).

Peterskirche (St. Peter's church), Peterskirchplatz. Fine Gothic church dating from the 13th century with 14th- and 15th-century additions. Valuable frescoes in the Eberler chapel and the right nave, dating from the 15th century. Open Tues. to Fri. 10–4.

Rathaus (Town Hall), Marktplatz. Built to commemorate Basel's entry into the Swiss Confederation in 1501, it is a marvelously colorful structure with rich murals. Guided tours by appointment. The courtyard is open to the public during the day.

SHOPPING. Strolling around Basel's shops may not be quite the glamorous experience it is in Geneva or Zürich, but it is by no means without its moments. Although shops are in general perhaps a little smaller, even cosier, many of the international couturiers have outlets here; similarly, there are numerous expensive jewelry and watch shops. Basel is very much the sort of place where you might suddenly find something you've been searching for for years, or just fall in love with at first glance. The Freiestrasse is the main shopping street, but there are many other streets and alleys in and around it worth exploring.

Among the specialty shops in the city is the **Läckerli-Huus** at Gerbergasse 57. Läckerli candy is very much a Basel specialty. Created in the 15th century for the sophisticated tastes of noble gentlemen attending the Ecumenical Council who turned up their noses at the city's plainer offerings, they have remained popular through the centuries. They are essentially a species of honey cookie, made with a delicious mixture of exotic spices, cherry brandy and orange peel.

For other souvenirs, try the **Basel Heimatwerk** at Freiestrasse 45. For Fasnacht carnival gifts try **Erwin Oesch** on Spalenvorstadt, or **Musik Hug** on Freiestrasse, with its wide selection of drums.

Basel is justly renowned for its antiquarian bookshops. They can be found on Klosterberg through Elisabethenstrasse to Aeschengraben. The coin and medal dealers Münzen und Medaillen AG at Malzgasse 25 are also worth a visit. Nosing around the alleyways and streets near the Münster is also a rich experience for antique book and furniture lovers.

On the Marktplatz a fruit-and-vegetable market is held most mornings from 7 to 12.30. A flea market takes place at the same venue on the second and fourth Wednesdays of each month. A clothing market on the Barfüsserplatz each Thursday from 1.30–9 P.M. can be fun. There's another flea market on the Petersplatz on Saturdays from 9–4.

MUSIC, MOVIES AND THEATERS. Music. Basel has a long and distinguished musical tradition, with a rich and varied offering of concerts. In recent years it has gained a considerable reputation for its contemporary approach to classical music. Among the leading concert venues are the following:

Stadtcasino, Steinenberg 14. You can book in advance at the Musikhaus au concert, Aeschengraben 24 (tel. 061–23 11 76) or buy tickets one hour in advance at the box office (tel. 061–23 66 57).

Musik-Akademie der Stadt Basel, Leonhardsgraben 4–6. An important European academy with international performers of great quality. Bookings as above.

Movies. Movies have the great advantage, as they do all over Switzerland, of usually being shown in the original language. Enlist help from your hotel in deciphering what's on from the newspaper and how to get to movie houses.

Theaters. Stadttheater, Theaterstr. 7. A high-quality theater with opera, musical comedy, ballet and drama. For advance bookings, tel. 061–22 11 33, from 10–1 and 3.30–6.45 (to 5 on Sun.). At the theater tickets are available 45 minutes before a performance.

Komödie, Steinenvorstadt 63. Lighter theater in an intimate atmosphere. Advance bookings as for Stadttheater, and at the theater.

NIGHTLIFE. Basel has a considerable range of nightspots. They are usually open till 2 A.M., with some closing at 3 A.M. Fridays and Saturdays. For those who do not find enough variety in Basel itself, there is plenty of after-midnight activity over the German border in Lörrach. Your hotel will tell you how to get there. You will find a list of the Basel discos and nightclubs in the tourist magazine *Basel Aktuell.*

Bora-Bora, Hilton Hotel, Aeschengraben 31 (tel. 061–22 66 22), is a popular disco in an exotic atmosphere. The **Frisco-Bar,** Untere Rebgasse 3 (tel. 061–25 07 00), is an intimate nightclub with the oldest striptease show in town. **Hazyland,** Heuwaage (tel. 061–23 99 82), has no strip, but a top orchestra and a show. **King's Club,** Hotel Drei Könige am Rhein, Blumenrain 8 (tel. 061–25 36 58), offers an attractive combination of show and dance. **Le Plaza Club,** Le Plaza Hotel, Messeplatz (tel. 061–32 32 06), offers a variety of music and show attractions. **Singerhaus,** Marktplatz (tel. 061–25 64 66), is a traditional nightclub with a good show; bar opens at 5 P.M., dancing from 9 P.M., old-time dancing on Sunday afternoons from 4–7.

SPECIAL EVENTS. The first Monday after Ash Wednesday is the time to be in Basel. That's when the famous carnival of Fasnacht begins and the city is transformed into a weird and gorgeous world with magically dressed groups whistling and drumming their way through the streets. It lasts for three days, beginning promptly at the unearthly hour of 4 A.M. on Monday. No carnival à la Rio this—though not without humor—but à ceremonial and serious event dating from the 16th century. Its origins are in fact half-pagan, half-Christian, a combined celebration of the end of winter and a massive pre-Lenten blow-out.

SPORTS. Golf. *Golf and Country Club Basel,* Hagenthal-Le-Bas in France (tel. 067–68 50 91), is open to visitors. This is one of the most beautiful golf courses in Europe, with attractive views of the Jura, Black Forest and the Vosges mountains; bring your passport.

Tennis. Courts can be reserved at the *Sporthalle St. Jakob:* Mon. to Fri. 10–5, tel. 061–41 75 55; Sat. and Sun. from 5 P.M., tel. 061–42 88 96.

Swimming. Possible at the *Hallenschwimmbad Rialto,* Birsigstr./Viaduktstr. (tel. 061–23 91 61). Open Tues. to Fri. 9 A.M.–9.30 P.M., Sat. and Sun. 10–5.30.

Squash. *Eglisee Squash-Courts,* Riehenstr. 315 (tel. 061–33 22 10). Open Mon. to Fri. 10 A.M.–11 P.M., Sat. and Sun. 9–6.30.

Skating. *Basler Kunsteisbahn,* Margarethenpark (tel. 061–35 95 95). Open Mon. to Fri. 9–5 and 8 P.M.–10 P.M., Sat. 9–5.30 and 8 P.M.–10 P.M., Sun. 10–5.30. Also at *Kunsteisbahn Eglisee,* tel. 061–32 89 50. Open Mon. to Sat. 9 A.M.–9.40 P.M., Sun. 9.30–5.30.

Cross-Country Skiing. Many possibilities in the nearby Jura area. Ask at your hotel or at the tourist office how to get to the right area.

Skiing. The Bernese Oberland, with some of the finest skiing in Europe, is within two hours of the city. See the *Bernese Oberland* chapter for further information, or ask at your hotel or the tourist office.

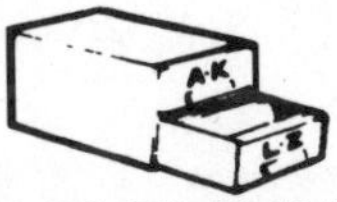

USEFUL ADDRESSES. Car Hire. *Avis,* Münchensteinstr. 73 (tel. 061–57 28 40). *Budget,* Bachlettenstr. 7 (tel. 061–54 28 00 and 54 28 05). *Europcar,* Peter-Merian-Str. 58 (tel. 061–23 85 55). *Hertz,* Gartenstr. 120 (tel. 061–22 58 22). All also have desks at Basel-Mülhausen airport.

Travel Agents. *American Express,* Aeschengraben 10 (tel. 061–23 66 90). *Wagon Lits/Cook's,* Freiestr. 3 (tel. 061–25 50 55). *British Rail,* Centralbahnplatz 9 (tel. 061–23 14 04). *Swissair,* central rail station (tel. 061–22 54 80).

Rail Information: Badischer Bahnhof (German), tel. 061–33 76 76; Französischer Bahnhof (French), tel. 061–22 50 33; Schweizerischer Bundesbahnhof (Swiss), tel. 061–21 23 21.

City Lost and Found Office, tel. 061–21 70 34.

HOTELS AND RESTAURANTS ELSEWHERE IN THE REGION

AARAU. *Aarauerhof* (M), tel. 061–24 55 27. Large and very comfortable. AE, DC, MC, V. *Anker* (I), tel. 061–22 74 18. Historic and quiet with facilities for the handicapped. AE, DC, MC.

BRUGG. *Rotes Haus* (I), tel. 056–41 14 79. Well-appointed hotel. Skittles. AE, DC, MC.

EGERKINGEN. *Motel AGIP* (M), tel. 062–61 21 21. Very quiet, in own grounds with facilities for the handicapped. AE, DC, MC, V.

LANGENBRUCK. *Landgasthof Bären* (M), tel. 062–60 14 14. Historic hotel where Napoleon is reputed to have stayed. With sauna; excellent restaurant. AE, DC, MC, V.

LAUFENBURG. *Adler* (I), tel. 064–64 12 32. Surprisingly low prices. AE, DC, MC, V.

LIESTAL. *Engel* (M), tel. 061–91 25 11. Comfortable family hotel in attractive surroundings. AE, DC, MC, V.

OLTEN. *Europe AG* (M), tel. 062–32 35 55. MC, V. *Schweizerhof* (I), tel. 062 –26 46 46. Central. AE, DC, V.

Restaurants. *Zollhaus* (I–E), tel. 062–26 36 28. Excellent. Closed Mon. AE, DC, MC. *Felsenburg* (I–M), tel. 062–26 22 77. Recommended. Closed Tues. AE, DC, MC, V.

RHEINFELDEN. *Eden Solbad* (L), tel. 061–87 54 04. Quiet, with cure facilities. AE, V. *Schwanen Solbad* (E), tel. 061–87 53 44. Sauna, gymnasium, cure facilities. AE, DC, MC, V. *Schiff am Rhein* (M), tel. 061–87 60 87. Quiet rooms; bowling. AE, DC, MC, V. *Schützen* (M), tel. 061–87 50 04. Indoor pool, cure facilities. AE, DC, MC, V. *Goldener Adler* (I), tel. 061–87 53 32. No showers; in historic building, central.

SOLOTHURN. *Astoria* (M), tel. 065–22 75 71. Splendid view. DC, MC, V. *Krone* (M), tel. 065–22 44 12. One of Switzerland's oldest inns, though now much modernized. AE, DC, MC, V. *Roter Turm* (M), tel. 065–22 96 21. Modern and bright; good food. Recommended. AE, DC, MC, V.

Restaurants. *Chez Derron* (M), tel. 065–22 25 31. *Misteli-Gasche* (I–M), tel. 065–22 32 81. Closed Sun. evening and Mon. *Tiger* (I), tel. 065–22 24 12. Closed Wed. V.

ZOFINGEN. *Engel* (M), tel. 062–51 50 50. Breakfast only. AE, DC, MC. *Zofingen* (M), tel. 062–50 01 00. Central, terrace and grill. AE, MC, V. *Römerbad* (I), tel. 062–51 12 93. No showers, very basic. AE, MC, V.

ZURZACH. *Zurzacherhof* (E), tel. 056–49 01 21. Quiet rooms. AE, DC, MC, V. *Turmhotel* (M), tel. 056–49 24 40. Pool and cure facilities.

Restaurant. *Ochsen* (I–M), tel. 056–49 23 30. Good hotel restaurant. AE, DC, MC, V.

BERN

Arcades, Bears and Fountains

Bern is a state capital where you can run into the country's president having a cup of coffee in a local cafe. He'll probably have arrived for work by tram or train. And if you're here during one of the regular meetings of the federal parliament, likely as not you'll see the parliamentarians plotting political strategy in their favorite small restaurants all over town. Bern, in short, though preeminently a city of government and diplomacy, retains exactly the same sort of down to earth, no-nonsense quality that Zürich prides itself on. There isn't even an official presidential residence. Indeed the seven members of the coalition government, each of whom serves a year as president, have to find their own places to live when in Bern.

What in fact, at any rate at a first glance, Bern really resembles is a prosperous country town rather than a major European capital. But then this is hardly a surprise when you consider that some of Switzerland's richest agricultural land is right on the city's doorstep, or that from no other European capital can you reach the countryside so quickly or so easily. Likewise, the streets regularly fill with powerfully built farmers and their families in town for the shopping and to sell their produce in the weekly markets. These markets help reinforce the rural flavor, as stalls piled high with vegetables, fruit and flowers fill the squares in front of the imposing Bundeshaus, the federal parliament. In the same vein, the city's principal festival, the Zibelemärit, is centered around the humble onion. Positively tons of them are lovingly arranged on stalls for Bern's housewives to buy.

The prevailing flavor imparted by all this agriculture and straightforwardness is underlined further by a near total absence of industry, or at any rate conspicuous industry, and—rare for Switzerland—banking. Likewise, the people of Bern have jealously guarded their medieval city center from modern development, in large measure accounting for the fact that it is today probably the most beautiful of all Switzerland's historic cities. Bern remains a delightful city to visit, not least for its unusual and charming *Lauben,* the medieval sandstone arcades that line the length of the Old Town's streets, still very much the heart of the city, all six kms. (four miles) of them. Goethe, Germany's 18th-century literary giant, remarked that, "Bern's cityscape is the most beautiful I have ever seen." A modern-day Goethe could say very much the same today.

Yet when all is said and done Bern remains first and foremost a city of government. Moreover, it always has been. Among the medieval streets today you'll notice countless elegant patrician townhouses, evidence of Bern's long history as an urban republic ruled by noble families who played a leading role on the stage of European power politics. For much of its history Bern has been fundamentally expansionary in intent, ruling large areas of Switzerland and, largely through the successes of her mercenary armies, exercising an influence out of all proportion to her size. Today of course it is business that makes Switzerland tick, meaning that Zurich, Geneva and Basel have become the driving forces in Swiss economic life. But Bern, despite her population of only 140,000, strategically sited between the country's two main linguistic and cultural groups, is still the place where the government of Switzerland is decided.

Bern Background

Bern was founded in 1191 by Berchtold V, Duke of Zähringen, a member of the German Alemanni tribes and one of the countless rulers of the Holy Roman Empire. To some extent, it is surprising that no previous settlement had be made here before the warlike Berchtold established his fortress. For Bern lies on a steep peninsula of rock, girdled on three sides by a U-bend in the swift flowing river Aare, a more or less impregnable stronghold. But to Berchtold the site possessed another invaluable advantage. It lay right on the western edge of the Alemanni's lands, almost on the border of the Burgundian Counts of Savoy's great kingdom that spread across much of France and into present-day French speaking Switzerland. This strategic location made it not only an ideal defensive spot, but perfect for attacks on the Burgundians.

Few doubt today that Bern's name came about as a result of the multitude of bears that roamed the wilderness along the Aare. Legend has embellished this somewhat with the oft-repeated story that Berchtold, out hunting, told his followers that the new town would be called after the first animal he killed. Predictably, it was a bear. And it's true that the name Bern differs only slightly from the German word for bear, Bär. At all events, the animal has long since been adopted as Bern's mascot, appearing on flags, the city coat of arms, buildings, statues, chocolates and, most famously, in the flesh in the city's celebrated bear pits.

From Berchtold's original Nydegg fortress (destroyed in 1295) the town grew gradually from East to West. By 1344 it had reached the spot where the rail station stands. At its Spitalgasse exit are the remains of the Christoffelturm, the Christoffel Tower, built that year as part of the town walls. By the 14th century, in fact, Bern had grown to become a strong urban republic, a powerful force in the land. Following the death of the last of the Zähringens, the Bernese defeated those nobles of the Holy Roman Empire who hoped to fill the vacuum left by the Zähringen and in 1353 became the eighth canton to join the by now rapidly growing Swiss Confederation. It was an unlikely union: aristocratic, urban Bern on the one hand; the strongly democratic, farming communities of Central Switzerland on the other. But it provided the Bernese with the necessary security against the Habsburg Holy Roman Empire to continue their westward expansion.

In 1405 a major fire swept through the city, destroying most of the houses, then made mainly of wood. It was rebuilt in sandstone, giving it the delightfully unified appearance it enjoys today. Later buildings barely disturb this uniformity. Even the stately 19th-century mansions of the diplomatic quarter blend in pleasingly with their older surroundings.

By the late 15th century Bern had become a power of European stature. This new found status was confirmed by three decisive victories over the Duke of Burgundy in 1476 and 1477. Aided by the other cantons of the Confederation, and prompted by Louis XI, king of France and bitter enemy of the Burgundians, the Bernese crushed Charles the Bold, Duke of Burgundy, driving him out of his Swiss lands. The consequences for Bern of these victories were great. Not only did her territories now extend all the way to Geneva, but the city acquired immense wealth, great treasures of gold, silver and precious textiles as well as new lands. To all intents and purposes Bern had assumed the leading role in Switzerland and Swiss affairs.

The city was not to avoid the religious strife which traumatized Europe in the 16th century, caught between the Protestantism of Zürich and the aggressive Catholicism of Central Switzerland. Attempts at mediation were to prove futile, however, and before the end of the century Bern too found herself swept along on the tide of the Reformed church.

Through the 17th and 18th centuries Bern's considerable prosperity was built not on commerce so much as on the export of troops and military know-how. The city and her territories were essentially a patrician state, ruled by a nobility that saw their *raison d'être* in politics, foreign policy, the acquisition of new lands and the forging of alliances. At the same time, her landed gentry continued to grow fat on the fruits of the city's rich agricultural lands.

By the middle of the 18th century Bern's smoothly functioning and prosperous system of government had become a source of some admiration in Europe. Frederick the Great, stern Emperor of Prussia, commented that Bern was, " . . . dignified in all its activities," while Edmund Burke, leading British Conservative and political philosopher, was moved to remark that Bern was, "One of the happiest, most prosperous and best governed countries on earth."

In 1798 Bern was invaded by Napoleon and its government swept away. It was to return after Napoleon's final defeat at Waterloo in 1815 but lasted only until the 1830s when a wave of popular discontent swept it away for a second and final time. In 1848 the present Swiss Confederation replaced the previous alliance of Swiss states. Bern was the natural choice as capital—or federal capital, as the Swiss correctly point out. The historic role of Bern as geographic and political center of a linguistically and culturally diverse nation was confirmed.

Exploring Bern

It is not difficult to cover the principal attractions of Bern in a comparatively short time, since the geography of the city has compressed its sights into a restricted area, albeit a hilly one. The Old Town is perched on a high rock that juts into a loop of the river Aare. Most of what the visitor wants is contained within this loop, and the few places outside it lie just on the far side of the bridges. For the unspoilt appearance of the medieval architecture on this peninsula, Bern has been granted World Landmark status by the United Nations (UNESCO).

As you stroll through the streets of the capital, three architectural features will almost certainly impress you—arcades, fountains and towers. The arcades—the *Lauben*—are a welcome asset in the main shopping streets. With their low, vaulted roofs, they extend to the edge of the pavement, where they are supported on sturdy 15th-century pillars so comfortable window shopping is possible even in the worst weather. Most of the arcades (and there are over eight kms./five miles of them) are in the Old Town; the most famous being on the Spitalgasse, Marktgasse, Kramgasse and Gerechtigkeitsgasse.

The brilliantly colored and skilfully carved fountains, their bases surrounded by flowers, are for the most part the work of Hans Gieng, and were set up between 1539 and 1546. They provide light relief from the often severe structure of the medieval houses that form their background. The Fountain of Justice might seem less than original with its figure of the blindfolded goddess with her sword and scales, perched on a high column, until you glance at the severed heads that lie at the base—not only those of the Holy Roman Emperor, the Sultan of Turkey and the Pope, but even, striking nearer home, of the mayor of Bern! The Ogre Fountain shows a giant enjoying a meal of small children. Then there are the Bagpiper, the Messenger, Moses, the Zähringer Fountain (with its harnessed bear and its cubs feasting on a bunch of grapes), Samson (overcoming a lion), and many others, some of them sculptured references to historical events. All the fountains have lately been restored and treated with a protective plastic paint.

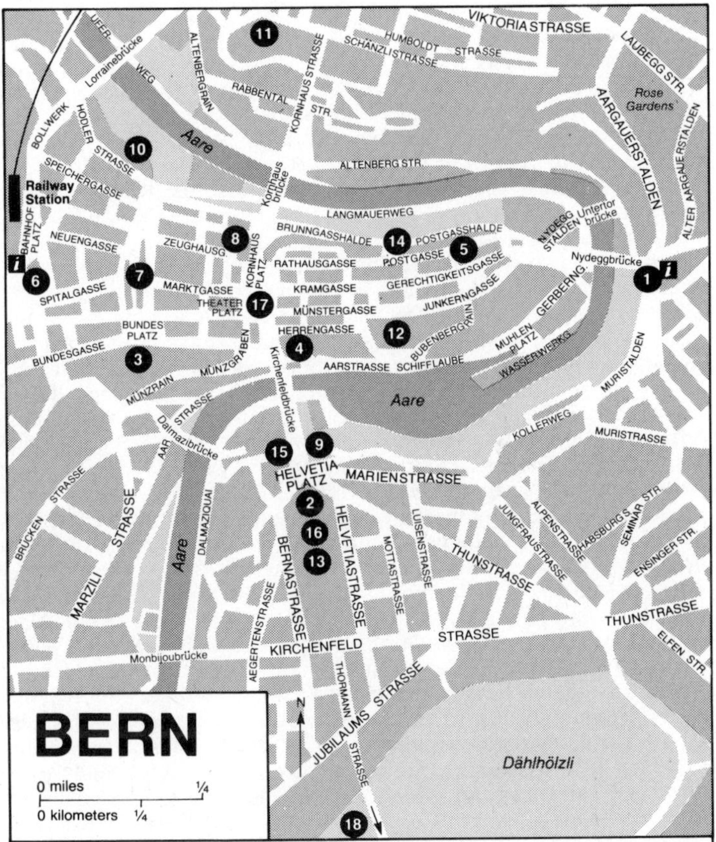

Points of Interest

1 Bärengraben (Bear Pit)
2 Bernisches Historisches Museum
3 Bundeshaus
4 Casino
5 Fountain of Justice
6 Heiliggeistkirche
7 Käfigturm
8 Kornhaus
9 Kunsthalle
10 Kunstmuseum
11 Kursaal
12 Münster
13 Naturhistorisches Museum
14 Rathaus
15 Schweizerisches Alpines Museum; P.T.T. Museum
16 Schweizerisches Schützenmuseum
17 Zeitglockenturm
18 Zoo

i Tourist Information

A Bern Walk

Start on busy Bahnhofplatz in front of the Schweizerhof hotel, facing the mirror-like walls of Bern's rail station. To your left, and at the top of Spitalgasse, is the Heiliggeistkirche (church of the Holy Ghost), finished in 1729 and now plainly uncomfortable amid the modernity and bustle of the '80s. If you now walk down Spitalgasse you will quickly come to samples of Bern's fountains and towers. The Bagpiper Fountain stands in the middle of the street with the Käfigturm (the prison gate), a city gate in the 13th and 14th centuries, beyond it. The Käfigturm now houses a small museum charting the economic and cultural life of Bern. Straight down Marktgasse and past the Anna Seiler and Marksman Fountains, you'll come to Kornhausplatz on the left and its Ogre Fountain. On the square is the imposing Kornhaus (granary) built in the 18th century. Its magnificent cellar, which once housed wine brought to town by the farmers as a tribute to the patrician city government, is today a popular restaurant. To your right is Theaterplatz and in front of you Bern's colorful showpiece and trademark: Zeitglockenturm (Clock Tower).

The "Zytgloggeturm" (as it is called in the local dialect) was originally built as a city gate by Berchtold V in 1191. In 1530 an astronomical clock and a series of mechanically operated puppets were installed on the eastern side; and every hour, when the clock strikes, they put on a delightful, and justly famous, performance.

To see the show it is best to take up position at the corner of Kramgasse and Hotelgasse at least five minutes before the hour. You won't be the only one there. For photographers, the best time in summer is 10 or 11 A.M. At about four minutes to the hour, heralded by a jester nodding his head and ringing two small bells, the puppet show begins. From a small arch on the left a couple of musically inclined bears—a drummer and a piper—appear, leading a procession of a horseman with a sword, a proud bear wearing a crown, and lesser bears, each carrying a gun, sword or spear. When the procession comes to an end a metal cockerel on the left crows and flaps his wings in delight, after which a knight in golden armor at the top of the tower hammers out the hour, while Father Time on a throne in the middle beats time with a scepter in one hand and an hour glass in the other.

From the Zeitglockenturm our route continues down Kramgasse. It's a lovely old street with many guildhouses, some particularly fine 18th-century houses the inevitable arcades and, needless to say, a couple more fountains—the Zähringer and the Samson. At the next intersection it is best to make a brief diversion and turn left down a short, narrow lane. This will bring you to Rathausplatz and the Rathaus (Town Hall) itself, seat of the cantonal government.

Originally built in the 15th century after the great fire which destroyed most of Bern, the Rathaus is a pleasingly simple late Gothic building. The markets once occupied the ground floor, while city business was conducted above. But today, after several restorations, it has become the center of both city and cantonal government, the council chamber being a really charming old room. In the courtyard is a lovely fountain which, although modern, shows a distinct affinity with the medieval ones outside. The Rathausplatz in front of the Town Hall is a beautiful little medieval square with delightful dimensions and lines. It contains the Venner (Ensign) Fountain.

If you now leave the Rathausplatz, return down the lane and turn left at the intersection, you will walk down Gerechtigkeitsgasse and past the Justice Fountain. Once again, this lovely street is lined with patrician houses. Note in particular two buildings that are now hotels. The Hospiz zur Heimat is at number 52. Constructed between 1760 and 1762, it has the best Louis XV facade in the city. At number 7 is the Gasthaus zum Goldenen Adler. Built between 1764 and 1766, it has a particularly captivating coat of arms by locksmith Samuel Rüetschi. A left turn at the bottom will take you steeply down Nydegg Stalden through one of the oldest parts of the city, past the fountain depicting a 16th-century messenger with his bear companion, and on to the 15th-century Untertor Bridge over the river Aare. On your way look into the Nydeggkirche (Nydegg Church). The chancel was built in the years 1341–46, the main aisle 1494–1500, the bell tower in 1480 and 1569–71. Intriguingly, the church is built on the foundations of Berchtold V's original fortress, which was destroyed in the 13th century.

From here it is a short, steep climb to the far end of the high Nydegg Bridge which will later take us back over the river. However, if you are feeling energetic it's well worth while crossing the road and then either climbing up the little path to the left, turning right at the top, or walking up Alter Aargauerstalden, and then turning left. Both will bring you to the entrance (free) of the splendidly arranged and kept Rose Gardens. Allow a little time here, to enjoy not only the 200 varieties of roses, and the fine plants and shrubs, but also the best panoramic view there is of the city tightly squeezed in the bend of the river. On a hot summer day, too, you'll find it difficult to resist a rest in the cool shade of the trees before returning to the Nydegg Bridge where, at the end on the left, you'll find the famous, but surprisingly drab, bear pits. Here Bern's mascots, alive and not made of metal or stone as on the Clock Tower or fountains, will put up a fine bit of clowning if you dangle a carrot above their heads.

Cathedrals and Casinos

Leaving the bears, now cross the Nydegg Bridge and at the far end turn left up Junkerngasse, a street notable for its fine old houses. Watch out for number 59. This is the elegant Béatrice v. Wattenwyl house where the Swiss government gives receptions for its famous guests. The facade of the building dates from the mid-15th century. At the top you come to the pride of the city—the magnificent Gothic Münster (Cathedral). Started in 1421 by master mason Matthias Ensinger on a site formerly occupied by an older church, it was planned on lines so spacious that half the population could worship in it at one time. Its construction went on for centuries. Even the Reformation, which converted it from a Catholic to a Protestant church, did not prevent work being continued. Daniel Heinz directed this for 25 years (from 1573 to

1598), completing the nave and the tower. The finishing touch, the tip of the 90-meter-high (300-ft.) steeple, was not added until 1893.

The cathedral has two outstandingly fine features, one on the outside and one inside. Outside is the main portal, with a magnificent sculptured representation of the Last Judgment (1490) whose 234 carved figures may distract attention from the admirable statues of the Wise and Foolish Virgins. This work was completed immediately before the Reformation, but fortunately escaped destruction by the iconoclasts who emptied the niches of the side portals.

Inside the church, while the elaborately carved pews and choir stalls are worth attention, of particular interest is the stained glass. Possibly the best are the 15th-century windows of the choir, but Bern has not been content to rest with the heritage of the past. Many fine windows have been added in recent years, like that of the Dance of Death which, though modern in execution, is old in design, for it was made from a sketch by Niklaus Manuel, Bern's artist-statesman-warrior of the 16th century. Before leaving the cathedral, walk across to the terrace at the back where, from the walls, there is a splendid view down on to the river. Look back in the direction from which you have come and you will see the gardens of the patrician houses along the Junkerngasse. In the little houses on the banks of the Aare the handworkers once lived. In those days this was the raucous part of town with many inns. There developed a bizarre dialect which you can still hear today if you are lucky. Known as Matten-English, it is spotted with Gypsy and Yiddish sounds. "Matten" stood for lowland and "English" for unintelligible. From the cathedral terrace, a little railway goes down to the Matten-English district.

If you walk from the cathedral up Herrengasse or Münstergasse, you will quickly reach the Casinoplatz and the Casino, which stands at the northern end of the Kirchenfeldbrücke. This contains a concert hall (frequent concerts), restaurants and banqueting rooms. Unlike most Swiss cities, Bern also has a Kursaal (usually they have one or the other), which lies on the northern side of the river and is devoted to rather lighter entertainment than the Casino. One of its attractions is a gaming room where boule is played to a five-franc limit. Further south on the same side of the river—opposite the Casino—is Helvetiaplatz, reached from the other bank by the Kirchenfeldbrücke. This historic square is surrounded by a cluster of Bern's most fascinating museums; including the Bernisches Historisches Museum (Bernese Historical Museum), Naturhistorisches Museum (Natural History Museum), Schweizerisches Schützenmuseum (Swiss Rifle Museum, Schweizerisches Alpines Museum (Swiss Alpine Museum) and the Kunsthalle (Art Gallery). Beyond Helvetiaplatz is the residential quarter of Kirchenfeld, and, a little further on still, the zoo.

Returning to the Casinoplatz, turn left down Münzgraben and then right along the terrace behind the Bundeshaus, the parliament building. Here there's another fine view across the river and, in good weather, to the distant Alps. At the bridge end of the parapet there is a diagram which will help you to pick out the principal peaks. You can walk round the end of the Bundeshaus into the Bundesplatz, and then into the traffic-free Bärenplatz. On Tuesday and Saturday mornings there is a colorful and lively market here and in some of the surrounding streets. It is at its best during the summer and fall.

PRACTICAL INFORMATION FOR BERN

GETTING TO BERN. Most people will arrive in Bern by train or car. However, there is a small airport—Belpmoos, nine kms. (six miles) south of the city—with flights from London, Paris, Nice, Venice and Lugano. A bus runs between the airport and the rail station; the fare is Fr. 8.

However, Bern's major links with the outside world are by train—and there are excellent rail connections with all the major Swiss cities—and by road. Again, the major Geneva–Zürich expressway runs by Bern. There is also a direct connection from Paris to Bern by superfast French train (TGV), 4½ hours.

TOURIST OFFICES. The Bern tourist office (Offizielles Verkehrsbüro Bern) is located in the Bahnhof, the rail station (tel. 031–22 76 76). The office is open in winter, Mon. to Sat. 8–6.30; and in summer, Mon. to Sat. 8–8.30 and Sun. 9–8.30. Services include hotel reservations, information about the city and the region, excursions, city sightseeing, guides and hostesses, and arranging congresses. The tourist office has a wide range of publications, most useful of which is *This Week in Bern,* with full listings of entertainment and events in the city. The tourist city transport card—full details under "Getting Around" below—is also available here. Additional information service at the bear pits during summer months.

HOTELS. Bern, with a large migrant population of parliamentarians and their staffs and foreign diplomats, has considerable numbers of good quality, moderately priced hotels, all for the most part comfortable and unpretentious, reflecting the town's homely quality. But this unfortunately also means that hotel space is often at a premium, especially during the four annual sessions of the Federal Parliament (March, June, September and December). Accordingly, you are well advised to make your reservations well in advance. Reservations and hotel list at the tourist office (electronic board outside, out of office hours).

Deluxe

Bellevue Palace, Kochergasse 3–5 (tel. 031–22 45 81). 250 beds. An exception to Bern's usual image as a city of unpretentious and cosy hotels, the Bellevue Palace is a luxury hotel with a vengeance. Excellently managed, it exudes an atmosphere of old-world comfort and boasts a number of fine restaurants. Its bar is a regular hangout for politicians from the Bundeshaus next door. AE, DC, MC, V.

Schweizerhof, Bahnhofplatz 11 (tel. 031–22 45 01). 175 beds. Opposite the rail station. Though less palatial than its rival, the Bellevue Palace, the accent here is nonetheless very much on comfort and elegance. With fine restaurants, plus a good bar, this too is popular among the politicos. AE, DC, MC, V.

Moderate

Alfa, Laupenstrasse 15 (tel. 031–25 38 66). 59 beds. Small hotel on the north bank of the river Aare, opposite the Old Town, but handy for the rail station. AE, DC, MC, V.

Ambassador, Seftigenstrasse 97 (tel. 031–45 41 11). 175 beds. Modern hotel with a good view of the city. Away from the center but reached easily by tram (number 9). AE, DC, MC, V.

Bären, Schauplatzgasse 4 (tel. 031–22 33 67). 91 beds. Pleasant, sturdy hotel in the heart of town with a fine-quality restaurant. A few minutes' walk from the rail station. AE, DC, MC, V.

Bern, Zeughausgasse 9 (tel. 031–21 10 21). 170 beds. Comfortable modern spot in the Old Town, with many facilities. AE, DC, MC, V.

Bristol, Schauplatzgasse 10 (tel. 031–22 01 01). 140 beds. Spacious and centrally located, just a few steps from the rail station. No restaurant. AE, DC, MC, V.

City-Mövenpick, Bubenbergplatz 7 (tel. 031–22 53 77). 73 beds. Reliable, modern chain hotel in good central location. Restaurant next door is part of the Mövenpick chain. AE, DC, MC, V.

Metropole, Zeughausgasse 28 (tel. 031–22 50 21). 100 beds. Comfortable modern hotel in the Old Town. Good food in all three restaurants. AE, DC, MC, V.

Savoy, Neuengasse 26 (tel. 031–22 44 05). 95 beds. No restaurant, but central location compensates. AE, DC, MC, V.

Inexpensive

Alpenblick, Kasernenstrasse 29 (tel. 031–42 42 55). 21 beds; no rooms with bath. Reasonably priced, small hotel. Away from the center, but easily reached by tram (number 9).

Continental, Zeughausgasse 27 (tel. 031–22 26 26). 65 beds. Pleasant hotel in the heart of historic Bern. No restaurant. AE, DC, MC, V.

Goldener Adler, Gerechtigkeitsgasse 7 (tel. 031–22 17 25). 40 beds. In lovely old building right in the center of the Old Town. AE, MC.

Goldener Schlüssel, Rathausgasse 72 (tel. 031–22 02 16). 48 beds. Loads of Old-Town atmosphere combined with competent service. AE, DC, MC.

Hospiz zur Heimat, Gerechtigkeitsgasse 50 (tel. 031–22 04 36). 70 beds. Fine Old-Town location and reasonable rates. AE, DC, MC, V.

Jardin, Militärstrasse 38 (tel. 031–40 01 17). 34 beds. Away from the center but easily reachable by tram (number 9). Rooms with shower at reasonable prices. AE, DC, MC.

Krebs, Genfergasse 8 (tel. 031–22 49 42). 70 beds. Centrally located, but with a wide range of room prices. No restaurant. AE, DC, MC.

Kreuz, Zeughausgasse 41 (tel. 031–22 11 62). 170 beds. Prices between moderate and inexpensive, depending on the room you get. Very centrally located for both shopping and sightseeing. AE, DC, MC.

Marthahaus, Wyttenbachstrasse 229 (tel. 031–42 41 35). 62 beds; no rooms with bath. Low rates. Away from the center but easily reached by bus (number 20).

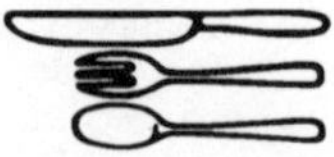

RESTAURANTS. The Bernese love to eat and drink, and have more than 150 restaurants, taverns and bars to prove it. From French cuisine, through Spanish, Chinese and Greek to American hamburgers, it is all here. But no one should leave without trying Bern's own specialties. They reflect a population with a hearty appetite and a rural tradition. Just to mention a few:

Bärner Platte (boiled beef, port, tongue, sausages and ham with sauerkraut and beans); *Berner Zungenwürst* (Bernese tongue sausage); *Buurehamme* (hot smoked ham); *Emmentaler Schafsvoressen* (Emmental lamb stew); *Berner Rösti* (grated potato and onion fried in butter); *Ratsherrentopf* (Rösti with roast veal, beef, liver and sausage); *Oepfelchüechli* (hot apple doughnuts); *Schlüferli* (twists of sweet batter deep fried and served cold); *Züpfe* (Bernese farmer's bread).

Expensive

Bären, Schauplatzgasse 4 (tel. 031–22 33 67). Excellent hotel-restaurant of the Bären hotel, with warm atmosphere. Prices are surprisingly reasonable. Bears feature heavily in the decor. AE, DC, MC, V.

Bellevue Grill, Kochergasse 3–5 (tel. 031–22 45 81). Outstanding food and excellent service have long made this hotel-restaurant a favorite among politicians, diplomats and businessmen. AE, DC, MC, V.

Della Casa, Schauplatzgasse 16 (tel. 031–22 21 42). This is where you could meet a member of the Swiss government out for lunch or dinner. Usually filled with politicians enjoying the French and Italian dishes as well as listening to the latest gossip from the Bundeshaus. DC, MC, V.

Du Théâtre, Theaterplatz 7 (tel. 031–22 71 77). Elegant establishment with a long tradition of fine food and wines. AE, V.

Ermitage, Marutgasse 15 (tel. 031–22 35 41). One of the most pleasant restaurants in town, with a wide choice of classical dishes. AE, DC, MC, V.

Mistral, Kramgasse 42 (tel. 031–22 82 77). Excellent specialties from Provence in the south of France; try the lamb. AE, DC, MC, V.

Räblus, Zeughausgasse 3 (tel. 031–22 59 08). Romantic atmosphere and excellent food. Pianist plays in the bar. AE, DC, V.

Schultheissenstube, in the Schweizerhof hotel, Bahnhofplatz 11 (tel. 031–22 45 01). Dignified and rather formal hotel-restaurant, with fine French cuisine.

Zum Rathaus, Rathausplatz 5 (tel. 031–22 61 83). On the historic Town Hall square. Loads of local atmosphere as well as fine food. AE, DC, V.

Moderate

Beaujolais, Aarbergergasse 52 (tel. 031–22 48 86). French bistro with good food. AE, MC.

Casino, Herrengasse 25 (tel. 031–22 20 27). Though sometimes expensive for the category, the Casino comes into its own in summer when the tables are moved outside; fine view over the river. AE, DC, MC, V.

Frohsinn, Münstergasse 54 (tel. 031–22 37 68). A small eating house with only 12 tables, but where the stress is very much on the excellent food. Rather more expensive than some of the other restaurants in this category, but worth it.

Kornhauskeller, Kornhausplatz 18 (tel. 031–22 11 33). In the cellar of the impressive 18th-century town granary. A visit here is a must if only for the impressively historic surroundings. Swiss specialties. AE, DC, MC, V.

Lorenzini, Marktgasse-Passage 3 (tel. 031–22 78 50). Excellent Italian food in a bistro atmosphere.

Morillon, Morillomstrasse 8–10 (tel. 031–45 96 96). Run by one of Switzerland's best-known chefs, Victor Imfeld. Prices can be high for this category, but standards remain consistently good.

Pinocchio, Aarbergergasse 6 (tel. 031–22 33 62). Friendly Italian restaurant, particularly popular among Social Democrat politicians. Fast service. AE, DC, MC, V.

Taverne Valaisanne, Neuengasse 40 (tel. 031–22 77 66). Excellent and reasonably priced Swiss specialties.

Zimmermania, Brunnengasse 19 (tel. 031–22 15 42). A charming restaurant in the Old Town with simple, high-quality food.

Zum Zähringer, Badgasse 1 (tel. 031–22 32 70). Part of a tiny old theater and accordingly long since a favorite of the theater-going crowd. Varied menu.

Inexpensive

Brasserie am Bärengraben, Muristalden 1 (tel. 031–41 42 18). Charming little restaurant with moderate to inexpensive dishes. Great pastries.

Fédéral, Bärenplatz 31 (tel. 031–22 16 24). Across the square from the Bundeshaus, and correspondingly popular with ministers, parliamentarians and farmers alike, despite—or possibly because of—the simple decor.

Gfeller, Bärenplatz 21 (tel. 031–22 69 44). Famous for its enormous range of fruit tarts. Popular with farmers' wives coming into town on market days.

Klötzlikeller, Gerechtigkeitsgasse 62 (tel. 031–22 74 56). More for drinking than eating, this is a lovely old wine cellar, one of the few to have survived. AE.

Vegetaris, Neuengasse 15 (tel. 031–22 46 16). A first-floor restaurant where, surprisingly, you can eat outside in a quiet garden. No alcohol.

GETTING AROUND. By Bus and Tram. Bern has an extensive network of buses and trams, most of which start from the main station. Fares range from 80 centimes, for the shortest trips, to Fr. 1.20. Tourist cards for an unlimited number of rides are available for the whole network: 1-day Fr. 3, 2-day Fr. 5, 3-day Fr. 7. There is a 24-hour season ticket, good for the entire network, which costs Fr. 4. These tickets are available from the public transport ticket office in the subway leading down to the main station (take the escalator in front of Loeb's department store and turn right through the Christoffel Tower) and from the tourist office. Ordinary tickets are available at tram and bus stops; you should buy your ticket before boarding the tram or bus. A map on the dispenser shows you which ticket to buy.

There is also a little railway that runs from the Bundesterrasse (the terrace behind the Bundeshaus) down to Marzili on the banks of the Aare. This is the Marzili cogwheel railway. It works on the water balance system. The track itself is only 105 meters (320 ft.) long, but during the one-minute trip it climbs 32 meters (70 ft.). The one-way trip costs 60 centimes.

By Taxi. These are plentiful in Bern, but, as elsewhere, are expensive.

By Car. For sightseeing you are better off leaving your car in the garage. Points of interest are close together. Streets are often narrow and sometimes closed to general traffic.

By Bicycle. These are available from the main rail station. However, unless you want to leave the center, getting around on foot is much easier.

On Foot. By far the most sensible way to get around. Ask for a map of the city at your hotel or the tourist office, which also has suggested tours on foot, including one in their *This Week in Bern* magazine.

TOURS AND EXCURSIONS. For further details of all tours in and around Bern, contact the Bern tourist office in the main rail station. A daily, two-hour tour around the Old Town is organized by the tourist office. This covers all the principal sights in the city (see pamphlet "Sightseeing").

Excursions from Bern. Bern, thanks to its central location and excellent road and rail links with the rest of the country, is an ideal base for day-trips to many other Swiss cities, Zürich, Geneva and Basel among them. However, the most popular trips from the city, and for good reasons, are to the alpine villages and towering peaks of the Bernese Oberland, or to the delightful and remote farming region of the Bernese Mittelland.

Probably the most popular trip of all is to the Jungfrau in the Bernese Oberland. Round-trip rail tickets cost Fr. 108 second class and Fr. 124 first class. The train goes through Interlaken, Lauterbrunnen, Wengen and Kleine Scheidegg to the Jungfraujoch, which, at 3,454 meters (11,333 ft.), has the highest rail station in Europe, located among the unforgettable peaks and eternal snows of the Bernese Alps. Full details are given in our *Bernese Oberland* chapter.

The Bernese Mittelland to the east of the city is accessible by train and bus. Among its many rustic highlights are the little town of Worb and the Emmental Valley, famous for its cheese and huge fortress-like farmhouses.

Closer to home is Gurten, Bern's "mountain," a peak some 850 meters (2,660 ft.) high and no more than 20 minutes from the city center by road and cable car. It's a lovely spot for walks and has fine views.

MUSEUMS AND GALLERIES. Opening hours vary so much and change so often that it's best to consult *This Week in Bern,* which gives full details of all museums. Entrance fees vary from Fr. 1 to 3. Some museums are free. All the principal museums can be reached on foot from the station in about ten minutes. There's a lot to see, so spread your museum visits out a bit to give yourself time to digest them comfortably.

Bernisches Historisches Museum (Bern Historical Museum), Helvetiaplatz 5 (tel. 031–43 18 11). One of the most important historical museums in Switzerland, with a renowned prehistoric collection, 15th-century Burgundian-Dutch tapestries, and engravings. Among the specifically Bernese works are the 15th-century sculptures from the west door of the Cathedral. Open Tues. to Sun. 10–5.

Einstein Haus, Kramgasse 49. The house where the physicist Albert Einstein lived during some of his seven years in Bern in the early years of the century. It was in Bern that he produced his special theory of relativity and started work on his general theory of relativity. Open Tues. to Sat. 10–5.

Käfigturm (Prison Tower), Marktgasse 67 (tel. 031–22 23 06). Erected as a prison tower between 1641 and 1643, it now serves as an exhibition center charting the economic and cultural life of Bern. Open Tues. to Sun. 10–1 and 2–6, also 7–9 P.M. on Thurs.

Kornhaus, Zeughausgasse 2 (tel. 031–22 31 61). An 18th-century granary in which alternating exhibitions show Bern's industry, commerce and arts and crafts. Open Tues. to Sun. 10–12 and 2–5, also 7–9 P.M. on Thurs.

Kunsthalle (Art Gallery), Helvetiaplatz 1 (tel. 031–43 00 31). Challenging and innovative exhibits of modern and contemporary works. Open Tues. 10–9, Wed. to Sun. 10–5.

Kunstmuseum (Fine Arts Museum), Hodlerstrasse 8–12 (tel. 031–22 09 44). Excellent and extensive collections from the Middle Ages to the present, though with a particularly strong modern department, including the largest and probably the finest collection of paintings by Paul Klee in the world. The turn-of-the-century building has lately been extensively renovated. Interesting temporary exhibits. Open Tues. 10–9, Wed. to Sun. 10–5.

Naturhistorisches Museum (Natural History Museum), Bernastrasse 15 (tel. 031–43 18 39). Magnificent natural history museum. Of particular interest is an extensive collection of Swiss alpine minerals, crystals and precious stones. But don't miss Barry, a stuffed St. Bernard dog who saved more than 40 people in the Alps during the last century. Open Mon. to Sat. 9–12 and 2–5, Sun. 10–12 and 2–5.

Schweizerisches Gutenbergmuseum (Swiss Gutenberg Museum), Zeughausgasse 2 (tel. 031–22 31 61). Charts the history of printing through the ages from hand presses to composing and bookbinding machines. Volumes from many different periods. Temporarily closed.

Schweizerisches P.T.T.-Museum (Swiss P.T.T. Museum), Helvetiaplatz 4 (tel. 031–44 92 88). A must for stamp collectors, with rare stamps from around the world, plus the history of Switzerland's postal system and, more up to date, telecommunications.

Schweizerisches Schützenmuseum (Swiss Rifle Museum), Bernastrasse 5 (tel. 031–43 01 27). Excellent museum tracing the development of firearms since 1817. Open Wed. to Fri. 10–12 and 2–4, Tues. and Sat. 2–4, Sun. 10:30–12 and 2–4.

HISTORIC BUILDINGS AND SITES. Bärengraben (Bear Pit), near Nydeggbrucke. The city's famous bear pit, here since 1856, though bears are believed to have been here in Bern since at least the 15th century.

Bundeshäuser (Houses of Parliament), Bundesplatz. 19th-century parliament buildings somewhat reminiscent of the Capitol building in Washington. Guided tours on weekdays at 9, 10, 11, 2, 3 and 4, and on Sundays at 9, 10, 11, 2 and 3. No tours during parliamentary sessions, on holidays or special occasions.

Münster (Cathedral), Münsterplatz. Begun in 1421 and largely completed during the following century, though the tower was finished only at the end of the 19th century. There are fine sculptures over the main entrance and a vaulted ceiling in the choir richly painted by Niklaus Manuel in the 16th century. Open Tues. to Fri. 10–12 and 2–4, Sat. 10–12 and 2–5, Sun. 11–12.

Rathaus (Town Hall), Rathausplatz. Fine Gothic Town Hall dating from 1406–17, rebuilt 1939–42, though the interior is largely untouched since the 15th century. Guided tours by arrangement; not otherwise open to the public.

Zeitglockenturm (Clock Tower), Kramgasse. Original west gate to the city, built by Berchtold V in 1191. Famous today principally for the Renaissance astronomical clock; begins about four minutes to the hour at 10 and 11 A.M. The inside of the clocktower can be seen daily at 4:30 P.M. (tickets from the tourist office in the main railway station).

ZOO. Dalmaziquai 149 (tel. 031–43 06 16). A short trip by tram (number 18) from the center. The 800 animals include wildlife rarely seen in a conventional zoo. There are bison, wolves, lynx, black grouse, roe deer, chamois, white hare, and bears, all to be seen in beautiful woodland. Open all year: in summer, daily 8–6.30; in winter, daily 9–12 and 2–5.

SHOPPING. Bern's proud boast is that its six kms. (four miles) of arcades make it Europe's largest all-weather medieval shopping center! The focal points for good shopping lie between the main station and the Clock Tower. You will find watchmakers and jewelers, clothing stores, shops specializing in leather goods, embroidery and stationery, department stores, cafes-cum-cake-shops, etc. The shops all lie so close together that the best thing to do is walk right down the town under the arcades on one side and then up the other to be quite sure not to miss anything.

There is a wide choice of department stores: **EPA** on the left half-way down Marktgasse (toiletries, tights, food department in the basement), **ABM** and **Globus** in Spitalgasse, both on the right going down the town, and **Migros** for more or less everything, again on the left going down Marktgasse. Here you will find the food department on the ground floor and everything else in the basement. Sports equipment, books and the music department are on the first floor next to a discount market that is good for wines.

But to get a real feel for Bernese shopping, you should wander in and out of the little shops. Antique shops and secondhand bookshops can be an adventure. The delicatessens, bread shops, butchers, chocolate and cheese shops are mouth-watering. Then there are very individual boutiques, music shops and all sorts of stores in the underground cellars.

Bern is also famous for its markets. In the Middle Ages the town was a great market center with four major markets lasting several days annually and attracting merchants from far away. The only one to survive is the Zibelemärit (Onion Market). This takes place on the fourth Monday in November. It is a very colorful event with onions braided together in long strips hanging from the stalls. Onions take on the shapes of dolls, animals, even alarm clocks. The market is said to date back to 1405 when a large part of the city was destroyed by fire. In gratitude for assistance given by Neuchâtel and Lake Murten country people after the tragedy, Bern granted the latter the right to sell their onions in the city's market square.

In May there is a geranium market. How would Bern look in summer without those poster-red flowers brightening up the facades? Bernese householders are very proud of the quality of their plants and there is quite a lot of competition between neighbors to see who has the best. For its unique flower decoration, Bern has been awarded the title "Europe's Most Beautiful Floral City" by the Entente Florale.

In addition, Bern has weekly markets on Tuesday and Saturday mornings. Farmers and market gardeners pour into town to sell fruit, vegetables and flowers to the city folk from stalls in front of the Bundeshaus. In the Münstergasse is the meat and dairy produce market.

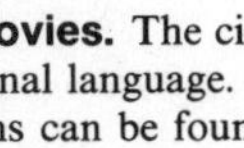

MUSIC, MOVIES AND THEATERS. Music. A number of churches in the city, including the Münster, have concerts, the latter every Tuesday evening in summer. Fine concerts take place also at the **Konservatorium für Musik,** Kramgasse 36, and at the **Radio Studio Bern,** Schwarztorstrasse 21. Consult *This Week in Bern* for ticket sales and starting times. Jazz is popular and reaches a peak with an International Jazz Festival in spring.

Movies. The city has some 20 movie theaters where films are shown in the original language. You will find a wide variety of English-language films. Programs can be found in the local press or on street posters.

Theaters. A unique aspect of Bern is its wide range of little theaters. Most are found in the cellars of the Old Town. Avant-garde plays, pantomime, and modern dance are performed in this underground world where the audience sits close together on folding chairs. For details of programs at the pocket theaters, which have wonderful names like **Theater am Zytglogge, Kleintheater, Atelier-**

Theater am Käfigturm, consult *This Week in Bern* or ask at your hotel. The usual language is German, so be prepared.

Stadttheater (Municipal Theater), Kornhausplatz 20. The city's leading traditional theater: operas, operettas, plays and ballet. Tickets are available at Predigergasse 3 (tel. 031–22 07 77), Mon. to Sat. 10–6.30, and Sun. 10–12.30.

NIGHTLIFE. Bern is not the liveliest of night spots, but there are a few venues to satisfy the night owls. The **Mocambo,** Genfergasse 10 (tel. 031–22 50 41) has dancing and is a fair bet for a good night out; **Jaylin's Club** at the Schweizerhof hotel, Bahnhofplatz 11 (tel. 031–22 45 01) is a pleasant disco and famous jazz club, and also has a bar with music; the **Cadillac,** Laupenstrasse 10 (tel. 031–25 34 34) serves food as well as providing a show and dancing; **Chikito,** Neuengasse 28 (tel. 031–22 26 80) is a haunt for the young; and the **Babalu,** Gurtengasse 3 (tel. 031–22 08 88) is another popular dance spot. Be prepared to pay quite a bit at any of these nightclubs, especially if you drink spirits. Clubs are open till around 2–2:30 A.M., later on Fri. and Sat.

For jazz, try the **Mahogany Hall,** Klösterlistutz 18 (tel. 031–41 60 00). For Swiss folk music and dancing, and where you can also eat, there is the **Swiss Chalet,** Rathausgasse 75 (tel. 031–22 37 71). **Mr. Pickwick Pub,** Speichergasse 37 (tel. 031–22 91 93) is a friendly drinking spot where you can also get something to eat. It is open until midnight. And for those who want to round off the evening with a quiet nightcap in elegant surroundings, there is the bar of the **Bellevue Palace** hotel, Kochergasse 3–5 (tel. 031–22 45 81) or the bar of the Schweizerhof hotel, Bahnhofplatz 11 (tel. 031–22 45 01).

SPORTS. Golf. *The Golf and Country Club Blümisberg,* 18 kms. (11 miles) west of Bern on the road to Fribourg (tel. 037–36 13 80). 18 holes. Only for members of a golf club: membership cards required. Clubhouse with restaurant, bar, showers and swimming pool. Green fees: weekdays Fr. 35, Sat. or Sun. Fr. 50, per week Fr. 200. Open end of Mar. to beginning of Nov.

Swimming. There are many public swimming pools in the Bern area. Right in the center is *Hallenbad Hirschengraben,* Maulbeerstr. 14 (tel. 031–25 36 56). This is an indoor pool. But for a great experience in summer—if you are a good swimmer—go to the Marzili river bath below the Bundeshaus (tel. 031–22 00 46). There you can undress, walk a couple of kilometers along the Aare, and then swim down, getting out at the Marzili. Later the swimming gets tough.

Tennis. Bern has a number of courts where you can play. Ask at the tourist office or your hotel for details.

Riding. The *Riding School Eldorado,* Gurtentäli, is easily reached by bus (number 17), tel. 031–53 48 40. Open Mon. to Fri. 8–9:30 P.M. and Sat. 8–12.

Cycling. There are about 300 kms. (185 miles) of marked trails around Bern. Ask for information from the tourist office.

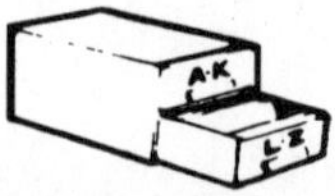

USEFUL ADDRESSES. Travel Agents. *Thomas Cook Reisebüro,* von Werdt-Passage 3–5 (tel. 031–22 35 45).

Embassies. *American Embassy,* Jubiläumsstrasse 93 (tel. 031–43 70 11). *British Embassy,* Thunstrasse 50 (tel. 031–44 50 21). *Australian Embassy,* Alpenstrasse 29 (tel. 031–43 01 43). *Canadian Embassy,* Kirchenfelder 88 (tel. 031–44 63 81).

Car Hire. *Avis,* Effingerstr. 20 (tel. 031–25 10 25); *Hertz,* Kasinoplatz (tel. 031–22 33 13); *Europcar,* Laupenstr. 15 (tel. 031–25 75 55).

THE BERNESE OBERLAND

Aristocrat of Alpine Scenery

It was the Bernese Oberland, more than any other area of Switzerland, that put Switzerland on the tourist map. Its towering peaks, massive glaciers, lakes and waterfalls attracted the famous and fashionable from the end of the 18th century onwards, leading to the great explosion of tourism to Switzerland in the 19th century.

It was the Romantics who wrought this great change. What for generations had been considered a wild, terrifying and inhospitable region became for the poets, painters and writers of the late 18th and early 19th centuries an awe inspiring and magnificent landscape. The great German writer Goethe was moved to write one of his most celebrated poems, *Gesang der Geister über den Wassern* ("Song of the Spirits Over the Waters"), in 1779 after contemplating the Staubbach Falls. Rousseau was another early and admiring visitor, paving the way for fashionable Parisian society in the early 19th century which flocked to Interlaken to see these magnificent natural phenomena for themselves. Thereafter the list of those who visited the Bernese Oberland reads like a 19th century Who's Who: Byron, Shelley, Thackeray, Ruskin, Queen Victoria, Matthew Arnold, Brahms, Turner, and that indefatigable traveler Mark Twain. A more recent traveler to the Bernese Oberland, Joanna Lumley, there to play one of James Bond's girls in *On Her Majesty's Secret Service,* said of the view from Piz Gloria, the restaurant at the peak of the Schilthorn, "Ringed by range after range of mountains, the view was unparaleled, perfect; too perfect—it looked like a painted backcloth. A props man was given the task of enticing birds to fly around to show it was real."

Today, tourism remains the region's most important industry in both summer and winter. For in addition to the famous summer lakeside resorts of Interlaken, Thun, Spiez and Brienz, the Bernese Oberland also boasts some of the best and most popular winter resorts in Switzerland: Wengen, Grindelwald, Mürren and Gstaad among them.

Bernese Oberland Overview

The Bernese Oberland covers an area of around 4,600 sq. kms. (1,800 sq. miles), and comprises nine major valleys and two major lakes, the Thunersee and the Brienzersee (the lakes of Thun and Brienz). There are also a number of very much smaller lakes in the heart of the mountains, namely the Bachalpsee, at a height of 2,254 meters (7,400 ft.), located just below the summit of the Faulhorn, and the Öeschinensee above Kandersteg. But the major attraction remains of course the mountains themselves, the Eiger at 3,970 meters (13,022 ft.), the Mönch at 4,099 meters (13,022 ft.) and, most famous of all, the Jungfraujoch at 4,158 meters high (13,638 ft.).

The wide variety in altitude between the resorts in the north of the Bernese Oberland and the mountains to the south creates a great diversity of scenery. Around the Thunersee you will see fig trees, vineyards, and positively Mediterranean-like vegetation; in two hours' time you will reach the region of Alpine plants, and an hour and a half later you are in the land of eternal snow and ice. On an early July morning you can swim in the Thunersee, and in the afternoon ski on the slopes of the Jungfrau.

Even the two neighboring lakes, Thunersee and the Brienzersee, vary greatly in character. The former has a mild climate and a relatively open situation, although the hills rise steeply along the northern shore. It is surrounded by fertile land, flowers, orchards, vineyards and fig trees, the whole sprinkled with ancient villages, castles, and manors. But the Brienzersee on the other hand is encircled by wild mountain ranges, rocky cliffs, and dark forests. While traveling around it you will constantly hear the thunder of waterfalls. Lake Thun is much the larger, 20 kms. (13 miles) long, and about three kms. (two miles) wide. The lake of Brienz is just over 13 kms. (over eight miles) long, and two and a half kms. (one and a half miles) wide.

However fascinated you are by the natural beauty of the district, keep an eye on the little towns and villages you pass, for in architectural charm the Bernese Oberland is almost unsurpassed. Whether you travel by bus, car, or train, you will see enchanting houses with terraces and graceful little towers, their gardens bursting with color in summer.

On Sundays you might see women and children dressed in local costume; but the thick, boned bodices are not very comfortable and are infrequently worn these days. However, the Swiss Society for the Preservation of Historic Sites is increasingly concerning itself with the

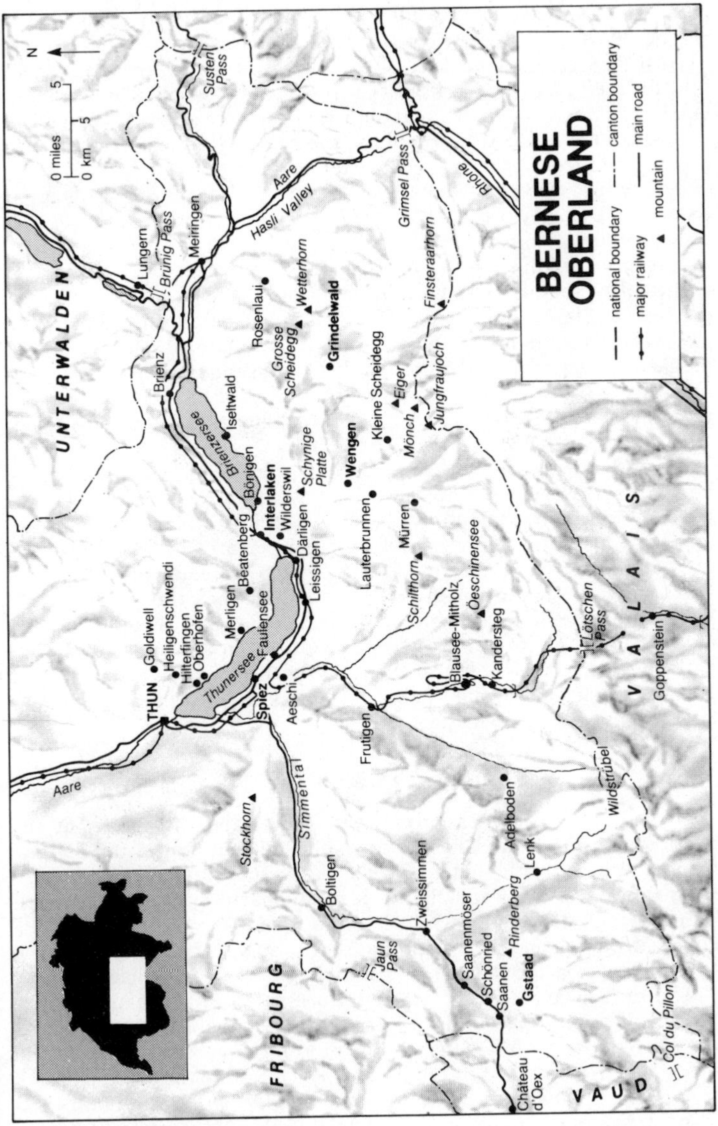
BERNESE OBERLAND
national boundary
canton boundary
major railway
main road
mountain
0 miles 5
0 km 5
N
UNTERWALDEN
FRIBOURG
VAUD
VALAIS
Aare
Rhône
THUN
Goldiwell
Heiligenschwendi
Hilterfingen
Oberhofen
Merligen
Beatenberg
Faulensee
Thunersee
Spiez
Aeschi
Leissigen
Därligen
Interlaken
Wilderswil
Bönigen
Iseltwald
Brienzersee
Brienz
Lungern
Brünig Pass
Meiringen
Hasli Valley
Susten Pass
Grimsel Pass
Rosenlaui
Grosse Scheidegg
Wetterhorn
Grindelwald
Schynige Platte
Wengen
Kleine Scheidegg
Eiger
Mönch
Jungfraujoch
Finsteraarhorn
Lauterbrunnen
Mürren
Schilthorn
Öeschinensee
Blausee-Mitholz
Kandersteg
Lötschen Pass
Goppenstein
Frutigen
Stockhorn
Simmental
Boltigen
Zweissimmen
Adelboden
Lenk
Wildstrubel
Saanenmöser
Schönried
Rinderberg
Saanen
Gstaad
Jaun Pass
Château d'Oex
Col du Pillon

conservation of the national dress, and its branches organize festivals and pageants to encourage its use.

The men's traditional dress has almost entirely disappeared—except in a few of the most inaccessible villages and on special occasions—but the women's is much better preserved. There are girls who still possess a *Hasli,* a shirt with starched sleeves, worn in white on Sundays and blue for the rest of the week. With it goes a heavy woollen ankle length skirt, fastening at the front, and blue or purple stockings. A small black cap, known as a *Zitterli,* completes the outfit. But the costume varies a great deal throughout the Bernese Oberland.

The Bernese Oberland is known also for its woodcarving. This originated at Brienz in the last century. A man named Fischer started carving pipes of horn and later of maple. Soon he applied his knowledge to carving napkin-rings, boxes, egg-cups and cigarette holders and eventually experimented with figures—first trying William Tell, of course. Gradually his neat, artistic work gained a following, and Fischer's whim became a vast industry. Today the industry has grown to include cabinetwork, and although these large and impressive pieces of furniture may not be particularly comfortable or easy to clean, they are nicely designed. Another form of woodworking takes place at Frutigen, where matches and matchboxes are made.

Among other traditional crafts here is lacemaking, while handweaving is still practised on a small scale. The handmade "torchon" lace of the Lauterbrunnen valley is well known and justly admired. First-rate fancy leather articles are manufactured by a firm in Spiez, and the artistic and lovely pottery made at Steffisburg is gaining popularity.

Apart from the craftsmen and the hotel-keepers, the remaining inhabitants of the Bernese Oberland are mostly farmers. If you are traveling by car, you have to stop every now and then to let the cows pass, and wherever you go you hear the tinkle of the bells hung around their necks. Even in the elegant streets of Interlaken you will meet the herd coming home every evening.

Exploring the Bernese Oberland

At the point where the river Aare leaves the Thunersee, at the northern end of the lake, lies the town of Thun, gateway to the Bernese Oberland, a picturesque place which has managed to retain much of its medieval character and charm. It is dominated by the four-turreted Zähringen Castle, which with the church and the town hall forms a coherent photogenic group approached by steep streets and flights of stairs. Down on the lakeside is another castle, called Schadau.

The town is an excellent center for a number of fascinating walks. Within pleasant walking distance are the heights of Goldiwil, Heiligenschwendi and the Grusisberg. A morning's walk will take you to several small resorts around the end of the lake, or to the bird sanctuary at Einigen. If you are a glutton for exercise (although you don't need to be a mountaineer), you can make the pleasantly tiring climb up Stockhorn (2,163 meters, 7,100 ft.). Alternatively, if walking doesn't appeal, there are good boat services from Thun, bus services around the lake, and trains along the southern shore.

On the northern shore of the Thunersee, betweem Thun and Interlaken, are a string of interesting villages, all of them fairly well known resorts. During the summer these places are filled to capacity, but being smaller and less worldly than either Interlaken or Thun, they are quieter and, of course, less expensive. Hilterfingen, the nearest resort to Thun, has a yachting school and, like adjacent Oberhofen, is notable for its gardens and lush vegetation. Oberhofen, on a lovely bay, has a picturesque 12th-century castle on the waterside. Next comes Gunten, a waterskiing center, which is also well known for its rich southern vegetation and mild climate. From here, you can take a bus to the hillside resort of Sigriswil. A little bit farther on is Merligen, a lakeside resort at the entrance to the Justis valley where every September cheese produced during the summer is gathered together for solemn division between the dairymen and cattle-owners of the district at the ceremony known as the *Kästeilet.* Just beyond, at the shore terminal of Beatenbucht, you can take the funicular up to Beatenberg (1,157 meters, 3,800 ft.) and then a chairlift on to Niederhorn (1,919 meters, 6,300 ft.), both of them winter and summer resorts with remarkable views. Farther on still is the entrance to the illuminated Beatus caves.

Spiez

Heading along the southern shore of the Thunersee from Thun, the first important town is Spiez. Here you can still breathe the air of ancient poetry and hear the songs of troubadours. It was Rudolph II, King of Burgundy, who built the present castle of Spiez, then called "The Golden Hall of Wendelsee." Afterwards it belonged to the Strättliger family one of whom, Heinrich, was a great troubadour. But the poets and troubadours of the 13th century frequently fell upon hard times, and Heinrich von Strättliger was forced to sell his castle. It was bought by a nobleman called Adrian von Bubenberg, whose stout defense of Murten against the Burgundians in the 1470s was to make him a Swiss hero. The castle, with its lovely Romanesque choir and massive crypt, was later acquired by the von Erlach family, to whom it belonged from 1516 to 1875. Now it is the property of a public foundation. Concerts and open-air theatrical performances are periodically held here.

Leaving Spiez, you pass through some villages that are less well known and less popular with visitors than the resorts on the opposite shore. They include Leissigen, Darligen, the small sailing resort of Faulensee, and behind it (at 850 meters, 2,800 ft.), Aeschi, which caters for both winter and summer visitors.

Interlaken

Gateway to the Bernese Oberland, for generations Interlaken has had one purpose only: to attract tourists. Interlaken, as its name implies, is situated "between the lakes"—the Thunersee and the Brienzersee. On a strip of flat, grassy land bisected by the River Aare, it is surrounded by a superb mountain panorama. The west and east sections of the town are connected by the Höheweg, a central esplanade lined with trees, formal gardens, hotels and shops. A quaint touch is given by the horse-drawn carriages as they clip-clop alongside today's monster tourist buses, but it's a nostalgic touch, too, for they are a reminder of 19th-century and Edwardian Interlaken. Many older hotels have been pulled down or modernized and new ones have arisen, such as the skyscraper Metropole with its breathtaking views from the upper floors. However, if you want to sink into the last century, there is the beautifully renovated Hotel Victoria-Jungfrau, full of memories of yesteryear.

Halfway along the Höheweg on the north side, and almost hidden behind shops, is Interlaken's Casino, standing in beautiful gardens with a gigantic flowerbed clock. In the Casino, a building of curiously mixed styles both inside and out, you can try your luck at the gaming tables (maximum stake Fr. 5), or listen to a constantly changing program of symphony concerts, dance bands, even yodeling.

During the summer Interlaken has a tradition of open-air performances (but the audience sits in a splendid covered grandstand) of Schiller's *Wilhelm Tell,* a drama with a large cast which perpetuates the memory of the legendary hero and the historic overthrow of the house of Habsburg. The resort also has an outstandingly fine 18-hole golf course at Unterseen, close to the Thunersee, but golfers claim that they are put off by the magnificent scenery.

Interlaken as an Excursion Center

Obviously Interlaken has many restaurants, cafés, bars, dance halls, movie theaters, and all the trappings that go to make a successful resort but, first and foremost, it is a center for excursions, and as such has few rivals in Europe.

The Swiss are justly famous for their remarkable engineering ability. Throughout the Bernese Oberland they have fully developed this special skill in providing mountain transport. It seems, in fact, as if every peak and crag has been tunneled for trains or elevators, or bound with the cables of aerial cabins and chairlifts. Cogwheel trains scurry up and down mountains; buses add a touch of contrasting color to winding roads; cable cars and chairlifts soar silently aloft. Thus sightseers can alight at heights varying from around 500 meters (about 2,000 ft.) to the Jungfraujoch's 3,475 meters (11,400 ft.). The latter is possibly the finest excursion in Switzerland—some say in Europe—and maybe the most expensive one, too. But first let's take a look at something more modest.

Only five minutes' walk from Interlaken's West station is the lower terminal of the funicular railway up to Heimwehfluh (669 meters, 2,200 ft.), from where there are magnificent views of towering Jungfrau, Eiger and Mönch. At the top, there's an elaborate scale-model railway. On the other side of the town, not much farther away, is the funicular which will take you on the 15-minute ride up to Harder Kulm (1,310 meters, 4,300 ft.), and so to an even finer mountain and lake panorama. There are splendid walks along prepared paths, and you may even see a wild ibex, for they wander freely hereabouts. Just a short distance from the top station is an attractive restaurant with a terrace where you can drink in both the view and something stronger.

Now let's venture farther afield and a trifle higher. From Interlaken East station the Bernese Oberland Railway will take you in six minutes to Wilderswil, a charming little spot with a view of the Jungfrau that, according to Ruskin, is one of the three great sights of Europe. At Wilderswil you change to a cogwheel train for the steep, 50-minute climb to Schynige Platte (1,965 meters, 6,450 ft.). Even by Bernese Oberland standards the view from here is remarkably beautiful and fully justifies its fame. Almost as famous is the Alpine Botanical Garden near the summit station, where hundreds of different Alpine plants have been laid out in natural surroundings. If you are looking for a really memorable evening there are moonlight walks organized along the ridge from Schynige Platte. All you need is to be reasonably fit, well shod, and suitably clothed. Check with the Interlaken tourist office for details.

The Schilthorn and Mürren

The excursion described here—up the Schilthorn and the Jungfraujoch—should not be attempted by anyone susceptible to mountain sickness, which, though it affects few people, is an unpleasant experience at best and can be dangerous, or those suffering from heart trouble, weak lungs or high blood pressure. If you are in *any* doubt about whether you should attempt either of these excursions consult a doctor beforehand.

It takes about one and a half hours to get from Interlaken to the top of the Schilthorn; starting with a train journey to Lauterbrunnen and then a ten-minute coach ride to Stechelberg, where you'll see the Mürrenbach, said to be Europe's highest waterfall, tumbling over the cliff. Incidentally, even more impressive and famous are the Staubbach Falls near Lauterbrunnen, and the Trümmelbach Falls some three km. (nearly two miles) away. At Stechelberg the real trip begins—a four-stage cable car journey lifting you silently in little more than a half-hour to the summit of the Schilthorn, some 2,970 meters (9,750 ft.) above sea level. And if you go into the circular Piz Gloria restaurant above the cable-car terminal, you can sit and watch an Alpine panorama—so grand that it seems faintly unreal—slowly roll past your window, for the whole restaurant revolves continuously. Sit here 50 minutes, and you'll have gone the full circle.

On the way up one of the cable-car stations is Mürren (1,663 meters, 5,400 ft.), the highest village in the Bernese Oberland. Impressively perched among clifftop pastures almost 800 meters (2,600 feet) above the Lauterbrunnen valley, Mürren enjoys an incomparable view of the Jungfrau and its snow capped colleagues. It's a first-rate resort, tailor made for those yearning to escape from the noise and hurly-burly of city life since it is inaccessible by road, leaving the streets blessedly traffic-free. For winter sports, Mürren is world-famous. Especially notable is the funicular to Allmendhubel (1,910 meters, 6,270 ft.), where a bobsleigh run begins, and descends through hairpin bends to the finish over 300 meters (1,000 ft.) below.

Instead of going by cable car, a slightly quicker and more interesting way to reach Mürren is by train from Interlaken to Lauterbrunnen, then by funicular up the steep cliff to Grütschalp, and finally by mountain railway along the cliff edge to the resort itself.

The Jungfraujoch

From Interlaken the journey to the Jungfraujoch is in two parts, the first via Lauterbrunnen or Grindelwald to Kleine Scheidegg, and the second from there to the summit station. The usual outward route is from Interlaken East station (578 meters, 1,900 ft.), past Wilderswil and Zweilütschinen to Lauterbrunnen (791 meters, 2,600 ft.), noted for its mountain torrents, beautiful waterfalls and lace. You may not see the latter but you will certainly notice plenty of rushing and falling water. Just before Zweilütschinen, if you look to the right of the train, you'll get a glimpse of the confluence of the rivers Schwarze (Black) Lutschine and Weisse (White) Lutschine, and where the waters join you'll clearly see the difference in color. The "white" is glacier water and the "black" comes from rocks.

At Lauterbrunnen you join the green cogwheel trains of the Wengernalp Railway, popularly known as WAB, and the steep climb to the top really begins. The train twists and turns through tunnels and over viaducts, giving a succession of camera-clicking views of yet more mountain torrents and waterfalls, of the Lauterbrunnen valley down below with the funicular to Mürren up the other side, and of an unending, constantly changing vista of peaks. In early summer the track is lined with a superb display of wild flowers.

The first main stop is at Wengen, 1,150–1,350 meters (3,772–4,429 ft.), a famous, long established, and well equipped all-year resort which is still no more than a mountainside plateau village at the foot of the Jungfrau. Nor is its peaceful atmosphere disturbed by cars, since it cannot be reached by road. The sunset is one of Wengen's claims to fame. You may have admired many sunsets, but here the glow which bathes surrounding peaks and slopes and casts a pink and flame-red light over the entire scene is unique.

Rocks, Snow and Ice

The train which takes you onwards from Wengen must be classified as one of the miracles of Swiss engineering. It seems incredible that the steeply climbing train can find a route through the rocks, snow, and ice.

At 1,873 meters (6,150 ft.) you pass through Wengernalp, where Byron stayed in 1816 and is reputed to have conceived the idea for *Manfred.* Soon afterwards, at a height of 2,059 meters (6,760 ft.), you will reach Kleine Scheidegg, a quiet little winter and summer resort. It doesn't quite belong to the land of eternal snow but it is high enough for skiing right into late spring.

At Kleine Scheidegg you change over to the smart little brown-and-cream train of the Jungfrau Railway which climbs more than 1,370 meters (4,500 ft.) over the next nine and a half kms. (six miles), which leads to the summit station. Over seven kms. of this distance (four and a half miles) is in a tunnel which runs through the Eiger and Mönch mountains. The line took 16 years to build and was opened in 1912. Even today it is still one of the marvels of the world's railway systems.

Leaving Kleine Scheidegg, where there is a good moderately priced station restaurant, the train passes through pastures with views of Mönch and Grindelwald, as well as the treacherous north face of the Eiger, which you'll see better on the way down. Just before the next station, Eigergletscher (2,318 meters, 7,610 ft.) which has a small hotel and restaurant, you'll see on the right-hand side of the track the kennels of the husky dogs which pull the sleighs at the summit, and next to them a pen containing a colony of the small, furry marmots which inhabit the high Alps.

Now the train plunges into the long tunnel which leads steeply up to the Jungfraujoch—a 40-minute journey. The next station is Eigerwand (2,864 meters, 9,400 ft.), which lies only a few meters inside the precipitous north face. From the station platform short tunnels lead to enormous windows cut into the north face, and all trains stop long enough for passengers to walk across to take in the view. Given fine weather, you'll see a magnificent panorama of Grindelwald far below, the Thunersee in the distance, and a multitude of mountains, valleys, fields and forests. At the next station—Eismeer (3,154 meters, 10,350 ft.)—windows are also cut into the mountain face a few yards from the platform, but here the view is very different and even more impressive. Here for the first time you realize you are in a white world of ice, glaciers and snow.

On Top of the Jungfraujoch

From Eismeer it is only about 11 minutes to the Jungfraujoch terminus at 3,475 meters (11,400 ft.). Remember that from Interlaken you have risen a total of 2,887 meters (9,470 ft.), and that the air, however pure, is also rarefied. Those who move around too quickly before they are adjusted to the altitude may feel giddy, or even become ill. So take it easy; move slowly. Or, as the Swiss guide said, "For the first 15 minutes, please forget that you are young."

From the trainside of the Jungfraujoch station—the highest in Europe—a rocky corridor used to lead to the Berghaus, Europe's highest hotel and restaurant. Alas, this was all burned down in 1972, but it has been replaced by the fine Inn-above-the-Clouds restaurant and cafeteria, seating 290.

If, when you leave the train, you take the free elevator behind the post office and souvenir shop, it will take you to the corridor leading to the Ice Palace. It's quite a long one, much of it cut through a glacier, its walls, ceiling and floor of solid ice. On the way you'll pass a full size car sculptured out of ice, and a replica of a bar complete with tables, chairs, counter and a whiskey barrel. Down a few steps at the end is the great hall, also cut out of ice.

Back at the station, another corridor—the Sphinx Tunnel—leads from the lower end of the platform to yet another free elevator, this one whisking you up 111 meters (367 ft.) in 90 seconds to the famous

Sphinx Terrace. Here there's not only a research institute and astronomical observatory but, from the observation terrace, an incomparable panorama of rock, snow, ice and clouds that is one of the wonders of Europe. Facing south you'll see the primeval Aletsch Glacier, a 16 km. (ten mile) ribbon of shattered ice, divided into strips by thin traces of black. To the southwest, apparently little more than arm's length away, is the 4,160 meter (13,647 ft.) peak of the Jungfrau, and behind you, to the northeast, the peaks of the Mönch and the Eiger. On a fine day you may see the Jura and Vosges, the Black Forest, and the lakes of Central Switzerland.

If you have never been on skis before, but want to try just for fun, you can do so on top of the Jungfraujoch at the summer ski school. The school is reached along a path from the Sphinx Tunnel exit. The services of an instructor and rental of skis and boots will set you back about Fr. 12 an hour. But although there's a skilift, it's a simple slope and of little interest to serious skiers. Should you want something a little less strenuous, near the ski school, for Fr. 4, you can have a five-minute sleigh ride, weather permitting, pulled by the husky dogs that live down at Eigergletscher.

Grindelwald

To vary the homeward journey, at Kleine Scheidegg you can get a train which goes via Grindelwald (your ticket is valid both ways), giving you, as it descends steeply around the Eiger, superb views of the north face towering above. The north face was first climbed in summer in 1938, but it was not until 1961 that the first group of climbers successfully conquered in winter the almost vertical rock face, braving sub-zero temperatures, and falls of rock, ice and snow. It took them six days to reach the top. As you look up from the comfort of the Jungfrau Railway train, the surprise is not that about 40 people should have lost their lives on the north face, but that anyone, even in summer, should have succeeded. If your eyes are good, from near Alpiglen station you can just see, almost in the center of the north face and about halfway up, the windows of the Eigerwand station.

Grindelwald (1,050 meters, 3,445 ft.) is a fairly large, year-round resort noted for its glaciers and views. From it the Wetterhorn (3,701 meters, 12,139 ft.), the Eiger (3,970 meters, 13,025 ft.), the Finsteraarhorn (4,274 meters, 14,019 ft.), and countless other peaks can be seen, as can the Lutschine valley. Perhaps the greatest attraction is the Firstbahn, Europe's longest lift, which in half an hour carries you from Grindelwald to an altitude of 2,163 meters (7,100 ft.) at First. In summer it's the views which are spectacular; in winter, the skiing, although Grindelwald also has skating, curling and ice hockey. From Grindelwald it is only about 40 minutes back to Interlaken.

The trip up the Jungfraujoch breaks many records. It has the highest railway in Europe; and the world's highest underground rail station; Europe's highest mountain observation terrace gives a view of the largest glacier in the Alps, the Aletsch; and includes the world's most expensive rail line. But, like some 400,000 people every year, it's a fair bet you'll think it was worth every franc.

The Brienzersee

The journey round the Brienzersee, bordered by steeply rising mountains, is of considerable interest. Heading along the wild southern shore of the lake from Interlaken, the small lakeside road goes only as far as Iseltwald, about halfway along the lake and set among green hilly meadows. (You can also take the new expressway, the N6, that cuts through the steep hills bordering the lake to the eastern end of the Porienzersee.) Iseltwald is a charming, unsophisticated village resort, located partly on a picturesque peninsula jutting out into the quiet waters of the lake, and partly around a small bay formed by the peninsula itself. From Iseltwald, a beautiful forest walk of about an hour and a half brings you to the Giessbach Falls, where 14 cascades rush down through the rocky cliffs to the lake.

Alternatively, take the road along the north shore of the lake, passing through several small resorts, to Brienz. Although only a small town, Brienz is the largest place on the lake, and as well as being a popular resort it is also the home of the Swiss woodcarving industry, as you will gather from the shop windows. Switzerland's last steam-driven cogwheel train also runs from here, up to the summit of Brienzer-Rothorn —346 meters (7,700 ft.) above the town. Many artists have settled here, and the town's school of woodcarving is subsidized by the government. Of particular interest here are the lovely wooden houses, dating from the 17th, 18th and 19th centuries, near the church at the eastern end of the town.

Brienz again represents the milder beauties of the Oberland. Its climate—though not quite so mild and southern as the Thunersee's Gunten—is much warmer than that of neighboring regions.

Just outside Brienz, at Ballenberg, is the Freilichtmuseum Ballenberg, a substantial park containing characteristic Swiss houses from many parts of the country and from many periods, carefully dismantled and transported here and illustrating many aspects of rural life in Switzerland over the years. Crafts such as linen weaving, basket making and baking are demonstrated here during the summer.

About 12 kilometers (eight miles) beyond Brienz, is Meiringen, the main town in the Hasli valley, and the center of the valley's weaving industry. It is popular with mountaineers and particularly with tourists, for roads lead north to the Brünig Pass and Luzern east over the Susten Pass to Andermatt, and south along the Hasli valley to the Grimsel, Furka and St. Gotthard Passes.

The rocky Hasli valley is renowned for its dramatic scenery, for the one and a half kms. (a mile) of the Aarschlucht (an eerie 180 meters/ 600 ft. deep gorge, about 25 minutes' walk from Meiringen), and for the Reichenbach Falls. Sherlock Holmes enthusiasts won't need reminding that Conan Doyle recounts in *The Final Problem* how the villainous Dr. Moriarty tried to fling the famous detective down these very falls. The faithful will also remember that it was at nearby Rosenlaui that Holmes spent the night before the fateful struggle. American author Sam Rosenberg, in a book about Holmes, has put forward the theory that Conan Doyle modeled Moriarty on the famous, but somewhat sinister, German philosopher Nietzsche. Part of the evidence for this comes from the hotel register at Rosenlaui, which shows that Nietzsche had a holiday there in 1877. It is also known that when, at the suggestion of Sir Henry Lunn, Conan Doyle visited the falls a few years later to see whether they would be suitable for the intended demise of Holmes, he also went to Rosenlaui, where he must have learned of Nietzsche's visit.

The Simmental and Gstaad

From Spiez, on the Thunersee, the highway leads southwest into the Simmental, or Simmen valley. Weissenburgbad, a short distance north of Weissenburg on the main Simmen valley road, is hidden in a romantic gorge. Its mineral water, famous since the 15th century, achieves excellent results in curing respiratory troubles. Higher up in the Simmen valley, we reach Boltigen, just beyond which the Jaun Pass road leads off to the right. This is a most attractive and not unduly difficult side trip, although there are many hairpin bends up to the summit and on the descent. You'll be rewarded, too, just before you reach Bulle, by a splendid view of Gruyères, in the middle distance to the left, standing proudly on top of its rocky pinnacle.

Zweisimmen is the main town of the Simmen valley, and although it is primarily important as a cattle market, it is also a winter sports resort, with a gondola cableway (said to be Europe's longest) to the splendid skiing slopes on Rinderberg (2,010 meters, 6,600 feet high). Pleasant short walks lead to the Mannenberg ruins and the Simmen Falls.

From Zweisimmen, still following the river Simme, you can reach Lenk by railway or secondary road. Lenk, situated at 1,110 meters (3,650 ft.), is surrounded by wild glaciers and thundering waterfalls, and dominated by the mighty Wildstrübel mountain. From two glaciers, seven torrents rush down to the valley, which is popularly called Siebental ("Valley of the Seven"). Lenk is both a spa, founded on one of the strongest sulphurous springs in Europe, and a beautiful and popular winter sports resort. Being in a rather isolated position, it is comparatively inexpensive.

If, instead of turning at Zweisimmen up to Lenk, you continue along the main road, passing the resorts of Saanenmöser and Schönried, you come to Saanen, a winter sports and summer resort. Spare a little time here to turn off the main road into the village, for its streets contain many particularly fine old wooden chalets. Some date from the 16th century and their projecting gables and facades are beautifully carved, ornamented and inscribed. At Saanen, the road forks. One branch goes along the beautiful Sarine valley, through Château d'Oex and the Pays d'Enhaut (both of them in canton Vaud). The other turns south to go through Gstaad and then over the Col du Pillon to Aigle, in the Rhône valley.

Gstaad has long been famous as one of Switzerland's most chic and modish winter resorts, easily the equal of St. Moritz, say, in Graubünden. It is by some way the most fashionable winter resort in the Bernese Oberland, and certainly the most expensive. It has an impressive location, surrounded by forests, hills, glaciers and small mountain lakes well stocked with trout. There are golf and tennis tournaments every summer, though the winter remains perhaps its most glamorous season. Chalet owners here have included Prince Rainier, the Aga Khan, Elizabeth Taylor and Julie Andrews. Yehudi Menuhin is a frequent visitor, not least for the famous Menuhin Festival each August.

Blausee and Kandersteg

Again using Spiez on the Thunersee as a jumping off point, there's one further magnificently dramatic excursion offered by the Bernese Oberland. Head south from Spiez, either by road or on the superb Lötschberg rail line. You pass by the ruins of Tellenberg Castle and a massive stone viaduct before arriving at Blausee-Mitholz (974 meters, 3,200 ft.). The lovely little lake here, as its name suggests, is a deep blue color. Algae and fossilized trees lie at the bottom of the lake and are clearly visible in the crystal clear water, as are the famous Blausee blue trout. The water is supposed to come underground from the Oeschinensee and some scientists maintain that its extraordinary color is due to chemical effects of the minerals as it runs deep in the earth. An alternative suggestion is that it is due to the algae in the water.

From Mitholz the road goes only as far as Kandersteg, about five miles further on. The trip is much more easily continued by rail. Leaving Blausee-Mitholz, the train begins to traverse wilder and wilder regions; it goes on climbing and passing across many bridges and through long tunnels. Sometimes, as it twists and turns, you can see the tracks at three different levels. The next stop is Kandersteg, surrounded by mountains and scenery as magnificent as you can ever hope to see. Situated at a height of 1,176 meters (3,858 ft.), it enjoys a rare advantage, being built on a plateau that extends for several kilometers. In consequence, visitors not keen on alpine climbing can spend their holiday on high ground and still be able to take pleasant walks on almost flat country. Those who wish to make longer excursions can reach the famous and much admired Öeschinensee in about an hour and a half. This is a superb and romantic sight, with an amphitheater of rocks and glaciers in the background. The Kander Falls are also accessible. Kandersteg possesses the usual amenities for winter and summer holidays, including an indoor skating rink, which is now also open in July and August.

Walking in the Bernese Oberland

The Bernese Oberland is a rambler's paradise. Here are a few suggestions, arranged by districts, both for shorter and longer walks:

Eastern Oberland. *Meiringen–Brünig Pass–Lungern.* Three and three-quarter hours. On this route you pass the Alpbach Gorge, which is a remarkable wonder of nature. The Brünig Pass itself is one of the best-known and lowest passes in Switzerland. *Meiringen–Grosse Scheidegg–Grindelwald.* This is for the most ambitious rambler, as the walk takes six and a half hours. You will see the river Aare, you will be impressed by the mighty walls of the Wetterhorn, and have a magnificent view of the mountains encircling Grindelwald. Grindelwald itself is a world famous glacier village, with mild, green slopes on one side, and almost perpendicular mountains on the other.

Central Oberland. *Interlaken–Grünenbergpass–Inner Eriz.* Six hours. The route takes you amid rich and exotic rocks and wild forests. You pass the Seefeld and Tropfstein caves. Inside the caves are a maze of intersecting passages, and at the entrance you will be advised to unroll a ball of string, so that you will be able to find your way out again. In the Eriz region you will see the Zulg stream, which has many other streams and ditches running into it and gives the district a wild appearance. *Spiez–Rengglipass–Wilderswil.* Eight hours. On this route you reach the broad and high Aeschi chain with its widely scattered and picturesque wooden huts and houses. At Aeschi-Allmend there's a particularly beautiful view: to the north the lake and behind it chains of mountains. Between Wilderswil and Interlaken—if you continue—you will see the ruins of Unspunnen, restored.

West Oberland. *Goppenstein–Lötchenpass–Kandersteg.* Nine and three-quarter hours. The Gastern valley is easily one of the greatest and finest of the high mountain valleys of the Alps. The easiest route is from the Goppenstein area, overnighting at the simple inn at Kummenalp above Wiler. There are a great many steep, rocky cliffs with thundering waterfalls, most particularly the snowy giants of the Valais. The Bietschhorn is the highest among the mountains: its glistening peaks, capped with glaciers, are an impressive and unforgettable sight. From Kandersteg, take the chair-lift to Oeschinensee for a spectacular view of this mountain lake.

PRACTICAL INFORMATION FOR THE BERNESE OBERLAND

TOURIST OFFICES. The principal tourist office for the Bernese Oberland is the Verkehrsverband Berner Oberland (the Bernese Oberland tourist office), Jungfraustr. 38, Interlaken (tel. 036–22 26 21). It is open Mon. to Fri 8–12 and 2–6, Sat. 8–12.

In addition all the major towns and villages of the Bernese Oberland also have their own local tourist offices. The principal offices are located at: **Adelboden** (tel. 033–73 22 52); **Frutigen** (tel. 033–71 14 21); **Grindelwald** (tel. 036–53 12 12); **Gstaad** (tel. 030–4 10 55); **Interlaken** (tel. 036–22 21 21 for town information); **Lauterbrunnen** (tel. 036–55 19 55); **Mürren** (tel. 036–55 16 16); **Spiez** (tel. 033–54 21 38); **Thun** (tel. 033–22 23 40); **Wengen** (tel. 036–55 14 14).

As a general rule these offices have similar opening hours to the Bernese Oberland office in Interlaken.

HOTELS AND RESTAURANTS. With some of the oldest and most famous resorts in the country, the Bernese Oberland boasts a large number of superb luxury hotels, both old and new. But budgeters are equally well catered for in this highly tourist-oriented region, with a wide range of less expensive hotels, especially in some of the smaller, less accessible towns and villages.

ADELBODEN. *Parkhotel Bellevue* (E), tel. 033–73 16 21. 100 beds. Quiet, with indoor pool, sauna and facilities for children. V. *Alpenrose* (M), tel. 033–73 11 61. Comfortable. DC, MC, V. *Huldi and Waldhaus* (M), tel. 033–73 15 31. 80 beds. Quiet and comfortable. AE, DC, MC, V. *Kreuz* (M), tel. 033–73 21 21. 26 beds. AE, DC, MC, V. *Nevada Palace* (M), tel. 033–73 21 31. Indoor pool, tennis, skating. DC, MC, V.

AESCHI. *Baumgarten* (I), tel. 033–54 41 21. 40 beds. Very quiet hotel in its own grounds. AE, DC, MC, V. *Niesen* (I), tel. 033–54 36 26. 60 beds. Has facilities for the handicapped.

BEATENBERG. *Kurhaus Silberhorn* (M), tel. 036–41 12 04. 55 beds. A very quiet hotel in its own grounds; sauna. MC, V. *Favorita* (I), tel. 036–41 12 04. 12 beds. Quiet and central; breakfast only.

BIEL (BIENNE). *Continental* (M), tel. 032–22 32 55. 140 beds. Modern, centrally located and quiet. AE, DC, V. *Elite* (M), tel. 032–22 54 41. 100 beds. Comfortable and well appointed. AE, DC, MC, V. *Baren en ville* (I), tel. 032–22 45 73. 24 beds. Small and central, with breakfast only. AE, DC.

Restaurant. *Bielstube* (M), tel. 032–22 65 88. Excellent. AE, DC, V.

BONIGEN. *Seiler au Lac* (E), tel. 036–22 30 21. 80 beds. Splendid views from this quiet hotel. AE, V. *Park Hotel* (M), tel. 036–22 71 06. 55 beds. Centrally located by the lake. AE, V.

BRIENZ. *Bären* (I), tel. 036–51 24 12. 50 beds. Quiet hotel by the lake with its own beach. AE, DC, MC, V. *De La Gare* (I), tel. 036–51 27 12. 22 beds. AE, DC, MC, V.

BURGDORF. *Touring-Bernerhof* (I), tel. 034–22 16 52. 55 beds. Quiet and central with facilities for the handicapped. Extremely good value. AE, DC, MC, V.

FAULENSEE. *Strandhotel Seeblick* (I), tel. 033–54 23 21. 40 beds. Lakeside hotel and restaurant. AE.

GRINDELWALD. *Grand Hotel Regina* (L), tel. 036–54 54 55. 180 beds. Indoor and outdoor pools, tennis and sauna, and dancing in the evenings. *Alpina* (E), tel. 036–53 33 33. 60 beds. Comfortable and quiet. AE, DC, MC, V. *Derby-Bahnhof* (E), tel. 036–54 54 61. 110 beds. Centrally located family hotel. AE, DC, MC, V. *Parkhotel Schoenegg* (E), tel. 036–53 18 53. 100 beds. A quiet hotel on its own grounds, with indoor pool, gymnasium and sauna. AE, DC, MC, V. *Lauberhorn* (M), tel. 036–53 10 82. 50 beds. Riding available; situated in its own grounds. MC, V. *Sporthotel Jungfrau* (M), tel. 036–53 13 41. 55 beds. Tennis available. AE, DC, MC, V. *Schweizerheim* (I), tel. 036–53 10 58. 34 beds. Simple and small but very reasonably priced.

GSTAAD. *Palace* (L), tel. 030–8 31 31. 200 beds. One of Switzerland's great hotels, with indoor and outdoor pools, sauna, dancing, gardens and all possible amenities. MC, V. *Alpina Grand Hotel* (E), tel. 030–4 57 25. 70 beds. Comfortable, and with magnificent food. V. *Bellevue Grand Hotel* (E), tel. 030–8 31 71.

85 beds. A quiet location, facilities for children, and no less than three restaurants. AE, V. *Olden* (E), tel. 030–4 34 44. 25 beds. Central, with dancing in the evenings. Very popular. AE, DC, MC, V. *Park Hotel Reuteler* (E), tel. 030–8 33 77. 87 beds. Tennis and skating. AE, V.

Alphorn (M), tel. 030–4 45 45. 30 beds. Quiet and rustic, ideal for children. AE, MC, V. *Posthotel Rössli* (M), tel. 030–4 34 12. 35 beds. Atmospheric and attractively located in an historic building. DC, MC, V.

INTERLAKEN. *Victoria-Jungfrau Grand Hotel* (L), tel. 036–21 21 71. 400 beds. Justifiably famous; indoor pool and tennis. AE, DC, MC, V. *Bellevue-Garden Hotel* (E), tel. 036–22 44 31. 100 beds. Quiet, comfortable. AE, DC, MC, V. *Du Lac* (E), tel. 036–22 29 22. 70 beds. Located near the Brienzersee boat landing stage, and highly recommended. AE, MC, V. *Metropole* (E–L), tel. 036–21 21 51. 225 beds. High rise building with superb views from the top floor; indoor pool. AE, DC, MC, V. *Royal St. Georges* (E), tel. 036–22 75 75. 170 beds. AE, DC, MC, V. *Stella* (E), tel. 036–22 88 71. 55 beds. Exceptionally pleasant and highly recommended; indoor pool. AE, DC, MC, V.

Chalet Oberland (M), tel. 036–22 94 31. 60 beds. Excellent ratings for both the hotel and its cuisine. AE, DC, MC, V. *Park-Hotel Mattenhof* (M), tel. 036–21 61 21. 120 beds. Tennis, pool, and facilities for children. AE, MC. *Alpina* (I), tel. 036–22 80 31. 60 beds. Simple but inexpensive; no rooms with bath. DC, V. *De la Paix* (I), tel. 036–22 70 44. 40 beds. Superior hotel for this price catagory; sauna. AE, DC. *Gasthof Hirschen* (I), tel. 036–22 15 45. 32 beds. In an historic and attractive building; no rooms with bath. DC.

Restaurants. *La Terrasse* (M–E), at Victoria Jungfrau Grand Hotel (see above); exceptionally good food. AE, DC, MC, V. *A la Fine Gueule* (I–M), in Carlton Hotel (tel. 036–22 38 21). AE, DC, MC, V. *Krebs* (I–M), tel. 036–22 71 1. AE, MC. *Metropole* (I), in hotel of same name (tel. 036–21 21 51). First class. AE, DC, MC, V. *Schuh* (I) is Interlaken's number one spot for morning coffee or afternoon tea. V.

KANDERSTEG. *Royal Bellevue* (L), tel. 033–75 12 12. 60 beds. Very quiet, with riding, tennis, water skiing, two pools. DC, MC, V. *Victoria and Ritter* (E), tel. 033–75 14 44. 130 beds. Indoor pool, tennis; ideal for children. AE, DC, MC, V. *Alpenblick* (I), tel. 033–75 11 29. 30 beds. Breakfast only. AE, DC, MC, V. *Alpenrose* (I), tel. 033–75 11 70. 50 beds. Quiet and comfortable. DC, MC, V. *Parkhotel Gemmi* (I), tel. 033–75 11 17. 60 beds. Indoor pool and an attractive location. AE, DC, MC, V.

KLEINE SCHEIDEGG. *Scheidegg* (E), tel. 036–55 12 12. 120 beds. Quiet, with fine views. AE, DC, MC, V.

LENK. *Kreuz* (E), tel. 030–3 13 87. 160 beds. Indoor pool, sauna and facilities for the handicapped. AE, DC, MC. *Kurhotel Lenkerhof* (E), tel. 030–3 14 24. 160 beds. Tennis and cure facilities. AE, DC, MC, V. *Waldrand* (M), tel. 030–3 32 32. 50 beds. Quiet, a lovely garden, and dieters will appreciate the availability of low-cal meals. AE, DC, MC, V. *Sternen* (I), tel. 030–3 15 09. 28 beds. Centrally located.

MEIRINGEN. *Du Sauvage* (M), tel. 036–71 41 41. 94 beds. A good family hotel in a quiet location; riding available. AE, DC, MC, V. *Sherlock Holmes* (M), tel. 036–71 42 42. 90 beds. Indoor pool, gymnasium and sauna in this quiet hotel. AE, MC, V. *Tourist* (I), tel. 036–71 10 44. 25 beds. Small and central.

MERLIGEN. *Beatus* (L), tel. 033–51 21 21. 140 beds. Very comfortable with a splendid lakeside location; water skiing, indoor pool and sauna. AE, DC, MC, V. *Du Lac* (I), tel. 033–51 15 24. 40 beds. Very quiet lakeside hotel in its own grounds; pool. AE, DC, MC, V.

MÜRREN. *Eiger* (E), tel. 036–55 13 31. 85 beds. Traditional family hotel with indoor pool and sauna. AE, DC, MC, V. *Mürren* (E), tel. 036–55 24 24. 98 beds. Good family hotel with beautiful views; a center of winter social life. DC, MC, V. *Alpenruh* (M), tel. 036–55 10 55. 52 beds. Newly renovated. DC, MC, V. *Blumental* (M), tel. 036–55 18 26. 30 beds. With a wonderful specialty restaurant. DC, V. *Jungfrau Lodge* (M), tel. 036–55 28 24. 34 beds. Quietly located, with tennis facilities. AE, DC, MC, V. *Sporthotel Edelweiss* (M), tel. 036–55 26 12. 50 beds. Splendid views. AE, DC, V. *Alpina* (I), tel. 036–55 13 61. 55 beds. Tennis and marvelous views. AE, DC, MC, V.

SAANENMOSER. *Bahnhof* (E), tel. 030–4 15 06. 27 beds. V. *Golf and Sport Hotel* (E), tel. 030–4 32 22. 60 beds. Curling, tennis, skating and golf. MC, V. *Hornberg* (E), tel. 030–4 44 40. 70 beds. Quiet and comfortable hotel with indoor and outdoor pools and sauna. AE, MC, V.

SPIEZ. *Bahnhof Terminus* (M), tel. 033–54 31 21. 100 beds. Centrally located. AE, DC, MC, V. *Belvédère Silence* (M), tel. 033–54 33 33. 55 beds. Excellent vistas and serene location. AE, DC, MC, V. *Edenhotel* (M), tel. 033–54 11 54. 80 beds. Pool and tennis. *Bellevue* (I), tel. 033–54 23 14. 25 beds. Good views, and quiet.

Restaurant. *Welle* (M), tel. 033–54 40 43. The perfect summer spot, with a large terrace on the lakeside just beside the boat dock. Excellent fish specialties.

SUNDLAUENEN. *Beatus* (I), tel. 036–41 16 24. 10 beds. Modest but reasonable. AE, DC, MC, V.

THUN. *Beau-Rivage* (M), Aare-Quai (tel. 033–22 22 36). 50 beds. Indoor pool; breakfasts only. AE, DC, MC, V. *Freienhof* (M), Freienhofgasse 3 (tel. 033–21 55 11). 105 beds. In a beautiful 14th-century building in the Old Town; quiet. AE, DC, MC, V. *Holiday* (M), Gwattstr. 1 (tel. 033–36 57 57). 114 beds. Lakeside hotel with bar, terrace and swimming. AE, DC, MC, V. *Krone* (M), Rathausplatz (tel. 033–22 82 82). 64 beds. Historic building with indoor pool and facilities for children. AE, DC, MC, V.

Restaurants. *Casa Barba* (I–M), tel. 022–22 22 27. Specializes in Spanish foods. AE, DC, V. *Simmenthalerhof* (I–M), tel. 033–22 22 03. Very good. *Steinbock* (I–M), tel. 033–22 40 51. Well recommended. AE, DC, V.

WENGEN. *Parkhotel Beausite* (L), tel. 036–56 51 61. 102 beds. With indoor pool and sauna. *Regina* (E), tel. 036–55 15 12. A splendid family hotel, and very quiet. AE, MC, V. *Silberhorn* (E), tel. 036–56 51 31. 140 beds. Sauna and gymnasium. AE, DC, MC, V. *Victoria Lauberhorn* (E), tel. 036–56 51 51. 120 beds. Central, with quiet rooms. AE, DC, MC, V. *Alpenrose* (M), tel. 036–55 32 16. 80 beds. Quiet, with a specialty restaurant. AE, DC, MC, V. *Eiger* (M), tel. 036–55 11 31. 62 beds. Central, with a good restaurant. AE, DC, MC, V. *Falken* (M), tel. 036–55 14 31. 80 beds. Centrally located, quiet. AE, DC, MC, V.

Bären (I), tel. 036–55 14 19. 26 beds. Breakfast only. DC, MC, V. *Belvédère* (I), tel. 036–55 24 12. 120 beds. A good family hotel. *Bristol* (I), tel. 036–55 15 51. 60 beds. With good views. AE, V. *Eden* (I), tel. 036–55 16 34. 30 beds. AE, DC, MC, V.

WILDERSWIL. *Jungfrau* (M), tel. 036–22 35 31. 65 beds. A quiet, well appointed hotel in its own grounds. AE, MC, V. *Alpenblick* (I), tel. 036–22 07 07. 55 beds. Quiet and comfortable, at extremely reasonable prices. AE, DC, MC, V. *Bären* (I), tel. 036–22 35 21. 80 beds. Comfortable and central. AE, DC, MC, V.

ZWEISIMMEN. *Sonnegg* (M), tel. 030–2 23 33. 20 beds. Offering diet meals. AE, DC, MC, V. *Krone* (I), tel. 030–2 26 26. 50 beds. The ideal quiet family hotel. AE, DC, MC, V. *Sport-Motel* (I), tel. 030–2 12 31. 50 beds. Golf available. AE, MC, V.

GETTING AROUND. Public transport in the Bernese Oberland is very well organized. Even if you don't have a car you should have little difficulty in getting around. In addition to the excellent train and bus network, there are also cable cars, chair lifts, gondolas and mountain railways galore, all helping make otherwise remote towns, villages and, of course, mountains readily accessible. Tourist offices have full details of all schedules and fares.

The Bernese Oberland issues an excellent value holiday season-ticket. In view of the expense of the trip up to the Jungfraujoch, for example, this can prove an unbeatable bargain. The ticket is valid for 15 days, giving unlimited free travel on all rail lines, cable cars, chair lifts, buses and lake boats for five days, and half-price travel for the remaining ten days. The ticket currently costs Fr. 134 in first class and Fr. 102 in second (this may change before 1988). A number of other reduced value tickets are also available; details from tourist offices.

By Train. Around 20 train routes thread through the Bernese Oberland, linking all the main resorts and connecting with cable cars. The Bernese Oberland also boasts the highest rail station in the world, that on the summit of the Jungfraujoch at 3,475 meters (11,400 ft.). The region also has the last steam-driven cogwheel railway in the country, running to the summit of the Brienzer Rothorn at an elevation of 2,350 meters (7,710 ft.).

By Bus. Postal buses complete much of the public transport otherwise not served by trains, serving in particular many of the smaller mountain towns. In addition, a number of bus excursions cover many of the main points of interest. Details of schedules are available from tourist offices.

By Boat. There are regular boat trips around the Thunersee and Brienzersee. The round trip from Interlaken to Thun, for example, takes about four hours; the trip to Spiez takes around two hours. The round trip from Interlaken to Brienz takes around two and a half hours, to Iseltwald about an hour and a quarter.

Details of sailings are available from all major tourist offices.

By Cable Car. More than 30 major cableway and lift systems climb up to the Bernese Oberland's many peaks. They include the largest cableway in the world, stretching up to the Schilthorn above Mürren. Likewise, the Grindelwald–First chair lift is also the longest of its type in the world. The real bonus of all these cable cars is provided by the spectacular scenery they straddle.

On Foot. The Bernese Oberland is a magnificent region for hiking. Tourist offices can provide maps of major hiking routes. Most principal trails pass by a convenient number of restaurants and inns, both hotels will generally provide picnic lunches.

SIGHTSEEING DATA. The Bernese Oberland's most spectacular and popular attractions are its mountains, waterfalls and lakes. But there are also a number of other places of interest, particularly castles and a few small museums. Excursions taking in many of the places listed here are operated regularly; details from tourist offices.

BALLENBURG. Freilichtmuseum Ballenberg (Swiss Open Air Museum of Rural Building and Home Life). One hundred-and-twenty acres of parkland dotted with typical houses from the various regions of Switzerland, illustrating rural Swiss life over the centuries. Reached by train over the Brienz railway station with direct bus connections to the museum. By car take Route 6 via Spiez. Open daily mid-Apr. through Oct.; Apr., May and Oct. from 10–5, June through Sept. 9:30–5:30.

BEATENBURG. St. Beatus Höhlen. Fascinating series of caves inhabited thousands of years ago. Legend has it that in the 6th century an Irish missionary, the holy Beatus, lived in here, having previously had to overcome a dragon. About 20 minutes by road from Interlaken; also reachable by boat on the Thunersee. Open daily 9:30–5:30, Palm Sun. to mid-Oct.

HILTERFINGEN. Museum Schloss Hünegg (Castle Hünegg Museum), tel. 033–43 19 82. Fine late 19th-century castle with fascinating period furnishings. Open Mon. to Sat. 2–5, Sun. 10–12 and 2–5 June through Sept.

INTERLAKEN. Touristik-Museum der Jungfrau-Region (Jungfrau Tourist Museum), Obere Gasse 26 (tel. 036–22 98 39). Intruiging museum charting the development of tourism in the Jungfrau region from the 18th century to the present. Open Tues. to Sun. 10–12:30 and 1:30–5 May to mid-Oct.

OBERHOFEN. Schloss Oberhofen (Oberhofen Castle), tel. 033–43 12 35. Seven centuries of Swiss architecture are illustrated in this typically massive castle, parts of which date from the 12th century. Interiors chart the evolution of interior styles and fashions from the Middle Ages to the late 19th century. Open daily 10–12 and 2–5 mid-May to mid-Oct.; closed Mon. mornings.

SPIEZ. Schloss Spiez (Spiez Castle), tel. 033–54 15 06. Attractive early-Norman church dating from around the beginning of the 11th century. The tower dates from the 12th century. During the summer plays are enacted in the castle grounds which can be worth checking out. Open daily 9:30–12 and 2–6 Easter to mid-Oct.; closed Mon. mornings.

THUN. Schloss Thun (Thun Castle), tel. 033–23 20 01. The huge tower around which the building centers was probably built by the Zähringers at the end of the 12th century. Now used as an historical museum, the major point of interest is the knights' hall with an impressive fireplace. Open 10–5 Apr., May and Oct.; 9–6 June and Sept.

NIGHTLIFE. There is no shortage of winter nightlife in the Bernese Oberland. Well-known resorts such as Gstaad, Grindelwald and Wengen all have a wide range of bars and discos. Lesser-known resorts also have their own lively après-ski haunts. Things quieten down in the summer, however, though Interlaken comes through with a wide variety of entertainment which lasts throughout the summer months.

All the following are in Interlaken. For folklore performances try the **Zentrum Casino Kursaal,** Congress-Centre-Casino (tel. 036–22 25 21), which has regular weekly performances, though check locally for times. Other like spots are **Harderkulm Restaurant** (tel. 036–22 34 44) and **Heimwehfluh Restaurant** (tel. 036–22 89 33), both occupying panoramic locations reached by cable railway. Shows are one night a week; check locally for days and times. The **Barbarella,** at the Grand Hotel Victoria-Jungfrau (tel. 036–22 12 38), is a disco/nightclub with show bands which doesn't shut its doors until 3 A.M. or thereabouts. The **Cabaret** nightclub, in the same hotel, features show girls. Other discos are the **Black & White,** in the Hotel Metropole (tel. 036–21 21 51); **High Life,** near West railway station (tel. 036–22 15 50); and **Johnny's Club,** in the Hotel Carlton (tel. 036–22 38 21). If you like your music light, there is the **Casino-Bar-Dancing,** at the Congress-Centre-Casino (tel. 036–22 25 21), with orchestral music and soft disco. Most of these nightspots are open from 9 P.M. and close between 1 and 3 A.M.

During summer there are also romantic evening cruises on the Thunersee and Brienzersee, with dancing on the outer decks or in the saloons. For further information contact the cruise organizers at 033–36 02 58, or check at any tourist office.

SHOPPING. If you've always had a yen for a cuckoo clock, this is the time to act on it. Woodcarvings are also extremely popular, with Brienz in particular famous for its wood craftwork. You will have not the slightest difficulty in finding the traditional Swiss buys such as Swiss army knives, excellent cheeses and mouth-watering chocolates.

Interlaken and the resort towns of Gstaad, Grindelwald and Wengen have shops which cater for sophisticated needs (anyone for leiderhosen?), while the smaller villages also have shopping facilities, though somewhat lacking the variety of larger towns. For crafts and souvenirs try **Heimatwerk Interlaken,** Höheweg 115.

SPECIAL EVENTS. Tell Open Air Theater. Since 1912, Friedrich Schiller's play above the Swiss freedom fighter and ace archer *William Tell,* has been performed in the Rugen woods near Interlaken. The season runs during July and Aug., with performances usually falling on Thurs. and Sat. at 8 P.M. Ticket sales are at Tell Box Office, Bahnhofstr. 5, Interlaken (tel. 036–22 37 22).

Interlaken Festival Weeks. This excellent classical music festival got its start over 20 years ago, and is now going strong. Details of the program can be obtained from Secretary of the Interlaken Festival Weeks, P.O. Box, CH–3800 Interlaken (tel. 036–22 22 19).

In summer there are any number of alpine and *Schwinger* (wrestling) festivals, and it's worthwhile asking at tourist offices if there are any on during your visit. Of particular note are *Alpaufzüge,* when the cows are moved up into the mountains for summer grazing, and *Alpabfahrten,* when the herds are brought down. The festivals take place in May/June and Sept./Oct. respectively.

SPORTS. If weather permits, the Bernese Oberland is a paradise for summer sports. This is one of the great mountain climbing regions, but don't try it unless you are a trained mountain climber; the great peaks claim a tragic number of victims. Mountain climbing is a dangerous sport meant for the trained, fit and well equipped. Better to stick to the **hiking** trails which will undoubtedly provide you with plenty of exercise. Most villages offer a multitude of attractive trails. For example Gstaad has over 300 kms., Lenk 200 kms., Zweisimmen 200 kms., Kandersteg 350 kms., Grindelwald 300 kms., Wengen 500 kms., Mürren 100 kms., and Hasliberg 300 kms. If you manage to hike through all of what's available, maybe you should climb a mountain!

Golf. Beautifully situated at Interlaken-Unterseen is the 18-hole golf course of the same name with trained caddies, a clubhouse (tel. 036–22 21 21), and restaurant. Three kms. (two miles) from the center of Interlaken, it is easily reached by bus or boat. The course is open from Apr. through Oct.

Riding. The area between the Thunersee and Brienzersee offer a number of scenic bridle paths through woods, over fields and by streams. Accompanied rides are also possible. Contact the Voegeli Riding School, Scheidgasse 66 in Unterseen (tel. 036–22 74 16) or the Häsler Riding Stables, Alpenstr. 21-B in Bönigen (tel. 036–22 52 70). Stables are also found in Gstaad and Saanen.

Sailing. One of the world's most beautiful lakes to sail must be the Thunersee. It has a sailing school which is open daily from mid-Apr. to mid-Oct. 9–12 and 2–5. Information is available from the Interlaken Tourist Office (tel. 036–22 21 21). Sailing is also possible on the nearby Brienzersee.

Swimming. There are several beaches around the Thunersee and one at Ringgenberg/Goldswil on the Brienzersee. Apart from that, major towns and many resort villages have pools. Ask at the Tourist Office for details.

Tennis. This has become a very popular sport in Switzerland, and almost all resorts have courts. Gstaad, in particular, hosts a major international tennis competition in July to which many top names come.

Wind Surfing. Once again the Thunersee is the place. The Lake of Thun Wind Surfing School is at Steindlerstr. 28, 3800 Unterseen (tel. 036–22 97 10 or 22 22 95).

WINTER SPORTS. The Bernese Oberland is, of course, one of the world's most celebrated winter sports areas. A separate book would be required to do full justice to the winter activities of the resorts of the Oberland, but here is a brief rundown on the principal centers. Remember, every one of these resorts has its own tourist office; a postcard will bring you detailed information concerning any of them.

Grindelwald, 1,050 meters (3,445 ft.); 2 funicular railways, 1 cable car, 19 lifts, 165 kms. of downhill runs, 32 kms. of cross-country trails, 45 kms. of ski-hiking trails, 7.5 kms. of tobogganing trails, 10 kms. of special ski bob runs; skating, curling, ski schools.

Gstaad, 1,110 meters (3,650 ft.); 8 cable cars, 7 lifts, 250 kms. of downhill runs, 21 kms. of cross-country trails, 50 kms. of hiking trails, 6 kms. of ski bob trails; skating, curling, ski schools.

Interlaken, 580 meters (1,900 ft.); skating on either a natural or artificial ice rink; ski-bus brings you in 20 minutes to Lauterbraunnen, starting point for Jungfrau skiing region's mountain railways.

Hasliberg, 1,050 meters (3,445 ft.); 7 cable cars, 4 lifts, 50 kms. of downhill runs, 10 kms. of cross-country trails, 20 kms. of hiking trails; ski school.

Kandersteg, 1,176 meters (3,858 ft.); 3 cable cars, 4 lifts, 13 kms. of downhill runs, 55 kms. of cross-country trails, 20 kms. of hiking trails; tobogganing, skating, curling, ski-schools.

Lenk, 1,110 meters (3,650 ft.); 5 cable cars, 8 lifts, 200 kms. of downhill runs (with Adelboden, which has 21 lifts), 53 kms. of cross-country trails, 30 kms. of hiking trails; skating, ski bob, ski schools.

Mürren, 1,110 meters (5,400 ft.); 2 funicular railways, 4 cable cars, 7 lifts, 50 kms. of downhill runs, 24 kms. of cross-country trails not far from Mürren, 3 kms. of prepared tobogganing trails; curling, skating, ski schools.

Wengen, 1,150–1,350 meters (3,772–4,429 ft.); 3 funicular railways, 1 cable car, 1 gondola, 17 lifts, 90 kms. of downhill runs, 1.5 kms. of prepared tobogganing trails, 25 kms. of ski bob trails, 12 kms. of cross-country skiing at the bottom of the valley; skating, curling, ski schools.

Zweisimmen, 960 meters (3,150 ft.); 2 cable cars, 4 lifts, 250 kms. of downhill runs within easy reach with additional lifts in the region, 42 kms. of cross-country trails, 25 kms. of hiking trails, 7 kms. of toboggan trails; ski schools.

THE JURA, NEUCHÂTEL AND FRIBOURG

Where "East ist Ost" and "West est Ouest"

Although the subtitle of this chapter is roughly correct, you will find there is no sharply defined geographical boundary with "German" Switzerland on one side and "French" on the other. However, for the sake of convenience, if you draw a line from Montreux to Fribourg, extending it to Neuchâtel, then up through Biel (Bienne) and due north to Delémont, you can say fairly confidently that the country is mainly French-speaking to the west and German-speaking to the east. The western half of the upper valley of the Rhône is also predominantly French-speaking but differs in character from the Jura and is described in the Valais chapter.

But bear in mind that there exists a shaded area on either side of the "language frontier," where French and German influences are rather delicately balanced. Along the imaginary line it is not unusual to hear towns referred to by either their French or German names: Bienne = Biel; Morat = Murten; Neuchâtel = Neuenburg; Soleure = Solothurn; and you may find your "thank you" answered by a bilingual *Merci vielmal.*

One of the most unusual areas in Switzerland, this region includes the old walled university town of Fribourg, plunging to the river from its hilltop railroad station; the historic city of Neuchâtel, entrance to the region of watchmakers, and a considerable educational center in its own right, and with the lake for warm-weather pleasures; and the Jura region, little known to visitors but enjoyed by the Swiss who vacation here. The Jura is the horse country of Switzerland, with meadows, rolling hills and excellent bicycling routes through small rural villages. The region has particularly active hiking organizations. In the canton of Neuchâtel alone there are 2,212 kms. (1,375 miles) of marked footpaths, maintained by local organizations.

Fribourg's Unique Role

Between the rich pasturelands of the Swiss plateau and the alpine foothills, Fribourg exudes a feeling of happy satisfaction, produced by centuries of prosperity and the knowledge of its importance in the Roman Catholic world. The city was founded in 1157 when Berthold of Zähringen decided that the rocky cliffs of twisting river Sarine exactly met his idea of security. The House of Zähringen died out in 1218, and Fribourg then passed first into the hands of the counts of Kyburg and next to Count Habsburg-Laufenburg, who sold it a few years later to his cousin Rudolph of Habsburg. In the first half of the 15th century the city saw many battles between Bern on the one side, and Savoy on the other, receiving little help in the process from the Habsburgs, who had other fish to fry. Eventually, in 1452, Fribourg came under Savoy's "protection."

During this time, however, the city had won many rights and liberties, and extended its territory, absorbing the estates of neighboring feudal lords. The Burgundian Wars, in which Fribourg supported the confederate states, brought further spoils in the form of more estates and municipalities. In 1481, thanks to the intervention of Niklaus von Flüe, Fribourg was admitted to the Confederation as a sovereign canton. Thereafter, skillful purchases brought Fribourg still more estates and municipalities while, externally, its history merged with that of the Confederation. Its citizens resisted the Reformation, making their state a stronghold of Catholicism. This was further strengthened by the foundation of the Catholic College of St. Michael in 1584 and, three centuries later, of Fribourg's university, the only Catholic *and* bilingual university in Switzerland.

Six centuries of peace were broken when, on 1 March 1798, French troops occupied the city, bringing to a sudden end almost two centuries of patrician self-government. In 1814, with the loosening of France's grip on Switzerland, a patrician government was restored in Fribourg, only to be replaced once again in 1830 by a democratic regime.

Architecturally, Fribourg is a delight. The ancient houses in the old quarter around the cathedral are elegant and well-preserved. The city hall has all the pristine glory of its 16th-century origin, and the picturesque Bernese-style fountains add a lighter note to the winding streets. It is a city of memorable views. From the Zähringen viaduct you can look down to the river Sarine far below, with the ancient covered wooden bridge of Bern, and the high-arched Gottéron Bridge beyond: and from the Gottéron Bridge itself, or from the Chapelle de Lorette, or the Milieu or St.-Jean bridges, you will get a splendid view of the town.

Dominating the old town is the Cathedral of St. Nicholas, dating from the 13th century. It is a magnificent building, now fully restored, and its organ is famous throughout the world. Equally fine is the 18th-century Church and Convent of the Cordeliers, built on the site of an earlier edifice. Its treasures include a 16th-century triptych on the high altar by the anonymous Nelkenmeisters (two artists who signed their works only with a red and white carnation), a carved wood triptych believed to be Alsatian, a notable side altar, and a 16th-century retable by the Fribourg artist, Hans Fries. The Church of the Augustines possesses a magnificent 17th-century altar by Peter Spring, the sculptor-monk. In complete contrast to this are the modern university buildings in the new quarter, reached from the cathedral area by the rue de Romont and the rue de Lausanne.

Wednesday and Saturday are market days, when you may find the farmers and their wives in national dress. For the men this means a white, shortsleeved shirt under a linen jacket, and a skull cap of embroidered velvet or straw; for women, a dainty blouse under a tight-waisted, sleeveless cotton dress, with full ankle-length skirt ornamented by a colorful apron; the whole set off with a draped neck square and a wide-brimmed straw hat. This is weekday dress; Sunday costumes are more elaborate.

Even more ornate costumes abound during the International Folklore Festival at the end of August. The festival includes processions, open-air folklore displays, and much singing and dancing in the streets.

Fribourg to Gruyères

The canton of Fribourg is bilingual because it straddles the language frontier. But as two-thirds of its inhabitants speak French and only one-third German, it may be considered French. Its lush pasturelands, particularly around Gruyères, are rich in milk and cream yielded by the Fribourg cows, black-and-white like the cantonal coat of arms. Gruyère cheese, home-cured hams, bacon and sausage, *Vacherin* (a delicious creamy cheese made in Alpine pastures during the summer and preserved for winter in cherrywood boxes)—these are all products of Fribourg's agricultural hinterland. By the way, the town is spelled with a final "s", the region—and the cheese—without one.

Gruyères itself is one of the most picturesque villages in the whole of Europe. To reach it you can either take a train from Fribourg (changing at Bulle for the final stage of the journey), or take the longer route by car. In either case you will pass through Romont, a delightful, sleepy little township, surrounded by cool meadowlands. It is worth leaving the highway for a while to climb into this 13th-century town (composed of two broad streets) to enjoy the magnificent view from the castle terrace. This fortress was originally built by Peter II of Savoy, and its 13th-century ramparts completely surround the town forming a belvedere from which the Alps—from Mont Blanc to the Bernese Oberland—can be seen. In 1581 the government of Fribourg added a new wing to the castle, and today it houses the Musée du Vitrail, a museum of stained glass. From this high point you can see two other notable buildings in the town, the 12th-century Cistercian convent, and the 17th-century Capuchin monastery.

As you continue on to Gruyères look at the architecture of the farms and outbuildings; it is different from that of Bern and from the modified Bernese style of Vaud. Instead, Fribourg farmsteads are composed of two units, the stone-built living quarters and the wooden barns, both under the same roof. The eaves are wide and peaked, and shelter from the cold is provided by a lean-to on the windward side.

You will find Gruyères enchanting if you are here when bus tours are *not.* Closed to automobile traffic, it stands high on a rocky crag, its medieval houses and single main street cozy within its ramparts. It is a perfect specimen of the medieval stronghold, and was once capital of the idyllic Alpine estates of the counts of Gruyères (whose crest bears a crane, from the French word *grue*), vassal lords of the Kingdom of Burgundy.

In all there were 19 counts, who from 1080 to 1554 fought, went on Crusades, and lorded it over their serfs. Michael of Gruyères, the last of them, was a lover of luxury and spent lavishly. Fribourg and Bern did not mind his extravagances, for when at last he fled from his creditors, these two powerful cantons divided up his estates between them. Fribourg and Bernese bailiffs succeeded each other in the old castle until 1848, when the castle was bought by a wealthy Genevan family, whose members were patrons of the arts. One of their guests was Corot, and there are several panels by him in the drawing room.

The one real street in Gruyères is lined with Renaissance houses in perfect condition, their façades dating from the 15th to the 17th centuries. From the ramparts and the castle terrace, the view extends to Broc, the place where Peter-Cailler-Kohler chocolate is made. Beyond is the artificial Lake of Gruyères, built to feed the powerful hydroelectric plants. In the town itself is a cheese dairy which is open to the public and well worth a visit.

Southeast of Gruyères is one of Switzerland's newer resorts, Moléson-Village. From there, you can go by aerial cableway to Plan Francey (1,493 meters, 4,900 ft.) and thence to Mount Moléson (2,010 meters, 6,600 ft.) or to Vudella (1,645 meters, 5,400 ft.). Moléson-Village offers several lifts, several kilometers of marked ski-runs, and no less than four mountain restaurants seating a total of 1,000 people. A post bus runs between Moléson-Village and Bulle.

There is an interesting regional museum at Bulle, the Musée Gruérien, near the castle in a new building. The collections include paintings (a number of Courbets among them), engravings, and documents—all brought to life by an audio-visual show which illustrates the life and traditions of the Gruyère area. During the summer, a folklore market is held on Thursday mornings in Bulle town center.

Gruyères to Château d'Oex

From Gruyères it is a 25-minute train ride to Montbovon, where you change trains for the quarter-hour trip which follows the glorious river Sarine to Château d'Oex, the gateway to the Pays d'Enhaut ("the highlands"), one of the most scenic regions of southwestern Switzerland. Château d'Oex, actually in the canton of Vaud, is a growing winter sports and summer resort. Within a few kilometers, there are a couple of dozen assorted lifts and cableways, the latter leading up to La Montagnette at 1,700 meters (5,600 ft.). If you are interested in peasant handicrafts, a visit to the local museum will be worthwhile but, on a clear day, let nothing interfere with an hour's postal bus ride to the Col des Mosses. This will be one of your most unforgettable experiences in Switzerland. You will see the entire panorama of the Alps, extending into both France and Italy, and there will be no more doubt as to why this region is called the "Pays d'Enhaut."

An alternative excursion from Fribourg is north to the lovely lakeside town of Murten (or Morat), a half-hour by train. This bilingual town is in the canton of Fribourg; and it was here that in 1476 Charles the Bold, Duke of Burgundy, suffered his second defeat at the hands of the Swiss Confederation. The Confederates in fact lost only 410 men while 8,000 Burgundians perished. A fascinating model of the battle is on display at the Landesmuseum, the Swiss national museum, in Zürich. Every year on the first Sunday in October, thousands of runners participate in a 17-kms. (11-mile) road-race from Morat to Fribourg, the route a Swiss courier is said to have run to bring the news of the victory to the residents of Fribourg.

Murten and Avenches

Murten has retained all its medieval charm. The modern highway enters and leaves the old part of the town through the 13th-century gates; and the houses and shops which line the broad main street (Hauptgasse) look out from under deep, vaulted arcades. The town was founded by the dukes of Zähringen in the 12th century, and became an Imperial city in the 13th before passing into the hands of Savoy, whose dukes built the imposing castle and ramparts. Its diminutive namesake lake is fed by the river Broye and its outflow goes into Lake Neuchâtel. The renovated town mill houses the Musée Historique de Morat, complete with two water-powered mill wheels. Also on view are prehistoric finds, ancient military exhibits, and trophies from the Burgundian Wars. The town walls, with their numerous towers, are extremely well preserved and are accessible to the public.

It is a pleasant 15-minute drive to the southwest, at first along the lakeside, to Avenches in the canton of Vaud, the old Celtic capital of the Helvetians. Later, as Aventicum, it became an important Roman city of 40,000 (about 20 times its present population), until the Alamanni destroyed it in the 3rd century. You can still see the remains of a Roman forum, bathhouse and amphitheater—today the Musée et Théâtre Romains—where 12,000 bloodthirsty spectators watched the games. The collection of Roman antiquities at the museum is noteworthy although the famous bust of Marcus Aurelius, unearthed at Avenches a few years ago, has been moved to Lausanne.

A bare 20 minutes on the smooth-running electrified Swiss Federal Railways mainline, or a 12-kms. (eight-mile) drive along the Lausanne road, will take you to Payerne. Here you should visit the carefully restored 11th-century Romanesque abbey church, one of the finest in Switzerland, before returning to Fribourg, a half-hour's journey.

Neuchâtel

The story of Neuchâtel really begins in 1011, for in that year it is first mentioned in a deed of gift made by King Rudolph III of Burgundy to his wife Irmengarde. The township was then probably little more than a fortified village. In 1034, two years after the death of Rudolph, Neuchâtel was given by the German Emperor Conrad II in fief to a local lord whose descendants, using the title "count," greatly developed their domains, encouraging both agriculture and industry. Three centuries later the direct line of the house died out, and thereafter Neuchâtel came under the rule of several dynasties, until in 1707 it passed to Frederick I, Prussia's first king. But although in theory a Prussian principality, this made little difference to the life of the people because their sovereign left them to manage their own affairs. Neuchâtel retained its French culture, and the 18th century saw the rise of a new and lucrative craft—watchmaking. From 1806 Napoleon inevitably loomed into the picture, and for the next eight years the town was held by his Chief of Staff, Maréchal Berthier.

In 1815, Neuchâtel became a member of the Swiss Confederation, and a very odd member too. With the fall of Napoleon it had reverted to the King of Prussia and was, in consequence, the only non-Republican canton in a republican confederation. Its loyalties were therefore divided between the King of Prussia, Frédéric-Guillaume III and the Federal Parliament in Bern, who were themselves not wholly on speaking terms. The events which shook the great European powers at the beginning of 1848 allowed the people of Neuchâtel to become a republic without bloodshed, and in 1857 the king formally acknowledged Neuchâtel's independence.

Throughout the 18th century, watchmaking progressed rapidly from a home craft to the status of an industry, and a number of allied trades sprang up, absorbing the canton's labor. During the present century, watchmaking has become increasingly scientific, and the city has helped manufacturers by placing an observatory and an Institute for Horological Research at their service. The observatory provides the official time for all of Switzerland. Astronomical observations, research into metals, and improved manufacturing techniques have turned watchmaking from an industry into a science. Not everyone in this region is a watchmaker of course. There are also farmers and vintners along the sunny shore of the lake, but scientific horology is the main source of the canton's wealth.

Exploring Neuchâtel

Located at the foot of the Jura, flanked by vineyards and facing southeast, Neuchâtel enjoys incredible views across its lake to the whole crowded range of the middle Alps, from the majestic mass of Mont-Blanc to the Bernese Oberland. Lake Neuchâtel, at 38 kms. (24 miles) long and eight kms. (five miles) wide, is the largest in the country. A prosperous city, Neuchâtel possesses an air of almost tangible dignity. In the lower part of the town, bordering the placid lake, are broad avenues lined with imposing butter-colored sandstone buildings, giving an overall effect of unruffled but compact grandeur. The influence of Prussia has not left so much as a scratch on its culture and way of life, and it is one of the citizens' boasts that they speak "the best French in Switzerland." This in turn is one reason why so many finishing schools have been established here, and why Neuchâtel and its university (founded in 1838) have won such fame in educational circles.

Sightseeing in Neuchâtel should include the Collegiate Church—in the old quarter of the city—a handsome Romanesque and Gothic structure dating from the 12th century; and grouped around it the castle (mainly 15th and 16th centuries), ramparts, cloisters and a shady terrace. The influence of French architectural styles predominates in the city. In the rue des Moulins, for example, are two perfect specimens of the Louis XIII period; and there is a fine Louis XIV house in the Market Square (place des Halles), also notable for its turreted 16th-century Maison des Halles. The Renaissance has left its mark at the Croix du Marché, while in the City Hall Square (place de l'Hôtel de Ville) the 18th century prevails. There are several fine patrician houses, such as the mansion of Du Peyrou, the friend, protector, and publisher of Jean-Jacques Rousseau. But almost anywhere in the old town you will find picturesque buildings, and strolling among them is all the more enjoyable now that many of the streets are closed to traffic. Among the museums, the interesting Musée d'Art et d'Histoire is of interest. If you get tired of walking you can relax in the shade of the trees lining Neuchâtel's lively, lengthy quays, five kms. (three miles) in all, while looking across the water to the distant Alps. Here too, changes are taking place. A large sports area and small port have been built, and a landscaped lake-side walk linking the wine-growing village of Colombier with St.-Blaise is nearing completion. Excursions to the summits of Chaumont, La Vue des Alpes and Tête de Ran offer more views.

La Tene at the eastern tip of the lake was the site of excavations whose finds gave their name to a whole period of European Iron Age culture. Today the finds can be seen in the town's Musée Cantonal d'Archéologie.

The Jura

Straddling the French frontier, from Geneva almost all the way to Basel, lie the Jura Mountains, an impressive range although one very different in character from the Alps. By alpine standards the mountains are relatively low, and few peaks exceed 1,500 meters (5,000 ft.). It is a region of pine forests, lush pastures, and deeply-cleft, often craggy, valleys where the farmers lived in relative isolation until the invasion of railways and roads. In winter some parts of the Jura can be very cold. At La Brévine, a windswept hamlet between Le Locle and Les Verrières on the Franco-Swiss frontier, the temperature sometimes drops as low as minus 34 degrees Centigrade (minus 30 degrees Fahrenheit), leading some to call it "Swiss Siberia."

The Jura also has a number of thriving winter sports resorts, although most are comparatively small, with local rather than international appeal. Surprisingly it is a region which is relatively uncluttered with tourists, since travelers usually bypass it in favor of more famous places. This makes the Jura one of the most reasonably priced regions in Switzerland.

Strangely, the Jura has a number of pockets of industry. Occasionally, without warning and in the middle of nowhere, one comes to a large, white factory—probably bearing a world-famous name. If you look at your watch face you may well see the same name, for watchmaking—one of Switzerland's most important industries—has long been one of the principal occupations of the region.

The Jura is divided into several well-defined districts: Franches-Montagnes, with its chief town, Saignelégier; the French-speaking Bernese Jura, including St.-Imier; Delémont, Porrentruy, the Ajoie area and the Neuchâtel Jura, with the great watchmaking centers of La Chaux-de-Fonds and Le Locle.

To La Chaux-de-Fonds and Ste.-Croix

From Neuchâtel, take the main highway north to Valangin, where the beautiful mountain road known as the Vue des Alpes begins. As the highway rises, the view extends over Lake Neuchâtel towards the Savoy Alps and into the Bernese Oberland.

La Chaux-de-Fonds, which lies in a hollow, is not a picturesque town. Its straight, broad streets and avenues lie stiffly at right angles, and are bordered by stone houses. All the buildings are relatively new, since the old town was destroyed by fire at the end of the 18th century; and recently an ultramodern industrial and residential sector has sprung up among the pastures on the western side of La Chaux-de-Fonds. As you pass through the town you will see on the factories the names of many internationally famous makes of watches; and if you wish to learn more about the craft, the Musée International d'Horlogerie in the rue des Musées is truly outstanding.

Leaving La Chaux-de-Fonds, you should turn off southwest to reach Le Locle, another important watchmaking center. From here it is worth continuing on for a few kilometers to Col des Roches, and then through the tunnel—for on the other side you will have a magnificent view of France. From here you will be able to see the river Doubs as it runs through high cliffs, a small lake, and finally to a waterfall. Next, backtrack to Le Locle, turn right and continue through meadows and pine covered hills to Les Petits-Ponts. There, another right turn will take you to Fleurier along the Val de Travers; the winding gorges of this valley are extremely picturesque. Beyond Fleurier you climb up to Ste.-Croix where, from the pine-covered ridge above the village (which, incidentally, makes music boxes) there's a splendid view. If you're a glutton for views, turn left here to Les Rasses—it's only a couple of kilometers—for another fine one. From Ste.-Croix you drive down towards Yverdon and then return along the lake shore to Neuchâtel.

To Moutier and Delémont

From Neuchâtel, take the Vue des Alpes route to La Chaux-de-Fonds and bear northeast (right) along the pretty valley of St.-Imier, a small watchmaking center which lies at the foot of Mont Soleil (1,219 meters, 4,200 ft.) and faces Mont Chasseral (1,615 meters, 5,300 ft.), the Jura's highest mountain. St.-Imier is a modern town, but not blatantly so, and legend has it that it was founded by a holy hermit from Burgundy. A trip by funicular up Mont Soleil is worthwhile, especially if you have time to spend a night there to see the sunrise the following morning. On winter Sundays Mont Soleil is a favorite haunt of skiers from Basel.

From St.-Imier it is about 40 kms. (25 miles) to the medieval town of Moutier, which produces a special cheese called *Tête de Moine* (Monk's Head), the only reminder of the once renowned monastery of Bellelay. At Moutier, you turn north to Delémont, the chief town of the Bernese Jura, located in a wide picturesque valley. It has an ancient story and is first mentioned in history in 727. In the 11th century, Delémont was annexed by the bishop-princes of Basel, who often used it as a summer residence. At the beginning of the 18th century they built a castle for this purpose, but they had left things too late, for in 1793 the town was seized by France and later, in 1815, given to Bern under the Treaty of Vienna. Visitors will find that even today Delémont retains an 18th-century charm.

The round trip from Delémont northwest to Porrentruy and back is about 55 kms. (35 miles) long, and is a beautiful run along part of the Corniche du I. If you have time for a side-trip, take the secondary road on the left just beyond Les Rangiers. After about six kms. (four miles) you will come to the charming fortified town of St.-Ursanne, where time seems to have stood still. At the far end of the narrow bridge there's a picturesque view of the old houses lining the side of the river Doubs. There's also a fine Romanesque church here. Porrentruy, at 425 meters (1,400 ft.), has about 8,500 inhabitants and is the chief center of the Ajoie district. Its splendid castle, above the town, was yet another residence of the bishop-princes of Basel and it can boast several fine 18th-century buildings. Like many of the Jura towns, Porrentruy has an excellent watchmaking school where for generations skilled craftsmen have been trained; but thanks to the lovely surrounding countryside and excellent local food, the district is also a popular holiday center in summer. Year round, it organizes special horseback riding holidays, trekking from village to village in the region. At the local airfield, you can learn to fly or glide, and if you aspire to be a balloonist you can make a trip over the Jura with an expert pilot.

Saignelégier to Bienne

From St.-Ursanne a delightful picturesque drive takes you along the secondary road which leads southwest into the Franches-Montagnes, past the villages of Soubey and Les Enfers, to Saignelégier.

Saignelégier is the center of a horse-breeding area, and also, on the second weekend in August, the scene of a fascinating horse show and market with races that attract large crowds. The Franches-Montagnes horse is used chiefly for military purposes and agriculture.

The district has typical Jura scenery: rolling hills, long valleys and pine-capped hummocks, although the grazing land is mostly poor. Peat is dug in certain areas, and the roots of the yellow gentian are used for making a powerful liqueur, said to have medicinal properties.

From Saignelégier continue to Le Noirmont, a typical Jura village, through La Chaux-de-Fonds, and so down again to Neuchâtel.

At Neuchâtel the vineyards begin. Their wines, chiefly white, are light, somewhat sparkling, and have a distinct bouquet. They are bottled before the second fermentation begins, so have a rather high carbonic acid content. These wines are exported, as well as consumed on the home market. The annual harvest of the grapes is celebrated on the last weekend of September with parades and fanfares in the city center.

About six kms. (four miles) southwest of Neuchâtel, and well worth a visit, is the medieval village of Colombier. It lies just to the right of the main road and is approached through a massive stone gateway beside the impressive 16th-century castle.

The lakeside village of Grandson (in the canton of Vaud) is about 25 kms. (16 miles) further on. It is said that a member of the Grandson family accompanied William of Normandy (better known as the Conqueror) to England in 1066, where he founded the English barony of Grandison. Otto I of Grandson took part in the Crusades, and one of his descendants, so legend has it, was a troubadour whose poems were praised by Chaucer. When the Burgundian Wars broke out in the late 15th century, Grandson castle, much rebuilt in the 13th and 15th centuries, was in the hands of Charles of Burgundy. In 1475 the Swiss won it by siege, but early the next year their garrison was surprised by Duke Charles, and 418 of their men were captured and hanged from the apple trees in the castle orchard. A few days later the Swiss returned to Grandson and, after inflicting a crushing defeat on the Burgundians, retaliated by stringing their prisoners from the same apple trees. After being used for three centuries as a residence by the Bernese bailiffs, the castle was bought in 1875 by the de Blonay family, who restored it.

Just under five kms. (three miles) beyond Grandson is the busy market and industrial town of Yverdon, also something of a spa. It was here that the famous Swiss educationalist Pestalozzi (born in 1746), opened an experimental school in the castle, an enterprise which attracted other reformers from both Germany and England, (one of his visitors was the poet Southey). The castle, built by Peter II of Savoy in the middle of the 13th century, has been restored and modernized, and in front of Yverdon's town hall, notable for its Louis XV façade, is a monument to commemorate Pestalozzi. From Yverdon you can return to Neuchâtel by the other side of the lake, the road passing alongside the mini-lake of Morat (Murtensee). On the way you will pass the ancient lakeside townlet of Estavayer, almost every corner of which has some special charm of its own, not least of which is the well kept, moated castle.

Only about 11 kms. (seven miles) from Lake Neuchâtel is Lake Bienne (Lac de Bienne or Bielersee), its smaller but sprightly neighbor. Projecting from the southern shore, like a long thin finger pointing to the city of Bienne at the other end of the lake, is the extraordinary St. Peter's Isle. On the island's lumpy wooded headland you will find an old monastery, now a small hotel, where Jean-Jacques Rousseau stayed in 1765.

Bienne (or Biel) itself is a busy industrial and commercial city, which also has a tourist eye-opener—the well-preserved and restored old town. This can best be seen by walking from the busy junction of the rue du Canal and rue de Nidau up rue du Bourg, past the fine Gothic town hall with its 17th-century fountain, and taking one of the streets on the right to the famous "Ring," a medieval architectural gem. The focal point of ancient Bienne, the Ring is a picturesque little square with a 15th-century church, arcaded houses and, in the center, a fountain. Almost adjacent to the Ring is the main street (Obergasse), again with lovely old arcaded buildings and, of course, the inevitable fountain.

Today watchmaking is one of Bienne's main industries, but the town has much to entertain the tourist, from theater to water sports, and it's a good excursion center with boat trips down the lake or up the river Aare to Solothurn. Both French and German are spoken with equal ease and, indeed, are often mixed together in conversation. Such is the language frontier of Switzerland.

PRACTICAL INFORMATION FOR THE JURA, NEUCHÂTEL AND FRIBOURG

TOURIST OFFICES. Bulle, Office du Tourisme de la Gruyère, av. de la Gare 4 (tel. 029–28022); open Mon. to Fri. 8–12 and 2–6, Sat. 9–12. **La Chaux-de-Fonds,** Office du Tourisme, rue Neuve 11 (tel. 039–28 13 13); open Mon. to Fri. 9–6, Sat. 9–12. **Delémont,** Office Jurassien du Tourisme, Pl. de la Gare 12 (tel. 066–229778); open Mon. to Fri. 9–6, Sat. 9–4. **Fribourg,** Office du Tourisme, Square des Places 1 (tel. 037–81 31 75); open Mon. to Fri. 8–6, Sat. 9–12. **Morat,** Office du Tourisme, Schlossgasse 5 (tel. 037–71 51 12); open Mon. to Fri. 9–12 and 2–5.30, Sat. 9–12. **Neuchâtel,** Office du Tourisme, rue de la Place d'Armes 7 (tel. 038–25 42 42); open Mon. to Fri. 9–6, Sat. 9–12. **Saignelégier,** Office du Tourisme, pl. du 23 Juin 1 (tel. 039–51 21 51); open Mon. to Fri. 9–12 and 2–6, Sat. 9–12.

HOTELS AND RESTAURANTS. The Jura-Neuchâtel-Fribourg region is among the least expensive in Switzerland, but services are still good, true to the best Swiss traditions. Fribourg, with 40,000 inhabitants, has all the advantages of a small city, while at the same time offering all tourist and commercial services. Similarly, Neuchâtel and La Chaux-de-Fonds offer a broad range of hotels and restaurants. These are all good bases from which to make excursions to more rural areas, rarely more than an hour's drive away.

In the smaller towns, the choice of hotels and restaurants is significantly reduced, but again service is almost always reliable, and the setting often spectacular. It's also possible to rent chalets or apartments for group or family accommodations throughout much of the region. Contact tourist offices for more information.

Many hotels have a wide variety of rooms, with price ranges that do not fit neatly into the general gradings given in our listings. For specific prices and information, it's best to check with the hotel beforehand. The gradings are made on a regional basis, but an expensive hotel in Neuchâtel might be considered medium-priced or even inexpensive by Geneva or Zürich standards.

Many hotels have their own restaurants, and a light breakfast is often included in the hotel price. Restaurant portions are usually large, and the atmosphere, especially in some out-of-the-way places, is warm and friendly. Some restaurants are closed on Sundays.

Food here is influenced by both French and German traditions. Cheese dishes such as *raclette* and *fondue* are found throughout the region. *Fondue fribourgeoise,* or *moitié-moitié* (half-and-half), calls for a combination of Gruyère and Fribourg Vacherin cheeses. Fribourg's agricultural tradition is celebrated in most homes and restaurants with the "Bénichon," an annual thanksgiving meal for the harvest. It consists of three meat dishes, an abundance of vegetables, and sweets of all kinds. The date of the Bénichon feast varies from community to community, but usually falls on a Sunday in September or October.

BULLE. *Des Alpes et Terminus* (I), tel. 029–2 92 92. 60 beds. Quiet rooms, restaurant. DC. *Le Rallye* (I), tel. 029–2 84 98. 35 beds. Splendid view, bar and dancing. DC, MC, V. *Du Tonnelier* (I), tel. 029–2 77 45. 35 beds. Simple and central, restaurant. AE, MC, V.

Restaurants. *Café de la Gare* (I–M), av. de la Gare 6 (tel. 029–2 76 88). Try the *fondue au Vacherin. De l'Hôtel de Ville* (I–M), Grand-Rue 7 (tel. 029–2 78 88). Actually in the town hall. AE, DC.

CHARMEY. *Cailler* (M), tel. 029–7 10 13. 90 beds. Tennis, sauna, fitness room, indoor pool. AE, DC, MC.

CHATEL-ST.-DENIS/LES PACCOTS. *Corbetta* (I), tel. 021–56 71 20. 30 beds. Quiet and attractive. No showers. *Ermitage* (I), tel. 021–56 75 41. 48 beds. Bowling. AE.

Restaurant. *Tivoli* (I–M), tel. 021–56 70 39. Excellent *Fondue fribourgeoise.*

LA CHAUX-DE-FONDS. *Club* (M), rue du Parc 71 (tel. 039–23 53 00). 80 beds. AE, DC, MC. *Fleur-de-Lys* (M), av. L.-Robert 13 (tel. 039–23 37 31). 54 beds. Quiet, with restaurant. AE, DC, MC, V. *Moreau* (M), av. L.-Robert 45 (tel. 039–23 22 22). 60 beds. Good family hotel with restaurant, and facilities for the handicapped. AE, MC.

Restaurants. *Aérogare* (M), blvd. des Eplatures 54 (tel. 039–26 82 66). Terrace. MC, V. *Channe Valaisanne* (M), av. L.-Robert 17 (tel. 039–23 10 64).

Good for *raclette* and *fondue*. AE, DC, MC. *Le Provencal* (M), rue Jaquet-Droz 60 (tel. 039–23 19 22). French cuisine. V. *Coop City* (I), rue de la Serre 37–43 (tel. 039–23 89 01). Self-service, hot meals, open 11–1.45 and 3–5.

CRESUZ. *Vieux Chalet* (I), tel. 029–7 12 86. 10 beds. Quiet and very small.

DELEMONT. *City* (M), rte. de Bâle 38 (tel. 066–22 94 44). 30 beds. Grill and restaurant. AE, DC, MC, V. *Le National* (M), rte. de Bâle 25 (tel. 066–22 96 22). 54 beds. Piano bar, Chinese restaurant. AE, DC, MC, V.

ESTAVAYER-LE-LAC. *Du Château* (I), rue du Château (tel. 037–63 10 49). 9 beds. Small but attractive and very reasonable. No showers. *Du Lac* (I), pl. Port 1 (tel. 037–63 13 43). 17 beds. Lakeside hotel, excellent restaurant. AE, DC, V.

FRIBOURG. *Eurotel* (M–E), Grands-Place 14 (tel. 037–81 31 31). 200 beds. Central, indoor pool and dancing. DC, MC, V. *Alpha* (M), rue du Simplon 13 (tel. 037–22 72 72). 60 beds. Quiet rooms, gymnasium. AE, DC, MC, V. *Duc Bertold* (M), rue des Bouchers 112 (tel. 037–81 11 21). 60 beds. In the old town. Hotel bar. AE, DC, MC. *Hôtel de la Rose* (M), pl. Notre Dame 179 (tel. 037–22 46 07). 71 beds. Central location, restaurant and night club. AE, DC, MC. *Elite* (I–M), rue du Criblet 7 (tel. 037–22 38 36). 69 beds. Near railway station. Recommended. AE, DC, MC. *Touring* (I), rue de Lausanne 25 (tel. 037–22 32 19). 28 beds. Central location. AE, DC, MC.

Restaurants. *Aigle Noir* (M–E), rue des Alpes 58 (tel. 037–22 49 77). DC, MC, V. *Buffet de la Gare* (M–E), rail station (tel. 037–22 28 16). French restaurant. Highly recommended. AE, DC, MC. *De la Gérine* (M), at Marly (3 kms./1½ miles), tel. 037–46 14 98. Recommended for its excellent fish, among other dishes. *Trois-Rois* (M), Samaritaine 2 (tel. 037–22 16 45). Specialty is *la charbonnade,* meat grilled at the table. DC, MC. *Café du Midi* (I–M), rue de Romont 25 (tel. 22 31 33). All things cheesy; excellent. AE, DC, MC, V. *Le Soleil-Blanc* (I–M), in the old town, tel. 037–22 15 63. Known for its *fondue. Fleur de Lys* (I), rue des Forgerons 18 (tel. 037–22 79 61). In the old town. Inexpensive and good, jazz some evenings.

GRUYÈRES. *Hostellerie des Chevaliers* (M), tel. 029–6 19 33. 70 beds. Quiet. First-class restaurant. AE, DC, MC, V. *Hostellerie St. Georges* (M), tel. 029–6 22 46. 34 beds. Quiet area. Restaurant with view, bar. AE, DC, MC, V. *Hôtel de Ville* (I), tel. 029–6 24 24. 23 beds. Terrace restaurant. Historic building. AE, DC, MC, V.

Restaurant. *Le Chalet* (I), tel. 029–6 21 54. Right near château. Cheese specialties and delicious thick Gruyère double cream. AE, DC, MC.

LE LOCLE. *Hôtel des Trois Rois* (I), rue du Temple 27 (tel. 039–31 65 55). 40 beds. Excellent restaurant. AE, DC, MC, V.

MURTEN/MORAT. *Le Vieux Manoir au Lac* (M–E), tel. 037–71 12 83. 40 beds. 3 kms. (1½ miles) from town center. Old house in charming setting with park and private harbor on the lake. Excellent but expensive grill room. AE, DC. *Schiff* (M), tel. 037–71 27 01. 30 beds. Right on the lake, quiet and comfortable. Famous restaurant with bar and dancing. AE, DC, MC, V. *Krone* (I–M), Rathausgasse 5 (tel. 037–71 52 52). 65 beds. Central, but with quiet rooms. Hotel bar, lakeside terrace restaurant. DC, V. *Weisses Kreuz* (I–M), Rathausgasse 31 (tel. 037–71 26 41). 60 beds. With lake view, bowling. MC, V.

NEUCHÂTEL. *Beaulac* (M–E), quai L.-Robert 2 (tel. 038–25 88 22). 92 beds. Lakeside location near the port. Three restaurants. AE, DC, MC, V. *Eurotel* (M–E), av. de la Gare 15–17 (tel. 038–21 21 21). 200 beds. Modern and a little antiseptic, indoor pool and sauna. AE, DC, MC, V. *City* (I–M), pl. Piaget 12 (tel. 038–25 54 12). 70 beds. Central location. French and Chinese restaurants, hairdresser. AE, DC, MC, V. *Touring au Lac* (I–M), pl. Numa-Droz 1 (tel. 038–25 55 01). 80 beds. Next to port but quiet. AE, DC, MC, V.

Restaurants. *Au Vieux Vapeur* (E), tel. 038–24 34 00. Floating restaurant in the port. Fresh fish daily, bar and dancing. AE, DC, MC. *Maison des Halles* (M), pl. des Halles (tel. 038–24 31 41). Pizzeria and 2nd-floor restaurant. *Buffet de la Gare* (I–M), Gare CCF (tel. 038–25 48 53). First class, fish specialties. DC, MC, V. *Bagatelle* (I), Fog. de l'Hôpital 5 (tel. 038–25 82 52).

At **St.-Blaise,** five kms. (three miles) away, is *Chez Norbert* (M), av. Bachelin 11 (tel. 038–33 36 80). Probably the best food in the district. V.

NEUCHÂTEL-THIELLE. *Novotel Neuchâtel-Thielle* (M), autoroute Neuchâtel–Bienne (tel. 038–33 57 57). 160 beds. Six kms. (four miles) from city center. Quiet hotel with pool, restaurant, garden. AE, DC, V.

PORRENTRUY. *Belvédère* (I), rte. de Bure 61 (tel. 066–66 25 61). 15 beds. Small and budget value. Quiet location. Restaurant with grill. AE.

SAIGNELEGIER. *Bellevue* (I), rue de la Gruère 13 (tel. 039–51 16 20). 100 beds. Sauna, stables, restaurant. AE, DC, MC, V. *De la Gare et du Parc* (I), tel. 039–51 11 21. 56 beds. Good restaurant, indoor tennis. AE, MC, V.

GETTING AROUND. By Train. Connections between larger towns and cities are good and fairly frequent, but outlying areas are often beyond the reaches of the national rail network. Several private lines exist, which are just as comfortable, and these can get you to some smaller villages and the countryside. The Neuchâtel mountain railroad, for example, offers 21 kms. (12 miles) of track and often shuttles hikers and skiers. For more information, inquire at the local tourist office or train station.

By Car. Traveling by car is ideal in this part of Switzerland because much of the sightseeing is in the countryside and villages. Roads are good, and wandering around on the back roads is recommended. The major highway connects Fribourg with Bern and Lausanne.

By Bus. Where the trains don't run, postal buses often do, but they may make trips only a couple of times a day. Plan your trip having consulted the official Swiss transportation timetable, available at any train station.

By Boat. There are boat trips on the lakes of Neuchâtel, Murten/Morat and Biel/Bienne, as well as on the Aare river and the Broye Canal (a national wildlife sanctuary). Schedules vary according to season, but in summer tours are frequent and include evening trips.

Sightseeing Data

AVENCHES. Musée et Théâtre Romains (Roman Museum and Theater), tel. 037–75 17 27. Sculpture, pottery and other remains from the Roman period in Switzerland. Open daily 9–12 and 1–5. During Nov. to Mar. closed on Mon.

BOUDRY. Musée de l'Areuse (Areuse Museum), tel. 038–42 30 46. Open May to Sept., Sun. 2–5.

BROC. Chocolate factory visits; Société des Produits Nestlé, tel. 029–6 12 12. By appointment only. Film on chocolate making, guided tour of the factory, and a chance to sample the finished products. Open Mar. to Oct. (not July), Tues. to Thurs.

BULLE. Musée Gruérien (Gruyère Museum), pl. du Cabalet (tel. 029–2 72 60). Regional museum with a collection of paintings, costumes and furniture, plus displays of traditional living and working quarters. Open Tues. to Sat. 10–12 and 2–5, Sun. 2–5.

LA CHAUX-DE-FONDS. Musée des Beaux-Arts (Fine Arts Museum), rue des Musées 33 (tel. 039–23 04 44). Excellent collection of contemporary paintings, sculpture and tapestries. Includes works by Le Corbusier and Léopold Robert, both of whom were born in La Chaux-de-Fonds. Open Tues. to Sun. 10–12 and 2–5. On Wed. free entrance, open until 8 P.M.

Musée d'Histoire et Médaillier (Museum of History and Medals), Parc des Musées (tel. 039–23 50 10). Housed in an ancient patrician residence, this collection includes etchings, armor and medals. Open Mon. to Fri. on request, Sat. and Sun. 10–12 and 2–5.

Musée d'Histoire Naturelle (Natural History Museum), av. L.-Robert 63 (tel. 039–23 39 76). Gallery of Swiss fauna, exhibitions of birds, reptiles and African animals. Open Tues. to Sat. 2–5, Sun. and holidays 10–12 and 2–5.

Musée International d'Horlogerie, "L'Homme et le Temps" (International Clock Museum, "Man and Time"), rue des Musées 29 (tel. 039–23 62 63). Founded in 1902, this museum houses an important collection of more than 300 exhibits connected with watchmaking. In the restoration center, craftsmen can be seen at work. Open Tues. to Sun. 10–12 and 2–5.

Musée Paysan et Artisanal (Arts and Crafts Museum), les Eplatures (tel. 039–26 77 42). Regional tools, furniture and clothing housed in a restored 17th-century farmhouse. Open Nov. to Apr., Wed., Sat. and Sun. 2–5, May to Oct., daily 2–5, closed Fri.

DELEMONT. Musée Jurassien (Jura Museum), tel. 066–22 80 77. Open Sun. 2–5.

ESTAVAYER-LE-LAC. Musée Regional (Regional Museum), tel. 037–63 10 40. Open Nov. to Feb., Sat. and Sun. 2–5, Mar. to Oct., Tues. to Sun. 9–11 and 2–5.

FRIBOURG. Musée d'Art et d'Histoire (Art and History Museum), rue Pierre-Aeby 227 (tel. 037–22 85 71). Housed in a Renaissance building, this collection includes medieval and 16th-century paintings and sculpture, some remarkable archeological finds, and grand furniture. Open Tues., Wed., Fri., Sat. and Sun. 10–5, Thurs. 10–5 and 8–10 P.M.

Musée d'Histoire Naturelle (Natural History Museum), Pérolles, chemin du Musée (tel. 037–82 63 91). Open daily 2–6.

LES GENEVEZ. Musée Rural des Genevez (Rural Museum of Genevez), tel. 032–91 97 88. Open Easter to 1 Nov., Sun. 2–5.

GRUYÈRES. Château de Gruyères, tel. 029–6 21 02. Most of the castle dates from the late 15th century, though the 13th-century dungeon remains. The Chapel of St. John shelters within the castle walls. Collection includes three copes bearing the heraldry of Charles the Bold, and part of the booty from the battle of Morat. Open June to Sept., daily 9–6; March to May and Oct. 9–12 and 1–5; Nov. to Feb. 9–12 and 1–4:30.

Musée de Cire (Wax Museum), tel. 029–6 11 70. Small exhibition of Swiss personalities. Open daily 10:30–6.

Cheese dairy visits, tel. 029–6 14 10. Observe the three-month process of making cheese that involves heating, pumping, pressing, salting and turning the cheese. The main vat produces 32 wheels of cheese a day, each weighing 35 kilos. Excellent audiovisual presentation. Cheese products for sale. Open daily 6–6.

HAUTERIVE (seven kms.—four miles—from Fribourg). **Cistercian monastery** by the river Sarine, tel. 037–24 17 83. Founded in 1138. Abbey church with Gothic facade. Open Easter to mid-Sept., Mon. to Sat. 2:30–5, Sun. and holidays 10:45–11:30 and 2:45–4:45; mid-Sept. to Easter, Mon. to Sat. 2–4, Sun. and holidays 10:45–11:30 and 2–4. Closed the first Sunday of every month.

LE LOCLE. Musée d'Horlogerie (Museum of Horology), Château des Monts (tel. 039–31 62 62). Open May to Oct., Tues. to Sun. 10–12 and 2–5; Nov. to April on Sun. 2–5 and on demand.

MOTIERS. Musée Régional d'Histoire et d'Artisanat, Musée Jean-Jacques Rousseau, Musée de la Forêt (Museum of History and Crafts, Rousseau Museum, Forest Museum), Grand-Rue (tel. 038–61 28 22). Group of three museums. Open Tues. to Fri. 2–5, Sat. (Apr. to Sept.) 2–5.

MURTEN/MORAT. Musée Historique de Morat (Morat Historical Museum), tel. 037–71 30 00. In town mill near the castle. Regional history, archeological finds and folklore art; diorama slide show of the battle of 1476. Open May to Sept., Tues. to Sun. 10–12 and 1:30–6; Oct. to Apr., Tues. to Sun. 10–12 and 1:30–5.

MURTEN-MUNTELIER. Equestrian hall, tel. 037–71 46 46. One of Europe's largest, with shows, exhibits, and a riding school.

NEUCHÂTEL. Musée d'Art et d'Histoire (Art and History Museum), quai L.-Robert (tel. 038–25 17 40). Rich collection including clocks, coins, ceramics, works by Swiss artists, French Impressionists and 18th–20th-century French artists. Open Tues., Wed., Fri., Sat. and Sun. 10–12 and 2–5, Thurs. 10–12 and 2–9.

Musée Cantonal d'Archéologie (Cantonal Archeological Museum), av. Du Peyrou 7 (tel. 038–25 03 36). Regional archeological finds going back 50,000 years. Open Tues. to Sun. 2–5.

Musée d'Ethnographie (Ethnographical Museum), rue Saint-Nicholas 4 (tel. 038–24 41 20). Important Far Eastern collection. Remarkable toys and musical instruments. Open Tues. to Sun. 10–12 and 2–5.

Musée d'Histoire Naturelle (Natural History Museum), rue des Terreaux 14 (tel. 038–25 68 72). Displays of Swiss fauna. Open Tues. to Sun. 2–5.

Fête des Vendanges (festival of the grape harvest), last weekend in Sept.; music, markets, parades and dancing.

PAYERNE. Abbatiale Roman (Romanesque Abbey). Open in summer, Mon. to Sat. 9–12 and 2–6, Sun. and holidays 10.30–12 and 2–6; in winter, Mon. to Sat. 10–12 and 2–5, Sun. and holidays 10–12 and 2–5.

PORRENTRUY. Musée de Porrentruy (Porrentruy Museum), Hôtel-Dieu (tel. 066–65 11 21). Open Wed. and Fri. 3–5, and the last Sunday of every month 3–6.

ROMONT. Musée de Vitrail (Museum of Stained-Glass), tel. 037–52 10 95. Old and contemporary church windows and other art works within the superb setting of the Savoyard castle. Open 15 May to Sept., Tues. to Sun. 10–12 and 2–6; Oct. to 15 May, Sat. and Sun. 10–12 and 2–6.

ST.-URSANNE. Musée Lapidaire (Lapidary Museum), next to church cloisters. Museum of sculpture with sarcophagi from the 7th century. Open Sat. and Sun. 10–12 and 2–6.

SAIGNELEGIER. Fête des Chevaux (national horse festival), second weekend in Aug.; parades, races, markets. **Intl. Dog-Sled Races,** beginning of Feb.

TAFERS. Sensler Heimatmuseum, tel. 037–44 25 31. Regional museum. Open Apr. to Oct., Tues., Sat. and Sun. 2–6; Nov. to Mar., Sat. and Sun. 2–6.

VALANGIN. Fortress Château and Museum, route des Gorges du Seyon et de La Chaux-de-Fonds (eight kms., five miles, from Neuchâtel), tel. 038–36 11 51. Open Mar. to Dec., Tues. to Sun. 10–12 and 2–5, closed Fri. afternoons.

WINTER SPORTS. Bugnenets-Savagnières, 1,430 meters (4,692 ft.); 7 lifts, 40 kms. (24 miles) of prepared trails. Ski school, restaurants. Ten minutes from St.-Imier.

Charmey, 1,626 meters (5,335 ft.); 7 lifts including gondola, 30 kms. (18 miles) of downhill runs, 15 kms. (9 miles) of cross-country trails including one lighted trail. Ski school, heated indoor pool.

Châtel-St.-Denis/Les Paccots, 1,486 meters (4,875 ft.); 9 lifts, 15 kms. (nine miles) of downhill runs, 12 kms. (seven miles) of cross-country trails, eight kms. (5 miles) of ski-hiking trails. Ski school.

La Chaux-de-Fonds, 1,120 meters (3,675 ft.); 18 lifts, 27 kms. (16 miles) of downhill runs, cross-country skiing, tobogganing, curling, skating. Ski schools.

Gruyères/Moléson, 2,002 meters (6,568 ft.); 3 cable cars, 2 lifts, 30 kms.(18 miles) of downhill runs, eight kms. (five miles) of cross-country trails. Ski school.

Schwarzsee/Lac Noir, 1,160–1,751 meters (3,806–5,745 ft.); 3 ski areas, 10 lifts, 25 kms. (15 miles) of downhill runs, 12 kms. (seven miles) of cross-country trails. Ski school.

THE VALAIS AND THE ALPES VALAISANNES

A Journey up the Rhône

Extending along the valley of the upper Rhône from Lac Léman to the river's source, the scenic canton of Valais (Wallis in German) is one of the most magnificent regions in Europe. The river valley itself is roughly L-shaped, with the angle resting on the town of Martigny, where the Val d'Entremont branches off to lead to the Great St. Bernard Pass. It is the right, or long, leg of the "L" that is the most characteristic and imposing part of the region.

But the Valais is far more than the riverbed of the Rhône and its cliff-like walls. It is an alpine network with a score or more of narrow valleys that wind left and right into even more remote areas. Mark Twain wrote in *A Tramp Abroad* of meeting British tourists in Zermatt at the end of one of the side valleys—they had made the journey by mule—but with a few hardy exceptions, such encounters used to be rare. Until quite recent times, only the feet of the mountain folk and their animals could negotiate the precipitous hillsides. Even today some of the more remote districts rarely see a tourist.

Exploring the Valais

The Rhône enters Lac Léman just a few kilometers west of Villeneuve, itself just west of Montreux and easily reached on the N9 expressway that runs along the northern shore of Lac Léman. From Villeneuve, you can take either the N9 into the Rhône valley, or the slower but more scenic route 9. Excellent train links also extend into the Valais from Lac Léman to the important rail junction at Brig (where you can also catch the aptly named "Glacier Express" that claws its way over the Alps to Graubünden).

The Rhône valley at Villeneuve is broad and alluvial. But heading up the valley, by the time you reach Aigle, about 11 kms. (seven miles) away, the mountains are already beginning to crowd in on either side. Here, you are still in canton Vaud. An interesting detour from the main Valais road is to Chesières and Villars, the latter especially one of the Vaud's most popular summer and winter resorts with splendid views and a nine-hole golf course. From Villars a mountain railway climbs up to Bretaye (1,858 meters, 6,100 ft.), at the foot of Chamossaire, from which lifts fan out in all directions to the surrounding heights, where you can find wonderful ski-runs in winter and fine walks in summer. There is also a cable car to Roc d'Orsay at 2,010 meters (6,600 ft.).

If you have made this detour, instead of returning to Aigle, you can continue beyond Villars. Almost immediately, the road begins its long winding descent, offering a succession of glorious views and passing through several picturesque villages before bringing you back to the main highway at Bex, just under 10 kms. (six miles) beyond Aigle. The whole detour from Aigle to Bex will take rather less than an hour of gentle, if hilly, driving. But try to allow more. It's difficult to resist stopping to admire views, inspect villages, particularly on the downward run, and explore Villars. At Bex you will find a complete contrast to all this: thanks to its sheltered location on the valley floor this long-established brine spa enjoys a very mild climate—pomegranates, figs and grapes grow here.

Champéry and the Val d'Illiez

Another detour, this time to the southwest, starts from Bex. You cross the Rhône (passing out of the Vaud into the Valais), go through the industrial center of Monthey, five kms. (three miles) west, and then turn up the valley which opens before you. After a couple of kilometers a sharp right fork at Troistorrents leads up to Morgins, a mountain and ski resort just on the French border.

Another excursion is to Champéry, an all-year resort perched 1,066 meters (3,500 ft.) up in the Val d'Illiez. To reach it, take the left fork at Troistorrents and head up the little valley, bordered to the south by the dramatic Dents du Midi, the final escarpment of the Mont Blanc range. From Champéry, a cable car swings you a good kilometer higher to Planachaux at 1,767 meters (5,800 ft.) where a collection of lifts give access to some splendid ski runs, including one to Avoriaz in France.

From Champéry, it's about 20 kms. (12 miles) back down to the Rhône and St.-Maurice, the next important town on our route.

St.-Maurice and Martigny

St.-Maurice is where the two main routes from Lac Léman, which have hugged each side of the wide Rhône valley, converge. It is here that both the valley and the river begin to change character. The mountains have closed in. The Rhône, although still a king-sized river, gradually loses its placidity, giving a foretaste of the mountain torrent it will become as we get nearer its source.

St.-Maurice owes its name, according to tradition, to Maurice, the leader of the Theban Legion who, with most of his men, was massacred here in A.D. 302 for refusing to acknowledge the pagan gods of Rome. To commemorate the martyrdom an abbey was built, rapidly growing in importance and wealth. Excavations near the Baroque abbey church have revealed the foundations of this original building.

Just before you reach Martigny, 14 kms. (nine miles) further up the valley, another mountainous side trip beckons. A right-hand fork will take you west and then south along a narrow road that weaves through the gorges of the river Trient. Salvan is the first village in this remote valley. Though popular as a summer resort since the days of the Romans, many of its old traditions have survived, including an unusual and beautiful dress worn by the women on festival days. The next village, Les Marecottes, is a charming little resort set in the pinewoods and, for some reason, very popular with the Dutch, many of whom have built vacation homes here. The skiing is quite good, but the summer walking is outstanding.

Martigny, back on the valley floor, was in ages past a Roman camp called Octodorum. It sits squarely astride the historic crossroads at the sharp angle of the Rhône, where it bends west. From Martigny, roads head south to the Great St. Bernard Pass to Italy, the Forclaz Pass to France, and along the upper Rhône to the Simplon Pass and beyond.

The Great St. Bernard Pass

The Great St. Bernard Pass is the oldest and most famous of the great Alpine crossings. Known and used centuries before the birth of Christ, it has watched an endless stream of emperors, knights and simple travelers. In the 11th century Frederick Barbarossa, the German king and Roman emperor, became almost a commuter over the pass as he went from one country to another to settle the problems which constantly beset him. Napoleon took an army of 40,000 across it en route to Marengo, where he defeated the Austrians in 1800. In somewhat greater comfort than Frederick or Napoleon, you will almost certainly want to explore the pass to the summit, either by car or, better still (because you can watch the scenery while someone else does the driving), by the Swiss postal buses that run to the famous hospice several times a day in summer.

Almost immediately after leaving Martigny, the road to the Grand St. Bernard Pass starts to climb up the valley of the Drance to the village of Sembrancher. Here, a road branches off to the left up the Bagnes valley to the modern, exceptionally well-equipped resort of Verbier, at 1,490 meters (4,900 ft.). Verbier, though something of an unplanned and generally unattractive sprawl of modern, box-like chalets, is nonetheless a chic skiing resort par excellence, particularly popular with Geneva's international community, who flock here at weekends. The skiing is in fact magnificent, with a vast network of lifts, cable cars and ski runs. Towering over Verbier is Mont Gelé, over 3,000 meters (9,900 ft.) high.

At Sembrancher, the St. Bernard Pass road enters the valley of Entremont. About six kms. (four miles) from here you come to Orsières, from where a road to the right leads up the Val Ferret. It then forks right again to Champex, set on its miniature lake. This is one of the most outstandingly beautiful spots in the Valais. There is adequate skiing as well.

Back on the main St. Bernard Pass road again, from Orsières you begin to appreciate the formidable character of the Great St. Bernard. Rocks and mountains close in on all sides as you reach Bourg-St. Pierre, whose inn was stayed in by Napoleon (the chair he is said to have used is on display). Except when the winters are unusually severe, the road is kept open to this point so that postal buses can continue to bring mail and food supplies for the monastery at the top of the pass. From here, whenever the pass is blocked with winter snows, the lay brothers and monks have to carry everything up to the hospice on their backs.

But for travelers today the romantic but formidable old pass, which for centuries has been impassable for more than half of each year, has lost much of its fear. For the splendidly engineered new road, which branches off the old road, is the approach to the new five-and-a-half-kilometer (three and a half miles) St. Bernard Tunnel. This burrows through the mountain to emerge in Italy, thus enabling road traffic to use this important international route all the year round.

The hospice itself, bypassed by the new tunnel, is a gaunt block of grey stone which stands at the highest point on the old road (2,468 meters, 8,100 ft.), since its founder wanted to make sure that it could be seen from a distance. For centuries it was a stopping-off point for pilgrims and weary travelers who were offered accommodations without charge, whether for one night or many. (Now you are directed to a nearby hotel—the Grand St. Bernard.)

There is an interesting story about the foundation of the hospice. In the year 1048 Bernard of Menthon, who was Bishop of Aosta, in answer to a request by Hugues of Provence, set out to clear the Mons Jovis—as the St. Bernard was then called—of brigands and highway robbers. It is said that on reaching the summit of the pass the good bishop found a pagan temple, over which he threw his chasuble. The shrine immediately crumbled to dust and, by the same power, the bandits were utterly defeated. Then Bernard, with the help of the canons of his diocese, established the hospice.

The service rendered to travelers by the canons of St. Bernard through the Middle Ages was invaluable. Kings and princes rewarded the hospice by showering estates upon the order. By the 12th century it owned 79 estates in England and elsewhere, among which were Priors Inn and the site of the present Savoy Hotel in London, as well as the Hospice of St. Nicholas and St. Bernard at Hornchurch (Essex).

The canons of St. Bernard are splendid athletes. Their training covers a period of seven years and includes not only the study of theology but also intensive physical preparation, for the priests must pass the official examinations for mountain guides, and ski instructors.

The St. Bernard dogs have for centuries been the surefooted helpers of the order. In 1949, after two years' travel on foot in Tibet, Canon Détry, of the St. Bernard Hospice, brought back proof that these dogs originated from Central Asia. The canon believed that in Greek and Roman times, Tibetan dogs were brought to Asia Minor with the silk caravans and used by the Romans as war dogs. When the Romans crossed the Alps the dogs found their natural climate, and those that escaped from the Roman armies reverted to their original state.

From near the hospice there is a lift—said to be one of the highest in the world—which will take you to La Chenalette at 2,800 meters (9,200 ft.), from which, if you are lucky with the weather, you will have a view that includes no less than 27 glaciers.

Beyond the hospice you will quickly come to the customs post, and from there the road winds down into the Great St. Bernard Valley where it joins up once more with the tunnel route. Before Aosta (Italy) is reached, you will notice that the vegetation is distinctly Mediterranean in character, and you will find it difficult to imagine that in winter the hospice from which you have just come becomes utterly isolated from the world, with snow drifts that rise over three meters (12 ft.), as high as the second story of the building.

Isérables and Sion

After allowing your senses to recover from the remarkable trip and sobering views of the St. Bernard, continue up the Rhône Valley, with terraced vineyards on its northern slopes and apricot trees in the middle. About 14 kms. (nine miles) from Martigny you'll come to the village of Riddes, the terminus of the cable car up to Isérables.

This is an unforgettable excursion. The cable car rises in a straight line high above the meadows, depositing you on a platform at the entrance to the village, which is built out of the sheer rock like an eyrie, at a height of 1,035 meters (3,400 ft.). A single rough street, lined with flower-decked chalets, leads to a venerable Romanesque church. The village has some good examples of ancient barns, or *mazots* as they are called in French-speaking Switzerland, raised on mushroom-shaped blocks to prevent mice and rats from marauding among the winter food supplies and to ensure good air circulation.

The inhabitants of this ancient village have long had the curious nickname "Bedjuis." Some say it is derived from Bedouins and that the people are descended from the Saracen hordes who, after the battle of Poitiers in 732, overran some of the high Alpine valleys. Certainly the people here seem different from many of those in Canton Valais, being stocky, swarthy, and dark eyed.

Back at Riddes on the valley floor, those with children in tow may like to head over to Saillon, just on the north side of the Rhône. Here, a brand-new swimming pool complex has been built, its waters fed from one of a series of thermal springs that run along the Rhône valley. The whole lavish complex—enormous toboggan run and all—is an excellent place to break a car journey.

From Riddes, it is another 14 kms. (nine miles) to Sion, the capital of the Valais. The town is marked by two rocky hills that materialize in front of you like a fairytale landscape. Crowning the first, Tourbillon, you'll see a ruined castle; on the other, Valère, there is a church. Both indicate the age and ecclesiastical importance of Sion which has been a bishopric for nearly 1,500 years. Valère's church of Notre Dame, looking more like a fortified castle, dates from the 11th century, or even earlier. Its organ is believed to be the oldest still in use in the world. The ruins on Tourbillon are those of a bishop's residence built in the 13th century. From either hill there is a splendid view of the city below. Don't miss Sion's late Gothic cathedral, notable for its 9th-century Romanesque tower, nor the 17th-century town hall, with its gracious carved doors and ancient clock, and the early 16th-century Supersaxo house. The latter is a superb example of deliberately ostentatious luxury carried out with impeccable taste.

Sion's ancient streets once rang with the echoes of pageantry and ecclesiastical pomp. But the town today is a market center, sharing with nearby Sierre the task of collecting the produce of a prosperous agricultural region where fruit, vegetables and the vine provide a lucrative income. Valais strawberries and asparagus are flown to markets in London and Paris, the apricots are superb, and the canton produces some of the best wines in Switzerland. In April the mass of blossom in the orchards is not only a beautiful sight, but gives some indication of the immense amount of fruit to come.

The Valais, however, is not all fertile, and it has its share of rocks, mountain torrents and remote valleys; all of which are difficult to cultivate. Many of the women wear national costume on holidays: a long-sleeved black dress with a tight bodice and full skirt, and depending on the valley, a white blouse, black shoes and stockings, a colorful apron or one made of lace, and a black straw hat trimmed with velvet or a bonnet. All very picturesque.

Anzère and Thyon

Just north of Sion is Anzère, one of the few purpose-built ski resorts in Switzerland, constructed on what used to be a bare but sunny mountainside plateau. Today, Anzère is a deluxe holiday center with hotels, chalets, apartment blocks, skating rink, shops, and all the other trappings of a successful modern ski center.

To the southwest, on the other side of the Rhône, lies Haute Nendaz, originally a simple Alpine village but today a bustling ski resort with accommodations for up to 12,500 visitors. Like Anzère, Haute Nendaz is one of only a handful of purpose-built ski resorts, as indeed are neighboring Thyon 2000 and Super Nendaz. What these resorts lack in charm, they more than make up for in magnificent skiing, however, not least as a result of the extensive links between them, allowing the adventurous skier more or less unlimited access to a wide range of slopes and runs. You can even, if you are feeling particularly hardy, ski all the way from Thyon to Verbier.

Up the Val d'Hérens to Evolène

From Sion a good road strikes south up the beautiful Val d'Hérens, past the curious, boulder-capped "pyramides" of Euseigne, to Evolène and Les Haudères. Before the road was built the people of this valley had to be almost self-supporting and life was frugal. They developed a special local craft—the spinning and weaving of wool. Nowadays Evolène homespun, coarse and warm, is popular throughout Switzerland as knitting wool.

Evolène's charm lies not only in its scenic beauty but also in the old brown chalets and the national costume of the women. From here, the valley and road continue via Les Haudères, its picturesque old chalets overshadowed by the heights of the Dents du Veisivi, to tiny Arolla, which at 2,010 meters (6,600 ft.) is one of the highest resorts in the Valais, making it popular with mountaineers.

Excursions from Sierre

If you continue up the valley of the Rhône for about 16 kms. (10 miles) beyond Sion you reach Sierre, which boasts of being the sunniest place in what is Switzerland's driest region. It is a busy market town which has thrived on the adjacent aluminum plant at Chippis, and this modern influence can be seen in the buildings, particularly around the station and the terminal of the funicular that runs to Montana. From the town there are three attractive side trips.

The first leads up the northern slope to the adjoining, sophisticated resort complex of Crans-Montana, attractively perched over 1,500 meters (5,000 ft.) up on a spacious sunny plateau among woods, grassland and small lakes. Film stars, tycoons and other celebrities are two-a-penny in the excellent hotels, modern apartment blocks and fashionable shops. There is a golf course, casino, several cable cars and a whole assortment of chairlifts and skilifts. Among the trees on the surrounding mountain slopes are several large hospitals, where various Swiss cantons and cities send their patients to recuperate—an indication of the health-giving properties of the region. The approach to Montana from Sierre is either by funicular or by an excellent road. But if you prefer, you can turn off the main Rhône highway just beyond St. Leonard (about eight kms., five miles, from Sierre) to visit Montana and Crans, and then drop down into Sierre without any backtracking.

The second sidetrip leads northeast through Leuk to Leukerbad, an important health-spa and winter resort set in a huge amphitheater of mountains at an altitude of 1,400 meters (4,600 ft.). It boasts the hottest springs in Switzerland, with many therapeutic properties. The complex has been largely rebuilt, and contains a remarkable range of pools: very hot pools, baby pools, indoor and outdoor pools, even pools which start indoors and from which you can swim outside, thus enjoying the sensation of being outdoors and surrounded by snow and ice while remaining perfectly warm. From Leukerbad, there are cable cars to Gemmi and Torrent at 2,300 meters (7,600 ft.), from where there are superb views and, especially at Gemmi, a famous selection of mountain hikes.

The third excursion is of a very different character. You turn south from Sierre and plunge into the high alpine valley of Anniviers. Here live perhaps the only remaining nomadic people of Europe, the name of the valley being derived from the Latin "anni viatores" (year-round travelers).

The year of wandering starts in the spring when men, women, and children leave their headquarters in the villages, taking with them their priest and schoolmaster. Only one man is left in each hamlet—as the firewatcher. The migrants first descend to the slopes of the valley around Niouc, where they stay a few weeks, living in barns, and mazots, to till communal land and plant wheat, maize, and potatoes. This done, they move down the valley to Sierre where they cultivate collectively owned vineyards under an almost feudal statute-labor system: every man resident in the commune is obliged to put in so many days' work. The work in the vineyards is done to the accompaniment of fife and drum (usually six players), which roll out tuneless little airs all day long. In late summer the nomads move back up the high valley to gather in the crops and then go down again for the grape harvest. When the year's work on the land is over, they return to their mountain villages and remain there, snowed in all the winter.

Things have changed, however, in the picturesquely sited old village of Zinal, at the head of the valley, once only accessible over a very bad road. Now, with a road kept open throughout the winter it has become a small, carefully planned all-year resort with a cableway to Serebois at 2,430 meters (8,000 ft.). But the charming, rustic character of the village, with its ancient barns and chalets, has been retained since all the new structures have, by law, to blend in with the old.

About halfway between Sierre and Zinal, at the mountainside village of Vissoie with its strategically placed old tower, a road branches off to Grimentz, a simple little winter sports and summer resort notable for its particularly picturesque old chalets. On the other side of Vissoie a short road climbs steeply up to St.-Luc, a smallish but appealing year-round resort.

Zermatt and the Matterhorn

From Sierre, the Rhône road continues for 29 kilometers (18 miles) up to Visp. At the halfway point, just beyond Gampel-Steg, it passes a left-hand turnoff to the beautiful Lötschen valley, the Lötschental. Visp is the junction for the spectacular railway which, helped by rack-and-pinion, climbs up gradients as steep as 1 in 8 on its one-and-a-half-hour journey to Zermatt. Past picturesque mountain pastures, across rushing torrents, and through steep-sided narrow valleys, it curves and climbs up into the realm of snowy peaks and glaciers. When opened in 1891, it was considered one of the major engineering feats of the time, and even today it is a railway marvel. There is no public road to

Zermatt but from Visp you can drive as far as Täsch (vast car lot at the station). There you have to take one of the frequent electric trains for the remaining five kms. (three miles) to Zermatt itself—where no private cars are allowed.

Despite its huge fame, Zermatt has a permanent population of only 3,500, though at the height of the season up to 16,000 visitors flood into the little town. With an absolute ban on cars, strolling down Bahnhofstrasse, the main street, the only dangers are the silent, electric mini-taxis which ply between the station and the hotels, a few horse cabs, and a herd of about 80 goats which trot ceremoniously through the town, their bells clanging loudly, at 8:30 each morning.

At an altitude of 1,615 meters (5,300 ft.), Zermatt is set in a hollow of meadows and trees ringed by mighty mountains, which include the unmistakable triangular mass of Matterhorn (4,477 meters, 14,690 ft.), or Le Cervin as the French-speaking Swiss call it (the Italian resort on the other side of the mountain is called Cervina; you can ski to it from Zermatt). In winter skiing is the great attraction, lasting until April on the more accessible runs and right through the summer in the Theodul Pass area. There are cable cars, lifts galore, nearly a score of skating and curling rinks, and every possible facility for mountain climbing. Indeed, the name Zermatt is synonymous with mountaineering. Over the last 100 years or more, Zermatt's guides have become world famous and have accompanied expeditions to the Himalayas and other great mountain ranges of the world.

At 5:30 A.M. on Friday July 13 1865, in the then tiny hamlet of Zermatt, a certain Alexander Seiler stood at the door of his newly acquired hotel waving goodbye to a party of seven men starting off on a dangerous and historic climb. They were Edward Whymper, the Rev. Charles Hudson, Douglas Hadow, Lord Francis Douglas, and three guides, two Swiss—Peter Taugwalder and his son—and one French, Michel Croz. The next day, at 1:40 P.M., Whymper and his party achieved their objective by becoming the first people ever to set foot on the summit of the Matterhorn. But disaster followed: on the way down, Hadow slipped, a rope broke, and all except Whymper and the Taugwalders were killed by falling over 1,200 meters (4,000 ft.) down the North Wall.

Alexander Seiler, the man who waved farewell to the ill-fated party, also had a distinguished, if less glamorous, career. He was new to Zermatt, having just purchased the tiny village's original hotel—Lauber's Inn—which he renamed Monte Rosa Hotel. It became merely the first of the famous Seiler group of hotels.

From Zermatt to Gornergrat runs one of the highest cogwheel railways in Europe. Gornergrat has inspired so many grandiloquent descriptions that it is enough to say that among all your memories of Switzerland one of the most vivid will be of standing here at an altitude of over 3,100 meters (10,200 ft.), gazing across glistening glaciers to Monte Rosa (the mountain, not the hotel!), the Matterhorn, and about 50 almost equally majestic peaks; as well as a grand total of 32 glaciers.

Another excellent excursion from Zermatt, this time a three-stage one, starts by taking the lift to Sunnega at 2,285 meters (7,500 ft.), the gondola car to Blauherd (2,590 meters, 8,500 ft.), and lastly the cable car for the final climb of 217 meters (1,700 ft.) to Findeln Rothorn, where once again—if you're lucky with the weather—the view will make you forget the cost. You can also go to Schwarzsee, nearly 2,600 meters (8,500 ft.) high, by cableway. From there the awe-inspiring Matterhorn seems almost near enough to touch. Or you can take the cable car to Trockener Steg and Klein-Matterhorn (2,956 meters, 9,700 ft.), where there's the largest summer skiing area in the Alps.

Saas-Fee and Grächen

Zermatt is at the head of one of the two valleys that lead south from Visp. In the other (the road forks at Stalden) at a height of nearly 1,800 meters (5,900 ft.) is the important winter and summer resort of Saas-Fee; another car-free town. Besides a number of lifts there are cable cars to Längfluh, a good starting point for skiing and walking tours which lies at the foot of the Dom (a peak even higher than the Matterhorn); and to Felskinn (2,986 meters, 9,800 ft.). There are also gondola cars to Hannig (2,376 meters, 7,800 ft.) and Plattjen (2,529 meters, 8,300 ft.). Saas-Fee now boasts the highest subway in the world, running from Felskinn to the Mittelallalin, 3,500 meters (11,500 ft.) high. It has opened up large new skiing areas, extending the season well into the summer as well.

Another fine resort is at Grächen, a sunny village lying on a magnificent mountain terrace 1,615 meters (5,300 ft.) high. You can reach it by car or on the postal bus from St. Niklaus station. Grächen has all the facilities for a summer and winter resort, with an aerial cableway that brings the tourists up to the splendid skiing fields on the Hannigalp. So much new has been built here in recent years that it is difficult to find the old heart of town.

Brig and the Simplon Pass

Back at Visp, if you continue up the Rhône Valley, you come quickly to the important rail and road junction of Brig. This small town has for centuries been a center of trade with Italy, for not only does it guard the Simplon route, but it also lies at the foot of the high valley of the Rhône. The latter leads past the Aletsch Glacier to Gletsch and the Grimsel Pass (for the route north to Meiringen and the Bernese Oberland) or the Furka Pass (towards Andermatt and Central Switzerland).

Brig has one particularly interesting and curious feature—the Stockalper Castle, Switzerland's largest private residence. It was built between 1658 and 1678 for Gaspard Stockalper, a 17th-century Swiss tycoon who was the first to recognize the importance of the Simplon Pass for trade with Italy, and who amassed immense wealth by exploiting it to the full. But he also made much money from salt and other monopolies, and from a host of shrewd enterprises and deals. Likeable as well as rich, and speaking five languages, Stockalper was apparently quite a character and was welcomed at the courts of kings, the palaces of popes, and the salons of international society. He not only made money in vast quantities, but poured it in the same way into his fabulous new home—the Stockalperpalast. But the people of the Valais gradually came to resent their uncrowned king and his wealth. Eventually, and rather tragically, he had to flee in disguise to Italy over the very pass which had brought him much of his wealth. After six years of exile he returned, only to die shortly afterwards in his palatial home. This huge structure, instantly recognizable by its trio of onion-topped towers, has a gigantic central courtyard surrounded by elegant cloisters, and is certainly worth a visit. Nearby is Brigerbad, where there is a very pleasant open-air thermal bath.

Just above the eastern outskirts of Brig is the entrance to the twin Simplon Tunnels, through which famous international trains disappear into dank darkness to emerge almost 20 kilometers (12 miles) later into Italian daylight on the southern side of the Alps. The first of the twin tunnels—the world's longest railway tunnels—was started in 1898 and took six years to complete.

The Simplon Pass road also begins just outside Brig, meandering through deep gorges and wide, barren, rock-strewn pastures, and across the mountains' flanks. As the highway slowly rises, there are glimpses of Brig in the Rhône Valley below, giving an excellent view of these grim historic routes: at one point the Aletsch Glacier can be seen shimmering in the distance.

At the top of the pass stands the Simplon-Kulm Hotel (2,010 meters, 6,600 ft.) and, just beyond it, the Simplon Hospice of the monks of St. Bernard, built 150 years ago at Napoleon's request. A little farther on, cupped in a hollow to the right of the main road, is the Alter Spital. A square, tall building with a church-like bell tower, this hospice was built in the 17th century by Gaspard Stockalper. Beside it you can still see parts of the old road of the merchant princes and Napoleon, and it is easy to imagine the hardships which travelers of those times had to bear in crossing the pass. The road drops rapidly from the summit, passing through Simplon village and then Gondo, the last village before the Italian border.

The Simplon Pass is an impressive gateway to Italy, with a succession of splendid views and lots of stopping places from which to admire them. The addition of extensive new tunnels and snow galleries means that it is now open throughout the year. If, however, exceptionally heavy snowfalls temporarily close the road your car can be taken by train through the Simplon rail tunnel between Brig and Iselle (the first village on the Italian side).

From Brig up the Rhône to Gletsch

We should not leave the neighborhood of Brig without mentioning one of the most remarkable trains in Europe, the "Glacier Express." Starting from Zermatt, it runs through Brig, up the Rhône Valley, through the Furka Tunnel, past Andermatt, over the Oberalp Pass, and then down through Disentis and Chur in Graubünden to terminate in St. Moritz. From Andermatt onwards it carries a restaurant car. This famous train struggles across the backbone of Europe, running through places where a mountain goat would be hard pressed to find a footing. For miles it toils up gradients so severe that cogwheels are necessary and goes round curves so sharp that it seems in danger of tying a knot in itself. Much of the time it is above the timber line. Unfortunately, the most spectacular mountain section of the line over the Furka Pass via Gletsch has been closed. However, sights of a feat of nature have been replaced by the experience of a feat of man—the longest meter gauge railroad tunnel in the world, from Oberwald to Realp, at some 15.4 kms. (10 miles). This masterpiece of engineering provides a direct all year connection between the resorts of the Valais, Central Switzerland and Graubünden.

From Brig, closely following the route taken by the "Glacier Express," the main road continues up the valley of the Rhône, before going underground at Oberwald. To the north of the turbulent river is the great mass of the Bernese Oberland, with some of the highest mountains in Europe—Aletschhorn, Jungfrau, Mönch, Eiger, Schreckhorn, Finsteraarhorn and many others. Life in this part of the valley is especially hard, the soil poor and the road approach to Gletsch blocked by snow from November until about June. But it is a journey well worthwhile, one in which grimness, beauty and grandeur combine in a superb and powerful symphony, a fitting farewell to the Valais.

PRACTICAL INFORMATION FOR THE VALAIS AND THE ALPES VALAISANNES

TOURIST OFFICES. The principal regional tourist office for the Valais is L'Union Valaisanne du Tourisme, 1951 Sion (tel. 027–22 31 61). There are local tourist offices in practically every town and resort in the Valais, the majority open year-round. For a full list write to the Valais regional office in Sion.

HOTELS AND RESTAURANTS. The Valais rivals the Bernese Oberland as the leading tourist region of a country which has long since prided itself as second to none as a tourist destination. Accordingly, the region is packed with hotels and restaurants of all types. Indeed our listing here represents no more than the tip of the iceberg. Prices vary greatly from resort to resort. The Zermatts, Verbiers and Montanas, for example, are every bit as expensive as their reputations might lead you to believe, with a premium on wall-to-wall comfort. It's not impossible to find inexpensive hotels in these places, but it isn't easy. At the smaller and less well-known resorts on the other hand—try Saas Almagell rather than the more famous Saas Fee for instance—your room will cost no more than you would pay for lunch in the expensive resorts.

Nearly all hotels will provide packed lunches if you want to spend the day hiking or sightseeing, but make a point of giving plenty of notice; it's best to ask the night before. Likewise, don't be inhibited about asking for a very early breakfast if you plan to spend a long day in the mountains.

Not listed here are the Alpine huts, or *cabanes,* scattered around the Valais. Many belong to mountaineering clubs and are only open to members. But there are many others that welcome all guests. Luxury is not generally their style, but solid shelter is guarranteed. Full lists are available from tourist offices.

ANZÈRE. *Des Masques* (E), tel. 027–38 26 51. 80 beds. Quiet and comfortable, with good restaurant. AE, DC, MC, V. *Grand Roc* (I), tel. 027–38 35 35. 44 beds. Central but quiet. AE, MC, V.

BRIG. *Victoria* (M), tel. 028–23 15 03. 72 beds. Central, with restaurant and terrace. AE, DC, MC, V. *Glisserallee* (I), tel. 028–23 11 95. 8 beds. Very small and inexpensive. *Schlosshotel* (I), tel. 028–23 64 55. 45 beds. Breakfast only; quiet and facilities for the handicapped. AE, V.

CHAMPÉRY. *De Champéry* (E), tel. 025–79 10 71. 133 beds. Quiet, with sauna and facilities for children. AE, MC, V. *Beau Séjour Vieux Chalet* (M), tel. 025–79 17 01. 45 beds. Quiet; with good restaurant. AE, DC, MC, V. *Rose des Alpes* (I), tel. 025–79 12 18. 45 beds. Quiet; with facilities for children.

CHAMPEX. *Des Alpes et Lac* (M), tel. 026–4 11 51. 100 beds. Tennis and facilities for children. AE, DC, MC, V. *Auberge de la Forêt* (I), tel. 026–4 12 78. 30 beds. Quiet and central. *Du Glacier Sporting* (I), tel. 026–4 14 02. 60 beds. Quiet and ideal for children. AE, V.

CRANS. *Du Golf et des Sports* (L), tel. 027–41 42 42. 150 beds. Tennis, indoor pool and sauna; very expensive. AE, DC, MC, V. *Alpina et Savoy* (E), tel. 027–41 21 42. 100 beds. Gymnasium, indoor pool and sauna. AE, DC, MC, V. *Grand Hotel Beauséjour* (E), tel. 027–41 24 46. 100 beds. Indoor pool and sauna. AE, DC, MC, V. *De l'Etrier* (E), tel. 027–41 15 15. 200 beds. Two pools, riding and sauna. AE, DC, MC, V. *Excelsior* (E), tel. 027–40 11 61. 100 beds. Quiet and comfortable. AE.

Belmont (M), tel. 027–41 11 71. 50 beds. Quiet rooms. AE. *Elite* (M), tel. 027–41 43 01. 50 beds. Pool and facilities for the handicapped; ideal for children. AE, DC, MC, V. *Etoile* (M), tel. 027–41 16 71. 60 beds. Central. AE, DC, MC, V. *Les Mélèzes* (M), tel. 027–43 18 12. 42 beds. Quiet hotel in own grounds. AE, DC, V. *Tourist* (M), tel. 027–41 32 56. 72 beds. Breakfast only; central and in own grounds. AE, DC, MC, V. *Centrale* (I), tel. 027–41 37 67. 38 beds. Central. AE, DC, MC, V. *Du Télèférique* (I), tel. 027–41 33 67. 20 beds. Small and simple. V.

GRACHEN. *Elite* (M), tel. 028–56 16 12. 48 beds. Quiet rooms. AE, DC, MC, V. *Hannigalp & Valaisia* (M), tel. 028–56 25 55. 50 beds. Indoor pool, gym and sauna. AE, MC, V. *Waldheim* (M), tel. 028–56 19 48. 36 beds. Quiet family hotel with gym and sauna. MC, V. *Wallisherhof* (M), tel. 028–56 11 22. 50 beds. With skittle alley. MC, V. *Alpina* (I), tel. 028–56 26 26. 30 beds. Central, but quiet rooms. AE, V.

GRIMENTZ. *Marenda* (M), tel. 027–65 11 71. 78 beds. Large hotel in own grounds with excellent food; very quiet. AE, V. *De Moiry* (I), tel. 027–65 11 44. 25 beds. Inexpensive and quiet.

HAUTE-NENDAZ. *Mont-Calme* (M), tel. 027–88 11 56. 40 beds. In own grounds. AE, DC, MC, V. *Sourire* (M), tel. 027–88 26 16. 58 beds. Central and quiet. AE, V.

LEUKERBAD. *Badehotel Bristol* (L), tel. 027–61 18 33. 150 beds. Substantial hotel with riding, tennis, indoor pool and gym as well as cure facilities. AE, DC, MC, V. *Badehotel des Alpes* (E), tel. 027–62 11 51. 90 beds. Spa hotel, tennis and indoor pool, central. MC, V. *Badehotel Grand-Bain* (E), tel. 027–62 11 61. 75 beds. Spa hotel, tennis. AE.

Dala (M), tel. 027–61 12 13. 25 beds. Breakfast only; central, facilities for the handicapped. AE, DC, MC, V. *Escher* (M), tel. 027–61 14 31. 35 beds. Small and comfortable. AE, MC, V. *Wallisherhof* (M), tel. 027–61 14 24. 50 beds. Centrally located and with facilities for the handicapped. *Zayetta* (M), tel. 027–61 16 46. 75 beds. Central and quiet, sauna. AE, V. *Chamois* (I), tel. 027–61 13 57. 11 beds. Breakfast only; small and simple.

LES MARECOTTES. *Aux Milles Etoiles* (E), tel. 026–6 15 89. 54 beds. Ideal family hotel with indoor pool, gym and sauna; very quiet. V. *Jolimont* (I), tel. 026–6 14 70. Skating, tennis and outdoor pool; central and in own grounds.

MARTIGNY. *De la Poste* (M), tel. 026–2 14 44. 65 beds. Central and with quiet rooms. Breakfast only. AE, DC, MC, V. *Du Rhône* (M), tel. 026–2 17 17. 100 beds. Central with very quiet rooms and facilities for the handicapped. AE, DC, MC, V.

Du Grand St. Bernard (I), tel. 026–2 26 12. 40 beds. AE, DC, MC, V.

MONTANA. *Crans Ambassador* (L), tel. 027–41 52 22. 135 beds. Excellent hotel with indoor pool, facilities for children, fine views and good restaurant. AE, DC, MC. *Super Crans* (L), tel. 027–41 29 15. 50 beds. Comfortable hotel in own grounds with tennis, indoor pool and restaurant. DC. *Mirabeau* (E), tel. 027–41 39 12. 100 beds. Superior hotel with bowling; central. AE, DC, MC, V. *St. Georges* (E), tel. 027–41 24 14. 75 beds. Very quiet but central hotel in own grounds; pool. AE, DC, MC, V.

Curling (M), tel. 027–41 12 42. 70 beds. Pool and sauna; very quiet rooms. AE, MC, V. *De la Forêt* (M), tel. 027–41 36 08. 140 beds. Indoor pool and sauna in this well-appointed hotel. AE, DC, MC, V. *Du Lac* (M), tel. 027–41 34 14. 50 beds. Very quiet and in own grounds. AE, DC, MC. *Cisalpin* (I), tel. 027–41 24 25. 71 beds. Good family hotel. DC, MC. *Weisshorn* (I), tel. 027–41 21 52. 12 beds. Very small and very quiet hotel in own grounds. Extremely reasonable.

MORGINS. *Bellevue* (E), tel. 025–78 11 71. 260 beds. Superior hotel with facilities for children, indoor pool and sauna. AE, MC, V. *Beau Site* (I), tel. 025–77 11 38. 30 beds. Good value, breakfast only. No rooms with bath.

SAAS-FEE. *Beau-Site* (E), tel. 028–57 11 22. 88 beds. Central, with indoor pool and sauna. AE, DC, MC, V. *Grand Hotel* (E), tel. 028–57 10 01. 100 beds. Comfortable and luxurious; pool and tennis. AE, DC, MC, V. *Saaserhof* (E), tel. 028–57 15 51. 100 beds. Facilities for the handicapped along with sauna and quiet rooms in this, the smartest hotel in town. AE, DC, MC, V.

Allalin (M), tel. 028–57 18 15. 80 beds. Central and quiet with marvelous view. AE, DC, MC, V. *Burgener* (M), tel. 028–57 15 22. 30 beds. Central but quiet and with superb view. AE, DC, MC, V. *Britannia* (M), tel. 028–57 16 16. 46 beds. AE, MC, V. *Dom* (M), tel. 028–59 11 01. 17 beds. Quiet; with sauna. AE, DC, MC, V. *Sonnenhof* (M), tel. 028–57 26 93. 35 beds. Quiet and good. AE, DC, MC, V. *Des Alpes* (I), tel. 028–57 15 55. 57 beds. Quiet rooms, sauna. Breakfast only. AE, DC, MC, V.

SAAS-GRUND. *Monte Rosa* (I), tel. 028–57 25 70. The oldest hotel in the valley, still in same family. Friendly and old-fashioned with excellent food.

SIMPLON. *Bellevue* (I), tel. 028–29 13 31. 70 beds. Quiet rooms, restaurant. AE, DC, MC, V.

SION. *Du Rhône* (M), tel. 027–22 82 91. 80 beds. Central and quiet. AE, DC, MC. *Touring* (M), tel. 027–23 15 51. 40 beds. Facilities for the handicapped and quiet rooms. DC, MC, V.

VERBIER. *Farinet* (E), tel. 026–7 66 26. 50 beds. MC, V. *Rosalp* (E), tel. 026–7 63 23. 30 beds. With outstanding restaurant. DC, MC, V.

Grand-Combin (M), tel. 026–7 55 15. 52 beds. Central and quiet and with facilities for the handicapped. AE, DC, MC, V. *Le Mazot* (M), tel. 026–7 68 12. 46 beds. In own grounds. AE, DC, MC, V. *Rhodania* (M), tel. 026–7 01 21. 75 beds. Comfortable and central. AE, DC, MC, V. *Catogne* (I), tel. 026–7 51 05. 18 beds. Small and simple. AE, MC, V. *Rosa-Blanche* (I), tel. 026–7 44 72. 57 beds with facilities for children. AE, DC, MC.

ZERMATT. *Grand Hotel Zermatterhof* (L), tel. 028–66 11 01. 155 beds. Tennis, indoor pool, sauna and gym in this desirable hotel. AE, DC, MC, V. *Mont Cervin* (L), tel. 028–66 11 21. 252 beds. Famous and luxurious; tennis, indoor pool, sauna; central. AE, DC, MC, V.

Monte Rosa (E), tel. 028–66 11 31. 95 beds. Atmospheric and comfortable. AE, DC, MC, V. *Follux* (E), tel. 028–67 19 46. 65 beds. Quiet; sauna. *Butterfly* (M), tel. 028–67 37 21. 70 beds. Central and quiet. AE, DC, MC, V. *Carina* (M), tel. 028–67 17 67. 36 beds. In own grounds; sauna. AE, MC, V.

Alphubel (I), tel. 028–67 30 03. 50 beds. Central and quiet. AE, MC, V. *Tannenhof* (I), tel. 028–67 31 88. 35 beds. Breakfast only; reasonable. *Touring* (I), tel. 028–67 11 77. 38 beds. Quiet. MC, V.

GETTING AROUND. The Valais exemplifies the very best of Swiss public transport. Indeed, unless you plan to hire a car for the whole of your stay, the interlinked train and bus network is so good that driving seems largely redundant.

By Train and Bus. As we say, the train and bus service here is excellent. Trains run to practically every major town, with buses filling the few gaps. The Horaire du Valais (Valais Timetable) available free from tourist offices and all rail stations gives full details of all services; bus schedules are posted outside all post offices.

A wide range of special offers are available. Sion, for example, has a weekly tourist ticket (Fr. 44) which gives you unlimited travel to all the major places of interest in and around the town. Again, details from tourist offices.

If you travel with children the new (1987) rail pass is worthwhile. For Fr. 100 you can travel half-price (1st or 2nd class) for a year on trains, postal buses, some ski and scenic trains and some lake steamers. You get given a family pass as well which means children under 16 travel free. Imagine getting to the Gornergrat with two children for the price of one half fare!

By Car. Despite the excellent bus and train network, roads throughout the Valais are first class and extensive, reaching every resort (with the exception of

Zermatt and Saas-Fee, in both of which cars are banned, though good parking facilities are provided outside each).

Mountain roads are all well graded. Likewise, the terrifying bends that were once common are now very much a thing of the past. Nonetheless, anyone new to Alpine roads should take great care, even in the summer. Likewise winter driving here should not be taken lightly. Though all roads are regularly sanded and swept, venturing out during or immediately after a snow storm can be dangerous and should not be attempted. Winter tires, with or without studs, are essential; similarly, the locals all accept the unpleasantness of using chains during bad weather.

SIGHTSEEING DATA. Sightseeing in the Valais means, first and foremost, the region's magnificent natural scenery rather than plodding round museums and churches. Nonetheless, the area does have a number of small museums and galleries, the best known of which we list below.

Otherwise, for those here in search of natural beauty, there are one or two useful points to make. The first concerns the magnificent Alpine flowers that grow in such abundance in the spring and summer. To anyone whose knowledge of Alpine flowers does not extend beyond the wrapper of a box of chocolates, the first sight of a field of flowers, up to a third of which can be orchids and other protected species, may be a mind-blowing experience, especially when further consideration makes you realise that the whole lot will be lunch for some unappreciative cows in a week or two. The flowers start about May at low altitudes and as summer progresses you have to go higher and higher. Despite its reputation, the edelweiss is relatively easy to find—although you may have to do some walking first.

The second point is an obvious one. The best way really to appreciate the beauty of an area is to walk it: the view from a restaurant can be spectacular, but a half hour plod away and the car fumes and noise can be left behind and a totally different kind of beauty makes an appearance. The Valais Tourist Office has produced an excellent map with walking tours planned (and timed) called *A Pied à Travers le Valais.* It's in French and German.

BISCHOFSSCHLOSS. Heimat-Museum Bischofsschloss Leuk (National Museum), tel. 027–63 12 23. Open June 15 to Oct. 20, Sat. 2–4.

BRIG. Museum in Stock-Alper-Schloss, tel. 028–23 25 67. Hourly guided tours in summer over the castle and its contents. Call for details.

BURGERHAUS. Regionalmuseum Binn, tel. 028–71 14 50/20. Displays minerals and local traditions. Open in summer Mon. and Thurs. 4–5.

EGGERBERG. Weinbaumuseum, Bei der Kirche, tel. 028–46 43 70. A 1750 wine press. Call for appointment.

ERNEN. Kirchenmuseum und Museum in Zendenrathaus (Church Museum), tel. 028–71 18 65 and 028–71 15 62. Guided tours every Tuesday in summer through the village and museum. Call for details.

ST. GINGOLPH. Musée—Archives du Vieux St. Gingolph (Archives of Old St. Gingolph) in the castle, tel. 025–71 66 22/3. Exhibits of lake-life and boats;

other local traditions. Open July and Aug. Sat. 3–5; otherwise first Sat. in month only.

GRAND ST.-BERNARD. Musée du Grand St.-Bernard (St. Bernard Museum) in the Hospice, tel. 026–4 92 36. Open June 9–12, July and Aug. 9–6, Sept. 1–5.

LES HAUDERES. Resto-Musée "Au Vieux-Pays" (Museum of Yesteryear), tel. 027–83 11 37. Furniture and tools illustrate the history of the valley. Open 8–12.

ISERABLES. Musée Folklorique d'Iserables (Iserables Museum of Folklore) at the bottom of the cable car, tel. 027–86 28 40. Exhibits of local life and agriculture. Ring for appointment.

KIPPEL. Lötschentaler Museum, tel. 028–23 21 27 and 028–49 14 44. Local history. Open June to Sept., Tues. to Sun. 10–12 and 2–6.

MARTIGNY. Musée des Amis de Plan-Cerisier (Museum of the Friends of Plan-Cerisier) at Plan-Cerisier, tel. 026–2 14 44. Devoted to wine and its culture. Open Easter to Oct. 1, Sat. 3–5 and Sun. 10–12.

Musée Gallo-Romain d'Octodure, Fondation Pierre Gianadda, rue du Forum, tel. 026–2 39 78. Spectacular museum built over the remains of a Gallo-Roman temple. Upper gallery devoted to Roman remains, lower gallery hosts a first-class art exhibit every summer; the annex houses a collection of veteran cars. Open Tues. to Sun. 10–12 and 1:30–6, in winter 1:30–6 only.

ST. MAURICE. Musée Militaire Cantonal (Cantonal Military Museum), Château St. Maurice, tel. 025–65 24 58. Displays of arms, uniforms and flags illustrating Valais military history, plus a series of models of the Maginot line. Open summer Mon. to Sun, 10–12 and 2–6; in winter 10–12 and 2–5; closed Mon.

MONTHEY. Musée du Vieux Monthey (Museum of Old Monthey) in the castle, tel. 025–71 26 42. Temporary exhibitions showing the industrialization of Monthey. Open Mon. and Wed. 3–7, Wed. and Fri. 9–11.

PFARRHAUS. Pfarreimuseum Münster, tel. 028–73 11 62. Treasures of the church. Ring for appointment.

PRAZ-DE-FORT. Musée des Traditions et du Mobilier Rural (Museum of Rural Traditions and Furniture), Saleinazstr. Praz-de-Fort, tel. 026–4 17 32. Pictures and furniture. Open Tues. to Sun. 2–5:30, in winter Wed. and Sun. 2–5 only; closed Jan., Mar. and Nov.

REIDERALP. Alp-Museum, Alphütte, Nagelspalmen, tel. 028–27 13 65. Alpine artefacts and economy. Open June to mid-Oct., Tues., Thurs., and Sun. (Wed. and Fri. guided tours). Ring for details.

Naturschutzzentrum Aletschwald (Nature Studies Center), Villa Cassel, tel. 028–27 22 44. Natural history of the area. Open mid-June to mid-Oct. Ring for details.

SAAS-FEE. Saaser Museum, tel. 028–57 23 15 and 028–57 14 75. Devoted to the village and its environment. Open June to Oct. 10–12 and 2–6; closed Mon.; Dec. to Apr. 2–6; closed Sat. and Sun.

SAXON. Musée Vieux Saxon (Old Saxon Museum), in the Maison d'Ecole, tel. 026–6 27 46. Ring for appointment.

SIERRE. Musée des Etains (Pewter Museum), Château Bellevue (Hôtel de Ville), tel. 027–57 11 71. Rich in French and Swiss pewter. Open Mon. to Thurs. 8–12 and 2–5, 4:30 on Fri.

SION. Musée Cantonal d'Archeologie (Cantonal Museum of Archaeology), 12 Pl. de la Majorie, tel. 027–21 69 16. Newish museum in old farm buildings, mostly results of local excavations; plus the Guigoz collection. Open Tues. to Sun. 10–12 and 2–6; open Mon. in July and Aug.

Musée Cantonal des Beaux-Arts (Cantonal Art Museum), 15 and 19 Pl. de la Majorie, tel. 027–21 69 02. In the days when Sion was run by prince-bishops, their administrators lived in the 12th- and 13th-century buildings which now house collections dating from the 15th century to the present time. Exhibits mostly local artists or artists with local connections. Open Tues. to Sun. 10–12 and 2–5, 2–6 in summer; open Mon. in July and Aug.

Musée Cantonal d'Histoire et d'Ethnologie (Cantonal Museum of History and Ethnology), Château de Valère, tel. 027–21 69 22. Religious art from the Middle Ages; local costumes and artefacts housed in the old castle. Open Tues. to Sun. 9–12 and 2–5, 2–6 in summer; open Mon. in July and Aug.

Musée Cantonal d'Histoire Naturelle (Cantonal Museum of Natural History), 40 Av. de la Gare. Predictable, except for a room devoted to a dinosaur's footprints discovered in 1979 during the building of the dam at Vieux-Emosson. Open daily July and Aug., 2–6; rest of year Sun. only, 10–12 and 2–6.

VILLETTE. Musée Nos'astro Bon Bagna, Villette (Le Châble), tel. 026–7 13 86. Old home with costume exhibition. Ring for details.

VISSOIE. Musée Patoisants et Costumes (Museum of Local Life and Costumes), tel. 027–65 13 19. Kitchen and other life of the period. Ring for appointment.

ZERMATT. Alpines Museum, Dorfzentrum, tel. 028–67 27 22 and 028–67 41 00. The early days of mountaineering. Opening hours on display at Tourist Office.

WINTER SPORTS. Winter sports in the Valais are second to none, easily the equal of anywhere else in Europe. Facilities throughout are excellent. Our lists here give only a small idea of the full range on offer; full details from tourist offices.

Aminona. 1,500 meters (4,500 ft.). Tel. 027–41 57 56. 24 tows, 5 chairlifts, 8 telecabines. 17 kms. (over 10 miles) of cross-country trails, curling, skating, dancing. Links to Crans/Montana.

Anzere. 1,525 meters (4,500 ft.). Tel. 027–38 25 19. 7 tows, 4 chairlifts, 1 telecabine. 12 kms. (8 miles) of cross-country trails; most other facilities.

Bettmeralp. 1,956 meters (6,435 ft.). Tel. 028–27 12 91. 16 tows, 4 chairlifts, 5 cable cars. 10 kms. (6 miles) of cross-country trails. Heated swimming pool, mountaineering school.

Super St.-Bernard. 1,930 meters (over 6,000 ft.). Tel. 026–4 91 41. Not a resort in itself but well worth driving up the pass to use the 2 tows, 1 chairlift and 1 cable car. (No ski school.)

Champéry. 1,035 meters (3,400 ft.). Tel. 025–79 11 41. 77 tows, 28 chairlifts, 6 cable cars. Skating, curling; kindergarten. One of the growing linked ski areas of the French-speaking alps.

Champex. 1,470 meters (4,823 ft.). Tel. 026–4 12 27. 2 tows, 2 chairlifts, 20 kms. (12 miles) of cross-country trails.

Crans-Montana. 1,525 meters (5,000 ft.). Tel. 027–41 21 32. 25 tows, 7 chairlifts, 8 cable cars. 25 kms. (16 miles) of cross-country trails. One of the world's most famous resorts.

Evolene. 1,370 meters (4,500 ft.). Tel. 027–83 12 35. 6 tows, 1 chairlift. 15 kms. (over nine miles) of cross-country trails. Very pretty.

Fiesch. 1,050–2,900 meters (nearly 9,000 ft.). Tel. 028–71 14 66. 21 tows, 3 chairlifts, 5 cable cars. Connects to Riederalp and Bettmeralp.

Grachen. 1,635 meters (5,360 ft.). Tel. 028–56 13 00. 10 tows, 2 chairlifts, 2 cable cars. 25 kms. (16 miles) of cross-country trails. Very picturesque.

Grimentz. 1,600 meters (5,250 ft.). Tel. 027–65 14 93. 8 tows, 2 chairlifts, skibobbing and lovely scenery.

Haute-Nendaz/Super-Nendaz. 1,300–1,700 meters (4,300 ft. plus). Tel. 027–88 14 44. 46 tows, 21 chair lifts, 15 cable cars. 23 kms. (over 14 miles) of cross-country trails. Skiers' paradise.

Leukerbad. 1,415 meters (4,650 ft.). Tel. 027–62 11 11. 11 tows, 2 chairlifts, 3 cable cars. Some of the 20 kms. (over 12 miles) of cross-country trails go round the sewage plant but forget all, ease your aching bones in the hot pools.

Les Marecottes. 1,110 meters (3,650 ft.). Tel. 026–6 15 89. 5 tows, 1 cable car. Good place to teach beginner children.

Mayens-de-Riddes/La Tzoumaz. 1,500 meters (5,000 ft.). Tel. 027–86 18 51. Shares same 46 tows as Haute-Nendaz (see above).

Montana (see Crans-Montana above).

Morgins. 1,430 meters (4,700 ft.). Tel. 025–77 23 61. 52 tows, 19 chairlifts, 5 cable cars. Connects to Champéry etc.

Riederalp. 1,200–2,700 meters (4,000 ft. and up). Tel. 028–27 13 65. 16 tows, 3 chairlifts, 5 cable cars. Rapidly growing. Connects to Bettmeralp and Fiesch.

Saas-Fee. 1,800 meters (5,980 ft.). Tel. 028–57 14 57. 16 tows, 2 chairlifts, 5 cable cars and the world's highest—and newest—metro which at last puts Saas-Fee into the world-class it has long been claiming.

Saas-Grund. 1,560 meters (5,000 ft.). Tel. 028–57 24 03. 8 tows, 1 chairlift, 2 cable cars. Another resort which has recently invested heavily in new facilities.

Thyon 2000/Les Collons. 1,780–2,000 meters (up to 6,500 ft.). Tel. 027–81 16 08. 9 tows, 3 chairlifts plus Haute-Nendaz complex. You start at the top and ski down.

Val d'Illiez/Crosets/Champoussin. 948–1,668 meters (up to 5,500 ft.). Tel. 025–77 20 77. 52 tows, 19 chairlifts, 5 cable cars. All fairly new.

Verbier. 1,525 meters (5,000 ft.). Tel. 026–7 62 22. Shares the 46 tows and other facilities of Haute-Nendaz. Rightly regarded as one of the greatest ski resorts.

Veysonnaz. 1,233 meters (4,000 ft.). Tel. 027–22 03 53. Shares Haute-Nendaz's 46 tows and facilities.

Zermatt. 1,616 meters (5,360 ft.). Tel. 028–67 10 31. 18 tows, 2 chairlifts, 13 cable cars, 1 train, 1 metro. Many would claim this the greatest of all the resorts. Recent investment has brought it back up to standard.

SPECIAL EVENTS. The Valais, as in much of Switzerland, has a passion for brass bands, fifes and drums and the like. During May there are lots of processions concerts and other performances.

The Valais also has a strong farming tradition and apart from fruit and wine all the farming is linked with cows. To survive in Alpine conditions the cows have to be tough and for decades there have been cow fights to establish the strongest cow (allegedly they never hurt each other—just show who is boss-person). These combats take place from April to October.

The Tibor Varga festival is the highlight of the classical music year in the Valais. It takes place (mostly in Sion) during July and August and attracts musicians from all over the world.

On August 1 (Swiss National Day) every resort, village and town puts on a splendid show of fireworks, dancing, food and drink.

Several resorts have 4,000-meter (13,120-ft.) peak-bagging "races," others have grueling high-altitude runs; every grape-growing area has some form of celebration after the harvest and the heaviest milker leads the other cows down from the pastures bedecked in flowers at the end of the season.

The Tourist Office in Sion will give you precise dates and also head you towards suitable places to taste wine and cheese and watch them being made if it is the right time of year.

THE LAC LÉMAN REGION

Lausanne, Vevey and Montreux

One of the joys of Lac Léman, or Lake Geneva as it is known outside Switzerland, is that when you travel along either side (much of the southern side of the lake is in France), the roads never stray very far from the shore and provide an unending succession of lovely views: of the lake, the mountains, and the steep vine-covered hillsides. You can take either the lake-side road or the expressway, which runs the length of the Swiss shore. The views from the expressway, particularly of the distant French Alps, are, if anything, even better than from the lake-side road, while its landscaping is a lesson to any engineer. (But don't forget to switch on your headlights in the tunnels, however short. It is not unusual for the police to wait at the far end and fine you on the spot if you have transgressed.)

From Geneva to Rolle, about one-third of the way along the lake, the shore road is bordered by fine parklands and estates strikingly reminiscent of the English countryside, a likeness which is more than mere coincidence. In the late 18th century the sons of wealthy Genevan and Vaud families often became tutors to prosperous English families. They returned with money in the bank and new ideas, planning their gardens in the style they had admired in England.

La Côte

Heading east from Geneva along the shores of Lac Léman there is little to see until you reach Coppet, 12 kms. (eight miles) from Geneva. Thereafter, the 40-kms. (25-mile) stretch between Coppet and Morges, just outside Lausanne, is known simply as La Côte, the coast. Its sunny slopes provide excellent conditions for vine-growing and, indeed, the light white wines of La Côte are among the best in Switzerland, though sadly little is exported.

Coppet itself is famous principally for the lovely old Château where the remarkable Madame de Staël spent many years in exile. She was the daughter of Suzanne Curchod, whose father was a Vaud parson. Suzanne had been jilted by the youthful Edward Gibbon in 1756 and, on the rebound, did very well for herself by accepting the hand of Jacques Necker, a Genevan banker who later became financial adviser to Louis XVI. The far-sighted Necker bought the mansion at Coppet as a retreat, and he was glad to take refuge there when the French Revolution broke out. At the château, Madame de Staël established an intellectual court whose literary salons were attended by giants of the early Romantic period: Byron, Benjamin Constant, Sismondi, August Schlegel, the faithless Edward Gibbon, and others. The château, still kept as it was in Madame's time, may be visited every day except Monday. There is now a charming little museum of Vieux Coppet over the "Copétane" in the Grand-Rue. The music room in particular is intriguing, not least for the bizarre part-piano, part-violin it boasts.

Nyon, some eight kms. (five miles) from Coppet, was founded by Julius Caesar in about 56 B.C. as a camp for war veterans. The Romans called it Noviodunum, and the splendid basilica they built here is today the site of an impressive museum—the Basilique et Musée Romain—with many remains from the Roman period. There is an excellent, three-dimensional artist's impression of the basilica building on the outside wall of the museum that makes clear its size and sophistication.

Nyon also lays claim to a fine medieval castle. It was built by Louis, first Baron of Vaud, but was subsequently captured by the Bernese in 1570. Today it houses a museum noted for its collection of Nyon china, the Musée de la Porcelaine. In the 17th and 18th centuries Nyon was the center of a flourishing chinaware craft; its flowersprigged tea sets, vases, and bowls were in great demand and today are still sought by collectors. Nyon motifs are now used by Swiss manufacturers and for hand-painted craftwork.

If you leave the road to visit the town center you'll find one good view from the gardens and another from the castle. Down by the shore, with its delightful promenade, the Maison du Léman features models of the lake's boats through the ages.

All in all, Nyon, with its excellent shops, good bistros, beautifully laid out parks, and little harbor, is well worth a visit. While the Geneva area is well served with covered swimming pools, during a heat wave the lack of sufficient outdoor pools becomes apparent. The best complex is at Nyon, where there is an Olympic-sized pool, a large play pool with a shoot and a separate area for babies, the whole set in landscaped

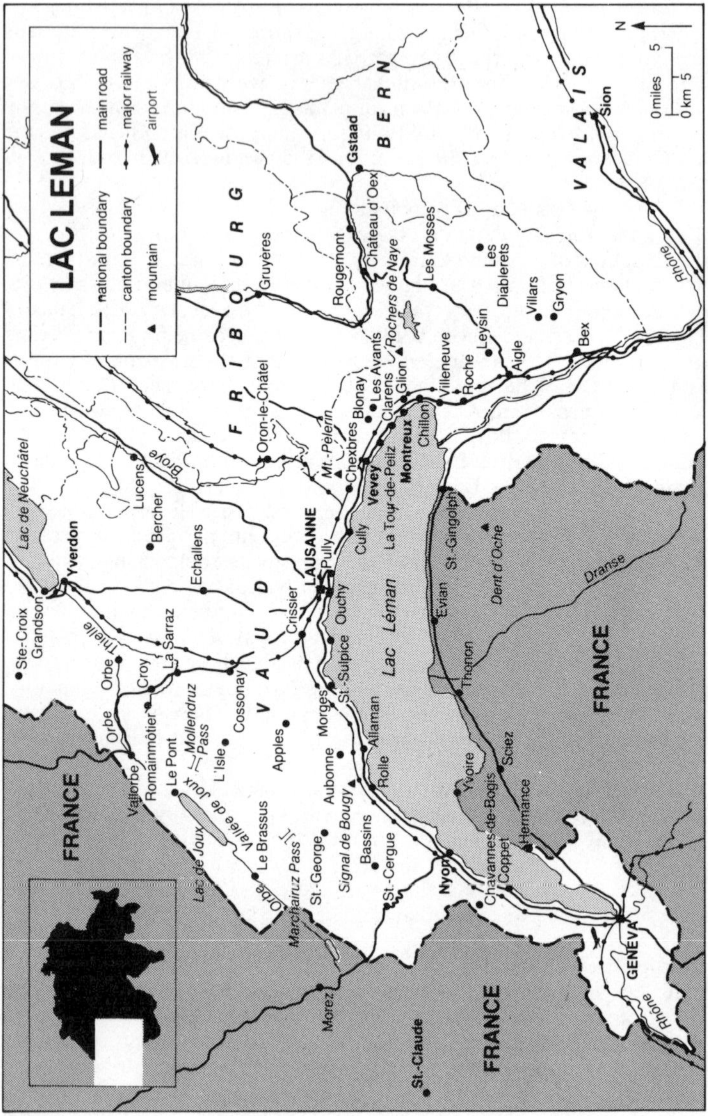
LAC LEMAN
national boundary
canton boundary
mountain
main road
major railway
airport
FRANCE
FRANCE
FRANCE
VAUD
FRIBOURG
BERN
VALAIS
Lac Léman
Lac de Neuchâtel
Lac de Joux
Vallée de Joux
Yverdon
Grandson
Ste.-Croix
Thielle
Orbe
Orbe
Croy
La Sarraz
Romainmôtier
Vallorbe
Le Pont
Mollendruz Pass
L'Isle
Cossonay
Echallens
Bercher
Lucens
Broye
Oron-le-Châtel
Gruyères
Rougemont
Château d'Oex
Gstaad
Les Mosses
Les Diablerets
Villars
Gryon
Bex
Aigle
Leysin
Roche
Villeneuve
Chillon
Rochers de Naye
Glion
Les Avants
Clarens
Blonay
Montreux
La Tour-de-Peilz
Vevey
Chexbres
Mt.-Pèlerin
Cully
Pully
LAUSANNE
Ouchy
Crissier
St.-Sulpice
Morges
Apples
Allaman
Aubonne
Rolle
Signal de Bougy
St.-George
Bassins
St.-Cergue
Nyon
Le Brassus
Marchairuz Pass
Orbe
Morez
St.-Claude
Coppet
Chavannes-de-Bogis
Hermance
Yvoire
Sciez
Thonon
Evian
St.-Gingolph
Dent d'Oche
Dranse
GENEVA
Rhône
Rhône
Sion
0 miles 5
0 km 5
N

grounds beside the lake. The trees are mature enough to provide shade, and there is a cafeteria. But don't forget that swimming caps are mandatory—even, in theory, for babies.

From Nyon you can take a little mountain railway up to St.-Cergue, 20 kms. (12 miles) to the north, and beyond. The ride is beautiful, and the contrast between the old rolling stock, museum pieces in themselves, and the brand new coaches is startling. St.-Cergue is a charming little resort in both summer and winter. The downhill skiing is adequate, with outstanding facilities for the very young. But the cross-country skiing has to be among the best in the world. In summer the walking, flowers and views make St.-Cergue totally delightful.

Twelve kms. (seven miles) along the lake is Rolle, a pleasant, small town with a castle by the water's edge. If you have time it is worth heading inland at Allaman—about five kms. (three miles) beyond Rolle—to visit Aubonne, which has remained virtually unchanged since the 16th century. The Château d'Allaman has been restored and furnished with antiques—all of which are for sale which makes this the biggest permanent antique market in Switzerland. The 12th-century castle in Rolle was bought in 1670 by the eccentric J. B. Tavernier, a great French traveler who visited the courts of Persia and Turkey and wrote entertaining accounts of his journeys.

Morges, a further 12 kms. (seven miles) from Rolle, is a peaceful little lake port, popular among sailing enthusiasts. It too has a castle, in this instance built by the Duke of Savoy in about 1286 as a defense against the bishop-princes of Lausanne. It now houses the Vaud Military Museum, the Musée Militaire, full of weapons, uniforms, models and a collection of 8,000 lead soldiers. Morges is one of the Vaud's principal wine-producing centers, and has an exuberant and joyful wine festival every year on the first weekend in October. It lasts for three days and the whole town throws itself into the merry making with floats, parties and, naturally, more than a little serious wine tasting. However, the festival has become very popular so if you want to join in the fun book your hotel well in advance.

About six kms. (four miles) from Lausanne you'll come to St.-Sulpice, site of the best preserved 12th-century Romanesque church in Switzerland, a charming little building. It was built by monks from the famous Cluny Abbey in Burgundy. Three original apses remain, although the nave has disappeared. The short bell tower is built of small stone blocks that were probably brought from the ruined Roman township at nearby Vidy. The adjoining priory was converted into a private residence during the 16th century.

Lausanne

While Lausanne, which is two-thirds of the way along the north shore of Lac Léman, may not be quite as famous as Geneva, it is a town with as long and illustrious a history. Traces of prehistoric man have been found in and around the city, and when Julius Caesar arrived at the end of the first century B.C. he found settlements of lake dwellers and a primitive stronghold. The Romans established a military camp and relay point by the lake at Vidy, on the western fringe of present-day

Lausanne (or Lousonna, as the Romans called it) and the place became an important junction of routes into Gaul and over the Great St. Bernard Pass into Italy. Four centuries later the Alemanni, a German tribe, burned the township, and its citizens took refuge at another smaller settlement already established a bit higher up the hill. To this refuge came Bishop Maire (or Marius) fleeing from his burnt-out see of Aventicum (now the town of Avenches), near the eastern shore of Lake Neuchâtel. A church was built and trade began, merchants climbing with their pack mules to the developing town on the hill.

In the 12th century Italian, Flemish and French architects, with the encouragement of Pope Innocent IV, set about building a cathedral. By 1275, this beautiful Burgundian Gothic edifice—today considered one of the finest medieval churches in Switzerland—was ready for consecration. Another Pope, Gregory X, came expressly to perform the ceremony. To mark the occasion, the ubiquitous Rudolph of Habsburg brought his wife, eight children, seven cardinals, five archbishops, 17 bishops, four dukes, 15 counts, and a multitude of lesser lords, spiritual and temporal; for the Pope was to make it a double event by crowning him Emperor of Germany and the Holy Roman Empire.

With such a flying start, Lausanne's Cathedral of Notre Dame could not fail to become a pilgrimage center—and so it did. Merchants, traders and innkeepers thrived, their houses spreading down the hillside and into the two rocky valleys surrounding the crag on which the cathedral stood. The bishops in their palace-fortress waxed powerful and wealthy, building themselves a summer island-castle at Ouchy, the growing town's lake port and fishing village. Although the House of Savoy owned most of the neighboring territory, Lausanne itself was ruled firmly by the bishops.

Towards the end of the 15th century tension between the citizens of Lausanne and the all-powerful bishop mounted, with the result that in 1525, in order to assert its right of franchise, the city council concluded a treaty of "fellow burgership" with the powerful cantons of Bern and Fribourg. Bern proved a fickle friend however, and in the summer of 1536 she declared war on Savoy and invaded the Pays de Vaud, the region around Lausanne which was a vassal territory of Savoy. Then, claiming that Sebastian of Montfaucon, the Bishop of Lausanne, was a partisan of Savoy, Bern also marched into this city, where the invading army was greeted as a liberator. But the conquering force chose to treat both Vaud and Lausanne as occupied territory, putting a bailiff in the bishop's castle and reducing the power of the city fathers to zero. That August, the city council felt compelled to renounce Catholicism and accept the reformed faith. Catholic churches were ransacked and the cathedral's treasures sent to fill Bernese coffers.

However, the culture of Lausanne remained intact and, despite the stern glances of Bernese society in the 18th century, grew particularly brilliant. The élite of the district offered warm-hearted hospitality to the cream of European society and intellect. From many countries aristocrats and literary celebrities, such as the historian Edward Gibbon, the Duke of Württemberg, and Voltaire, were drawn to Lausanne and caught up in a social whirl of parties, amateur theatricals and picnics. But revolt seethed behind this glittering facade, and it erupted in January 1798 when the Liberal Party, led by Fréderic César de la Harpe, proclaimed the independence of the Vaud and threw out the Bernese. Years of bickering followed until, in 1803, Napoleon Bonaparte introduced the Act of Mediation. Among other things this document, which for the first time in history used the word "Switzerland" as the name of the whole country, created the independent canton of Vaud, making Lausanne its capital.

The Modern City

As a prosperous market town, renowned as a center of culture, and with a romantic attraction for English travelers and residents, Lausanne began to take itself seriously towards the end of the 19th century. Construction of roads, avenues and bridges went on apace.

Lausanne today is as nearly picturesque as a modern, bustling city can be. Rising in tiers from the lakeside at Ouchy (360 meters, 1,200 ft. above sea level) to over 600 meters (2,000 ft.), it is situated on three hills. Two small rivers used to flow through gorges between the hills, but they are now entirely covered over and the valleys spanned by several handsome bridges carrying the flow of modern traffic high over the streets and houses beneath.

Today, Lausanne's importance stems from a number of disparate roles. Politically, it is important as the site of the Tribunal Federal, the highest court of appeal in Switzerland. Commercially, though by no means in the same league as Zürich or even Bern, Lausanne is nevertheless headquarters for a great many multinational organizations. Similarly, located on a major international rail route and an important national junction, most of the surrounding agricultural regions and the expanding industrial towns of the Vaud channel their trade through Lausanne. But pride of place in Lausanne is reserved for the city's role as the Olympic city. The I.O.C., the International Olympic Committee, has been based here since 1915, steering the Olympic movement through times of crisis and success alike. Fittingly, the city is now also the site of the new Court of Arbitration for Sport.

Over the years Lausanne has become the home of many royal families, either reigning, deposed, or abidcated; but the general tone of the city owes much more to the hard-headed and humorous country people, from whom even some of the "best" families have sprung. Moreover, many of the leading business families are descended from 17th-century French Huguenots. There has never been an oligarchy in Lausanne as in Fribourg, Geneva or Neuchâtel; and as a result less stress is laid on the quality of the family tree. An old farmstead or winegrower's vault is almost equal to a castle in terms of importance as a family seat.

Exploring Lausanne

1987 marks a special moment for Lausanne, the 100th anniversary of the opening of the city's first tourist office. By way of commemorating the event, a brand new tourist office has been opened at Ouchy on the lakeside.

The city today is a curious combination of the old and the new. The first 20 years or so after the war saw an immense building boom, with old buildings and whole quarters being pulled down to make way for shining new office blocks and apartment buildings. This architectural exuberance has given Lausanne a rather lopsided air. A hillside skyscraper (17 stories on one side and 15 on the other) contrasts brutally with the beautiful proportions of the cathedral rising in majesty on the crest of its hill. Atmospheric, although possibly unhygienic, alleys and narrow streets have been ruthlessly demolished, yet the old town clustered around Notre Dame has been painstakingly and attractively restored and refurbished.

Most of the shopping and sightseeing in Lausanne can be done within 550 meters (600 yds.) of the place St. François, the hub of the city and a veritable traffic maelstrom. North of the place and close to the cathedral is the 15th-century castle of St. Maire, formerly the bishop's palace; and the university (Palais de Rumine) with its fine museums: the Musée Cantonal des Beaux Arts, the Musée Cantonal d'Histoire Naturelle, and the Musée Cantonal d'Archéologie et d'Histoire. To the left, on the way from the place to the cathedral, is the charming 17th-century City Hall, its clock tower looking down onto the bustling, colorful market in the place de la Palud. To the west of St. François, beyond the terminal of the funicular (which goes all the way down to Ouchy), are the 19th-century Law Courts. To the east, in the Park of Mon Repos are the handsome, modern buildings of the Supreme Court of Appeal, the Tribunal Federal.

But almost any walk around the hilly streets, steep alleys and stairways is rewarding for it will take you past a succession of charming old buildings and incongruous, often impressive, new ones. You will get a hundred different views of the lake across rooftops, between buildings, or from the gardens. Perhaps the two finest views in Lausanne are from the Park of Montriond, a short walk from the station down avenue W. Fraisse, and from Le Signal, a justly famed viewpoint 640 meters (2,100 ft.) high, which lies just over a kilometer north of the cathedral.

For those who enjoy walking, there are innumerable day and half-day trips to be made in the wooded hills of Jorat, about 820 meters (2,700 ft.) high, above the city. A little lower, at Sauvabelin, just beyond Le Signal, there is a fine park, a charming little lake and a restaurant. Down by the waterside is Ouchy, with its long, elegant, tree-lined promenades that offer splendid views of both lake and mountains. You will also find colorful gardens and a wide range of hotels, including a number in the super-deluxe class. Ouchy is Lausanne's port, although it is far from being a conventional one. True, it's quite a busy spot, but its activity is mainly with the smart white steamers; more call here than at any other place on the lake. So it makes a fine starting point for excursions as well as being an international resort.

The Lavaux Region

To the east of Lausanne is the Lavaux, a remarkably beautiful region of vineyards, which rise up the hillsides all the way from Pully, on the outskirts of Lausanne, to Montreux—a distance of 24 kms. (15 miles).

Brown-roofed stone villages in the Savoy style, old defense towers and small baronial castles stud the green and brown landscape. The vineyards, enclosed within low stone walls, slope so steeply that all the work there has to be done by hand. Insecticides, fungicides, manures, and even soil washed down by summer storms are carried in baskets and containers strapped to men's backs. No wonder harvest in mid-October is a period for rejoicing! The grapes, picked by cheerful looking girls and women, are carried down by the men to the nearest road, emptied into vats and taken by tractor to the nearest press. Some Lavaux vintages are excellent and in great demand, but unfortunately, as in so much of Switzerland, the yield is small.

At Cully, about eight kms. (five miles) east of Lausanne, the motorist has a choice of roads just before entering the village. Straight on will take you along the main coastal road to Vevey. If instead you fork right, you will eventually come to the beautiful Corniche Road leading to Chexbres, a spick-and-span summer resort around 600 meters (2,000 ft.) above sea level. Winding high above the lake through delightful, narrow-streeted villages among steeply sloping vineyards, the Corniche Road offers a succession of fabulous views across the lake. From Chexbres, the Corniche Road winds down through the Dézaley (whose vineyards produce a light white wine) to rejoin the lake highway just before it enters Vevey.

Vevey to Montreux

Vevey needs no introduction to globetrotters. Together with neighboring Montreux it has been a popular resort since the early 19th century. Facing the lofty Dent d'Oche peak across the lake, its romantic appearance exercises a great attraction. It's also the center of an important wine-producing region which, four or five times a century, celebrates the fact with a prodigious, world-famous Fêtes des Vignerons (winegrowers' fair). The last one was held 30 July to 14 August 1977; there will probably not be another before the year 2000. However, you can get just a little of the feel of the great festival during the summer when a delightful market is held in the main square every Saturday morning. Wine tasters will not be disappointed.

On the heights above Vevey and Montreux lie several delightfully quiet summer or winter resorts accessible by road or rail: Les Pléiades, Les Avants, Mont-Pèlerin, and Blonay. Between Blonay and Chamby there is a railway, worked by 50-year-old steam locomotives, which runs for around five kms. (three miles) through delightful country side during summer weekends. The neighboring mountain slopes and valleys, particularly at Les Avants, are famous for the wonderful spring display of wild narcissi, usually in bloom from about mid-May to mid-June.

At the eastern end of Vevey's lakeside promenade is La Tour-de-Peilz, named after a castle built here in 1280 by Peter of Savoy.

Exploring Montreux

Montreux, one of Europe's most beautifully situated resorts and the most popular vacation spot on Lac Léman, is a French-style Edwardian town. Its population is predominently elderly and rich, and indeed the town has long had a reputation as an ultra-desirable retirement home. Nonetheless, Montreux is far from being just a place for millionaires to wile away their remaining years. The town has a series of internationally famous jazz festivals every year, as well as the Golden Rose of Montreux, an influential festival of television comedy. Further proof of the sprightliness of Montreux is provided by the presence of Le Club, a new and very expensive nightclub where the gilded youth of the area come to drink, dine and dance. In addition, like all the other towns along Lac Léman, Montreux has a thriving port, and all the water sports you could wish for.

It enjoys a remarkably mild climate thanks to mountains which protect it from cold north and east winds. Mulberries, magnolias and palm trees grow in its lush, well-tended gardens. Yet, despite the sheltering mountains, Montreux has a fine open situation, looking across the vast expanse of the lake, and eastwards up the wide Rhône Valley to a magnificent background of snowcapped peaks.

On the main Simplon railway line, Montreux is also the terminus of several mountain railways, not least the scenically splendid Montreux Oberland Bahn, whose comfortable little trains will take you on a winding journey among the mountains of the Bernese Oberland to Saanenmöser, Gstaad, Zweisimmen, and the Simmen Valley.

While at Montreux, a trip by mountain railroad (the trains leave from the main station) to the Rochers de Naye is imperative. There, at 1,040 meters (6,700 ft.) above sea level, you can enjoy the splendid view of Lac Léman, the Savoy, and the Swiss Alps; and ski between December and April.

Another lovely trip from Montreux is the drive to Glion and Caux, just above the town, both also accessible by train. The area around Caux is particularly memorable in May and June with—as long as it hasn't snowed—millions of white narcissi as far as the eye can see. The tourist offices at Lausanne or Montreux can advise on the optimum time to visit. At the top of the winding road is a memorable view, and, in Caux, the vast Mountain House formerly the Palace Hotel and now the international conference center of the Moral Re-Armament movement (MRA).

About two and a half kms. (one and a half miles) from Montreux is the castle of Chillon. Although only a few meters from the shore the castle forms an island, and the romantic atmosphere is enhanced by the deep blue-green water which reflects it. Nearby the modern highway and the overhead cables of the electric railway provide a strange contrast.

As it stands today, Chillon was built under the direction of Duke Peter of Savoy in the 13th century with, it is said, the help of military architects from Plantagenet England. For a long period it served as a state prison, and one of the many unfortunate "guests" was François

Bonivard. As Prior of St. Victor in Geneva he had supported the Reformation, an act which infuriated the Catholic Duke of Savoy. To ponder on the error of his ways Bonivard was sent to Chillon, where he spent six gloomy years, much of the time chained to a pillar in the dungeon, before being released by the Bernese in 1536. Up to the 17th century, Chillon was the scene of many trials for such things as sorcery, the wretched victims coming to a gruesome end in the castle courtyard.

When he was in Clarens, on the other side of Montreux, in 1816, the poet Byron visited Chillon. He learned of Bonivard's incarceration and wrote his famous poem, *The Prisoner of Chillon.* If you visit the castle, usually open from mid-morning to late afternoon or early evening, you will see that Byron, like a true tourist, carved his name on a pillar in Bonivard's dungeon. You will also be able to see the great hall and torture chamber, and a fine collection of medieval furnishings and decorations.

Beyond Chillon the road curves round the end of the lake to the small town of Villeneuve, guarding the estuary of the river Rhône and the long narrow plain which lies beyond. Until 1940, most of this area was considered unsuitable for agriculture. It was covered with reeds and horsegrass and was swampy, but wartime food problems provided the spur to drastic action. Drainage and irrigation were undertaken by private enterprise, and vast areas of land were reclaimed.

Return to Geneva

At Villeneuve, your tour of the Swiss playground along Lac Léman is almost ended, but if you wish, you can return to Geneva along the southern (French) shore. Just over six kms. (four miles) from Villeneuve the road crosses the Rhône, here a muddy river which discolors the water where it enters the lake. A right turn soon after the bridge will bring you quickly to the lakeside village of St.-Gingolph, half Swiss, half French.

The first large township in France is the popular resort and spa of Evian-les-Bains, 17 kms. (10 miles) from St.-Gingolph, which the Swiss often visit; crossing the lake on one of the busy little steamers to spend an afternoon shopping or, more likely, an evening trying their luck at the casino. Thonon, about nine kms. (six miles) beyond Evian, is not only an important agricultural center but, like Evian, is a popular lakeside resort and spa. At Sciez, a further nine kms. (five miles) beyond Thonon, you can either go straight along the direct main road to Geneva or turn right for the more interesting secondary road along the lake through the little resort of Yvoire, crossing the frontier to reenter Switzerland at Hermance, 14 kms. (nine miles) from Geneva.

Excursions North from Geneva

There are several interesting side-trips from the road along the northern shore of Lac Léman. The first is from Nyon, past the little resort of St.-Cergue. From St.-Cergue a secondary road cuts away to the northeast, passing through Bassins and St. George, and then over the Marchairuz Pass, closed in winter to motor traffic (1,447 meters, 4,745 ft.), to Le Brassus, a watchmaking center in the Vaud Jura. The hotel on the Marchairuz (which is over 100 years old) is an excellent stopping point for cross-country skiing. You can go the whole length of the Jura on skis in winter and on foot in summer. Allow seven to 14 days depending on how far you go.

In a cleft of the straight Valley of Joux, so typical of Jura scenery, lies the Lake of Joux, ideal for sailing and windsurfing. You can drive along either shore, for both roads converge at Le Pont at the far end of the lake. The road then climbs over the Mollendruz Pass, 1,066 meters (3,500 ft.) high. Halfway down the other side there is a magnificent panoramic view of Lac Léman, with Lausanne in the foreground. From L'Isle, a village at the bottom, you can return to Nyon through Apples, Aubonne and Rolle.

Another pleasant little sidetrip—one you can complete in an afternoon—leads northwards from Lausanne or Morges, both roads joining up at the village of Cossonay. A few kilometers beyond Cossonay is La Sarraz, whose castle, on a rocky promontory, was originally built in the 11th century by the Burgundian kings. Reconstructed in the 13th century, it was destroyed by the Confederates in 1475 and once again rebuilt. Its last owner, Henri de Mandrot, gave the Castle of La Sarraz to the Canton of Vaud in 1920. Today, it is a national monument and houses a splendid furniture collection.

About six kms. (four miles) from La Sarraz on the Vallorbe road is Croy, and if you take the left fork here you will quickly come to the charming old Jura village of Romainmotier, noted for its 11th-century Romanesque church. Returning through Croy it is only eight kms. (five miles) to Orbe, once the Roman town of Urba. Quaint rather than beautiful, Orbe was later an important focal point in Charlemagne's Europe; and it was here that the Emperor's sons met to divide his estates. According to legend the cruel Queen Brunhilda of Burgundy also held court in Urba during the 9th century.

At Bossaye, about two kms. (one mile) from Orbe along the road to Yverdon, are the ruins of several Roman villas from the 1st and 2nd centuries. Apart from Zofingen, near Olten, this is the only place in Switzerland where Roman mosaics can be viewed on their original sites. From here, you can either return via La Sarraz or go on to Yverdon and back via Echallens.

Any of the roads which lead up into the hills and valleys behind Vevey or Montreux are worth exploring. In only a few minutes they will bring you to splendid views and, in the late spring or early summer, to fields of wild flowers.

Quite different but equally lovely views can be seen from the fleet of smart, white paddle-steamers, diesel motor boats and even a hydrofoil, which ply busily around and across the lake, calling frequently at all the towns and many of the lakeside villages.

PRACTICAL INFORMATION FOR LAUSANNE

GETTING TO TOWN FROM THE AIRPORT. Getting to Lausanne from Geneva's Cointrin airport is simplicity itself. A brand new rail station, opened in late '86, has regular connections to all parts of the country. The journey time to Lausanne is 42 minutes.

TOURIST OFFICE. Lausanne's Office du Tourisme et des Congres is at 2 av. de Rhodanie (tel. 021–27 73 21). They produce a regularly updated guide to the city, written in English, French and German, and detailing events, exhibits, excursions, etc., and listing hotels and restaurants.

Lausanne is also the site of the Office du Tourisme de Canton de Vaud (O.T.V.), 3 av. de Mon Repos (tel. 021–22 77 82). They issue a similar publication, the *Guide Touristique,* which is also written in three languages.

HOTELS. Lausanne's hotels are renowned for their quiet elegance, air of luxury (even in the more moderately priced ones), huge size, and, above all, excellent service. Nearly all the hotels in our listings have a wide range of rooms, a good many of which may well fall into a lower grading than that given here. The best advice is always to check in advance with the hotel.

The tourist office can help with accommodations, if you arrive without reservations, but generally try to make reservations well in advance. The tourist office at the rail station is open late (to 10 P.M. in summer), but when it's closed the notice board outside the downtown tourist office lists places to stay, and there are two phone booths alongside.

Deluxe

Beau Rivage Palace, pl. Gen.-Guisan (tel. 021–26 38 31). 320 beds. Stands in its own grounds facing the lake at Ouchy; this is one of the great hotels of Europe. The many facilities include sauna, tennis and indoor pool. AE, DC, MC, V.

Lausanne Palace, 7–9 rue du Grand-Chêne (tel. 021–20 37 11). 270 beds. In the city center beside pleasant gardens and with a superb view from the terrace restaurant. All facilities. AE, DC, MC, V.

Expensive

Bellerive, 99 av. de Cour (tel. 021–26 96 33). 78 beds. Down the hill between the city center and Ouchy. AE, DC, MC, V.

Alpha-Palmiers, 34 rue du Petit Chêne (tel. 021–23 01 31). 240 beds. In the city center. Two good restaurants, quiet rooms. AE, DC, MC, V.

Continental, 2 pl. de la Gare (tel. 021–20 15 51). 180 beds. Near the station. Quiet, good, many facilities. AE, DC, MC, V.

Mirabeau, 31 av. de la Gare (tel. 021–20 62 31). 100 beds. Quiet and central; in own grounds. AE, DC, MC, V.

De la Paix, 5 av. B. Constant (tel. 021–20 71 71). 210 beds. Quiet, central hotel; well-appointed and comfortable. AE, DC, MC, V.

La Résidence, 15 pl. du Port (tel. 021–27 77 11). 96 beds. By the lake at Ouchy. Tennis, gym, pool and sauna. AE, V.

Royal-Savoy, 40 av. d'Ouchy (tel. 021–26 42 01). 180 beds. By the lake at Ouchy. Comfortable and well-appointed. AE, DC, MC, V.

Victoria, 46 av. de la Gare (tel. 021–20 57 71). 100 beds. Large hotel near the station. Comfortable if a little faded. DC, MC, V.

De Ville et du Rivage, tel. 021–39 12 61. 60 beds. At Lutry, six kms. (four miles) from the center.

Moderate

Angleterre, 9 pl. du Pont, Ouchy (tel. 021–26 41 45). 55 beds. Quiet hotel overlooking the lake. DC, MC, V.

City, 5 rue Caroline (tel. 021–20 21 41). 110 beds. Central and well-appointed, with facilities for the handicapped. AE, DC, MC.

Elite, 1 av. Ste.-Luce (tel. 021–20 23 61). 58 beds. In the city center, but quiet; in own grounds. Breakfast only. AE, DC, MC, V.

Novotel, rte. de Sullens (tel. 021–89 28 71). 200 beds. Seven kms. (four miles) out of town at Bussigny. AE, DC, MC, V.

Pré-Fleuri, 1 rue du Centre (tel. 021–34 72 73). 40 beds. Six kms. (three miles) out of town at St.-Sulpice. AE, MC.

Des Voyageurs, 19 rue Grand-St.-Jean (tel. 021–89 28 71). 50 beds. Central, with bar. Breakfast only. AE, V.

Inexpensive

De la Fôret, 75 route du Pavement (tel. 021–37 92 11). 24 beds. Small, with good restaurant.

Logement Pres de Vidy, Ch. du Bois de Vaux (tel. 021–24 24 79). Bargain rates for bed and breakfast: fr. 23 per night per person.

Près-Lac, 16 av. Gen. Guisan (tel. 021–28 49 01). 70 beds. At Pully. AE, DC, MC.

Regina, 18 rue Grand-St.-Jean (tel. 021–20 24 41). 55 beds. Central, but quiet. Breakfast only.

RESTAURANTS. You will be spoilt for choice by the quality of Lausanne's restaurants. We can provide little more than the tip of the iceberg in our listings, but further information is available from the city's tourist office.

Prices—like quality—are high, but a number of supermarkets and department stores have excellent inexpensive restaurants and cafeterias. But wander through the back streets and you will see that the less affluent in Lausanne eat well too—and if all else fails there are numerous fast food outlets and cafes throughout the city.

Expensive

Le Beaujolais, 2 pl. de la Gare (tel. 021–20 15 51). Restaurant of the hotel Continental; extremely good. AE, DC, MC, V.

La Grappe d'Or, 3 rue Chencau-de-Bourg (tel. 021–23 07 60). Excellent French cuisine. AE, DC, V.

Kwong Ming, 74–76 av. de Cour (tel. 021–27 78 25). Excellent Peking duck. DC, MC.

Le Mandarin, 7 av. du Théâtre (tel. 021–23 74 84). Good Chinese specialties. DC, MC, V.

Du Mont d'Or, 1 Chemin de Contigny (tel. 021–26 74 60). Fine French food. AE, DC, MC.

Le Relais, tel. 021–20 37 11. Restaurant of the Lausanne Palace hotel; excellent. AE, DC, MC, V.

Le Richelieu, 4 av. de Cour (tel. 021–26 32 35). Restaurant of the Carlton hotel and generally considered one of the best in town. AE, DC, MC, V.

San Marino, 20 av. de la Gare (tel. 021–22 93 69). Italian restaurant and brasserie. AE, MC.

Trattoria Toscana, 2 rue Belle Fontaine (tel. 021–23 41 61). Italian. DC, MC.

Voile d'Or, 9 av. E.-Jacques-Delacroze (tel. 021–27 80 11). Glorious location on a clear day. Lakeside restaurant where you can dine in the excellent grill room (marvelous view), eat in the more moderately priced snack bar, or spend the whole day sunbathing, swimming or dancing. DC, MC, V.

Wellingtonia, tel. 021–26 38 31. Restaurant of the Beau Rivage Palace. AE, DC, MC, V.

Moderate

Auberge de Lac de Sauvabelin—follow the signs to Sauvabelin (tel. 021–37 39 29). Set in a lovely forest just above Lausanne, this restaurant specializes in game, especially *chamois.*

Café de Jorat, 1 pl. de l'Ours (tel. 021–20 22 61). Unpretentious spot with excellent food. DC, MC.

Chaumière, 23 rue Centrale (tel. 021–23 53 64). Rustic setting; American specialties. MC, V.

Chez Pitch, at Pully, tel. 021–28 27 43. Steak and fish specialties on attractive outdoor terrace.

White Horse Pub, 66 av. d'Ouchy (tel. 021–26 75 75). Try this place for surprisingly good steaks; relaxed atmosphere. AE, DC, V.

Inexpensive

Le Chalet Suisse, 40 route du Signal (tel. 021–22 23 12). Typical Swiss food in attractive setting. AE, DC, MC.

Du Théâtre, 12 av. du Théâtre (tel. 021–23 38 27). AE, MC, V.

GETTING AROUND LAUSANNE. By Bus. The city has an excellent bus network: timetables and routes are available at the tourist office. All tickets cost Fr. 1.50, and each ticket gives you one hour's run of the system. Buy your ticket from the slot machine at all bus stops.

By Metro. The city has a miniature metro (subway) system from the rail station down to the lake front at Ouchy, and from the station up to the place St.-François. Services are frequent, fast and inexpensive.

MUSEUMS AND GALERIES. Cinémathèque Suisse (Swiss Film Archives), Casino de Montbenon, 3 allée Ernest-Ansermet (tel. 021–23 75 56). Daily showings of old and new movies at 3, 6:30 and 8:30 (see local press for details). Closed Sun.

Collection d'Art Brut, Château de Beaulieu, 11 av. des Bergières (tel. 021–37 54 35). Permanent exhibition of Art Brut (art by non-artists) presented by Jean Dubuffet. Open Tues. to Fri. 10–12 and 2–6, Sat. and Sun. 2–6. Admission Fr. 5 (students Fr. 3).

Fondation de l'Hermitage, 2 route du Signal (tel. 021–20 50 01). Series of outstanding temporary art exhibitions. Beautiful house and grounds and lovely view. Cafeteria. Open Nov. to Mar., daily 2–6; Apr. to Oct., daily 10–1 and 2–6 and Thurs. 8–10 P.M. when the grounds are floodlit.

Forum de l'Hôtel de Ville, pl. de la Palud. Temporary exhibits at the town hall. Admission free.

Musée des Arts Décoratifs de la Ville de Lausanne (Decorative Arts Museum), 4 av. Villamont (tel. 021–23 07 56). Temporary exhibitions of graphics, textiles, photography, etc. Open daily 10–12 and 2–6 and Tues. 8–10 P.M.

Musée Cantonal d'Archéologie et d'Histoire (Museum of History and Archeology), Palais de Rumine, 6 pl. de la Riponne (tel. 021–22 83 34). Neolithic, Bronze Age, Iron Age and Roman periods well represented. Open daily 10–12 and 2–5.

Musée Cantonal des Beaux-Arts (Fine Arts Museum), Palais de Rumine, 6 pl. de la Riponne (tel. 021–22 83 32/3). Mostly 18th–20th-century local artists. International Biennial of Tapestry and other changing exhibits. Open daily 10–12 and 2–5 (8 on Thurs.). Closed Mon. A.M.

Musée Cantonal de l'Elysée, 18 av. de l'Elysée (tel. 021–27 48 21). 18th century mansion housing prints and photographs. Open Tues. to Sun. 2–6.

Musée Cantonal d'Histoire Naturelle (Natural History Museum), Palais de Rumine, 6 pl. de la Riponne. There is a geological section (tel. 021–22 83 31) and a zoological section (tel. 021–22 83 86) that includes six extinct species of birds. Open daily 10–12 and 2–5. Admission free.

Musée de la Cathédrale (Cathedral Museum), Ancien Evêché, 2 pl. de la Cathédrale. Every aspect of the cathedral. Open Nov. to Mar., daily 2–5 (7 on Thurs.); Apr. to June and Sept. to Oct., daily 10–12 and 2–6 (8 on Thurs.); July and Aug., daily 10–6 (8 on Tues. and Thurs.). Closed Mon.

Musée Historique de l'Ancien-Evêché (Bishops' Palace Museum), 2 pl. de la Cathédrale (tel. 021–22 13 68). Permanent and temporary exhibitions of old Lausanne. Open Nov. to Mar., daily 2–5 (7 on Thurs.); Apr. to June and Sept. to Oct., daily 10–12 and 2–6 (8 on Thurs.); July and Aug., daily 10–6 (8 on Tues. and Thurs.). Closed Mon.

Olympic Museum, 18 av. Ruchonnet (tel. 021–20 93 31). All about the Olympic Games. Temporary building until new purpose-built museum is finished at Ouchy. Open Mon. 2–6:30, Tues. to Sat. 9:30–6:30, and Sun. 2–6:30.

Musée de la Pipe et Objets du Tabac (Pipe and Tobacco Museum), 7 rue de l'Académie (tel. 021–23 43 23). More than 2,500 exhibits from 50 pipe-smoking countries. Open daily 9–12 and 2–6. Admission Fr. 3.50.

Musée de Pully, 2 chemin Davel (tel. 021–28 33 11). Exhibits of paintings with the focus on Pully. Open daily 2–5. Closed Mon. Admission free.

Musée Romain de Vidy (Vidy Roman Museum), chemin du Bois-de-Vaux (tel. 021–25 10 84). Exhibits proving that Vidy dates back B.C. Open Wed. and Sat. 2–5 (4 in winter), Sun. 10–12 and 2–4. Admission free.

Musée de la Villa Romain du Pully (Pully Roman Villa Museum), pl. du Prieuré (tel. 021–28 33 04). Reconstruction of Roman ruins with 1st-century fresco. Audiovisual displays in three languages. Open daily 2–5 (Sat. and Sun. only in winter). Closed Mon. Admission free.

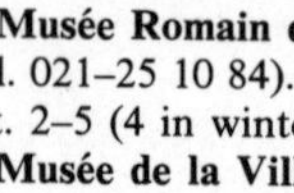

PARKS AND ZOOS. Jardin Botanique de Lausanne (Lausanne Botannical Gardens), 14 av. de Cour (tel. 021–26 24 09). The alpine section has rock plants from all over the world, and there is a small arboretum and a hothouse. **La Thomasia** at Pont-de-Nant above Bex at 1,250 meters (4,100 ft.) is the mountain section of the Botannical Gardens. It opens about May, depending on the snow conditions. Here you can see alpine plants in an area much closer to their natural habitat. In Lausanne the gardens are open Mar. to Oct., daily 8–12 and 1:30–5:30. Admission free.

Vivarium, 82 chemin de Boissonet (tel. 021–32 72 94). One of Europe's largest collections of live poisonous snakes. Also crocodiles, tortoises and birds of prey. Open Mon., Wed., Thurs. and Fri. 2–6:30, Sat. and Sun. 10–12 and 2–6:30. Admission Fr. 4 (children under 16 Fr. 2, senior citizens Fr. 2:50).

Zoo de Servion, tel. 021–93 16 71. Above Lausanne in the Jorat forest. (Take no. 22 bus from the city terminal at pl. du Tunnel.) 350 animals including lions, tigers, bison and tropical birds in glasshouses. Restaurant. Open 9 until dusk. Admission Fr. 6 (children under 16 Fr. 3).

SHOPPING. Elegant Lausanne can be a delightful, if distinctly expensive, place to shop, with plenty of tempting spots for the discriminating. The best places for luxury goods are in the rue de Bourg and around the place St.-François. Less expensive shops are found around the Geneva side of the Grand Pont.

If the city has any one specialty it is probably chocolate. True, there are few places in Switzerland where you can't buy excellent chocolate, but Lausanne really does seem to have the edge. The place to head for is **Moujonnier** in the av. de Chailly. They lay strong claim to producing the best chocolate in the country.

The other great shopping treat in Lausanne is the market, held every Wednesday and Saturday morning in the town center. Though nothing if not picturesque, the market is very much more than a tourist trap. Rather it is a vital part of life in Lausanne, and as such makes only too clear the importance the city places on fresh food of the highest quality. The fruits, cheeses and vegetables are all super-fresh and super-delicious.

MUSIC AND THEATERS. The **Beaulieu** and **Municipal** theaters present opera, operetta, concerts and plays all year round. The world-famous Orchestre de la Suisse Romande performs regularly, dividing its time between Geneva and Lausanne. The Beaulieu is also an enormous conference and exhibition center with something going on virtually all year round. The Comptoir Suisse (National Fair) is a September highlight, featuring everything from cows to computers—and lots of wine.

Full details of performances and what's on are available from the tourist office.

NIGHTLIFE. Brummell, 7 rue Grand-Chêne (tel. 021–22 09 20). Elegant. Closed Sun.

Cabaret Montparnasse, pl. Bel-Air (tel. 021–20 83 13). Strip show. Closed Sun.

Darling, Galeries St.-François (tel. 021–22 09 35). Closed Mon. and Tues.

Le Paddock, 46 av. de la Gare (tel. 021–20 57 75). In the Victoria hotel. Disco. Closed Mon.

La Tomate, Chalet Suisee, Signal de Sauvabelin (tel. 021–22 23 12). Disco in attractive setting.

Voile d'Or, av. E.-Jacques-Delacroze (tel. 021–27 80 11). Smart; outdoors in hot weather.

USEFUL ADDRESSES. Car Hire. *Avis,* 50 av. de la Gare (tel. 021–20 66 81); *Europcar,* 12 pl. de la Riponne (tel. 021–23 71 42); *Hertz,* 34 chemin de Mornex (tel. 021–20 66 51); *Lococar,* 30 av. Ruchonnet (021–20 30 80). **Scooter Hire.** *Auto-Location,* 2 av. Ruchonnet (tel. 021–23 47 22).

PRACTICAL INFORMATION FOR THE REST OF THE REGION

TOURIST OFFICES. The principal tourist office for the entire Lac Léman region is the Office du Tourisme de Canton de Vaud (O.T.V.), 3 av. de Mon Repos, Lausanne (tel. 021–22 77 82). In addition, there are local tourist offices in the following towns: **Aubonne,** Société de développement d'Aubonne et environs, tel. 021–76 57 25. **Château-d'Oex,** Office du Tourisme, tel. 029–47 78 8. **Les Diablerets,** Office du Tourisme, tel. 025–53 13 58. **Gryon,** Office du Tourisme, tel. 021–68 14 22. **Lavey-les-Bains,** Etablissement thermal cantonal vaudois (Vaud thermal baths association), tel. 025–65 11 21. **Leysin,** Office du Tourisme, tel. 025–34 22 44. **Montreux,** Office du Tourisme, 5 rue du Théâtre (tel. 021–63 12 12). **Morges,** Office du Tourisme, 80 Grand Rue (tel. 021–71 32 33). **Les Mosses,** Office du Tourisme, tel. 025–55 14 66. **Nyon,** Office du Tourisme, 7 av. Viollier (tel. 022–61 62 61). **Orbe,** Office du Tourisme, tel. 024–41 31 15. **St.-Cergue,** Office du Tourisme, tel. 022–60 15 05. **Vallée de Joux,** Office du Tourisme, tel. 021–85 62 57. **Vallorbe,** Office du Tourisme, tel. 021–83 25 83. **Vevey,** Adive, 5 pl. de la Gare (tel. 021–51 48 25). **Villars,** Office du Tourisme, tel. 025–35 32 32. **Villeneuve,** Office du Tourisme, 10 Grand Rue (tel. 021–60 22 86). **Yverdon-les-Bains,** Cité des Bains (tel. 024–21 44 56).

HOTELS AND RESTAURANTS. Hotels throughout the Vaud are generally excellent. Montreux, like Lausanne, boasts a number of world-famous names, renowned for comfort and luxury. Similarly, many of the lakeside resorts have excellent and extremely well-run hotels. Away from major centers advance reservations are advisable if not essential, particularly for the peak periods around Christmas and the New Year and in June, July and August.

Local inns *(auberges)* in almost all villages are frequently worth trying, and offer good food and comfortable rooms often at astonishingly low prices.

LES BIOUX. *Des Trois Suisses* (I), tel. 021–85 55 08. 25 beds. Lakeside family hotel with excellent food. Recommended.

LE BRASSUS. *De la Lande* (M), tel. 021–85 44 41. 64 beds. Very comfortable. Sauna. AE, DC, MC, V.

CHATEAU D'OEX. *Résidence la Rocaille* (E), tel. 029–46 21 5. 50 beds. Very comfortable hotel in own grounds. AE, DC, V. *Beau-Séjour et Taverne* (M), tel. 029–47 42 3. 70 beds. Central but very quiet. AE, MC, V. *Ermitage* (M), tel. 029–46 00 3. 42 beds. Good restaurant as well. AE, DC, V. *Hostellerie Bon-Accueil* (M), tel. 029–46 32 0. 30 beds. Quiet family hotel in historic building in its own grounds. AE, DC, MC, V. *De l'Ours* (M), tel. 029–46 33 7. 86 beds. Quiet and central. AE, DC, MC, V. *La Printanière* (I), tel. 029–46 11 3. 18 beds. Small hotel in own grounds; very quiet. No rooms with bath.

CHAVANNES-DE-BOGIS. *Motel* (I), tel. 022–76 47 11. Claims to be the biggest in Europe, ten minutes from Geneva airport. Tennis courts, sauna, and various restaurants. Within walking distance the same owner has a slightly older, less luxurious, but even cheaper *Motel de Founex,* tel. 022–76 25 35.

CHEXBRES. *Du Signal* (E), tel. 021–56 25 25. 132 beds. Quiet with splendid view. Tennis and pool; good restaurant. *Cecil* (I), tel. 021–56 12 92. 42 beds. Pool. Good restaurant. MC, V.

COPPET. *Du Lac* (E), tel. 022–76 15 21. 38 beds. Good position, good restaurants. AE, DC, MC, V. *Orange* (I), tel. 022–76 10 37. 22 beds. Also with restaurant. AE, MC, V.

Restaurant. *La Petite Marmite* (I–M), tel. 022–76 18 54. Hot and cold buffet and lots of it.

CRISSIER. Restaurant. *Girardet* (E), tel. 021–34 15 14. Switzerland's best restaurant. Count on at least Fr. 100 per person and book well in advance. Remember the meal for ever!

LES DIABLERETS. *Ermitage* (E), tel. 025–53 15 51. 150 beds. Sauna, gymnasium and indoor pool. AE, MC. *Eurotel* (E), tel. 025–53 17 21. 220 beds. Indoor pool and sauna. AE, DC, MC, V. *Mon Abri* (M), tel. 025–53 14 81. 50 beds. Comfortable and quiet. AE, MC, V. *Les Lilas* (I), 025–53 11 34. 20 beds. Small. AE, MC.

GLION. *Victoria* (E), tel. 021–63 31 31. 80 beds. Gracious and appropriately Victorian. Pool and excellent food. AE, DC, MC, V. *Des Alpes Vaudoises* (M), tel. 021–63 20 76. 90 beds. Medium-sized hotel in own grounds; pool. AE, DC, MC, V. *Mont Fleuri* (I), tel. 021–63 52 81. 60 beds.

Restaurant. *Jaman* (M). Friendly bar and restaurant with tasty food and an exceptional stock of Belgian beers.

LEYSIN. *Central-Résidence* (E), tel. 025–34 12 11. 200 beds. Large and superior hotel with indoor pool, sauna and gymnasium. AE, DC, MC, V. *Relais-Regency* (E), tel. 025–34 24 24. 100 beds. Well-appointed and central. DC, MC, V. *Mont Riant* (I), tel. 025–34 12 35. 36 beds. Quiet hotel in own grounds. AE, DC, MC, V. *Les Orchidées* (I), tel. 025–34 14 21. 27 beds. Very quiet and good value. AE, DC, MC, V.

MONTREUX. *Excelsior* (L), tel. 021–63 32 31. 120 beds. Sauna, pool, water sports, beauty treatments. Chinese, French and health-food restaurants. AE, DC, MC, V. *Montreux Palace* (L), tel. 021–63 53 73. 450 beds. Vast hotel with golf, tennis and outdoor pool. AE, DC, V. *Bonivard* (E–L), tel. 021–63 43 41. 180 beds. Quiet. DC. *Eden au Lac* (E), tel. 021–62 55 51. 210 beds. Quiet, with pool. AE, DC, MC, V. *Eurotel Riviera* (E), tel. 021–62 29 51. 270 beds. Lakeside hotel with indoor pool. Kitchenette in every room. MC, V. *Hyatt Continental* (E), tel. 021–63 51 31. 326 beds. Highly recommended. AE, MC, V. *Suisse et Majestic* (E), tel. 021–63 51 81. 250 beds. Sauna and gymnasium. Facilities for children. AE, DC, MC, V. *Bon Accueil* (M), tel. 021–63 05 51. 78 beds. Central but down steep stairs from the station; superb view. Breakfast only. AE, DC, MC, V. *Masson* (I), tel. 021–63 15 37. 20 beds. Quiet. Facilities for children.

MORGES. *Du Léman* (M), tel. 021–71 21 88. Excellent. V. *Du Mont-Blanc au Lac* (M), tel. 021–71 63 71. 80 beds. Recommended. AE, DC, MC, V.

NYON. *Du Clos de Sadex* (E), tel. 022–61 28 31. 30 beds. Small hotel on the lake; quiet, with waterskiing. AE, DC, MC, V. *Beau Rivage* (M–E), tel. 022–61 32 31. 85 beds. Splendid view; good food. AE, DC, MC, V. *XVIe Siècle* (I), tel. 022–61 24 41. 29 beds. With good restaurant. MC.

Restaurant. *Le Léman* (M–E), tel. 022–61 22 41. Excellent. Fish and nouvelle cuisine. AE, DC, MC, V.

ROCHERS DE NAYE. *Rochers de Naye* (I), tel. 021–63 74 11. 15 beds. Simple and very inexpensive hotel beside the summit station, more than 2,000 meters (6,560 ft.) up; spectacular location. No rooms with bath.

ROLLE. *Rivesrolle* (E), tel. 021–75 34 91. 64 beds. Recommended. AE, DC, MC, V. *La Tête Noire* (I), tel. 021–75 22 51. 30 beds. In own grounds; central. AE, DC, V.

Restaurant. *Du Marché* (M), tel. 021–75 17 54. Good fish—some caught by the owner.

ST.-CERGUE. *De la Poste* (I), tel. 022–60 12 05. 22 beds. Small and simple. AE.

VEVEY. *Trois Couronnes* (L), tel. 021–51 30 05. 120 beds. Somewhat Victorian interior, but a lot of character and comfort. Open-air restaurant overlooking lake. AE, DC, MC, V. *Du Lac* (E), tel. 021–51 10 41. 90 beds. Lakeside location, with swimming pool. AE, DC, MC, V. *De Famille* (I), tel. 021–51 39 31. 100 beds. Central, with indoor pool and sauna. AE, MC, V.

Restaurant. *Du Raisin* (M–E), tel. 021–51 10 28. First class. V.

VILLARS. *Eurotel* (L), tel. 025–35 31 31. 250 beds. Central, with indoor pool and sauna. AE, DC, MC, V. *Grand Hôtel du Parc* (L), tel. 025–35 21 21. 140 beds. Quiet, with indoor pool and tennis. Ideal for children. V. *Du Golf et Marie-Louise* (E), tel. 025–35 24 77. 118 beds. Quiet and central. Tennis. AE, DC, MC, V. *Chalet Henriette* (I), tel. 025–35 21 63. 35 beds. Facilities for the handicapped. MC.

GETTING AROUND. By Train. Good train links connect all major towns around Lac Léman. The postal buses serve the smaller towns and villages off the main rail routes. (See "By Bus" below.)

In addition to main rail lines, a number of privately operated scenic rail lines run through parts of the region. These are:

Bière–Apples–Morges line, from the lake into the Jura. Schedules are such that you can combine a scenic ride with some lovely walks away from many of your fellow tourists.

Blonay–Chamby line is run by enthusiasts. This tourist railway, with a mixture of electric and steam engines, also has a small museum. Tel. 021–53 21 21 for details. Open May to Oct., Sat. and Sun.

Lausanne–Echallens–Bercher (L.E.B.) line passes through some glorious countryside. The timetable allows you to combine the train rides with short or longer walks. Steam engines are run in the summer. Ask for the timetable from the tourist office or tel. 021–81 11 15/6 for details.

Montreux–Oberland–Bernois. Spend a day on this line and see some of the loveliest spots—Les Avants, Château-d'Oex, Rochers-de-Naye, etc.—or use it to move on to the Bernese Oberland. Ask the tourist office for timetable.

Nyon–St.-Cergue–Morez line goes from busy Nyon into the heart of holiday-land. Again, use it purely to view the scenery or to gain access to the skiing. There is a wonderful contrast between carriages that are almost museum pieces and brand new rolling stock.

By Car. Roads throughout the Vaud and the Lac Léman region are excellent, both highways and expressways. Visiting the region by car is in fact by far the best way to get the most out of it; it is difficult to see how any visitor, however determined, would be able to take in any of the more remote areas without a car.

By Bus. Postal buses visit a number of towns and villages off the rail network, though many of the smaller places have perhaps only a couple of services daily. Schedules are available from tourist offices and rail stations.

By Boat. Lake steamers ply the length and breadth of Lac Léman, and just about any lakeside town and village has a landing stage. Schedules and fares are available from all tourist offices or from the *Compagnie Générale de Navigation sur le Lac Léman* (C.G.N.),

Sightseeing Data

AIGLE. Château et Le Musée Vaudois de la Vigne et du Vin (Castle and Wine Museum), tel. 025–26 21 30. 13th-century fortress and the history of wine-making. Open Apr. to Oct., daily 9–12:30 and 2–6. Admission Fr. 3 (children Fr. 2).

ALLAMAN. Château, tel. 021–76 38 05. A beautiful old castle that has been restored and turned into a show place for furniture and prints, all for sale. Open Wed. to Fri., 2:30–6:30, Sat. 10–5, and the first and last Sun. of the month, 2:30–6.

BEX. La Mine de Sel (Salt mine), tel. 025–63 24 62. Go down a salt mine in an electric train and see both old and modern methods of operation. Open Apr. to Nov., 9–2. Telephone on a Thurs. to book a visit.

CHÂTEAU-D'OEX. Le Chalet, tel. 029–46 67 7. Everything you ever wanted to know about alpine-style cheese-making. The process is demonstrated daily, 1:30–5. Exhibitions, shop and restaurant, open daily 9–6.

CHILLON. Château, tel. 021–63 39 11/2. This has been painted, photographed and written about, notably by Byron, for centuries. Open Apr. to Sept., daily 9–6:30; Oct. to Mar., daily 10–12:45 and 1:30–4:45.

COPPET. Château, tel. 022–76 10 28. Still owned by the family of Mme. de Staël and Jacques Necker, Louis XVI's finance minister. Open Mar. to Oct., daily 10–12 and 2–6. Closed Mon.

Musée du Vieux Coppet (Museum of Old Coppet), tel. 022–76 36 88. Restored family house. Note in particular the music room with its combination violin/keyboard. Same opening hours as the château.

GRANDSON. Château et Musée d'Automobiles (Castle and Car Museum), tel. 024–24 29 26. Medieval castle plus Greta Garbo's Rolls Royce. Open Mar. to Oct., daily 9–6; Nov. to Feb., daily 2–5, also Sat. and Sun. 10–12, closed Mon.

LUCENS. Château, tel. 021–95 80 32. Once the holiday home of the bishops of Lausanne, the castle has now been restored and furnished by Galerie Koller. All the contents are for sale. Open Apr. to Oct., daily 10–4; Nov. to Mar., daily 10–5; closed Mon. and Jan. and Feb. Admission Fr. 4.40.

MORGES. Musée Militaire (Military Museum), tel. 021–71 26 15. In the castle. Armory, toy soldiers and more. Open Feb. to Dec., daily 10–12 and 1:30–5, Sat. and Sun. afternoons only.

NYON. Musée de la Porcelaine (Porcelain Museum), tel. 022–61 58 88. For a brief period after the French Revolution Nyon was the porcelain center of the world, and there are some excellent examples here. Open Apr. to Oct., daily 9–12 and 2–6; Nov. to Mar., daily 2–5. Closed Mon. Admission Fr. 2 or Fr. 3 for this and the two museums below (children Fr. 1).

Maison du Léman (House of the Lake), tel. 022–61 09 49. Includes fishing, boats and ecology. Opening hours as above.

Basilique et Musée Romain (Basilica and Roman Museum), tel. 022–61 75 91. Nyon was a Roman colony and there is an impressive collection of Roman remains. Same opening hours as above.

ORON-LE-CHATEL. Château, tel. 021–93 72 22. Good furniture. Open daily 9–12 and 2–6 (5 from Nov. to Apr.). Closed Mon.

ROCHE. Musée Suisse de l'Orgue (Swiss Organ Museum), tel. 021–60 22 00. Devoted to organs and housed in an old monastery. Open May to Sept., daily 10–6.

STE.-CROIX-LES-RASSES. Musée Baud à l'Auberson (Baud Museum at Auberson), tel. 024–61 24 84. Unique collection of old mechanical musical instruments. Open 7 July to 15 Sept., daily 2–5; Sun. 9–12 and 2–6 all year round.

Centre International de la Mécanique d'Art (International Centre for Mechanical Art), 2 rue de l'Industrie (tel. 024–61 44 77). Another collection of mechanical musical instruments. Brand new. There are guided tours Tues. to Sat., 1:30–6:30, Sun. and public holidays 9–6:30. Admission Fr. 7 (children Fr. 4).

Musée de Ste.-Croix, tel. 024–61 31 89. Local exhibits from industry and crafts to fossils. Open Oct. to Apr., Sun. 3–5; May to Sept., Sun. 10–12.

SALAVAUX. Château, tel. 037–77 25 26. Biggest carillon in Europe, and a memorial to Dr. Albert Schweitzer and his life. Open Mar. to Nov., daily 10–6.

SIGNAL DE BOUGY. Parkland, with much-painted view of the lake. The supermarket chain Migros runs the whole place (including the alcohol-free restaurant). Children's playground is probably the best in Switzerland. Lots of special events during the holidays. Open Mar. to Nov. daily 9–10 P.M.

VEVEY. Alimentarium, Musée de l'Alimentation (Food Museum), 1 rue de Léman (tel. 021–52 77 33). All about food and everything to do with it. Open daily 10–12 and 2–5. Closed Mon.

Musée de Vieux Vevey (Museum of Old Vevey), 43 rue d'Italie (tel. 021–51 07 22). In the castle. All about life in the area. Open daily 10–12 and 2–5 (11–12 on Sun.). Closed Mon. Admission free.

Musée Suisse d'Appareils Photographiques (Swiss Camera Museum), 5 pl. du Marché (tel. 021–51 94 60). Only one of its kind in Switzerland. Open daily 2–5. Closed Mon. Admission free.

Musée Jenisch, 2 av. de la Gare (tel. 021–51 29 50). Paintings. Open Nov. to Apr., daily 2–5 (11–12 on Sun.); May to Oct. 10–12 and 2–5. Closed Mon. Admission free.

YVERDON-LES-BAINS. Château, tel. 024–21 01 21. Rich in history, good furniture and an interesting collection of costumes. Pestalozzi spent 20 years in the castle. Open Oct. to May, daily 2–5; June to Sept., daily 10–12 and 2–5. Closed Mon.

Musée, tel. 024–21 93 10. Good on archeology and natural history. Same opening hours as above.

SPORTS. Watersports. Sailing and windsurfing are possible from just about every lakeside town or village. If you haven't brought your own equipment (wetsuits are recommended for most of the summer; Lac Léman comes from the glaciers of the Alps and is freezing all year round) it is reasonably easy to hire on the spot. Details from any tourist office.

Wintersports. This area has a pleasant mixture of challenging and easier ski resorts. Cross-country skiing is becoming more popular each year, and there are plenty of road and rail links to the mountains that are kept open. The list highlights the better known resorts, but any, however small, are well worth an afternoon's exploration.

Alpe des Chaux, 1,550 meters (4,800 ft.). New resort linked to Villars.

Château-d'Oex, 1,015 meters (3,330 ft.); 2 cable cars, 10 lifts, 35 kms. (21 miles) of downhill runs, 40 kms. (24 miles) of cross-country trails, skating, six kms. (three miles) of ski bob trails. Ski schools. Now the Swiss hot-air ballooning center.

Les Diablerets, 1,220 meters (4,000 ft.); 6 cable cars, 14 lifts, 60 kms. (37 miles) of downhill runs, 15 kms (nine miles) of cross-country trails, eight kms. (four miles) of prepared tobogganing trails, skating, curling. Ski schools.

Leysin, 1,275 meters (4,185 ft.); more than 48 kms. (29 miles) of sign-posted and highly varied ski-runs served by 30 lifts, all inter-linked, and including a fast shuttle train service and 2 cable cars. Indoor and heated outdoor pools, skating, curling, ski bob, golf, hiking and indoor games.

Rougemont, 1,000 meters (3,000 ft.). The ski-pass links into Gstaad and Château-d'Oex.

St.-Cergue, 1,050 meters (3,340 ft.); 30 lifts, outstanding cross-country skiing, floodlit run. Sunny spot with varied skiing and excellent facilities for very young learners.

La Vallée de Joux, 1,000–1,680 meters (3,000–4,500 ft.); more than 240 kms. (150 miles) of prepared pistes. The whole valley is a cross-country skier's paradise. Adequate downhill skiing as well. Le Brassus is the center.

Villars, 1,398/1,450 meters (4,585/4,755 ft.); 60 kms. (37 miles) of downhill runs, 15 kms. (nine miles) of cross-country trails, 30 kms (18 miles) of ski-hiking trails (vast skiing area for all levels), 19 lifts. Curling, swimming, tennis, golf, fishing, hiking (180 kms./111 miles of marked paths), skittles.

WINETASTING. Many famous wines are produced from grapes grown on the hills above the lake, and indeed the region is dotted with signs saying "Route de Vignoble." Follow these and you will find yourself among the vines. For more information about the science, skill and sheer hard work that goes into making good wines, as well as details about which wine merchants welcome visitors (and many do), write to Office des Vins Vaudois, 58 av. de Tivoli, 1007 Lausanne (tel. 021–25 04 46), and ask for the *Guide to the Vaudois Vineyards* in English. You will also be supplied with the annually updated *Guide de Vignoble Vaudois,* which gives practical information about opening hours, tastings etc., but only in French.

GENEVA

Cosmopolitan Corner of the Lake

Geneva is an international and cosmopolitan city *par excellence*—even perhaps *the* most international and cosmopolitan city in the world, New York notwithstanding. European headquarters of the United Nations and global headquarters of a multitude of international organizations—the World Health Organization, the International Labor Office, the Red Cross, even the Boy Scouts, to name only a handful—there are times when it can be hard to find anyone here who isn't a foreigner, and times when you are hard put to it to realize that you are actually in Switzerland at all. The population more often than not appears to consist exclusively of businessmen, diplomats, tourists, waiters and, presumably, spies from every corner of the globe. In addition, the city is home to a host of multinational corporations, as well as being the second most important banking center in the country: when the money was flowing from the oil wells, Geneva was widely believed to contain more Arab money than anywhere else in the world, including the Middle East. This international role is underlined further by the scores of gatherings and meetings, many of global significance, held here, the Reagan–Gorbachev Fireside Summit in the fall of 1985 being just the latest in a long line. (The U.S.–Soviet disarmament talks have been taking place here for longer than most people care to—or can—remember).

The people of Geneva do not always look with pleasure on the international shenanigans that go on in their midst. A much-heralded get-together like the Fireside Summit can virtually bring the city to a standstill while Russian and American security forces move in to protect their respective leaders. Likewise, the vast influx of foreign business and internationally employed personnel does dire things to restaurant prices and makes it wellnigh impossible to find an apartment for rent at anything but a millionaire's ransom. The slight zenophobia which has shown itself lately in voting patterns for local elections and referenda about such matters as foreign workers (called guest workers, a name that cloaks their down-to-earth usefulness to the community) has been strengthened by the presence of this vast international workforce in Geneva. It is not a problem that affects other Swiss cities to anything like the same extent.

Appropriately, the city is immensely accessible, with excellent transport links to the rest of Switzerland and, indeed, the world. More unusually, but in keeping with its international flavoring, Geneva is something of an enclave in a foreign country, France. Located at the southwestern end of Lac Léman (Lake Geneva), the city is almost entirely surrounded by French territory, the Pays de Gex to the north and the Haute Savoie to the south, the former now something of a dormitory area for Geneva. Like Basel, which lies at the meeting place of France, Germany and Switzerland, border formalities here are, if not nonexistent, certainly not much more than minimal. Accordingly, trips into France, even just for a meal, are very much part of the pattern of life. At the time of writing, in a determined effort to control the spread of terrorism, all foreigners except Swiss and nationals of the European Community need visas to visit France—even for lunch. Apply to your local French consul before you leave home.

Geneva Background

Although today Geneva is very much a city of the 20th century, it is nonetheless an ancient place, with a history that fades back into the mists of time. The crest of the hill on which the Cathédrale St.-Pierre now stands offered an excellent strategic position, first for primitive tribes; next for the Romans, who stayed there for 500 years (until A.D. 443); and then for the early Burgundians and their later kings. In the first part of the 5th century Geneva became a bishopric, and by the end of the 11th century its prince-bishops had developed a See both rich and powerful. But they had to fight hard to defend it against the territorially greedy house of Savoy, and the conflicts between the two rumbled on through the 12th and the 14th centuries. In the meantime, the merchant classes were gradually gaining in wealth and power, building up their independence by freeing themselves whenever possible from the feudal lordship of the bishops.

This prosperity was given a boost at the beginning of the 15th century by a close commercial alliance between Geneva and the cloth-manufacturing town of Fribourg, about 135 kms. (85 miles) to the northeast. Fribourg textiles found a ready market at Geneva's fairs, the medieval city's greatest source of trade and revenue. But in 1462 Louis

XI of France and his nephew, the Duke of Savoy, put a stop to that by forbidding French merchants to attend the fairs, and at the same time switching the dates of the Lyon fairs to coincide with those at Geneva; steps which virtually brought an end to the city's prosperity.

Almost ruined commercially, torn by internal strife and threatened continually by the increasingly aggressive new Duke of Savoy, Geneva at last appealed for aid to the Swiss Confederation. The Swiss intervened and in 1530 the Duke of Savoy signed a treaty by which, in effect, he agreed to trouble the city no longer. Geneva then concluded an alliance with the cantons of Fribourg and Bern and began to rebuild its economic stability.

But along with this newly found independence came William Farel—a fervent disciple of Zürich's great reformer Zwingli—and with him he brought from Bern all the constricting religious zeal of the Reformation. By 1536, the city had enthusiastically switched from Catholicism to the Protestant faith, said goodbye to the last of the Catholic prince-bishops, and was already under the influence of John Calvin, a French refugee who came to visit Farel and stayed to eclipse him.

Calvin turned Geneva from a lively city into one where theaters were closed, entertainment frowned upon, dancing forbidden, and food and drink regarded only as necessities of life to be taken without indulgence or enjoyment. Banquets, the wearing of jewels, and all forms of finery were forbidden by the Sumptuary Laws. But despite all this Geneva owes a lot to Calvin, for he also made it into a center of French learning, the academy he founded in 1599 being today's university. He also did much to restore the city's commercial prosperity.

All this time, the Duke of Savoy was still coveting Geneva and hoping to restore Catholicism. On the night of December 11th–12th, 1602, he made a surprise attack on the city, in an operation known as the Escalade, since his men attempted to scale the city walls with ladders. They were ignominiously defeated when a housewife, seeing the Savoyards attempting to scale the walls, poured her hot soup over their heads and gave the alarm. This event is commemorated every year by the Festival of the Escalade when uniforms are taken out of museums and worn in reenactments of the battle all over the Old Town. A chocolate version of the soup pot, or *marmite,* is filled with marzipan vegetables for the children, and anyone not in costume will be in fancy dress—despite the cold this is usually one of the liveliest weekends in Geneva!

Although many left the city to escape the narrow austerity and bigotry of Calvinism, a great many others fled *to* the city, principally English, French and Italian refugees, escaping persecution in their own countries. Geneva formed the kind of haven that the New World was to be later. These refugees introduced to the city something of the cosmopolitan atmosphere it has today, as well as bringing with them new crafts and trades, and a keen business sense. Since the 16th century, Geneva has been one of Europe's leading watchmaking and jewelry centers, and the Reformation (which left citizens few leisure activities and little on which to spend their money) allowed for concentration on work and an accumulation of wealth. The city also became one of the main intellectual centers of Europe. Throughout this period,

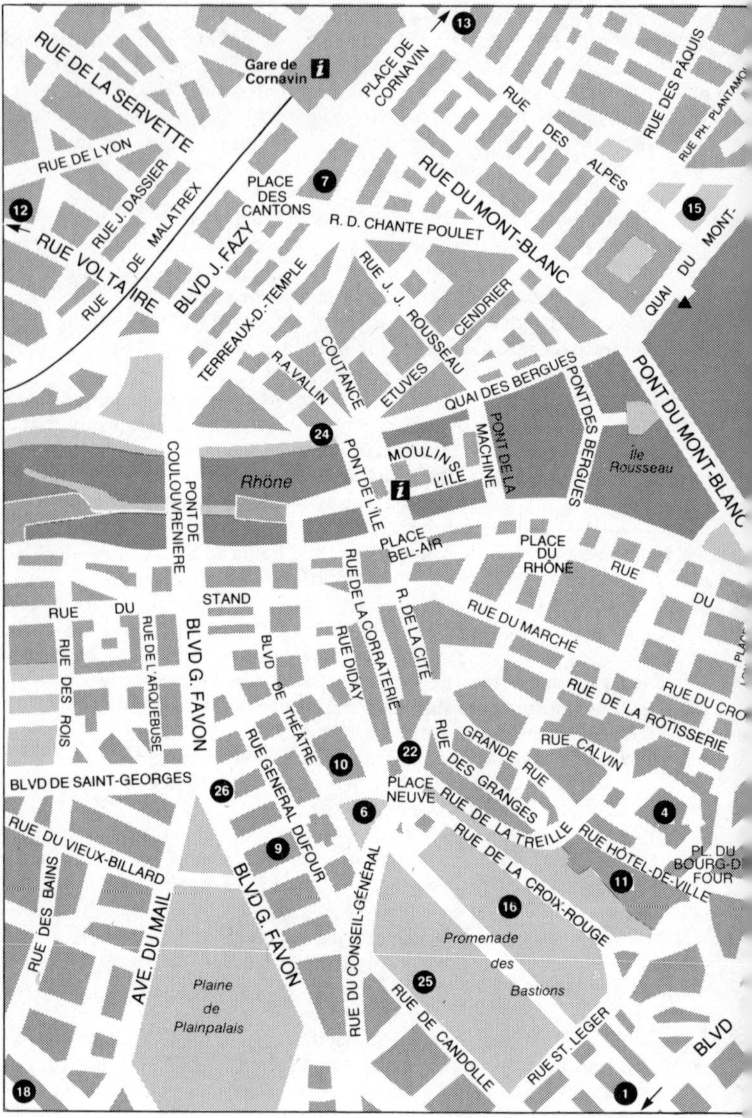
Gare de Cornavin
PLACE DE CORNAVIN
RUE DE LA SERVETTE
RUE DE LYON
RUE J. DASSIER
RUE DE MALATREX
RUE VOLTAIRE
BLVD J. FAZY
PLACE DES CANTONS
R. D. CHANTE POULET
RUE DES ALPES
RUE DU MONT-BLANC
RUE DES PAQUIS
RUE PH. PLANTAMOUR
QUAI DU MONT-
TERREAUX-D.-TEMPLE
RUE J. J. ROUSSEAU
CENDRIER
R. A. VALLIN
COUTANCE
ETUVES
QUAI DES BERGUES
PONT DES BERGUES
PONT DU MONT-BLANC
Île Rousseau
PONT DE LA MACHINE
MOULINS
L'ILE
PONT DE L'ILE
Rhône
PONT DE COULOUVRENIERE
PLACE BEL-AIR
PLACE DU RHÔNE
RUE DU
STAND
RUE DU
RUE DES ROIS
RUE DE L'ARQUEBUSE
BLVD G. FAVON
BLVD DE THÉÂTRE
RUE DIDAY
RUE DE LA CORRATERIE
R. DE LA CITE
RUE DU MARCHÉ
RUE DE LA RÔTISSERIE
RUE DU CRO
RUE CALVIN
GRANDE RUE
RUE DES GRANGES
RUE GENERAL DUFOUR
PLACE NEUVE
RUE DE LA TREILLE
RUE HÔTEL-DE-VILLE
PL. DU BOURG-DE-FOUR
BLVD DE SAINT-GEORGES
RUE DU VIEUX-BILLARD
RUE DES BAINS
AVE. DU MAIL
BLVD G. FAVON
RUE DU CONSEIL-GÉNÉRAL
RUE DE LA CROIX-ROUGE
Promenade des Bastions
Plaine de Plainpalais
RUE DE CANDOLLE
RUE ST. LEGER
BLVD
1
4
6
7
9
10
11
12
13
15
16
18
22
24
25
26

Points of Interest

1 Barbier-Müller Collection
2 Baur Collection
3 Cabinet des Estampes
4 Cathédrale de St. Pierre
5 Collège Calvin
6 Conservatoire de Musique
7 Eglise de Notre Dame
8 Eglise de St. Joseph
9 Eglise du Sacré Coeur
10 Grand Théâtre
11 Hôtel de Ville (City Hall)
12 Institut et Musée Voltaire
13 Jardin Botanique; International Complex
14 Jet d'Eau
15 Monument Brunswick
16 Monument de la Reformation
17 Musée d'Art et d'Histoire
18 Musée d'Ethnographie
19 Musée d'Histoire Naturelle
20 Musée de l'Horlogerie et de l'Emaillerie
21 Musée des Instruments Anciens de Musique
22 Musée Rath
23 Petit Palais
24 Tour de l'Ile
25 Université
26 Victoria Hall

i Tourist Information

▲ Sightseeing Boats (Débarcadère)

however, the city grew less democratic, with the government passing into the hands of a few wealthy aristocrats.

But this was checked in 1798, when this rich but melancholy city was annexed by France during the Revolution, to become the capital of the French Department of Léman. It remained in French hands until 1814, after the fall of Napoleon; and in the following year the city was admitted to the Swiss Confederation as a canton in its own right.

Since then most of the major landmarks in Geneva's history have been connected with international affairs. In 1863 the Red Cross was founded. 1864 saw the first Geneva Convention for the care of war casualties. The city became the home of the League of Nations and the International Labor Office in 1919. In 1946, the United Nations made the city its European headquarters, to be followed by the flood of other international organizations that so distinguish Geneva today.

Exploring Geneva

You can see a considerable part of Geneva's attractions in a single walk by starting off along the broad rue du Mont-Blanc from the Cornavin railroad station to the lake. Here you will be rewarded with a lovely view which, if you are lucky with the weather, includes a distant glimpse of Mont Blanc. It's visible from Geneva about one day out of three. Directly ahead of you, if you are there at the right time, the Jet d'Eau rises like a gigantic plume from a jetty thrusting out into the lake. On a sunny day this towering stream of water, over 130 meters (400 ft.) high, can be seen for miles. Weather permitting it plays daily from March until September.

A right turn takes you along the quai des Bergues, beside the Rhône, which leaves the lake at this point. Beneath the water alongside the opposite bank is a four-story, electronically controlled parking lot capable of taking 1,500 cars. In the center of the river is Rousseau Island, with a statue of the French philosopher Jean-Jacques Rousseau, who was born in Geneva and did so much to popularize both the city and Switzerland in the 18th century. His proud boast was that he was a "citizen of Geneva." Just beyond you will pass the pont de la Machine. Here the crystal-clear Rhône, its waters having lost the mud they carried when entering the eastern end of the lake, tumbles in a tumult of foam over the dam which regulates the level of the lake. By crossing the river at the next bridge, the pont de l'Île, you will pass the Tour de l'Île, a one-time prison dating from the epoch of the bishopric. Today it is almost swallowed up by more modern buildings on either side. The very helpful Tourist Office stands here on the island.

This brings you to the place Bel-Air, the center of the banking and business district. You are now passing into the Vieille Ville, the Old Town, Geneva's historic heart, crowded with lovely old buildings and full of atmosphere. If you cross the place you can follow the rue de la Corraterie to the place Neuve, which is the site of the Grand Théâtre, the Musée Rath, and the Conservatoire de Musique. Just in front of you is the entrance to a park and on your left, bordering the square, a high wall (part of the ancient ramparts) above which is a row of fine old buildings. Enter the park, which contains the university, and keep to your left.

Almost immediately, at the foot of the ramparts, you will come to Geneva's most famous monument, the international memorial to the Reformation. Built between 1909 and 1917, the Reformation Monument is a gigantic wall, over 90 meters (300 feet) long, as impressive for its simplicity and clean lines as for its sheer size. It is worth sitting down on the terrace steps—made of Mont–Blanc granite—which face the wall, to take it all in. The central group consists of four statues of the great leaders of the Reformation—Bèze, Calvin, Farel, and John Knox—each over 4.5 meters (15 feet) high. On either side of these giants are smaller statues (a mere 2.7 meters, 9 feet tall) of other personalities, such as Oliver Cromwell. Between the smaller figures are bas reliefs and inscriptions which tell the story of important events connected with the Reformation. Carved in the wall to the right of Cromwell, you'll see the presentation by the English Houses of Parliament of the Bill of Rights to King William II, in 1689. Above it, in English, are listed the Bill's main features—the guiding principles of democracy. To the left of Cromwell is a bas relief of the Pilgrim Fathers praying on the deck of the *Mayflower* before signing the Mayflower Compact; and further left again another relief shows John Knox preaching with obvious passion in St. Giles Cathedral, Edinburgh.

Museums and Churches

If you leave the park by the gate just beyond the monument and turn left into rue St. Léger, passing under an ivy-hung bridge, and then climb up the winding street, you'll come to the charming place Bourg-de-Four. This dreamy little place was once the crossroads of some important routes which led to southern France via Annecy and Lyon, to Italy, to the Chablais, and elsewhere. Before that it served as a Roman Forum and as a cattle and wheat market. If, in the place, you turn right down rue des Chaudronniers you'll find, not far away on the left, Calvin's College, sponsored by the stern reformer himself in 1559 and now the Cantonal Grammar (High) School.

Straight on down Chaudronniers it's only a short walk to the somewhat formal Musée d'Art et d'Histoire and the Baur Collection, while on the left, looking like a part of Moscow's Red Square, are the golden, onion shaped cupolas of the Russian Church. The Musée d'Art et d'Histoire has excellent temporary exhibitions, and is a good place to come to grips with some of the quiet riches of Swiss art. There is a great tradition of landscape painting, not surprising when you think of the possible subjects roundabout. Even as far back as the 15th century, Konrad Witz, the greatest Swiss painter before Holbein, depicted a scene which is recognizably Lac Léman as a background to an altarpiece now here in the museum. The Baur is especially noted for its Japanese and Chinese collections.

From the place Bourg-de-Four turn left along any of the narrow streets, ramps, and staircases leading up to the Cathédrale St.-Pierre, whose stubby stone towers and green spire will be your guide. The severe interior of the cathedral has undergone extensive restoration, but can now be visited. Climb up the north tower and admire the splendid view. Architecturally, perhaps the most intriguing feature of the building is the extraordinary contrast between the façade, a stern and rather beautiful classical portico, and the splendid Gothic of the rest of the building—a startling juxtaposition of architectural styles. Beneath the cathedral is the St. Pierre archeological site, one of the biggest in Europe and perhaps the most important north of the Alps. It dates from A.D. 1000 with 4th-century mosaics, baptisteries for total immersion and other expressions of early Christian life.

Opposite, the City Hall, dating from the 16th century but restored and enlarged in later years, houses the famous Alabama Hall where, on August 22nd 1864, the Geneva Convention was signed by 16 countries, laying the foundation of the International Red Cross. Eight years later in 1872, a court of arbitration was convened in this same room to settle the Alabama dispute between Great Britain and the United States, easing the latter's unhappiness over British support to Confederate ships during the Civil War.

The winding, cobbled streets leading from the cathedral to the modern city are picturesque and full of antique shops, booksellers, shops specializing in rugs and sculpture, paintings and objets d'art, all of them elegantly expensive. Rue Calvin has a number of 18th-century *hôtels,* the town residences of noble families; No. 11 is on the site of Calvin's house. In rue du Puits-Saint-Pierre, No. 6, the Maison Tavel, is now a museum. The Grand rue is the oldest street in Geneva, mostly medieval. The rue Hôtel-de-Ville, once the headquarters of Italian religious refugees, is lined by 17th-century dwellings built with the craftsmanship typical of their former owners.

On the subject of shopping, at the bottom of the hill below the cathedral, beside the lake and the Jardin Anglais with its flower clock, is Geneva's main shopping district. This centers on the quai Générale-Guisan, rue du Rhône, rue du Croix d'Or, and rue du Marché, where superb shops, fashionable boutiques and the dazzling window displays of jewelers are an irresistible magnet for even the most budget conscious tourist. For those not on a budget, a visit to the glamorous and glittering new Confederation Center in the rue de la Confederation (three levels of boutiques, shops, restaurants, cinemas and the Geneva Stock Exchange) may well be a must. But don't neglect the side streets, where the prices are often noticeably lower.

Parks and the International Complex

From the Jardin Anglais you have two choices. You can turn right along the lakeside, and wander down past the Jet d'Eau, following the quai Gustave-Ador, passing one of the docking points for the sightseeing boats, the Parc de la Grange with its lovely rose gardens, and the Parc des Eaux-Vives, until you reach the marina and swimming place of the Genève-Plage.

Or you could cross over the pont du Mont-Blanc, and turn right onto the quai du Mont-Blanc. Here the lake is bordered by distinguished hotels and more swish boutiques. A little way along is the Monument Brunswick, the tomb of a Duke of Brunswick who died in the city in

1873, left his fortune to Geneva, and had his memorial modeled in high-Victorian style on the Scaglieri monument in Verona. On the right are two embarcation points (Débarcadère) for the boats which ply around the lake, crisscrossing as they go, and which make a wonderful half-day's trip. A little further on a swimming area (the Pâquis-Plage) has been built out over the lake, with changing rooms, restaurants and plenty of space both to swim and sunbathe. Contrary to belief, the summer in Geneva can be very hot, and when it is these pools and terraces are crammed solid.

Your walk could continue, taking in the small parks and modern sculpture—there's a particularly lovely one of a young boy and a horse—until you get to the gardens of the excellent Perle du Lac restaurant.

Here you could turn inland, up the avenue de la Paix. On the right is the Jardin Botanique (Botanical Gardens), open all day, admission free, with interesting collections of Alpine rock plants, hothouses and a deer park. This road will lead you eventually to the international complex—or you could reach it by taxi or bus (0) from the rail station. Take them to the place des Nations. A combined stroll through the attractive grounds and visits to some of the buildings could take several instructive hours. Apart from the main buildings of such organizations as the W.H.O.—with fine arts and crafts donated by member countries—I.C.R.C. (Red Cross), U.N.O.—with a cafe-restaurant looking out onto its park—there are two museums, the Ariana, in a lovely 19th-century house, with a collection consisting mainly of porcelain and ceramics, and the Château de Penthes, the Museum of the Swiss Overseas, also with a cafe-restaurant and a magnificent park.

PRACTICAL INFORMATION FOR GENEVA

GETTING TO TOWN FROM THE AIRPORT. Simple. Geneva's Cointrin airport, located just to the north of the city, has a brand new rail station with regular and fast services into Geneva itself, and on to the rest of the country. Taxis into town, though plentiful, are very expensive and no faster.

TOURIST OFFICES. The city has an excellent and well-organized tourist office (Office du Tourisme de Genève) located in the Cornavin rail station (tel. 022–45 52 00); open Mon. to Sun. 8–10 (July to Sept.), and Mon. to Fri. 8.15–7.30, Sat. 9–6 and Sun. 4–8 during the rest of the year. The station itself is currently being extensively renovated, with shopping malls, restaurants, car park and airport check-in point all being built. Construction work is scheduled to last until 1988.

The office can supply information on all aspects of the city, including the useful *This Week in Geneva* and a quarterly guide to exhibits in the city.

In addition, the Geneva English Language Coordinating Service (GELCOS) produces two excellent publications, the monthly *What's On in Geneva,* giving details of all upcoming events, and the annual *Guide to the English-Speaking Community in Geneva.* Both are available from Philippe Reverdin, 11 rue

Massot, 1206 Geneva (tel. 022–47 25 21). Send a large, stamped self-addressed envelope (50 ct.), or, if writing from abroad, an international reply coupon.

HOTELS. Hotels in Geneva can be a problem. Not that there's any shortage of deluxe and expensive hotels catering for businessmen, diplomats and delegates that crowd the city year round, though even so it's important to make reservations well in advance. The real problem is that there's an alarming lack of more moderately-priced and inexpensive hotels, meaning that it can be necessary to book many months ahead. One solution is to try neighboring France. Both Annemasse in the Haute Savoie and the Ferney/Divonne/St.-Genis area on the French side of the airport have built, and are building, a lot of new hotel accommodations. Call the Syndicat d'Initiative (tourist office) at Gex (tel. 023–50–41–53–85) or Divonne (tel. 023–50–20–12–22) for information.

Both Geneva airport and station have free telephone booths from where you can check on available hotel space and book.

Deluxe

Beau-Rivage, 13 quai du Mont Blanc (tel. 022–31 02 21). 180 beds. One of the world's great hotels, with a marvelous restaurant on the lake *(le Chat Bottée).* Airconditioning and every luxury. AE, DC, MC, V.

Des Bergues, 33 quai des Bergues (tel. 022–31 50 50). 173 beds. Another distinguished and beautifully-run hotel; also overlooks the lake. AE, DC, MC, V.

Bristol, 10 rue de Mont Blanc (tel. 022–32 38 00). 200 beds. Plush and luxurious. Facilities include a health club, and a video in every room. AE, DC, MC, V.

Intercontinental, 7–9 Petit-Saconnex (tel. 022–34 60 91). 704 beds. Vast modern hotel with private suites, pool, sauna, and smart shops; 18 floors and 400 rooms. AE, DC, MC, V.

Metropole, 34 quai Général-Guisan (tel. 022–21 13 44). 206 beds. Elegant and comfortable modern hotel built inside the shell of the original 19th-century Metropole. Excellent food complements the many facilities. AE, DC, MC, V.

Noga-Hilton, 19 quai du Mont Blanc (tel. 022–31 98 11). 446 beds. Part of the fairly new complex on the lake which includes the Grand Casino theater and some very tempting shops. Opposite the American church. Every luxury. AE, DC, MC, V.

Président, 47 quai Wilson (tel. 022–31 10 00). 374 beds. Well decorated, airconditioned, fantastic views from lakeside rooms. AE, DC, MC, V.

Ramada Renaissance, 19 rue de Zürich (tel. 022–31 02 41). 357 beds. Large modern hotel; central, with a nice bistro. AE, DC, MC, V.

La Réserve, 301 route de Lausanne (tel. 022–74 17 41). 110 beds. Just out of town and set in parkland with pool and tennis courts. Quiet, elegant and luxurious. AE, DC, MC, V.

Du Rhône, quai Turretini (tel. 022–31 98 31). 410 beds. Substantial and elegant hotel, with fine restaurant and, as the name suggests, a good view of the river. AE, MC, V.

Le Richemond, Jardin Brunswick (tel. 022–31 14 00). 200 beds. Classy, family-run spot overlooking the lake and boasting every luxury. AE, MC, V.

Expensive

California, 1 rue Gevray (tel. 022–31 55 50). 100 beds. Central but quiet; breakfast only. AE, DC, MC, V.

Cornavin, 33 blvd. James-Fazy (tel. 022–32 21 00). 175 beds. Close to the station—as the name implies—but surprisingly quiet. Breakfast only. AE, MC, V.

Grand-Pré, 35 rue du Grand-Pré (tel. 022–33 91 50). 150 beds. Quiet and efficient. Breakfast only. AE, DC, MC, V.

Rex, 44 av. Wendt (tel. 022–45 71 50). 143 beds. Central, unpretentious. AE, DC, MC, V.

Royal, 41 rue de Lausanne (tel. 022–31 36 00). 300 beds. Ask for a quiet room; near the station. AE, DC, MC, V.

Moderate

Amat-Carlton, 22 rue Amat (tel. 022–31 68 50). 190 beds. T.V. in all rooms. AE, DC, MC, V.

Athénée, 6 route de Malagnou (tel. 022–46 39 33). 80 beds. Good value; central. AE, DC, MC, V.

Drake, 32 rue Rothschild (tel. 022–31 67 50). 60 beds. Central but quiet. AE, DC, MC, V.

Eden, 135 rue de Lausanne (tel. 022–32 65 40). 80 beds. Near the Palais des Nations. AE, DC, MC, V.

Inexpensive

Astoria, 6 pl. Cornavin (tel. 022–32 10 25). 95 beds. Handy for the station. Breakfast only. AE, DC, MC, V.

Bernina, 22 pl. Cornavin (tel. 022–31 49 50). 110 beds. Good value. Recommended. AE, MC, V.

International et Terminus, 20 rue des Alpes (tel. 022–32 80 95) 80 beds. With good grill restaurant. AE, DC, MC, V.

Lido, 8 rue Chantepoulet (tel. 022–31 55 30). 60 beds. Centrally located, but quiet. Breakfast only. AE, DC, MC, V.

Rivoli, 6 rue des Pâquis (tel. 022–31 85 50). 85 beds. Central, well managed and comfortable. Studios with kitchenette. Gardens. Breakfast only. AE, MC, V.

RESTAURANTS. Geneva is a veritable gourmet's paradise—indeed it is almost impossible to eat badly here. The range of restaurants is vast: French—both classical and *nouvelle*—Italian, Indian, Chinese, Japanese—even Swiss! Prices can, however, be high; in the top spots excessively so, though, as we say, standards are superb.

But this does not mean that you can't eat well and inexpensively. Nearly all restaurants, including the really expensive ones, offer a *plat du jour,* or daily dish, that will be both nourishing and good value. Best places to try are the little bistrots on just about any street. Also good value, although more expensive, is the *menu,* the fixed-price meal, that most restaurants offer for lunch.

For other inexpensive meals try the canteens of the international organizations: you'll find good food, low prices, and, often as not, excellent wines. The Migros chain also offers good-value, alcohol-free meals in their larger restaurants: the outdoor terrace in the Balexert shopping mall is particularly good in the summer. Finally, anyone yearning for home can be consoled by the knowledge that Geneva also boasts three McDonalds.

Our lists here are no more than the tip of the iceberg. We have not, for example, listed hotel restaurants; not because they are not to be recommended—most are outstanding—but because they are easy to identify. Similarly, the adventurous might well be tempted to visit France for a meal. Full lists of restaurants are available from the tourist office or from the Elm Book Shop—an English-language book store—at 5 rue Versonnex (tel. 022–36 09 45).

Expensive

Auberge des Trois Bonheurs, 39 route Florissant (tel. 022–47 25 23). Many locals claim this has the best Chinese food in town. AE, V.

Cheval-Blanc, 1 route de Meinier, Vandoeuvres (tel. 022–50 14 01). Excellent Italian food, outstanding dessert trolley where it is quite in order to ask for a selection of fatmanizers!

Moulin des Evaux, 50 chemin François-Chavaz, Onex (tel. 022–93 22 55). Hard to believe you are so near the city center as the countryside stretches in all directions around you. Comfortable and good food. AE, MC, V.

A l'Olivier de Provence, 13 rue Jacques-Dalphin, Carouge (tel. 022–42 04 50). Good French food, outdoors in summer. AE, DC, MC, V.

Moderate

Les Armures, 1 rue Puits-St.-Pierre (tel. 022–28 34 42). Traditional Swiss food and atmosphere right by the canons in the Old Town. MC.

Cent Suisses, 18 rue de Pregny (tel. 022–34 48 65). Opposite the U.S. mission. Excellent *plats du jour* and outstanding open pies for dessert. Only disadvantage is the local birds who know there is a delicious salad bar outside in the summer.

Creux de Genthod, 29 route de Creux de Genthod (tel. 022–74 10 06). Right on the lake where you can share the view of the Alps with the swans and eat outside when it is fine. Perfect setting for the Geneva specialty of *filets de perche* (lake fish).

La Matze, 7 rue Chaponnière (tel. 022–32 79 61). Eat *charbonnade* here—thin slices of beef charcoal-grilled at the table with sauces (similar to *fondue bourguinogne* but less heavy on the stomach). AE, DC, MC, V.

Pavillon de Ruth, quai Cologny (tel. 022–52 14 38). Old-fashioned and delightful. Overlooking the lake.

Vieux-Bois, 12 av. de la Paix (tel. 022–33 03 30). At one of the entrances to the U.N. You get good food in pretty surroundings and it should be perfectly served as this is a hotel school.

Inexpensive

Des Banques, 6 rue Hesse (tel. 022–21 44 98). Particularly good for the welcome it gives people wanting to dine very early or very late because of the nearby Grand Theater and Victoria Hall.

Cave Valaisanne et Chalet Suisse, 23 blvd. Georges-Favon (tel. 022–28 12 36). Large, cheerful and a lot of fun. DC, MC.

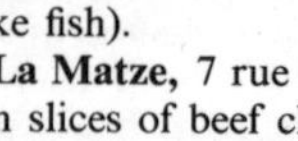

GETTING AROUND. By Public Transport. Geneva has an excellent network of trams, buses and trolley buses, the whole extremely efficient and remarkably inexpensive. Every bus stop has a machine selling tickets, and for Fr. 1.50 you can use the system for one hour, changing as often as you want. If you plan to travel frequently, buy a card (there's usually a newsstand displaying a *TPG* sign near the stop); this costs Fr. 8 for six trips. You put the card into a machine to have it validated just before you get onto a bus or a tram. Fines for not having a ticket are hefty, and the driver only sells tickets in country areas where there are no machines. Fares into the country are a bit more expensive. Politeness, cleanliness and reliability are commonplace throughout the system, and maps of the network are clear and easy to understand.

By Taxi. Taxis, too, are immaculate and the drivers polite, but Geneva residents often complain that they have the most expensive taxi system in the world—and they may well be right. Call 022–21 22 23 or 94 71 11, or simply 141. It won't be cheap.

On Foot. On a nice day (and there are plenty in both winter and summer) Geneva is a perfect city to walk around. It's not too big, and the lake and dozens of parks absorb traffic noise. And don't be afraid of being mugged—even little old ladies are perfectly happy to walk alone in the dark!

TOURS AND EXCURSIONS. City Tours. For further details of all tours in and around the city contact the tourist office in the rail station. For Fr. 5 the tourist office will provide audio-cassette tours of the Old Town, complete with map; a returnable deposit of Fr. 50 is payable on all cassette machines. These tours last as long as you want them too, and take in all the major sites of the Old Town.

Guided bus tours around the city are operated by Key Tours (tel. 022–31 41 40) and leave from the bus station in the pl. Dorcière behind the English church. Tours leave at 9.30, 10, 2 and 2.30 (2 only in winter) and last two hours. Cost Fr. 19.

Private guides are also available. Rates are generally Fr.90 for two hours, but daily rates may also be arranged. Call 022–45 52 00 or contact the tourist office.

The U.N. runs a highly professional visitor service with guided tours around the Palais des Nations. Enter by the Pregny Gate in the av. de la Paix. Tours are given regularly from 10–12 and 2–4 (9–12 and 2–6 in July and Aug.) and last around an hour. Fr. 5 per person.

Excursions. Trips on Lac Léman are one of the perennial pleasures of Geneva, though *not* if the weather is bad. A vast variety of sailings is available, from a quick tour round the city end of the lake, lasting less than an hour, to a day-long trip around almost the whole lake. All the longer sailings make frequent stops, allowing you to get off the boat for sightseeing, shopping or lunch and then catch a later boat. Full details from Mouettes Genevoises (tel. 022–32 29 44), Swiss Boat (tel. 022–32 47 47); Compagnie Générale de Navigation (tel. 022–21 25 21); or the tourist office.

An exotic—and expensive—variation on the everyday business of sightseeing is provided by Air-Glaciers (tel. 022–98 92 76). For Fr. 60 per person, they offer brief flights over the city, or, for Fr. 1,350 for seven people, they will fly you down the lake to the Théodule Glacier under the Matterhorn.

Regular bus tours out of town are numerous—to Lausanne, Mont Blanc, the Château de Chillon and elsewhere in and around Lac Léman.

MUSEUMS AND GALLERIES. Geneva is rich in museums, the most important of which we have listed here. Most have temporary exhibits, public lectures, slide shows, etc. A monthly publication available from the tourist office—though, unfortunately, only in French—called *Musées, Bibliotèques, Musique, Spectacles, Expositions* details all major exhibits and art shows.

Museums in Geneva are surprisingly inexpensive, and many are free.

Barbier-Müller Collection, 4 rue Ecole de Chimie (tel. 022–20 02 53). Primitive art. Open Tues. to Sat. 2:30–5:30.

Baur Collection, 8 rue Munier-Romilly (tel. 022–46 17 29). Fine collection of Chinese and Japanese ceramics, jades, prints, etc. Open daily 2–6. Closed Mon.

Cabinet des Estampes (Print Room), 5 Promenade du Pin (tel. 022–20 10 77). Marvelous series of contemporary exhibits. Open daily 10–12 and 2–6. Closed Mon. Admission Fr. 3.

Centre d'Art Contemporain (Contemporary Art Center), Palais Wilson, 52 rue des Paquis (tel. 022–31 39 56). Changing exhibits. Open Tues. to Fri. 2–7, Sat. 1–5. Closed Mon.

Centre Genèvois de l'Artisant (Geneva Crafts Center), 26 Grand Rue (tel. 022–21 29 41). Changing exhibits. Open Mon. 2–6:30, Tues. to Fri. 10–6:30, and Sat. 10–5. There is also a shop at 2 av. du Mail (tel. 022–29 11 44) which is open 9–6:45 (Mon. from 2).

Centre Genèvois de Gravure Contemporaine (Geneva Center for Comtemporary Prints), 17 route de Malagnou (tel. 022–35 12 60). Open Mon. and Tues. 2–9, Wed. to Fri. 2–6.

Centre Genèvois de la Photographie (Geneva Photographic Center), Salle Simon-I.-Patino, Cité Universitaire, 46 av. de Miremont (tel. 022–47 50 33). Changing exhibits. Open daily 2–6.

Château de Penthes, 18 chemin de l'Impératrice, Chambesy. Two museums: **Musée des Suisses à l'Etranger** (Museum of the Swiss Overseas), tel. 022–34 90 21. What the Swiss have been doing abroad since the Middle Ages; and the **Musée Militaire Genèvoise** (Geneva Military Museum), tel. 022–33 53 81. Particular emphasis on local hero General Dufour.

Halles de l'Ile (Covered Marketplace), 1 pl. de l'Ile, pl. Bel-Air. There are three exhibition halls in this recently converted group of buildings: **Halle Sud** and **Espece Un** (same tel. 022–28 46 20). The exhibitions change regularly and include sculpture, photographs, etc. Open Tues. to Fri. 11–5. Closed Sun. and Mon. Also the **Centre d'Art Visuel** (Visual Arts Center), tel. 022–29 60 00.

Institut et Musée Voltaire (Voltaire Museum), 25 rue des Délices (tel. 022–44 71 33). Voltaire's home. Open Mon. to Fri. 2–5.

Maison Tavel (Tavel House), 6 rue du Puits-St.-Pierre (tel. 022–28 29 00). Town life during the 14th–16th centuries. Open daily 10–5. Closed Mon.

Musée Ariana, 10 av. de la Paix (tel. 022–34 29 50). The land on which the Palais des Nations was built was the garden of this beautiful house. It is now a porcelain museum in the process of being restored. The work should be finished by 1988: call to find out.

Musée d'Art et d'Histoire (Art and History Museum), 2 rue Charles-Galland (tel. 022–29 00 11). Fine permanent collection of archeological objects, paintings and sculpture; particularly strong in the decorative arts. Temporary shows, lectures, etc. Open daily 10–5. Closed Mon.

Musée d'Ethnographie (Ethnographic Museum), 65 blvd. Carl-Vogt (tel. 022–28 12 18). Permanent and temporary exhibits. Open daily 10–12 and 2–5. Closed Mon.

Musée d'Histoire Naturelle (Natural History Museum), route de Malagnou (tel. 022–35 91 30). Everything you would expect to find in a large, purpose-built museum of this kind. Regular film shows, cafeteria. Open daily 10–5. Closed Mon.

Musée de l'Horlogerie et de l'Emaillerie (Watch, Clock and Enamels Museum), 15 route de Malagnou (tel. 022–36 74 12). Permanent exhibit of good timepieces and enamels. Open daily 10–12 and 2–6. Closed Mon. morning.

Musée des Instruments Anciens de Musique (Old Musical Instrument Museum), 23 rue Lefort (tel. 022–49 95 65). Three hundred 16th–19th-century musical instruments. Also, ask for details about the costumed concerts. Open Tues. 3–6, Thurs. 10–12 and 3–6, and Fri. 8–10 P.M. or by appointment. Admission Fr. 1.

Musée Rath, pl. Neuve (tel. 022–28 56 16). Temporary exhibits of the highest quality. Open daily 10–12 and 2–6 (also 8–10 P.M on Wed.). Closed Mon. morning. Admission never more than Fr. 5 (depending on the exhibit).

Petit Palais, 2 terrasse Saint-Victor (tel. 022–46 14 33). Modern art from the 19th century onwards. Also loan exhibits. Open daily 10–12 and 2–6. Closed Mon. morning. Admission Fr. 5.

PARKS. Conservatoires et Jardin Botaniques (Botanical Gardens), 192 rue de Lausanne (tel. 022–32 69 69). One of the best of its kind, with a tiny zoo. Many of the buildings have recently been replaced. Gardens open during daylight hours; buildings 9–11 and 2–4.30 (not Fri.).

SHOPPING. Geneva is a shopper's paradise. Clothes? Of course. It is alleged that every major European couturier has an outlet here; and it may be true. Certainly, if it is high fashion you want, start at **Bon Genie,** 34 rue de Marché, a luxury department store filled with lovely things. After that, you can walk in every direction and find ever more tempting possibilities. The top of the heap is probably **Anita Smaga** on the rue de Rhône which sells Saint Laurent and the like. At the cheaper end of the market there are plenty of **Benettons,** while, cheaper still, there are several **Hennes et Mauritz.** Leather goods are of excellent quality, the bookshops are good, and cameras are often cheaper than in the Far East. Happy shopping!

But, of course, most shoppers here want at least three of Switzerland's specialties—chocolate, army knives and watches. Geneva's chocolate shops are outstanding: **Du Rhone** at 3 rue de la Confederation, **Teuscher** in the Confederation Center, **Mont Blanc** at 4 rue de Mont Blanc, **Haefliger** at 27 rue Lamartine, **Bergues** at 27 quai Bergues, and, in particular, **Rohr** at 3 pl. Molard and in the covered passageway at 42 rue du Rhône. Rohr's windows are memorable: at circus time there are masses of chocolate elephants, in the fall there are chestnuts and so on. While in the complex of passageways aim for **Passage Malbuisson;** as the clock strikes the hour a marvelous mechanical timepiece comes into action with soldiers and horses crossing the terrain to the sound of a carillon. Swiss army knives are on sale at all department stores, stationers, etc.

Watches can be bought everywhere: Swatches are cheaper in Switzerland than overseas. The latest present to take home is a Clip. Designed in Geneva there are masses of pretty designs to choose from—all at Fr. 50 each. Another status symbol in timekeeping is the rather more expensive Rockwatch—made from a piece of Swiss rock. After these, you have to go to ever more exclusive jewelers to buy ever more expensive watches. You can, of course, also buy beautiful jewelry—all the famous makes are here, but visit **Gilbert Albert** at 24 rue Corraterie. His peers consider him one of the best in the world.

Legislation in Britain several years ago required offshore vendors to pay duty and sales tax on all modern items offered for auction. As a result, Switzerland became a duty-free marketplace for the major British auction houses: Christie's, Sotheby's and Phillip's all set up in Geneva to sell jewels, watches, silver, small enamels and the like. There are major auctions held every year in May and November. It's all very glamorous and lots of fun. And, as at all auctions, prices can vary enormously. Call Christie's, 8 pl. Taconnerie (tel. 022–28 25 44); Sotheby's, 24 rue de la Cité (tel. 022–21 33 77); and Phillip's, 6 rue de la Cité (tel. 022–28 68 28) for more detailed information about dates.

All the best shopping is in the Old Town and in or off the rue du Rhône. In summer you can sit outside, sipping a cooling drink and watching the flower market in the pl. du Môlard; in winter you can warm your hands on hot chestnuts, the smell of which wafts from every corner. All very pleasant.

For inexpensive and cheerful presents, the department stores and supermarkets both have a lot to offer. The Swiss want you to spend your money so they make it as attractive as possible to linger in their stores. There are lots of places to eat, drink, sit, change the baby, leave the baby; and carts can be pushed to your car in underground car lots so you don't even get wet. It definitely beats fighting your way down Fifth Avenue.

MUSIC, MOVIES AND THEATERS. Music. Geneva boasts a rich and varied musical life. The Orchestre Suisse Romande has its home here and gives weekly concerts throughout the season. The usual venue is the **Victoria Hall,** rue Joseph-Hofnung (tel. 022–28 35 73). The **Grand Casino,** 19 quai de Mont Blanc (tel. 022–32 06 00) is a relatively new concert hall and theater in which the world's top musicians give concerts on a regular basis. **Radio-Suisse Romande** at 66 blvd. Carl Vogt (tel. 022–29 23 33) has a concert hall, and audiences are welcome at the live broadcasts. Concerts also take place at the **Conservatoire de Musique,** pl. Neuve (tel. 022–21 89 71).

Most glamorous of all venues is the **Grand Theâtre,** also in the pl. Neuve (tel. 022–21 23 18), home of Geneva's opera, some of the best in Europe. Tickets are very hard to come by, however, and are often booked up months in advance, though you may sometimes be able to get returns. More accessible are the chamber music concerts held in its foyer on Sunday mornings in the season.

In the summer the city sponsors an open-air concert season in the Old Town, and there are organ recitals in the cathedral and other churches, particularly at the Temple de la Fusterie every Saturday at 5.

The Swiss love brass bands and there are plenty of concerts in the parks during the summer. Jazz is also very popular and the concerts every Saturday night at the **Halles de l'Ile,** pl. de l'Ile are well worth a visit.

Movies. Geneva has numerous movie theaters. Most films are shown in their original language; look for the letters "v.o.", meaning *version originale.* Listings are given in the tourist office's *This Week in Geneva.*

Theater. Though the theater plays an important part in Geneva's cultural scene, most visitors will find it somewhat difficult of access, as performances are in French. But full details are available from the tourist office. Ballet has been growing in importance over the last five years. Visiting companies are a regular feature—they usually perform at the Grand Casino—while the ballet company at the Grand Thêatre also gives performances.

English theater is surprisingly lively in Geneva. There are three different groups which present 11 full-stage productions between September and June, plus all sorts of other events. Their leaflet *Theater in English* is available at the tourist office and most hotels. Though amateur, productions are of high quality.

NIGHTLIFE. Despite a strong Protestant tradition, there is plenty of sophisticated nightlife in Geneva, with cabarets, discos and places to dance to suit every reasonably well-stuffed purse and every taste, however exotic. The best known are the **Ba-Ta-Clan,** 15 rue de la Fontaine (tel. 022–29 64 98), **Maxim's,** 2 rue Thalberg (tel. 022–32 99 00) and **La Garconnière,** 15 rue de la Cité (tel. 022–28 21 61).

Most of Geneva's young, with the not-so-young in hot pursuit, would rate **La Macumba** in St. Julien-en-Genèvois just over the French border (cross at Perly) as the most lively nightspot. It claims to be the biggest disco in Europe, which indeed it might be. Attractions change so call 023–50–49–23–50 for details.

Bars are everywhere and some of the best are to be found in hotels. **La Coupole,** 116 rue du Rhône (tel. 022–36 16 82) is an attractive venue with piano music from 7 P.M. **L'Arbalète,** 3 rue Tour Maîtresse (tel. 022–28 41 55) is now open on Sunday evenings. Geneva's newest yuppy rendezvous is the **Cactus Club,** tel. 022–32 63 98, underneath **Mañana** at 3 rue Chaponnière (tel. 022–32 21 31). It was started as a marketing exercise by two students at the Geneva campus of Webster University and serves magnificent cocktails at all hours of the day or night.

Geneva does now have a casino in the Grand Casino complex but, as everywhere in Switzerland, the maximum stake is Fr. 5. If you want to live a little more dangerously cross the border to Divonne, which has the biggest turnover of all casinos in France. Evian, also in France on the southern shore of Lac Léman, likewise has a casino.

SPORTS. Winter Sports. Though Geneva itself is no winter sports center, there are plenty of skiing opportunities within an hour or so of the city center. Nearest is the village of Crozet in France. While not in the international class, it is well worth the 15-minute drive. The Col de la Faucille, above Gex, is slightly further, has some good runs, connects with the area on the other side of the Jura and, with luck, offers a most stunning panorama of the Alps from the restaurant at the top.

Otherwise, choose between some of the world's best skiing: take the expressway toward Chamonix and turn left or right to Megève, Flaine, Les Gets, Les Carroz, etc., etc.

Skating. There are two skating rinks open from October to March: Patinoire des Vernets, quai des Vernets (tel. 022–43 88 50) and Patinoire de Meyrin (open-air), chemin Louis Rendu (tel. 022–82 13 00).

Windsurfing. Windsurfing *(planche à voile)* is the current passion. You can hire equipment or take lessons from many places including Ecole de Voile du Léman, opposite 44 quai Gustave Ador (tel. 022–35 22 63).

Sailing. This is also very popular. Both the Ecole Club Migros, 3 rue du Prince (tel. 022–28 65 55) and the Centre Culturel Coop, 35 rue des Pâquis (tel. 022–31 26 50) offer courses.

Hang-gliding. This is another sport that has its addicts. If you want to do more than watch (top of the Salève is a good place) call the tourist office to find out how to make your appointment with fear!

Golf. The Golf Club de Genève at 70 route de la Capite, Cologny (tel. 022–35 75 40) accepts visitors and will hire out all equipment.

Riding. You can ride at plenty of venues including Société de Nouveau Manège de Genève, La Pallanterie, route de Thonon, Vesenaz (tel. 022–52 38 44), or have a lesson in English at the Club Hippique International de St. Georges at Naz Dessus, near Gex, in France (tel. 023–50–41–02–56).

Swimming. When high summer hits Geneva it rapidly becomes obvious that there are nothing like enough open-air swimming pools. The best complex is the one at Meyrin (a skating rink in winter) in chemin Louis Rendu (tel. 022–82 13 00). Geneva residents are firmly divided into two camps: those who swim in the lake and have done so for years, and those filled with dire predictions about the cystitis, strep throat and such like that you'll get from entering its polluted waters. Choose as you will. Divonne has a lush pool complex and also a small lake, made from the gravel pits created during the construction of the expressway. First on the right after customs.

Tennis. The whole of Europe has gone tennis-mad in the last ten years or so, and even in Geneva, where every square meter of empty terrain is considered primarily for its potential to support a bank or an apartment building, there are plenty of tennis courts being built. However, there are nothing like enough to meet the demand. Even so, visitors are welcomed at some clubs, particularly the New Sporting Club, 51 route de Collex, Bellevue (tel. 022–74 15 14) and the Tennis du Bois Carré, 204 route de Veyrier, Carouge (tel. 022–84 30 06).

Jogging. The days when American businessmen trying to jog off their jet lag were refused reentry to their fancy hotels for breakfast are over. Genevans of all nationalities are addicted to jogging and pound their way up and down the shores of the lake. Join them in their fun.

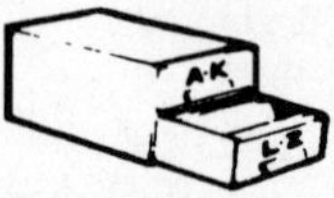

USEFUL ADDRESSES. Consulates. *Canada,* 8 av. de Budé (tel. 022–33 90 00); *U.K.,* 37 rue de Vermont (tel. 022–34 38 00); *U.S.,* 11 route de Pregny (tel. 022–99 02 11).

Travel Agents. *American Express,* 7 rue de Mont Blanc (tel. 022–31 76 00) and elsewhere; *Cooks,* 64 rue de Lausanne (tel. 022–31 32 85) and elsewhere.

Car Hire. *Avis,* 42 rue de Lausanne (tel. 022–31 90 00); *Budget,* 35 rue de Zürich (tel. 022–32 04 07); *Hertz,* 60 rue de Berne (tel. 022–32 83 28). All also have desks at the airport.

Emergencies. *Hôpital Cantonal,* 24 rue Micheli-du-Crest (tel. 022–22 61 11).

THE TICINO

Canton of Contrasts

There is one thing of which you can be sure in the Ticino. It will be different. This is where Switzerland suddenly becomes Italian, but stays Swiss just the same, where the cuisine is Italian flavored, where the language is Italian, where the church architecture and the villages seem to have been imported from Lombardy, where one can imagine that someone has uprooted the azaleas and rhododendrons from Italian gardens and replanted them, where even the climate seems to have been borrowed from the Mediterranean.

It is the only Swiss canton to lie entirely south of the Alps, the one where exuberant Italian *brio,* love of life and boisterous participation in it, has been blended with the disciplining of Swiss efficiency. It has more hours of sunshine than any other part of Switzerland, Locarno topping the league with nearly 2,300.

Color, color all the way, and most of it unspoiled. Statistics tell the story. It is the fourth Swiss canton in size, but only tenth in order of population. That means that here, more than most other regions of Switzerland, nature is unbruised by human hand. Yet you are never far from modern sophistication. You can be alone amid the primitive wonders of the mountains at mid-day and strolling along the fashionable boulevards or in the shopping complexes by Lugano's blue lake in the afternoon. And the ride will have taken you through a glorious panorama of Alpine scenery.

The Ticino is contradictions and contrasts. High amid the silence of the mountains, it is impossible to believe that banking is one of its principal occupations. But it is. Lugano is Switzerland's fourth most important financial center after Zürich, Geneva and Basel. Contrasts? The seasons tumble over each other. In early October, you will find summer flowers still flourishing in full glory along the lakeside walks of Lugano and Locarno while the russet leaves of fall form a carpet and, above, the winter snows are already gleaming white on the mountains, turning softly to pink as the sun goes down.

Sometimes the contrasts in the mountains tell a story. In the 19th century there was a mass emigration from the valleys to France, Italy and beyond in search of employment. Even today, some of these valleys have a population only half that of the 1850s. But the call of the homeland was too much for some, who came back bringing a higher standard of living and a new way of life with them. There is a building in the Val Blenio which tells the story at a glance, a handsome villa on to which abuts a working class dwelling. Two brothers once lived there. One emigrated to France and then came back. The other stayed home.

Those emigrants brought back more than personal prosperity. They cast their influence on the language as well. In the valleys not only is the dialect quite different from the Italian spoken elsewhere. There are words that are unique, brought home by those returning families. Some are French in derivation, some even have their roots in English. English itself is not widely spoken in the valleys, although it is naturally in general use in the resorts. But its very scarcity opens the window on another charming characteristic of the Ticino, the spontaneous kindness of its people. Wait a moment, and they will produce somebody who *can* speak English, and all is explained. And this is often the passport to friendship. The Ticinese enjoy getting to know people, and it can be fun.

Ticino Approaches

The Ticino belonged to Italy until 1512, when the Swiss Confederation took it, and dominated it until 1803. Then, during the confusion of Napoleon's campaigns, it emerged as a free canton, before rejoining the Confederation.

In shape, it is like a triangle standing on its head and digging into Italy. The easiest approach by air used to be to fly to Milan, and then travel the short distance north by road or rail. But the development of Crossair's services, linking Lugano's small airport with the international Swiss airports of Basel, Bern, Geneva and Zürich with daily flights, means you can now get to the Ticino with one change.

If you approach the Ticino from the north by road or rail, you will take the historic St. Gotthard route. This, indeed, is in some ways preferable to an approach from the south, because it throws in your face at once the dramatic change of culture. By road, you will pass through the longest motorway tunnel in the world, nearly 17 kms. (10 miles) of it, carrying that superb highway that now runs all the way from

Hamburg in north Germany to Reggio Calabria in southern Italy, Mediterranean and Baltic linked.

Ticino, in short, is a canton of variety, whose rich foliage bears witness to its climate, its resorts to a well-organized tourist industry, its castles to a turbulent history, its numerous folk museums to an affection for its way of life, then and now.

EXPLORING THE TICINO—Lugano

The view from Lugano's waterfront on a fine day (and most of them are) is unforgettable. No wonder they call it "the Queen of the Ceresio" and "the Rio de Janiero of the old world." The lake is a shimmering blue, studded with white sails, ruffled by the wakes of the launches that ply from shore to shore. Flowers and tropical plants abound. The mountains, tipped with white, are a dramatic backcloth. Close at hand, flanked with green meadows, Monte Brè and Monte Salvatore stand like jealous guards of the treasures beneath.

Lugano has superb hotels and restaurants and as enticing a shopping center as you could wish. Opportunities for all holiday sports are plentiful. But there is little of the noisy clamor you expect of a top holiday resort. Lugano is leisurely. There are really two Luganos. Sophisticated, modern Lugano is one. Lugano of the old-world charm is the other, its arcades and twisting streets so reminiscent of a small Italian town.

It has long been inhabited. The Liguri were here 2,300 years ago, and the Romans followed. By the Middle Ages it was under the lordship of Como. Then the Swiss Confederation got their hands on it, and a not always easy relationship followed. It became part of the canton of Ticino in 1803.

It has entertainment of all types. One of the most distinguished is the *Primavera Concertistica* throughout April and May, a music festival which attracts the world's top orchestras. There is jazz at Easter, plus theaters, cinemas, and nightclubs.

Exploring Lugano

Start from the piazza Riforma, with its neo-Classical town hall, built in 1844. From here, thread your way through old streets to the cathedral of San Lorenzo, where, from the terrace you have a fine view of city and lake. The cathedral has a Renaissance exterior but more important is Santa Maria degli Angioli in the piazza Luini (junction of the via Nassa and the lakeside promenade). Bernardino Luini's greatest work, his *Crucifixion* fresco (1520), faces you as you enter.

But the essential visit for all art lovers is the Villa Favorita at Castagnola, a short tram ride from the center. A 10-minute walk from the entrance through well kept gardens prepares one for the treasures within. Here is the collection of Baron Heinrich von Thyssen, one of the world's finest private galleries. In 20 well-lit rooms are numerous masterpieces from the Middle Ages to the present day. Look particularly for van Eyck's *Annunciation* and Dürer's *Jesus Among the Scribes.*

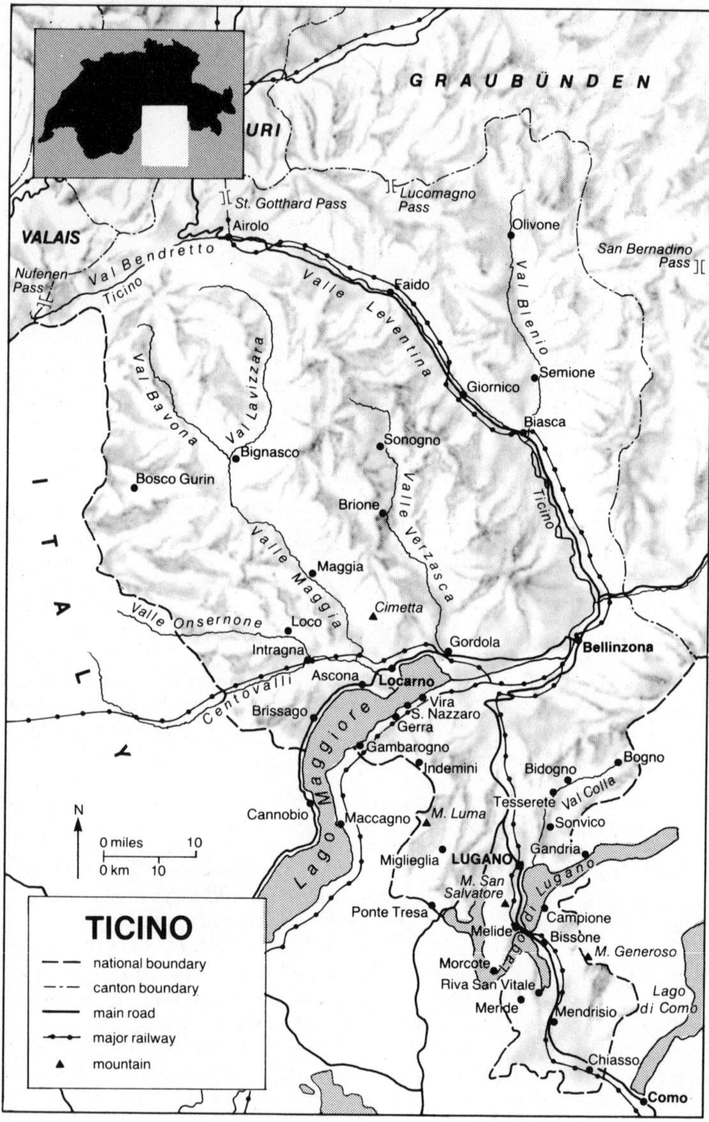
GRAUBÜNDEN
URI
VALAIS
St. Gotthard Pass
Lucomagno Pass
San Bernadino Pass
Nufenen Pass
Airolo
Olivone
Val Bendretto
Ticino
Valle Leventina
Faido
Val Blenio
Val Bavona
Val Lavizzara
Semione
Giornico
Biasca
Sonogno
Bignasco
Bosco Gurin
Brione
Valle Verzasca
Valle Maggia
Maggia
Cimetta
Valle Onsernone
Loco
Gordola
Bellinzona
Intragna
Ascona
Locarno
Centovalli
Brissago
Vira
S. Nazzaro
Gerra
Gambarogno
Indemini
Bidogno
Bogno
Val Colla
Tesserete
Sonvico
Gandria
ITALY
Cannobio
Lago Maggiore
Maccagno
M. Luma
Miglieglia
LUGANO
M. San Salvatore
Lago di Lugano
Ponte Tresa
Campione
Melide
Bissone
M. Generoso
Morcote
Riva San Vitale
Meride
Mendrisio
Lago di Como
Chiasso
Como
N
0 miles 10
0 km 10
TICINO
national boundary
canton boundary
main road
major railway
mountain

Lugano is rightly proud of its parks. The Parco Civico is close to the center. Spreading lawns are fringed by multi-colored flower beds and handsome trees. Concerts are given in the summer, but the park is ideal for relaxation at all times. Located in the park is the Villa Ciani, housing visiting exhibits. The Belvedere garden is smaller, but a little gem. Palms, camellias, oleander, roses and magnolia are the background for 12 modern sculptures purchased by Lugano after an exhibit in 1977. There are also wonderful views of the bay and the mountains. Rose lovers cannot afford to miss the Tassino Park behind the rail station. Deer welcome you as you enter, while inside there are 300 bushes representing 80 varieties. Again, there are the same splendid views. The lakeside is one and a half tree-shaded miles. There is a bust of George Washington, who was never actually in Lugano. One Angelo Brunere sculpted it in 1859 for a Swiss engineer who made a fortune in America. Lugano has a vast lido on the Cassarate side of the Parco Civico. It includes nightclub, gaming room, cinema and theater.

Excursions from Lugano

Monte Generoso is 1,700 meters (about 5,600 ft.) high, and a must. Take the boat to Capolago, then the cogwheel train to the top station. From here there's an easy 250 ft. walk to the summit along a path. There are fabulous views of the Po valley and the Apennines to the south, and of the Alps to the north.

Monte Salvatore (912 meters, about 3,000 ft.) is reached by funicular from Paradiso and offers fine views of the Ticino mountains and valleys. The funicular operates from March to November.

Monte Brè (950 meters, about 3,050 ft.) is Switzerland's sunniest mountain. There are buses every 10 minutes from the center of town to Cassarate, from there a mountain railway. This operates all year.

The Ceresio, the Collina d'Oro and the Malcantone

The Ceresio lies to the southwest of Lugano. This is pastoral Switzerland. There are plenty of holiday amenities, but you will remember it most for its charming villages, leisurely strolls through green woods crisscrossed by footpaths, and the sweetness of its air. Since the Collina d'Oro and the Malcantone have similar characteristics and are adjacent, it's convenient to treat them together.

Immediately west of Lugano, a peninsula runs south like a probing finger. There are parallel ridges, the more spectacular of which is the eastern one starting at Monte San Salvatore and plunging into the lake at Morcote. The western ridge is the more gentle Collina d'Oro, the Golden Hill. If you want to make them separate excursions, then explore the eastern one by leaving Lugano at Paradiso and following the twisting road up to Monte San Salvatore and the western one by taking the road to Sorengo on the outskirts of Lugano, thence to Gentilino.

Gentilino is worth a stop for the view, and for a visit to the cemetery where are buried Bruno Walter, one of the greatest of all conductors, and Nobel prize winner and poet Hermann Hesse who lived in nearby Montagnola.

In either case, go on to Carona, where from the car lot there is one of the finest views of many offered by both journeys. Carona has a distant link with Leonardo da Vinci, for its Romanesque church houses *The Death of John the Baptist* by Solari, one of his pupils. In general, the town is a pleasant vacation center, with delightful botanical gardens.

It is recommended, however, that you make the discovery of this region one complete excursion. In which case, go on through the sheltered woods of the steep road that takes you down to Morcote. Decorated houses and a picturesque waterside setting suggest that Morcote is the sort of place that ought to have an artists' colony. It has.

Allow time to absorb Morcote. Then follow the road round the west side of the peninsula north to Ponte Tresa. If you've left your passport behind, don't cross the bridge. Italy lies ahead. Turn right, follow the river Tresa and make for Monteggio. You are in the Malcantone. This is a lovable, unspoiled area of tiny villages set on hill tops, delicate woodlands and green valleys nestling under a mountainous ridge reaching its peak at Monte Luma, 1,625 meters (5,330 ft.), accessible by chair lift from Miglieglia. From there, you have a choice of roads back to Lugano.

Valli di Lugano

Several quiet valleys invite leisurely discovery north of Lugano. Tesserete, eight kms. (five miles) from Lugano, is the starting point. The villages are drowsy, and there are scores of spots for picnics amid lush meadows dotted with multi-colored wildflowers. There are sign-posted walks through chestnut woods, and the pure air is famous.

Before starting out from Tesserete, it is worth turning west for the nearby village of Ponte Capriasca where the church of Sant' Ambrogio has a fresco which is almost a copy of Leonardo's *Last Supper.* But not quite. It differs in many details, and the artist added two scenes (Christ on the Mount of Olives and the Sacrifice of Abraham). Who was he? Probably Francesco Melzi.

The drive along the Val Colla is full of atmosphere. From Tesserete, the road hugs the mountain side to Bidogno and Bogno at the head of the valley. Turn back on your tracks to return to Lugano, through Sonvico, with its 15th-century church of San Giovanni Battista, and Dino where the church is 12th century.

Campione

This is where the police cars have Swiss number plates, but the policemen inside are Italian; where they pay their taxes to Italy but do it in Swiss francs. In other words, a little bit of Italy that seems to have been left stranded on a Swiss lake, overlooked in all the sordid frontier share-outs of history.

It is directly across the lake from Lugano. In the 8th century, the Lord of Campione gave it to St. Ambrosius of Milan as a present.

Despite all the wars that went on around it, Campione stayed Italian until somebody remembered it at the end of the 18th century. Then it was incorporated in the Cisalpine Republic. Later, it became part of the new Kingdom of Italy. And that's how it has stayed. There are no border frontiers between Campione and Switzerland. Although the territory is politically Italian, the currency, customs, postal and telephone services are all Swiss.

Tiny it may be, but it has exercised an influence out of all proportion to its size. In the Middle Ages the *Maestri Comaceni* were internationally renowned. They were a group of stonemasons, sculptors and architects who came from Campione before emigrating to Milan, there to found an important school whose work included a considerable share in the cathedrals of Milan, Verona, Cremona, Trento and Modena, and even Santa Sofia in Constantinople.

Today, Campione is a magnet for gamblers. Its large, glittering casino winks out its invitation nightly across the water. At Campione, you can squander all you like on roulette, *chemin de fer, baccara* and the rest. In Switzerland, the stakes are limited. Here, they are not.

Gandria, Lake Como and Italy

Somehow, there's a fascination about smuggling even if you've never brought so much as a single cigarette over your allowance through the green Nothing-to-Declare channel. It comes to life at Gandria, a village on the remote shore to the east of Lugano. Here they have opened a smugglers' museum bristling with souvenirs of the days when there was a flourishing smuggling trade between Italy (very close at hand) and Switzerland. There is a certain piquant justice in the fact that the museum is located in a former customs house.

But Gandria hardly needs its museum to attract visitors. It is a picturesque village rising in tiers of narrow alleys from the water's edge. Though tourist orientated, its attraction cannot be denied. A pleasant round trip is to go by boat from Lugano (30 minutes) and walk back by the lakeside path to Castagnola (about 45), from where there are regular trams to Lugano.

From Gandria, you can be in Italy in a few minutes. Just like the smugglers in fact. The road runs from above the village. Alternatively, go by boat from Lugano to Porlezza at the Italian end of Lake Lugano. Then by road to Menaggio, hardly any distance. Close at hand are the glorious gardens of the Villa Carlotta (open all year).

Other visits to Italy are also easy, but remember your passport. To Como itself (frequent trains from Lugano); to Ponte Tresa (see the section on the Malcantone); to Cannobio (short journey on the lakeside road from Ascona or Locarno); or Luino (short drive from Ponte Tresa). Inquire locally about market days; they are always fun in Italy.

The Mendrisiotto and Lower Ceresio

The Mendrisiotto has many claims for attention. It holds a mirror to Ticinese history, right back to prehistoric times. It has the Ticino's oldest building. It has wine. And it has a village which was one of the shortest-lived republics in history.

To reach it, cross the causeway from Melide and pause at Bissone, an entirely delightful little place. First enjoy a lakeside coffee or aperitif, then visit the Casa Tencalla (Tencalla House), a lovely Italian Renaissance building acquired by the Ticino Crafts and Artists Society, and now furnished in the regional style of the 17th century.

Tencalla himself was born here in 1623. He left for Vienna, where he founded a school of painting and architecture, then came back to Bissone where he died in 1685. You can see his frescoes in the church of San Carpoforo. Francesco Borromini, leading architect of the Baroque in Rome, also came from Bissone.

There is more art at Ligornetto. Here was born Vincenzo Vella, whose sculptures decorate many Italian cities, as well as Paris, Lisbon and Istanbul. Much of his work has been assembled in his former home, now the Vincenzo Vella Museum. But before Ligornetto comes Mendrisio, the principal town of the area. Mendrisio has a reputation as the friendliest town in the Ticino, credible because it is the center of the wine industry, and wine towns and wine people in any country are usually warm and happy. Mendrisio lives up to its reputation. But its past has frequently been troubled. It was caught up in the protracted medieval row between the Guelphs and the Ghibellines, respectively supporters of Pope and Emperor. The local ruling Torriani family were Guelphs, frequently battling with the Ghibellines. They won in the end, but only after much bloodshed and slaughter.

Mendrisio has an enchanting atmosphere and is famous for its colorful processions. On Maundy Thursday, that depicting Christ's journey to Calvary is held, with knights on horseback, Roman soldiers and Biblical characters, all passing under archways of 17th-century banners hung from windows and balconies. That on Good Friday is a deeply moving torchlight parade recalling the events of the Crucifixion. There are historic monuments including the Chiesa di San Giovanni and the Palazzo Torriani-Fontana.

But something much older than anything Mendrisio can offer can be found in Riva San Vitale. This is the 5th-century baptistery, with a large stone baptismal font for baptism by immersion from the same century. Riva San Vitale gets into the book of records for another reason. Its people objected to the boundaries drawn up in 1798, and the village declared itself an independent republic. Nobody seems to have noticed or cared for 14 days. Then the news seeped through, and a small cantonal army was sent to sort things out. They did, and the brief republic was no more.

Nearby Monte San Giorgo has yielded fossils thousands of years old. They are on show at Melide. The Mendrisiotto and the lower Ceresio countryside shelter many Italianate villages clustered around ancient bell towers. Fall is particularly lovely here. Monte Generoso (1,700 meters, about 5,600 ft.) has quite wonderful views, and is reached by cogwheel railway from Carpolago.

Locarno

Locarno has style. Romance, too. It has a subtropical climate, it is kissed by the blue waters of Lake Maggiore, an enchanting background for its riotously varied flowers. Behind it, the vineyards rise in terraced discipline. It has more hours of sunshine than any other town in Switzerland. It makes a mockery of seasonal divisions. When the grapes have ripened, the bathers are still bathing. When the spring flowers are at their zenith, at Cardada above the town, the skiers are still skiing.

It does everything a resort ought to do, but does it with discretion. Its most valuable characteristic is its gift for taking a leisured view of life. The old streets recall a Lombardic past. But it has a sense of occasion as well. It welcomes many international artists during its music weeks in the gracious setting of the church of San Francesco, and the summer Locarno Film Festival against the backdrop of the piazza Grande is famous. The pilgrim's church of the Madonna del Sasso nearby is a pearl.

It is steeped in tradition, and has many folk festivals. Steeped in history, too, and not just medieval history. Here, in 1925, Briand, Stresseman, Mussolini and Chamberlain signed the Locarno Pact. It might easily have been called something different, for the story goes that it was to have been held elsewhere but the French minister's mistress insisted on Locarno. If so, one admires her taste. Locarno has known bravery, disaster and hardship. In the 16th century, 60 of her most illustrious families fled to Zürich and Basel (where they started the silk industry) rather than take the Roman Catholic faith. There were disastrous floods, and in 1576 a plague which left only 700 out of a population of 5,000.

Exploring Locarno

Italianate indeed is the handsome piazza Grande, with its gracious sweep of Lombard style houses and arcades, and shops specializing in both antiques and contemporary art, fashions and local handicrafts. Along the lakeside promenade, there are cafes where visitors mingle with the locals engaged in the time-honored mid-morning Italian habit of putting the world right, though they do it less noisily here than in Italy itself. Wisteria and orange blossom line the waterfront.

It makes a refreshing start to a Locarno exploration. The little streets winding tantalisingly down to the piazza or promenade quickly transport you from today and sophistication into old-world corners. If you go for the Baroque, you will find it at its extravagant best in the 17th-century Chiesa Nuova with its giant statue of St. Christopher outside and exuberant angels within. If you are moved by simplicity, the frescoes of Santa Maria in Selva, painted in 1400, will hold you enthralled.

But the most moving experience Locarno has to offer is a visit to the Madonna del Sasso sanctuary, high on a rock but reached in five minutes by funicular from the center of town. Here, in 1480, Brother

Bartolomeo da Ivrea saw a vision of the Virgin. The sanctuary was begun seven years later, and gradually enlarged. Today, it is a haven of peace and contemplation and contains some beautiful 15th-century paintings, including two by Bernadino de Conti and Bramantino's *Flight into Egypt.*

Romanesque and Baroque blend happily in Locarno's churches. Perhaps the most striking is the basilical San Vittore, started in the 11th century. The bas-relief of the saint by Martino Berazione (1462) was found in nearby Muralti castle, partly restored in 1926. Legend has it that the church of San Franceso was founded by St. Anthony of Padua. Rebuilding began in 1538. The emblems of the Renaissance facade show that Locarno was firmly convinced about social distinctions at the time. The eagle represents the aristocrats, the ox the citizens (unkind, surely) and a lamb the countrymen.

Excursions from Locarno

You can be whisked into another world right from the center of Locarno. The funicular takes you to the Madonna del Sasso, its tranquility and panoramic terraces. From there, take the cable car to Cardada, then the chair lift to Cimetta (1,508 meters, about 5,000 ft.). As the lake gradually falls away beneath, you sail over flowery meadows and wooded hills. Always the prospect is changing. From Cardada, there are numerous walks, so too from Cimetta (in winter a busy sports center). There are good restaurants at both, and superb views of Monte Rosa and the Italian Apennines from the top. It's a hiker's paradise.

The Centovalli has the Ticino's highest bell tower (San Gottardo at Intragna, where the valley starts, on the road due west of Locarno) and one of its strangest legends, though, to be accurate, Rè, where it originated, is slightly over the border in Italy. They say that one day the ball from a game of *boccia* (traditional in these parts) struck the face of the Madonna painted on the church wall. A stream of blood appeared. The player responsible fled and became a hermit in the mountains. Italian Rè may be, but on April 30 every year, the people of the Swiss Centovalli join the procession of pilgrims there. It's an easy run by car. But you can also wander through the Centovalli by the little trains that run from Locarno through superb scenery and over gushing rivers, past tumbling waterfalls, to join the classic Milan–Simplon Pass –Paris line at Domodossola.

Centovalli really means "valley of a hundred valleys." Somebody may have got his arithmetic wrong, but there are certainly several gorges branching off into remote corners.

Ascona

How, one might ask, does a small town so close to Locarno (just four kms., two and a half miles) preserve its own unique identity? Ascona has done it very well, partly by emphasising its role as a center of arts and crafts. Tucked away behind its waterfront is a labyrinth of old streets, where bookbinders, artists and craftsmen compete to catch the eye. For Ascona is the place to which they come. In the adjacent valleys they make woven cloths, baskets, mats, pottery, rugs and *zoccoli* (characteristic wooden clogs). And Ascona is where they sell them.

Painters, poets and composers have all fallen in love with the place. They still do. Not only do the local painters display their wares here (*Painters on the Piazza* every July). Famous musicians perform from August to October in the Ascona International Music Festival and there is a festival of New Orleans jazz in June and July. Ascona's lakeside promenades have splendid views and a thriving life. Most vacation amusements are available. The wide range of excursions—by boat, car, train or bus—is the same as from Locarno.

Valle Maggia, Valle Onsernone and Valle Verzasca

Like most of the valleys of the Ticino, the web leading off from Locarno has good roads and is served faithfully by the yellow postal buses.

The Valle Maggia climbs steadily northwest from Locarno. Make Maggia itself the first stop for the church of Santa Maria delle Grazie di Campagna, its elegant frescoes contrasting sharply with the rustic wood-beamed ceiling, and its paintings executed by country people in gratitude for prayers answered; naive yet somehow touching in their expression of an unquestioning faith.

They have conquered and harnessed an old enemy in the Valle Maggia. Shortly before reaching Maggia you will pass through Avegno. It was almost totally destroyed by a flood in 1747. Similar disasters wreaked similar havoc in the 19th century. But today the dangerous mountain waters have been diverted into a network of hydroelectric plants built inside the mountains. Sometimes the rock walls of the valley hide something more delectable. Behind them are stored the wines of the Ticino ready for serving at the *grotti,* the simple restaurants whose characteristic meals, mostly of cold meats, can be so delightful during long walks in the open air.

The road from Maggia rises to Bignasco, then the valley splits. To the right is the Val Lavizzara, noted for its cheeses, to the left the Val Bavona. Both have tiny stone-walled mountain villages, splashes of primitive grandeur, and frothing waterfalls.

For the Valley Onsernone, head for Verscio, Cavigliano and Loco. All that has been written about its neighbors applies: thrilling gorges, dominating mountain ridges, sudden homely villages, and stimulating air every time you stop the car to sample it. The Valle Onsernone still has a straw industry, though down the centuries many of its craftsmen emigrated to take their skills to Italy and Belgium.

Connoisseurs will declare that the Valle Verzasca is the most lovely of those leading from Locarno. Wild and awe-inspiring, it is still relatively undeveloped. There is a spectacular road running up the valley from Gordola, east of Locarno, to Sonogno.

You may want to stop on the way at Brione to visit the castle and the church which has the remains of frescoes in the style of Giotto surviving from the 14th century. You will certainly want to stop many times to breathe the clean air, thrill at the panorama, or wonder at a silence broken only by the clicking of the camera.

Riviera del Gamborogno and Indemni

The green slopes of Monte Gamborogno are relatively undiscovered. Similarly unspoiled, despite expanding tourism, is the bracelet of delectable little villages that embrace the northern end of Lake Maggiore beneath. Together they offer a day out in charming contrast to the wild beauty of the valleys.

From Locarno go round the north side of the Lake to Vira, turn left for a road that winds (but is excellent) round the slopes of Monte Gamborogno. The views of Lake Maggiore become ever more exciting the higher you climb. You reach Indemni, a picturesque village where steep paths replace streets. Definitely a place to linger.

Drive on into Italy, dropping down to Maccagno, and then back to Locarno through Gerra, St. Nazzaro and Vira, all neat resorts with lakeside walks and cafes, ideal for a relaxed stop. The scent of mountain flowers, the cobbled village paths, and walks through chestnut woods are characteristics of this area, easily explored by postal buses as well.

Brissago and Its Islands

Alpine drama and subtropical colors make an exotic background for Brissago. Behind the town Gridone (2,187 meters, about 7,000 ft.) rises like a sentry post guarding the frontier with Italy. Yet Brissago beneath is the lowest point in Switzerland, just 193 meters (680 ft.) above sea level. Alpine roses and gentian on the heights, camelia, azalea and mimosa down by the lake. The journey from either Locarno or Ascona is brief, but is a constant reminder of how close Italy is, with its Lombard style villas in cosy gardens.

The Brissago islands are set like jewels in the lake. They are nationally preserved botanical gardens with more than 1,000 species. The boats from Locarno and Ascona call at the larger island regularly.

Bellinzona

From almost any point in Bellinzona you will see a castle. Most of the time, more than one. There are actually three of them, and they sum up in a single glance the history of Bellinzona. It has been hotly disputed. Spread out the map, take a quick look, and all is made clear. It is not just that Bellinzona is the capital of the Ticino canton. Strategically, it has always been at the crossroads. And the roads to the north led to the historic passes of St. Gotthard, St. Bernardino and Lucomagno. Who controlled them commanded not only military and political destinies, but the rich trade routes from northern and central Europe to Italy.

Feudal lords fought and argued over Bellinzona. Bishops whose interests were often more of this world than the next sent their armies, and so did emperors. Bellinzona was always in the firing line, and the valleys around rang to the clash of sword on sword. And when the battle was won, Bellinzona and its people usually changed landlords. But once it happened without a blow being struck. In the 15th century, the canton of Uri bought it for 2,400 florins, which sounds like a bargain. Much good it did them. They surrendered it at the battle of Arbedo three years later. But in 1503 the men of Uri had it back, sharing overlordship with Schwyz and Unterwalden. That began three centuries of hard oppression for the Ticinese, ending in 1803 with the creation of the new canton of Ticino.

Frontiers change, geography does not. Bellinzona still stands astride arteries important to trade, and now important to the new industry of tourism as well. The expresses of the famed St. Gotthard route call here, linking it with all Europe. The Bellinzona section of the great expressway that runs from north Germany to south Italy was the last to be completed, in 1986. To the passes of St. Gotthard (gateway to central Switzerland), St. Bernardino (to the Grisons) and Lucomagno (to eastern Switzerland) has been added Nufenen (to the Rhône valley).

The castles, dating from the 13th, 14th and 15th centuries, look down on a busy and welcoming town. The Castello Grande is on a hillock near the center. On another hill overlooking the rail station is the Castello di Montebello, well restored and now an important museum. Higher on the same hill, the Castello di Sasso Carboro has terraces offering impressive views of town and valley. Respectively, they are also known as the castles of Uri, Schwyz and Unterwalden, names celebrated in Bellinzona today not in fear, but as partners in a united nation.

Val Blenio

Biasca is in one respect a miniature Bellinzona. It, too, stands at a meeting place of highways, giving it rather more importance and civilized facilities than one might usually expect of a town of around 5,000 people. And those roads delve into valleys rich in natural beauty, folk traditions jealously guarded, old churches, picturesque mountain villages and breathtaking mountain scenery so that Biasca really unlocks the door on an enthralling experience. Among the most characteristic of all the Ticinese valleys is the Val Blenio which gets ever more wild, ever more superb, as it approaches the aloof isolation of the Lucomagno pass. The upper reaches are sometimes closed in winter.

Yet they call it the Sun Valley, and rightly so. The climate for most of the year is benevolent, as witness the plant life. In this valley, you will see not only the gentian, narcissi and anenomes of the mountains. There are palms which might have been uprooted from Lugano. The scent of mint is sweet in the air. In the spring the valley is ablaze with rhododendron, the chestnut trees are heavy with bloom. This in a valley of formidable rocky heights, glistening snow, plunging waterfalls and bubbling mountain streams.

Drive north up the east side of the valley, calling at the friendly and interesting folk museum of Lottinga, pause for a break at a conveniently sited terrace cafe with a panoramic view. Return on the western side to wonder at a Roman bridge near Porto Valentino, and if you fancy a walk (20 minutes uphill) park your car at Frugiasco or Leontice and visit the remote church of St. Ambrose at Negrentino, where there are remarkable old frescoes. It's worth an early start so as to be back in

Biasca in time for lunch. There the restaurants make a specialty of Ticinese dishes. Ask if they are not on the menu. They will be happily proud if you do.

Valle Leventina

Road and rail play hide and seek with each other as this valley climbs steadily north towards the St. Gotthard Pass. But for all its busy traffic, the Valle Leventina (apart from one small industrial blot) has kept its character, with its chestnut forests and conifers, granite-walled cottages with orange tiles, the sudden surprise of Romanesque churches and snowcapped ridges radiant against a blue sky.

Biasca is again the starting point. Make an early stop at Giornico, where the carefully restored 12th-century church of St. Nicolao has unusual carvings of animals and mythical beasts. The bridge nearby is 14th century. A little to the north is the site of the battle of Sassi Grossi, where in 1478 a few hundred Swiss put to flight several thousand well-armed Milanese by the simple but highly effective method of standing on a ridge above the road and dropping boulders on them.

Airolo is at the head of valley, the last town before the St. Gotthard. But if you have a taste for further adventure, take the road to the left through the Val Bedretto, the way to the Nufenen pass. Near there the Ticino river rises. It is a fitting climax to a Ticino journey.

PRACTICAL INFORMATION FOR THE TICINO

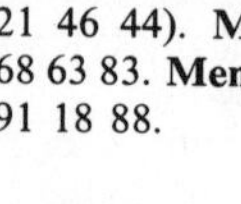

TOURIST OFFICES. The principal tourist authority for the Ticino is the Ente Ticinese per il Turismo, Villa Turrita, Bellinzona (tel. 092–25 70 56). In addition, there are also local tourist offices in the following places: **Ascona,** viale Papio (tel. 092–35 55 44). **Bellinzona,** Palazzo Municipio, piazza Nosetto (tel. 092–25 21 31). **Brissago,** tel. 093–65 11 70. **Gamborogno,** tel. 093–61 18 66. **Locarno,** tel. 093–31 86 33. **Lugano,** riva Abertolli 5 (tel. 091–21 46 44). **Malcantone,** piazza Lago (tel. 091–71 29 86). **Melide,** tel. 091–68 63 83. **Mendrisio,** tel. 091–46 57 61. **Tesserete** (for Lugano valleys), tel. 091–91 18 88.

HOTELS AND RESTAURANTS. As always in Switzerland, hotels in the Ticino cover a wide range of prices and facilities. The following guide is accurate at the time of going to press, but gradings change, and it is wise to check first. So, too, with restaurants. And in addition to those we list, remember that there are numerous *Grotti,* stone buildings sometimes isolated in the woods, sometimes carved deep into the adjoining rock, where they serve simple meals (mostly assorted cold meats) and bring the wine in a *boccalino* (small jug). Most open only in the summer. Good for atmosphere, good for a snack.

You would expect a canton so strongly Italianate in its culture to be Italy-orientated in its cuisine. Many Ticinese specialties are variations on traditional Lombardy dishes, spiced with local flavor. Characteristic items to watch out for (and ask for if you don't see them on the menu) are *busecca* (vegetable soup with tripe), *trota in carpine* (trout marinaded in red wine and vinegar and sometimes served as a cold hors d'oeuvre), *polenta con carne in umido* (maize pudding with stew), and the Ticinese *zabaglione* (whipped egg in marsala). Typical of the Ticino are the numerous game dishes from the mountains: rabbit, hare or roast kid.

Most of the Ticino wines are produced by the *cantina sociale* (wine cooperatives) since the vineyards are small. There are two of these, at Giubiasco, and Mendrisio. An excellent red, ruby-shaded, is the *Alba* from Giubiasco, based on the Merlot grape, and a recommended white is the *Bianco del Mendrisiotto.* A Ticinese liqueur is *Ratafia,* made from grapes, sugar, coffee, vanilla and nutmeg.

AIROLO. *Delle Alpi* (I), tel. 094–88 17 22. 57 beds. Central and comfortable. AE, DC, MC, V. *Motta e Poste* (I), tel. 094–88 23 88. 50 beds. Central and quiet. AE, MC, V.

ASCONA. *Albergo Giardino* (L), 093–35 01 01. 150 beds. Recently opened spacious hotel in own grounds. Sauna, indoor swimming pool, facilities for the handicapped. *Castello del Sole* (L), tel. 093–35 02 02. 125 beds. Quiet, indoor tennis and pool, swimming, hairdresser, fitness room. *Delta* (L), tel. 093–35 11 05. 90 beds. Garden, indoor swimming pool, sauna, fitness room. AE, DC, MC, V. *Eden Roc* (L), tel. 093–35 01 71. 100 beds. Luxurious lakeside hotel in own grounds. Tennis, three pools and sauna. AE, DC, MC, V.

Acapulco au Lac (E), tel. 093–35 45 21. 84 beds. Quiet hotel by the lake with water-skiing and indoor pool. AE, DC, MC, V. *Ascolago* (E), tel. 093–35 20 55. 45 beds. Luxury hotel by the lake. Sauna, indoor swimming pool, facilities for the handicapped and for children. Own garden. AE, MC. *Casa Berno* (E), tel. 093–35 32 32. 100 beds. Quiet hotel in own grounds with pool and sauna. AE. *Europe au Lac* (E), tel. 093–35 28 81. 80 beds. Quiet, lakeside hotel with two pools, garden. *Sasso Boretto* (E), tel. 093–35 71 15. 93 beds. Good family hotel. Sailing and indoor pool. AE, MC, V.

Castello-Seeschloss (M), tel. 093–35 18 03. 65 beds. Central but quiet and comfortable. Pool. *Romantik Tamaro* (M), tel. 093–35 02 82. 78 beds. Atmospheric and quiet. *Luna* (I), tel. 093–35 36 07. 45 beds. Quiet and central. Facilities for the handicapped. Breakfast only. AE, MC. *Mulino* (I), tel. 093–35 36 92. 61 beds. Ideal family hotel. Quiet, and in own grounds. AE, MC, V. *Villa Veratum* (I), tel. 093–35 35 77. 15 beds. Small, central and atmospheric. Pool. Breakfast only.

Restaurants. *Ascolago* (E), tel. 093–35 20 55. Elegant hotel restaurant; international cuisine. AE, MC. *Da Ivo* (M), via Collegio (tel. 093–35 10 31). Recommended.

BELLINZONA. *International* (M), tel. 092–25 43 33. 45 beds. Close to the station. All rooms recently renovated. Breakfast only. AE, DC, MC, V. *Unione* (M), tel. 092–25 55 77. 75 beds. Conveniently central but quiet and in own grounds; excellent restaurant. AE, DC, MC, V. *Croce Federale* (I), tel. 092–25 16 67. 29 beds. Near the station but quiet. Sauna. AE, DC, MC, V.

Restaurants. *Locanda Lessy* (E), tel. 092–29 19 41. Characteristic restaurant at Gnosca, just outside Bellinzona. Ticinese cooking; kid a specialty. AE, DC. *Corona* (M), via Comminata 5 (tel. 092–25 28 44). AE, DC, MC.

BIASCA. *Al Giardinetto* (I), tel. 092–72 17 71. 35 beds. Simple, but welcoming and friendly. AE, DC, MC. *Della Posta* (I), tel. 092–72 21 21. Efficient and reasonable. AE, DC, MC. Both with excellent (E) restaurants.

BISSONE. *Lago di Lugano* (E), tel. 091–68 85 91. 160 beds. Lakeside location, private beach, sauna, outdoor swimming pool, water-skiing; very quiet location. AE, DC, MC.

BRISSAGO. *Villa Cäsar* (L), 093–65 27 66. 62 beds. Quiet lakeside location, sauna, indoor and outdoor pools, private beach. AE, DC, MC, V. *Mirto au Lac* (M), tel. 092–65 13 28. 46 beds. Lakeside hotel with sailing and water-skiing. Very quiet. *Camelia* (I), tel. 092–65 12 41. 42 beds. Central, but quiet and in own grounds. AE.

Restaurant. *Giardino* (E), tel. 093–65 13 41. Reputedly one of the finest restaurants in the Ticino. Many specialties, not all Ticinese.

CHIASSO. *Corso* (M), tel. 091–44 57 01. 50 beds. Well-appointed hotel with terrace restaurant. AE, DC, MC. *Touring Mövenpick* (M), tel. 091–44 53 31. 120 beds. Comfortable. AE, DC, MC, V.

Restaurant. *Touring Mövenpick* (E). Hotel restaurant; much recommended by locals. AE, DC, MC, V.

FAIDO. *Milano* (M), tel. 094–38 13 07. 70 beds. Medium-size hotel in own grounds. Very quiet. AE, DC, MC, V. *Faido* (I), tel. 094–38 15 55. 38 beds. Central and small.

GANDRIA. *Moosman* (I), tel. 091–51 72 61. 50 beds. Small, but quiet and with lakeside location. AE, DC, MC, V.

Restaurant. *Antico* (M), tel. 091–51 48 71. Recommended hotel lakeside restaurant. AE, DC, MC.

LOCARNO. *La Palma au Lac* (L), tel. 093–33 01 71. 128 beds. Beautiful lakeside situation with water-skiing, indoor pool, sauna, hairdresser, and swimming. AE, DC, MC, V.

Arcadia al Lago (E), tel. 093–31 02 82. 180 beds. Recently built hotel in own grounds, close to lake with outdoor swimming pool, sauna and apartment service. AE, DC, MC. *Dellaville* (E), tel. 093–33 01 21. 85 beds. Hillside position, with swimming pool, sauna, fitness room, tennis and apartment service. *Esplanade* (E), Minusio (tel. 093–33 21 21). 120 beds. Traditional style hotel with tennis and pool. Extensive gardens. AE, DC. *Muralto* (E), tel. 093–33 01 18. 145 beds. Splendid lake view, central, facilities for the handicapped, swimming pool. AE, MC, V. *Quisisana* (E), tel. 093–33 01 41. 110 beds. Splendid view from this hotel above the town. Indoor pool, fitness room, gardens. AE, DC, V. *Reber au Lac* (E), tel. 093–33 02 02. 130 beds. Lakeside location with tennis, indoor swimming pool and garden. AE, DC, V.

Beau-Rivage (M), tel. 093–33 13 55. 90 beds. Central and quiet. AE, DC, MC, V. *Remorino* (M), tel. 093 33 10 33. 44 beds. Quiet in own grounds; ideal for children. Breakfast only. *Zurigo* (M), tel. 093–33 16 17. 50 beds. Reader recommended. AE, DC, MC, V. *Dell 'Angelo* (I), tel. 093–31 81 75. 100 beds. Atmospheric and central. AE, MC, V. *Du Lac* (I), tel. 093–31 29 21. 53 beds. Central. Facilities for the handicapped. AE, DC, V. *India* (I), tel. 093–31 12 10. 30 beds. Quiet family hotel in own grounds.

Restaurants. *Le Coq d'Or* (E). Attached to the hotel La Palma au Lac. One of Switzerland's most distinguished restaurants. AE, DC, MC, V. *Centenario* (M–E), tel. 093–33 82 22. Another restaurant with an international reputation. AE, DC. *Mövenpick-Oldrati* (M), via Verbano 1 (tel. 093–33 85 44), at Lungo-Lago, Muralto. First class. AE, DC, MC, V.

LUGANO. *Eden Grand Hotel* (L), Riva Paradiso 7 (tel. 091–55 01 21). 230 beds. Quiet lakeside location. Two indoor pools, sauna, water-skiing, cure facilities, swimming. AE, DC, V. *Spendide Royale* (L), riva Caccia 7 (tel. 091–54 20 01). 204 beds. Old-fashioned elegance but modern facilities. Indoor swimming pool, sauna, facilities for children. AE, DC, MC, V.

Admiral (E), via Geretta 15 (tel. 091–54 23 24). 150 beds. Two swimming pools, sauna, fitness room, facilities for the handicapped. AE, DC, V. *Alba* (E), via delle Scuole (tel. 091–54 37 31). 42 beds. Quiet location in own grounds. AE, V. *Arizona* (E), via S. Gottardo 58 (tel. 091–22 93 43). 100 beds. Close to rail station with outdoor swimming pool. AE, MC. *Bellevue au Lac* (E), riva Caccia 10 (tel. 091–54 33 33). 120 beds. Central and with pool. AE, V. *PLM Commodore* (E), riva Caccia 6 (tel. 091–54 39 21). 130 beds. Lakeside location with fine view. AE, DC, MC, V. *Du Lac-Seehof* (E), riva Paradiso 3 (tel. 091–54 19 21). 90 beds. Lakeside location, sauna, pool, water-skiing. AE, DC. *De La Paix* (E), via Cattori 18 (tel. 091–54 23 31). 140 beds. Swimming pool. AE, DC, MC, V. *Europa au Lac* (E), via Cattori 3 (tel. 091–54 36 21). 170 beds. Handsome lakeside hotel with indoor pool, garden and hairdresser. AE, DC, MC, V.

Béha (M), via G. Mazzini (tel. 091–54 13 31). 100 beds. Central and with facilities for the handicapped. AE, DC, MC, V. *Meister* (M), via San Salvatore 11 (tel. 091–54 14 12). 130 beds. Fine family hotel. AE, DC, MC, V. *Park Hotel Nizza* (M), via Guidino 14 (tel. 091–54 17 71). 70 beds. Park location with heated pool and excellent views. Panorama bar; recommended. *Walter au Lac* (M), piazza Rezzonico 7 (tel. 091–22 74 25). 64 beds. Central and quiet. AE, DC, MC, V. *Rio* (I), via Cantonale 9 (tel. 091–22 81 44). 28 beds. Small, simple and reasonably priced; breakfast only. AE, MC, V.

Restaurants. *Locanda del Boschetto* (E), via al Boschetto 8 (tel. 091–54 24 93). Fish dishes a specialty at this fine restaurant. DC, MC, V. *Al Portone* (E), viale Casserate 3 (tel. 091–23 59 95). Excellent international cuisine. AE, DC, V.

Bianchi (M–E), via Pessina 3 (tel. 091–22 84 79). Another restaurant with a consistently high standard. V. *Galleria* (M–E), via Vegezzi (tel. 091–23 62 88). High quality and comprehensive menu. AE, DC, MC.

Cina (M), piazza Riforma 9 (tel. 091–23 51 73). Excellent Chinese cooking. AE, MC. *Gambrinus* (M), piazza Riforma (tel. 091–23 19 55). AE, MC. *Huguenin* (M), riva Abertolli 1 (tel. 091–22 88 01). DC, MC.

Grotto Grillo (I–M), via Ronchetti 6 (tel. 091–51 18 01). DC, V. *La Tinera* (I–M), via dei Gorini 2 (tel. 091–23 52 19). AE, V.

Parco-Ciani Mövenpick (I), piazza Indipendenza 4 (tel. 091–23 86 56). Moderately priced. AE, DC, MC, V. *Scala* (I), via Nassa 29 (tel. 091–22 09 58). Moderately priced. DC.

MELANO. *Motel Lido* (M), tel. 091–68 79 71. 80 beds. Lakeside hotel in own grounds. Pool and facilities for the handicapped. AE, DC, MC, V.

MENDRISIO. *Coronado* (M), tel. 091–46 56 51. 106 beds. In own grounds with outdoor pool. AE, DC, MC. *Milano* (M), tel. 091–46 57 41. 55 beds. Outdoor swimming pool. AE, DC, MC. *Morgana* (I), tel. 091–46 23 55. 35 beds. Quietly situated with outdoor swimming pool and terrace restaurant. AE, DC, MC. *Stazione* (I), tel. 091–46 22 44. 50 beds. Central with facilities for the handicapped. AE, DC, MC, V.

Restaurant. *La Pignatta* (M), tel. 091–46 57 41. Hotel restaurant of the Milano. AE, DC, MC.

MORCOTE. *Olivella au Lac* (L), tel. 091–69 10 01. 150 beds. Superior lakeside hotel with indoor and outdoor swimming pools, sauna, sailing and water-skiing. Facilities for children. AE, DC, MC, V. *Carina* (M), tel. 091–69 11 31. 40 beds. Lakeside hotel with fine views. Historic building. Terrace restaurant and outdoor pool. Water-skiing, garden. AE, DC, MC, V. *Rivabella* (I), tel. 091–69 13 14. 30 beds. Small lakeside hotel. In own grounds and very quiet. AE, DC, MC, V.

Restaurants. *Carina* (E), hotel restaurant. Typical Ticinese cuisine of a particularly high standard. AE, DC, MC. *Voile d'Or* (M). Restaurant of the hotel Olivella au Lac. AE, DC, MC, V.

ORIGLIO. *Origlio Country Club* (L), tel. 091–93 19 21. 110 beds. Quietly situated in a countryside location and in own ground. Tennis, indoor and outdoor pools, terrace restaurant. AE, DC, MC, V.

PONTE TRESA. *Del Pesce* (M), tel. 091–71 11 46. 44 beds. Lakeside hotel with pool and water-skiing. Facilities for the handicapped.

VIRA GAMBAROGNO. *Touring Bellavista* (M), tel. 093–61 11 16. 110 beds. Wonderful views from this hotel standing in its own grounds. MC, V. *Viralgo* (M), tel. 093–61 15 91. 68 beds. Lakeside hotel with fitness room, indoor pool, tennis, sauna and facilities for children.

GETTING AROUND. There is a wide range of concessions for foreign visitors. Lugano and Locarno both offer Holiday Season Tickets giving unlimited first class local and lake travel, plus reductions in entrance fees to places of interest and other advantages. Inquire at the local tourist offices for details.

By Bus. Though some of the most dramatic and picturesque corners of the Ticino are mercifully removed from the busy highways of tourism, they are readily accessible by public transport. The famous yellow postal buses of which the Swiss are justly proud probe diligently into them. Details of services and timetables are available from rail stations and all post offices.

By Car. The superb new motorway, Strada Nazionale SN2, completed only in 1986, runs from the St. Gotthard tunnel right through the Ticino like a sturdy backbone, on into Italy and the south. The main valley roads are excellent, and their branches leading to the heights are constantly improving.

By Boat. The steamers and motor launches of lake Lugano, and those operating on the Swiss end of lake Maggiore are leisurely but convenient links between attractive little lakeside villages. The services are reduced in winter.

By Air. The services of Crossair link Lugano's airport with the principal Swiss cities, such as Basel, Bern, Geneva and Zürich.

Sightseeing Data

ASCONA. Monte Verita. Chinese collection of Baron von der Heycht. Open daily 8–6.

BELLINZONA. Museo Civico, Castello di Montebello. Collection illustrating local history. Open daily June 1 to Sept. 30, 9:30–12 and 2–5:30, closed Mon.; Oct. 1 to May 31, daily 10–12 and 2–5, closed Mon.

BISSONE. Casa Tencalla. Italian Renaissance building housing furnishings from the Ticinese 17th century. Open Apr. to Oct., 10:30–12 and 2–5.

BOSCO GURIN. Walserhaus. Ticino country life. Utensils for woodwork and the manufacture of hemp, linen and wool. Open daily June 1 to Oct. 31, 9–11 and 2–5, closed Mon.

CASTAGNOLA. Villa Favorita. The finest private art collection in Switzerland, and one of the most impressive anywhere in Europe. In over 20 beautifully appointed rooms is displayed the collection of Baron von Thyssen, including masterpieces from the Italian, Dutch, Spanish, French and German schools. Open Good Friday to the second Sunday in Oct., Fri. and Sat. 10–12 and 2–5, Sun. 2–5.

GANDRIA. Cantine di Gandria. Museo delle Dogane (Smugglers' Museum). Fascinating exhibition recalling the days when there was a healthy smuggling trade around lake Lugarno. Short boat ride from Lugano. Open Easter to Oct. 15, 2:30–5:30.

GIORNICA. Museo di Leventina (Museum of Leventina). Ticinese country life. Utensils, documents, sculptures, paintings, old prints, photographs. Open April to Sept., Sat. and Sun. 3–5.

LIGORNETTO. Museo Vela (Vincenzo Vela Museum). Sculptures by this 19th-century artist. Open daily March to Nov., 9–12 and 2–5; closed Mon.

LOCARNO. Museo Civico/ Museo d'Arte Contemporanea (Civic Museum and Museum of Contemporary Art), piazza Castello 2. Comprehensive collection of exhibits illustrating Locarno's colorful history, and a display of modern art. Open April to Oct. 10–12 and 2–5; closed Mon.

LOCO. Museo Onsernonese (Museum of the Onsernone Valley). Traditional handicrafts including pewter, copper and furniture. Open daily Apr. 1 to Oct. 31, 10–11:30 and 2–5.

LOTTIGNA. Museo di Blenio (Local History Museum of the Blenio Valley). Agricultural and artistic crafts and wine production are illustrated. Religious art and an important armory collection. Open daily Easter to Nov. 1, Tues. to Fri., 2–5, and Sat. and Sun., 10–12 and 2–5.

LUGANO. Archivio Storico (Historical Archives), Strada di Gandria 4, Castagnola. Italian writer Carlo Cattaneo and Latvian poets Janis Rainis and Aspazija have a room each. Open all the year Mon. to Fri., 10–12 and 2:30–5:30.

Museo Cantonale di Storia Naturale (Cantonal Museum of Natural History), viale Cattaneo 4. Zoological and botanical exhibition. Open daily all year 9–12 and 2–5, closed Sun. and Mon.

Villa Ciani. In the municipal park. Art collection includes important exhibitions on loan and paintings and sculptures by Ticinese artists. Open daily all the year 10–12 and 2–6, closed Mon.

Villa Malpensata, riva Caccia 5. Houses national and international exhibitions. Open all the year 10–12 and 2–6, closed Mon.

MELIDE. Swissminiatur. A remarkable concentration of Swiss life in miniature. Models of castles, villas, farms, trains, steamers and characteristic buildings from all parts of the land. Open Mar. to Oct. 8–6. In July and Aug. until 10 P.M.

MENDRISIO. Museo d'Arte (Art Museum). The Grigioni collection. Works of the Italian, Flemish and German schools from the 16th century onwards and also contemporary art. Open Wed., Sat., Sun. 2–6.

MERIDE. Museo Paleontologico (Paleontological Museum). Monte San Giorgio yielded some remarkable fossils, collected here in a fascinating exhibition. Open daily 8–6.

OLIVONE. Museo di Sant Martino (Museum of Saint-Martin), Ca da Rivöi. An old priory housing the museum of the churches of the upper valley of the Blenio. Religious art and costumes, agricultural implements and crafts. Open April to Oct., Tues. to Sun. 2–5.

RANCATE. Pinacotech Cantonale Giovanni Züst (Picture Gallery Züst). Paintings by Ticinese artists from 16th century to present day. Open daily Mar. 1 to Nov. 1, 9:30–12 and 2–5, closed Mon.

SEMIONE. Collezione di Minerali e Fossili (Museum of Minerals and Fossils), Casa San Carlo. Important collection of 25,000 items. Open daily Easter to Nov. 1, 3–5. For information call 092–76 11 88.

SONOGNO. Museo di Val Verzasca (Museum of the Verzasca Valley). Rural arts and crafts, also religious exhibits and costumes. Open daily July 1 to Sept. 30, 1:30–4:30.

SPORTS. Fishing. River fishing in the valleys, lake fishing from the lake resorts. For tourist fishing permits apply to the Lugano Tourist Office (see above).

Golf. There are 18-hole courses open all the year at Ascona (tel. 093–35 21 32) and Lugano (tel. 093–71 15 57).

Riding. Numerous centers throughout the canton, including **Origlio,** Scuderia San Giorgio (tel. 091–56 52 12), Scuderia Hubertus (tel. 091–93 15 44) and at **Stabio,** Ranch Club Santa Margherita (tel. 091–47 33 84).

Tennis. Plenty of courts in the principal centers both outdoor and under cover, including some illuminated at night. Professional coaching at Lugano Lido (tel. 091–51 56 36). Inquire further at local tourist offices (see above).

Water Sports. The principal lakeside resorts have facilities for all of them including swimming, rowing, underwater sports, water-skiing, sailing, windsurfing. **Lugano Lido** (tel. 091–51 40 41) is a well-developed bathing resort surrounded by green lawns, with several pools for adults and children, heated in spring and autumn. Open-air terrace restaurant.

WINTER SPORTS. Until recently, the Ticino had hardly kept pace with other areas of Switzerland in the development of winter sports facilities, but now expansion is going ahead rapidly, making it difficult to provide an up-to-date guide. Resorts which have led in this field are:

Ascona. 205 meters (670 ft.). Skating and curling.

Locarno. 205 meters (670 ft.). Funicular railway, 1 cable car, 4 lifts, 13 kms. (8 miles) of downhill runs, 3 km. of cross-country trails, ski school.

Lugano. 275 meters (900 ft.). Two funiculars, 1 cable car, 1 cogwheel railway, 10 kms. (6 miles) of downhill runs, skating.

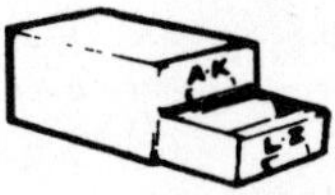

USEFUL ADDRESSES. Lugano. *Alitalia,* via Nassa 40 (tel. 091–23 45 65). *American Express,* c/o Danzas Viaggi, piazza Manzoni 8 (tel. 091–22 17 82). *Cooks Wagons-Lits Turismo,* riva Caccia 1C (tel. 091–54 77 51). *Crossair,* Aeroporto Lugano-Agno (tel. 091–50 50 01). *Swissair,* via Pretorio 9 (tel. 091–23 63 31).

ENGLISH-FRENCH-GERMAN-ITALIAN VOCABULARY

ENGLISH-FRENCH-GERMAN-ITALIAN VOCABULARY

ENGLISH	FRENCH	GERMAN	ITALIAN
Come in!	Entrez! (ahn'tray)	Herein!	Avanti!
Can anyone here speak English?	Y a-t-il ici quelqu'un qui parle anglais?	Spricht jemand hier englisch?	C'è qualcuno che parla inglese?
Do you speak English?	Parlez-vous anglais?	Sprechen Sie englisch?	Parla inglese?
Do you understand?	Comprenez-vous?	Verstehen Sie?	Capisce?
I don't understand	Je ne comprends pas	Ich verstehe nicht	Non capisco
Don't mention it	Pas de quoi	Bitte sehr	Di niente
I beg your pardon	Pardon	Verzeihung	Mi scusi
Good morning	Bonjour	Guten Morgen	Buon giorno
Good day	Bonjour	Guten Tag	Buon giorno
Good evening	Bonsoir	Guten Abend	Buona sera
Good night	Bonne nuit	Gute Nacht	Buona notte
Good-bye	Au revoir	Auf Wiedersehen	Arriveder La, Arrivederci
How are you?	Comment allez-vous?	Wie geht es Ihnen?	Come sta?
How much . . . many?	Combien?	Wieviel?	Quanto . . . quanti?
I don't know	Je ne sais pas	Ich weiss nicht	Non so
No	Non	Nein	No
Yes	Oui	Ja	Si
Please speak more slowly	Parlez plus lentement, s'il-vous-plait	Bitte, sprechen Sie langsamer	Parli più lentamente, per favore
Sit down	Asseyez-vous	Setzen Sie sich	S'accomodi
Thank you very much	Merci bien	Danke sehr	Grazie mille
There is, there are	Il y a	Es gibt	C'è, ci sono
Very good . . . well	Très bien	Sehr gut	Molto bene
What is this?	Qu'est-ce-que c'est?	Was ist das?	Che cosa è questo?
What do you want?	Que voulez-vous?	Was wünschen Sie?	Cosa desidera?
Please	S'il vous plaît (silvooplay)	Bitte (bi'teh)	Per piacere, per favore

ENGLISH	FRENCH	GERMAN	ITALIAN
What is your name?	Comment vous appelez-vous?	Wie heissen Sie?	Come si chiama?
With pleasure	Avec plaisir	Mit Vergnügen	Con piacere
You are very kind	Vous êtes bien aimable	Sehr freundlich	Lei è molto gentile
Sunday	dimanche	Sonntag	domenica
Monday	lundi	Montag	lunedí
Tuesday	mardi	Dienstag	martedí
Wednesday	mercredi	Mittwoch	mercoledí
Thursday	jeudi	Donnerstag	giovedí
Friday	vendredi	Freitag	venerdí
Saturday	samedi	Samstag	sabato
Is there . . .	Y-a-t'il . . .	Gibt es . . .	C'è . . .
—a bus for . . . ?	—un autobus pour . . . ?	—einen Autobus nach . . . ?	—un autobus per . . . ?
—a dining car?	—un wagon-restaurant?	—einen Speisewagen?	—una carrozza ristorante?
—an English interpreter?	—un interprète anglais?	—einen englischen Dolmetscher?	—un interprete inglese?
—a guide?	—un guide?	—einen Führer?	—una guida?
—a good hotel at . . . ?	—un bon hôtel à . . . ?	—ein gutes Hotel in . . . ?	—un buon albergo a . . . ?
—a good restaurant here?	—un bon restaurant ici?	—ein gutes Restaurant hier?	—un buon ristorante qui?
—a sleeper?	—une place dans le wagon-lits?	—einen Schlafwagen?	—una cuccetta nel vagone letto?

ENGLISH	FRENCH	GERMAN	ITALIAN
Is there . . .	Y-a-t'il . . .	Hat man . . .	C'è . . .
—time to get out?	—le temps de descendre?	—Zeit auszusteigen?	—tempo di scendere?
		Gibt es	
—a train for . . . ?	—un train pour . . . ?	—einen Zug nach . . . ?	—un treno per . . . ?
Thank you	Merci	Danke	Grazie
Where is . . .	Où est . . .	Wo ist . . .	Dov'è . . .
—the airport?	—l'aéroport?	—der Flugplatz?	—l'aeroporto?
—a bank? (money exchange?)	—une banque? (change?)	—eine Bank? (Wechselstube?)	—una banca (un ufficio di cambio)?
—the bar?	—le bar?	—die Bar?	—un bar?
—the barbershop?	—le coiffeur?	—ein Coiffeur/Friseur?	—un barbiere?
—the bathroom?	—la salle de bains?	—das Badezimmer?	—la sala da bagno?
—the ticket (booking) office?	—le guichet?	—der Billettschalter?	—lo sportello?
—a chemist's shop (drug store)?	—une pharmacie?	—eine Apotheke?	—la farmacia?
—the movies (cinema)?	—le cinéma?	—das Kino?	—il cinema?
—the checkroom?	—la consigne?	—die Gepäckaufbewahrung?	—il deposito bagagli?
—the British (American) Consulate?	—le consulat (américain) d'Angleterre?	—das englische (amerikanische) Konsulat?	—il consolato (d'America) d'Inghilterra?
—the Customs office?	—la douane?	—das Zollamt?	—la dogana?
—a garage?	—un garage?	—eine Garage?	—un autorimessa?
—a hairdresser?	—un coiffeur?	—ein Coiffeur?	—un parrucchiere?

ENGLISH	FRENCH	GERMAN	ITALIAN
—the lavatory?	—les toilettes?	—die Toilette?	—i gabinetti?
—the luggage?	—les bagages?	—das Gepäck?	—i bagagli?
—the museum?	—le musée?	—das Museum?	—il museo?
—the police station?	—le poste de police?	—die Polizei?	—la polizia?
—the post office?	—le bureau de poste?	—das Postamt?	—l'ufficio postale?
—the theater?	—le théâtre?	—das Theater?	—il teatro?
—the railway station?	—la gare?	—der Bahnhof?	—la stazione?
—a tobacconist?	—un tabac?	—ein Tabakladen?	—una tabaccheria?
When . . . (At what time . . .)	Quand . . . (A quelle heure est)	Wann . . .	Quando . . . (a che ora)
—is lunch?	—le déjeuner est-il servi?	—ist das Mittagessen?	—è il pranzo?
—is dinner?	—le dîner est-il servi?	—ist das Abendessen?	—si cena?
—is the first (last) bus?	—part le premier (dernier) autobus?	—geht der erste (letzte) Autobus?	—parte il primo (l'ultimo) autobus?
—is the first (last) train?	—part le premier (dernier) train?	—geht der erste (letzte) Zug?	—è il primo (l'ultimo) treno?
—does the train leave (arrive)?	—le train part-il (arrive-t-il)?	—geht der Zug ab (kommt der Zug an)?	—parte (arriva) il treno?
—does the theater open?	—ouvre-t-on le théâtre?	—wird das Theater geöffnet?	—si apre il teatro?
—will it be ready?	—sera-t-il-(elle) prêt?	—wird es fertig sein?	—sarà pronto?
—does the performance begin (end)?	—la séance commence-t-elle(finit-elle?)	—beginnt (endet) die Aufführung?	—comincia (finisce) la rappresentazione?

ENGLISH	FRENCH	GERMAN	ITALIAN
—can I have a bath?	—pourrai-je prendre un bain?	—kann ich ein Bad nehmen?	—posso fare il bagno?
Which is . . .	Quel est . . .	Welches ist . . .	Qual'è . . .
—the way to . . . street?	Par où va-t-on à la rue . . .?	Wie komme ich zur . . . Strasse?	—la strada per . . . ?
—the best hotel at . . .?	—le meilleur hôtel de . . . ?	—das beste Hotel in . . . ?	—il migliore albergo di . . . ?
—the train (bus) for . . . ?	—le train (autobus) pour . . . ?	—der Zug (Autobus) nach . . . ?	—il treno (l'autobus) per . . . ?
What is . . .	Quel est . . .	Was ist . . .	Qual'è
—the fare to . . . ?	—le prix du voyage à . . . ?	—der Fahrpreis nach . . . ?	—il prezzo per . . . ?
—the single fare?	—le prix d'aller?	—der einfache?	—il prezzo per?
—the round trip (return) fare?	—le prix d'aller et retour?	—der Preis der Rückfahrkarte?	—il prezzo per andata e ritorno?
—the price?	—le prix?	—der Preis?	—il prezzo?
—the price per day?	—le prix par jour?	—der Preis pro Tag?	—il prezzo per giorno?
—per week?	—par semaine?	—pro Woche?	—per settimana?
—the price per kilo?	Combien le kilo?	—der Preis pro Kilo?	—il prezzo al kilo?
—the price per meter?	Combien le mètre?	—der Preis pro Meter?	—il prezzo al metro?
—the matter?	Qu'est-ce qui se passe?	—los?	—Che c'è?
—this?	Qu'est-ce que c'est?	—das?	—Che e questo?
—the French (etc.) for?	Comment dit-on . . . en français?	Wie sagt man . . . auf deutsch?	—Come si dice . . . in Italiano?

ENGLISH	FRENCH	GERMAN	ITALIAN
Have you . . .	Avez-vous . . .	Haben Sie . . .	Ha . . .
—any American (English) cigarettes?	—des cigarettes américaines (anglaises)?	—amerikanische (englische) Zigaretten?	—delle sigarette americane (inglesi)?
—a timetable?	—un indicateur des chemins de fer?	—einen Fahrplan?	—un orario?
—a room to let?	—une chambre à louer?	—ein Zimmer zu vermieten?	—una camera libera?
—anything ready? (food)	—quelque chose de prêt?	—etwas fertig?	—qualcosa di pronto?
—any fruit?	—des fruits?	—etwas Obst?	—della frutta?
How long?	Combien de temps?	Wie lange?	Quanto tempo?
How often?	Combien de fois?	Wie oft?	Quante volte?
I want . . . would like . . . need	Je désire . . . je voudrais	Ich brauche . . . Ich möchte . . . Ich bitte um	Vorrei . . .
—my bill	—mon compte	—meine Rechnung	—il conto
—the chambermaid	—parler avec la femme de chambre	—Ich möchte mit dem Zimmermädchen sprechen	—parlare con la cameriera
—a dentist	—consulter un dentiste	Ich brauche einen Zahnarzt	—consultare un dentista
—a dictionary	—un dictionnaire	Ich brauche ein Wörterbuch	—un dizionario
—a doctor	—consulter un médecin	Ich brauche einen Arzt	—consultare un medico
—to buy . . .	—acheter . . .	Ich möchte . . . kaufen	—comprare . . .
—something to drink	—prendre quelque chose à boire	Ich möchte etwas trinken	—qualcosa da bere

Index

Romont, 259
Rorschach, 114, HR117